Rav

Bed & Breakfast U.S.A.
from the press:

"Today *Bed & Breakfast U.S.A.* is a best-selling travel book that is updated every year and contains descriptions of over 600 places to stay, as well as reservation services that can book an additional 10,000 homes."—***Reader's Digest***

"The best source of nationwide information"—***Changing Times***

"The most comprehensive B&B guide"—***Sylvia Porter's Personal Finance***

"The most comprehensive B&B guide"—***Savvy***

"One of the best"—***Akron Beacon Journal***

"Your best bet"—***Philadelphia Inquirer***

"Makes enjoyable reading"—***Country Living***

"Extremely useful, well-organized guide"—***American Library Association Booklist***

"The best source for B&Bs throughout the country"—***Let's Go USA***

"Many a first-time B&B guest vows never again to stay in a motel . . . business travelers—particularly women traveling alone—have found this personal touch just the ticket."—**Karen Cure, *TWA Ambassador***

"Bed and breakfast lodging has been sweeping the United States by storm. . . . *Bed & Breakfast USA* is one of the bibles of the business. . . ."—***Chicago Tribune***

"Squeezed budgets get relief at B&Bs. . . . *Bed & Breakfast USA* [is] an extensive list of establishments. . . ."—***United Press International***

"The best overall view . . . Betty Rundback is so enthusiastic that she even gives readers pointers on how to start their own B&Bs."—***Detroit News***

"Fills a need for travelers who are watching their wallets. . . . Especially helpful . . . especially valuable."—***New York Daily News***

"For those who have embraced the B&B way to travel, there is no going back to hotel highrises and motel monotony."—***Time***

"America's newest and hottest accommodations trend is B&B."—***Boston Globe***

Rave reviews from hosts and guests:

Our guests write: "I feel I must write to you to express my complete satisfaction with your book—*Bed & Breakfast U.S.A.*"

"You should be ashamed—keeping me up half the night reading that super book of yours!! It's the stuff dreams are made of!"

"All B&Bs exceeded our expectations and all hosts were very friendly. Thank you for a marvelous guide."

"I feel I must write to express my complete satisfaction with your book."

"Our B&B in New York was an excellent experience. . . . It was our home away from home."

"We were completely satisfied and will never stay any place but a B&B. Can't say enough about our delightful stay."

"The B&B was immaculate, comfortable and inviting. Our hosts were absolutely charming. . . . It felt like a visit with friends."

"It's not just the fact that the accommodations are comfortable, attractive, and reasonable—but it's the pleasant, gracious touch. It's being able to get directions, find out about current attractions. . . ."

"We, being English, have stayed at many B&Bs in Europe and we can truthfully say that we have never experienced such hospitality and kindness anywhere."

"We were complete strangers when we arrived, and departed a few days later as good friends. Absolutely beautiful accommodations and exceptional hospitality."

Our hosts report: "Travelers continue to flock to our house in response to your book. We are also getting many guests for a second, third, and fourth visit."

"We've had the most interesting people in the world come up our driveway clutching *Bed & Breakfast U.S.A.* as though it were a passport to heaven."

"Your book is, without a doubt, the most widely used and the most trusted by our guests."

"Each guest has been a real joy for us and there is a sadness when they leave. We have been so impressed with your book—year after year it has improved and is so attractive. It is evident that you put a great amount of thought and work into the best bed & breakfast book in the U.S.A."

"I have had wonderful responses to my listing. Many people have never been to a B&B and ask me all sorts of questions."

"Thanks once again for writing *Bed & Breakfast U.S.A.* It is definitely the best of the B&B guides."

Bed & Breakfast U.S.A.

A GUIDE TO
Tourist Homes
AND
Guest Houses

Betty Revits Rundback
and
Nancy Kramer

Tourist House Association of America

E. P. Dutton • New York

With love to Bob Rundback
because this whole project was his idea,
and to Ann Revits,
ever the proud mother and grandma.

Front cover photo: Cliff Harbor, Bandon, Oregon, by Doris Duncan.
Back cover photos: living room, Cliff Harbor, Bandon, Oregon, by Doris Duncan; bedroom, White Lace Inn, Sturgeon Bay, Wisconsin, by Fran Klotz; kitchen, Yankees' Northview Bed & Breakfast, Plainfield, Vermont, by Tom Sparrow.

Published in the United States by E. P. Dutton, a division of NAL Penguin Inc., 2 Park Avenue, New York, N.Y. 10016

Published simultaneously in Canada by Fitzhenry & Whiteside Limited, Toronto

ISBN: 0-525-48353-5

Editor: Sandra W. Soule

Designer: Stanley S. Drate/Folio Graphics Co. Inc.

10 9 8 7 6 5 4 3 2 1

Contents

Reservation service organizations appear here in boldface type.

Preface

If you have read earlier editions of *Bed & Breakfast U.S.A.*, you know this book has always been a labor of love. It is personally gratifying to see how it has grown from the first 16-page edition, titled *Guide to Tourist Homes and Guest Houses*, which was published in 1975 and contained 40 individual listings. Thirteen years later, the twelfth revised edition lists 857 homes and 145 reservation agencies, giving travelers access to over 11,000 host homes. This spectacular success indicates how strongly the revived concept of the guest house has recaptured the fancy of both travelers and proprietors.

On the other hand, what was welcomed as a reasonably priced alternative to the plastic ambience of motel chains has, in some instances, lost its unique qualities. Our mailbox is crammed with letters from grand hotels, condominium rental agencies, camp-group compounds, and chic inns with nightly tariffs topping the $100 mark. All share a common theme—they all serve breakfast and they all want to be listed in *Bed & Breakfast U.S.A.* Who can blame them? Since 1976, over 500,000 people have read this best-selling guide.

We also receive a substantial amount of mail from our readers, and we have tailored our book to meet their needs. We have given a great deal of thought to what we feel a B&B should be and are again focusing on our original definition: an owner-occupied residence with breakfast included at a fair rate, where the visitor is made to feel more like a welcome guest than a paying customer.

Based on personal experience, and comments from our readers, several key problems are apparent in some B&Bs: Waiting your turn to use a bathroom shared with five other guests is unpleasant, especially when you're paying upward of $40 a night. Nor is it enjoyable to pay $90 and up simply for staying in someone's home, no matter how exquisite the decor. Finally, when paying $35 or $40, no one wants to go out to a restaurant for breakfast—no matter how close it may be, it's just not the same as breakfast "at home."

As a result of these problems, we have regretfully deleted several listings that have been on our roster for years. This does not imply, in any way, that these B&Bs aren't nice; it simply means that, *in our opinion*, they do not fit the traditional B&B experience. We've had a goodly share of irate letters from several "old friends" disputing our opinion and pointing out that rising operating expenses must be reflected in their charges. Newcomers to the business decry our stand and tell us of their high costs that must somehow be recouped. While we sympathize and understand fully their positions, we must, in all fairness, be firm.

This is not a project where listings are compiled just for the sake of putting a book together; bigger isn't necessarily better. *Bed & Breakfast U.S.A.* is a product of a membership organization whose credo is "Comfort, Cleanliness, Cordiality, and fairness of Cost." We solicit and rely on the comments of readers. For this purpose, we include a tear-out form on page 697. If we receive negative reports, that member is dropped from our roster. We genuinely appreciate comments from guests . . . negative if necessary, positive when warranted. *We want to hear from you!*

All of the B&Bs described in this book are members of the Tourist House Association of America. THAA dues are $20 annually. We share ideas and experiences by way of our newsletter, and arrange regional seminars and conferences. To order a list of B&Bs that joined after this edition went to press, use the form at the back of this book.

Betty R. Rundback
Director, Tourist House Association of America
RD 2, Box 355A Greentown, Pennsylvania 18426

January 1988

Acknowledgments

A special thanks to Michael Frome, who saw promise in the first 16-page "Guide" and verbally applauded our growth with each subsequent edition. And many thanks to all the other travel writers and reporters who have brought us to the attention of their audience.

Many hugs to family and friends who lovingly devoted time to the "office" chores: Mike and Peggy Ackerman, John Rundback, Betty Neuer, Theresa Mennella, Harry Revits, Susie Scher, Elinor Scher, Harriet Frank, Joan Smith, Lorrie Vining, Theresa Mennella, and Karen Zane. We are most grateful to Joyce and James McGhee for their artwork.

Our appreciation goes to our editor, Sandy Soule. She exhausted her supply of blue pencils but never her patience.

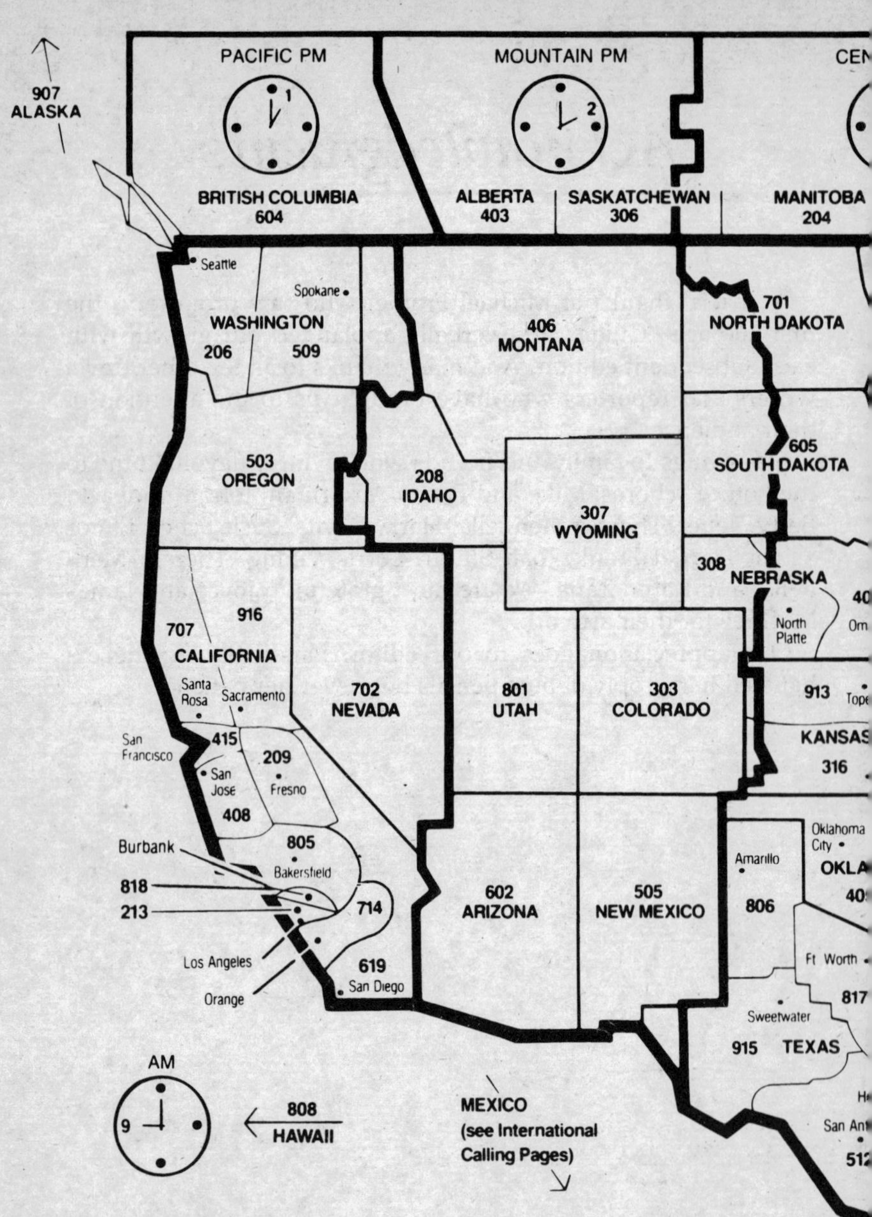
907
ALASKA
PACIFIC PM
MOUNTAIN PM
BRITISH COLUMBIA
604
ALBERTA
403
SASKATCHEWAN
306
MANITOBA
204
Seattle
Spokane
WASHINGTON
206
509
406
MONTANA
701
NORTH DAKOTA
503
OREGON
208
IDAHO
605
SOUTH DAKOTA
307
WYOMING
308
NEBRASKA
North Platte
916
707
CALIFORNIA
Santa Rosa
Sacramento
702
NEVADA
801
UTAH
303
COLORADO
913
KANSAS
316
San Francisco
415
209
San Jose
Fresno
408
805
Bakersfield
Burbank
818
213
714
Los Angeles
Orange
619
San Diego
602
ARIZONA
505
NEW MEXICO
Amarillo
806
Oklahoma City
Ft Worth
817
Sweetwater
915
TEXAS
AM
9
808
HAWAII
MEXICO
(see International
Calling Pages)

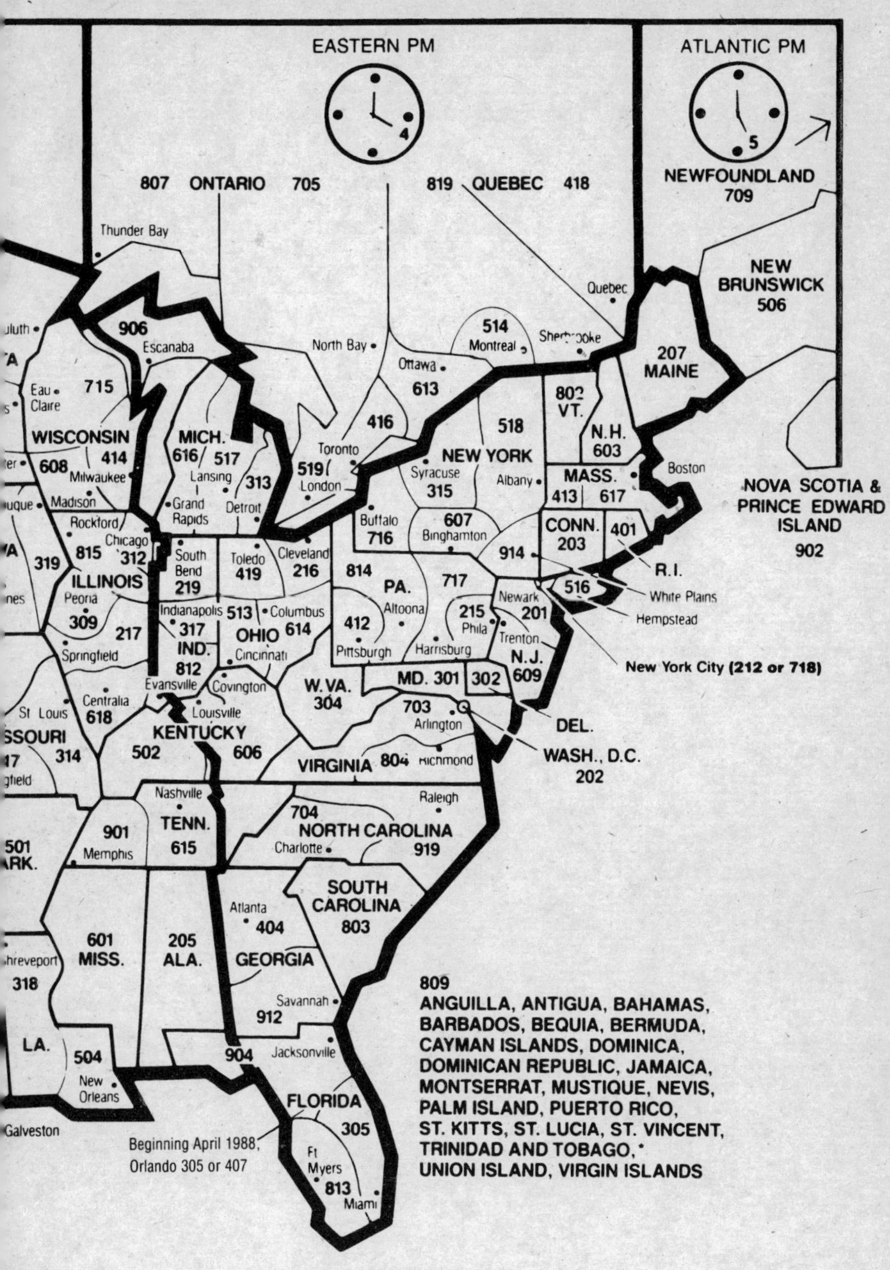
EASTERN PM
ATLANTIC PM
4
5
807 ONTARIO 705
819 QUEBEC 418
NEWFOUNDLAND
709
Thunder Bay
NEW
BRUNSWICK
506
Quebec
514
Montreal
906
Escanaba
North Bay
Ottawa
613
207
MAINE
715
Eau Claire
WISCONSIN
414
608
Milwaukee
Madison
MICH.
616
517
Lansing
313
Grand Rapids
Detroit
416
Toronto
519
London
518
NEW YORK
Syracuse
315
Albany
VT.
N.H.
603
MASS.
413
617
Boston
NOVA SCOTIA &
PRINCE EDWARD
ISLAND
902
Rockford
815
Chicago
312
319
ILLINOIS
Peoria
309
217
Springfield
South Bend
219
Toledo
419
Cleveland
216
Buffalo
716
607
Binghamton
CONN.
203
401
R.I.
914
814
PA.
717
Altoona
412
Pittsburgh
215
Phila
Harrisburg
Newark
201
516
White Plains
Hempstead
Trenton
N.J.
609
New York City (212 or 718)
Indianapolis
317
IND.
812
513
OHIO
Columbus
614
Cincinnati
Covington
Evansville
W.VA.
304
MD. 301
302
703
Arlington
DEL.
WASH., D.C.
202
Centralia
618
St Louis
314
KENTUCKY
502
606
Louisville
VIRGINIA
804
Richmond
Nashville
TENN.
615
901
Memphis
704
NORTH CAROLINA
Charlotte
919
Raleigh
SOUTH
CAROLINA
803
Atlanta
404
GEORGIA
601
MISS.
205
ALA.
318
LA.
504
New Orleans
Galveston
Savannah
912
904
Jacksonville
FLORIDA
305
Ft Myers
813
Miami
Beginning April 1988,
Orlando 305 or 407
809
ANGUILLA, ANTIGUA, BAHAMAS,
BARBADOS, BEQUIA, BERMUDA,
CAYMAN ISLANDS, DOMINICA,
DOMINICAN REPUBLIC, JAMAICA,
MONTSERRAT, MUSTIQUE, NEVIS,
PALM ISLAND, PUERTO RICO,
ST. KITTS, ST. LUCIA, ST. VINCENT,
TRINIDAD AND TOBAGO,
UNION ISLAND, VIRGIN ISLANDS

1

Introduction

Bed and Breakfast is the popular lodging alternative to hotel high rises and motel monotony. B&Bs are either private residences where the owners rent spare bedrooms to travelers, or small, family-operated inns offering a special kind of warm, personal hospitality. Whether large or small, B&Bs will make you feel more like a welcome guest than a paying customer.

The custom of opening one's home to travelers dates back to the earliest days of Colonial America. Hotels and inns were few and far between in those days, and wayfarers relied on the kindness of strangers to provide a bed for the night. Which is why, perhaps, there is hardly a Colonial-era home in the mid-Atlantic states that does not boast: "George Washington Slept Here!"

During the Depression, the tourist home provided an economic advantage to both the traveler and the host. Travelers always drove through the center of town; there were no superhighways to bypass local traffic. A house with a sign in the front yard reading "Tourists" or "Guests" indicated that a traveler could rent a room for the night and have a cup of coffee before leaving in the morning. The usual cost for this arrangement was $2. The money represented needed income for the proprietor as well as the opportunity to chat with an interesting visitor.

In the 1950s, the country guest house became a popular alternative to the costly hotels in resort areas. The host compensated for the lack of hotel amenities, such as private bathrooms, by providing comfortable bedrooms and bountiful breakfasts at a modest price. The visitors enjoyed the home-away-from-home atmosphere; the hosts were pleased to have paying houseguests.

The incredible growth in international travel that has occurred over the past 30 years has provided yet another stimulus. Millions of Americans now vacation annually in Europe and travelers have become enchanted with the bed and breakfast concept so popular in Britain, Ireland, and other parts of the continent. In fact, many well-traveled Americans are delighted to learn that we "finally" have B&Bs here. But, as you now know, they were always here . . . just a rose by another name.

Bed and breakfasts are for:

- **Parents of college kids:** Tuition is costly enough without the added expense of "Parents' Weekends." Look for a B&B near campus.
- **Parents traveling with children:** A family living room, play room, or backyard is preferable to the confines of a motel room.
- **"Parents" of pets:** Many proprietors will allow your well-behaved darling to come too. This can cut down on the expense and trauma of kenneling Fido.
- **Business travelers:** Being "on the road" can be lonely and expensive. It's so nice, after a day's work, to return to a home-away-from-home.
- **Women traveling alone:** Friendship and conversation are the natural ingredients of a B&B.
- **Skiers:** Lift prices are lofty, so it helps to save some money on lodging. Many mountain homes include home-cooked meals in your room rate.
- **Students:** A visit with a family is a pleasant alternative to camping or the local "Y."
- **Visitors from abroad:** Cultural exchanges are often enhanced by a host who can speak your language.
- **Carless travelers:** If you plan to leave the auto at home, it's nice to know that many B&Bs are convenient to public transportation. Hosts will often arrange to meet your bus, plane, or train for a nominal fee.
- **Schoolteachers and retired persons:** Exploring out-of-the-way places is fun and will save you money.
- **History buffs:** Many B&Bs are located in areas important to our country's past. A number have the distinction of being listed on the National Register of Historic Places.

- **Sports fans:** Tickets to championship games are expensive. A stay at a B&B helps to defray the cost of attending out-of-town events.
- **Antique collectors:** Many hosts have lovely personal collections, and nearby towns are filled with undiscovered antique shops.
- **House hunters:** It's a practical way of trying out a neighborhood.
- **Relocating corporate executives:** It's more comfortable to stay in a real home while you look for a permanent residence. Hosts will often give more practical advice than professional realtors.
- **Relatives of hospitalized patients:** Many B&Bs are located near major hospitals. Hosts will offer tea and sympathy when visiting hours are over.
- **Convention and seminar attendees:** Staying at a nearby B&B is less expensive than checking into a hotel.

And everyone else who has had it up to here with plastic motel monotony!

What It Is Like to Be a Guest in a B&B

The B&B descriptions provided in this book will help you choose the places that have the greatest appeal to you. A first-hand insight into local culture awaits you; imagine the advantage of arriving in New York City or San Francisco and having an insider to help you sidestep the tourist traps and direct you to that special restaurant or discount store. Or explore the countryside, where fresh air and home-cooked meals beckon. Your choice is as wide as the U.S.A.

Each bed and breakfast listed offers personal contact, a real advantage in unfamiliar environments. You may not have a phone in your room or a TV on the dresser. You may even have to pad down the hall in robe and slippers to take a shower, but you'll discover little things count:

- In Williamsburg, Virginia, a visitor from Germany opted to stay at a B&B to help improve her conversational English. When the hostess saw that she was having difficulty understanding directions, she personally escorted her on a tour of Old Williamsburg.

- In Pennsylvania, the guests mistakenly arrived a week prior to their stated reservation date and the B&B was full. The hostess made a call to a neighbor who accommodated the couple. (By the way, the neighbor has now become a B&B host!)
- In New York City, the guest was an Emmy Award nominee and arrived with his tuxedo in need of pressing. The hostess pressed it; when he claimed his award over nationwide TV, he looked well groomed!

Expect the unexpected, like a pot of coffee brewed upon your arrival or fresh flowers on the nightstand. At the very least, count on our required standard of cleanliness and comfort. Although we haven't personally visited all the places listed, many have been highly recommended by Chambers of Commerce or former guests. We have either spoken to or corresponded with all the proprietors; they are a friendly group of people who enjoy having visitors. They will do all in their power to make your stay memorable.

Our goal is to enable the traveler to crisscross the country and stay only at B&Bs along the way. To achieve this, your help is vital. Please take a moment to write us of your experiences; we will follow up on every suggestion. Your comments will serve as the yardstick by which we can measure the quality of our accommodations. For your convenience, an evaluation form is included at the back of this book on page 697.

Cost of Accommodations

Bed and Breakfast, in the purest sense, is a private home, often referred to as a "homestay," where the owners rent their spare bedrooms to travelers. These are the backbone of this book.

However, American ingenuity has enhanced this simple idea to include more spectacular homes, mansions, small inns, and intimate hotels. With few exceptions, the proprietor is the host and lives on the premises.

There is a distinction between B&B homestays and B&B inns. Inns are generally defined as a business and depend upon revenue from guests to pay expenses. They usually have six or more guest rooms, and may have a restaurant that is open to the public. The tariff at inns is usually higher than at a "homestay" because the owners must pay the mortgage, running expenses, and staff, whether or not guests come.

Whether plain or fancy, all B&Bs are based on the concept that people are tired of the plastic monotony of motels and are disappointed that even the so-called budget motels can be quite expensive. Travelers crave the personal touch and they sincerely enjoy "visiting" rather than just "staying."

Prices vary accordingly. There are places in this book where lovely lodging may be had for as low as $10 a person a night and others that feature a gourmet breakfast in a canopied bed for $85. Whatever the price, if you see the sign ✪, it means that the B&B has guaranteed its rates through 1988 to holders of this book, so be sure to mention it when you call or write! (If there is a change in ownership, the guarantee may not apply. Please notify us in writing if any host fails to honor the guaranteed rate.)

Accommodations vary in price depending upon the locale and the season. Peak season usually refers to the availability of skiing in winter and water sports in summer; in the sunbelt states, the winter months are usually the peak season. Some B&Bs require a two-night weekend minimum during peak periods, and three nights on holiday weekends. Off-season rate schedules are usually reduced. Resorts and major cities are generally more expensive than out-of-the-way places. However, B&Bs are always less expensive than hotels and motels of equivalent caliber in the same area. A weekly rate is usually less expensive than a daily rate. Special reductions are sometimes given to families (occupying two rooms) or senior citizens. Whenever reduced rates are available, you will find this noted in the individual listings.

Meals

Breakfast: "Continental" refers to fruit or juice, rolls, and a hot beverage. Many hosts pride themselves on home-baked breads, homemade preserves, plus imported teas and cakes, so their Continental breakfast may be quite deluxe. Several hosts have regular jobs outside the home so you may have to adjust your schedule to theirs. A "full" breakfast includes fruit, cereal and/or eggs, breakfast meats, breads, and hot beverage. The table is set family-style and is often the highlight of a B&B's hospitality. Either a Continental breakfast or full breakfast is included in the room rate unless otherwise specified.

Other Meals: If listed as "available," you can be assured that the host takes pride in his or her cooking skills. The prices for lunch or dinner are usually reasonable but are not included in the quoted room rate unless clearly specified as "included."

Making Reservations

- Reservations are a MUST or you may risk missing out on the accommodations of your choice. Reserve *early* and confirm with a deposit equal to one night's stay. If you call to inquire about reservations, please remember the difference in time zones. When dialing outside of your area, remember to dial the digit "1" before the area code.
- Many individual B&Bs now accept charge cards. This information is indicated in the listings by the symbols "MC" for Master Card, "AMEX" for American Express, etc. A few have a surcharge for this service, so inquire as to the policy.
- Cash or traveler's checks are the accepted method of paying for your stay. Be sure to inquire whether or not tax is included in the rates quoted so that you will know exactly how much your lodging will cost.
- Rates are based on single or double occupancy of a room as quoted. Expect that an extra person(s) in the room will be charged a small additional fee. Inquire when making your reservation what the charge will be.
- If a listing indicates that children or pets are welcome, it is expected that they will be well behaved. All of our hosts take pride in their homes and it would be unfair to subject them to circumstances where their possessions might be abused or the other houseguests disturbed by an unruly child or animal.
- Please note that many hosts have their own resident pets. If you are allergic or don't care to be around animals, inquire before making a reservation.
- In homes where smoking is permitted, do check to see if it is restricted in any of the rooms. Most hosts object to cigars.
- Where listings indicate that social drinking is permitted, it usually refers to your bringing your own beverages. Most hosts will provide ice; many will allow you to chill mixers in the refrigerator, and others offer complimentary wine and snacks. A few B&B inns have licenses to sell liquor. Any drinking should not be excessive.
- If "Yes" is indicated in the listings for airport/station pickup, it

means that the host will meet your plane, bus, or train for a fee.
- Feel free to request brochures and local maps so you can better plan for your visit.
- Do try to fit in with the host's house rules. You are on vacation; he isn't!
- A reservation form is included at the back of this book for your convenience; just tear it out and send it in to the B&B of your choice.

Cancellations

Cancellation policies vary from one B&B to another, so be sure to read the fine print on the reservation form. Many require a 15-day notice to refund the entire deposit, after which they will refund only if the room is rebooked. When a refund is due, most keep a "processing fee" and return the balance. A few keep the deposit and apply it to a future stay.

While the above may seem harsh, please keep in mind that B&Bs are not hotels, which commonly overbook and where no-show guests can easily be replaced. Your host may have turned down a prospective guest and may have bought special breakfast food in anticipation of your visit and should not be penalized. If you feel you've been unfairly treated in a cancellation situation, please do let us know.

B&B Reservation Services

There are many host families who prefer not to be individually listed in a book, and would rather have their houseguests referred by a coordinating agency. The organizations listed in this book are all members of the Tourist House Association. They all share our standards regarding the suitability of the host home as to cordiality, cleanliness, and comfort.

The majority do a marvelous job of matching host and guest according to age, interests, language, and any special requirements. To get the best match, it is practical to give them as much time as possible to find the host home best tailored to your needs.

Many have prepared descriptive pamphlets describing the homes on their rosters, the areas in which the homes are located, and information regarding special things to see and do. *Send a self-addressed, stamped, business-size envelope to receive a descriptive directory by return mail along with a reservation form for you to complete.* When returning the form, you will be asked to select the home or homes listed in the brochure that most appeal to you. (The homes are usually given a code number for reference.) The required deposit should accompany your reservation. Upon receipt, the coordinator will make the reservation and advise you of the name, address, telephone number, and travel instructions for your host.

A few agencies prepare a descriptive directory and *include* the host's name, address, and telephone number so that you can contact the host and make your arrangements directly. They charge anywhere from $2 to $5 dollars for the directory.

Several agencies are *membership* organizations, charging guests an annual fee ranging from $5 to $25 per person. Their descriptive directories are free to members and a few of them maintain toll-free telephone numbers for reservations.

Most reservation services have a specific geographic focus. The coordinators are experts in the areas they represent. They can often make arrangements for car rentals, theater tickets, and touring suggestions, and offer information in planning a trip best suited to your interests.

Most work on a commission basis with the host, and that fee is included in the room rates quoted in each listing. Some make a surcharge for a one-night stay; others require a two- or three-night minimum stay for holiday periods or special events. Some will accept a credit card for the reservation but the balance due must be paid to the host in cash or traveler's checks.

All of their host homes offer Continental breakfast and some may include a full breakfast.

Many reservation services in the larger cities have, in addition to the traditional B&Bs, a selection of apartments, condominiums, and houses *without hosts in residence.* This may be appealing to those travelers anticipating an extended stay in a particular area.

The statewide services are listed first in the section for each state. City or regionally based organizations are listed first under the heading for that area. For a complete description of their services, look them up under the city and state where they're based.

NOTE: When calling, do so during normal business hours (for that time zone), unless otherwise stated. Collect calls are not accepted.

2

How to Start Your Own B&B

What It's Like to Be a Host

Hosts are people who like the idea of accommodating travelers and sharing their home and the special features of their area with them. They are people who have houses too large for their personal needs and like the idea of supplementing their income by having people visit. For many, it's a marvelous way of meeting rising utility and maintenance costs. For young families, it is a way of buying and keeping that otherwise-too-large house and furnishing it, since many of the furnishings may be tax deductible. Another advantage is that many state and local governments have recognized the service that some host families perform. In browsing through this book you will note that some homes are listed on the National Historic Register. Some state governments allow owners of landmark and historical houses a special tax advantage if they are used for any business purpose. Check with the Historical Preservation Society in your state for details.

If you have bedrooms to spare . . . if you sincerely like having overnight guests . . . if your home is clean and comfortable . . . this is an opportunity to consider. It is a unique business because *you* set the time of the visit and the length of stay. (Guest houses are not boarding homes.) You invite the guests at *your* convenience, and the extras, such as meals, are entirely up to you. You can provide a cup of coffee, complete meals, or just a room and shared bath. Remember that your income may be erratic and should not be depended upon to pay for monthly bills. However, it can afford you some luxuries.

Although the majority of hosts are women, many couples are finding pleasure in this joint venture. The general profile of a typical host is a friendly, outgoing, flexible person who is proud of his or her home and hometown. The following information and suggestions represent a guideline to consider in deciding whether becoming a B&B host is really for you.

There are no set rules for the location, type, or style of a B&B. Apartments, condos, farmhouses, town houses, beach houses, vacation cottages, houseboats, mansions, as well as the traditional one-family dwelling are all appropriate. The important thing is for the host to be on the premises. The setting may be urban, rural, or suburban; near public transportation or in the hinterlands. Location is only important if you want to have guests every night. Areas where tourism is popular, such as resort areas or major cities, are often busier than out-of-the-way places. However, if a steady stream of visitors is not that important or even desirable, it doesn't matter where you are. People will contact you if your rates are reasonable and if there is something to see and do in your area, or if it is near a major transportation route.

Setting the Rates

Consider carefully four key factors in setting your rates: location, private vs. shared bath, type of breakfast, and your home itself.

Location: If you reside in a traditional resort or well-touristed area, near a major university or medical center, or in an urban hub or gateway city, your rates should be at least 40% lower than those of the area's major motels or hotels. If you live in an out-of-the-way location, your rates must be extremely reasonable. If your area has a "season"—snow sports in winter, water sports in summer—offer off-season rates when these attractions are not available. Reading through this book will help you to see what is the going rate in a situation similar to yours.

The Bath: You are entitled to charge more for a room with private bath. If the occupants of two rooms share one bath, the rate should be less. If more than five people must share one bathroom, you may have complaints, unless your rates are truly inexpensive.

The Breakfast: Figure the approximate cost of your ingredients, plus something for your time. Allow about $1 to $2 for a Continental breakfast; $2 to $3 for a full American breakfast; then *include* it in the rate.

Your Home: Plan on charging a fair and reasonable rate for a typical B&B home, one that is warm and inviting, clean and comfortable. If your home is exceptionally luxurious, with king-size beds, Jacuzzi baths, tennis courts, or hot tubs, you will find guests who are willing to pay a premium. If your home is over 75 years old, well restored, with lots of antiques, you may also be able to charge a higher rate.

The Three B's—Bed, Breakfast, and Bath

The Bedroom: The ideal situation for a prospective host is the possession of a house too large for current needs. The children may be away at college most of the year or may have left permanently, leaving behind their bedrooms and, in some cases, the extra bath. Refurbishing these rooms does not mean refurnishing; an extraordinary investment need not be contemplated for receiving guests. Take a long, hard look at the room. With a little imagination and a little monetary outlay, could it be changed into a bedroom *you'd* be pleased to spend the night in? Check it out *before* you go any further. Are the beds comfortable? Is the carpet clean? Are the walls attractive? Do the curtains or shades need attention? Are there sturdy hangers in the closet? Would emptying the closet and bureau be an impossible task? Is there a good light to read by? A writing table and comfortable chair? A mirror? Peek under the bed and see if there are dust balls or old magazines tucked away. While relatives and friends would "understand" if things weren't perfect, a paying guest is entitled to cleanliness and comfort.

If the idea of sprucing up the room has you overwhelmed, forget the idea and continue to be a guest rather than a host! If, however, a little "spit and polish," replacement of lumpy mattresses, sagging springs, and freshening the room in general presents no problem . . . continue!

Mattresses should be firm, covered with a mattress pad, attrac-

Jackson Street Inn
Janesville, Wisconsin

tive linens, and bedspread. Although seconds are OK, good quality linens are a wise investment, since cheap sheets tend to pill. Offer a selection of pillows of different firmnesses—a choice of down or fiberfill is the ultimate in consideration! Twin beds are often preferred, since many people do not wish to share a bed. Sofa beds are really not comfortable and should be avoided. Is there a bedside lamp and night table on each side of the bed? Bulbs should be 75 watts for comfortable reading. A luggage rack is convenient for guests and keeps the bedspread clean. Provide a varied assortment of books, current magazines in a rack, a local newspaper, and some information on what's doing in your town along with a map. If yours is a shared-bath accommodation, do provide a well-lit mirror and convenient electric outlet for makeup and shaving purposes. It will take the pressure off the bathroom! A fresh thermos of ice water and drinking glasses placed on an attractive dresser tray is always appreciated. Put it in the room while the guest is out to dinner, right next to the dish of hard candy or fruit. A fancy candlestick is a pretty accessory and a useful object in case of a power failure. Dresser drawers should be clean and lined with fresh paper. A sachet, flashlight, and a pad and pencil are thoughtful touches. For safety's sake, prohibit smoking in the bedroom. Besides, the odor of tobacco clings forever. Always spray the bedroom with air freshener a few minutes before the guest arrives. On warm or humid days, turn on the air-conditioner as well.

From time to time sleep in each guest room yourself. It's the best test.

The Breakfast: Breakfast time can be the most pleasant part of the guest's stay. It is at the breakfast table with you and the other guests that suggestions are made as to what to see and do, and exchanges of experiences are enjoyed. From a guest's point of view, the only expected offering is what is known as Continental breakfast, which usually consists of juice, roll, and coffee or tea.

Breakfast fare is entirely up to you. If you are a morning person who whips out of bed at the crack of dawn with special recipes for muffins dancing in your head, to be drenched with your homemade preserves followed by eggs Benedict, an assortment of imported coffee or exotic tea . . . hop to it! You will play to a most appreciative audience. If, however, morning represents an awful intrusion on sleep and the idea of talking to anyone before noon is difficult, the least you should do is to prepare the breakfast table the night before with the necessary mugs, plates, and silverware. Fill the electric coffee pot and leave instructions that the first one up should plug it in; you can even hook it up to a timer, so that it will brew automatically!

Most of us fall somewhere in between these two extremes. Remember that any breakfast at "home" is preferable to getting dressed, getting into the car, and driving to some coffee shop. Whether you decide upon "Continental breakfast" or a full American breakfast, consisting of juice or fruit, cereal or eggs, possibly bacon or sausage, toast, rolls, coffee, or tea, is up to you. It is most important that whatever the fare, it be included

The Bayberry Inn
Peebles, Ohio

in your room rate. It is most awkward, especially after getting to know and like your guests, to present an additional charge for breakfast.

Some Suggestions:

- Don't have a messy kitchen. If you have pets, make sure their food dishes are removed after they've eaten. If you have cats, make sure they don't walk along the counter tops, and be certain that litter boxes are cleaned without fail. Sparkling clean surroundings are far more important than the decor.
- Let guests know when breakfast will be served. Check to see if they have any allergies, diet restrictions, or dislikes. Vary the menu if guests are staying more than one night.
- Do offer one nonsweet bread for breakfast.
- Consider leaving a breakfast order sheet in each room with a request that it be returned before guests retire. It might read:

We serve breakfast between 7 AM and 10 AM. Please check your preference and note the time at which you plan to eat.
☐ Coffee ☐ Tea ☐ Milk ☐ Decaf ☐ Muffins ☐ Sweet Rolls
☐ Toast ☐ Orange Juice ☐ Tomato Juice ☐ Fruit Cup

The Bath: This really is the third "B" in "B&B." If you are blessed with an extra bathroom for the exclusive use of a guest, that's super. If guests will have to share the facilities with others, that really presents no problem. If it's being shared with your family, the family must always be "last in line." Be sure that they are aware of the guest's importance; the guest, paying or otherwise, always comes first. No retainers, or used Band-Aids, or topless toothpaste tubes are to be carelessly left on the sink. The tub, shower, floor, and toilet bowl are to be squeaky clean. The mirrors and chrome should sparkle and a supply of toilet tissue, fresh soap, and unfrayed towels go a long way in reflecting a high standard of cleanliness. Make sure that the grout between tiles is free of mildew and that the shower curtain is unstained; add nonskid tape to the tub. Cracked ceilings should be repaired, the paint free of chips, and if your bath is wallpapered, make certain no loose edges mar its beauty.

Although it is your responsibility to check out the bath at least twice a day, most guests realize that in a share-the-bath situation they should leave the room ready for the next person's use. It is a thoughtful reminder for you to leave tub cleanser, a cleaning towel or sponge, and bathroom deodorant handy for this purpose. A wastepaper basket, paper towels, and paper cups should be part of your supplies. Needless to say, your hot water and septic systems should be able to accommodate the number of guests you'll have without being overtaxed. Call the plumber to fix any clogged drains or dripping faucets. Make sure that there are enough towel bars and hooks to accommodate the towels. Extra bathroom touches:

- Use liquid soap dispensers in lieu of bar soap on the sink.
- Provide a place for guests' personal toilet articles; shelves add convenience and eliminate clutter.
- Give different colored towels to each guest.
- Supply each guest room with its own bath soap in a covered soap dish.
- Provide guests with one-size-fits-all terry robes.

The B&B Business

Money Matters: Before embarking upon any business, it's a good idea to discuss it with an accountant and possibly an attorney. Since you'll be using your home for a business enterprise there are things with which they are familiar that are important for you to know. For instance, you may want to incorporate, so find out what the pros and cons are. Ask about depreciation. Deductible business expenses may include refurbishing, furnishings, supplies, printing costs, postage, etc. An accountant will be able to guide you with a simple system of record keeping. Accurate records will help you analyze income and expense, and show if you are breaking even, or operating at a profit or a loss.

Taxes: Contact your state department of taxation requesting specific written information regarding tax collection and payment schedules. Get a sales tax number from your county clerk. If you rent rooms less than 15 days a year, you need not report the B&B income on your federal return. Income after the fourteenth day is taxable, and you can take deductions and depreciation allowances against it. If the revenues from running the B&B are insignificant, you can call it "hobby income" and avoid taxes. However, you can't qualify as a business and may lose other tax advantages.

Record Keeping: Open a B&B checking account and use it to pay expenses and to deposit all income, including sales tax. Write checks whenever possible for purchases; get dated receipts when you can. Estimate the cost of serving breakfast and multiply it by the number of guests you feed annually; keep track of extra expenses for household supplies and utilities.

The Case for Credit Cards: Many guests prefer to stay now and pay later; business travelers like the easy record keeping for their expense sheets. Even if you don't wish to accept them on a regular basis, credit cards give you the opportunity to take a deposit over the phone when there isn't time to receive one by mail. The cost is negligible, generally 4%.

If you do accept a last-minute reservation without a credit card number to guarantee it, make certain the caller understands that if they don't show up, and you have held the room for them, you will have lost a night's rent. You may also remind them that if they aren't there by a mutually-agreed-upon time, you may rent the room to someone else. Needless to say, it is equally important for you to remain at home to receive the guests or to be on hand for a phone call should they get lost en route to your home.

Insurance: It is important to call your insurance broker. Many home-owner policies have a clause covering "an occasional overnight paying guest." See if you will be protected under your existing coverage and, if not, what the additional premium would be. As a member of the THAA, you may participate in our group liability policy under the auspices of Brown, Schuck, Townshend, and Associates.

Every home should be equipped with smoke detectors and fire extinguishers. All fire hazards should be eliminated; stairways and halls should be well lit and kept free of clutter. If you haven't already done so, immediately post prominently the emergency numbers for the fire department, police, and ambulance service.

Regulations: If you have read this far and are still excited about the concept of running a B&B, there are several steps to take at this point. As of this writing, there don't seem to be any specific laws governing B&Bs. Since guests are generally received on an irregular basis, B&Bs do not come under the same laws governing hotels and motels. And since B&Bs aren't inns where emphasis is on food rather than on lodging, no comparison can really be made in that regard either. As the idea grows, laws and regulations will probably be passed. Refer to the back of *Bed & Breakfast U.S.A.* and write to your state's office of tourism for information. The address and phone number are listed for your convenience. You might even call or write to a few B&Bs in your state and ask the host about his or her experience in this regard. Most hosts will be happy to give you the benefit of their experience, but keep in mind that they are busy people and it would be wise to limit your intrusion upon their time.

If you live in a traditional, residential area and you are the first in your neighborhood to consider operating a B&B, it would be prudent to examine closely the character of houses nearby. Do physicians, attorneys, accountants, or psychologists maintain offices in their residences? Do dressmakers, photographers, cosmeticians, or architects receive clients in their homes? These professions are legally accepted in the most prestigious communities as "Customary House Occupations." Bed and breakfast has been tested in many communities where the question was actually brought to court. In towns from La Jolla, California, to Croton-on-Hudson, New York, bed and breakfast has been approved and accepted.

Zoning boards are not always aware of the wide acceptance of the B&B concept. Possibly the best evidence that you could present to them is a copy of *Bed & Breakfast U.S.A.*, which indicates that it is an accepted practice throughout the entire country. It illustrates the caliber of the neighborhoods, the beauty of the homes, and the fact that many professionals are also hosts. Reassure the zoning board that you will accept guests only by advance reservation. You will not display any exterior signs to attract attention to your home. You will keep your home and grounds properly maintained, attractive, and in no way detract from the integrity of your neighborhood. You will direct guests to proper parking facilities and do nothing to intrude upon the privacy of your neighbors.

After all, there is little difference between the visit of a family friend and a B&B guest, because that is the spirit and essence of a B&B. Just as a friend would make prior arrangements to be a houseguest, so will a B&B guest make a reservation in advance of arriving. Neither would just "drop in" for an overnight stay. We are happy to share letters from hosts attesting to the high caliber, honesty, and integrity of B&B guests that come as a result of reading about their accommodations in this book. There are over 12,000 B&Bs extending our kind of hospitality throughout the United States and the number is increasing geometrically every day.

You should also bring along a copy of *Bed & Breakfast U.S.A.* when you go to visit the local Chamber of Commerce. Most of them are enthusiastic, because additional visitors mean extra business for local restaurants, shops, theaters, and businesses. This is a good time to inquire what it would cost to join the Chamber of Commerce.

The Name: The naming of your B&B is most important and will take some time and consideration because this is the moment when dreams become reality. It will be used on your brochures, stationery, and bills. (If you decide to incorporate, the corporation needs a name!) It should somehow be descriptive of the atmosphere you wish to convey.

Brochure: Once you have given a name to your house, design a brochure. The best ones include a reservation form and can be mailed to your prospective guests. The brochure should contain the name of your B&B, address, phone number, best time to call, your name, a brief description of your home, its ambience, a brief history of the house if it is old, the number of guest rooms, whether or not baths are shared, the type of breakfast served, rates, required deposit, minimum stay requirement if any, dates when you'll be closed, and your cancellation policy. Although widely used, the phrase "Rates subject to change without notice" should be avoided. Rather, state the specific dates when the rates will be valid. A deposit of one night's stay is acceptable and the promise of a full refund if cancellation is received at least two weeks prior to arrival is typical. If you have reduced rates for a specific length of stay, families, senior citizens, etc., mention it.

If you can converse in a foreign language, say so, because many visitors from abroad seek out B&Bs; it's a marvelous plus to be able to chat in their native tongue. Include your policy regarding children, pets, or smokers, and whether you offer the convenience of a guest refrigerator or barbecue. It is helpful to include directions from a major route and a simple map for finding your home. It's a good idea to include a line or two about yourself and your interests, and do mention what there is to see and do in the area as well as proximity to any major university. A line drawing of your house is a good investment since the picture can be used not only on the brochure, but on your stationery, postcards, and greeting cards as well. If you can't have this taken care of locally, write the Tourist House Association. We have a service that can handle it for you.

Take your ideas to a reliable printer for his professional guidance. Don't forget to keep the receipt for the printing bill since this is a business expense.

Confirmation Letter: Upon receipt of a paid reservation, do send out a letter confirming it. You can design a form letter and have it offset by a printer, since the cost of doing so is usually nominal. Include the dates of the stay, number of people expected, the rate including tax, the cancellation policy, as well as explicit directions by car and, if applicable, by public transportation. A simple map reflecting the exact location of your home in relation to major streets and highways is most useful. It is a good idea to ask your guests to call you if they will be traveling and unavailable by phone for the week prior to their expected arrival. You might even want to include any of the house rules regarding smoking, pets, or whatever.

Successful Hosting

The Advantage of Hosting: The nicest part of being a B&B host is that you aren't required to take guests every day of the year. Should there be times when having guests would not be convenient, you can always say you're full and try to arrange an alternate date. But most important, keep whatever date you reserve. It is an excellent idea at the time reservations are accepted to ask for the name and telephone number of an emergency contact should you have to cancel unexpectedly. However, *never* have a guest come to a locked door. If an emergency arises and you cannot reach your prospective guests in time, do make arrangements for someone to greet them and make alternate arrangements so they can be accommodated.

House Rules: While you're in the "thinking stage," give some thought to the rules you'd like your guests to adhere to. The last thing you want for you or your family is to feel uncomfortable in your own home. Make a list of House Rules concerning arrival and departure during the guests' stay and specify when breakfast is served. If you don't want guests coming home too late, say so. Most hosts like to lock up at a certain hour at night, so arrange for an extra key for night owls. If that makes you uncomfortable, have a curfew on your House Rules list. If smoking disturbs you, confine the area where it's permitted.

Some guests bring a bottle of their favorite beverage and enjoy a drink before going out to dinner. Many hosts enjoy a cocktail hour too, and often provide cheese and crackers to share with the guests. B&Bs cannot sell drinks to guests since this would require licensing. If you'd rather no drinks be consumed in your home, say so.

Many hosts don't mind accommodating a well-behaved pet. If you don't mind or have pets of your own, discuss this with your guests before they pack Fido's suitcase. Your House Rules can even be included in your brochure. That way both the host and the guest are aware of each other's likes and dislikes, and no hard feelings are made.

Entertaining: One of the most appealing features of being a guest at a B&B is the opportunity of being able to visit in the evening with the hosts. After a day of sightseeing or business, it is most relaxing and pleasant to sit around the living room and chat. For many hosts, this is the most enjoyable part of having guests. However, if you are accommodating several people on a daily basis, entertaining can be tiring. Don't feel you'll be offending anyone by excusing yourself to attend to your own family or personal needs. The situation can be easily handled by having a room where you can retreat and offering your guests the living room, den, or other area for games, books, magazines, and perhaps the use of a television or bridge table. Most guests enjoy just talking to each other since this is the main idea of staying at a B&B.

The Telephone: This is a most important link between you and your prospective guests. As soon as possible, have your telephone number included under your B&B name in the White Pages. It is a good idea to be listed in the appropriate section in your telephone directory yellow pages. If your home phone is used for a lot of personal calls, ask the local telephone company about call-waiting service, or think about installing a separate line for your B&B. If you are out a lot, give some thought to using a telephone answering device to explain your absence and time of return, and record the caller's message. There is nothing more frustrating to a prospective guest than to call and get a constant busy signal or no answer at all. Request that the caller leave his name and address, "at the sound of the beep," so you can mail a reservation form. This will help eliminate the necessity of having to return long-distance calls. If the caller wants further information, he will call again at the time you said you'd be home.

B&B guests don't expect a phone in the guest room. However, there are times when they might want to use your phone for a long-distance call. In your House Rules list, suggest that any such calls be charged to their home telephone. Business travelers often have telephone charge cards for this purpose. In either case, you should keep a telephone record book and timer near your instrument. Ask the caller to enter the city called, telephone number, and length of call. Thus, you will have an accurate record should a charge be inadvertently added to your bill. Or, if you wish, you can add telephone charges to the guest bill. The telephone operator will quote the cost of the per-minute charge throughout the country for this purpose.

Maid Service: If you have several guest rooms and bathrooms, you may find yourself being a chambermaid as part of the business. Naturally, each guest gets fresh linens upon arrival. If a guest stays up to three days, it isn't expected that bed linen be changed every day. What is expected is that the room be freshened and the bath be cleaned and towels replaced every day. If you don't employ a full-time maid you may want to investigate the possibility of hiring a high school student on a part-time basis to give you a hand with the housekeeping. Many guests, noticing the absence of help, will voluntarily lend a hand, although they have the right to expect some degree of service, particularly if they are paying a premium rate.

Keys: A great many hosts are not constantly home during the day. Some do "hosting" on a part-time basis, while involved with regular jobs. There are times when even full-time hosts have to be away during the day. If the guests are to have access to the house while you are not on the premises, make extra keys and attach them to an oversize key chain. It is also wise to take a key deposit of $50 simply to assure return of the key. Let me add that in the 11 years of my personal experience, as well as in the opinions of other hosts, B&B guests are the most honest people you can have. No one has ever had even a washcloth stolen, let alone the family treasures. In fact, it isn't unusual for the guest to leave a small gift after a particularly pleasant visit. On the other hand, guests are sometimes forgetful and leave belongings behind. For this reason it is important for you to have their names and addresses so you can return their possessions. They will expect to reimburse you for the postage.

Registering Guests: You should keep a regular registration ledger for the guest to complete before checking in. The information should include the full name of each guest, home address, phone number, business address and telephone, and auto license number. It's a good idea to include the name and phone number of a friend or relative in case of an emergency. This information will serve you well for other contingencies, such as the guest leaving some important article behind, or an unpaid long-distance phone call, or the rare instance of an unpaid bill. You may prefer to have this information on your guest bill, which should be designed as a two-part carbon form. You will then have a record and the guest has a ready receipt. (Receipts are very important to business travelers!)

Settling the Bill: The average stay in a B&B is two nights. Since a deposit equal to one night's lodging is the norm, when to collect the balance is up to you. Most guests pay upon leaving, but if they leave so early that the settling of the bill at that time is inconvenient, you can request the payment the previous night. You might want to consider the convenience of accepting a major credit card but contact the sponsoring company first to see what percentage of your gross is expected for this service. If you find yourself entertaining more business visitors than vacationers, it might be something you should offer. Most travelers are aware that cash or traveler's checks are the accepted modes of payment. Accepting a personal check is rarely risky but again, it's up to you. You might include your preference in your brochure.

Other Meals: B&B means that only breakfast is served. If you enjoy cooking and would like to offer other meals for a fee, make sure that you investigate the applicable health laws. If you have to install a commercial kitchen, the idea might be too expensive for current consideration. However, allowing guests to store fixings for a quick snack or to use your barbecue can be a very attractive feature for families traveling with children or for people watching their budget. If you can offer this convenience, be sure to mention it in your brochure. (And, be sure to add a line to your House Rules that the guest is expected to clean up.) Some hosts keep an extra guest refrigerator on hand for this purpose.

It's an excellent idea to keep menus from your local restaurants on hand. Try to have a good sampling, ranging from moderately priced to expensive dining spots, and find out if reservations are required. Your guests will always rely heavily upon your advice and suggestions. After all, when it comes to your town, you're the authority! It's also a nice idea to keep informed of local happenings that might be of interest to your visitors. A special concert at the university or a local fair or church supper can add an extra dimension to their visit. If parents are visiting with young children they might want to have dinner out without them; try to have a list of available baby-sitters. A selection of guide books covering your area is also a nice feature.

The Guest Book: These are available in most stationery and department stores, and it is important that you buy one. It should contain designated space for the date, the name of the guest, home address, and a blank area for the guest's comments. They generally sign the guest book before checking out. The guest book is first of all a permanent record of who came and went. It will give you an idea of what times during the year you were busiest and which times were slow. Secondly, it is an easy way to keep a mailing list for your Christmas cards and future promotional mailings. You will also find that thumbing through it in years to come will recall some very pleasant people who were once strangers but now are friends.

Advertising: Periodically distribute your brochures to the local university, college, and hospital, since out-of-town visitors always need a place to stay. Let your local caterers know of your existence since wedding guests are often from out of town. If you have a major corporation in your area, drop off a brochure at the personnel office. Even visiting or relocating executives and salesmen enjoy B&Bs. Hotels and motels are sometimes overbooked; it wouldn't hurt to leave your brochure with the manager for times when there's no room for their last-minute guests. Local residents sometimes have to put up extra guests, so it's a good idea to take an ad out in your local school or church newspaper. The cost is usually minimal. Repeat this distribution process from time to time, so that you can replenish the supply of brochures.

Check the back of this book for the address of your state tourist office. Write to them, requesting inclusion in any brochures listing B&Bs in the state.

The best advertising is being a member of the Tourist House Association since all member B&Bs are fully described in this book, which is available in bookstores, libraries, and B&Bs throughout the U.S. and Canada. In addition, it is natural for THAA members to recommend each other when guests inquire about similar accommodations in other areas. The most important reason for keeping your B&B clean, comfortable, and cordial is that we are all judged by what a guest experiences in any individual Tourist House Association home. The best publicity will come from your satisfied guests who will recommend your B&B to their friends.

Additional Suggestions

Extra Earnings: You might want to consider a few ideas for earning extra money in connection with being a host. If guests consistently praise your muffins and preserves, you might sell attractively wrapped extras as take-home gifts. If you enjoy touring, you can plan and conduct a special outing, off the beaten tourist track, for a modest fee. In major cities, you can do such things as acquiring tickets for theater, concert, or sports events. A supply of *Bed & Breakfast U.S.A.* for sale to guests is both a source of income and gives every THAA member direct exposure to the B&B market. Think about offering the use of your washer and dryer. You may, if you wish, charge a modest fee to cover the service. Guests who have been traveling are thrilled to do their wash or have it done for them "at home" rather than wasting a couple of hours at the laundromat.

Several hosts tell me that a small gift shop is often a natural offshoot of a B&B. Items for sale could include handmade quilts, pillows, potholders, and knitted items. One host has turned his hobby of woodworking into extra income. He makes lovely picture frames, napkin rings, and footstools that many guests buy as souvenirs to take home. If you plan to do this, check with the Small Business Administration to inquire about such things as a resale license and tax collection; the Chamber of Commerce can advise in this regard.

Transportation: While the majority of B&B guests arrive by car, there are many who rely on public transportation. Some hosts, for a modest fee, are willing to meet arriving guests at airports, train depots, or bus stations. Do be knowledgeable about local transportation schedules in your area and be prepared to give explicit directions for your visitors' comings and goings. Have phone numbers handy for taxi service, as well as information on car rentals.

Thoughtful Touches: Guests often write to tell us of their experiences at B&Bs as a result of learning about them through this book. These are some of the special touches that made their visit special: fresh flowers in the guest room; even a single flower in a bud vase is pretty. One hostess puts a foil-wrapped piece of candy on the pillow before the guest returns from dinner. A small decanter of wine and glasses, or a few pieces of fresh fruit in a pretty bowl on the dresser are lovely surprises. A small sewing kit in the bureau is handy. Offer guests the use of your iron and ironing board, rather than having them attempt to use the bed or dresser. Writing paper and envelopes in the desk invite the guest to send a quick note to the folks at home. If your house sketch is printed on it, it is marvelous free publicity. A pre-bed cup of tea for adults and cookies and milk for children are always appreciated.

By the way, keep a supply of guest-comment cards in the desk, both to attract compliments as well as to bring your attention to the flaws in your B&B that should be corrected.

Join the Tourist House Association: If you are convinced that you want to be a host, and have thoroughly discussed the pros and cons with your family and advisers, complete and return the membership application found at the back of this book. Our dues are $20 annually. The description of your B&B will be part of the next issue of the book *Bed & Breakfast U.S.A.*, as well as in the interim supplement between printings. Paid-up members receive a complimentary copy of *Bed & Breakfast U.S.A.* You will also receive the THAA's newsletter; regional seminars and conferences are held occasionally and you might enjoy attending. And, as an association, we will have clout should the time come when B&B becomes a recognized industry.

Affiliating with a B&B Reservation Agency: Over 145 agencies are listed in *Bed & Breakfast U.S.A.* If you do not care to advertise your house directly to the public, consider joining one in your area. Membership and reservation fees, as well as the degree of professionalism, vary widely from agency to agency, so do check carefully.

Prediction for Success: Success should not be equated with money alone. If you thoroughly enjoy people, are well organized, enjoy sharing your tidy home without exhausting yourself, then the idea of receiving compensation for the use of an otherwise dormant bedroom will be a big plus. Your visitors will seek relaxing, wholesome surroundings and unpretentious hosts who open their hearts as well as their homes. Being a B&B host or guest is an exciting, enriching experience.

3

How to Start Your Own B&B Reservation Service Organization

by Megan Backer

About Megan: In 1980 Megan Backer founded *Megan's Friends*, the first and only private membership B&B/Reservation Service Organization in San Luis Obispo County, California. She devised simple and economical methods to operate the service as an informal part-time home hobby-business. Now, *Megan's Friends* has new owners and Megan is a B&B consultant, speaker, and fiction writer. Our thanks to her for contributing this chapter.

What's an RSO?

A Bed & Breakfast *Reservation Service Organization* (B&B/RSO) represents a group of B&B home owners or renters who have listed their lodgings with an RSO. The RSO owner (or manager or director or coordinator) arranges guest bookings in host homes. The RSO owner is in personal contact by telephone and/or letter with both guest and host. The guest does not arrange his own booking, but selects a home from the RSO's list, either weeks in advance by letter, or, more typically, during a telephone consultation with the owner several days to two weeks before his expected arrival.

Note: Read Chapter 2, *How to Start Your Own B&B*, again. You and your hosts need this information.

A Reservation Service Organization is just that. It is different from a B&B directory that is compiled, sold for a fee, and contains listings of B&B homes, owners' names, addresses, telephone numbers, and sometimes prices. If guests use this method of securing B&B reservations, they telephone hosts directly and arrange their own reservations. The homes on such a list may or may not be inspected by the compiler. A true RSO not only arranges bookings for the guests after detailed consultation, but promises dependable quality of accommodations and hospitality of hosts. Some RSOs charge a fee for their directory to help cover expenses; this amount should then be applied as a credit when reservations are made.

A local concentration of homes seems to be the best guarantee of individual, caring B&B service. The ideal number of homes for an RSO varies according to both the owner's and the hosts' available time, and the volume of guests. Generally, 10 to 25 homes usually permit the owner to maintain control of standards and know every host and home.

If the B&B/RSO grows too large, personal attention to each guest's needs may give way to automated efficiency. A small, well-organized RSO may net as much income for the time invested as a vast empire of homes in faraway places, without the tension of grueling hours, paid employees, and competition with motels.

Here is a typical RSO structure. (*Megan's Friends* differs in some respects, which will be noted parenthetically.)

1. Hosts pay a listing fee to their RSO: typically $50 to $75. (*Megan's Friends* had no host listing fee.)
2. The RSO retains 20% commission for each night's guest stay.
3. The RSO often requires a two-night minimum stay. (*Megan's Friends* accepted one-night stays.) The desirability of this requirement depends on your location. Is it a "pass-through" area or does it have attractions that detain travelers? An efficiently organized RSO can make money on one-night stays and often gains valuable goodwill and business otherwise lost.
4. The RSO provides hosts with screened guests, publicity, and bookkeeping assistance.
5. The RSO offers guests ease of booking, centralized information, and assurance of inspected homes.

The RSO owner maintains two relationships: one with hosts,

and the other with guests. Trust is an integral part of the business. Once lost, it is hard to rebuild. Nothing is more to be prized than the confidence of your hosts and guests.

Is It for You?

Several personal qualities are essential to a successful RSO owner: management and organizational skills, the ability to get along with a diverse group of people, and tact.

You will be the *manager* of a group of hosts and their homes. As such, your responsibilities are different from and greater than those of an individual host.

You advise prospective guests and help them make appropriate selections. Often you do this during a long-distance telephone call lasting five to ten minutes. You are responsible for quality control, complaints, compliments, and everything else you, the hosts, and the guests can think of; you must handle it using all the good taste and tact you can muster.

Do you have organizational ability? Do you have experience in working with people? Do you have, or can you obtain, helpful community contacts that will bring you hosts and guests? (For instance, a Chamber of Commerce membership, participation in your PTA, church, local sports.) Can you develop your own PR, becoming known locally through friendly community contacts, such as schools, banks, supermarkets, other businesses, and nationally, through letters and telephone calls to other B&B and RSO owners?

A useful background for a B&B/RSO owner could include interviewing skills (have you been a receptionist? teacher? survey-taker? counselor?), a friendly, trust-inspiring telephone voice, and good recordkeeping ability (do you balance the family checkbook, make appointments, write letters?). Success will come easily if you are efficient and have friendly good manners and enthusiasm for B&B.

Does It Make Sense in Your Area?

Educate yourself about the local attitudes toward B&Bs generally and about your proposed B&B/RSO specifically. Follow the usual sensible guideline for any beginning small business: be discreet. You do not want possible competitors to become established first; you do not want to instigate a rash of unnecessary restrictive local rulings; you do not want to alarm anyone's neighbors.

If you decide that local attitudes are benign and informed—or at least neutral—proceed to the next step. Does the volume of tourists and other travelers through or to your area warrant a B&B/RSO? Your Chamber of Commerce has these figures. Look at its brochures. What are the area attractions and how many visitors do they have? Are the motel/hotel rooms in your area fully booked? Is your area growing or declining in number of residents and tourists? Are other B&Bs already operating? Busy? Why? Why not? Is there a need for an RSO?

There are no formula numbers to answer these questions. Every location is unique. You must make a decision based on your own judgment and acquired knowledge, or consult an expert. (If you talk with a local business person, bank president, or Chamber of Commerce officer, be sure your discussion is confidential. Everyone is eager to tell a friend about a good new business idea.)

Getting Started

This list of needs is for present and future reference. Some items can wait until you've been in business for a few months. Save money and time until you know that your new B&B/RSO will succeed. Needs depending on your specific situation:

1. Equipment: Telephone with call-waiting and call-forwarding, or two telephone lines. Answering machine (with a friendly, informative message). Two ledgers.
2. Descriptive listing of B&Bs, guest and host applications, maps, and directions to host homes.
3. Business cards.
4. A rubber stamp with your business name, address, telephone.
5. Chamber of Commerce membership. One major, active, tourist-oriented group.
6. Business license. City, county, as applicable. Required.
7. Bank account under business name.
8. Membership in a *few* large B&B organizations for referrals. (First choice is the Tourist Home Association of America, Box 355A, RD 2, Greentown, Pennsylvania 18426. See page 691 for an application.)

9. Letters of introduction to other B&Bs enclosing your brochure and business card. (For example, write to selected B&B owners from this book.) Mail only to those who are apt to send referrals to you.
10. Fictitious business name statement. Required by the state for any business name that does not include the owner's surname. You must file this statement with your county clerk's office, and publish it for four consecutive weeks in a local newspaper. If your name is Kathy Jones and you decide to call your RSO "Seaside B&B," you'll need to file a statement. If you prefer to call it "Jones B&B," the name is not "fictitious" and no statement is needed.
11. Service mark, logo. Register with state. Optional, for protection of your name and logo.

Start very simply by signing up a few local homes (probably friends of yours) on your host application forms. Make yourself known at the local tourist centers and have a minimum order of business cards made.

Alone or with a Partner: A B&B/RSO is ideally operated by a couple who live on the premises—a mom-&-pop business. There is better telephone coverage and relief time for the partner who is not on duty. However, successful RSOs exist with one owner, or with two partners who do not live together. It can be difficult to find a compatible partner, and you may not want to halve your profits.

Start-up Expenses: Some RSOs have spent $10,000 on initial equipment, office rent, advertising, brochures, and so on. My own RSO started five years ago with $10! A reasonable sum might be $200 if you have the basic equipment already mentioned, and plan to work in your home.

Finances

Try out tax preparers—preferably an accountant—until you find one who is careful, honest, and knowledgeable. An accountant's advice and work for you will more than cover the (deductible) fee. He or she will know all of the tax deductions that apply to your part-time home business and can show you how to keep simple records during the year.

Open a special B&B bank account in your business name. There is usually no charge for this, although the bank may ask to see your fictitious business name statement. It is very convenient to have a rubber stamp made by the bank with your business name and account number on it for use in endorsing your numerous guests' checks for deposit.

Keep your income-expense ledger up-to-date daily to maintain an accurate record of payments and commissions. Sometimes your hosts or guests will challenge you about payments made; you cannot afford to be slipshod. Keep a record of all checks received (name, number, bank, date, amount) and sent as well as cash payments.

Establish a deposit-and-refund policy for guests and stick to it. Always quote your listed prices. Some guests will try to cut the price by requesting bed without breakfast or other options. Unless you have a resort situation in which guests typically stay a week or more, keep the price the same for each night. On request, quote special prices for group reservations, such as wedding parties, which are negotiated individually in advance with the host(s) involved.

Credit card use is optional. It increases your costs 2% to 5% and requires more record keeping. In my area, a famous large inn does not accept credit cards, but many businesses do. You may decide it is worthwhile to accept credit cards as a way of guaranteeing telephone reservations or for payment in full.

Legalities

Insurance coverage is still generally unregulated, and you will need to investigate your own state's rules. It is advisable to consult a lawyer to be sure you have correct wording on your host and guest forms that places liability responsibility on them, as you are only a booking agency. Setting up as a "private membership" organization may give you some legal protection, as you are then not in the business of serving the general public. (You must collect membership fees and retain signed member applications in your files.)

B&B regulations still vary widely, and government officials may not even be familiar with the term *B&B.* If yours is such a community, organize your RSO as simply, carefully, and legally as you can and wait for your local government to become informed. When the time comes, you may need to supply them with helpful information, so start collecting precedents and examples of how B&B is done elsewhere. For example: a large, well-known B&B/RSO successfully won a court case rescinding the collection of bed tax from B&B homes in that state.

Zoning requirements may apply to your B&B homes. You need to check local rules. This still seems to be a "point of view" question. There may be some B&B homes operating in local areas that are prohibited to you, but continue because they are listed with out-of-town RSOs and locations are unknown to local officials.

Check out your health department rules regarding the serving of food and drink. For example, serving liquor may require a special license. Let your host know this. It is best to avoid potential problems!

Host Relationships

Your hosts become your friends, since you talk with them often. Take a genuine interest in them. Treasure and appreciate them, for you are exchanging trust, confidence, and loyalty. Value your business relationship, but respect your friendship, too.

Signing Up Hosts: To get your first hosts, if you do not already have eager friends, do some local PR work. *Talk* about B&B and your new RSO *everywhere* to *everybody*. This is "word-of-mouth" awareness. Also, try to be interviewed (phone the newspaper's "new business" editor) for an article favorable to you, B&B, and B&B/RSO. Publicize your RSO by speaking about B&B to local groups who are always looking for new speakers and new topics. Visit the senior citizen's center, libraries, banks, churches, schools, stores, offices—leave your business card and your smile everywhere you go.

Avoid placing newspaper ads for hosts. You will find that you get many replies from unsuitable hosts with substandard homes. This will waste your time and test your tact in saying no gracefully.

Exclusive Listings: Exclusive listings are those homes that accept paying guests only through one RSO. If you opt for exclusive listings (some or all), try to keep them local. It's hard to know whether a less-used host of yours is "filling in the chinks" by accepting outside reservations. List, describe, and price your exclusive listings. List nonexclusives and referrals only by the name of their city.

Exclusive listings are a boon to you, for you have absolute knowledge of availability and can often complete a reservation on the first call. You use your exclusives more often; you know them well and you can count on the hosts' willingness, interest, and hospitality. Guests tend to choose homes that are described and priced, so will favor your exclusives. An RSO without some dependable exclusives obviously incurs more expense and frustration.

Sometimes B&B hosts are unhappy with their RSOs. They have told me that some RSOs are inconsiderate, inefficient, dishonest, send very few guests, require host fees, share no deposit money on cancellations, and so on! These hosts often ask to be added to your listings. Emphasize the need for new hosts to inform their former agencies if they have signed an exclusive agreement with you.

The Ideal Host: The ideal hosts are generally middle-aged or retired, well-educated world travelers. They enjoy having house guests and consider the money a bonus, not a necessity. They are usually available and flexible, so they naturally earn more money than those who often travel, or have headaches or other reasons for not taking guests. A host's popularity with guests will be enhanced by reasonable prices, fine beds, private baths, excellent breakfasts, and unflagging hospitality.

When you interview a prospective host, be direct and clear about your rules. *This* is the time to test the bed, check the bath and general housekeeping, and be assertive in speaking up about anything that does not meet your standards. Give second chances if there is an outstanding plus in the listing, such as an ocean view, scrumptious food, or charming hosts, but be sure the dirty windows are clean and the spiders are gone on your second visit. Reinspect host homes occasionally, with only a same-day telephone appointment with the host. The host whose room and bath are always ready is a habitual good housekeeper. Encourage it.

Host Instructions: When you enroll a new host, provide a list of requirements and suggestions similar to the following:

Memo to All Host Families

Required: Freshly laundered sheets (change every third day or with each new guest) and towels (change daily). Spotless room and bath. No personal items of yours in sight. Each guest room needs: a nightstand, a lamp to turn on from bed, two pillows and a wastepaper basket. Bed must be standard size (no hideabed, trundle, etc., for primary accommodation), firm, and used less than five years. Please, no used soaps, spiders, or other bugs! No pets are permitted in the guest room.

For breakfast: juice or fruit, protein (perhaps eggs), starch (perhaps a sweet bread), and a beverage. (Examples: pancakes, combining starch and protein, ham and eggs, or simply cold breakfasts. This is your choice.)

Suggested: Make up room same day guest departs; always be prepared for new guest, except for dusting, fresh flowers, and airing.

Stock freezer with staples such as breads, rolls, waffles, juices, instant coffee, ice cubes, etc. Stock a cold cereal and a hot cereal, fresh milk or half and half, tea, etc.

You may put a card with a typed list of your rules in each guest room. (Example: 8–9 AM breakfast, please close shower door when showering.) Some hosts think this is too intimidating and use no list. You need only be available for one hour in the morning to serve and talk with your guests. If you wish, volunteer help-yourself breakfast before or after the hour, or prepare a cold breakfast tray. Don't rattle around in the kitchen or house earlier than one hour prior to arranged breakfast time! Your guest's sleep WILL be disturbed.

Keep a calendar near phone for reservations. Mark unconfirmed reservations with a question. Always treat your guests as you would expect to be treated in a B&B home.

Note: Shy guests will appreciate being told which areas of your home and garden they may use.

Call RSO when you have a problem, and remember that everyone makes mistakes!

Undesirable Hosts: How can you turn away unwanted hosts tactfully? There is always a telephone conversation prior to home inspection. If you determine over the telephone that this home is not suitable—for example, it has a shared bath or old bed or grumpy host—you can graciously explain why the house does not meet the requirements of your RSO, but, "thank you very much for calling."

On the other hand, if the house sounds desirable, say that although you have no immediate need for another home, the situation may unexpectedly change, so you would like to come to see the home and meet the hosts.

Once there, if you want to list it, do so! Explain your system, especially the seniority preference you give to hosts who have been with you longer, if there are two similar homes available.

If you do not want the home, give praise anyway and repeat that there is no immediate need, but that you will call if the situation changes. (Of course, you never call.)

Rates: How do you arrive at the right price for a B&B rental? One helpful guideline is this: ask the prospective host—and yourself—how much you really would be willing to pay for a similar accommodation in someone's home when traveling. Also, how much are similar B&B homes in the area renting for? How busy are they? (Many overpriced B&B inns are now up for sale.) New hosts need to familiarize themselves with local prices and amenities offered by B&B homes, B&B inns, motels, and hotels. What can the prospective host offer? Color TV in the room? Private bath? King-size bed? Full or Continental breakfast? Children free? Swimming pool? Nearby restaurant?

Negotiating a fair price with your host is a delicate matter. It is up to you to understand human nature, to encourage hosts to comparison-shop fairly (not quote the price of the fanciest motel in town!), and to hold the line on prices. With a few hosts, greed eventually corrupts original intent.

Of course you should be fair to your hosts and list their rooms at the best price possible. With the standard commission, for every dollar your hosts earn, you receive 20 cents. If the price becomes too high, you will have a much harder job of "selling" the room, followed by complaints from your host that you aren't sending as many guests anymore!

RSO/Host Agreement: Sometimes a host will become a problem to you. Perhaps housekeeping or cooking inadequacies develop, or perhaps the host turns out to be either overbearing or indifferent, or perhaps the host inspects the guests' belongings during their absence from the home. Whatever the fatal flaw, you need to be aware of it and decide whether to keep the hosts and educate them or, if the problems—or hosts!—are intractable, to stop sending guests.

An RSO/host agreement clarifies your relationship. Here is one I devised, which is brief enough not to annoy new hosts, yet informative and protective to the RSO.

Host Application

This is a private membership B&B/RSO group. I will not accept paying guests from other sources. I will not refuse guests solely on the basis of color, creed, or marital status. I understand that (RSO name), its agents and employees, do not warrant the suitability of guests or vouch for their conduct. Accordingly, I hereby release and hold harmless (RSO name) from all liability arising out of my participation as a host member. I certify that I have homeowner's or renter's liability insurance covering my paying guests and I am responsible for obtaining and paying for any license, bed tax, etc. required by any government agency. For services, I will pay 20% of my rental fees, due weekly, to (RSO name).

SIGNATURE ______________________ DATE __________

ADDRESS ______________________________________

TELEPHONE ____________________________________

Price for one_____ Bed size_____ Price for two_____ Bed size_____
three_____ _____ four_____ _____

Specify your limitations, such as no children under a certain age, nights not available on a regular basis, etc.

List special features such as a wheelchair ramp. Resident dog or cat? Special treat always ready, such as fresh room flowers, new magazines, books, local tourist brochures? Tea?

Describe your home and yourself for listing guideline, mentioning features such as nearby attractions, garden, Jacuzzi, ocean view, beach, room features such as balcony, TV, breakfast specialties, areas of home that your guests may use, your occupation, hobbies, interests (tour guide, cooking, local flora and fauna, history, business, shopping, recreation).

Concise road directions to your home from major highway.

This agreement may be terminated in writing and with good cause with 30 days' notice by host or by (RSO name).

Host Finances

Advise your hosts (verbally and in writing) that it is wise to accept only cash or traveler's checks from the guests. If the host allows guests to write personal checks, they are to be made out to the host, not to the RSO. You do not need to take the (small) risk of a bad check from someone you haven't met. Also, tell your hosts to have change for $50 or $100; some guests do not have small bills. Guests usually pay cash at the host home or send personal checks in advance to the RSO.

If time has not allowed for any advance deposit, and you do not interview the guests at your office before their arrival at your host's home, the host may ask for payment on arrival. (My RSO policy was to ask for an advance deposit of 20% only, the balance being due on arrival. This greatly simplified bookkeeping and saved time.) Payment on arrival rather than at departure ensures a relaxed host. One "skip" and a host becomes sufficiently assertive and creative in getting payment promptly and pleasantly. Unless prepaid, guest payment is the host's responsibility.

Pay your hosts regularly. My RSO checks were sent every Monday and hosts agreed to send commissions due to the RSO every Monday. Most RSOs pay monthly or even bimonthly. Let your host know what to expect.

"Delayed payments" were the most frequent complaint I heard from hosts listed with other agencies, followed by resentment of the RSO owners' callous attitude or even neglect to notify the host when a guest cancelled. B&Bs have far fewer "no shows" than commercial travel agencies, but it does happen. If a deposit has been made but the guest does not materialize, it was my policy to split the amount equally with the host, to provide us both some compensation for our preparations. If no deposit had been made, we were both out of luck. So far as I know, sharing a forfeited deposit was unique with my RSO.

A price break I always gave was to forfeit my commission when my own hosts traveled and booked my RSO homes.

These generosities will be appreciated by your hosts. Fairness and concern for them results in their loyalty and best efforts for you. Don't take advantage of their good nature and let them do work that is really your responsibility as RSO owner. If you are consistently open and honest, and frankly admit your mistakes, you will maintain comfortable, cooperative relations with your hosts, guests, and other B&Bs.

Organizing Your Information

Simplicity and uniformity are the keys to good organization. Physically, your work area needs a typewriter, telephone, answering machine, pens and pencils, paper, your ledgers and a file cabinet with suspended hanging files, headed "Guest Applications," "Host Applications," "Brochures," "Maps," "PR," "Correspondence with guests, with RSO, with hosts," etc. (You can start with a cardboard box and manilla folders before investing in a file cabinet.)

After using individual host calendars, then recipe card files for two years, I devised a ledger system. At a glance, all the needed information about guests and hosts is available on an opened "double" page. Buy two inexpensive hard-bound simple ledgers (the other is for your expenses). Make your own headings, rule vertical lines as indicated. Examples are on the following pages.

LEDGER FOR BOOKINGS—COMMISSIONS

Month	Reserved Date	1st Call	Host Name	Guest Name & Phone	Address	Occupation	Referred By	Advance Deposit
Jan 1								
2								
3								
4								

If you have a small RSO, at bottom of each page list your regular host names and dates not available.

Smith 1, 4
Allen
Jones 1
Brown 2, 4

Donovan
Baker 1, 2, 4
etc.

LEDGER FOR EXPENSES

Date	Item	Paid Out	Travel, Entertainment	Outside Labor	Telephone	Office Supplies, Postage	Advertising
Jan 1							
2							
3							
4							

Host Nets	RSO Owes Host	RSO Commission	Total Fee	Application	List	Membership	Map	ETA

(ETA = estimated time of arrival. Check off the last four items after mailing them. Or write "H" if the host supplies on arrival.)

Automobile	Legal, Professional Fees	Taxes, Licenses	Equipment, Repairs	Referral Fees Paid Out	Dues, Publications

RSO/Guests Relationships

When guests call an RSO, they expect to be given a choice of suitable homes with detailed information about each so that they can comparison-shop, then make a selection over the telephone. If they are planning an extensive trip and have confidence in you, they will also make reservations for distant homes of yours or for your referral homes. Occasionally, guests will ask *you* to make the lodging selections for them.

Quote the same price for every guest reserving the same lodging. This evidences your reliability and fairness. Do not dicker or haggle, or agree to add on charges when cooperating with another B&B on a reservation. Be honest and friendly, but be firm about your listed prices.

If potential guests call only to "shop," ask if they would like to receive your brochure and application. Many future reservations will result.

Later on, if you can afford it, all the names and addresses you have collected make a fine bulk mailing list for sending out updated brochures.

Brochures and Printed Materials

Contrary to popular belief, I learned that guests in all income brackets trust a "homespun" simple copied listing sheet more than an expensive "commercial" brochure featuring, for example, lithography on parchment paper. Pass the savings on to the guests.

Many B&Bs are failing because they are overpriced. Most travelers look for a guarantee of CLEANLINESS, COMFORT, and CORDIALITY. Stress this in your brochure and forgo the chocolate on the bedpillow or the Victorian wallpaper, unless it is included at a reasonable price.

Your brochure should provide essential information for the guest, such as office hours, location and description of listings (partial or complete), your special rules, payment procedures, and of course, your own telephone and address. Most RSOs absorb mailing and printing costs and send their brochures at no charge. Next to your vocal salesmanship, appealing listings attract customers. Guests will happily mull over their choices. A honeymoon cottage on the ocean? A room and bath in town? Describe the advantages of each listing, including special features. Hire a writer if necessary. Beware of sounding like you're selling real estate. Think of what you, as a traveler, would want to know. Here is an excerpt of *Megan's Friends'* listing sheet:

Inspected Referrals
(not exclusive)

Angwin, Napa area, kitchen
Pebble Beach, kitchen
Orosi, Fresno-Sierras
Incline Village, Lake Tahoe
Santa Barbara, kitchen
Carpenteria
Ojai
Rancho Palos Verdes
Laguna Niguel
Newport Beach
El Cajon, pool
Sausalito, S. F. houseboat
San Diego, kitchen

Suggested Calling Hours

3:30 to 8:30 PM on school days; other hours when available, or messages taken. Weekends OK.

No Smoking Inside

Full breakfasts free at your option. Children, supervised, by permission. Usual check-in after 2, check-out by 10. Otherwise by arrangement. Notify if delayed over an hour. Reservations held 7 days pending receipt of deposit. Unpaid last-minute reservations held until 4 PM.

Payment: Personal check in advance for total amount or for $10 one-time membership plus 20% deposit for each night's stay. The balance is due in cash or traveler's checks *on arrival,* to host. (Membership and deposits *not* refundable but may be applied to a later date at any M.F. home if canceled at least 2 days ahead and reservation rescheduled within a 30-day limit.) Membership is waived for foreign guests—passport number requested. Gift certificates valid for 6 months. Personal help gladly given to members for U.S.A., Canada. Access to over 10,000 B&B accommodations of various types.

Sample Listings:

Monterey Area about 2 miles from Carmel center
Pines frame this floor-to-ceiling Bay view from inviting bed-sitting room with shower and tub bath, sliding glass door entrance from private deck, king or twin beds, small TV. Thoughtfully decorated, fresh and airy, breakfast in the solarium. 1/$50, 2/$60. Trundle bed for 3rd person in same room, add $10.

Cambria Area 7 miles south of Hearst Castle
Love seat, color TV, private patio with furniture, private entrance, twin beds; or, king bedroom. 1 mile to beach, easy drive to swimming pools, Moonstone Beach and Gardens, Hwy 46 to wineries, Cambria center's quaint shops. Quiet home at end of the road, flower garden, wildlife. 1/$40, 2/$50.

San Luis Obispo Area
Quiet neighborhood near hills and golf course. Cozy queen room or king master bedroom with glass doors onto patio-garden. Friendly, English hospitality. Local attractions include Old Mission San Luis Obispo de Tolosa (1772), Madonna Inn, historic tour of town, winery, lakes, and parks. Hearst Castle 45 min. No children. 1/$40, 2/$50 for queen.

Most RSOs require guest applications. By now, new RSOs generally copy established RSO forms, so most are similar. Your forms should contain information essential to the guest, such as your RSO policy on delays and cancellations, children, breakfasts, payment by cash, check, credit card, travelers check, and the amount of deposit. Essential to you are the guests' signatures, date signed, date of reservation, selected home, guests' address, telephones, employer, occupation, reference, allergies, special needs, arrival and departure times and dates.

Include a disclaimer of liability. This deters the possibility of lawsuits. To my knowledge, there have been none as of this writing—a great testimonial to both hosts and guests who "do" B&B. B&B/RSO insurance policies are just beginning to be written. Word your guest application carefully to afford you the greatest protection. Here is a sample *Megan's Friends* guest application:

Application

EXCLUSIVE LISTINGS
NO SMOKING INSIDE

PRINT NAME: ______________________________
Last First

Reservation
Dates: ______________________________________

First Word of Listing:
1st choice ________ 2nd ________ Host ________

Full breakfasts free at your option. Children by permission, supervised. Usual check-in after 2 PM, check-out by 10 AM. Other hours by arrangement. Notify if delayed over an hour. Reservations held 7 days pending receipt of deposit. Last-minute unpaid reservations held until 4 PM.

Payment: Personal check in advance for $10 membership fee + 20% deposit for each night's stay. Balance due to host in cash or traveler's check on arrival. (Membership and deposits not refundable, but may be applied to a later date at any home if you cancel at least 2 days in advance and reschedule your reservation within a 30-day limit.) Membership waived for foreign guests on presentation of passport. Personal help and referrals gladly given upon request. Thank you!

PRINT: NAME ______________ HOME ADDRESS ______________

CITY & STATE ___________________________ ZIP ____________

TELEPHONE: HOME _____________ BUSINESS _____________

OCCUPATION ______________ EMPLOYER ______________

PERSONAL REFERENCE (someone who knows you well—minister, teacher, employer—who would welcome you as a guest in his own home) NAME, ADDRESS, TELEPHONE: (Print)

____

ALLERGIES? ______________ SPECIAL NEEDS? ______________

APPROX. ARRIVAL TIME ________ ARRIVAL DATE ________

DEPARTURE ____

DISCLAIMER: MEGAN'S FRIENDS, agents or host families, shall not be responsible for any damage, injury, or loss incurred by any person as a result of the act, or omission, whether negligent, or not, of any person rendering accommodations offered by this agency. MEGAN'S FRIENDS does not warrant the suitability of hosts or their homes, or vouch for the conduct of participating guests. Accordingly, I hereby release and hold harmless MEGAN'S FRIENDS from all liability arising out of each occurrence of my participation as a guest member. Signature of each party indicates an acceptance of the terms and conditions listed above.

Signatures	**Date Signed**	**Each Member of Your Party**
______________	Date ______	______________ Date ______
______________	Date ______	______________ Date ______

If you are already a member, date of your membership: ________
Please enclose a stamped envelope for reservation confirmation, membership card, and directions to your host home. If all arrangements have been made, just mail back this application.

How Did You Discover Megan's Friends? ______________

After you receive a guest application returned by mail with a deposit or a check in full, make the appropriate notations in your booking ledger. Then call the host to confirm the reservation. Then send a confirmation letter to the guest, acknowledging the amount paid and the balance due, repeating the reservation date and enclosing a map and directions to the house. Here is a chance to convey your personal interest—wish them a safe journey, or a happy anniversary, or reassure them that grandmother will have no steps to climb to reach her room, or whatever is appropriate.

It is a good idea to supply guest evaluation postcards for your hosts to leave in their guest rooms, prepaid (P.O. cards) and addressed to your RSO. Many guests will use these to provide you with compliments or complaints.

Telephones

If you anticipate a busy RSO, you need two lines; one for personal and host calls, and the other for guest and business calls. Or, you may be able to manage with one number featuring call-forwarding and call-waiting. These features are worth their extra cost.

The skillful use of the telephone is most important. You need to extract considerable information from callers, select appropriate homes, convince the callers that this is what they want, and do it all with charm and speed. Callers dislike answering machines; more hurried guests will hang up and dial another B&B. Here is the recorded telephone message I used when I had to be absent from my desk: "Hello! Megan here. I *would* like to talk to you so will you please leave your name, number, address, and message? If this is long distance, may I return your call collect? Regular office hours are . . . (time zone) daily. Thank you!"

Your message needs to be businesslike, informative, short, and friendly. Your prospective guests risk their money and comfort on how you sound over the phone, so you had better sound good. *How* you say it (your tone and manner) is just as important as what you say. It is wise to check your tape occasionally to be sure your message is clear and your voice inviting, relaxed, happy, and efficient. Get a frank evaluation from an objective friend—or stranger!—about this.

Your request for collect return calls will keep your phone bill low. The callers say yes or tell you they'll call again. The caller's message generally includes reservation dates, desired types of lodging, and special needs. Before you call back, do some research.

If you are well organized, you can often nail everything down with the caller's long-distance call followed by your local call to your host. Naturally, whenever possible, you will use "smart phoning" such as evening and weekend calls, to reduce your costs; shop around to see which long-distance phone company offers the best deal.

For a new business, the more live telephone coverage you have, the better. When the other B&Bs are not answering their phones, you can build up your business by keeping *long* hours daily.

Guests often travel on the spur of the moment and pick up the phone from Anywhere, U.S.A., to call your agency for a reservation date *today,* or *tomorrow.* You have no time for a written letter of reference, advance deposit, or applications. In these cases, you need to have people-intuition. Collect as much personal information about the caller as you can.

Here is an example of a typical call from a guest. Have your booking ledger ready and either write directly in it or transfer information from your work pad of paper as soon as you hang up.

1. Listen; answer questions.
2. Get names, address, phone, booking date, occupation, reference if needed.
3. If booking date is far enough ahead, offer to send listings and application.
4. Explain your special rules, like private membership, no smoking, or whatever.
5. After determining guests' preferences, suggest a specific home, describe, make a tentative confirmation pending arrival by the deposit (and membership fee, if applicable).
6. Inform the caller that as soon as his check arrives, you will send a map, directions, host's name, address, and firm confirmation of his reservation. Also a list of your B&Bs and application if the guest does not already have one.

Don't increase the caller's long-distance charges with your inefficiency or with long-winded anecdotes. If the caller *wants* to chat, you will sense it. It is good telephone etiquette to let the originator of the call determine its length. (If you are very busy, of course you can graciously excuse yourself after collecting the necessary data.)

You may reduce inconvenience and lost income if you accept credit card numbers over the phone to confirm deposits on last-minute phone bookings. Decide whether the extra bookkeeping time is worth it.

Publicity and Promotion

Follow the advice given in Chapter 2 for individual B&Bs. Extra ideas for RSO publicity and promotion would include correspondence with far-flung B&Bs, your agency name in publications, inquiries for "hosting" of hosts or from guests who want to become your hosts "back home," and your addition of sidelines using your agency name, such as a recipe book, speeches, paperweights, dolls, etc.

Referrals

Sometimes the honor system of commission-splitting with another B&B works, post guest-stay. Some agencies collect their commission in advance, then refer the guest to you for the remaining payment. Others provide free referrals to save record-keeping time. You may find that you are boosting someone else's business by sending them referrals but not getting any referrals *or* split commissions in return. Keep a short list of reliable B&Bs who will send you 10% per night's stay (the travel industry standard) and concentrate on these referrals.

Write down the names of callers requesting referrals, then give them the appropriate phone number to call, advising them to say at once that you referred them. This record of names, dates, and referred B&Bs will let you determine which B&Bs will reliably send commissions. But realize that some guests will forget to mention you, mistakenly believe they will get a lower price if they don't, or will not follow through on your recommendation.

You may (sweetly!) tell the inquiring callers that you don't have time to research referrals unless the callers make a deposit. If they demur, suggest that they stop at your office to browse through your reference materials.

You will occasionally get a request to arrange an extended tour covering several states. Obtain an advance deposit to cover the cost of your time in case the traveler cancels.

Conclusion

Honesty, reliability, resourcefulness, and courtesy are good management, essential to the continuing success of any business. Most of your B&B problems can be solved with common sense. If not, pretend that *you* are the guest, or the host, and you will gain insight. If you have the combination of personality and skills needed, you are bound to succeed in this fascinating, personal endeavor.

4

B&B Recipes

The recipes that follow are not to be found in standard cookbooks. Some are original and the measurements are sometimes from the school of "a smidgen of this," "according to taste," and "till done." But they all indicate the host's desire to pamper guests with something special. The most important ingredient is the heartful of love that is as unmeasured as the handful of flour.

We had an overwhelming response to our request for host-contributed favorite breakfast recipes. Although we could not publish them all this time, we will use most of them in future editions. The following represent, as much as possible, regional or ethnic recipes that impart the flavor and variety of B&Bs across the country.

BREADS AND CAKES

Any Fruit Coffee Cake

4 c. chopped apples, apricots, peaches, pineapples, blueberries, or raspberries
1 c. water
2 tbsp. lemon juice
1½ c. sugar
⅓ c. cornstarch

3 c. flour
1 c. sugar
1 tbsp. baking powder
1 tsp. cinnamon
¼ tsp. mace
1 tsp. salt
1 c. butter/margarine
2 slightly beaten eggs
1 c. milk
1 tsp. vanilla

Topping
½ c. sugar
½ c. flour
¼ c. butter
½ c. walnuts

In covered saucepan combine and simmer fruit and water for five minutes. Stir in lemon juice. Stir 1½ cup sugar and cornstarch slowly into fruit mixture; cook, stirring continuously until mixture thickens. Cool. Stir together flour, sugar, baking powder, cinnamon, mace, and salt. Cut in 1 cup butter until mixture is crumbly. Combine eggs, milk, and vanilla, and add to flour mixture and blend. Spread half the batter into one or two pans. Spread fruit mixture over batter. Spread rest of batter over fruit. Combine first three topping ingredients until crumbly, then add nuts and sprinkle over batter. Bake at 350° for 45 to 50 minutes in a 13″ × 9″ × 2″ pan, or 40 to 45 minutes in two 8″ × 8″ × 2″ pans. Cool and remove from pans.

Isaiah B. Hall House, Dennis, Massachusetts

Cranberry Coffee Cake

½ c. margarine
1 c. sugar
2 eggs
1 c. sour cream
1 tsp. vanilla
1 tsp. baking powder
1 tsp. baking soda
½ c. flour
16 oz. cooked whole cranberries, canned or homemade

Cream margarine and sugar. Add eggs, one at a time, then sour cream and vanilla. Beat well. Add dry ingredients and mix well. Put ½ batter into greased tube pan. Spoon cranberries on top. Pour remaining batter and spoon more berries on top. Bake at 375° for 45 minutes. May be topped with a mixture of powdered sugar, warm water, and almond flavoring.

The Marlborough, Woods Hole, Massachusetts

Grandma Nettie's Bread Pudding

4 kaiser rolls or half-loaf challah
4 eggs, beaten
½ c. golden raisins
1 tart apple, grated
5 tsp. cinnamon sugar
1 quart milk
6 c. cornflakes
½ c. sugar
1½ tsp. vanilla
boiling and cold water

Soak bread in water and cover. Pour boiling water over raisins and cover. Squeeze water from bread and add eggs. Add sugar, milk, cornflakes, grated apple, and vanilla. Drain raisins and add. Mix together. Spread into 9″ × 13″ well-greased baking pan. Sprinkle with cinnamon sugar and bake for one hour at 350°. Serve warm with sweet cream.

Bit o' the Apple, New York City

Plum Nut Bread

1 c. butter
1 tsp. vanilla
3 c. flour
1 tsp. cream of tartar
3/4 c. plain yogurt
2 c. diced purple or prune plums in 1/2″ pieces
1 c. chopped walnuts
2 c. sugar
4 eggs
1 tsp. salt
1/2 tsp. baking soda
1 tsp. grated lemon rind

Cream butter with sugar and vanilla until fluffy. Add eggs, one at a time; beat after each egg. Sift flour, salt, cream of tartar, and baking soda. Blend yogurt and lemon rind. Add to creamed mixture, alternating with dry ingredients. Stir until well blended. Add plums and nuts, mix. Place in 2 greased and floured bread pans. Bake at 350°, 50 to 55 minutes or until done. Loosen sides of bread from pan with a knife and let cool 10 minutes in pan before turning out.

The Colonial House, Weston, Vermont

Strawberry Jam Bread

3 c. all-purpose flour
1 tsp. salt
3/4 tsp. cream of tartar
1/2 tsp. baking soda
1 1/2 c. sugar
1 c. butter or margarine, softened
1 tsp. vanilla extract
1/4 tsp. lemon juice
4 eggs
1 c. strawberry jam
1/2 c. buttermilk
1 c. chopped nuts

Combine flour, salt, cream of tartar, and soda; set aside. Combine sugar, butter, vanilla, and lemon juice in a large mixing bowl; cream until light and fluffy. Add eggs, one at a time, beating well after each addition. Stir together jam and buttermilk; add to creamed mixture alternately with dry ingredients, mixing just until blended. Stir in nuts. Spoon batter into 2 greased 9″ × 5″ × 3″ loaf pans. Bake at 350° for 55 minutes or until bread tests done. Cool 15 minutes; remove from pans onto cooling racks. Yield: 2 loaves.

Parkview House, Amarillo, Texas

Vermont Honey Loaf

1½ c. flour
½ c. brown sugar
½ tsp. salt
½ tsp. baking powder
1 tsp. baking soda
1 tsp. cinnamon
¼ tsp. cloves
½ c. honey, mixed with 1 tbsp. hot water
1 tbsp. molasses
½ c. buttermilk
1 egg

Mix all ingredients together until "satiny." Pour into greased bread pan. Bake at 325° for one hour. Slice and toast before serving.

The Little Lodge at Dorset, Dorset, Vermont

Zucchini Bread

3 eggs
1¼ c. oil
1½ c. sugar
1 tsp. vanilla extract
2 c. grated, unpeeled, raw zucchini
2 c. flour
2 tsp. baking soda
1 tsp. baking powder
1 tsp. salt
1 tsp. cinnamon
½ tsp. cloves
¼ tsp nutmeg
1 c. raisins
1 c. walnuts (optional)

Preheat oven to 350°. Butter five miniloaf pans. Beat eggs, oil, sugar, and vanilla until light and thick. Fold grated zucchini into egg/oil mixture. Sift dry ingredients, stir into zucchini mixture. Fold in raisins and nuts. Pour batter into pans. Bake for 1¼ hours. Cool slightly. Remove and cool completely on racks. Serve with butter, marmalade butter, or whipped cream cheese.

Candlewick Inn, Woodstock, Virginia
The Kingsleigh, Southwest Harbor, Maine

EGGS AND CASSEROLES

Apple-Sausage Ring

2 lbs. bulk sausage, cooked & drained
2 eggs, slightly beaten
½ c. milk
1½ c. herb stuffing
¼ c. minced onion
1 c. apples, pared and finely chopped

Preheat oven to 350°. Combine sausage, eggs, milk, stuffing, onion, and apples. Mix thoroughly and press into greased mold. Bake 1 hour. This can be made the day before and partially baked for 30 minutes. Finish baking before serving. Serves 8 to 10.

The Oakwood Inn, Raleigh, North Carolina

Cheese Strata

8 slices day-old bread, cubed
1½ c. cheddar cheese, grated
8 eggs
2 c. milk
4 tbsp. butter, melted
½ tsp. dry mustard

Layer oven-proof Pyrex dish with bread and cheese, ending with cheese. Combine milk, eggs, melted butter, and mustard in blender and blend for 20 seconds. Pour over bread-and-cheese mixture and refrigerate overnight. Bake at 350° until firm in center (about 45 to 60 minutes). Variations: Add minced onion, chopped green chilies, diced ham, cooked and drained bulk sausage, sautéed mushrooms, chopped chives, or scallions.

Chili Cheese Casserole

4 eggs
¼ c. flour
½ tsp. baking powder
1½ tsp. dry mustard
1 c. cottage cheese
1 c. Monterey jack cheese, shredded
1 c. cheddar, shredded
¼ c. margarine, melted
14 oz. can chopped green chilies

Beat eggs. Add dry ingredients and beat well. Blend in remaining ingredients. Batter will be lumpy. Lightly grease casserole dish and bake at 350° for 25 to 35 minutes, or until center is firm and top is nicely browned.

La Posada de Chimayó, Chimayó, New Mexico

Orange French Toast—Ahif Style

½ c. melted butter
⅓ c. orange juice
1 tbsp. honey
4 eggs
1 loaf French bread, unsliced

Slice bread into 1" slices. Pour melted butter in jelly roll pan. Tilt to cover bottom evenly. Place in refrigerator to chill. Whisk orange juice, honey, and eggs in large bowl. Dip bread slices into egg mixture and lay out on jelly roll pan that has been chilling. Cover and refrigerate overnight. Next morning, preheat oven to 400°. Bake 8 to 10 minutes, turn over, and bake 7 to 8 minutes until browned nicely on the bottom. Serves 4 to 6.

The Ahif House, Grants Pass, Oregon

Puffed Sliced Apple Dish

6 large eggs
1½ c. milk
1 c. flour
3 tbsp. sugar
1 tsp. vanilla extract
1 tsp. cinnamon
¼ tsp. nutmeg
1 stick butter or margarine
2–4 apples
1–2 tbsp. lemon juice
2–3 tbsp. brown sugar

Preheat oven to 350°. Mix eggs, milk, flour, (white) sugar, vanilla, cinnamon, and nutmeg. Core and slice apples; sprinkle with lemon juice. Melt butter in 12" quiche dish in oven. Add apple slices and return to oven until butter sizzles, but does not brown. Remove from oven and pour batter over apples. Sprinkle brown sugar on top, and bake until brown and puffed, about 30 minutes.

Four Seasons B&B, Branchport, New York

Shaw Casserole

1 c. hot cooked grits
1 box jiffy cornbread mix
4 eggs (beaten)
1¾ c. hot milk
1 stick of butter
salt & pepper to taste

Mix all ingredients together.

1 c. grated cheese
2 lbs. hot bulk sausage, cooked, drained

Layer sausage, grits mixture, top with cheese. Bake 45 minutes at 325°.

The Shaw House, Georgetown, South Carolina

Shirred Egg in Bread Basket

Bread Baskets
Use square white sandwich bread. For each basket: trim crusts, roll flat with rolling pin, butter one side of the bread, place butter side down in muffin tin, and bake at 350° till brown (10 to 15 minutes).

Cheese Sauce
One part butter, melted with one part flour. Whisk in four parts of milk and heat until thickened. Add mustard powder (1/6 part). Add favorite cheese and stir till melted.

(Prepare bread baskets and cheese sauce ahead.)
Put bread basket in greased muffin tin. Place slice of ham or smoked turkey in bread basket. Ladle 1 tbsp. of cheese sauce over meat. Carefully crack egg into bread basket. Top with another tbsp. of cheese sauce and bake at 350° for 15 minutes or till yolk is set. Serve topped with cheese sauce.

Beechmont, A Bed and Breakfast Inn, Hanover, Pennsylvania

MUFFINS

Bran Muffins

1/2 package All-Bran cereal, crushed
2 c. honey
5 c. unbleached white flour or combined whole wheat and white
5 tsp. baking soda
1 tsp. salt
3 tsp. cinnamon
4 eggs, beaten
1 c. vegetable oil
3 c. buttermilk

Combine first 6 ingredients in large bowl. Mix. Add remaining ingredients. Mix. Bake in preheated oven 15 to 20 minutes at 375°. Store in tight container for up to 6 weeks. Makes about 60 muffins.

Watercourse Way, South Strafford, Vermont

Hearty Blueberry Muffins

1½ c. unsifted all-purpose flour
½ c. unsifted whole wheat flour
½ c. brown sugar (packed)
1 tbsp. baking powder
½ tsp. salt
½ tsp. ground cinnamon
1 c. fresh or frozen (unthawed) blueberries
½ c. (1 stick) butter, melted
½ c. milk
2 large eggs
1 tsp. vanilla

Preheat oven to 425°. Grease 12 muffin cups (or use muffin papers). Makes about a dozen. Combine all dry ingredients in a bowl and blend well. In a separate small bowl, toss 1 tablespoon of the dry ingredients with berries. Cool melted butter a little, then add milk, eggs, and vanilla, and stir. Add wet mixture to dry mixture and stir until just moist. Stir in berries. Spoon batter into muffin cups and sprinkle sugar on top. Bake about 15 minutes until brown on top.

White Lace Inn, Sturgeon Bay, Wisconsin

Jalapeño Muffins

3 c. corn bread mix
2½ c. milk
½ c. salad oil
3 eggs, beaten
1 large onion, grated
2 tbsp. sugar
½ c. finely chopped peppers
1½ c. sharp cheese, shredded
¼ lb. bacon, fried and crumbled
¼ c. chopped pimientoes
½ clove garlic, crushed

Mix first four ingredients, then add remainder. Bake in heavily greased or lined muffin tins. Bake at 400° for approximately 35 minutes. (Yields 4 dozen muffins; freezes well.) Variation for supper use: Decrease milk by ¼ c. and add 2 c. cream-style corn.

Betty Hyde, Dallas, Texas

Morning Glorious Muffins

2 c. flour
1¼ c. sugar
2 tsp. baking soda
2 tsp. cinnamon
1½ c. shredded carrots
1½ c. chopped apples
¾ c. coconut
½ c. chopped pecans
3 beaten eggs
1 c. vegetable oil
1 tsp. vanilla
½ tsp. salt

Combine flour, sugar, baking soda, cinnamon. In a separate bowl, combine carrots, apples, coconut, and nuts. Stir in eggs, oil, vanilla, and salt. Add dry ingredients and blend. Fill muffin tins 3/4 full. Bake 18 to 20 minutes in 375° oven. Good warm or cold; keeps well in sealed container.

Ramblewood at Lake of the Ozarks, Camdenton, Missouri

Peach Mountain Muffins

2 c. flour
1/3 c. brown sugar
1 tbsp. baking powder
1/4 tsp. baking soda
1/8 tsp. nutmeg
1/4 tsp. salt

Stir together in bowl, make well in center.

Combine:
1 egg
1/4 c. cooking oil
1 c. chopped peaches (fresh, frozen, or canned)

Add peach mixture all at once to flour mixture. Stir until just moistened. Spoon into greased muffin pan. Temperature: 400°. Bake: 20 to 25 minutes. Yield: 12 muffins.

The Bayberry Inn B&B, Peebles, Ohio

Sara's French Puffs

3 c. flour
1 tbsp. baking powder
1 tsp. salt
1/2 tsp. ground nutmeg
1 c. sugar
2/3 c. shortening
2 eggs
1 c. milk

Topping
3/4 c. melted butter
2 tsp. cinnamon mixed with
1 c. sugar

Stir together flour, baking powder, salt, and nutmeg and set aside. In mixer bowl, cream together the first cup of sugar, shortening, and eggs. Add flour mixture to creamed mixture alternately with milk, beating well after each addition. Fill greased muffin cups 2/3 full. Bake at 350° for 20 to 25 minutes. Dip in melted butter, then in cinnamon-sugar mixture.

Stranahan House, Mercer, Pennsylvania

PANCAKES

Apple Rings

pancake batter
4 McIntosh apples
maple syrup

Prepare one recipe pancake batter (regular or whole wheat). Peel (if desired) and core 4 McIntosh or other soft apples; cut the apples into slices about 1/4 inch thick. Use a fork in the center of each apple piece to dip the ring into the pancake batter. Let any excess drip off. Fry the apple rings in butter, margarine, or vegetable oil in a skillet until golden brown on one side. Turn and brown on the other side. Serve hot with maple syrup.

Goose Creek Guesthouse, Southold, New York

Corn Fritters

2 c. sweet corn
3 eggs, separated
2 tbsp. butter
6 tbsp. white or whole wheat flour
dash nutmeg

Beat egg yolks until light and stir into corn. Add flour. Fold in stiffly beaten egg whites. Sauté on hot griddle in 2 tablespoons butter. Turn over gently and cook until lightly browned. Serve with real maple syrup or homemade fruit syrup.

Meadow Spring Farm, Kennett Square, Pennsylvania

Strawberry Blintzes

1 c. all-purpose flour
3 tbsp. granulated sugar
1/4 tsp. salt
3 eggs
1 1/3 c. milk
2 eggs
2 (8 oz.) cartons strawberry yogurt
1/2 c. strawberry preserves
butter/margarine
powdered sugar
strawberry preserves

In medium bowl, mix flour, sugar, and salt. In another medium bowl, mix 3 eggs and milk. Gradually add milk mixture to flour mixture. Beat with electric mixer (medium speed) until blended. Cover and chill 2 to 3 hours. Prepare crêpe pan or shallow skillet. Brush with oil, use 2 tbsp. batter for each crêpe. Cook until brown on bottom. Remove crêpe, stack crêpes between waxed paper. In medium bowl, slightly beat 2 eggs with fork. Stir in yogurt and 1/2 cup strawberry preserves. Place crêpe brown side up and spoon 1 1/2 tbsp. yogurt mix on center of crêpe. Fold crêpe over—first bottom, then sides, and top—envelope style. Melt butter in pan. Brown blintzes over medium heat on both sides. Sprinkle blintzes with powdered sugar and top with spoonful of strawberry preserves. Makes 10 servings.

The Brafferton Inn, Gettysburg, Pennsylvania

SCONES

Maine Blueberry Scones

2 c. flour
2 tbsp. sugar
3 tsp. baking powder
nutmeg (dash)
3/4 tsp. salt
1/2 stick sweet butter
1 egg, beaten
1 c. blueberries
1/2 c. medium cream
1/2–3/4 c. milk

Sift dry ingredients. Cut in shortening. Add berries. Combine egg with milk. Add to dry ingredients. Stir just enough to moisten. Pat out dough quickly and gently into a circle about 3/4″ thick. Cut into pie-shaped wedges. Brush with cream and sprinkle with sugar. Place on cookie sheet and bake in 450° oven for 15 minutes or until golden brown. Serve warm.

Bed & Breakfast Down East, Eastbrook, Maine

Scottish Oat Scones

2/3 c. butter or margarine (melted)
1/3 c. milk
1 egg
1 1/2 c. all-purpose flour
1 1/4 c. quick Quaker oats, uncooked
1/3 c. sugar
1 tbsp. baking powder
1 tsp. cream of tartar
1/2 tsp. salt
1/2 c. raisins or currants

Add butter, milk, and egg to combined dry ingredients; mix until just moist. Stir in raisins. Shape dough to form ball; pat out on lightly floured surface to form 8″ circle. Cut into 8 to 12 wedges; bake on greased cookie sheet in preheated 425° oven 12 to 15 minutes or until light golden brown. Serve warm with butter, preserves, or honey.

Oak Shores, Swampscott, Massachusetts

FRUITS

Baked Pears

d'Anjou pears
brown or cinnamon sugar
cream

Peel and halve small d'Anjou pears. Generously butter baking dish just large enough to hold desired number of pears. Sprinkle dish with 1/2 tablespoon brown sugar or cinnamon sugar per pear. Put pears cut side down in dish and sprinkle with additional 1/2 tablespoon sugar per pear. Bake in 375° oven for 20 minutes. Remove and pour one tablespoon cream over each pear half. Bake an additional 15 minutes. Serve hot or warm.

The Heirloom, Ione, California

French Clafouti

3 c. fresh ripe fruit (sliced peaches, cherries, pears, blueberries—or mixture; don't use strawberries)
1/2 c. sifted flour
1/2 c. sugar
3 eggs
1 1/3 c. half 'n' half

Mix flour and sugar. Make a well, add eggs, and mix. Add half 'n' half as you mix. Butter a rectangular baking dish and line with the fruit. Pour batter over fruit. Bake until golden and puffed for 30 to 35 minutes at 425°. Dust with powdered sugar when cold. Serve warm or cold.

Le Clos Normand Bed & Breakfast, Kennett Square, Pennsylvania

Fruit Crisp

1 qt. of berries (or any mixture of fruit sliced thinly)
1/3 c. water
1/3 c. flour
1/3 c. brown sugar
3/4 c. oatmeal
1/4 c. lemon juice (over the fruit)
6 tbsp. butter

Cream sugar and butter. Beat in oatmeal. Toss fruit in flour and water. Place in greased baking dish. Crumble oatmeal mixture over the top. Bake 40 minutes at 375°—serves 4 to 6.

The Whistling Swan, Stanhope, New Jersey

Voss Inn
Bozeman, Montana

5

State-by-State Listings

KEY TO LISTINGS

✪ This star means that rates are guaranteed through December 31, 1988 to any guest making a reservation as a result of reading about the B&B in *Bed & Breakfast U.S.A.*—1988 edition.

Location: As indicated, unless the B&B is right in town, or its location is clear from the address as stated.

Best time to call: When indicated, the time when the host is usually home to accept calls. Some have telephone answering machines or answering services to cover other times. Remember the differences in time zones when calling. *NOTE:* Reservation services are available during normal business hours (9 A.M.–5 P.M., Monday through Friday) unless otherwise indicated.

No. of rooms: Number of *guest* bedrooms.

Double: Rate for two people in one room. Double rooms may be furnished with a standard double bed, queen- or king-size bed, or twin beds.

Single: Rate for one person in a room.

Suite: Can be either two bedrooms with an adjoining bath, or a living room and bedroom with private bath.

Guest cottage: A separate building that usually has a mini-kitchen and private bath.

pb: Private bath and/or shower.

sb: Shared bath and/or shower.

Max. no. sharing bath: Maximum number of people that might be sharing one bathroom. Keep in mind that some B&Bs have sinks in each bedroom.

Double/pb: Room for two with private bath.

Single/pb: Room for one with private bath.

Double/sb: Room for two with shared bath.

Single/sb: Room for one with shared bath.

NOTE: There is usually an extra charge for an additional person occupying the same room.

Open: As indicated. Keep in mind that many B&Bs are closed for Thanksgiving, Christmas, and Easter.

Breakfast: Included in the room rate unless otherwise stated. A Continental breakfast consists of juice, bread, and hot beverage. Some hosts provide a gourmet breakfast with homemade cakes, breads, and preserves. A full breakfast consists of juice, cereal, eggs, breakfast meat, bread or rolls, and hot beverage. Some are so special, you may not be hungry for lunch!

Credit cards: When reservation services accept them, the deposit can be made with a credit card but the host will still require that the balance due be paid in cash or by check.

Pets: Keep in mind that the host may have resident pets. Always ask if it is convenient to bring yours, to make certain there won't be a conflict with other guests. If you are allergic to animals, inquire before reserving.

Children: If "crib" is noted after the word "welcome," the host can accommodate children under the age of three.

Smoking: If permitted, this means it is allowed *somewhere* inside the house. Some hosts discourage smoking in the breakfast room for the comfort of other guests; some prohibit smoking in bedrooms for safety's sake. Most do not allow cigars or pipes.

Social drinking: Some hosts provide a glass of wine or sherry; others provide setups for bring-your-own.

Airport/station pickup: If "yes" is indicated, the host will pick you up from the closest airport or station for a fee.

Minimum Stay: A two-night minimum stay is sometimes required.

Please enclose a self-addressed, stamped, business-sized envelope when contacting reservation services.

Always mention *Bed & Breakfast U.S.A.* when making reservations!

ALABAMA

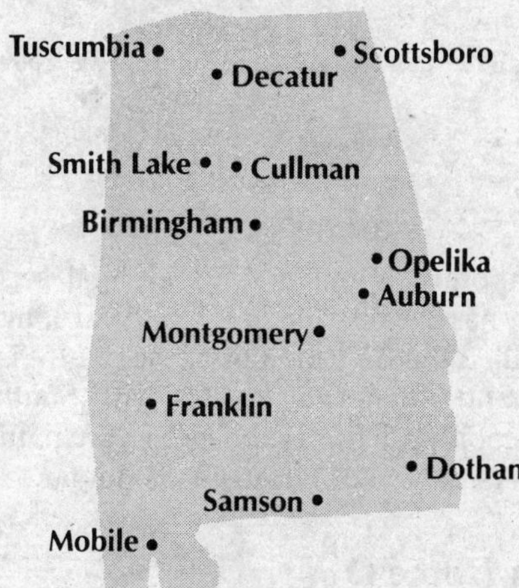

Bed & Breakfast—Birmingham ✪

P.O. BOX 31328, BIRMINGHAM, ALABAMA 35222

Tel: **(205) 591-6406**
Coordinators: **Ruth Taylor**
States/Regions Covered: **Auburn, Birmingham, Cullman, Decatur, Dothan, Franklin, Montgomery, Tuscumbia**

Rates (Single/Double):
Modest: **$28–$36**
Average: **$38–$55**
Luxury: **$65–$85**
Credit Cards: **No**

Ruth specializes in making compatible placements in host homes where southern hospitality is assured. Her listings range from an exquisite cottage to a classic contemporary. There are antebellum Federalist homes, Victorian farmhouses, or cozy vacation hideaways. They are located in a variety of settings: close to lakes, rivers, downtown, in suburbs, or convenient to I-65. All are comfortable accommodations in homes where hosts balance friendliness with respect for privacy.

Kraft's Korner ✪
90 CARLILE DRIVE, MOBILE, ALABAMA 36619

Tel: **(205) 666-6819**
Best Time to Call: **6-8 AM**
Host(s): **Estelle and Allen Kraft**
Location: **5 mi. from I-10**
No. of Rooms: **2**
No. of Private Baths: **1**
Max. No. Sharing Bath: **2**
Double/pb: **$30**
Single/pb: **$25**
Double/sb: **$25**
Single/sb: **$20**
Suites: **$50 (for 4)**
Open: **Feb. 1–Oct. 31**
Reduced Rates: **10%, seniors**
Breakfast: **Full**
Other Meals: **Available**
Pets: **No**
Children: **Welcome**
Smoking: **No**
Social Drinking: **No**
Airport/Station Pickup: **Yes**

This is a contemporary home in a residential section, where the temperate climate has flowers blooming all year long. Nearby Bellingrath Gardens, called the Charm Spot of the South, is a must on your itinerary. Estelle and Allen spoil guests with Southern hospitality. Estelle is a fine cook and the emphasis is on natural and healthy dining. The University of South Alabama is not far.

Vincent-Doan Home ✪
1664 SPRINGHILL AVENUE, MOBILE, ALABAMA 36604

Tel: **(205) 433-7121**
Host(s): **Betty M. Doan**
No. of Rooms: **3**
No. of Private Baths: **3**
Double/pb: **$50**
Single/pb: **$40**
Open: **All year**
Reduced Rates: **10%, seniors**
Breakfast: **Full**
Credit Cards: **MC, VISA**
Pets: **Welcome**
Children: **Welcome**
Smoking: **Permitted**
Social Drinking: **Permitted**
Airport/Station Pickup: **Yes**

The Vincent-Doan Home, built circa 1827, is one of the area's last remaining "summer houses" and the only known example of French Creole architecture in the city. The area, known as the Old Dauphin Way District, is listed on the National Register of Historic Places. The furnishing and decor are subtle but elegant, and reflect the history of the home. It is 15 minutes to Bellingrath Gardens, 10 minutes to Battleship Park, and 30 minutes to deep-sea fishing. Betty will welcome you with a refreshing beverage.

Montgomery Bed & Breakfast

P.O. BOX 886, MILLBROOK, ALABAMA 36054

Tel: **(205) 285-5421**
Best Time to Call: **Before 9 AM; after 6 PM**
Coordinator: **Helen Maier**
States/Regions Covered: **Lowndesboro, Millbrook, Montgomery, Mt. Meigs, Prattville**

Rates (Single/Double):

	Single	Double
Average:	**$35**	**$40**
Luxury:	**$40**	**$40–$45**

Credit Cards: **No**

If you are a history buff, you are sure to love Montgomery, the Cradle of the Confederacy. Helen Maier can put you within easy reach of the sights as a guest in one of her 15 homes. Accommodations range from antebellum to country contemporaries with a typical farmhouse in between. Interesting hosts are waiting to welcome you to a cottage in historic Lowndesboro or a luxury home with a swimming pool. Southern hospitality abounds in each of these diverse homes.

Under the Oaks ✪

707 GENEVA STREET, OPELIKA, ALABAMA 36801

Tel: **(205) 745-2449**
Best Time to Call: **8 AM–5 PM**
Host(s): **Daniel and Donna Tankersley**
Location: **1/2 mi. from I-85, Exit 60**
No. of Rooms: **6**
No. of Private Baths: **6**
Double/pb: **$58**
Single/pb: **$50**
Suites: **$65**

Open: **All year**
Breakfast: **Continental**
Credit Cards: **AMEX, MC, VISA**
Pets: **No**
Children: **Welcome**
Smoking: **Permitted**
Social Drinking: **Permitted**

The luxurious guest rooms of this Greek Revival antebellum house are furnished individually with antiques or white wicker. Some rooms have fireplaces; all have lovely homemade quilts or down comforters on the beds. Small refrigerators are convenient for storing midnight snacks. The large couches and green plants make the living room an inviting place to get together with the other guests. Sports fans are pleased with the proximity of Auburn University's football field.

Jola Bama Guest Home

201 EAST STREET, SAMSON, ALABAMA 36477

Tel: **(205) 898-2478**
Host(s): **Jewel M. Armstrong**
Location: **40 mi. W of Dothan**
No. of Rooms: **5**
No. of Private Baths: **2**
Max. No. Sharing Bath: **2**
Double/pb: **$26**
Single/pb: **$20**
Double/sb: **$18**
Single/sb: **$15**
Open: **All year**
Breakfast: **Continental**
Pets: **Welcome**
Children: **Welcome**
Smoking: **Permitted**
Social Drinking: **Permitted**
Foreign Languages: **Spanish**

This comfortable clapboard Victorian boasts a collection of interesting antiques. It is 85 miles directly south of Montgomery, "the Cradle of the Confederacy." The north Florida beaches, the Army Aviation Museum, and Troy State College are nearby. Jewel is a tree farmer and cattle rancher, and looks forward to welcoming you all.

The Brunton House ✪

112 COLLEGE AVENUE, SCOTTSBORO, ALABAMA 35768

Tel: **(205) 259-1298**
Host(s): **Norman and Jerry Brunton**
Location: **1 mi. from Rte. 72**
No. of Rooms: **5**
Max. No. Sharing Bath: **5**
Double/sb: **$29**
Single/sb: **$24**
Suites: **$35–$42**
Open: **All year**
Reduced Rates: **10%, Nov. 30–Mar. 1; weekly**
Breakfast: **Full**
Other Meals: **Available**
Pets: **Sometimes**
Children: **Welcome**
Smoking: **Permitted**
Social Drinking: **Permitted**
Airport/Station Pickup: **Yes**

This fine old home is located on historic College Avenue. At Courthouse Square, two blocks away, an old-time drugstore operates its original soda fountain. Swimming, boating, and fishing are close by on the Tennessee River. Norman and Jerry invite you to watch TV in the living room, or use the kitchen for light snacks. The first Monday of every month (and the Sunday preceding) feature Monday Trade Day, an extravaganza of antique dealers from all over the country.

ALASKA

Accommodations Alaska Style—Stay with a Friend ✪

SUITE 173-3605 ARCTIC BOULEVARD, ANCHORAGE, ALASKA 99503

Tel: **(907) 344-4006**
Coordinator: **Jean Parsons**
States/Regions Covered: **Anchorage, Hatcher Pass, Homer, Juneau, Kenai, Palmer, Valdez, Wasilla, Willow**

Rates (Single/Double):

Modest:	**\$35–\$40**	**\$45–\$55**
Average:	**\$40–\$45**	**\$50–\$60**
Luxury:	**\$50–\$55**	**\$70–\$80**

Credit Cards: **MC, VISA**

Anchorage is an eclectic mix of tall buildings, Mt. McKinley, glaciers, and rush hour traffic. Its frontier spirit and contemporary style always take visitors by surprise. Accommodations include a B&B near a small park with views of the port and Sleeping Lady Mountain; another overlooks Cook Inlet; and a third is an elegant suite where breakfast may be enjoyed on the large deck. Jean will be happy to send you her free descriptive directory describing host homes in the towns she serves.

Alaska Private Lodgings ✪

1236 WEST 10TH AVENUE, ANCHORAGE, ALASKA 99511

Tel: **(907) 258-1717**
Best Time to Call: **8 AM–8:30 PM**
Coordinator: **Mary Reardon**
State/Regions Covered: **Anchorage, Homer, Kenai, Palmer, Seward, Talkeetna, Willow**

Rates (Single/Double):
Modest: **$35–$43**
Average: **$40–$45**
Luxury: **$50–$60**
Credit Cards: **MC, VISA**

Alaska hosts are this state's warmest resource! Mary's accommodations range from an original log house of a pioneer's homestead where the host is in the antique-doll business, to a contemporary home with guest quarters on the entire lower level, to a beautiful country guest home offering a spectacular view of the Anchorage bowl and Cook Inlet. Many are convenient to the University of Alaska and Alaska Pacific University. There's a $5 surcharge for one-night stays during May 1–Sept. 30.

The Green Bough ✪

3832 YOUNG STREET, ANCHORAGE, ALASKA 99508

Tel: **(907) 562-4636**
Best Time to Call: **7 AM–10 AM; 4 PM–8 PM**
Host(s): **Jerry and Phyllis Jost**
Location: **20 min. from airport**
No. of Rooms: **4**
Max. No. Sharing Bath: **4**
Double/sb: **$40–$45**
Single/sb: **$35–$40**

Open: **All year**
Reduced Rates: **Families**
Breakfast: **Continental**
Pets: **Sometimes**
Children: **Welcome**
Smoking: **No**
Social Drinking: **No**

Even on the coldest days, you'll forget about the outside temperature in this comfortable home filled with family furnishings, needlework, and local artifacts. Breakfast features a choice of homemade breads, muffins, and scones served with seasonal fruit and plenty of hot coffee. The Green Bough is located in a quiet residential area close to colleges, shopping, bike trails, and buses. A large yard and deck are available for reading and relaxing. Your hosts have 20 years of experience in this part of the country and they will gladly help you discover its charms. Special arrangements can be made for storing fishing and camping gear.

Porter House Bed & Breakfast ✪

P.O. BOX 868, 624 FIRST AVENUE, BETHEL, ALASKA 99559

Tel: **(907) 543-3552**
Best Time to Call: **9 AM–9 PM**
Host(s): **Rosie Porter**
No. of Rooms: **4**
Max. No. Sharing Bath: **4**
Double/sb: **$65**
Single/sb: **$45**
Open: **All year**
Reduced Rates: **No**
Breakfast: **Full**
Credit Cards: **MC, VISA**
Pets: **Sometimes**
Children: **No toddlers**
Smoking: **Permitted**
Social Drinking: **Permitted**
Airport/Station Pickup: **Yes**

If you were under the impression that an Alaskan B&B is an igloo with spartan accouterments, you haven't been to the Porters'. Located on the banks of the Kuskokwim River, Porter House is a warm combination of contemporary and country with living room furniture cleverly grouped for conversation. The bedrooms are cozy and comfortable, with such thoughtful touches as flannel sheets in winter, a candy dish on the dresser, and imported wool fat soap for your bath. Breakfast features reindeer sausage, gourmet omelets, fresh croissants, imported jams, and real cream for the fresh-ground coffee. It is beautifully served on fine china with lovely silverware.

Wilson's Hostel ✪

BOX 969, BETHEL, ALASKA 99559

Tel: **(907) 543-3841**
Best Time to Call: **Before 8 PM**
Host(s): **Gail and Tom Wilson**
No. of Rooms: **4**
Max. No. Sharing Bath: **4**
Double/sb: **$79**
Single/sb: **$59**
Open: **All year**
Reduced Rates: **Weekly**
Breakfast: **Full**
Credit Cards: **MC, VISA**
Pets: **Sometimes**
Children: **Welcome**
Smoking: **No**
Social Drinking: **No**
Airport/Station Pickup: **Yes**

A third *B* could be added to this B&B: banana splits (!) because Tom and Gail frequently serve them at bedtime as an example of the pampering guests receive here. This is in addition to refrigerator raiding, access to the family library, TV and stereo, laundry facilities, safety pins, and writing paper. You are encouraged to make yourself at home with all the privileges and responsibilities that implies. "Home," accessible only by air to the Bethel jetport, is a chalet made cozy by a fire in the wood stove and comfortable furnishings. Your hearty breakfast might be shared with a family from an Eskimo village, a business traveler, or a vacationer en route to the salmon streams along the nearby Kuskokwim River.

Glacier Bay Country Inn

BOX 5, GUSTAVUS, ALASKA 99826

Tel: **(907) 697-2288**
Best Time to Call: **9 AM–5 PM**
Host(s): **Al and Annie Unrein**
Location: **50 mi. W of Juneau**
No. of Rooms: **5**
No. of Private Baths: **5**
Double/pb: **$45–$76**
Open: **May 15–Sept. 30**
Breakfast: **Full**
Other Meals: **Included**
Pets: **No**
Children: **Welcome**
Smoking: **No**
Social Drinking: **Permitted**
Airport/Station Pickup: **Yes**

The Glacier Bay Country Inn is a rambling wood structure with log-beamed ceilings, dormer windows, and large porches. It is situated on a 160-acre farm, surrounded by forests of towering trees, meadows, and near a tranquil pond. You will find cozy wood stoves and handcrafts, and charming rooms, each with a view of gardens, hay-fields, and spectacular mountains. A special highlight of this private retreat is the cooking, featuring home-baked breads, and for dinner, garden produce and local seafood. The inn is just outside the Glacier Bay National Park. Your hosts can arrange for boat trips, fishing charters, and flight tours.

Alaska Bed and Breakfast ✪

P.O. BOX 1321, JUNEAU, ALASKA 99802

Tel: **(907) 586-2959**
Best Time to Call: **9 AM–4 PM**
Coordinator: **Stephen Hamilton**
States/Regions Covered: **Haines, Juneau, Petersburg, Sitka, Wrangell**
Rates (Single/Double):
Luxury: **$40** **$55**
Credit Cards: **MC, VISA**

Visitors can enjoy southeast Alaskan hospitality in a historic inn, a log cabin in the woods, a modern home overlooking the water, or an old Indian village. Mendenhall Glacier, Glacier Bay, and the University of Alaska are nearby. The area is known for fine fishing and great hiking.

Kodiak Bed & Breakfast ✪

P.O. BOX 1729, KODIAK, ALASKA 99615

Tel: **(907) 486-5367**
Best Time to Call: **Evenings; weekends**
Coordinator: **Mary Monroe**
State/Regions Covered: **Kodiak**
Rates (Single/Double):
Average: **$44–$55**
Credit Cards: **No**

Kodiak is one of the nation's top fishing ports, a hunting and sport fishing paradise, the home of the first Russian settlement in America and of the famous Kodiak bear. The people are warm and friendly and look forward to receiving you.

North Pole B&B

3045 TAXI LANE A, NORTH POLE, ALASKA 99705

Tel: **(907) 488-4163**
Best Time to Call: **Evenings**
Host(s): **John and Joyce Ashworth**
Location: **13 mi. S of Fairbanks**
No. of Rooms: **3**
Max. No. Sharing Bath: **3**
Double/sb: **$45**
Single/sb: **$35**
Open: All year
Reduced Rates: **25%, Oct.–Apr.**
Breakfast: **Full**
Credit Cards: **MC, VISA**
Pets: **No**
Children: **Welcome, over 12**
Smoking: **Permitted**
Social Drinking: **Permitted**
Airport/Station Pickup: **Yes**

This ranch-style, cedar-sided home is on an acre of wooded property situated next to a private airstrip. The Chena Lakes Recreation Area is four miles away. You are welcome to use the TV, laundry facilities, Ping-Pong table, and dart board. Joyce will prepare a box lunch for a reasonable fee. John will be pleased to share his interests in model railroading and model boat building with you.

Russell's Bed & Board

SRA BOX 6229-R, PALMER, ALASKA 99645

Tel: **(907) 376-7662**
Best Time to Call: **Mornings**
Host(s): **Evelyn and John Russell**
Location: **38 mi. N of Anchorage**
No. of Rooms: **4**
Max. No. Sharing Bath: **4**
Double/sb: **$45**
Single/sb: **$35**
Open: **All year**
Reduced Rates: **15%, weekly**
Breakfast: **Full**
Other Meals: **Available**
Pets: **No**
Children: **Welcome, over 5**
Smoking: **Permitted**
Social Drinking: **Permitted**
Airport/Station Pickup: **Yes**

Discover Alaska's countryside while staying in a modern home in the heart of the Matanuska Valley. The house offers beautiful views, modern furnishings, an art studio, and a two-story glass solarium. Guests may choose from clean, quiet accommodations with twin or full beds. In the morning enjoy a breakfast of reindeer sausage, homemade breads, and hot coffee. Your hosts will gladly pack you a lunch to take along while you visit nearby Bradly Lake Barn, Hatcher Pass, and Independence Mine. If you wish, a reasonably priced hearty dinner will be waiting when you return. The catch of the day will be cheerfully cooked to order.

ARIZONA

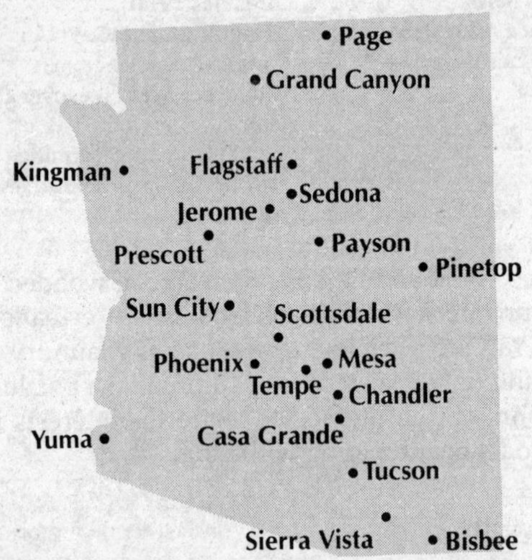

Bed & Breakfast in Arizona ✪

4533 N. SCOTTSDALE ROAD 5108, SCOTTSDALE, ARIZONA 85251

Tel: **(602) 995-2831**
Best Time to Call: **7:30 AM–4:30 PM**
Coordinator: **Jo Cummings**
States/Regions Covered: **Arizona (statewide)**

Rates (Single/Double):

Modest:	**$20–$30**	**$30–$40**
Average:	**$35–$55**	**$45–$65**
Luxury:	**$55 up**	**$65 up**

Credit Cards: **AMEX, MC, VISA**

Jo offers you local color and local customs explained by friendly hosts. Arizona is a spectacular state with every kind of scenery and climate you can imagine. This is the land of the spellbinding Grand Canyon, Indian and Mexican cultures, cowboys and cattle ranches, gold mines, ghost towns, majestic mountains, and awesome deserts. Plan to spend several days to truly get the most out of your visit. A two-day minimum stay is preferred on holiday weekends. There is a $5 surcharge for one-night stays.

Mi Casa–Su Casa Bed & Breakfast ✪

P.O. BOX 950, TEMPE, ARIZONA 85281

Tel: **(602) 990-0682**
Best Time to Call: **8 AM–8 PM**
Coordinator: **Ruth T. Young**
States/Regions Covered: **Flagstaff, Jerome, Mesa, Payson, Pinetop, Prescott, Scottsdale, Sedona, Show Low, Sierra Vista, Sun City, Tempe, Tucson, Yuma**

Rates (Single/Double):

Modest:	**$25**	**$35**
Average:	**$35**	**$40**
Luxury:	**$100**	**$125**

Credit Cards: **MC, VISA**

Ruth's guest houses are located statewide; the above is only a partial listing. They are located in cities, suburbs, and rural settings, all of which are within easy driving range of canyons, national parks, Indian country, Colorado River gem country, the Mexican border area, historic mining towns, and water recreation areas. Send $3 for her detailed directory. Arizona State University and the University of Arizona are convenient to many B&Bs. $5 surcharge for one night.

Cone's Tourist Home ✪

2804 WEST WARNER, CHANDLER, ARIZONA 85224

Tel: **(602) 839-0369**
Best Time to Call: **After 5 PM**
Host(s): **Howard and Beverly Cone**
Location: **18 mi. SE of Phoenix**
No. of Rooms: **1**
No. of Private Baths: **1**
Double/pb: **$30**
Single/pb: **$30**
Open: **Sept. 1–May 31**
Breakfast: **Continental**
Pets: **Sometimes**
Children: **Welcome**
Smoking: **Permitted**
Social Drinking: **Permitted**

This beautiful contemporary home is situated on two acres. Howard and Beverly offer a large guest room with phone and television, a large parlor for relaxing, and kitchen and barbecue facilities. It is 3 miles from fine restaurants and 12 miles from Sky Harbor airport.

Arizona Mountain Inn ✪

685 LAKE MARY ROAD, FLAGSTAFF, ARIZONA 86001

Tel: **(602) 774-8959**
Host(s): **The Wanek family**
Location: **1 mi. from I-17**
No. of Rooms: **6**
No. of Private Baths: **2**
Max. No. Sharing Bath: **2–4**
Double/sb: **$60**
Single/sb: **$50**
Guest Cottage: **$50–$90 (sleeps 2–4)**
Suites: **$100**
Open: **All year**
Reduced Rates: **10%, seniors**
Breakfast: **Full**
Credit Cards: **MC, VISA**

Pets: **No**
Children: **Cottage only**
Smoking: **No**
Social Drinking: **Permitted**
Airport/Station Pickup: **Yes**

The Wanek family invites you to their New England–style Tudor home in the heart of the Southwest. Arizona Mountain Inn is secluded on 13 acres of ponderosa pines. The Inn is surrounded by the Coconino National Forest and offers a perfect view of the San Francisco Peaks. Inside, you'll find comfortable rooms with a rustic look, complemented by oak furnishings and antiques. Each morning, enjoy a hearty meal of fruit, juice, ham or bacon, toast, and plenty of hot coffee or tea, all served in a cozy breakfast room. Guests are welcome to relax in the gazebo, stroll the grounds, or cook out on the barbeque. This lovely Inn is two miles from Flagstaff; the Grand Canyon, Oak Creek Canyon, Lake Powell, the Painted Desert, and the Petrified Forest are just some of the sights in the Flagstaff area.

Cedar Bed and Breakfast

425 WEST CEDAR, FLAGSTAFF, ARIZONA 86001

Tel: **(602) 774-1636**
Best Time to Call: **Mornings**
Host(s): **Mary Pickett**
Location: **3 mi. from I-40**
No. of Rooms: **2**
No. of Private Baths: **1**
Max. No. Sharing Bath: **3**
Double/pb: **$35–$45**
Single/pb: **$25**
Open: **All year**
Breakfast: **Full**
Pets: **No**
Children: **Welcome, over 8**
Smoking: **Permitted**
Social Drinking: **Permitted**
Airport/Station Pickup: **Yes**

This attractive contemporary is set among ponderosa pine and gambel oak. The house has a native Malpais stone exterior, with oak floors and wood paneling throughout the interior. Guests are welcome to relax in the large living room, which has plenty of comfortable seating and interesting motifs of glass, Indian rugs, and artifacts. In the colder weather, a fire is always going in the large stone hearth. When the temperatures climb back up, all are welcome to take in the sun on the deck or patio. In the morning your hostess offers homemade fruit-nut muffins, fresh seasonal fruit, and coffee. Flagstaff is the hub of popular tourist attractions, including the Grand Canyon, Sunset Crater, Meteor Crater, Walnut Canyon, and Wupatki Indian Ruins. Lowell Observatory, Northern Arizona University, and a branch of the U.S. Geological Survey are located nearby.

Dierker House ✪

423 WEST CHERRY, FLAGSTAFF, ARIZONA 86001

Tel: **(602) 774-3249**
Host(s): **Dorothea Dierker**
No. of Rooms: **3**
Max. No. Sharing Bath: **5**
Double/sb: **$35**
Single/sb: **$25**
Open: **All year**
Breakfast: **Full**
Pets: **Sometimes**
Children: **Welcome, over 12**
Smoking: **Permitted**
Social Drinking: **Permitted**

After a day of touring the Grand Canyon and Indian sites, return to Dorothea's Victorian home and enjoy a glass of wine and fresh fruit in the evening, by the fire in winter or in the pretty garden room. You are welcome to borrow a good book and snuggle in bed under a cozy down comforter. Activities might include a Colorado River raft trip in summer and skiing in winter.

Walking L Ranch ✪

RR 4 BOX 721B, FLAGSTAFF, ARIZONA 86001

Tel: **(602) 779-2219**
Best Time to Call: **8–10 AM; 5–9 PM**
Host(s): **Jerry and Susan Ladhoff**
Location: **7 mi. from I-40 and I-17**
No. of Rooms: **3**
No. of Private Baths: **3**
Double/pb: **$45–$60**
Single/pb: **$30**
Open: **All year**
Breakfast: **Full**
Other Meals: **Available**
Pets: **No**
Children: **Welcome, over 12**
Smoking: **Permitted**
Social Drinking: **Permitted**
Airport/Station Pickup: **Yes**

Nestled in the pines of the Coconino National Forest, this ranch house features a lovely plant-filled spa room with hot tub, redwood deck, and patio. The homey, inviting rooms are accented with antiques, collectibles, Indian art, and Susan's handicrafts. Jerry is a professor at nearby Northern Arizona University and his hobbies are gardening and woodworking. Riding, hiking, skiing, and walking are popular pastimes after you've had your fill of the Grand Canyon.

Bed 'n' Breakfast in Arizona ✪

5995 EAST ORANGE BLOSSOM LANE, PHOENIX, ARIZONA 85018

Tel: **(602) 994-3759**
Best Time to Call: **Mornings, evenings**
Host(s): **Marjorie Ann Lindmark**
Location: **5 mi. from airport**
No. of Rooms: **2**
No. of Private Baths: **1**
Double/pb: **$50**
Double/sb: **$45**
Single/pb: **$45**
Single/sb: **$40**
Suite: **$75**
Open: **All year**
Reduced Rates: **Weekly**
Breakfast: **Full**
Pets: **No**
Children: **No**
Smoking: **Permitted**
Social Drinking: **Permitted**

Marjorie's charming trilevel home is located in the exclusive Arizona Country Club area. It is furnished in an eclectic mix of contemporary and Indian artifacts. You are welcome to use the swimming pool. The delicious breakfast often features four-egg omelets or unusual quiche. Arizona State University is nearby. There's a $5 surcharge for a one-night stay.

Ford's Bed & Breakfast ✪

212 SOUTH PLEASANT, PRESCOTT, ARIZONA 86301

Tel. **(602) 776-1564**
Host(s): **David and Joan Ford**
Location: **30 mi. from I-17, Exit Hwy. 69**
No. of Rooms: **2**
Max. No. Sharing Bath: **4**
Double/sb: **$40**
Single/sb: **$25**
Open: **All year**
Breakfast: **Continental**
Pets: **No**
Children: **Welcome**
Smoking: **No**
Social Drinking: **Permitted**
Airport/Station Pickup: **Yes**

The Fords live in a turn-of-the-century frame house surrounded by a picket fence on a tree-lined street. Guest rooms are located on the first floor and share a large connecting bath. Antique furnishings and

handmade quilts accent the beauty of the original wood floors and hardcarved woodwork. It's a short walk to the lovely park that surrounds the town courthouse, or to several nice shops and good restaurants. Prescott College is nearby.

Lynx Creek Farm ✪

P.O. BOX 4301, PRESCOTT, ARIZONA 86302

Tel. **(602) 778-9573**
Host(s): **Greg and Cathy Temple**
Location: **30 mi. from I-17**
No. of Rooms: **2**
No. of Private Baths: **2**
Suites: **$60–$75**
Open: **All year**
Breakfast: **Full**
Credit Cards: **MC, VISA**
Pets: **Sometimes**
Children: **Welcome**
Smoking: **No**
Social Drinking: **Permitted**
Airport/Station Pickup: **Yes**
Foreign Languages: **Spanish**

From June till October, you are welcome to pick your own fruit and vegetables from the farm's harvest. Both guest suites and their decks are situated above the barn overlooking the creek. Greg and Cathy are avid cyclists and hikers. They'll be happy to lend a tent and sleeping bags to your older children who might enjoy a camping experience. You may use the swimming pool, laundry facilities, and piano. Breakfast frequently features huevos rancheros and chorizo sausage or Dutch Baby pancakes with fresh apple topping. Homemade granola with fruit from the orchards is always available.

Bed & Breakfast Scottsdale ✪

P.O. BOX 624, SCOTTSDALE, ARIZONA 85252

Tel: **(602) 998-7044**
Best Time to Call: **7 AM–10 PM**
Coordinator: **Lois O'Grady**
State/Regions Covered: **Scottsdale, Cave Creek, Fountain Hills, Paradise Valley, Pinnacle Peak**

Rates (Single/Double):

	Single	Double
Modest:	**$20**	**$30**
Average:	**$30**	**$35**
Luxury:	**$40**	**$45–$110**

Credit Cards: **No**

Lois wants to make your visit to Scottsdale as special as possible. She has a roster of friendly hosts with homes that have a relaxed atmosphere to complement the easygoing Southwestern life-style. Her list of accommodations includes pretty bedrooms opening onto sunny patios, suites with fireplace and balcony to enhance a romantic setting, or a hideaway cottage on a private estate. Many are in historic adobe homes secluded in the foothills, yet minutes to Paolo Soleri's Bell Foundry, Taliesin West, fine restaurants, shops, galleries, and lively entertainment. Take along plenty of color film to capture the panoramic desert sunset.

Valley O' the Sun Bed & Breakfast

P.O. BOX 2214, SCOTTSDALE, ARIZONA 85252

Tel: **(602) 941-1281**
Best Time to Call: **9 AM–5 PM**
Host(s): **Kay Curtis**
Location: **2 mi. E of Phoenix**
No. of Rooms: **3**
No. of Private Baths: **1**
Max. No. Sharing Bath: **4**
Double/pb: **$40**
Double/sb: **$35**
Single/sb: **$25**
Open: **Al year**
Reduced Rates: **Weekly**
Breakfast: **Full**
Minimum stay: **2 days**
Pets: **No**
Children: **Welcome**
Smoking: **No**
Social Drinking: **Permitted**
Airport/Station Pickup: **Yes**

Kay Curtis has an attractive yellow-brick house with two stately palm trees on the front lawn. Guests may choose from rooms decorated in white and blue or floral pastel colors. Both have full-size beds and television sets. In the morning, guests may choose from a full or Continental breakfast. Omelets and home fries are the breakfast specialties. The house is ideally located in the college area of Tempe, but is close enough to Scottsdale to enjoy its fine shops and restaurants. From the patio, you can enjoy a beautiful view of the Papago Buttes and McDowell Mountains. Local attractions include swimming at Big Surf, the Phoenix Zoo, and the Scottsdale Center for the Arts.

Barbara's Bed and Breakfast ✪

P.O. BOX 13603, TUCSON, ARIZONA 85732

Tel: **(602) 790-2399**
Best Time to Call: **9 AM–7 PM**
Coordinators: **Rena Kiekebusch and Dorna Nelson**
State/Regions Covered: **Tucson**

Rates (Single/Double):

Modest:	**$20**	**$30**
Average:	**$35**	**$45**
Luxury:	**$50**	**$65**

There is a wide variety of homes in Tucson proper, close to the desert, in outlying towns, and in more remote desert locations, ranging from "nothing pretentious" to foothills elegance and charm. Most fall into the comfortable middle range. Rena and Dorna will match you with a host home where you'll feel perfectly at home. The weather is always good and you'll find many interests to keep you busy, from playing golf, to visiting Indian missions, to taking a trip south of the border to Nogales, Mexico. The University of Arizona is nearby.

The Bird's Nest ✪

6201 N. PIEDRA SECA, TUCSON, ARIZONA 85718

Tel: **(602) 299-9164**
Best Time to Call: **Evenings**
Host(s): **Vic and Betty Hanson**
Location: **10 mi. from I-10**
No. of Rooms: **1**
No. of Private Baths: **1**
Double/pb: **$35**
Single/pb: **$30**
Open: **Jan. 1–Apr. 30; Oct. 1–Nov. 30**
Breakfast: **Continental**
Pets: **No**
Children: **No**
Smoking: **No**
Social Drinking: **Permitted**

Located in the foothills of the Catalina Mountains, this one-story adobe home has a patio. It's furnished in a pleasant blend of Colonial and Southwestern styles, decorated with lovely plants and original art, and it features beautiful views. Vic and Betty enjoy people and will be happy to help you with your touring plans. They'll also identify the large variety of birds that visit their backyard. The University of Arizona is nearby.

Desert Dream ✪

825 VIA LUCITAS, TUCSON, ARIZONA 85718

Tel: **(602) 297-1220**
Best Time to Call: **Evenings**
Host(s): **Ken and Nell Putnam**
Location: **6½ mi. from I-10, Exit Ina Rd.**
No. of Rooms: **1**
No. of Private Baths: **1**
Double/pb: **$35**
Open: **All year**
Breakfast: **Continental**
Pets: **No**
Children: **No**
Smoking: **No**
Social Drinking: **Permitted**

Designed to complement its Catalina Mountains setting, this adobe ranch-style house commands a spectacular view of the city in the valley below. The Desert Museum, Sabino Canyon, Pima Air Museum, and the San Xavier Mission are but a few of the not-to-be-missed nearby sights. You are welcome to use the kitchen for light snacks and the spacious patio for your relaxing pleasure.

Myers' Blue Corn House ✪

4215 EAST KILMER, TUCSON, ARIZONA 85711

Tel: **(602) 327-4663**
Best Time to Call: **After 5 PM**
Host(s): **Barbara and Vern Myers**
Location: **5 mi. from I-10**
No. of Rooms: **2**
Max. No. Sharing Bath: **4**
Double/sb: **$35**
Single/sb: **$25**
Open: **Sept. 1–May 31**
Reduced Rates: **Families, seniors**
Breakfast: **Full**
Pets: **Sometimes**
Children: **Welcome (crib)**
Smoking: **No**
Social Drinking: **Permitted**
Airport/Station Pickup: **Yes**

Located on a quiet residential street, it's convenient to downtown Tucson and the University of Arizona via city buses. The family room, decorated with Indian arts and crafts, and filled with history books, has bumper pool and TV. Close to seasonal recreation, it is also handy for tours of Old Tucson, Saguaro National Monument, Kitt Peak Observatory, and Nogales, Mexico. You may use the kitchen for light snacks, and the washing machine, dryer, and barbecue. The University of Arizona is nearby.

Redbud House Bed & Breakfast ✪

7002 EAST REDBUD ROAD, TUCSON, ARIZONA 85715

Tel: **(602) 721-0218**
Best Time to Call: **10–11 AM**
Host(s): **Ken and Wanda Mayer**
Location: **7 mi. from Rte. 10**
No of Rooms: **1**
No. of Private Baths: **1**
Double/pb: **$42**
Single/pb: **$36**
Open: **All year**
Breakfast: **Full**
Pets: **No**
Children: **No**
Smoking: **No**
Social Drinking: **Permitted**
Airport/Station Pickup: **Yes**
Foreign Languages: **German, Polish**

The Mayers' comfortable ranch-style brick home is on a residential street bordered by tall pines and palm trees. There is a view of the Catalina Mountains from the porch. Local attractions are the Saguaro National Monument, the Arizona Sonora Desert Museum, Kitt Peak National Observatory, and Sabino Canyon. You are welcome to use the bicycles, barbecue, TV, and laundry facilities. Several fine restaurants and a dinner theater are nearby.

Springview ✪

5708 EAST HOLMES STREET, TUCSON, ARIZONA 85711

Tel: **(602) 790-0664**
Best Time to Call: **After 5 PM**
Host(s): **Alec and Elizabeth Payne**
No. of Rooms: **2**
Max. No. Sharing Bath: **4**
Double/sb: **$45**
Single/sb: **$35**
Open: **All year**
Breakfast: **Full**
Pets: **No**
Children: **No**
Smoking: **Permitted**
Social Drinking: **Permitted**

Alec and Elizabeth have a lovely home in a fine neighborhood. It is clean, homey, and comfortably furnished, and you are welcome to relax on the large patio and swim in their pool. It is convenient to golf, shopping malls, the University of Arizona, and Nogales, Mexico.

For key to listings, see inside front or back cover.

✪ This star means that rates are guaranteed through December 31, 1988 to any guest making a reservation as a result of reading about the B&B in *BED & BREAKFAST U.S.A.*—1988 edition.

Please enclose a self-addressed, stamped, business-sized envelope when contacting reservation services.

For more details on what you can expect in a B&B, see Chapter 1.

Always mention *Bed & Breakfast U.S.A.* when making reservations!

If no B&B is listed in the area you'll be visiting, use the form on page 698 to order a copy of our "List of New B&Bs."

We want to hear from you! Use the form on page 697.

ARKANSAS

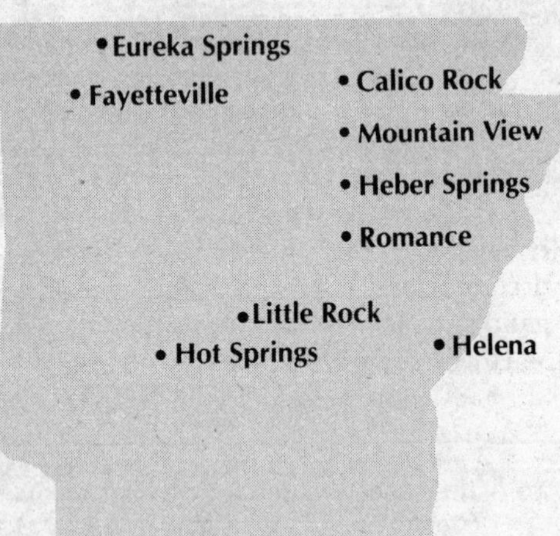

Bed & Breakfast of the Arkansas Ozarks ✪

ROUTE 1, BOX 38, CALICO ROCK, ARKANSAS 72519

Tel: **(501) 297-8764**
Best Time to Call: **7–11 AM**
Coordinator: **Carolyn S. Eck**
State/Regions Covered: **Calico Rock, Des Arc, Fort Smith, Harrison, Mountain Home, Mountain View, Norfolk**

Rates (Single/Double):

Modest:	$23	$35
Average:	$30	$65
Luxury:	$45	$85

Credit Cards: **No**

North-central Arkansas boasts an enviable combination of natural scenic beauty in its forests, rivers, and caves as well as the homespun fun of hootenannies, square dancing, and craft shops. Carolyn's homes include the small-town residence of a teacher-turned-social-worker, close to the river for fine trout fishing, and a new house on a tree farm where the host is a retired USMC officer and the hostess is a ceramic crafts teacher. All are warm and hospitable and echo the motto "Come home to the Ozarks."

Bridgeford Cottage B&B

263 SPRING STREET, EUREKA SPRINGS, ARKANSAS 72632

Tel: **(501) 253-7853**
Best Time to Call: **Mornings**
Host(s): **Ken and Nyla Sawyer**
No. of Rooms: **2**
No. of Private Baths: **1**
Max. No. Sharing Bath: **4**
Double/pb: **$65**
Single/pb: **$55**
Double/sb: **$50**
Single/sb: **$25**
Open: **All year**
Reduced Rates: **10% less, Jan.–Mar.**
Breakfast: **Full**
Pets: **No**
Children: **No**
Smoking: **Permitted**
Social Drinking: **Permitted**
Airport/Station Pickup: **Yes**

A stay at the cottage is a step into the quiet elegance of yesterday. It is located in the historic district, where Victorian homes line the charming streets, horse-drawn carriages wind along the avenue, and old-fashioned trollies carry guests to and fro. Ken and Nyla will pamper you with coffee, tea, and homemade cakes in the afternoon or evening. Breakfast is a real eye-opener of fresh fruit, homemade cinnamon rolls, Ozark ham, and delicious egg casseroles. There's a two-night minimum required on weekends and holidays.

Crescent Cottage Inn ✪

211 SPRING STREET, EUREKA SPRINGS, ARKANSAS 72632

Tel: **(501) 253-6022**
Best Time to Call: **9 AM–8 PM**
Host(s): **Ron and Brenda Bell**
Location: **On Rte. 62**
No. of Rooms: **4**
No. of Private Baths: **3**
Max. No. Sharing Bath: **4**
Double/pb: **$65**
Double/sb: **$55**
Open: **Apr.–Dec.**
Breakfast: **Full**
Credit Cards: **MC, VISA**
Pets: **No**
Children: **No**
Smoking: **No**
Social Drinking: **Permitted**

Crescent Cottage Inn was built in 1881 by Powell Clayton, the first governor of Arkansas. He would still be pleased today with the antique-filled rooms overlooking breathtaking scenes of the valley and East Mountain. Ron and Brenda provide special extras such as nightly turndown service, fresh flowers, and surprise snacks. In the morning they serve homemade rolls, jams, and jellies with a variety of egg dishes. Historic downtown Eureka Springs is just a short walk from here, past lovely springs and shade trees.

Harvest House ✪

104 WALL STREET, EUREKA SPRINGS, ARKANSAS 72632

Tel: **(501) 253-9363**
Best Time to Call: **10 AM–noon; 5–9 PM**
Host(s): **Margaret Conner**
No. of Rooms: **3**
No. of Private Baths: **3**
Double/pb: **$45**
Single/pb: **$35**
Open: **All year**
Breakfast: **Full**
Other Meals: **Available**
Pets: **Sometimes**
Children: **Welcome**
Smoking: **Permitted**
Social Drinking: **Permitted**

This green-and-white Victorian house is furnished with antiques, collectibles, and family favorites. The guest rooms are downstairs, with private entrances. Located in the Ozark Mountains, the scenery is lovely. Homemade surprise snacks are always available. Margaret is a wonderful host and will do everything possible to make your stay pleasant.

Sally's Bed and Breakfast ✪

RR 3, BOX 540, EUREKA SPRINGS, ARKANSAS 72632

Tel: **(501) 253-8340**
Best Time to Call: **9 AM–10 PM**
Host(s): **Sally Mason**
No. of Rooms: **2**
Max. No. Sharing Bath: **4**
Double/sb: **$45**
Single/sb: **$30**
Open: **All year**
Reduced Rates: **Dec.–May**
Breakfast: **Full**
Pets: **Small dogs welcome on leash**
Children: **Welcome**
Smoking: **No**
Social Drinking: **No**

Set in the rolling hills of the Ozarks, this B&B is equipped to accommodate wheelchair-bound guests with a ramp on the front porch and a shower large enough for a chair. The great Passion Play and live country-and-western music shows are performed in the area from May to October. Table Rock Lake is popular for fishing, boating, and swimming. There are many walnut trees on the five acres surrounding the large cedar home. A swing set is in the back yard for your children's pleasure. Breakfast often features sausage with gravy, hash browns, eggs, and biscuits. Evening snacks of cake and ice cream are offered along with interesting conversation.

Singleton House Bed & Breakfast ✪

11 SINGLETON, EUREKA SPRINGS, ARKANSAS 72632

Tel: **(501) 253-9111**
Host(s): **Barbara Gavron**
No. of Rooms: **4**
No. of Private Baths: **2**
Max. No. Sharing Baths: **4**
Double/pb: **$55–$65**
Single/pb: **$55**
Double/sb: **$45–$55**
Single/sb: **$45**
Suites: **$55–$65**
Open: **All year**
Reduced Rates: **After 3rd night**
Breakfast: **Full**
Credit Cards: **MC, VISA**
Pets: **No**
Children: **Sometimes**
Smoking: **No**
Social Drinking: **Permitted**

On a hillside overlooking Eureka Springs' historic district, Singleton House is whimsically decorated with an eclectic collection of comfortable antiques and folk art. Each guest room is decorated with handmade quilts, brass-and-iron bedsteads, ceiling fans, and fresh flowers. Breakfast is served on a balcony overlooking a garden with stony paths, a lily-filled fish pond, and flower-covered arches and arbors. This enchanting setting is credited to a one-of-a-kind designer who claims to be an elf. A secret footpath leads through the woods to quaint shops, cafés, and an active artists' colony. A convenient trolley provides transportation, and guided walking tours are available. Your hostess will help you discover all the best buys and will gladly direct you to popular local attractions, including Beaver Lake.

Eton House ✪

1485 ETON, FAYETTEVILLE, ARKANSAS 72701

Tel: **(501) 521-6344; 443-5481**
Best Time to Call: **10 AM–10 PM**
Host(s): **Patricia Parks**
Location: **65 mi. N of Ft. Smith**
No. of Rooms: **4**
No. of Private Baths: **4**
Double/pb: **$40**
Single/pb: **$35**
Open: **All year**
Breakfast: **Continental**
Pets: **Sometimes**
Children: **Sometimes**
Smoking: **Permitted**
Social Drinking: **Permitted**
Airport/Station Pickup: **Yes**

This buff brick ranch-style home has a cathedral ceiling and is furnished in an eclectic blend of white Victorian wicker and more staid European pieces. Patricia is an enthusiastic hostess and will be happy to direct you to the University of Arkansas, the Museum of Prehistoric Animals, Beaver Lake, Prairie Grove and Pea Ridge battlefields, plus a wealth of cultural and intellectual events. This area is rich in crafts and antique shops, folk art, and authentic mountain music.

Oak Tree Inn ✪

VINEGAR HILL, HIGHWAY 110 WEST, HEBER SPRINGS, ARKANSAS 72543

Tel: **(501) 362-8870/6111**
Host(s): **David and Freddie Lou Lodge**
Location: **60 mi. N of Little Rock**
No. of Rooms: **5**
No. of Private Baths: **5**
Double/pb: **$55–$65**
Single/pb: **$50–$60**
Open: **All year**
Reduced Rates: **Available**
Breakfast: **Full**
Pets: **No**
Children: **No**
Smoking: **No**
Social Drinking: **Permitted**
Airport/Station Pickup: **Yes**

The Oak Tree Inn is set amid Arkansas oaks next to a 45,000-acre lake. The house was designed for bed and breakfast guests, with all the comforts and elegance of a country retreat. Four of the bedrooms have fireplaces, three have queen-size beds, and each has its own whirlpool bath. Rooms are individually decorated in Oriental, Victorian, and English styles. In town and beyond, taste the renowned mineral waters, visit craft shops, and tour scenic roads; Greers Ferry Lake offers scuba diving, fishing, and boating. In the evening enjoy complimentary desserts with your hosts.

Stillmeadow Farm ✪

111 STILLMEADOW LANE, HOT SPRINGS, ARKANSAS 71913

Tel: **(501) 525-9994**
Host(s): **Gene and Jody Sparling**
Location: **4 mi. S of Hot Springs**
No. of Rooms: **4**
No. of Private Baths: **2**
Max. No. Sharing Bath: **4**
Double/pb: **$45–$50**
Single/pb: **$40–$45**
Double/sb: **$40**
Single/sb: **$35**
Suites: **$75–$80**
Open: **All year**
Breakfast: **Continental**
Pets: **No**
Children: **Welcome, over 6**
Smoking: **Permitted**
Social Drinking: **Permitted**

Stillmeadow Farm is a reproduction of an 18th-century New England saltbox, set in 75 acres of pine forest. The decor is of early country antiques. Your hosts provide homemade snacks and fruit in the guest rooms. For breakfast, freshly baked pastries and breads are served. Hot Springs National Park, Lake Hamilton, the Mid-America Museum, and a racetrack are nearby.

Williams House Bed & Breakfast Inn ✪

420 QUAPAW, HOT SPRINGS, ARKANSAS 71901

Tel: **(501) 624-4275**
Host(s): **Mary and Gary Riley**
Best Time to Call: **9–11 AM; evenings**
Location: **50 mi. SW of Little Rock**
No. of Rooms: **6**
No. of Private Baths: **4**
Max. No. Sharing Bath: **4**
Double/pb: **$55–$70**

Single/pb: **$50–$65**
Double/sb: **$50**
Single/sb: **$45**
Suites: **$65–$70**
Guest Cottage: **$135, sleeps 6 (2 baths; 3 bedrooms)**
Open: **All year**
Breakfast: **Full**
Pets: **No**
Children: **Welcome, over 7**
Smoking: **Permitted**
Social Drinking: **Permitted**

This Victorian mansion, with its stained-glass and beveled glass windows, is a nationally registered landmark. The atmosphere is friendly, and the marble fireplace and grand piano invite congeniality. Breakfast menu may include quiche, toast amandine, or exotic egg dishes. Gary and Mary will spoil you with special iced tea, snacks, and mineral spring water. World health experts recognize the benefits of the hot mineral baths in Hot Springs National Park. The inn is within walking distance of Bath House Row. There's a two-night minimum stay on weekends during February, March, and April.

The Commercial Hotel—A Vintage Guest House ✪

P.O. BOX 72, ON THE SQUARE, MOUNTAIN VIEW, ARKANSAS 72560

Tel: **(501) 269-4383**
Host(s): **Todd and Andrea Budy**
Location: **100 mi. N of Little Rock**
No. of Rooms: **8**
No. of Private Baths: **3**
Max. No. Sharing Bath: **5**
Double/pb: **$46**
Single/pb: **$42**
Double/sb: **$34–$38**
Single/sb: **$30–$35**
Suites: **$56**
Open: **All year**
Reduced Rates: **10% discount on 4th night**
Breakfast: **No**
Credit Cards: **AMEX**
Pets: **No**
Children: **Welcome (crib)**
Smoking: **No**
Social Drinking: **Permitted**

Listed on the National Register of Historic Places, there is nothing commercial about this elegant yet homey country inn. The name dates back to the early 1900s when it was originally built to attract business travelers. Completely and lovingly restored, the bedrooms have iron beds and antique dressers, and are air-conditioned for your summer comfort. There is a bakery on the premises where you may buy coffee and pastries. It is a mile to the Ozark Folk Center and close to Blanchard Springs Caverns. From November through March, accommodations are by reservation only.

CALIFORNIA

DESERT AREA

Cornwell's Corner

48-100 DESERT GROVE DRIVE #12, INDIO, CALIFORNIA 92201

Tel: **(619) 342-3151**	Open: **Sept.–May**
Best Time to Call: **7–9 AM; 7–9 PM***	Reduced Rates: **Seniors**
Host(s): **The Cornwell family**	Breakfast: **Continental**
Location: **3 mi. S of I-10**	Minimum Stay: **2 days**
No. of Rooms: **1**	Pets: **No**
No. of Private Baths: **1**	Children: **No**
Double/pb: **$50**	Smoking: **Permittted**
Single/pb: **$50**	Social Drinking: **Permitted**

The Cornwell family welcomes you to their comfortable home, located in the Palm Springs area. The guest room has a private entrance and is furnished with a queen-size bed, large bureau, and a TV with remote control. A private door leads onto the patio, where you can enjoy your morning coffee and pastry. Your hosts invite you to relax in the fireplaced living room, the den, or use the kitchen facilities for a quick snack. They are located next door to the Indian Palms Country Club, where President Eisenhower used to spend the winter months. Guests are welcome to take advantage of the many activities offered at the club, such as swimming, tennis, and golf.

Hotel Nipton ✪

72 NIPTON ROAD, NIPTON, CALIFORNIA 92364

Tel: **(619) 856-2335**
Best Time to Call: **9 AM–7 PM**
Host(s): **Jerry and Roxanne Freeman**
Location: **10 mi. from I-15**
No. of Rooms: **4**
Max. No. Sharing Bath: **4**
Double/sb: **$42**
Open: **All year**
Reduced Rates: **Group**
Breakfast: **Full**
Other Meals: **Available**
Credit Cards: **MC, VISA**
Pets: **No**
Children: **Welcome**
Smoking: **Permitted**
Social Drinking: **Permitted**
Foreign Languages: **Spanish**

The population of Nipton is 30! The recently restored hotel with its foot-thick adobe walls was built in 1904 and located in the East Mohave National Scenic Area. Nipton is in the heart of gold-mining territory, 30 minutes from Lake Mohave's Cottonwood Cove, and 20 minutes from Searchlight. You are welcome to relax on the porch or in the outdoor Jacuzzi. A home-cooked breakfast including eggs, sausage, hash browns, juice, toast, and coffee is served at the small café next door.

GOLD COUNTRY

The Heirloom ✪

P.O. BOX 322, 214 SHAKLEY LANE, IONE, CALIFORNIA 95640

Tel: **(209) 274-4468**
Host(s): **Melisande Hubbs and Patricia Cross**
Location: **35 mi. E of Sacramento**
No. of Rooms: **6**
No. of Private Baths: **4**
Max. No. Sharing Bath: **4**
Double/pb: **$65–$75**
Single/pb: **$55–$60**
Double/sb: **$50–$65**
Single/sb: **$40**
Open: **All year**
Reduced Rates: **Weekly**
Breakfast: **Full**
Pets: **No**
Children: **Welcome, over 10**

Smoking: **Permitted**
Social Drinking: **Permitted**
Airport/Station Pickup: **Yes**

Nestled in the Sierra foothills yet close to the historic gold mines, wineries, antique shops, and museums, this 1863 mansion, with its lovely balconies and fireplaces, is a classic example of antebellum architecture. It is furnished with a combination of family treasures and period pieces. Patricia and Melisande's hearty breakfast includes such delights as quiche, crêpes, soufflé, and fresh fruits. Afternoon refreshments are always offered.

The Pelennor, Bed & Breakfast at Bootjack ✪

3871 HIGHWAY 49 SOUTH, MARIPOSA, CALIFORNIA 95338

Tel: **(209) 966-2832**
Host(s): **Dick and Gwendolyn Foster**
Location: **45 mi. E of Merced**
No. of Rooms: **6**
Max. No. Sharing Bath: **4**
Double/sb: **$35**
Single/sb: **$30**
Open: **All year**
Breakfast: **Full**
Other Meals: **Available**
Pets: **Sometimes**
Children: **Welcome**
Smoking: **Permitted**
Social Drinking: **Permitted**
Airport/Station Pickup: **Yes**

The Pelennor is at the foothills of the Sierra Mountains, at the southern tip of the Mother Lode Gold Country. Guest accommodations are offered in the main house and in a separate B&B building. The property is also home to a friendly cat, dog, and goose. Guests are welcome to relax on the porch or use the barbecue facilities. Your hosts offer homemade croissants, muffins, strawberry jam, and omelets for breakfast. They will gladly direct you to the oldest newspaper and courthouse in the state and Yosemite National Park, one hour away. Dick and Gwendolyn play the bagpipes and can be talked into an occasional performance.

LOS ANGELES AREA

Bed & Breakfast of Los Angeles ✪

32074 WATERSIDE LANE, WESTLAKE VILLAGE, CALIFORNIA 91361

Tel: **(818) 889-8870 or 889-7325**
Best Time to Call: **Evenings**
Coordinators: **Peg Marshall and Angie Kobabe**
States/Regions Covered: **30 communities in greater Los Angeles**

Rates: (Single/Double):

	Single	Double
Modest:	**$24**	**$30**
Average:	**$30**	**$50**
Luxury:	**$40**	**$85**

Credit Cards: **MC, VISA**

Peg and Angie can provide accommodations for you from Ventura in the north to Laguna Beach in the south. There's a guest house in Hollywood, a luxury suite in Beverly Hills, and a contemporary loft in Balboa, to name a few choices. Please send $2 for their directory. B&Bs are located near major colleges in Los Angeles, Orange, and Ventura counties.

California Houseguests International ✪

18533 BURBANK BOULEVARD #190, TARZANA, LOS ANGELES, CALIFORNIA 91356

Tel: **(818) 344-7878**
Best Time to Call: **Before 8 AM**
Coordinator: **Trudi Alexy**
State/Regions Covered: **Greater Los Angeles area, the beach cities, San Diego, San Francisco, Wine Country**

Rates (Single/Double):

Modest:	**$40**	**$45**
Average:	**$50**	**$55**
Luxury:	**$60–$120**	**$65 and up**

Credit Cards: **At some inns**
Minimum Stay: **2 nights**

Through Trudi's 1,000 listings, choose a private suite in a charming chalet overlooking Malibu Beach, or bask in luxury on an estate in the Hollywood Hills, or walk to Disneyland from an Anaheim condo, or steep yourself in atmosphere in a San Francisco Victorian.

El Camino Real Bed & Breakfast ✪

P.O. BOX 7155, NORTHRIDGE, CALIFORNIA 91327-7155

Tel: **(818) 363-6753**
Best Time to Call: **Evenings**
Coordinator: **Claire Reinstein**
State/Regions Covered: **Beverly Hills, Malibu, Marina del Rey, Ojai, Pasadena, San Fernando Valley**

Rates (Single/Double):

Modest:	**$28**	**$35**
Average:	**$40–$45**	**$50–$60**
Luxury:	**N/A**	**$115**

Credit Cards: **No**
Minimum Stay: **2 nights**

This service brings the tradition of California hospitality begun with the Franciscan missions to the present-day traveler. Homes are in beach communities conveniently located to such attractions as Disneyland, Knott's Berry Farm, and the movie studios. Average accommodations are in upper-middle-class homes with swimming pools/spas, except in hilly areas. Choose from a house overlooking the ocean in Malibu, a rustic home in the countryside, or a beautiful condo overlooking a harbor filled with boats. Claire offers modest apartments with simple furnishings and a luxurious private guest house on an estate with a hot tub and swimming pool. All hosts are longtime residents of California, familiar with the restaurants, tourist attractions, and the best ways of getting to them.

House Guests U.S.A., Inc.

P.O. BOX 1185, HUNTINGTON BEACH, CALIFORNIA 92647

Tel: **(714) 891-3736**
Coordinator: **Layne Neugart**
State/Regions Covered: **Los Angeles, Orange County area, Long Beach**

Rates (Single/Double):

Modest:	**$39**	**$49**
Average:	**$49**	**$59 and up**
Luxury:	**$59**	**$69 and up**

Credit Cards: **AMEX, DC, MC, VISA**
Minimum Stay: **3 nights**

Layne invites you to "Wish Upon a Star," and he may have your dream come true. Surely one of his more than 1,000 accommodations will fulfill your desire. Amenities may include a spa, tennis court, spectacular view, or in-room television, and they may be in a beachfront residence or a hillside home. Available at extra cost are a yacht, a car, a chauffeur, or a guide to lead you on a personalized tour. Entertainment and dining discounts are provided. Please note that credit card charges are subject to a 5% surcharge and 60-day advance payment. Hostless homes and condos are also available.

Belair ✪

941 NORTH FREDERIC STREET, BURBANK, CALIFORNIA 91505

Tel: **(818) 848-9227**
Best Time to Call: **7 AM–7 PM**
Host(s): **Harry Bell**
Location: **10 mi. N of Los Angeles**
No. of Rooms: **3**
No. of Private Baths: **3**
Double/pb: **$35**
Single/pb: **$25**
Reduced Rates: **Weekly**

Open: **All year**
Breakfast: **Full**
Pets: **No**
Children: **Welcome, over 8**
Smoking: **Permitted**
Social Drinking: **Permitted**
Airport/Station Pickup: **Yes**
Foreign Languages: **French**

Your host, Harry Bell, a retired teacher, musician, adventurer, world traveler, and collector of exotic art, is as interesting as his home is convenient and comfortable. Located in quiet, residential Burbank, it is only 2 miles from studio tours, 5 miles from Hollywood, and 30 miles to beach or mountain resorts. It is also convenient to public bus transportation. The upstairs has a double bed in one room and a dorm with four beds. It is ideal for a family or friends traveling together. The charge for the dorm is $12 per person.

Shroff Bed & Breakfast Home ✪

1114 PARK AVENUE, GLENDALE, CALIFORNIA 91205

Tel: **(818) 507-0774**
Best Time to Call: **8–10 AM; evenings**
Host(s): **Spencer and Gerry Shroff**
Location: **10 mi. NE of Los Angeles**
No. of Rooms: **1**
Max. No. Sharing Bath: **2**
Double/sb: **$35**
Single/sb: **$30**
Open: **All year**
Reduced Rates: **7th day free**
Breakfast: **Continental**
Pets: **No**
Children: **Welcome**
Smoking: **Permitted**
Social Drinking: **Permitted**

Friendly, helpful hosts look forward to making your visit the best ever. Their Spanish-style stucco house with its double bed in the guest room is furnished with 1930s motifs. It is comfortable in all seasons, being centrally heated and air-cooled. It is convenient to the movie studio tours, art galleries, ethnic restaurants, as well as to Forest Lawn Memorial Park. The Shroffs love to travel and will happily share tips with you on where to go. Personal checks are not accepted.

Casablanca Villa ✪

449 NORTH DETROIT STREET, LOS ANGELES, CALIFORNIA 90036

Tel: **(213) 938-4794**
Host(s): **Suzanne Moultout**
No. of Rooms: **1**
Max. No. Sharing Bath: **2–3**
Double/sb: **$35**
Single/sb: **$30**
Open: **All year**
Breakfast: **Continental**
Pets: **No**
Children: **Welcome**
Smoking: **No**
Social Drinking: **No**
Airport/Station Pickup: **Yes**

Suzanne Moultout welcomes you to her Spanish-style house located on a quiet, attractive street. Here guests can enjoy the convenience of being close to West Hollywood, downtown, and Beverly Center, while having a comfortable home base. Your hostess offers an attractive guest room and a shady yard with fruit trees. She will gladly direct you to such nearby sights as Hollywood Hills, CBS Studios, and the beaches. Even if you don't have a car, the area is quite convenient, with a bus stop located within walking distance.

Terrace Manor ✪

1353 ALVARADO TERRACE, LOS ANGELES, CALIFORNIA 90006

Tel: **(213) 381-1478**
Host(s): **Sandy and Shirley Spillman**
Location: **Downtown Los Angeles**
No. of Rooms: **5**

No. of Private Baths: **5**
Double/pb: **$55–$85**
Open: **All year**
Breakfast: **Full**
Credit Cards: **AMEX, MC, VISA**
Pets: **No**
Children: **Welcome, over 10**
Smoking: **No**
Social Drinking: **Permitted**
Airport/Station Pickup: **Yes**

Nestled in modern downtown Los Angeles, Terrace Manor is one of several historical landmarks surrounding a park. Built in 1902, the Manor contains its original stained-glass and leaded-glass windows, paneled walls, hardwood floors, and an Ionic-columned fireplace with a built-in clock that still chimes on cue. Choose from comfortable rooms each named for its special feature. The Sun Room Suite is decorated in authentic period paper in coral and turquoise and has a queen-size iron-and-brass bed and an attached porch with trundle. Lydia's Room is rich hunter green and mauve, with an ornate king-size bed and Victorian settee. Your hosts serve breakfast in the dining room or outside on the patio. Specialties include seasonal fruit, French toast, fritatta, quiche, and omelets, served with coffee or tea. They also invite you to gather in the parlor or library later for an afternoon social hour with complimentary wine and a light repast.

Casa Larronde ✪

P.O. BOX 86, MALIBU, CALIFORNIA 90265-0086

Tel: **(213) 456-9333**
Best Time to Call: **Mornings**
Host(s): **Jim and Charlou Larronde**
Location: **40 mi. NW of Los Angeles**
No. of Rooms: **1 suite**
No. of Private Baths: **1**
Suite: **$75**
Open: **All year**
Breakfast: **Full**
Pets: **Sometimes**
Children: **Sometimes**
Smoking: **Permitted**
Social Drinking: **Permitted**

The guest suite has a fireplace and color TV, but if you walk down the beach you may get to see the stars live; Rich Little, Ann-Margret, and the McEnroes are the neighborhood people here on Millionaires' Row. This house is 4,000 square feet of spectacular living space. It has floor-to-ceiling glass, ocean decks, a private beach, and a planter that's two stories high. Jim and Charlou, world travelers, enjoy entertaining, and their gourmet breakfast ranges from Scotch eggs to French toast made with Portuguese sweet bread. Champagne, cocktails, and snacks are complimentary refreshments. Pepperdine College is two miles away. The Getty Museum is a five-minute drive.

Hideaway House ✪

8441 MELVIN AVENUE, NORTHRIDGE, CALIFORNIA 91324

Tel: **(818) 349-5421**
Best Time to Call: **6–10 PM**
Host(s): **Dean and Dorothy Dennis**
Location: **20 mi. NW of Los Angeles**
No. of Rooms: **2**
No. of Private Baths: **1**
Max. No. Sharing Bath: **2**
Double/pb: **$55**
Single/pb: **$50**
Open: **All year**
Breakfast: **Full**
Other Meals: **Available**
Pets: **Sometimes**
Children: **Welcome, over 10**
Smoking: **No**
Social Drinking: **Permitted**
Airport/Station Pickup: **Yes**

Located in a beautiful Los Angeles suburb, this secluded country estate in the San Fernando Valley is a good base for exploring southern California. It's 30 minutes to the beach and 50 minutes to Disneyland. Dean and Dorothy welcome you to their art- and antiques-filled home and will provide local guide service by prior arrangement. Cal. State–Northridge is nearby.

By-the-Sea ✪

4273 PALOS VERDES DRIVE SOUTH, RANCHO PALOS VERDES, CALIFORNIA 90274

Tel: **(213) 377-2113**
Host(s): **Ruth and Earl Exley**
Location: **5 mi. SW of Los Angeles**
No. of Rooms: **2**
No. of Private Baths: **2**
Double/pb: **$50**
Single/pb: **$35**
Open: **All year**
Reduced Rates: **10%, seniors**
Breakfast: **Full**
Other Meals: **Available**
Pets: **Sometimes**
Children: **Welcome**
Smoking: **Yes**
Social Drinking: **Permitted**
Airport/Station Pickup: **Yes**

This gracious ranch-style home in suburban Los Angeles has an unobstructed ocean view. Ruth and Earl belong to a private beach club across the road, and you can use the facilities there. It is close to Marineland, Disneyland, and Hollywood. Ruth's breakfast specialties include honey-baked ham, French toast, or quiche. Your hosts offer you hors d'oeuvres with other pre-dinner refreshments. California State–Dominguez Hills is close by.

Sea Breeze Bed & Breakfast ✪

122 SOUTH JUANITA, REDONDO BEACH, CALIFORNIA 90277

Tel: **(213) 316-5123**
Best Time to Call: **6–10 PM**
Host(s): **Norris and Betty Binding**
Location: **19 mi. S of Los Angeles**
No. of Rooms: **2**
No. of Private Baths: **2**
Double/pb: **$40**
Single/pb: **$30**
Open: **All year**
Reduced Rates: **After 1 night**
Breakfast: **Continental**
Pets: **No**
Children: **Welcome, over 5**
Smoking: **Permitted**
Social Drinking: **Permitted**
Airport/Station Pickup: **Yes**

The welcome mat is out in front of the lovely stained-glass Colonial doors at Norris and Betty's modest home. A patio-garden is just outside the large guest room where you may relax after seeing the sights in the area. The Getty Museum, Marineland, and the Pasadena Rose Bowl are within easy reach. Their beach is the start of 22 miles of the Redondo-to-Pacific Palisades bicycle path, and tennis courts are within walking distance. Provisions are available if you prefer to fix breakfast yourself. You are welcome to use the Jacuzzi and TV. UCLA, USC, and Loyola Marymount are nearby.

Noone Guest House ✪

2755 SONOMA STREET, TORRANCE, CALIFORNIA 90503

Tel: **(213) 328-1837**
Host(s): **Betty and Bob Noone**
Location: **15 mi. SW of Los Angeles**
No. of Rooms: **1 cottage**
No. of Private Baths: **1**
Guest Cottage: **$35; sleeps 2**
Open: **All year**
Breakfast: **Continental**
Pets: **No**
Children: **Welcome, over 12**
Smoking: **Permitted**
Social Drinking: **Permitted**

This comfortable guest cottage has a bedroom, bath, kitchen, patio, TV, and laundry facilities, but the special plus is the warm hospitality offered by Betty and Bob. They'll direct you to Disneyland, Knott's Berry Farm, or the beach—all close to "home." The University of Southern California is nearby.

The Whites' House ✪

17122 FAYSMITH AVENUE, TORRANCE, CALIFORNIA 90504

Tel: **(213) 324-6164**
Host(s): **Russell and Margaret White**
Location: **15 mi. S of Los Angeles**
No. of Rooms: **2**
No. of Private Baths: **2**
Double/pb: **$30**
Single/pb: **$25**
Open: **All year**
Reduced Rates: **Weekly; monthly**
Breakfast: **Continental**
Pets: **No**
Children: **Welcome**
Smoking: **Permitted**
Social Drinking: **Permitted**
Airport/Station Pickup: **Yes**

This contemporary home with its fireplaces, deck, and patio is located on a quiet street in an unpretentious neighborhood. The airport and lovely beaches are 15 minutes away. Disneyland, Knott's Berry Farm, Universal Studio Tours, and Hollywood are 30 minutes from the door. Use the laundry facilities or kitchen; Russell and Margaret want you to feel perfectly at home.

The Wild Goose ✪

2732 WEST 232 STREET, TORRANCE, CALIFORNIA 90505

Tel: **(213) 325-3578**
Host(s): **Elaine Steinert**
Location: **15 mi. SW of Los Angeles**
No. of Rooms: **2**
No. of Private Baths: **1**
Max. No. Sharing Bath: **4**
Double/pb: **$50**
Single/pb: **$35**
Double/sb: **$40**
Single/sb: **$25**
Open: **All year**
Reduced Rates: **Available**
Breakfast: **Full**
Pets: **No**
Children: **Welcome**
Smoking: **Permitted**
Social Drinking: **Permitted**
Airport/Station Pickup: **Yes**

The Wild Goose is a charming contemporary with a lovely courtyard entrance. The house has a light, open feeling created with glass motifs overlooking a planted atrium. Your hostess enjoys gardening, traveling, and entertaining. She will gladly direct you to the beach, four miles away. Other nearby attractions include Marineland and Los Angeles. Disneyland and Knott's Berry Farm are a 45-minute drive from the house.

Hendrick Inn ✪

2124 E. MERCED AVENUE, WEST COVINA, CALIFORNIA 91791

Tel: **(818) 919-2125**
Host(s): **Mary and George Hendrick**
Location: **20 mi. E of Los Angeles**
No. of Rooms: **2**
No. of Private Baths: **1**
Max. No. Sharing Bath: **3**
Double/pb: **$40**
Single/pb: **$40**
Double/sb: **$30–$35**
Single/sb: **$25**
Suites: **$40**
Open: **All year**
Breakfast: **Full**
Other meals: **Dinner available**
Pets: **No**
Children: **Welcome, over 5**
Smoking: **Permitted**
Social Drinking: **Permitted**
Foreign Languages: **Spanish**

This lovely home is one hour from the mountains, seashore, and desert. It's less than an hour to Disneyland or busy downtown Los Angeles. The living rooms of this sprawling ranch-style house contain comfortable sitting areas and fireplaces where you may share a nightcap with your hospitable hosts. You will enjoy the backyard swimming pool and the Jacuzzi after a day of touring. There's a three-night minimum in the suite, a two-night minimum in the guestrooms.

Coleen's California Casa ✪

11715 SOUTH CIRCLE DRIVE, WHITTIER, CALIFORNIA 90608

Tel: **(213) 699-8427**
Best Time to Call: **6:30 AM–7:30 AM; 5 PM–9 PM**
Host(s): **Coleen Davis**
Location: **18 mi. E of Los Angeles**
No. of Rooms: **3**
No. of Private Baths: **3**
Double/pb: **$55**
Single/pb: **$45**
Suite: **$55**
Open: **All year**
Breakfast: **Full**
Other Meals: **Available**
Pets: **No**
Children: **Welcome**
Smoking: **Permitted**
Social Drinking: **Yes**
Airport/Station Pickup: **Yes**
Foreign Languages: **Spanish**

Only minutes from the freeway system, this tranquil home is nestled into a hillside overlooking the city. It is convenient to Disneyland, Knott's Berry Farm, and all of Los Angeles's attractions. After a day of sightseeing, you'll be welcomed home with wine and hors d'oeuvres. With ample notice, Coleen will be happy to prepare dinner. Otherwise, she'll be pleased to recommend one of the many ethnic restaurants in the neighborhood. Breakfast is served on the deck filled with many exotic plants Coleen has cultivated.

MENDOCINO/WINE COUNTRY/NORTH COAST

Bed & Breakfast Exchange

1458 LINCOLN AVENUE, CALISTOGA, CALIFORNIA 94515

Tel: **(707) 963-7756**
Best Time to Call: **9 AM–5 PM**
Coordinators: **Larry M. Paladini and Diane Byrne**
States/Regions Covered: **Napa and Sonoma counties, northern California coast, Gold Rush country**

Rates (Single/Double):
Modest: **$50–$60**
Average: **$65–$85**
Luxury: **$90–$300**
Credit Cards: **MC, VISA**

Some homes are located convenient to the wineries and vineyards. Wine-tasting tours are popular pastimes. Others are in the historic area where gold was discovered, and still others are in the spectacular locale of the Pacific. The more expensive accommodations are on fabulous estates with pools, spas, and special services. You may also call Saturday, from 10 AM–5 PM; Sunday, noon–3 PM.

Big Yellow Sunflower Bed & Breakfast ✪

235 SKY OAKS DRIVE, ANGWIN, CALIFORNIA 94508

Tel: **(707) 965-3885**
Best Time to Call: **Evenings**
Host(s): **Dale and Betty Clement**
Location: **60 mi. N of San Francisco**
No. of Rooms: **1 suite**
No. of Private Baths: **1**
Double/pb: **$65**
Single/pb: **$55**

Open: **All year**
Breakfast: **Full**
Other Meals: **Available**
Pets: **Sometimes**
Children: **Welcome, over 6**
Smoking: **No**
Social Drinking: **Permitted**

Located near the center of the Napa Valley wine area, the guest duplex, a completely private suite with kitchenette and sun deck, is part of Betty and Dale's wood-and-brick Colonial home. Charmingly decorated with some antiques, lots of plants, and flower baskets, it accommodates seven people. Complimentary snacks and beverages are offered when you arrive. They pride themselves on serving a more-than-you-can-eat breakfast.

Scarlett's Country Inn ✪

3918 SILVERADO TRAIL N., CALISTOGA, CALIFORNIA 94515

Tel: **(707) 942-6669**
Best Time to Call: **9 AM–5 PM**
Host(s): **Scarlett Dwyer**
Location: **75 mi. N of San Francisco; 30 mi. from I-80, Napa Exit**
No. of Rooms: **3**
No. of Private Baths: **3**
Double/pb: **$75**
Single/pb: **$60**
Suites: **$75–$95**
Guest Cottage: **$220, sleeps 6**
Open: **All year**
Breakfast: **Continental**
Credit Cards: **MC, VISA**
Pets: **No**
Children: **Welcome**
Smoking: **Permitted**
Social Drinking: **Permitted**
Foreign Languages: **Spanish**

This inn is an intimate retreat tucked away in a small canyon in the heart of the famed Napa Valley, just minutes away from wineries and spas. Tranquillity, green lawns, and a refreshing swimming pool await you in this peaceful woodland setting. An ample breakfast featuring freshly squeezed juice, sweet rolls, and freshly ground coffee is served on the deck, at poolside, or in your own sitting room. All rooms have separate entrances, queen-size beds, and luxurious linens.

Muktip Manor ✪

12540 LAKESHORE DRIVE, CLEARLAKE, CALIFORNIA 95422

Tel: **(707) 994-9571**
Host(s): **Elisabeth and Jerry Schiffman**
Location: **101 mi. N of San Francisco**
No. of Rooms: **1 suite**
No. of Private Baths: **1**
Suite: **$50**
Open: **All year**
Breakfast: **Full**
Pets: **Welcome**
Children: **No**
Smoking: **Permitted**
Social Drinking: **Permitted**
Foreign Languages: **French, Spanish**

Elisabeth and Jerry have traded the often-frenzied San Francisco lifestyle for an uncomplicated existence by the largest lake in the state. They do not offer Victoriana, priceless antiques, or gourmet food. They do provide comfortable accommodations in their unpretentious beach house, a place to relax on the deck, and the use of their private beach and bicycles. They enjoy windsurfing and canoeing and have been known to give instruction to interested guests. Their motto is "If you wish company, we're conversationalists; if you wish privacy, we're invisible."

Vintage Towers ✪

302 NORTH MAIN STREET, CLOVERDALE, CALIFORNIA 95425

Tel: **(707) 894-4535**
Host(s): **Dan and Lauri Weddle**
Location: **90 mi. N of San Francisco**
No. of Rooms: **8**
No. of Private Baths: **6**
Max. No. Sharing Bath: **4**
Double/pb: **$55**
Double/sb: **$45**
Suites: **$68–$80**
Open: **All year**
Breakfast: **Full**
Credit Cards: **MC, VISA**
Pets: **No**
Children: **Welcome, over 10**
Smoking: **No**
Social Drinking: **Permitted**
Airport/Station Pickup: **Yes**

On a quiet street, reminiscent of New England, is this grand Queen Anne Victorian mansion listed on the National Register of Historic Places. Each room has been restored with period pieces and decorated with individual themes. Dan enjoys serving a breakfast of varied egg dishes as well as freshly baked breads and cakes. On cool mornings, you'll be served by the dining room fireplace; on warm mornings on the veranda or in the garden gazebo.

The Carter House ✪

1033 THIRD STREET, EUREKA, CALIFORNIA 95501

Tel: **(707) 445-1390**
Best Time to Call: **Noon–5 PM**
Host(s): **Mark and Christi Carter**
No. of Rooms: **7**
No. of Private Baths: **4**
Max. No. Sharing Bath: **4**
Double/pb: **$65–$80**
Single/pb: **$50**
Double/sb: **$55–$70**
Single/sb: **$45**
Suites: **$120–$150**
Open: **All year**
Reduced Rates: **5%, seniors**
Breakfast: **Full**
Credit Cards: **AMEX, MC, VISA**
Pets: **No**
Children: **Welcome, over 12**
Smoking: **No**
Social Drinking: **Permitted**
Airport/Station Pickup: **Yes**
Foreign Languages: **French, German, Spanish**

In 1982, this Victorian mansion was precisely reproduced from architectural plans drawn in 1884. The exterior is redwood, and the interior is done in redwood and oak. All trims and moldings are handmade and the chimneys rise to 50 feet. The rooms, each with a view, are furnished with authentic antiques, down comforters, Oriental rugs, original art, and fresh flowers. Christi and Mark pamper you with breakfasts that often include eggs Benedict or unusual pastries, hors d'oeuvres and complimentary wine before dinner, cookies and cordials before bedtime, and (by special arrangement with Mark) limousine service in his 1958 Bentley. Wow! Humboldt State University is nearby.

The Marlahan Ranch House

9539 NORTH HIGHWAY 3, FORT JONES, CALIFORNIA 96032

Tel: **(916) 468-5527**
Host(s); **Gene and Pat Graham**
Location: **15 mi. from I-5**
No. of Rooms: **4**
Max. No. Sharing Bath: **5**
Double/sb: **$45–$65**
Open: **All year**
Reduced Rates: **10%, Jan.–Mar.**
Breakfast: **Continental**
Credit Cards: **MC, VISA**
Pets: **Sometimes**
Children: **Welcome, over 12**
Smoking: **No**
Social Drinking: **Permitted**

The unspoiled terrain of California's northernmost county is the backyard of this Victorian ranch dating back to 1899. Two large covered porches offer views of secluded Scott Valley and the Trinity, Salmon, and Marble mountains. The atmosphere is casual, with spacious rooms furnished in country pieces and antiques. Gene and Pat serve homemade muffins or coffee cake, fresh fruit, coffee, and herb teas for breakfast. They will gladly help you plan a variety of recreational activities including cross-country and downhill skiing, hiking, fishing, hunting, and white-water rafting. History buffs will be glad to know of nearby Indian lore and the Fort Jones Museum.

Camellia Inn ✪

211 NORTH STREET, HEALDSBURG, CALIFORNIA 95448

Tel: **(707) 433-8182**
Best Time to Call: **Mornings**
Host(s): **Ray and Del Lewand**
Location: **65 mi. N of San Francisco**
No. of Rooms: **7**
No. of Private Baths: **5**
Max. No. Sharing Bath: **4**
Double/pb: **$55**
Double/sb: **$55**
Single/sb: **$45**
Suite: **$90**
Open: **All year**
Reduced Rates: **Available**
Breakfast: **Full**
Credit Cards: **MC, VISA**
Pets: **No**
Children: **Welcome, over 10**
Smoking: **No**
Social Drinking: **Permitted**

This elegant Italianate Victorian town house (circa 1869) is an architectural delight. It is convenient to the Russian River, wineries, golf, tennis, and more. Ray and Del serve a hearty breakfast buffet in the dining room, and wine is served in the afternoon in the grand parlor or on the pool terrace.

Frampton House

489 POWELL AVENUE, HEALDSBURG, CALIFORNIA 95448

Tel: **(707) 433-5084**
Host(s): **Roland and Janette Wilkinson**
Location: **70 mi. N of San Francisco**
No. of Rooms: **3**
No. of Private Baths: **3**
Double/pb: **$50–$70**
Open: **All year**
Reduced Rates: **Available**
Breakfast: **Full**
Credit Cards: **MC, VISA**
Pets: **Sometimes**
Children: **Welcome**
Smoking: **No**
Social Drinking: **Permitted**
Airport/Station Pickup: **Yes**
Foreign Language: **Spanish**

This turn-of-the-century redwood home is in the heart of Wine Country. The guest rooms offer a choice of queen-size beds or extra-long beds, and two of the baths have tubs-for-two. On chilly evenings, a fire crackles in the fireplace and complimentary vintage wines and cheese are served in the social room. Breakfast might consist of a Finnish oven pancake or apple-sausage casserole, and may be enjoyed in the solarium or at poolside. The Napa and Sonoma valleys are within an easy drive.

The Victorian Farmhouse ✪

7001 NORTH HIGHWAY 1, P.O. BOX 357, LITTLERIVER, CALIFORNIA 95456

Tel: **(707) 937-0697**
Host(s): **George and Carole Molnar**
Location: **168 mi. N of San Francisco**
No. of Rooms: **6**
No. of Private Baths: **6**
Double/pb: **$69–$77**
Open: **All year**
Breakfast: **Continental**
Pets: **No**
Children: **Welcome, over 10**
Smoking: **Permitted**
Social Drinking: **Permitted**
Airport/Station Pickup: **Yes**
Foreign Language: **Hungarian**

Built in 1877, the farmhouse has been completely renovated and furnished in period antiques to enhance its original beauty and Victorian charm. It's close to Mendocino with its many galleries, boutiques, and restaurants. There's an apple orchard and gardens, and the ocean is a short walk away. Whale-watching in the winter months is popular. George and Carole will pamper you with breakfast brought to your room, and will invite you to join them for evening sherry. There's a two-night minimum on weekends; three nights on holiday weekends.

The Swiss Chalet ✪

5128 SWEDBERG ROAD, LOWER LAKE, CALIFORNIA 95457

Tel: **(707) 994-7313**
Host(s); **Robert and Ingrid Hansen**
Location: **60 mi. NE of Santa Rosa**
No. of Rooms: **2**
No. of Private Baths: **1**
Max. No. Sharing Bath: **2**
Double/pb: **$55**
Single/pb: **$45**
Double/sb: **$55**
Single/sb: **$45**
Open: **Apr.–Dec.**
Reduced Rates: **$5 less after 2 nights**
Breakfast: **Full**
Pets: **No**
Children: **No**
Smoking: **Permitted**
Social Drinking: **Permitted**
Airport/Station Pickup: **Yes**
Foreign Languages: **French, German, Italian, Spanish**

Stained-glass windows enhance this Bavarian gem that overlooks an 85-square-mile mountain lake. The interior is immaculate and tastefully furnished with handpainted tole pieces, antiques, and rich woods. The stone fireplace, deck, and private beach are fine sites for relaxation. All seasonal sports are available. Robert and Ingrid will spoil you with such goodies as eggs Benedict or blueberry pancakes. By the way, the second bedroom is available only to friends traveling together.

Wine Country Cottage ✪

400 MEADOWOOD LANE, ST. HELENA, CALIFORNIA 94574

Tel: **(707) 963-0852**
Best Time to Call: **Evenings**
Host(s): **Jan Strong**
Location: **In the Napa Valley**
Guest Cottage: **$85; sleeps 2**
Open: **All year**
Breakfast: **Continental**
Pets: **Sometimes**
Children: **Sometimes**
Smoking: **Permitted**
Social Drinking: **Permitted**

A private woodland retreat for two, with a patio under the pines, a comfortable bed-sitting room, private bath with shower, and complete kitchen. Jan will make reservations for you at the nearby spas. Napa Valley wineries, hot-air ballooning, tennis, golf, or swimming facilities are all close by. There are many galleries and renowned restaurants for you to enjoy.

The Hidden Oak

214 EAST NAPA STREET, SONOMA, CALIFORNIA 95476

Tel: **(707) 996-9863**
Host(s): **Barbara and Jacques Gasser**
Location: **10 mi. from Rte. 37, Exit Sonoma**
No. of Rooms: **3**
No. of Private Baths: **3**
Double/pb: **$80**
Single/pb: **$70**
Open: **All year**
Reduced Rates: **$10 less, Thanksgiving–Easter**
Breakfast: **Full**
Pets: **No**
Children: **Welcome, over 15**
Smoking: **No**
Social Drinking: **Permitted**
Foreign Languages: **French**

Barbara and Jacques remodeled this fine home, built in 1913, without sacrificing any of its original charm. Furnished in antiques, the guest rooms have queen-size beds covered with cozy comforters. Breakfast features exotic entrees and home-baked treats served either in the formal dining room or on the sunny deck. You are welcome to borrow a bike and head for the wineries, which are less than 3 miles away. Boutiques, restaurants, and historical sites abound in the neighborhood. The Sears Point Car Raceway is 10 miles away. When you return from your explorations, you're welcome to stretch out beside the pool or by the fire, depending on the weather. Wine and hors d'oeuvres are graciously offered before dinner.

Oak Knoll Bed & Breakfast ✪

858 SANEL DRIVE, UKIAH, CALIFORNIA 95482

Tel: **(707) 468-5646**
Best Time to Call: **8 AM–12 PM; 3 PM–6 PM**
Host(s): **Shirley Wadley**
Location: **½ mi. from Hwy. 101**
No. of Rooms: **2**
Max. No. Sharing Bath: **4**
Double/sb: **$50**
Single/sb: **$45**
Open: **All year**
Breakfast: **Full**
Pets: **No**
Children: **No**
Smoking: **No**
Social Drinking: **Permitted**

Every window of this redwood contemporary offers breathtaking views of the valley and vineyards of Mendocino wine country. Your hostess, Shirley Wadley, has decorated her lovely home with a mixture of modern elegance and rustic charm. The rooms feature exquisite chandeliers and colorful wall coverings. Bedrooms have queen-size beds and fresh flowers to enjoy. Relax on the spacious deck with some cheese, crackers, and a glass of local wine. Guests are welcome to unwind in the large solar spa, play the piano in the living room, or enjoy a movie on a 40-inch screen in the family room. Oak Knoll offers easy access to the coast, the redwoods, Lake Mendocino, and the wineries of Ukiah and Mendocino County.

MONTEREY PENINSULA

Happy Landing Inn ✪

P.O. BOX 2619, CARMEL, CALIFORNIA 93921

Tel: **(408) 624-7917**
Best Time to Call: **8:30 AM–9 PM**
Host(s): **Bob Alberson, Dick Stewart**
Location: **120 mi. S of San Francisco**
No. of Rooms: **7**
No. of Private Baths: **7**
Double/pb: **$70**
Single/pb: **$70**
Open: **All year**
Breakfast: **Continental**
Credit Cards: **AMEX, MC, VISA**
Pets: **Sometimes**
Children: **Welcome, over 12**
Smoking: **No**
Social Drinking: **Permitted**
Foreign Languages: **Japanese**

Located on Monte Verde between 5th and 6th, this early Comstock-style inn is a charming and romantic place to stay. Rooms with cathedral ceilings open onto a beautiful garden with gazebo, pond, and flagstone paths. Lovely antiques and personal touches, including breakfast served in your room, make your stay special. There's a two-night minimum on weekends.

SACRAMENTO AREA

Annie Horan's ✪

415 WEST MAIN STREET, GRASS VALLEY, CALIFORNIA 95945

Tel: **(916) 272-2418**
Host(s): **Ivan and Bette Nance**
Location: **45 mi. NW of Sacramento**
No. of Rooms: **4**
No. of Private Baths: **4**
Double/pb: **$50–$75**
Open: **All year**
Reduced Rates: **$40–$50, Jan. 1–Mar. 31**
Breakfast: **Continental**
Credit Cards: **MC, VISA**
Pets: **No**
Children: **No**
Smoking: **No**
Social Drinking: **Permitted**
Airport/Station Pickup: **Yes**
Foreign Languages: **Spanish**

Annie Horan's is an elegant Victorian of splendid design and workmanship. Its parlor, entry hall, and guest quarters appear as they did in the opulent Gold Rush days. Bette and Ivan have furnished this treasure with antiques that best depict that era. They invite you to enjoy the mountain air on the spacious deck. Nearby activities include panning for gold, swimming, golf, hiking, and nature trails.

Jean Pratt's Riverside B&B ✪

P.O. BOX 2334, OROVILLE, CALIFORNIA 95965

Tel: **(916) 533-1413**
Host(s): **Jean Pratt**
Location: **2 minutes from Hwy. 70**
No. of Rooms: **7**
No. of Private Baths: **7**
Double/pb: **$45**
Single/pb: **$30–$40**
Suite: **$50–$65**
Open: **All year**
Breakfast: **Continental**
Other meals: **Available**
Pets: **No**
Children: **Sometimes**
Smoking: **Permitted**
Social Drinking: **Permitted**
Airport/Station Pickup: **Yes**
Foreign Languages: **French**

Jean's Riverside is located at the gateway to the scenic Feather River Canyon (the only year-round through-route to Reno and Lake Tahoe), on the banks of the river itself. Swimming, fishing, goldpanning, and canoeing are available on the five-acre private waterfront. Jean will happily direct you to Feather Falls, Mount Lassen, Oroville Dam and Lake, the nationally recognized Chinese temple, and other historic sites. All rooms are handsomely decorated and most have window walls that overlook the river and friendly wildlife.

The Feather Bed ✪

542 JACKSON STREET, QUINCY, CALIFORNIA 95971

Tel: **(916) 283-0102**
Host(s): **Chuck and Dianna Goubert**
Location: **70 mi. NW of Reno, Nevada**
No. of Rooms: **7**
No. of Private Baths: **7**
Double/pb: **$55**
Single/pb: **$50**
Suite: **$60**
Separate Cottage: **$75, sleeps 3**
Open: **All year**
Reduced Rates: **10% less on 3rd night**
Breakfast: **Full**
Credit Cards: **AMEX, MC, VISA**
Pets: **No**
Children: **Welcome, over 12**
Smoking: **No**
Social Drinking: **Permitted**
Airport/Station Pickup: **Yes**

This charming Queen Anne was built in 1893 and renovated at the turn of the century. The rooms feature vintage wallpaper, antique furnishings, and charming baths; most have clawfoot tubs. Enjoy a glass of sherry in the parlor or a cool iced tea on the front porch. A breakfast of blended coffee, fresh juices, fruits, and home-baked breads can be served in your room, on the patio, or in the dining room. The inn is convenient to water sports, snowmobiling, hiking, tennis, and skiing. Your hosts offer complimentary bicycles to help you explore beautiful Plumas National Forest and historic downtown Quincy.

Bear Flag Inn ✪

2814 I STREET, SACRAMENTO, CALIFORNIA 95816

Tel: **(916) 448-5417**
Best Time to Call: **Evenings**
Host(s): **Dean and Lisa Wofford**
Location: **½ mi. from I-80**
No. of Rooms: **4**
No. of Private Baths: **4**
Double/pb: **$59**
Single/pb: **$54**
Open: **All year**
Reduced Rates: **15%, Sun.–Thurs in Dec.–Feb.**
Breakfast: **Continental**
Credit Cards: **AMEX, DC, MC, VISA**
Pets: **No**
Children: **Welcome, over 8**
Smoking: **No**
Social Drinking: **Permitted**

This European-style hostelry is located in a residential neighborhood of downtown Sacramento. It is a handsomely restored California "Arts and Crafts Style" bungalow decorated with Queen Anne furnishings and within walking distance of fine restaurants, Sutter's Fort, and "J" Street boutiques.

The Briggs House ✪

2209 CAPITOL AVENUE, SACRAMENTO, CALIFORNIA 95816

Tel: **(916) 441-3214**
Best Time to Call: **9 AM–noon; 4–9 PM**
Host(s): **Sue Garmston, Barbara Stoltz, Kathy Yeates, Paula Rawles, Leslie Hopper**
Location: **1 mi. from I-80**
No. of Rooms: **7**
No. of Private Baths: **5**
Max. No. Sharing Bath: **2**
Double/pb: **$65–$80**
Double/sb: **$55–$70**
Guest Cottage: **$90–$95**
Open: **All year**
Reduced Rates: **10% less, 6 days**
Breakfast: **Full**
Credit Cards: **AMEX, MC, VISA**
Pets: **No**
Children: **Cottage only**
Smoking: **Permitted**
Social Drinking: **Permitted**

Just a few blocks from the State Capitol, this is an elegantly restored Victorian house surrounded by stately trees. Antiques add to the splendor of the rich wood paneling, inlaid floor, Oriental rugs, and lace curtains. You'll be pampered with flowers in your room and English china and fine silver for your gourmet breakfast. Relax in the spa or sauna after a busy day of sightseeing. Evening treats include wine, fruit, nuts, and unhurried conversation in the living room. California State University–Sacramento is nearby.

SAN DIEGO AND ORANGE COUNTY AREA

American Historic Homes Bed & Breakfast

P.O. BOX 388, SAN JUAN CAPISTRANO, CALIFORNIA 92693

Tel: **(714) 496-6953**
Coordinator: **Deborah Sakach**
State/Regions Covered: **Nationwide; in California: Anaheim, Carmel, Cambria, Laguna Beach, Napa, San Diego, San Francisco**

Rates (Single/Double):

Modest:	**$20**	**$25–$35**
Average:	**$30–$35**	**$36–$55**
Luxury:	**$50–$60**	**$56–$105**

Credit Cards: **No**

All the homes on Deborah's roster are historically significant. They range from a three-story Victorian in San Francisco to a North Carolina plantation, including sea captains' houses, bayside retreats, Georgian mansions, and Early American Colonials. Many are designated National Landmarks and all share the common element of warmth and hospitality.

Hospitality Plus

P.O. BOX 388, SAN JUAN CAPISTRANO, CALIFORNIA 92693

Tel: **(714) 496-7050**
Best Time to Call: **9 AM–5 PM**
Coordinator: **Deborah Sakach**
States/Regions Covered: **Los Angeles, Laguna Beach, Napa, Pacific Grove, Redondo Beach, Santa Barbara, Solvang**

Rates (Single/Double):

Modest:	**$20**	**$30**
Average:	**$30**	**$45**
Luxury:	**$50**	**$85**

Deborah's computerized service has access to over 1,000 B&Bs throughout California. Her specialty is planning complete coastal, mountain, and desert tours, staying at B&Bs all the way. No matter what your price range, special attention will be given to your needs.

Bayside ✪

1520 FIRST STREET, L-210, CORONADO, CALIFORNIA 92118

Tel: **(619) 435-1613**
Host(s); **Betty Soloff**
Location: **4 mi. W of San Diego; 1 mi. from 75, Glorietta Exit**
No. of Rooms: **1**
Max. No. Sharing Bath: **3**
Double/sb: **$35**
Single/sb: **$30**
Open: **All year**
Reduced Rates: **20% less on 6th night**
Breakfast: **Full**
Pets: **No**
Children: **No**
Smoking: **No**
Social Drinking: **Permitted**
Airport/Station Pickup: **Yes**

Bayside is located in the apartment complex of Oakwood Gardens, in the heart of Coronado, just over the bridge from San Diego. It is on the bay and overlooks the beautiful city skyline. Tennis, a swimming pool, and a hot tub are available on the premises. It's a short drive to Tijuana, Mexico, and a short walk to local shopping and restaurants. Betty has been affiliated with the local theater group and manned the information desk at the famed Balboa Park. She'll be glad to give you many insider tips on getting the most out of your stay in this delightful area.

The Blue Door ✪

13707 DURANGO DRIVE, DEL MAR, CALIFORNIA 92014

Tel: **(619) 755-3819**
Best Time to Call: **7 AM–10 PM**
Host(s): **Bob and Anna Belle Schock**
Location: **20 mi. N of San Diego**
No. of Rooms: **1 suite**
No. of Private Baths: **1**
Suites: **$40**
Open: **All year**
Reduced Rates: **After 5 nights**
Breakfast: **Full**
Pets: **No**
Children: **No**
Smoking: **No**
Social Drinking: **Permitted**

Enjoy New England charm in a southern California setting overlooking exclusive Torrey Pines Park. A garden-level suite with wicker accessories and king-size bed is yours; it opens onto a private garden patio. Breakfast is served in the spacious country kitchen or in the dining room warmed by the fire on chilly days. Anna Belle prides herself on creative breakfast menus featuring homemade baked goods. She will gladly direct you to the nearby racetrack, beach, zoo, or University of California at San Diego.

Gulls Nest ✪

12930 VIA ESPERIA, DEL MAR, CALIFORNIA 92014

Tel: **(619) 259-4863**
Best Time to Call: **Before 8:30 AM**
Host(s): **Connie and Mike Segel**
Location: **20 mi. N of San Diego**
No. of Rooms: **1**
No. of Private Baths: **1**
Double/pb: **$50**
Suite: **$65**
Open: **All year**
Breakfast: **Full**
Other meals: **Available**
Pets: **No**
Children: **Welcome**
Smoking: **No**
Social Drinking: **Permitted**

Gulls Nest is a contemporary wood home surrounded by pine trees. The house boasts a beautiful view of the ocean and a bird sanctuary from two upper decks. Guest accommodations consist of a comfortable, quiet room with queen-size bed, private bath, and patio. Breakfast is served outdoors, weather permitting, and features fresh-squeezed juice, eggs, ham or bacon, homemade breads, and coffee cake. The Segels can cook breakfast on their beach over an open fire, and will also be glad to serve guests an exotic Mongolian barbecue dinner. Great swimming and surfing are three blocks away at Torrey State Beach. Golf, shops, and restaurants are a 5-minute drive and Tijuana and the international border are 40 minutes away.

Lion's Head Guest House in Jamul ✪

P.O. BOX 21203, EL CAJON, CALIFORNIA 92021

Tel: **(619) 463-4271**
Best Time to Call: **7 AM–9 PM**
Host(s): **Ronald and Anneke Schieberl**
Location: **4 mi. from Hwy. 94**
No. of Rooms: **6**
No. of Private Baths: **6**
Double/pb: **$38**
Suites: **$50**
Guest Apartment: **$60–$80; sleeps 6**
Open: **All year**
Reduced Rates: **10%, weekly; 10%, seniors**
Breakfast: **Full**
Other Meals: **Available**
Pets: **Sometimes**
Children: **Welcome (crib)**
Smoking: **No**
Social Drinking: **Permitted**
Airport/Station Pickup: **Yes**
Foreign Languages: **Italian, Spanish**

The Shieberls' immense Spanish hacienda with its stucco walls and red tile roof overlooks San Diego and the Pacific. Ronald and Anneke are enthusiastic about meeting people and put a welcome basket of wine and fruit in each guest room. They can arrange for a TV and VCR for your room, and you may borrow from their extensive collection of films. You are free to use the microwave oven, laundry facilities, Jacuzzi, and grand piano. Breakfast treats come from the fruit trees and hen house on their eight acres. If you'd like a guide, or simply directions to nearby sights, your hosts will be happy to assist.

Julian Gold Rush Hotel ✪

P.O. BOX 856, 2032 MAIN STREET, JULIAN, CALIFORNIA 92036

Tel: **(619) 765-0201**
Best Time to Call: **8 AM–9 PM**
Host(s): **Steve and Gig Ballinger**
Location: **60 mi. NE of San Diego**
No. of Rooms: **16**
No. of Private Baths: **4**
Max. No. Sharing Bath: **4**
Double/pb: **$62–$75**
Double/sb: **$50–$65**
Single/sb: **$30–$35**
Guest Cottage: **$85–$105; sleeps 2**
Open: **All year**
Reduced Rates: **20%, seniors; families**
Breakfast: **Full**
Pets: **No**
Children: **Welcome, weekdays**
Smoking: **Permitted**
Social Drinking: **Permitted**

This century-old landmark is listed on the National Register of Historic Places, and it is furnished with American antiques lovingly restored by your hosts. The lobby has a wood-burning stove, books and games, and an original oak player piano. The historic town of Julian has been preserved to look much as it did 100 years ago and it has gold mine tours. Gig and Steve serve a man-size breakfast, and tea and coffee are always available.

Country Comfort Bed and Breakfast ✪

5104 EAST VALENCIA DRIVE, ORANGE, CALIFORNIA 92669

Tel: **(714) 532-2802**
Best Time to Call: **Evenings**
Host(s): **Geri Lopker and Joanne Angell**
Location: **5 mi. E of Anaheim**
No. of Rooms: **4**
No. of Private Baths: **1**
Max. No. Sharing Bath: **3**
Double/pb: **$60**
Single/pb: **$55**
Double/sb: **$50**
Single/sb: **$45**
Open: **All year**
Reduced Rates: **20% less after 3 nights**
Breakfast: **Full**
Other Meals: **Available**
Pets: **Sometimes**
Children: **Welcome**
Smoking: **No**
Social Drinking: **Permitted**
Airport/Station Pickup: **Yes**

Located in a quiet residential area, Geri and Joanne have furnished their home with your comfort and pleasure in mind. It is handicapped-accessible with adaptive equipment available. Amenities include a swimming pool, cable TV and VCR, an atrium, fireplace, and the use of bicycles including one built for two. Breakfast often features delicious cinnamon rolls, Scotch eggs, and sausages, along with fruits and assorted beverages. Disneyland and Knott's Berry Farm are less than seven miles away.

Jean's Retreat ✪

2308 CALLE LAS PALMAS, SAN CLEMENTE, CALIFORNIA 92672

Tel: **(714) 492-1216 or 492-4121**
Best Time to Call: **Before 10 AM, after 6 PM**
Host(s): **Jean Spain**
Location: **60 mi. S of Los Angeles**
No. of Rooms: **1**
No. of Private Baths: **1**
Double/pb: **$45**
Open: **All year**
Breakfast: **Full**
Pets: **No**
Children: **Welcome**
Smoking: **Permitted**
Social Drinking: **Permitted**

Jean's contemporary house, located in a quiet, exclusive area, is decorated in a comfortable blend of modern and antique pieces. The roses, exotic plantings, and vegetable garden attest to her green thumb. The house is two blocks from the beach, 10 minutes away from San Juan Capistrano, and 45 minutes from Disneyland. At home, there's a fireplace, spa, and large redwood deck for relaxing. Coffee, fruit, and snacks are always available.

Abigail

6310 RAYDEL COURT, SAN DIEGO, CALIFORNIA 92120

Tel: **(619) 583-4738**
Host(s): **Felix and Pearl Ammar**
Location: **200 yards from Freeway 8**
No. of Rooms: **1 suite**
No. of Private Baths: **1**
Suites: **$50–$68 (2–4)**
Open: **All year**
Breakfast: **Full**
Pets: **No**
Children: **No**
Smoking: **No**
Social Drinking: **Permitted**
Foreign Languages: **French, German, Greek, Italian, Spanish**

Felix and Pearl live on the first floor, and they have created a haven for two on the second floor, offering privacy in the exclusive Del Cerro section. There is a separate entrance to this one-bedroom apartment, which includes a kitchen where all the fixings for breakfast are provided; you can prepare what you wish, when you wish. San Diego Zoo, Balboa Park, Sea World, plus the Pacific Ocean and San Diego State University are all close by.

Betty Spiva Simpson's B & B ✪

3742 ARIZONA STREET, SAN DIEGO, CALIFORNIA 92104

Tel: **(619) 692-1385**
Best Time to Call: **Before noon; after 5 PM**
Host(s): **Betty Spiva Simpson**
Location: **2 mi. N of San Diego**
No. of Rooms: **1**
Max. No. Sharing Bath: **3**
Single/sb: **$25**
Open: **All year**
Reduced Rates: **15%, weekly**
Breakfast: **Full**
Pets: **No**
Children: **Welcome, infants (crib)**
Smoking: **Permitted**
Social Drinking: **Permitted**
Airport/Station Pickup: **Yes**

Betty offers clean, comfortable accommodations in an attractive bungalow. The guest room is furnished comfortably with tasteful pieces, carpeting, and a ceiling fan. You are welcome to relax in the den or the patio and can feel free to store snacks and beverages in the guest refrigerator. Betty will gladly direct you to nearby Balboa Park, San Diego Zoo, and tennis courts.

The Cottage ✪

P.O. BOX 3292, SAN DIEGO, CALIFORNIA 92103

Tel: **(619) 299-1564**
Best Time to Call: **9 AM–5 PM**
Host(s): **Robert and Carol Emerick**
Location: **1 mi. from Rte. 5**
Guest Cottage: **$45–$65; sleeps 3**
Open: **All year**
Breakfast: **Continental**
Credit Cards: **MC, VISA**
Pets: **No**
Children: **Welcome**
Smoking: **No**
Social Drinking: **Permitted**

Located in the Hillcrest section, where undeveloped canyons and old houses dot the landscape, this private hideaway offers a cottage with a king-size bed in the bedroom, a single bed in the living room, full bath, and fully equipped kitchen. Decorated with turn-of-the-century furniture, the wood-burning stove and oak pump organ evoke memories of long ago. It's two miles to the zoo, less to Balboa Park, and it is within easy walking distance of restaurants, shops, and theater. The University of California and the University of San Diego are nearby.

E's Inn

3776 HAWK STREET, SAN DIEGO, CALIFORNIA 92103

Tel: **(619) 295-5622**
Best Time to Call: **7:30 AM–11 AM, Mon.–Thurs.**
Host(s): **Erene Rallis**
Location: **½ mi. from US 5**
No. of Rooms: **2**
No. of Private Baths: **2**
Double/pb: **$45**
Single/pb: **$35**
Open: **All year**
Reduced Rates: **Weekly; 10%, seniors**
Breakfast: **Continental**
Other Meals: **Available**
Pets: **Sometimes**
Children: **Welcome (playpen, high chair)**
Smoking: **Porch and patio only**
Social Drinking: **Permitted**
Airport/Station Pickup: **Yes**
Foreign Languages: **Greek**

On a quiet street in Mission Hills, this gray-and-white cedar-sided home welcomes the visitor with its inviting pillared porch and French doors. Guests immediately feel at home here with a glass of sherry or a hot cup of coffee or tea. Bookcases flank the fireplace where a cozy fire is usually burning. The bedrooms are decorated with a blend of Greek antiques, armoires, and modern Dansk pieces, complemented by original paintings, ceramics, and enamels. Your hostess loves to cater to her guests and provides baskets of fresh fruit and flowers in each room. In the evening, she places a tiny surprise under each pillow. Breakfast specialties include bran muffins and Greek and Mexican omelets. E's is close to Balboa Park, the Gaslight District, Tijuana, and beautiful beaches.

Inn by the Park

1171 24TH STREET, SAN DIEGO, CALIFORNIA 92102

Tel: **(619) 232-1253**
Best Time to Call: **9 AM–1 PM**
Host(s): **Catherine Sarnat**
Location: **½ mi. from I-5**
No. of Rooms: **5**
Max. No. Sharing Bath: **5**
Double/sb: **$38–$58**
Open: **All year**
Reduced Rates: **Seniors**
Breakfast: **Continental**
Credit Cards: **MC, VISA**
Pets: **No**
Children: **Sometimes**
Smoking: **Permitted**
Social Drinking: **Permitted**
Foreign Languages: **Spanish**

Located one block from Balboa Park, this restored Victorian offers a pleasant journey back to the time of flapper girls and rumble seats. The house was once a showplace, and has been fully restored and decorated in 1920s furnishings. Elegant rooms feature fine linens, fluffy towels, and fresh flowers. Breakfast is served in the dining room where the player piano provides the sounds of the swing era. Specialties of the house include freshly ground coffee, tea, freshly squeezed orange juice, gourmet pastries, and seasonal fruit. This lovely inn is just a short walk from downtown and within five minutes from museum and the San Diego Zoo.

Vera's Cozy Corner

2810 ALBATROSS STREET, SAN DIEGO, CALIFORNIA 92103

Tel: **(619) 296-1938**
Best Time to Call: **Before 10 AM; after 5 PM**
Host(s): **Vera V. Warden**
No. of Rooms: **1**
No. of Private Baths: **1**
Double/pb: **$40**
Single/pb: **$30**
Open: **All year**
Breakfast: **Continental**
Pets: **No**
Children: **No**
Smoking: **No**
Social Drinking: **Permitted**
Foreign Languages: **German, French**

This crisp white Colonial with black shutters sits on a quiet cul-de-sac overlooking San Diego Bay. Guest quarters consist of a separate cottage with private patio entrance. Vera offers fresh-squeezed juice from her own fruit trees in season. The house is convenient to local shops and restaurants, and is a mile from the San Diego Zoo.

Friends-We-Haven't-Met ✪

10071 STARBRIGHT CIRCLE, WESTMINSTER, CALIFORNIA 92683

Tel: **(714) 531-4269**
Best Time to Call: **7–11 AM**
Host(s): **Bob and Sandy Runkle**
Location: **3 mi. S of Anaheim**
No. of Rooms: **3**
Max. No. Sharing Bath: **5**
Double/sb: **$35**
Single/sb: **$25**
Open: **All year**
Breakfast: **Full**
Pets: **No**
Children: **Welcome, over 12**
Smoking: **Permitted**
Social Drinking: **Permitted**
Airport/Station Pickup: **Yes**

The Runkles' two-story house offers a private den for reading, playing cards, or listening to music. The delightful backyard patio with flowers and barbecue is yours to enjoy. For those interested in physical fitness, Bob and Sandy are members of a private 17-acre sports club that you may utilize. You are welcome to help yourself to coffee, wine, and fresh fruit. Long Beach State and the U. of C. at Irvine are nearby.

SAN FRANCISCO AREA

American Family Inn ✪

P.O. BOX 349, SAN FRANCISCO, CALIFORNIA 94101

Tel: **(415) 931-3083**
Best Time to Call: **9 AM–5 PM**
Coordinators: **Susan and Richard Kreibich**
States/Regions Covered: **Carmel, Monterey, San Francisco, Marin County, Napa, Sonoma (Wine Country)**

Rates (Single/Double):

	Single	Double
Modest:	**$40**	**$50**
Average:	**$55**	**$75**
Luxury:	**$75**	**$125**

Credit Cards: **AMEX, DC, MC, VISA**

The San Francisco locations are near all the famous sights, such as Fisherman's Wharf and Chinatown. Many are historic Victorian houses. Some homes offer hot tubs and sun decks; a few are on yachts and houseboats where the tariff ranges $100–$120. There's a two-night stay required.

Bed & Breakfast International—San Francisco ✪

151 ARDMORE ROAD, KENSINGTON, CALIFORNIA 94707

Tel: **(415) 525-4569**
Best Time to Call: **8:30 AM–5 PM**
Coordinator: **Jean Brown**
States/Regions Covered: **California—Berkeley, Palo Alto, San Francisco and the Bay Area, Monterey, Napa Valley, Palm Springs, Lake Tahoe; Las Vegas; Hawaii; N.Y.C.**

Rates (Single/Double):
Modest: **$26–$32** **$32–$38**
Average: **$34–$50** **$40–$56**
Luxury: **$54–$90** **$60–$96**

Credit Cards: **AMEX, DC, MC, VISA**

Jean was the first to bring the concept of a bed and breakfast reservation service to America. Her accommodations range from a town house apartment to a villa above an ocean beach with a private pool. Others are located near the seashore, at a marina, in a redwood forest, by a mountain stream, in the middle of a vineyard, as well as in city neighborhoods and downtown areas. A minimum stay of two nights is required.

Burlingame B & B ✪

1021 BALBOA AVENUE, BURLINGAME, CALIFORNIA 94010

Tel: **(415) 344-5815**
Host(s): **Joe and Elnora Fernandez**
Location: **½ mi. from Rte. 101**
No. of Rooms: **1**
No. of Private Baths: **1**
Double/pb: **$40**
Single/pb: **$30**
Open: **All year**
Breakfast: **Continental**
Pets: **Sometimes**
Children: **Welcome**
Smoking: **No**
Social Drinking: **No**
Airport/Station Pickup: **Yes**
Foreign Languages: **Italian, Spanish**

Located in a pleasantly quiet neighborhood, with San Francisco only minutes away by good public transportation. The house offers the privacy of upstairs guest quarters with a view of a creek and native flora and fauna. It's all very clean and cheerfully decorated. Joe and Elnora will direct you to restaurants and shops to suit your budget.

Lore's Haus ✪

22051 BETLEN WAY, CASTRO VALLEY, CALIFORNIA 94546

Tel: **(415) 881-1533**
Host(s): **Lore Bergman**
Location: **25 mi. NE of San Francisco**
No. of Rooms: **2**
No. of Private Baths: **2**
Max. No. Sharing Bath: **4**
Double/pb: **$50**
Single/pb: **$45**
Double/sb: **$45**
Single/sb: **$35**
Open: **All year**
Reduced Rates: **10%, Nov.–Feb.**
Breakfast: **Full**
Pets: **Sometimes**
Children: **Welcome, over 14**
Smoking: **Permitted**
Social Drinking: **Permitted**
Airport/Station Pickup: **Yes**
Foreign Languages: **German, French**

Lore's Haus is an attractive ranch home on a quiet street, with a large, beautiful garden. Lore was born in Germany and has spent the last 30 years in Castro Valley. She prides herself on offering Americans a true European atmosphere with lots of plants, books, comfortable furnishings, and Oriental rugs. Breakfast includes French Brie, fresh German black bread, homemade jams, cold cuts, and eggs. If you like, tours of the Bay Area, Napa Valley, or anyplace else are available in German, French, or English. If you'd like to venture out on your own, the city center is 25 minutes away via car or rapid transit. After a day of touring, come back to Lore's and enjoy a glass of wine. A two-night stay is required.

Montara Bed & Breakfast ✪

P.O. BOX 493, MONTARA, CALIFORNIA 94037

Tel: **(415) 728-3946**
Best Time to Call: **Evenings**
Host(s): **Bill and Peggy Bechtell**
Location: **20 mi. S of San Francisco**
No. of Rooms: **1**
No. of Private Baths: **1**
Double/pb: **$55**
Single/pb: **$45**
Open: **All year**
Reduced Rates: **Weekly**
Breakfast: **Full**
Pets: **Sometimes**
Children: **No**
Smoking: **No**
Social Drinking: **Permitted**
Airport/Station Pickup: **Yes**

Relax in a California-style contemporary set in a coastal hamlet on scenic Highway 1. Montara is a rural area, yet it's just 20 miles from San Francisco. Guest accommodations are newly remodeled and feature a private entrance that opens onto a redwood deck. Guests have exclusive use of an adjacent sitting room with a fireplace and an ocean view. Breakfast is served in a solarium overlooking the garden. Your hosts serve a variety of specialties along with honey from their beehives. Local activities include playing in the waves at the state beach, wandering the hiking trails at McNee Ranch State Park, or riding on Miramar Beach. There are numerous seafood restaurants to choose from as well as cuisine from Italy, Germany, and Mexico.

Aurora Manor ✪

1328 16TH AVENUE, SAN FRANCISCO, CALIFORNIA 94122

Tel: **(415) 564-2480**
Host(s): **Saskia Thiadens**
No. of Rooms: **5**
No. of Private Baths: **1**
Max. No. Sharing Bath: **4**
Double/pb: **$55**
Single/pb: **$45**
Double/sb: **$44**
Single/sb: **$38**
Open: **All year**

Breakfast: **Full**
Credit Cards: **AMEX, MC, VISA**
Pets: **No**
Children: **Welcome (crib)**
Smoking: **Permitted**
Social Drinking: **Permitted**
Foreign Languages: **Danish, Dutch, French, German**

Aurora Manor was built in 1923 as a two-story San Francisco duplex. The interior is of rich oak wood accented with antiques. The private rooms are tastefully decorated and your hostess will make every effort to see that you feel at home. Hors d'oeuvres and sherry are offered in the living room for those gathering to read or chat. Aurora Manor is located close to the University of California Medical Center, Golden Gate Park, and Ocean Beach. There is easy transportation to downtown San Francisco.

Casa Arguello ✪

225 ARGUELLO BOULEVARD, SAN FRANCISCO, CALIFORNIA 94118

Tel: **(415) 752-9482**
Best Time to Call: **10 AM–6 PM**
Host(s): **Emma Baires**
No. of Rooms: **5**
No. of Private Baths: **2**
Max. No. Sharing Bath: **3**
Double/pb: **$50–$60**
Double/sb: **$45**
Suites: **$80 for 4**
Open: **All year**
Breakfast: **Continental**
Pets: **No**
Children: **Welcome, over 7**
Smoking: **No**
Social Drinking: **Permitted**
Foreign Languages: **Spanish**

This spacious duplex has an elegant living room, dining room, and cheerful bedrooms that overlook neighboring gardens. Tastefully decorated with modern and antique furnishings, it is convenient to Golden Gate Park, Golden Gate Bridge, Union Square, and fine shops and restaurants. Mrs. Baires allows her kitchen to be used for light snacks. The University of California Medical School is nearby. There is a two-night minimum stay. Excellent public transportation is close by.

Casita Blanca ✪

330 EDGEHILL WAY, SAN FRANCISCO, CALIFORNIA 94127

Tel: **(415) 564-9339**
Host(s): **Joan Bard**
No. of Rooms: **1 cottage**
No. of Private Baths: **1**
Guest Cottage: **$70; sleeps 2**
Open: **All year**
Pets: **No**
Children: **No**
Smoking: **Permitted**
Social Drinking: **Permitted**
Foreign Languages: **French, Spanish**

Perched on a hill, nestled among trees, and overlooking the city and bay, this unique cottage is separated from the main house, affording you the luxury of privacy. Every detail has been attended to, down to condiments in the kitchen. Though limited to two people at a time, there is a two-day minimum stay. Joan will be happy to direct you to all the nontourist spots that make this city so exciting. The University of California Medical Center is close by. Joan also offers B&B in Carmel Valley, Lake Tahoe, Sonoma, and Palm Desert.

Rancho San Gregorio ✪

ROUTE 1, BOX 54, SAN GREGORIO, CALIFORNIA 94074

Tel: **(415) 747-0810**
Host(s): **Bud and Lee Raynor**
Location: **35 mi. S of San Francisco**
No. of Rooms: **3**
No. of Private Baths: **1**
Max. No. Sharing Bath: **4**
Double/pb: **$60–$70**
Double/sb: **$50**
Open: **All year**
Reduced Rates: **Available**
Breakfast: **Continental; full, weekends**
Pets: **No**
Children: **Welcome, over 12 (limit 2)**
Smoking: **Outside only**
Social Drinking: **Permitted**
Airport/Station Pickup: **Yes**

Graceful arches and bright stucco characterize this Spanish Mission home set on 15 wooded acres. Rooms are decorated with American antiques and family pieces. Your hosts, Bud and Lee, are glad to share a snack and a glass of wine or champagne. On weekdays they serve a Continental breakfast; on Saturdays and Sundays a full feast features eggs or pancakes, fresh fruit and breads, and a variety of meats. The atmosphere is relaxing, and guests are welcome to use the hot tub, take a sauna, borrow a book from the library, or play the organ. Rancho San Gregorio is close to the beach, horseback riding, and golf. San Francisco, Half Moon Bay, and a variety of state parks and recreational areas are within an hour's drive.

Mrs. "K's" Retreat ✪

14497 NEW JERSEY AVENUE, SAN JOSE, CALIFORNIA 95124

Tel: **(408) 371-0593/559-3828**
Host(s): **Barbara and George Kievlan**
Location: **3 mi. E of Hwy. 17**
No. of Rooms: **3**
No. of Private Baths: **3**
Double/pb: **$45**
Single/pb: **$35**
Open: **All year**
Reduced Rates: **Weekly**
Breakfast: **Full**
Credit Cards: **AMEX, MC, VISA**
Pets: **No**
Children: **Welcome**
Smoking: **No**
Social Drinking: **Permitted**
Airport/Station Pickup: **Yes**

This sprawling ranch-style home is nestled at the base of Blossom Valley, once famous for its orchards. Guest rooms are furnished with flair and boast separate entrances. Your hosts invite you to enjoy the living room fireplace, family room, spa, and adjacent patio, with pool and spacious yard. Those interested in stained glass will surely want to visit the studio on the premises.

East Bay Bed and Breakfast

P.O. BOX 3365, SAN LEANDRO, CALIFORNIA 94578

Tel: **(415) 352-0234**
Best Time to Call: **10 AM–10 PM**
Host(s): **Robin Cowell**
Location: **30 mi. SE of San Francisco**
No. of Rooms: **1**
No. of Private Baths: **1**
Double/pb: **$34**
Single/pb: **$26**
Open: **All year**
Reduced Rates: **15%, weekly**
Breakfast: **Full**
Other Meals: **Available**
Pets: **No**
Children: **Welcome, over 5**
Smoking: **No**
Social Drinking: **Permitted**
Airport/Station Pickup: **Yes**

This contemporary condominium is ideally situated for touring the San Francisco Bay Area. Day trips to Wine Country, San Francisco, and the coastal parks and beaches are easily made from here. Robin will be glad to pack a picnic lunch. She loves entertaining and can accommodate those on low-cholesterol and high-fiber diets. Freshly ground coffee and homemade specialty breads are served each morning on the patio. Fresh fruits and nuts are always available, along with a glass of wine or juice, compliments of your hostess.

Madison Street Inn ✪

1390 MADISON STREET, SANTA CLARA, CALIFORNIA 95050

Tel: **(408) 249-5541**
Host(s): **Theresa and Ralph Wigginton**
Location: **1½ mi. from Rte. 880**
No. of Rooms: **5**
No. of Private Baths: **3**
Max. No. Sharing Bath: **4**
Double/pb: **$55–$75**
Double/sb: **$55**
Single/sb: **$50**
Open: **All year**
Reduced Rates: **15% for 4 nights; 15%, seniors**
Breakfast: **Full**
Other Meals: **Available**
Credit Cards: **AMEX, MC, VISA**
Pets: **Sometimes**
Children: **Welcome (crib)**
Smoking: **No**
Social Drinking: **Permitted**

This restored vintage Queen Anne is furnished with Oriental rugs and museum-quality antiques, including brass beds and tubs for two. Landscaped gardens, a swimming pool, and a hot tub grace the grounds, and a sunny meeting room is available for business gatherings. Belgian waffles or eggs Benedict are often on the breakfast menu. Exciting dinners can be arranged, prepared by Ralph, an accomplished cook. It is convenient to Santa Clara University and San Jose State University.

Glen Echo ✪

508 KILKARE ROAD, SUNOL, CALIFORNIA 94586

Tel: **(415) 862-2046**
Host(s): **Don and Jan Scheer**
Location: **2 mi. from I-680, Sunol Exit**
No. of Rooms: **2**
Max. No. Sharing Bath: **4**
Double/sb: **$35**
Single/sb: **$30**
Open: **All year**
Reduced Rates: **10%, seniors**
Breakfast: **Continental**
Pets: **No**
Children: **Welcome**
Smoking: **No**
Social Drinking: **No**
Airport/Station Pickup: **Yes**

This comfortable home is located in farm country, surrounded by woods with a creek flowing in front; a fine place to relax. Jan bakes delicious muffins or breads and serves them with fruit, cheese, and breakfast beverages. Don just acquired a 25-foot sloop and will be happy to make special arrangements if you would care to sail. San Francisco, Carmel, Yosemite, and Point Reyes National Seashore are some of the convenient sightseeing destinations.

Gasthaus zum Bären ✪

2113 BLACKSTONE DRIVE, WALNUT CREEK, CALIFORNIA 94598

Tel: **(415) 934-8119**
Best Time to Call: **After 3 PM**
Host(s): **Lois D. Martin**
Location: **33 mi. E of San Francisco**
No. of Rooms: **3**
No. of Private Baths: **1**
Max. No. Sharing Bath: **2**
Double/pb: **$50**
Single/pb: **$45**
Double/sb: **$40**
Single/sb: **$35**
Open: **All year**
Reduced Rates: **10%, seniors, families**
Breakfast: **Full**
Pets: **No**
Children: **Welcome, over 6 (must be swimmers)**
Smoking: **No**
Social Drinking: **Permitted**
Airport/Station Pickup: **Yes**
Foreign Languages: **German, Italian, Spanish**

This rambling ranch home is furnished with artifacts from around the world. A huge natural fireplace dominates the living and family rooms. In summer, the large swimming pool becomes the center of activity and a California-style breakfast is served in the garden. Guests are welcome to the Jacuzzi, grill, and bicycles. Your hostess will be happy to provide picnic suppers for performances at the nearby Concord Pavilion, an outdoor concert shell carved into Mount Diablo. Foreign-language tours of San Francisco, Sausalito, Muir Woods, and the Wine Country can be arranged on summer weekends. For nature lovers, Briones Regional Park and numerous wilderness areas are nearby. There's a two-night minimum stay.

SAN JOAQUIN VALLEY

Valley View Citrus Ranch ✪

14801 AVENUE 428, OROSI, CALIFORNIA 93647

Tel: **(209) 528-2275**
Host(s): **Tom and Ruth Flippen**
Location: **20 mi. N of Visalia**
No. of Rooms: **4**
No. of Private Baths: **3**
Max. No. Sharing Bath: **4 (washbasin in each bedroom)**
Double/pb: **$45**
Single/pb: **$42**
Double/sb: **$45**
Single/sb: **$42**
Open: **All year**
Breakfast: **Full**
Pets: **Sometimes**
Children: **Welcome**
Smoking: **Permitted**
Social Drinking: **Permitted**
Foreign Languages: **Spanish**

Located in the San Joaquin Valley (The Fruit Basket of the World), this modern, air-conditioned ranch home is set in the foothills of the Sierra Nevadas. The 70-foot-long porch provides some beautiful views. Tom and Ruth will be happy to plan your itinerary, which might include a visit to Sequoia National Park, Kings Canyon, Crystal Caves, Grants Grove, or you can play tennis on their clay court. Breakfast specialties are Belgian waffles served in the delightful gazebo. Complimentary beverages are always available, as is fresh fruit in season.

Tatum's Bed & Breakfast ✪

748 N. EAST AVENUE, REEDLEY, CALIFORNIA 93654

Tel: **(209) 638-4940**
Best Time to Call: **5:30–6 PM**
Host(s): **Dale and Mary Lee Tatum**
Location: **25 mi. S of Fresno**
No. of Rooms: **1 suite**
No. of Private Baths: **1**
Suites: **$50**
Open: **All year**
Reduced Rates: **Weekly**
Breakfast: **Continental**
Pets: **Sometimes**
Children: **Welcome, over 5**
Smoking: **No**
Social Drinking: **Permitted**
Airport/Station Pickup: **Yes**

The Tatums have lived in this brown stucco house for 20 years. Now that their three kids are grown and on their own, they have converted the upstairs into a suite that's cozy, private, and comfortable. Reedley is known as "The Fruit Basket of the World" because of the fruit farms that surround it, and is located midway between San Francisco and Los Angeles. Nearby, guests can enjoy the pleasures of the Kings River, which flows through the west side of town where fishing, picnics, boating, river rafting, and swimming are all appealing possibilities. The Tatums' hospitality has inspired guests to ask them "not to change a thing. We loved staying in your home."

Larson's Bed 'n' Breakfast ✪

718 PHILIPPINE STREET, TAFT, CALIFORNIA 93268

Tel: **(805) 765-2917**
Best Time to Call: **Before 9 AM; evenings**
Host(s): **Patricia Larson**
Location: **38 mi. SW of Bakersfield**
No. of Rooms: **3**
No. of Private Baths: **1**
Max. No. Sharing Bath: **2–4**
Double/pb: **$40**
Single/pb: **$30**
Double/sb: **$40**
Single/sb: **$30**
Open: **All year**
Reduced Rates: **Available**
Breakfast: **Continental**
Pets: **No**
Children: **No**
Smoking: **No**
Social Drinking: **Permitted**
Airport/Station Pickup: **Yes**

Larson's is a custom-built split-level located in the foothills of the San Joaquin Valley. The house is surrounded by three kinds of fruit trees and has a large sun deck overlooking the countryside. Your hostess takes pride in offering amenities such as complimentary wine and cheese and pillow mints. Guests are invited to relax by the Olympic-size swimming pool or enjoy a game of billiards in the fireplaced game room. After a lazy day, treat yourself to a manicure or pedicure; Patricia is a licensed manicurist with a business on the premises. For breakfast, a varying selection of freshly baked nut breads, muffins, Belgian waffles, and fresh orange and grapefruit juice are served. Taft is one of the great oil-producing centers of the world.

SAN LUIS OBISPO AREA

Megan's Friends

1776 ROYAL WAY, SAN LUIS OBISPO, CALIFORNIA 93401

Tel: **(805) 544-4406**
Best Time to Call: **8 AM–noon; 5–10 PM**
Coordinator: **Joyce Segor**
State/Regions Covered: **Atascadero, Baywood Park, Glendora, King City, Los Osos, Solvang, Sunset Palisades, San Luis Obispo**

Rates (Single/Double):
Average: **$30–$35** **$35–$40**
Luxury: **$40–$45** **$45–$65**

Credit Cards: **No**

Joyce has exclusive listings that no other reservation agency has. She is certain to accommodate you in a B&B best suited to your interests and purse; these range from a contemporary showplace to a cozy country cottage. A $10 annual membership is required, for which you receive a detailed list describing the accommodations.

Bayview House ✪

1070 SANTA LUCIA AVENUE, BAYWOOD PARK, CALIFORNIA 93402

Tel: **(805) 528-3098**
Host(s): **Jack and Frieda Murphy**
Location: **3 mi. S of Morro Bay**
No. of Rooms: **1 suite**
Suite: **$45–$55**
Open: **All year**
Breakfast: **Full**
Pets: **No**
Children: **Welcome**
Smoking: **Permitted**
Social Drinking: **Permitted**
Airport/Station Pickup: **Yes**
Foreign Languages: **Dutch, Indonesian**

If you enjoy sunsets from a private deck, a bird sanctuary, lovely flowers, and peaceful tranquillity, you will surely enjoy your stay in this spacious suite with its fully equipped kitchen and dining room. Breakfast features home-baked bread and homemade sausages. It's just a short drive to Hearst Castle, Montana de Oro State Park, and Cal. Poly.

Gerarda's Bed & Breakfast ✪

1056 BAY OAKS DRIVE, LOS OSOS, CALIFORNIA 93402

Tel: **(805) 528-3973**
Host(s): **Gerarda Ondang**
Location: **10 mi. from Hwy. 101**
No. of Rooms: **6**
No. of Private Baths: **2**
Max. No. Sharing Bath: **4**
Double/pb: **$41.34**
Single/pb: **$26.50**
Double/sb: **$41.34**
Single/sb: **$26.50**
Open: **All year**
Breakfast: **Full**
Pets: **Welcome**
Children: **Welcome**
Smoking: **No**
Social Drinking: **Permitted**
Airport/Station Pickup: **Yes**
Foreign Languages: **Dutch, Indonesian**

When you stay at Gerarda's, you are in for a veritable Dutch treat! Located in a pleasant, quiet neighborhood, the house is surrounded by interesting landscaping and lovely flower beds. This is a simple home comfortably furnished with charm and warmth. Breakfast features Dutch delicacies such as honeycake, jams, and breads. Hearst Castle, Morrow Bay, and San Luis Obispo are within a half hour's drive. A two-night minimum stay is required.

SANTA BARBARA AREA

D & B Schroeder Ranch ✪

1825 CRAVENS LANE, CARPINTERIA, CALIFORNIA 93013

Tel: **(805) 684-1579**
Best Time to Call: **7 AM–9 PM**
Host(s): **Don and Beverly Schroeder**
Location: **10 mi. E of Santa Barbara**
No. of Rooms: **1**
No. of Private Baths: **1**
Double/pb: **$50–$60**
Single/pb: **$50**
Open: **All year**
Breakfast: **Full**
Pets: **No**
Children: **Welcome (one only)**
Smoking: **No**
Social Drinking: **Permitted**

This wood-and-glass contemporary beauty is on a ten-acre lemon and avocado ranch and boasts ocean and mountain views. You may pick fruit, play a hand of bridge, or enjoy the use of Bev and Don's spa or bicycles. All the attractions of Santa Barbara are close by. You are welcome to play tennis at the Polo and Racquet Club where the guest fee is $5 per person.

George and Jean Harris ✪

1483 ANITA STREET, CARPINTERIA, CALIFORNIA 93013

Tel: **(805) 684-5629**
Host(s): **George and Jean Harris**
Location: **11 mi. E of Santa Barbara**
No. of Rooms: **1**
No. of Private Baths: **1**
Double/pb: **$35**
Single/pb: **$30**
Open: **All year**
Breakfast: **Full**
Pets: **No**
Children: **Welcome, over 11**
Smoking: **No**
Social Drinking: **Permitted**
Airport/Station Pickup: **Yes**

George and Jean have a one-story stucco home at the end of a quiet court. The guest room is decorated in Early American style and features a king-size bed and a mountain view. Special touches, such as a cookie jar filled with homemade goodies and fresh flowers in your room, are sure to help you feel at home. Outside, a spa surrounded by ferns awaits you in the garden. Breakfast specialties include orange-and-blueberry waffles, whole wheat pancakes, eggs, sausages, and fresh seasonal fruit. Carpinteria is known for its flower production, both in greenhouses and in open fields. The Harrises are 11 miles east of Santa Barbara, 1 mile from the beach, and ½ mile from the mountains.

Hidden Valley Home ✪

939 BARCELONA DRIVE, SANTA BARBARA, CALIFORNIA 93105

Tel: **(805) 687-8799**
Host(s): **Ellie and Kurt Pilgram**
Location: **¼ mi. from Rte. 101**
No. of Rooms: **1**
No. of Private Baths: **1**
Double/pb: **$50–$60**
Single/pb: **$45–$55**
Open: **All year**
Breakfast: **Continental**
Other Meals: **Available**
Pets: **No**
Children: **No**
Smoking: **No**
Social Drinking: **Permitted**
Airport/Station Pickup: **Yes**

The Pilgrams are self-confessed tennis addicts, and for guests who share their enthusiasm, they offer use of the tennis courts and swimming pool at the Tennis Club of Santa Barbara for a small guest fee. Ellie and Kurt live just one mile from the Arroya Burro Beach and four miles from downtown Santa Barbara. Bus service is convenient for those without a car. Guests are welcome to share Ellie's well-tuned piano and her knowledge of the area—she is a docent at the Santa Barbara Historical Museum.

Long's Seaview Bed & Breakfast ✪

317 PIEDMONT ROAD, SANTA BARBARA, CALIFORNIA 93105

Tel: **(805) 687-2947**
Best Time to Call: **Before 6 PM**
Host(s): **Bob and LaVerne Long**
Location: **1½ mi. from Hwy. 101**
No. of Rooms: **1**
No. of Private Baths: **1**
Double/pb: **$60**
Single/pb: **$50**
Reduced Rates: **Midweek; after 1 night**
Open: **All year**
Breakfast: **Full**
Pets: **No**
Children: **Welcome**
Smoking: **No**
Social Drinking: **Permitted**
Airport/Station Pickup: **Yes**

Overlooking Santa Barbara's prestigious north side, this ranch-style home is in a quiet residential neighborhood. Breakfast is usually served on the patio where you can see the ocean, Channel Islands, and citrus orchards. Convenient to the beach, Solvang, and Santa Ynez Valley, the large, airy bedroom is cheerfully furnished, with antiques and brass double bed. You are welcome to use the spa. The breakfast menu varies from Southern dishes to Mexican specialties.

Ocean View House ✪

P.O. BOX 20065, SANTA BARBARA, CALIFORNIA 93102

Tel: **(805) 966-6659**
Best Time to Call: **8 AM–5 PM**
Host(s): **Bill and Carolyn Canfield**
Location: **2 mi. from 101 Fwy.**
No. of Rooms: **2**
No. of Private Baths: **1**
Double/pb: **$40–$50**
Suites: **$60–$70 for 4**
Open: **All year**
Breakfast: **Continental**
Pets: **Sometimes**
Children: **Welcome**
Smoking: **No**
Social Drinking: **Permitted**
Airport/Station Pickup: **Yes**

This California ranch house features a guest room furnished with a queen-size bed and antiques. The adjoining paneled den, with double-bed divan and TV, is available together with the guest room as a suite. While you relax on the patio, you can look out at the sailboats on the ocean. It's a short walk to the beach and local shops. Hard-boiled eggs and cheese are always served. There is a two-night minimum.

Bed & Breakfast Approved Hosts ✪

10890 GALVIN, VENTURA, CALIFORNIA 93004

Tel: **(805) 647-0651**
Best Time to Call: **5–8 PM**
Coordinator: **Clara Hutton**
State/Regions Covered: **Ventura County**

Rates (Single/Double):

	Single	Double
Average:	**$35**	**$55–$85**
Luxury:	**$50**	**$55–$125**

Credit Cards: **No**
Minimum Stay: **No**

Clara has a small but select group of homes in this area known for its beaches, the Channel Islands, the Ojai Music Festival in spring, and the Shakespearean Festival in June. One large home known for its special Spanish architecture is hosted by an artist; another is a Southern-style Colonial hosted by a retired teacher and an engineer. All hosts serve a delicious full breakfast.

COLORADO

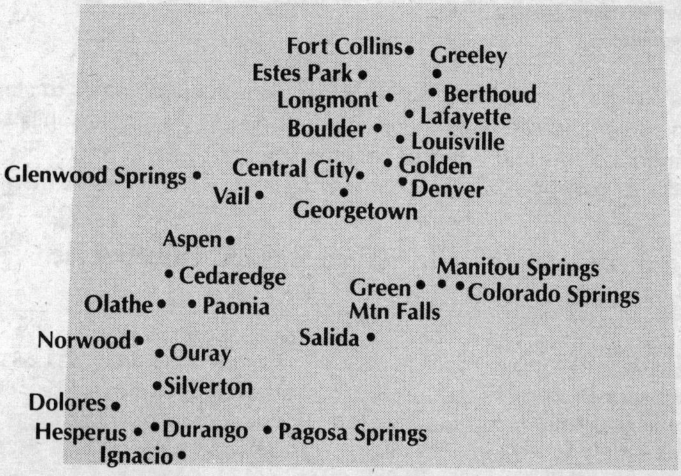

Fort Collins
Greeley
Estes Park
Longmont
Berthoud
Lafayette
Boulder
Louisville
Glenwood Springs
Central City
Golden
Denver
Vail
Georgetown
Aspen
Cedaredge
Manitou Springs
Green Mtn Falls
Colorado Springs
Olathe
Paonia
Norwood
Ouray
Salida
Silverton
Dolores
Hesperus
Durango
Pagosa Springs
Ignacio

Bed and Breakfast Colorado

P.O. BOX 6061, BOULDER, COLORADO 80306

Tel: **(303) 442-6664**
Best Time to Call: **1–6 PM**
Coordinator: **Lois LaCroix**
States/Regions Covered: **Colorado**

Rates (Single/Double):
Average: **$24** **$50**
Credit Cards: **MC, VISA**

Your home away from home could be a bedroom in an historic mansion overlooking a ski village, an apartment in the heart of Denver, or a small cottage all to yourself. Farm and ranch accommodations are available as well as homes in or near National Parks, including Mesa Verde. Major colleges and universities are convenient to many B&Bs. Just mention your interests, hobbies, and other requirements, and Lois will do her best to comply. Send $3 for the descriptive directory.

Bed & Breakfast—Rocky Mountains ✪

P.O. BOX 804, COLORADO SPRINGS, COLORADO 80901

Tel: **(303) 630-3433**
Best Time to Call: **9 AM–5 PM, May 15–Sept. 15; in winter, 12–5 PM**
Coordinator: **Kate Peterson Winters**
States/Regions Covered: **Colorado, Montana, New Mexico, Utah, Wyoming**

Rates (Single/Double):

	Single	Double
Modest:	**$20**	**$35**
Average:	**$28**	**$65**
Luxury:	**$50**	**$120**

Credit Cards: **MC, VISA**

Kate's roster covers the whole gamut, from modest homes to elegant mansions, log cabins to working cattle ranches, ski chalets with beamed ceilings and hot tubs to homes near lakes and rivers. Send $3 for the descriptive directory of over 100 unique homes and inns.

Bed & Breakfast—Ski Areas Reservation Service

P.O. BOX 491, VAIL, COLORADO 81658

Tel: **(303) 949-1212**
Best Time to Call: **Winter: 9 AM–6 PM; summer, noon—5 PM**
Coordinator: **Kathy Fagan**
States/Regions Covered: **Aspen, Avon, Breckenridge, Steamboat, Vail**

Rates (Single/Double):

	Single	Double
Average:	**$40–$45**	**$55–$85**
Luxury:	**$65–$85**	**$85-$100**

Located in the heart of the Rockies, Vail offers recreational activities in all seasons: the Nature Center helps the entire family know and understand this alpine environment; concerts, plays, and movies are regularly scheduled; and nightclubs provide entertainment and dancing nightly. There are over 70 restaurants, bars, and nightclubs, and more than 120 shops for all your needs and pleasures. Your host may be a local cowboy and his wife, who make sourdough pancakes on their wood-burning stove, and serve it with fresh maple syrup. Many homes are located on the mountain, convenient to skiing. Free shuttle buses are the best way to get around. There's a $5 surcharge for one-night stays in ski season.

Parrish's Country Squire ✪

2515 PARRISH ROAD, BERTHOUD, COLORADO 80513

Tel: **(303) 772-7678**
Host(s): **Donna and Jess Parrish**
Location: **30 mi. NW of Denver**
No. of Rooms: **2**
No. of Private Baths: **2**
Double/pb: **$45**
Single/pb: **$35**
Open: **Jan. 16–Dec. 14**

Reduced Rates: **10%, seniors**
Breakfast: **Full**
Pets: **No**
Children: **Welcome, over 5**
Smoking: **Permitted**
Social Drinking: **Permitted**
Airport/Station Pickup: **Yes**

Donna and Jess invite you to relax at their comfortable log ranch home located near Estes Park and Carter Lake. You are certain to enjoy the serenity and breathtaking scenery of this 1500-acre cattle ranch. Breakfast features homemade breads, wild plum or chokecherry jellies, as well as other delicious morsels. Horseback riding is available.

Bed and Breakfast of Boulder ✪

BOX 6061, BOULDER, COLORADO 80306

Tel: **(303) 442-6664**
Best Time to Call: **8 AM–5 PM**
Coordinator: **Lois LaCroix**
State/Regions Covered: **Boulder, Lafayette, Louisville, Longmont**

Rates (Single/Double):

	Single	Double
Modest:	**$23**	**$30**
Average:	**$32**	**$40**
Luxury:		**$75–$85**

Credit Cards: **MC, VISA**
Minimum Stay: **2 nights**

Lois's accommodations are quite select; listings range from a "modest" huge bedroom with a double bed, private bath, and separate entrance at the garden level to an "average" one with a living room with a fireplace and a deck overlooking the city. The "luxury" offering is a honeymoon cottage with fireplace, sauna, and hot tub. Don't miss Rocky Mts. National Park, the Shakespeare Festival, and great skiing. There is a $5 surcharge for a one-night stay. Please send $2 for her directory.

Melinda Meadows Bed and Breakfast ✪

ROUTE 2, BOX 304, 250 SW 11TH AVENUE, CEDAREDGE, COLORADO 81413

Tel: **(303) 856-6384**
Best Time to Call: **Evenings**
Host(s): **Jane and Dana Reed**
Location: **1/4 mi. off Hwy. 65**
No. of Rooms: **2**
No. of Private Baths: **2**
Double/pb: **$35**
Single/pb: **$25**
Separate Guest Apartment: **$35**
Open: **All year**
Reduced Rates: **10%, seniors**
Breakfast: **Continental**
Pets: **Sometimes**
Children: **Apartment only**
Smoking: **Permitted**
Social Drinking: **Permitted**

This country-style ranch home is located on ten acres of lawns and gardens. The rooms are furnished comfortably with a mixture of

Western and Oriental pieces. Guests may choose from tastefully furnished bedrooms or a separate apartment suitable for families. Breakfast is served in the backyard gazebo or the homey dining room. Cedaredge, at 6,000 feet, is on the south slopes of Grand Mesa; at 10,000 feet, it's the largest flat-top mountain in the country. This is the land of 200 lakes, minutes from fishing, hunting, picnicking, hiking, skiing, and snowmobiling. The area is famous for horse shows, rodeos, beautiful orchards, and friendly people.

Two Ten Casey ✪

BOX 154, 210 CASEY AVENUE, CENTRAL CITY, COLORADO 80427

Tel: **(303) 582-5906**
Best Time to Call: **6 AM–6 PM**
Host(s): **Esther Campbell**
Location: **35 mi. NW of Denver**
No. of Rooms: **1**
No. of Private Baths: **1**
Double/pb: **$35**
Single/pb: **$30**
Open: **All year**
Breakfast: **Continental**
Pets: **Sometimes**
Children: **Welcome, over 5**
Smoking: **Permitted**
Social Drinking: **Permitted**

The bay windows of this comfortable clapboard cottage overlook Gregory Gulch, where gold was discovered in 1859. Esther, a retired nurse, will be happy to point out the historic sights. She is an experienced hiker and will lead you along the old trails. Area attractions include ski slopes, museums, shops, and restaurants.

Griffins' Hospitality House ✪

4222 NORTH CHESTNUT, COLORADO SPRINGS, COLORADO 80907

Tel: **(303) 599-3035**
Best Time to Call: **Mornings**
Host(s): **John and Diane Griffin**
Location: **5 mi. N of Colorado Springs**
No. of Rooms: **4**
No. of Private Baths: **1**
Max. No. Sharing Bath: **4**
Double/pb: **$35**
Single/pb: **$25**
Double/sb: **$30**
Open: **All year**
Breakfast: **Full**
Pets: **No**
Children: **Welcome (crib)**
Smoking: **Permitted**
Social Drinking: **Permitted**
Airport/Station Pickup: **Yes**

The welcome mat is always out at Diane and John's house. It's close to Pike's Peak, the Air Force Academy, and the Garden of the Gods. You can use the picnic table, TV, washing machine, and dryer. You will enjoy a fine view of Pike's Peak while eating the bountiful breakfast. In the evening, you are invited to relax in the living room with wine and good conversation. The University of Colorado is four miles away.

Griffins Hospitality House
Colorado Springs, Colorado

Holden House ✪

1102 W. PIKE'S PEAK AVENUE, COLORADO SPRINGS, COLORADO 80904

Tel: **(303) 471-3980**
Best Time to Call: **Early AM; evenings**
Host(s): **Sallie and Welling Clark**
Location: **2 mi. from I-25**
No. of Rooms: **3**
No. of Private Baths: **3**
Double/pb: **$38–$44**
Single/pb: **$34–$38**
Open: **All year**
Breakfast: **Full**
Pets: **No**
Children: **No**
Smoking: **No**
Social Drinking: **Permitted**

This stately Victorian home, built in 1902, is located in the historic Old Colorado City area. It has been colorfully and lovingly furnished with many family heirlooms. A breakfast of homemade breads, muffins, jam, and freshly ground coffee is served in the lovely dining room, or on the veranda on warm, sunny mornings; wine and cheese are offered in the evening. Sallie and Welling will be pleased to help in planning your itinerary around the area's many attractions.

The Claim Jumper Inn ✪

704 WHITEROCK, CRESTED BUTTE, COLORADO 81224

Tel: **(303) 349-6471**
Host(s): **Jim and Nancy Harlow**
Location: **28 mi. from US Hwy. 50, Gunnison Exit**
No. of Rooms: **3**
No. of Private Baths: **1**
Max. No. Sharing Bath: **4**
Double/pb: **$50**
Double/sb: **$45**
Open: **All year**
Reduced Rates: **$5 less in spring and summer**
Breakfast: **Continental**
Pets: **No**
Children: **Welcome, over 12 (in sep. room)**
Smoking: **No**
Social Drinking: **Permitted**
Airport/Station Pickup: **Yes**

This beautiful old log home includes a Victorian parlor, breakfast room, and three bedrooms furnished with antiques and queen-size brass-and-iron beds. In addition, Jim and Nancy have added a complete plant-filled redwood hot tub room and sauna for your enjoyment. Some of the unusual antiques are a gramophone from the Arabian peninsula, model wooden sailing ships from the island of Mauritius in the Indian Ocean, and a gold-leaf mirror that hung in the home of the notorious Belle Starr. All were collected by your hosts during their travels throughout the world. From fine skiing in winter to fun at the Center for Performing Arts in summer, a variety of activities are yours for the asking.

Queen Anne Inn ✪

2147 TREMONT PLACE, DENVER, COLORADO 80205

Tel: **(303) 296-6666**
Best Time to Call: **8 AM–noon**
Host(s): **Anne and Charles Hillestad**
No. of Rooms: **10**
No. of Private Baths: **10**
Double/pb: **$65–$95**
Single/pb: **$55–$85**
Open: **All year**
Breakfast: **Continental**
Credit Cards: **MC, VISA**
Pets: **No**
Children: **Welcome, over 15**
Smoking: **No**
Social Drinking: **Permitted**

Located in the residential Clements Historic District, this three-story house built in 1879 faces Benedict Fountain and Park. Decorated in the Queen Anne style, the elegant bedrooms offer a choice of mountain or city views along with such touches as a unique aspen mural, a Roman tub with gold fixtures, a private third-floor deck, and antique writing desks. Fine art, good books, and unobtrusive chamber music provide a lovely backdrop. The Hillestads offer a generous breakfast including seasonal fruits, assorted breads, homemade granola, and a special blend of coffee. The Denver Center Arts Complex, the Denver Art Museum, a shopping mall, and diverse restaurants are within walking distance. You are always welcome to help yourself to fruit, candy, soft drinks, and a glass of sherry. Anne and Charles will be happy to lend you their bike for local touring.

"Little Southfork" Ranch B&B

15247 COUNTY ROAD 22, DOLORES, COLORADO 81323

Tel: **(303) 882-4259**
Host(s): **Gwen M. Taylor**
Location: **7 mi. N of Cortez**
No. of Rooms: **2**

No. of Private Baths: **1**
Max. No. Sharing Bath: **4**
Double/sb: **$30**
Single/sb: **$25**
Guest Cottage: **$40; sleeps 4**
Open: **All year**
Reduced Rates: **10%, off-season; families; weekly**
Breakfast: **Full**
Pets: **Sometimes**
Children: **Welcome, over 7**
Smoking: **Permitted**
Social Drinking: **Permitted**
Airport/Station Pickup: **Yes**

Enjoy a panoramic view of the Rockies in this picturesque rural section of southwestern Colorado. It's minutes to Mesa Verde National Park, Durango and the Silverton Train, river rafting on the Dolores River, the Painted Desert, aspen forests, lakes, and streams. Gwen is an active grandma who will make you feel at home. The cows, pigs, geese, and chickens will delight city slickers.

Simon Draw Guest House ✪

13980 COUNTY ROAD 29, DOLORES, COLORADO 81323

Tel: **(303) 565-8721**
Host(s): **Richard and Evelyn Wagner**
Location: **4½ mi. from Hwy. 160**
Guest Cottage: **$35 for 2; $50 for 5**
Open: **Apr.–Oct.**
Reduced Rates: **15%, weekly**
Breakfast: **Full**
Credit Cards: **MC, VISA**
Pets: **Yes**
Children: **Welcome (crib)**
Smoking: **Permitted**
Social Drinking: **Permitted**

This two-story cottage, complete with kitchen, living room, bedroom, and bath, is in the woods on the edge of a small canyon with a stream at the bottom. It contains two double beds and a twin-size couch in the living room. It is a charming home away from home while visiting Mesa Verde National Park.

Country Sunshine B&B ✪

35130 HIGHWAY 550 N., DURANGO, COLORADO 81301

Tel: **(303) 247-2853**
Best Time to Call: **Before 9 AM; after 3 PM**
Host(s): **Jim and Jill Anderson**
No. of Rooms: **4**
Max. No. Sharing Bath: **4**
Double/sb: **$45**
Single/sb: **$35**
Open: **All year**
Breakfast: **Full**
Credit Cards: **AMEX, MC, VISA**
Pets: **Sometimes**
Children: **Welcome**
Smoking: **No**
Social Drinking: **Permitted**
Airport/Station Pickup: **Yes**

Nestled below rocky bluffs, there's a spectacular view of the San Juan Mountains from this spacious ranch home. Breakfast of homemade breads, jams, and blackberry pancakes with pure maple syrup is served on the large deck in view of the narrow-gauge train. You may borrow a bicycle for riding the winding roads along the Animas River, which also has excellent trout fishing.

Elk Meadows Inn ✪

359 COUNTY ROAD 250, DURANGO, COLORADO 81301

Tel: **(303) 247-4559**
Best Time to Call: **7–9 AM; 4–6 PM**
Host(s): **Jo Ann and Gale Galbreath**
Location: **½ mile from Rte. 550**
No. of Rooms: **5**
No. of Private Baths: **2**
Max. No. Sharing Bath: **4**
Double/pb: **$45**
Single/pb: **$40**
Double/sb: **$35**
Single/sb: **$30**
Open: **Dec. 2–Sept. 1**
Reduced Rates: **$10 less in winter on p/b accommodations; 15%, seniors**
Breakfast: **Full**
Pets: **No**
Children: **Welcome**
Smoking: **No**
Social Drinking: **Permitted**
Airport/Station Pickup: **Yes**

This large, contemporary split-level has over 30 feet of picture windows overlooking the Animas River and red sandstone mountains. Elk herds graze all summer long in the valley. It's only minutes away from the Durango-Silverton narrow-gauge railroad, and the Mesa Verde Pueblo ruins, spectacular mountain vistas, and Purgatory Ski Area are all close by.

Scrubby Oaks Bed & Breakfast ✪

P.O. BOX 1047, DURANGO, COLORADO 81302

Tel: **(303) 247-2176**
Best Time to Call: **Early AM or PM**
Host(s): **Mary Ann Craig**
Location: **4 mi. from junctions 160 and 550**
No. of Rooms: **5**
No. of Private Baths: **1**
Max. No. Sharing Bath: **4**
Double/pb: **$55**
Single/pb: **$40**
Double/sb: **$45**
Single/sb: **$30**
Open: **All year**
Breakfast: **Full**
Pets: **No**
Children: **Welcome**
Smoking: **No**
Social Drinking: **Permitted**
Airport/Station Pickup: **Yes**

There's a quiet country feeling to this two-story home set on 10 acres overlooking the spectacular Animas Valley and surrounding mountains. Trees and gardens frame the patios where breakfast is apt to be served. All breads and preserves are homemade, and strawberry Belgian waffles are a specialty. On chilly mornings, the kitchen fireplace is the cozy backdrop for your wake-up cup of coffee or cocoa. You are made to feel part of the family and are welcome to play pool, take a sauna, read a book, watch a VCR movie, or simply take in the crisp air.

The Terraces

1281 HIGH DRIVE, MORAINE ROUTE, ESTES PARK, COLORADO 80517

Tel: **(303) 586-9411**
Host(s): **Don and Jackie Johnson**
Location: **70 mi. NW of Denver**
No. of Rooms: **2**
Max. No. Sharing Bath: **4**
Double/sb: **$44**
Single/sb: **$33**
Open: **May–Sept.**
Reduced Rates: **15%, weekly**
Breakfast: **Continental**
Pets: **No**
Children: **Welcome, over 14**
Smoking: **Permitted**
Social Drinking: **Permitted**
Airport/Station Pickup: **Yes**

This spacious home offers the charm of natural woodwork, Shaker furniture, hand-painted stenciling, and Jackie's handcrafted dolls. Each guest room has a comfortable queen-size bed and cedar-lined closet. Have morning coffee on the deck with the quiet splendor of the mountains before you. The house is adjacent to Rocky Mountain National Park, a hiker's paradise. Rejuvenate in the redwood hot tub overlooking majestic Long's Peak. Quaint shops, trout fishing, stables, lakes, and golf courses are minutes away.

Wanek's Lodge at Estes ✪

P.O. BOX 898, 560 PONDEROSA DRIVE, ESTES PARK, COLORADO 80517

Tel: **(303) 586-5851**
Best Time to Call: **Evenings**
Host(s): **Jim and Pat Wanek**
Location: **71 mi. NW of Denver**
No. of Rooms: **4**
Max. No. Sharing Bath: **4**
Double/sb: **$38**
Single/sb: **$31**
Open: **All year**
Breakfast: **Continental**
Other Meals: **Available**
Pets: **No**
Children: **Welcome, over 10**
Smoking: **No**
Social Drinking: **Permitted**

Jim and Pat invite you to share their modern mountain inn, located on a ponderosa pine-covered hillside, just minutes away from Rocky Mountain National Park. The wood beams, stone fireplace, plants, and beautiful scenery provide a comfortable and relaxed atmosphere.

Former educators, your hosts are people oriented, and staying with them is like being with old friends.

Elizabeth Street Guest House ✪

202 EAST ELIZABETH, FT. COLLINS, COLORADO 80524

Tel: **(303) 493-BEDS**
Host(s): **John and Sheryl Clark**
Location: **65 mi. N of Denver**
No. of Rooms: **3**
Max. No. Sharing Bath: **4**
Double/sb: **$39**
Single/sb: **$32**
Open: **All year**
Reduced Rates: **Weekly**
Breakfast: **Full**
Credit Cards: **MC, VISA**
Pets: **No**
Children: **Welcome, over 4**
Smoking: **Permitted**
Social Drinking: **Permitted**

This completely renovated and restored 1905 brick American four-square has leaded windows and oak woodwork. Family antiques, plants, old quilts, and handmade touches add to its charm. All the bedrooms have sinks. It is close to historic Old Town Square, Estes Park, Rocky Mountain National Park, and a block away from Colorado State University. John and Sheryl will spoil you with their special brand of hospitality and homemade treats.

Georgetown Bed & Breakfast

300 ROSE STREET, GEORGETOWN, COLORADO 80444

Tel: **(303) 569-2084**
Best Time to Call: **9 AM–10 PM**
Host(s): **Joe and Micky Lucas**
Location: **40 mi. W of Denver**
No. of Rooms: **2**
Max. No. Sharing Bath: **4**
Double/sb: **$35–$45**
Single/sb: **$25–$30**
Open: **All year**
Reduced Rates: **Available**
Breakfast: **Continental**
Pets: **Sometimes**
Children: **Welcome (playpen, high chair)**
Smoking: **Permitted**
Social Drinking: **Permitted**

The builder of this Italianate Victorian had each brick carted by wagon from Oklahoma in 1870. This was the first two-story home in town, and also the first to have the luxury of indoor running water. Many locals who profited from the nearby silver mines stayed here in bright rooms with 10-foot ceilings and lovely woodwork. Guests will find the atmosphere of the 1800s has been kept intact with antiques and period pieces including a player piano with candelabras. Plan your touring over wine and cheese or a cup of coffee. Joe and Micky will be glad to assist you in discovering the sights of this historic area, including Hamill House, Hotel De Pere, Georgetown Loop Railroad, and the silver and gold mines. Nearby recreational activities include camping, fishing, and skiing.

Hardy House

P.O. BOX 0156, GEORGETOWN, COLORADO 80444

Tel: **(303) 569-3388**
Best Time to Call: **After 10 AM**
Host)s): **Sarah M. Schmidt**
Location: **50 mi. W of Denver**
No. of Rooms: **3**
No. of Private Baths: **1**
Max. No. Sharing Bath: **3**
Double/pb: **$65**
Double/sb: **$45**
Single/sb: **$25**
Suites: **$45–$65**
Open: **All year**
Reduced Rates: **Weekly**
Breakfast: **Full**
Other Meals: **Available**
Pets: **Sometimes**
Children: **Welcome, over 10**
Smoking: **Permitted**
Social Drinking: **Permitted**

Back in the 1870s this bright red Victorian, surrounded by a white picket fence, was the home of a blacksmith. Inside you can relax by the potbelly parlor stove, sleep under feather comforters, and wake up to savory breakfast dishes such as waffle cheese strata and coffee cake. Guest quarters range from a two-bedroom suite to rooms with queen-size or twin beds. If you have a special birthday to celebrate, you can stay in the Victorian Suite and be served a candlelight dinner along with champagne, cake, and breakfast the next morning, for $125. In the evening, Sarah serves wine, coffee, and tea. She will also prepare fresh trout for breakfast if you happen to get lucky in the creek across the street. Hardy House is located in the heart of the Historic District, half a block from the shops of Main Street. It is also close to hiking, skiing, and is walking distance from the Loop Railroad. Perhaps the best way to explore the town is on Sarah's six-speed tandem mountain bike, which she will gladly lend.

Sojourner's Inn ✪

1032 COOPER AVENUE, GLENWOOD SPRINGS, COLORADO 81601

Tel: **(303) 945-7162**
Best Time to Call: **After 5 PM**
Host(s): **Clay and Darlene Carrington**
Location: **160 mi. W of Denver**
No. of Rooms: **4**
No. of Private Baths: **4**
Max. No. Sharing Bath: **4**
Double/pb: **$32–$45**
Single/pb: **$27**
Open: **All year**
Reduced Rates: **Available**
Breakfast: **Full**
Credit Cards: **MC, VISA**
Pets: **No**
Children: **Permitted**
Smoking: **Permitted**
Social Drinking: **Permitted**
Airport/Station Pickup: **Yes**

Sojourner's Inn is a large turn-of-the-century home in a quiet residential neighborhood. The house is a blending of different styles, but the prevailing one is comfort. Guest rooms are individually designed, featuring television and comfortable queen-size beds. Each morning, the cheerful dining room is the setting for a tempting breakfast, including homemade breads, fresh fruit, and specialty dishes. Hosts Clay and Darlene love their country surroundings and will gladly direct you to skiing, rafting, fishing, and hiking. Downtown Glenwood Springs and the world's largest hot springs pool are just a short walk from the house.

Sunnyside Bed and Breakfast ✪

925 PITKIN AVENUE, GLENWOOD SPRINGS, COLORADO 81601

Tel: **(303) 945-6203**
Best Time to Call: **Mornings; evenings**
Host(s): **Phil and Michaele Breidenbach**
Location: **160 mi. W of Denver**
No. of Rooms: **3**
No. of Private Baths: **1**
Max. No. Sharing Bath: **4**
Double/pb: **$42**
Single/pb: **$32**
Double/sb: **$32**
Single/sb: **$22**
Suites: **$54**
Open: **All year**
Breakfast: **Full**
Credit Cards: **MC, VISA**
Pets: **No**
Children: **Welcome, over 4**
Smoking: **No**
Social Drinking: **Permitted**
Airport/Station Pickup: **Yes**

Guests are welcomed to Sunnyside with a warm hello and a seasonal drink. The house is a 1905 frame with diverse furnishings and a friendly kitchen filled with copper, baskets, and collectibles. Breakfast specialties include fluffy omelets, homemade jam, and French toast. A sunny deck provides a comfortable spot for summer relaxing and birdwatching; separate cookout and picnic facilities are also available, as is a hot tub. Walk to hot springs pool, shops, restaurants, and the shuttle bus to Sunlight Ski area. Hiking, rafting, fishing, and boating are also nearby.

Talbott House ✪

928 COLORADO AVENUE, GLENWOOD SPRINGS, COLORADO 81601

Tel: **(303) 945-1039**
Host(s): **Cherry Talbott**
Location: **1 mi. from I-70, Exit 116**
No. of Rooms: **4**
Max. No. Sharing Bath: **4**
Double/sb: **$42**
Single/sb: **$27**
Guest Cottage: **$55 up; sleeps 2–5**
Open: **All year**
Breakfast: **Full**

Credit Cards: **MC, VISA**
Pets: **No**
Children: **Welcome**
Smoking: **Permitted**
Social Drinking: **Permitted**
Airport/Station Pickup: **Yes**

This Victorian dates back to the beginning of the century. It's been lovingly restored and features colorful wallpaper, Oriental rugs that cover fir floors, and an assortment of accessories collected from all over the world. Breakfast is served, family-style, in the dining room and typically includes homemade breads, burritos, potatoes, and fresh fruit. Cherry invites you to use the solar-powered outdoor hot tub in all seasons. Walk to the Hot Springs Pool, Vapor Caves, interesting shops, and restaurants. A free shuttle will whisk you to the slopes of nearby Ski Sunlight.

The Dove Inn ✪

711 14TH STREET, GOLDEN, COLORADO 80401

Tel: **(303) 278-2209**
Host(s): **Ken and Jean Sims**
Location: **10 mi. W of downtown Denver**
No. of Rooms: **5**
No. of Private Baths: **5**
Max. No. Sharing Bath: **4**
Double/pb: **$34–$55**
Single/pb: **$29–$49**
Open: **All year**
Reduced Rates: **10%, weekly**
Breakfast: **Full**
Credit Cards: **AMEX, DC, MC, VISA**
Pets: **Sometimes**
Children: **Welcome (crib)**
Smoking: **Permitted**
Social Drinking: **Permitted**
Airport/Station Pickup: **Yes**
Foreign Languages: **Spanish**

The Dove Inn is a charming Victorian on grounds beautifully landscaped with decks, walkways, and huge trees. The house has many bay windows, dormers, and angled ceilings; each room is individually decorated with pretty wallpapers and Victorian touches. Breakfast specialties such as cinnamon rolls and fresh-fruit compotes are served on the porch in the summertime. This delightful inn is located in the foothills of West Denver in one of the state's most beautiful valleys, yet it is just minutes from downtown Denver, historic Golden, and many other Rocky Mountain attractions. No unmarried couples, please.

Outlook Lodge ✪

BOX 5, GREEN MOUNTAIN FALLS, COLORADO 80819

Tel: **(303) 684-2303**
Host(s): **The Ahern family**
Location: **15 mi. W of Colorado Springs**
No. of Rooms: **11**
No. of Private Baths: **2**
Max. No. Sharing Bath: **6**
Double/pb: **$40**
Single/pb: **$35**
Double/sb: **$35–$37**
Single/sb: **$30–$32**
Open: **May 23–Sept. 1**
Breakfast: **Continental**
Credit Cards: **MC, VISA**
Pets: **Yes**
Children: **Welcome (crib)**
Smoking: **Permitted**
Social Drinking: **Permitted**
Foreign Languages: **German, Spanish**

This restored Victorian parsonage (1889) is set at the foot of Pike's Peak and is surrounded by pines on property fronted by a creek. The furnishings, stained glass, and rocking chair veranda all add to the feeling of "going to Grandma's." The gracious Aherns invite you to use the kitchen stove, refrigerator, barbecue, and picnic area. Located just a block away from a lake, pool, tennis court, stables, shops, and restaurants, it is also within easy driving of the Garden of the Gods, the Air Force Academy, Colorado College, Royal Gorge, and Cripple Creek.

Ute Creek Ranch B&B

2192 COUNTY ROAD 334, IGNACIO, COLORADO 81137

Tel: **(303) 563-4464**
Best Time to Call: **Evenings**
Host(s): **Peter and Peggy Welch**
Location: **20 mi. SE of Durango**
No. of Rooms: **6**
Max. No. Sharing Bath: **4**
Separate guest Cottage: **$55 for 2; $70 for 4; $85 for 6**
Open: **Nov. 10–Aug. 15**
Reduced Rates: **Weekly**
Breakfast: **Full**
Other Meals: **Available**
Credit Cards: **MC, VISA**
Pets: **Sometimes**
Children: **Welcome**
Smoking: **Permitted**
Social Drinking: **Permitted**
Airport/Station Pickup: **Yes**

The Welch family invites you to their 900-acre working cattle ranch, located in the San Juan Mountains. Choose from two completely furnished guest cottages, each with fully equipped kitchen and barbecue grill. The Pine River House is a secluded adobe on the riverbank with two bedrooms, one bath, and a large living room with an adobe fireplace. It has a fenced-in yard with an orchard and vegetable garden. The Ute Creek house is a two-story log cottage with four bedrooms, two baths, and a large living room with fireplace. The ranch-style breakfast includes farm-fresh eggs, homegrown fruit and vegetables, muffins, jams, and honey. Afternoon tea is also served along with fruit, cheese, and a variety of pastries. Ute Creek Ranch offers easy access to such attractions as the Durango-Silverton Narrow Gauge Railroad, Mesa Verde Cliff Dwellings, Pagosa Hot Springs, and Purgatory Ski Area. Horseback riding on the ranch can be arranged.

Back Narrows Inn ✪

1550 GRAND AVENUE, BOX 492, NORWOOD, COLORADO 81423

Tel: **(303) 327-4417**
Best Time to Call: **11 AM–6 PM**
Host(s): **Richard and Nancy Parker**
Location: **125 mi. SE of Grand Junction**
No. of Rooms: **11**
No. of Private Baths: **3**
Max. No. Sharing Bath: **6**
Double/pb: **$27–$32**
Single/pb: **$23–$28**
Double/sb: **$18–$26**
Single/sb: **$16–$23**
Open: **All year**
Breakfast: **Continental**
Other Meals: **Available**
Credit Cards: **MC, VISA**
Pets: **Welcome**
Children: **Welcome**
Smoking: **Permitted**
Social Drinking: **Permitted**

At the edge of the San Juan Mountains, the inn, built in 1880, retains a flavor of the past, with its antique furnishings. The lobby invites relaxation, conversation, darts, and other games. It's 33 miles to historic Telluride town and ski area for winter fun. There's marvelous local cross-country skiing too. Summer diversions are fishing, hiking, goldpanning, and music and film festivals.

Uncompahgre Cabin

8454 5700 ROAD, OLATHE, COLORADO 81425

Tel: **(303) 323-6789**
Best Time to Call: **Before 8 AM; after 8 PM**
Host(s): **Dean and Ellen Mosher**
Location: **15 mi. N of Montrose**
No. of Rooms: **2**
Max. No. Sharing Bath: **4**
Double/sb: **$27.50**
Single/sb: **$15**
Open: **All year**
Breakfast: **Continental**
Other Meals: **Available**
Pets: **Sometimes**
Children: **Welcome, over 2**
Smoking: **No**
Social Drinking: **Permitted**

This log cabin home is surrounded by the magnificent vistas of the Grand Mesa, the San Juan Mountains, and the Uncompahgre Plateau. Your hosts have created a rustic hunting lodge atmosphere overlooking the surrounding countryside. Natural, wholesome foods are served here, and guests are welcome to BYOB to a reasonably priced dinner topped off with a homemade dessert. In the morning choose from a Continental or full breakfast with home-baked breads. There is much to do close to home, such as fishing in the stocked ponds or visiting the many farm animals. Dean and Ellen will gladly pack a lunch for those who like to spend the day hunting, bird-watching, hiking, or skiing. After a busy day, watch the sunset from a porch rocker, or unwind in the hot tub.

The House of Yesteryear ✪

516 OAK STREET, P.O. BOX 440, OURAY, COLORADO 81427

Tel: **(303) 325-4277**
Host(s): **Raymond O'Brien**
Location: **76 mi. S of Durango**
No. of Rooms: **8**
No. of Private Baths: **2**
Max. No. Sharing Bath: **5**
Double/pb: **$45**
Single/pb: **$45**
Double/sb: **$35**
Single/sb: **$35**
Open: **June 10–Sept. 30**
Reduced Rates: **10%, June**
Breakfast: **Continental—$1.00**
Pets: **No**
Children: **Welcome (crib)**
Smoking: **Permitted**
Social Drinking: **Permitted**

Perched on a hill overlooking spectacular scenery, this spotless home is filled with many museum-quality antiques. Each room is individual in decor, an eclectic mix of old and new. Mount Abrams and Bear Creek Falls are nearby. Take a daytime drive on the Million Dollar Highway—the views are breathtaking.

The Main Street House ✪

334 MAIN STREET, OURAY, COLORADO 81427

Tel: **(303) 325-4317**
Host(s): **David Vincie**
Location: **80 mi. from I-70**
No. of Rooms: **3**
No. of Private Baths: **3**
Double/pb: **$35–$50**
Single/pb: **$30**
Suites: **$50**
Open: **All year**
Breakfast: **Continental**
Pets: **Sometimes**
Children: **Welcome**
Smoking: **Permitted**
Social Drinking: **Permitted**

The second-floor suite occupies an entire floor and features a fully equipped kitchen and two decks. The bedroom has a king-size bed and antique dresser. The living room is decorated in wood tones and the sofa converts to a double bed. One ground-floor suite has a studio room, small greenhouse, and a large deck overlooking Oak Creek Canyon. The other suite contains a double bed and futon couch that can sleep two. It is surrounded by a large deck with views of the San Juan Mountains. All guests are welcome to use the courtyard and children's play area. David is an avid outdoor enthusiast and will be happy to recommend ways for you to best enjoy his hometown.

Davidson's Country Inn ✪

BOX 87, PAGOSA SPRINGS, COLORADO 81147

Tel: **(303) 264-5863**
Host(s): **The Davidson Family**
Location: **On US Hwy. 160**
No. of Rooms: **10**
No. of Private Baths: **2**
Max. No. Sharing Bath: **4**
Double/pb: **$64**
Single/pb: **$52**
Double/sb: **$43.50**
Single/sb: **$36**
Open: **All year**
Breakfast: **Continental**
Credit Cards: **MC, VISA**
Pets: **Welcome (outside pen)**
Children: **Welcome**
Smoking: **No**
Social Drinking: **No**

You're sure to enjoy the beautiful Rocky Mountain scenery surrounding the 30 acres of the inn's grounds. Some months bring the deer and elk to graze nearby. There's a natural hot spring in town and the San Juan River flows close by. You are invited to browse in the gift shop, stocked with homemade items; play horseshoes or volleyball; or use the sun deck, solarium, and library. For the children, there's a full toy chest and sandbox. Family heirlooms, handmade quilts, and lovely paintings enhance the comfortable decor. Seasonal beverages are graciously offered.

E.T.'s Bed and Breakfast ✪

1608 SAGE LANE, PAONIA, COLORADO 81428

Tel: **(303) 527-3300**
Host(s): **Esther and Larry Taylor**
Location: **82 mi. SE of Grand Junction**
No. of Rooms: **2**
Max. No. Sharing Bath: **4**
Double/sb: **$35**
Single/sb: **$30**
Open: **All year**
Reduced Rates: **Available**
Breakfast: **Continental**
Other Meals: **Available**
Credit Cards: **MC, VISA**
Pets: **Sometimes**
Children: **Welcome**
Smoking: **No**
Social Drinking: **No**
Airport/Station Pickup: **Yes**

This one-story ranch sits on the side of a mountain overlooking the little town of Paonia. The guest rooms are furnished simply and cooled by mountain breezes. Your hosts prepare waffles and strawberries in the morning, but will gladly accommodate other requests. You can pursue just about any sport here in the foothills of the Colorado Rockies, including fishing, hunting, skiing, and just plain relaxing.

Sweet Adeline's ✪

949 F STREET, SALIDA, COLORADO 81201

Tel: **(303) 539-4100**
Best Time to Call: **9 AM–9 PM**
Host(s): **Bob and Adella Schulz**
Location: **132 mi. SW of Denver**
No. of Rooms: **3**
No. of Private Baths: **1**
Max. No. Sharing Bath: **4**
Double/pb: **$55**
Double/sb: **$45**
Single/sb: **$35**
Open: **All year**
Breakfast: **Full**
Credit Cards: **MC, VISA**
Pets: **No**
Children: **Welcome, over 8**
Smoking: **No**
Social Drinking: **Permitted**

Listed on the Colorado Inventory of Historic Sites, this Queen Anne home, vintage 1900, has been restored and decorated with country charm. Surrounded by the snow-capped peaks of the Rockies, the area abounds in every imaginable seasonal recreation. Adella enjoys catering to your appetite by serving family recipes that include a variety of homemade bread from Czech kolaches to Southern pecan rolls, as well as delicious pancakes or waffles served with homemade syrups. The bedrooms are beautifully decorated, and guests may choose from king, double, or extra-long twin beds. A game of croquet, pitching horseshoes, or just sitting in the porch swing are pleasant pastimes. Occasionally, everyone gathers 'round the player piano for a sing-along.

The Alma House ✪

220 EAST 10TH STREET, SILVERTON, COLORADO 81433

Tel: **(303) 387-5336**
Host(s): **Don and Jolene Stott**
Location: **50 mi. N of Durango**
No. of Rooms: **10**
Max. No. Sharing Bath: **5**
Double/sb: **$28**
Single/sb: **$28**
Open: **June 25–Sept. 7**
Breakfast: **Continental**
Credit Cards: **AMEX, MC, VISA**
Pets: **No**
Children: **No**
Smoking: **No**
Social Drinking: **Permitted**

This 1898 stone-and-frame building has been lovingly restored and comfortably updated. Each spacious room has a deluxe queen-size bed, luxurious linens, antique dressers, and special touches. The plumbing in the bathrooms is up-to-date but the brass-and-walnut fixtures are faithful to a day gone by. Don and Jolene have a large videotape library for your evening entertainment. Ride the Durango–Silverton Narrow Gauge Railroad. Silverton retains the flavor of the old Western town it is.

Wilson's Pinto Bean Farm ✪

BOX 252, YELLOW JACKET, COLORADO 81335

Tel: **(303) 562-4476**
Best Time to Call: **Before 8 AM**
Host(s): **Arthur and Esther Wilson**
Location: **18 mi. NW of Cortez**
No. of Rooms: **3**
Max. No. Sharing Bath: **6**
Double/sb: **$33**
Single/sb: **$26**
Open: **March–Nov.**
Reduced Rates: **Available**
Breakfast: **Full**
Other Meals: **Available**
Pets: **Sometimes**
Children: **Welcome**
Smoking: **Permitted**
Social Drinking: **Permitted**
Airport/Station Pickup: **Yes**

Wilson's Pinto Bean Farm is located in the dryland area, with mountains, alfalfa hay, and waving wheat visible in every direction. The farmhouse is surrounded by gardens and trees, with the biggest elm sheltering the backyard smokehouse and picnic table. This is a working farm with chickens, geese, ducks, and cows. Esther enjoys baking bread and has never bought a bakery cake or cookie mix. Breakfast specialties include blueberry or sourdough pancakes, hot cheese biscuits, fresh eggs, and homemade jams. The family would also be pleased to have you join them for supper. The Wilsons offer both a comfortable guest trailer and an antique-filled bedroom in the main house. They can show children of all ages the delights of farm animals and country living. The farm is 40 miles from Four Corners, where the southwestern states meet in one place.

CONNECTICUT

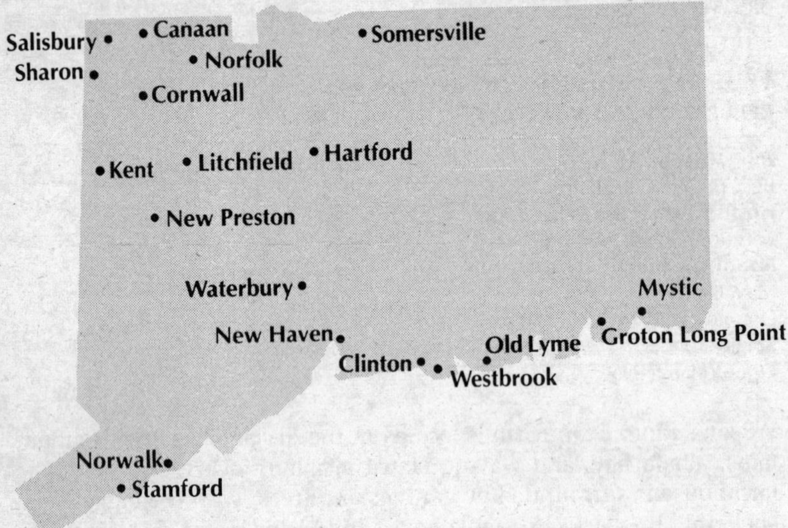

Bed and Breakfast, Ltd. ✪

P.O. BOX 216, NEW HAVEN, CONNECTICUT 06513

Tel: **(203) 469-3260**
Best Time to Call: **5–9 PM weekdays; anytime weekends**
Coordinator: **Jack Argenio**
State/Regions Covered: **Statewide; Rhode Island–Providence, Newport**

Rates (Single/Double):

Modest:	**$35**	**$45**
Average:	**$40**	**$50**
Luxury:	**$45**	**$55–$75**

Credit Cards: **No**

Whether you plan to visit one of Connecticut's many fine colleges including Trinity, Yale, Wesleyan, or the Coast Guard Academy, the Mystic Seaport, picturesque country villages, theater, opera, fine restaurants, it is always pleasant to return to one of Jack's homes-away-from-home with congenial hosts ready to extend warmth and hospitality.

Covered Bridge Bed & Breakfast ✪

P.O. BOX 701A, MAPLE AVENUE, NORFOLK, CONNECTICUT 06058

Tel: **(203) 542-5944**
Best Time to Call: **9 AM–7 PM**
Coordinator: **Diane Tremblay**
States/Regions Covered:
Connecticut—Cornwall, Essex, Kent, Litchfield, New Preston, Salisbury, Sharon; Massachusetts—The Berkshires

Rates (Single/Double):

	Single	Double
Modest:	**$45–$55**	**$45–$55**
Average:	**$55–$75**	**$55–$75**
Luxury:	**$75–$130**	**$75–$130**

Credit Cards: **No**
Minimum Stay: **2 days/holiday weekends**

If you enjoy historic homes, picture-postcard New England scenery, unsurpassed fall foliage, music festivals, theater, antiquing, auto racing, skiing, white-water rafting, or hiking, call Diane. Host homes are located primarily in the northwest corner of Connecticut, and the Berkshires in western Massachusetts. Williams College and Bennington College are nearby.

Captain Dibbell House ✪

21 COMMERCE STREET, CLINTON, CONNECTICUT 06413

Tel: **(203) 669-1646**
Host(s): **Ellis and Helen Adams**
Location: **21 mi. E of New Haven**
No. of Rooms: **3**
No. or Private Baths: **2 half-baths**
Max. No. Sharing Bath: **4**
Double/pb: **$60**
Single/pb: **$55**
Double/sb: **$50**
Single/sb: **$45**
Open: **All year**
Reduced Rates: **Weekly; 10%, seniors**
Breakfast: **Continental**
Pets: **No**
Children: **Welcome, over 12**
Smoking: **Permitted**
Social Drinking: **Permitted**
Airport/Station Pickup: **Yes**

Ellis and Helen fell in love with this piece of Connecticut shore years ago when they used to come from their home in New York to spend the weekend sailing. They liked it so much, in fact, that they bought this sea captain's home, located just one half mile from the shore and marinas and a short drive from the town beach, and converted it into a B&B. Clinton is ideally situated for exploring the Connecticut coast; not far away you'll find Hammonassett State Beach, Mystic Seaport and Aquarium, Gillette Castle, the Goodspeed Opera House, the Essex Steam Train, Long Wharf Theater, and Yale. In order to help you enjoy the Connecticut shore they love so much, the Adamses are happy to lend you their bicycles, beach chairs, beach umbrellas, and inflatable boat.

Shore Inne ✪

54 EAST SHORE ROAD, GROTON LONG POINT, CONNECTICUT 06340

Tel: **(203) 536-1180**
Best Time to Call: **8 AM–8 PM**
Host(s): **Helen Ellison**
Location: **3½ mi. W of Mystic**
No. of Rooms: **7**
No. of Private Baths: **3**
Max. No. Sharing Bath: **4**
Double/pb: **$55**
Single/pb: **$45**
Double/sb: **$45**
Single/sb: **$40**
Open: **Apr.–Oct.**
Reduced Rates: **20%, April, May**
Breakfast: **Continental**
Credit Cards: **MC, VISA**
Pets: **No**
Children: **Welcome**
Smoking: **Permitted**
Social Drinking: **Permitted**

Capturing the charm of the Connecticut coast, the inn's gracious rooms command water views. It is within a few miles of Mystic Seaport, the Marine Life Aquarium, Fort Griswold, and the U.S. Submarine Base and Memorial. Connecticut College and the U.S. Coast Guard Academy are close by. Swimming, fishing, biking, and tennis are a few steps from the door, and harbor and day cruises are available. Helen encourages you to enjoy the TV, library, and sunrooms.

Weaver's House ✪

GREENWOODS ROAD, NORFOLK, CONNECTICUT 06058

Tel: **(203) 542-5108**
Best Time to Call: **Before 8 AM**
Host(s): **Judy and Arnold Tsukroff**
Location: **39 mi. NW of Hartford**
No. of Rooms: **4**
Max. No. Sharing Bath: **4**
Double/sb: **$45**
Single/sb: **$40**
Open: **May 1–Nov. 1**
Breakfast: **Continental**
Pets: **No**
Children: **No**
Smoking: **No**
Social Drinking: **Permitted**
Airport/Station Pickup: **Yes**
Foreign Languages: **German**

Weaver's House is a turn-of-the-century Victorian facing the Yale Summer School of Music and Art Estate. In the 1930s, it was used as an annex to the Norfolk Inn. The guest rooms are simply decorated with handwoven curtains and rag rugs. Your hostess is a talented weaver, who will gladly display her loom for you. Norfolk is Connecticut's oldest town and offers many attractions. There are concerts and art shows in the summer and two state parks are nearby.

Janse Bed and Breakfast ✪

11 FLAT ROCK HILL ROAD, OLD LYME, CONNECTICUT 06371

Tel: **(203) 434-7269**
Best Time to Call: **Evenings**
Host(s): **Helen and Donald Janse**
Location: **1 mi. SW of New London**
No. of Rooms: **1**
No. of Private Baths: **1**
Double/pb: **$60**
Open: **All year**
Reduced Rates: **15%, seniors**
Breakfast: **Full**
Pets: **No**
Children: **Welcome, over 5**
Smoking: **Permitted**
Social Drinking: **Permitted**
Airport/Station Pickup: **Yes**

This Williamsburg-style saltbox is set on a quiet country road lined with vintage stone walls and century-old maples. The one-acre property includes a back patio and beautifully maintained gardens. Inside you'll find fresh flower arrangements, original art, Oriental rugs, and many antiques. Guest quarters feature pretty wallpaper, carpeting, wooden bed and bureau, and a sitting area with a Victorian love seat. Guests are welcome to relax in the library or living room with fireplace and grand piano. Your hosts serve fruit juice, ham or bacon, eggs, freshly baked muffins, and homemade jams for breakfast. Nearby points of interest include Mystic Seaport, the Goodspeed Opera House, and the Coast Guard Academy, home of the tall ship *Eagle*.

The Old Mill Inn ✪

63 MAPLE STREET, SOMERSVILLE, CONNECTICUT 06072

Tel: **(203) 763-1473**
Best Time to Call: **9 AM–9 PM**
Host(s): **Ralph and Phyllis Lumb**
Location: **10 mi. S of Springfield, Mass.**
No. of Rooms: **4**
No. of Private Baths: **2**
Max. No. Sharing Bath: **4**
Double/pb: **$50**
Single/pb: **$50**
Double/sb: **$45**
Single/sb: **$45**
Open: **All year**
Reduced Rates: **10%, seniors**
Breakfast: **Continental**
Credit Cards: **AMEX, MC, VISA**
Pets: **No**
Children: **Welcome**
Smoking: **No**
Social Drinking: **Permitted**
Airport/Station Pickup: **Yes**

Originally built in the 1850s, this comfortable home was enlarged and renovated many years later by the owner of the woolen mill next door. Today the old mill is a place to shop for gifts and furniture, while the house provides cozy lodgings for the traveler. Guest quarters are located on the second floor with bedrooms, baths, and a sitting room with cable TV, books, and a refrigerator. Bedrooms feature twin or full-size beds and comfortable furnishings. Downstairs in the gracious

guest living room, you may relax by the fire, read, or listen to the stereo. Breakfast is served in a beautiful dining room with hand-painted walls overlooking the lawn. The Old Mill Inn is minutes from golf, the Basketball Hall of Fame, museums, restaurants, and shops.

The Parsonage Bed & Breakfast ✪

18 HEWLETT STREET, WATERBURY, CONNECTICUT 06710

Tel: **(203) 574-2855**
Best Time to Call: **Mornings**
Host(s): **Lonetta Baysinger**
Location: **1½ mi. from I-84**
No. of Rooms: **4**
No. of Private Baths: **1**
Max. No. Sharing Bath: **5**
Double/pb: **$55**
Double/sb: **$55**
Suites: **$60**
Open: **All year**
Reduced Rates: **10%, seniors**
Breakfast: **Full**
Pets: **No**
Children: **Welcome (cradle)**
Smoking: **Permitted**
Social Drinking: **Permitted**
Airport/Station Pickup: **Yes**

Aptly named, the Parsonage was once a church rectory and is now listed on the National Register of Historic Places. With the Baysingers in charge, it has become a gracious bed and breakfast, welcoming travelers with its sweeping front porch, imposing central foyer, and winding stairway. Guests have a full or Continental breakfast—the choice is theirs—in a Victorian setting furnished with antiques. Located on a maple-lined street in a quiet residential neighborhood, the Parsonage is only five minutes from Interstate 84 and Route 8 and only minutes from the Waterbury business district.

Captain Stannard House ✪

138 SOUTH MAIN STREET, WESTBROOK, CONNECTICUT 06498

Tel: **(203) 399-7565**
Host(s): **Arlene and Ed Amatrudo**
Location: **25 mi. E of New Haven**
No. of Rooms: **7**
No. of Private Baths: **7**
Double/pb: **$60–$70**
Single/pb: **$55–$65**
Open: **All year**
Reduced Rates: **10%, seniors**
Breakfast: **Continental**
Credit Cards: **AMEX, DC, MC, VISA**
Pets: **No**
Children: **Welcome, over 6**
Smoking: **Permitted**
Social Drinking: **Permitted**

This Georgian Federal house with its fan window is the former home of a sea captain. Recapture the charm of yesteryear when you register in the country-store atmosphere. Play croquet or horseshoes, relax with a book, or browse through the on-premises antique shop. The village and the beach are close by. It is convenient to Mystic Seaport, Goodspeed Opera House, river cruises, fine restaurants, and charming shops. The U.S. Coast Guard Academy, Yale, and Wesleyan are nearby.

For key to listings, see inside front or back cover.

✪ This star means that rates are guaranteed through December 31, 1988 to any guest making a reservation as a result of reading about the B&B in *BED & BREAKFAST U.S.A.*—1988 edition.

Please enclose a self-addressed, stamped, business-sized envelope when contacting reservation services.

For more details on what you can expect in a B&B, see Chapter 1.

Always mention *Bed & Breakfast U.S.A.* when making reservations!

If no B&B is listed in the area you'll be visiting, use the form on page 698 to order a copy of our "List of New B&Bs."

We want to hear from you! Use the form on page 697.

DELAWARE

• Wilmington
• New Castle
• Smyrna
• Dover
• Lewes
• Rehoboth Beach
•Bethany Beach

The Sand Box & Sea-Vista Villas ✪

BOX 62, BETHANY BEACH, DELAWARE 19930

Tel: **(302) 539-3354 or (703) 820-7633**
Best Time to Call: **9 AM–5 PM**
Host(s): **Dale M. Duvall**
Location: **½ mi. from Rte. 1**
No. of Rooms: **3**
No. of Private Baths: **3**
Double/pb: **$60**
Single/pb: **$55**
Open: **May–Nov. 24**
Breakfast: **Full**
Pets: **Sometimes**
Children: **Welcome at the Sand Box**
Smoking: **Permitted**
Social Drinking: **Permitted**

Your cosmopolitan and most cordial host has two villas in a lovely wooded setting near Rehoboth Beach and Ocean City, Maryland. Guests will find the tennis court, swimming pool, terrace, and superb beach fine therapy after an urban winter. The Sand Box has two double bedrooms with baths, a deluxe kitchen, and a fireplace for chilly times. The Sea-Vista features a double bedroom and bath. Dale offers Happy Hour on the house.

Biddles Bed and Breakfast ✪

101 WYOMING AVENUE, DOVER, DELAWARE 19901

Tel: **(302) 736-1570**
Best Time to Call: **4–9 PM**
Host(s): **Millard and Hattye Mae Biddle**
Location: **½ mi. from US 13**
No. of Rooms: **3**
Max. No. Sharing Bath: **3**
Double/sb: **$40**
Single/sb: **$26**
Open: **All year**
Reduced Rates: **$30, Nov. 1–Apr. 1**
Breakfast: **Full**
Pets: **No**
Children: **No**
Smoking: **No**
Social Drinking: **Permitted**

At Biddles you will find old-fashioned hospitality in a contemporary setting. The guest rooms of this white frame house have been recently redecorated, with comfortable furnishings and special touches, such as fruit and mints. Breakfast features hot homemade muffins and biscuits. Your hosts will do all they can to make your stay in the capital city enjoyable. It's a short walk to the sights of the historic district. The beaches are 40 miles away. Dover Air Force Base is nearby.

Savannah Inn ✪

330 SAVANNAH ROAD, LEWES, DELAWARE, 19958

Tel: **(302) 645-5592**
Host(s): **Susan and Dick Stafursky**
Location: **120 mi. E of Washington, D.C.**
No. of Rooms: **7**
Max. No. Sharing Bath: **5**
Double/sb: **$35–$50**
Open: **Memorial Day–Labor Day**
Reduced Rates: **Available**
Breakfast: **Full, vegetarian**
Pets: **No**
Children: **Welcome**
Smoking: **Permitted**
Social Drinking: **Permitted**
Airport/Station Pickup: **Yes**

This brick Victorian, in the heart of historic Lewes, features a glassed-in, wraparound porch with wicker furniture and lots of plants. Furnishings are simple but comfortable. It's a short walk to the museum, bay beach, restaurants, and antique shops. It's a short drive to the state park, ocean beaches, and the Cape May–Lewes ferry. Susan and Dick are vegetarians so you can be sure of a delicious vegetarian breakfast. Dick, a naturalist, will be happy to arrange a variety of nature adventures, if you wish.

William Penn Guest House ✪

206 DELAWARE STREET, NEW CASTLE, DELAWARE 19720

Tel: **(302) 328-7736**
Best Time to Call: **After 5 PM**
Host(s): **Mr. and Mrs. Richard Burwell**
Location: **2 mi. from I-95**
No. of Rooms: **4**
Max. No. Sharing Bath: **4**
Double/sb: **$35**
Single/sb: **$35**
Open: **All year**
Breakfast: **Continental**
Pets: **No**
Children: **Welcome, over 3**
Smoking: **Permitted**
Social Drinking: **Permitted**
Foreign Languages: **Italian**

If you're a history buff, perhaps a stay in a 1682 house named for William Penn is what you've been seeking. Located in the heart of New Castle's historic district, the accommodations here are most comfortable. A lovely park for strolling and for the children to play in borders the Delaware shore, just two blocks away. The University of Delaware is 15 minutes from the house.

Tembo Guest House ✪

100 LAUREL STREET, REHOBOTH BEACH, DELAWARE 19971

Tel: **(302) 227-3360**
Host(s): **Don and Gerry Cooper**
Location: **3/4 mi. from US 1**
No. of Rooms: **4**
Max. No. Sharing Bath: **4**
Double/sb: **$50**
Single/sb: **$45**
Open: **All year**
Reduced Rates: **Seasonal**
Breakfast: **Continental**
Pets: **Sometimes**
Children: **Welcome (crib, high chair)**
Smoking: **No**
Social Drinking: **Permitted**
Airport/Station Pickup: **Yes**

This white two-story frame beach cottage, set among old shade trees, is one block from the Atlantic Ocean. The house is surrounded by brick walks and gardens, and a private yard with chaise longues for relaxing. The living room has a fireplace, hand-braided rugs, and an unusual collection of hand-carved shore birds and elephants. Each bedroom has an antique bureau, rocking chair, and either twin or full-size beds. Breakfast is served on a large enclosed front porch with rockers and swing. In colder weather, homemade muffins and scones are served in the kitchen, with its antique chandelier, butter churn, and coffee grinder. Don and Gerry will gladly direct you to local sights such as the restored Homestead, historic Port Lewes, and the Zwaanendael Museum.

The Main Stay ✪

41 SOUTH MAIN STREET, SMYRNA, DELAWARE 19977

Tel: **(302) 653-4293**
Best Time to Call: **After 5 PM**
Host(s): **Phyllis Howarth**
Location: **40 mi. S of Wilmington**
No. of Rooms: **2**
Max. No. Sharing Bath: **4**
Double/sb: **$35**
Single/sb: **$25**
Open: **Nov. 1–May 31**
Breakfast: **Continental**
Pets: **Sometimes**
Children: **Welcome**
Smoking: **No**
Social Drinking: **Permitted**

This traditional white clapboard Colonial town house is situated in the heart of the downtown historic area. It is decorated with Oriental rugs and antique furniture, and accented with Phyllis's needlework and handmade quilts. Depending on the season, you are welcome to relax on the open porch, in the sun room, or by the fireplace. You may use the laundry facilities, and coffee or tea are always on tap. It is 6 miles to the 5,000-acre Bombay Hook National Wildlife Refuge, and 15 miles to the Dover Air Force Base.

The Boulevard Bed & Breakfast ✪

1909 BAYNARD BOULEVARD, WILMINGTON, DELAWARE 19802

Tel: **(302) 656-9700**
Host(s): **Charles and Judy Powell**
Location: **½ mi. from I-95, Exit 8**
No. of Rooms: **6**
No. of Private Baths: **4**
Max. No. Sharing Bath: **3**
Double/pb: **$65**
Single/pb: **$60**
Double/sb: **$55**
Single/sb: **$50**
Open: **All year**
Reduced Rates: **Corporate; 10%, seniors**
Breakfast: **Full**
Credit Cards: **AMEX, MC, VISA**
Pets: **No**
Children: **Welcome**
Smoking: **Permitted**
Social Drinking: **Permitted**
Airport/Station Pickup: **Yes**

This beautifully restored city mansion was built in 1913 and has earned a place on the National Register of Historic Places. Upon entering, you'll be struck by the impressive foyer and magnificent staircase, leading to a landing complete with a window seat and large leaded-glass windows flanked by 15-foot fluted columns. Breakfast is served in the formal dining room or on the screened-in porch. Although Baynard Boulevard is a quiet and peaceful street, it's just a short walk away from the downtown business district. Parks are close by, and it's just a short drive to Hagley, Winterthur, the Delaware Natural History or Art Museum, or head for nearby Chadds Ford, Pennsylvania, and the famous Brandywine River Museum.

The Pink Door ✪

8 FRANCIS LANE, WILMINGTON, DELAWARE 19803

Tel: **(302) 478-8325**
Best Time to Call: **Noon–9 PM**
Host(s): **Frank and Mary Wehner**
Location: **4½ mi. N of Wilmington**
No. of Rooms: **2**
No. of Private Baths: **1**
Max. No. Sharing Bath: **3**
Double/pb: **$45–$50**
Single/pb: **$40–$45**
Open: **All year**
Breakfast: **Full**
Pets: **Sometimes**
Children: **Welcome, over 3**
Smoking: **Permitted**
Social Drinking: **Permitted**
Airport/Station Pickup: **Yes**

The Pink Door is a contemporary ranch home on a wooded cul-de-sac. Guests are welcomed with a carafe of wine or pot of tea, and a tray of cookies. The decor is eclectic, ranging from the romantic Queen Anne period to today's modern designs. After a long day of touring the Brandywine Valley, you will appreciate returning to the sounds of crickets and awakening to the chirping of the many birds. Breakfast is served in the dining room or on the screened deck facing the woods. Your hosts will gladly direct you to the nearby Brandywine River Museum, Longwood Gardens, and much more. By the way, pink is your hostess's favorite color.

Small Wonder B&B ✪

P.O. BOX 25254, WILMINGTON, DELAWARE 19899

Tel: **(302) 764-0789**
Best Time to Call: **After 4:30 PM**
Host(s): **Dot and Art Brill**
Location: **4 mi. from I-95, Exit 9**
No. of Rooms: **2**
No. of Private Baths: **1**
Max. No. Sharing Bath: **4**
Double/pb: **$55**
Single/pb: **$45**
Double/sb: **$50**
Single/sb: **$40**
Open: **All year**
Breakfast: **Full**
Other Meals: **Available**
Credit Cards: **MC, VISA**
Pets: **No**
Children: **Welcome, over 9**
Smoking: **No**
Social Drinking: **Permitted**
Airport/Station Pickup: **Yes**

The Brills describe their area—the Delaware and Brandywine valleys—as "a microcosm of American history and cosmopolitan trend—a blend of 17th-century Swedish and Dutch heritage and 20th-century innovation." They live in a quiet suburb surrounded by the things they love—a piano, an organ (Dot's a music teacher and organist), lots of books and original paintings by a Delaware artist. Outdoors they have a swimming pool (in use from May through September) and a hot tub set in an award-winning garden. Bellevue State Park, once the estate of William B. du Pont, is nearby—perfect, according to the Brills, for jogging or strolling or for a leisurely dinner served in the mansion on the property.

DISTRICT OF COLUMBIA

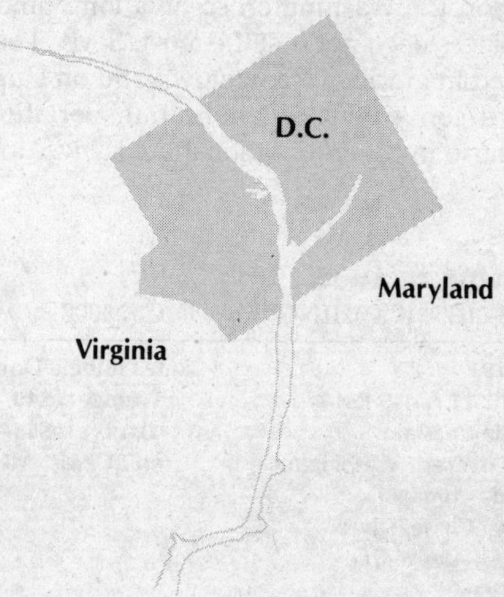

The Bed & Breakfast League, Ltd. ✪

3639 VAN NESS STREET, N.W., WASHINGTON, D.C. 20008

Tel: **(202) 363-7767**
Coordinator: **Millie Groobey**
States/Regions Covered: **Washington, D.C.; Annapolis, Baltimore**

Rates (Single/Double):

	Single	Double
Modest:	**$30–$35**	**$40–$45**
Average:	**$35–$45**	**$45–$55**
Luxury:	**$45–$60**	**$55–$70**

Credit Cards: **AMEX, MC, VISA**
Minimum Stay: **2 nights**

Millie's roster includes accommodations in apartment buildings, town houses, large homes, and small inns. Many are within easy walking distance of public transportation. Gracious hosts will cheerfully direct you to museums, fine restaurants, and interesting shops.

Bed 'n' Breakfast Ltd. of Washington, D.C. ✪

P.O. BOX 12011, WASHINGTON, D.C. 20005

Tel: **(202) 328-3510**
Best Time to Call: **10 AM–5 PM**
Coordinator: **Lisa Stofan**
States/Regions Covered: **Washington, D.C.; Virginia and Maryland suburbs**

Rates (Single/Double):

Modest:	**$30**	**$40**
Average:	**$35**	**$42–$45**
Luxury:	**$40–$65**	**$50–$75**

Credit Cards: **AMEX, MC, VISA**

This service boasts a network of homes in the city's historic districts. Lisa has been on the Washington scene a long time, and she knows that the best places need not cost the most. Several of her accommodations are located in gracious Georgetown and on Dupont Circle. All of the homes are convenient to public transportation. She caters to women and those in the international field. Five-dollar surcharge for one-night stay.

Sweet Dreams & Toast, Inc.

P.O. BOX 4835-0035, WASHINGTON, D.C. 20008

Tel: **(202) 483-9191**
Best Time to Call: **11 AM–5 PM**
Coordinator: **Ellie Chastain**
States/Regions Covered: **Washington, D.C.; Maryland—Annapolis, Bethesda, Chevy Chase, Silver Spring; Virginia—Alexandria, Arlington, McLean**

Rates (Single/Double):

Average:	**$40–$50**	**$53–$60**
Luxury:	**$55–$65**	**$65–$70**

Credit Cards: **MC, VISA**

The capital of the United States is awe-inspiring. You will want to spend several days to take it all in. This is your opportunity to watch history in the making and to visit the glorious monuments erected to memorialize those who shaped America's history. Ellie's hosts will direct you to restaurants and special shops that suit your taste and wallet. The agency is open January 6 to December 17. There's a two-night minimum stay.

The Reeds ✪

P.O. BOX 12011, WASHINGTON, D.C. 20005

Tel: **(202) 328-3510**
Best Time to Call: **10 AM–5 PM**
Host(s): **Charles and Jackie Reed**
No. of Rooms: **4**
Max. No. Sharing Bath: **4**
Double/sb: **$55**
Single/sb: **$30–$45**
Suite (apartment): **$60–$80 (4)**

Open: **All year**
Breakfast: **Continental**
Pets: **No**
Children: **Welcome**
Smoking: **Permitted**
Social Drinking: **Permitted**
Foreign Languages: **French**

This 100-year-old Victorian mansion boasts landscaped gardens, a terrace, and a fountain. The interior features original wood paneling, elaborate oak staircases, nine fireplaces, ornate mantels as well as Art Nouveau antiques, and is centrally air-conditioned in summer. Adjoining the Logan Circle Historic District, it is only 10 blocks from the White House. Charles is a real estate developer and Jackie was an interior designer, so it's no surprise that the house was featured on the Logan Circle House Tour.

For key to listings, see inside front or back cover.

✪ This star means that rates are guaranteed through December 31, 1988 to any guest making a reservation as a result of reading about the B&B in *BED & BREAKFAST U.S.A.*—1988 edition.

Please enclose a self-addressed, stamped, business-sized envelope when contacting reservation services.

For more details on what you can expect in a B&B, see Chapter 1.

Always mention *Bed & Breakfast U.S.A.* when making reservations!

If no B&B is listed in the area you'll be visiting, use the form on page 698 to order a copy of our "List of New B&Bs."

We want to hear from you! Use the form on page 697.

FLORIDA

A & A Bed & Breakfast of Florida, Inc. ✪

P.O. BOX 1316, WINTER PARK, FLORIDA 32790

Tel: **(305) 628-3233**
Best Time to Call: **9 AM–6 PM**
Coordinator: **Brunhilde (Bruni) Fehner**
States/Regions Covered: **Orlando area—Disney World, Epcot, Cape Kennedy, Sea World, Altamonte Springs, Winter Park, Maitland, New Smyrna Beach, Delray Beach, Ft. Myers, St. Augustine**

Rates (Single/Double):

Modest:	**$25**	**$35**
Average:	**$25–$35**	**$36–$45**
Luxury:	**$40**	**$65**

Credit Cards: **No**
Minimum Stay: **2 nights**

You should allow several days to really savor all this area has to offer. Bruni's hosts will suggest hints on getting the most out of the major attractions, wonderful un-touristy restaurants, and tips on where to shop for unique gifts to take home. All of her homes have a certain "touch of class" to make you delighted with your visit. Rollins College is close by. There is a surcharge of $5 for one night.

Bed & Breakfast Co.—Tropical Florida ✪

P.O. BOX 262, SOUTH MIAMI, FLORIDA 33243

Tel: **(305) 661-3270**
Coordinator: **Marcella Schaible**
States/Regions Covered: **Boca Raton, Delray Beach, Ft. Lauderdale, Miami, Palm Beach, Sanibel Island, The Keys**

Rates (Single/Double):

Modest:	**$25–$30**	**$32–$40**
Average:	**$30–$40**	**$40–$55**
Luxury:	**$40–$65**	**$50–$70**

Credit Cards: **MC, VISA**

Marcella's roster ranges from a restored Art Deco mansion on an island in Biscayne Bay to a 59-foot Hatteras yacht. Accommodations to suit all budgets, with or without swimming pools, hot tubs, spas, but all with comfortable furniture and traditional hospitality. Many are convenient to the University of Miami, Barry College, and the University of South Florida. Discount tickets are provided to many attractions. There's a $5 surcharge for one-night stays.

Bed & Breakfast Registry of Volusia County

P.O. BOX 573, DE LEON SPRINGS, FLORIDA 32028

Tel: **(904) 985-5068**
Coordinator: **Robin Johnstone**
States/Regions Covered: **Astor, Daytona Beach, De Bary, De Land, De Leon Springs, Deltona, Sanford**

Rates (Single/Double):

Average:	**$30**	**$35**
Luxury:	**$40**	**$45**

Credit Cards: **No**

Area attractions include the famed Daytona International Speedway and beach where the auto is king, Spring Garden Ranch where Thoroughbreds are trained, De Leon Springs State Park, and Blue Springs State Park, which is home to the manatee, an aquatic mammal. Summer rates are reduced by $10 nightly. Keep this in mind should you care to visit Disney World, Sea World, and Epcot, since they are an hour's drive from most host homes.

B&B Suncoast Accommodations

8690 GULF BOULEVARD, ST. PETERSBURG BEACH ISLAND, FLORIDA 33706

Tel: **(813) 360-1753**
Best Time to Call: **11 AM–2 PM; 4–7 PM**
Coordinator: **Danie Bernard**
State/Regions Covered: **Englewood, Ft. Myers, Naples, Sanibel, Sarasota, St. Pete Beach, Tampa**

Rates (Single/Double):

Modest:	**$35**	**$40**
Average:	**$40**	**$45–$55**
Luxury:	**$45**	**$50–$70**

Minimum Stay: **2 nights**

Florida, the land of sunshine, has always been a vacationer's dream. You can turn dreams into reality because Danie specializes in accommodations on the west coast and in Orlando. The above rates quoted are the in-season (December–May) rates. Off-season rates are reduced 20%.

Central Florida B&B Reservations ✪

719 S.E. 4TH STREET, OCALA, FLORIDA 32671

Tel: **(904) 351-1167**
Coordinator: **Marcie Gauntlett**
States/Regions Covered: **Ocala, Orange Springs, Oklawaha**

Rates (Single/Double):

Modest:	**$30**	**$35**
Average:	**$35**	**$40**
Luxury:	**$45**	**$65**

Credit Cards: **No**

One of Marcie's B&Bs is decorated with antiques and Oriental rugs bought in the Middle East and Europe. The hostess has a most interesting doll collection as well. Another is a farm located on Lake Fay where you are welcome to try your hand at fishing. The owner, a former horse trainer, has Arabians, quarter horses, and Thoroughbreds. Silver Springs, Wild Waters, the Museum of Drag Racing, and Cross Creek, the home of Marjorie Kinnan Rawlings, are some of the local attractions.

1735 House ✪

584 SOUTH FLETCHER, AMELIA ISLAND, FLORIDA 32034

Tel: **(904) 261-5878**
Best Time to Call: **9 AM–11 PM**
Host(s): **David and Susan Caples**
Location: **35 mi. NE of Jacksonville**
No. of Rooms: **5**
No. of Private Baths: **5**
Double/pb: **$65–$70**
Single/pb: **$55**
Guest Cottage: **$85–$115; sleeps up to 6**
Open: **All year**
Reduced Rates: **5%, seniors**
Breakfast: **Continental**
Credit Cards: **AMEX, MC, VISA**

Pets: **No**
Children: **Welcome**
Smoking: **Permitted**
Social Drinking: **Permitted**
Airport/Station Pickup: **Yes**

This quaint country inn is situated on the beach of beautiful Amelia Island. The house is furnished with wicker and rattan, and the bedrooms have interesting antiques. David and Susan allow you to use the kitchen for light snacks, and supply bags so you can take home your seashell collection. There's surf-casting right on the beach, and deep-sea fishing or boat charters can be arranged. Don't miss the private tour of Greyfield Inn.

The Barnacle ✪

ROUTE 1, BOX 780 A, LONG BEACH ROAD, BIG PINE KEY, FLORIDA 33043

Tel: **(305) 872-3298**
Best Time to Call: **Before 9 PM**
Host(s): **Wood and Joan Cornell**
Location: **33 mi. E of Key West**
No. of Rooms: **4**
No. of Private Baths: **4**
Double/pb: **$60–$65**
Guest Cottage: **$70–$80; sleeps 2**
Apartment: **$65–$75**
Open: **July–May**
Breakfast: **Full**
Pets: **No**
Children: **No**
Smoking: **Permitted**
Social Drinking: **Permitted**
Foreign Languages: **French**

The ultimate in privacy is the self-contained cottage—a tropical tree house with stained-glass windows and private terrace. The main house guest rooms have ocean views and one overlooks the atrium, hot tub, and lush plants; the mini-apartment has a private entrance and kitchenette. Every detail in and around their home reflects Wood and Joan's taste, attention to detail, and artistic flair. The structure was built to frame their outstanding collection of statuary, tapestries, and art. Their emphasis is on the sun and sea, with warm hospitality offered in abundance. You can scuba dive or fish right off "your own" beach. Bahia Honda State Park and Key West are close by. There's a two-night minimum stay in the guest rooms; three nights in the cottage and apartment.

Bed & Breakfast-on-the-Ocean "Casa Grande" ✪

P.O. BOX 378, BIG PINE KEY, FLORIDA 33043

Tel: **(305) 872-2878**
Host(s): **Jon and Kathleen Threlkeld**
No. of Rooms: **3**
No. of Private Baths: **3**
Double/pb: **$60**
Single/pb: **$55**
Open: **All year**
Breakfast: **Full**
Pets: **No**
Children: **No**
Smoking: **Permitted**
Social Drinking: **Permitted**

This spectacular Spanish-style home facing the water was custom-designed to suit the natural beauty of the Keys. The large landscaped garden patio is where you'll enjoy Jon and Kathleen's bountiful breakfast. It is also the site of the hot tub/Jacuzzi for relaxing by day or under a moonlit sky. The large and airy guest rooms are comfortably cooled by Bahama fans. Key deer and birds abound. You'll enjoy swimming, fishing, snorkeling, bicycling, and jogging. There's a picnic table, gas grill, hammock, and Windsurfer for guests to use, compliments of the gracious hosts.

Canal Cottage Bed & Breakfast

P.O. BOX 266, BIG PINE KEY, FLORIDA 33043

Tel: **(305) 872-3881**
Host(s): **Dean and Patti Nickless**
No. of Rooms: **1 suite**
No. of Private Baths: **1**
Suites: **$58 for 2**
Open: **All year**
Breakfast: **Full**
Pets: **No**
Children: **Welcome, over 10**
Smoking: **No**
Social Drinking: **Permitted**

Relax in the tropical atmosphere of this unusual wood stilt house. Your accommodations are nestled in the trees and consist of a bedroom with a queen-size bed, a bathroom, a living room with sleep space for two, and a kitchen stocked for your breakfast, which you can prepare at leisure and enjoy on the porch. You can dive, snorkel, and fish in the Gulf or the Atlantic. You can launch your boat at the neighborhood ramp and tie it up at your backyard dock, where you may also enjoy swimming. Dean and Patti live on the premises and will make every effort to ensure you a comfortable, enjoyable stay. Two-night minimum stay.

Deer Run ✪

LONG BEACH ROAD, P.O. BOX 431, BIG PINE KEY, FLORIDA 33043

Tel: **(305) 872-2015**
Best Time to Call: **7 AM–9 AM; 6 PM–10 PM**
Host(s): **Sue Abbott**
Location: **33 mi. E of Key West**
No. of Rooms: **2**
No. of Private Baths: **2**
Double/pb: **$75**
Single/pb: **$65**
Open: **All year**
Breakfast: **Full**
Pets: **No**
Children: **No**
Smoking: **No**
Social Drinking: **Permitted**
Airport/Station Pickup: **Yes**

Deer Run is a Florida Cracker-style home nestled among lush native trees on the ocean. The house is beautifully designed with skylights, high ceilings, and Bahama fans. The decor boasts many paintings, artifacts, and antiques to complement wicker and rattan furnishings. Each room has French doors that open onto a large veranda. Breakfast is served outside overlooking the water, where you may spot Key deer walking along the beach. Looe Key Coral Reef, Bahia Honda State Park, and Key West are all within easy reach, or you can relax and soak up the rays in the free-form deep spa where there's room for eight.

Feller House ✪

3684 SAYBROOK PLACE SW, BONITA SPRINGS, FLORIDA 33923

Tel: **(813) 992-4865**
Best Time to Call: **Evenings**
Host(s): **Wayne and Pat Feller**
No. of Rooms: **1**
No. of Private Baths: **1**
Double/pb: **$35**
Single/pb: **$30**
Open: **Oct. 1–June 1**
Breakfast: **Full**
Pets: **No**
Children: **Welcome, over 5**
Smoking: **Permitted**
Social Drinking: **Permitted**
Airport/Station Pickup: **Yes**
Foreign Languages: **German**

You are assured of a warm welcome in this attractive home on a lake in a quiet, residential neighborhood. Feel free to use the TV in the den; use the pool and patio, too. Gulf beaches are minutes away. Wayne and Pat, experienced travelers and home exchangers, will supply maps to take you to Everglades National Park and Corkscrew Bird Sanctuary, as well as directions to the fine shops and restaurants in town. Naples is 15 minutes away.

Bed & Breakfast of Tampa Bay ✪

3234 TERN WAY, FEATHERSOUND, CLEARWATER, FLORIDA 33520

Tel: **(813) 576-5825**
Best Time to Call: **Before 10 AM, after 6 PM**
Host(s): **Vivian and David Grimm**
Location: **7 mi. W of Tampa**
No. of Rooms: **3**
No. of Private Baths: **1**
Max. No. Sharing Bath: **4**
Double/pb: **$40**
Single/pb: **$30**
Double/sb: **$30**
Single/sb: **$20**
Open: **All year**
Breakfast: **Full**
Pets: **Sometimes**
Children: **Welcome**
Smoking: **Permitted**
Social Drinking: **Permitted**
Airport/Station Pickup: **Yes**

The lovely gardens of this fine stucco home have an Oriental flair, and the interior is graced with fine Oriental and European art. Whenever Vivian and David travel, they bring home souvenirs to enhance their decor. Busch Gardens, St. Petersburg Fine Arts Museum, and Tarpon Springs are 15 miles away; Disney World, Circus World, and Sea World are 65 miles away. If you want to stay close to home, the Grimms will lend you their bikes. You're welcome to use the pool, play the piano, or use the kitchen for light snacks. It's close to the University of South Florida and the University of Tampa.

Lakeside Inn Bed and Breakfast

P.O. BOX 71, EASTLAKE WEIR, FLORIDA 32632

Tel: **(904) 288-1396**
Best Time to Call: **Mornings, evenings**
Host(s): **Bill and Sandy Bodner**
Location: **20 mi. S of Ocala**
No. of Rooms: **6**
No. of Private Baths: **1**
Max. No. Sharing Bath: **4**
Double/pb: **$40**
Double/sb: **$38**
Single/sb: **$25**
Open: **All year**
Reduced Rates: **5%, families**
Breakfast: **Full**
Other Meals: **Available**
Pets: **Sometimes**
Children: **Welcome, over 5**
Smoking: **On porch only**
Social Drinking: **Permitted**
Airport/Station Pickup: **Yes**

If you enjoy fascinating homes filled with antiques and collectibles, this may be the vacation spot for you. This lovely Victorian Gothic home was built in the 1880s as a hotel. The house is set on beautiful Lake Weir and is complete with dock and sun deck. A huge veranda overlooks the lake on the first floor, as does the screened-in porch upstairs. The rooms are quaint and comfortable, featuring heart-of-pine paneling and floors, plus seven fireplaces. Enjoy a hearty Southern breakfast complete with home-baked goodies, then grab a fishing pole or go swimming right off their dock. Lakeside Inn is located in the Silver Springs area, which abounds with numerous lakes, streams, and rolling hills.

Dolan House

1401 N.E. 5 COURT, FT. LAUDERDALE, FLORIDA 33301

Tel: **(305) 462-8430**
Host(s): **Tom and Sandra Dolan**
Location: **5 mi. from I-95**
No. of Rooms: **4**
No. of Private Baths: **2**
Max. No. Sharing Bath: **4**
Double/pb: **$50**
Single/pb: **$45**
Double/sb: **$50**
Single/sb: **$45**
Open: **All year**
Breakfast: **Continental**
Pets: **No**
Children: **Welcome**
Smoking: **Permitted**
Social Drinking: **Permitted**
Airport/Station Pickup: **Yes**

All the comforts of home—if your home has a hot tub large enough to fit 19! Set right in the heart of Fort Lauderdale, and only two miles from the city's famed beach, the Dolan House offers privacy (it's completely fenced in) and convenience. When the weather's balmy, guests sit out on the large deck; when the nights are cool they can move indoors and enjoy the large coquina fireplace. The Dolans have lived in the area for 30 years and they're anxious to tell you all about it—ask them about the Galleria Shopping Center, the new Riverwalk historic section, Holiday Park, and all the nearby theaters and museums.

Windsong Garden ✪

5570-4 WOODROSE COURT, FORT MYERS, FLORIDA 33907

Tel: **(813) 936-6378**
Host(s): **Embe Burdick**
No. of Rooms: **2**
No. of Private Baths: **2**
Double/pb: **$45**
Single/pb: **$45**
Suite: **$45**
Open: **All year**
Reduced Rates: **$35, June–Oct.**
Breakfast: **Continental**
Pets: **No**
Children: **No**
Smoking: **No**
Social Drinking: **Permitted**

This modern cedar-shake-and-brick town house has a private courtyard and balcony for your enjoyment. The spacious combination bedroom-and-sitting room is most comfortable. Embe's varied interests include arts, crafts, and music. It's close to Sanibel and Captiva islands, fine shopping, good restaurants, and the University of Florida. You are welcome to use the barbecue and pool.

Country Meadows ✪

9506 SOUTH WEST 81 WAY, GAINESVILLE, FLORIDA 32608

Tel: **(904) 495-2699**
Best Time to Call: **4 PM–10 PM**
Host(s): **Allene and Orville Higgs**
Location: **10 mi. SW of Gainesville**
No. of Rooms: **2**
No. of Private Baths: **2**
Double/pb: **$30–$35**
Single/pb: **$26–$30**
Open: **All year**
Breakfast: **Continental**
Other Meals: **Available**
Pets: **No**
Children: **Welcome**
Smoking: **Permitted**
Social Drinking: **Permitted**
Airport/Station Pickup: **Yes**

Country Meadows is a Colonial-style home set on an acre and a half. The house is surrounded by pine trees and has a fenced-in yard for relaxing. The country-style decor consists of comfortable furnishings and lots of handmade craft items. The Higgses enjoy entertaining and are glad to prepare either a Continental breakfast or a larger meal for guests. They will gladly direct you to nearby nature parks, horse farms, and museums.

Hollywood Bed 'n' Breakfast ✪

P.O. BOX 768, HOLLYWOOD, FLORIDA 33022

Tel: **(305) 922-0930**
Best Time to Call: **Evenings**
Host(s): **Terri Garrison**
Location: **½ mile from I-95**
No. of Rooms: **1**
No. of Private Baths: **1**
Double/pb: **$30–$35**
Single/pb: **$25–$30**
Open: **All year**
Breakfast: **Full**
Pets: **Sometimes**
Children: **No**
Smoking: **Permitted**
Social Drinking: **Permitted**
Airport/Station Pickup: **Yes**

Terri likes to share her two-story town house condominium with people visiting southern Florida. She loves to cook and bake and practice the art of flower arranging—she just took a course in the latter, and you'll find evidence of it all over the house. Guests may take advantage of a lovely patio and heated swimming pool. When it's time to get out and explore the area, you can rely on getting good advice from your hostess. "People say this is a 'warm and cozy home' and that's the way I like it."

Meeks B&B on the Gulf Beaches ✪

19506 GULF BOULEVARD #8, INDIAN SHORES, FLORIDA 33535

Tel: **(813) 596-5424**
Best Time to Call: **7 AM–10 PM**
Host(s): **Greta Meeks**
Location: **10 mi. NW of St. Petersburg**
No. of Rooms: **7**
No. of Private Baths: **5**
Double/pb: **$60**
Single/pb: **$40**
Suites: **$75**
Open: **All year**
Breakfast: **Continental**
Pets: **No**
Children: **Welcome**
Smoking: **Permitted**
Social Drinking: **Permitted**
Airport/Station Pickup: **Yes**

This lovely beach cottage condo is located directly on the Gulf of Mexico. From your room you can step right onto lovely white sand beaches. Your hostess offers blueberry muffins or bagels and cream cheese in the morning. If you would like to bring lunch to the beach, picnic tables are available. This B&B is close to Gulf beach seafood restaurants and within walking distance of the Tiki Gardens. Greta is a local real estate agent who can easily guide you to the best sightseeing and dining.

Sunrise Sea House ✪

39 BAY DRIVE, BAY POINT, KEY WEST, FLORIDA 33040

Tel: **(305) 745-2875**
Best Time to Call: **Before noon**
Host(s): **Betty Collins**
No. of Rooms: **3**
No. of Private Baths: **1**
Max. No. Sharing Bath: **4**
Double/sb: **$70**
Suites: **$90**
Open: **Oct. 1–May 31**
Breakfast: **Full**
Pets: **No**
Children: **No**
Smoking: **Permitted**
Social Drinking: **Permitted**
Airport/Station Pickup: **Yes**

Decorated in the pretty salmon and turquoise hues that aptly typify its tropical ambience, guests wake to a sunrise and sea breezes. Perfect for those seeking privacy, each room has its own porch and patch of beach. The ocean is a few yards away and the canal in front of the house is a perfect place to swim. There's a boat ramp and dock for you to use in case you've brought your yacht or rowboat. Key West abounds with history, quaint houses, great shops, and marvelous restaurants and clubs. A minimum stay of two nights is required.

A Sunny Place Guest House ✪

121 NORTH OAK STREET, LANTANA, FLORIDA 33462

Tel: **(305) 586-3596**
Host(s): **Kent and Diane Hager**
Location: **1 mi. from I-95, Lantana Road Exit**
No. of Rooms: **1 apartment**
No. of Private Baths: **1**
Guest Cottage: **$65; sleeps 6**
Open: **All year**
Reduced Rates: **10%, weekly; seniors; 25% less, May 15–Sept. 15**
Breakfast: **Continental**
Pets: **Sometimes**
Children: **Welcome (crib)**
Smoking: **Permitted**
Social Drinking: **Permitted**
Airport/Station Pickup: **Yes**

A Sunny Place is a casual beach house located in the heart of Florida's Gold Coast, adjacent to South Palm Beach. It is within walking distance of a beautiful stretch of the beach that boasts its own snack bar and picnic and barbecue areas. The cottage is a private apartment, furnished in modern decor, with a bedroom, living room, full kitchen, bath, screened porch, and outdoor deck. It's a pleasant walk to restaurants, unique shops, boat rentals, scuba diving, snorkeling, and the Intracoastal Waterway. It's a short drive to posh Palm Beach and the exclusive shops of Worth Avenue.

Bette Lane

600 N.E. 36TH STREET, APARTMENT 1923, MIAMI, FLORIDA 33137

Tel: **(305) 576-6606**
Best Time to Call: **9–10 AM; 6–7 PM**
Host(s): **Bette Lane**
Location: **20 min. from airport**
No. of Rooms: **1**
No. of Private Baths: **1**
Double/pb: **$47**
Open: **All year**
Reduced Rates: **15%, Mar.–Sept.**
Breakfast: **Full**
Other Meals: **Available**
Pets: **No**
Children: **Sometimes**
Smoking: **No**
Social Drinking: **Permitted**

Bette lives on the 19th floor of a high-rise building overlooking downtown Miami and the Bay. The apartment has two bedrooms, two baths, and is furnished in comfortable Floridian style. Breakfast is your choice of pancakes, eggs, and hot or cold cereal, served with toast, coffee, and juice. Guests are welcome to take advantage of the tennis courts, swimming pool, and exercise room located on the premises. This lovely apartment is set at the foot of the bridge to Miami Beach and offers easy access to Miami International Airport, the major highways, and shopping areas.

The Allens ✪

2411 VIRGINIA DRIVE, ORLANDO, FLORIDA 32803

Tel: **(305) 896-9916 (use area code (407) after Apr. 16)**
Best Time to Call: **5:30 PM–9:30 PM**
Host(s): **Robert and Esther Allen**
Location: **2½ mi. from I-4**
No. of Rooms: **2**
Max. No. Sharing Bath: **4**
Double/sb: **$40**
Single/sb: **$35**
Open: **All year**
Reduced Rates: **10%, seniors**
Breakfast: **Continental**
Pets: **No**
Children: **No**
Smoking: **No**
Social Drinking: **Permitted**

The Allens have a single-story home with a vegetable garden in the front yard. They offer a comfortable suite consisting of a bedroom and sitting room with foldout couch. The house is attractively furnished and features lovely paintings and needlepoint. In the morning, enjoy a special array of homemade muffins, breads, or coffee cake. The Allens are close to the famous attractions of Disney World and Epcot. The Loch Haven Art Center, Winter Park shops, and Harry Leu Gardens are also nearby. You are welcome to enjoy the swimming pool.

Bed & Breakfast of Orlando ✪

8205 BANYAN BOULEVARD, ORLANDO, FLORIDA 32819

Tel: **(305) 352-9157**
Host(s): **Bobbie Jean Harlish**
Location: **2 mi. from I-4**
No. of Rooms: **2**
Max. No. Sharing Bath: **4**
Double/sb: **$50**
Single/sb: **$45**
Open: **All year**
Reduced Rates: **10%, seniors from Sept.–Nov.**
Breakfast: **Full**
Pets: **No**
Children: **Welcome**
Smoking: **Permitted**
Social Drinking: **No**
Airport/Station Pickup: **Yes**

Located in Sand Lake Hills, close to the country clubs of Bay Hills and Orange Tree, is Bobbie's lovely home. Weather permitting, breakfast is served in the screened-in Florida room overlooking orange groves. It is all very quiet and peaceful, yet minutes away from Epcot, Disney World, the Orange County Convention Center, and the Factory Outlet Mall. A two-night minimum stay is required.

Rinaldi House ✪

502 LAKE AVENUE, ORLANDO, FLORIDA 32801

Tel: **(305) 425-6549**
Best Time to Call: **Evenings**
Host(s): **Victor C. Brown**
No. of Rooms: **2**

Max. No. Sharing Bath: **4**
Double/sb: **$39**
Single/sb: **$33**
Guest cottage: **$33; sleeps 2**
Open: **All year**
Breakfast: **Full**
Other Meals: **Available**
Pets: **Welcome**
Children: **Welcome**
Smoking: **Permitted**
Social Drinking: **Permitted**
Airport/Station Pickup: **Yes**

A lovely 1895 restoration in the Lake Cherokee Historic District, this two-story Colonial is furnished with many antiques, including an 1886 reed organ. The landscaping features an ornate, Victorian-style gazebo. It's a 12-minute walk to downtown Orlando, Eola Park, the Historic Church Street Station Entertainment Complex, and fine restaurants. Disney World is a 30-minute drive. Complimentary wine and cheese are graciously served by Victor, whose hospitality is legend.

The Rio Pinar House ✪

532 PINAR DRIVE, ORLANDO, FLORIDA 32825

Tel: **(305) 277-4903; (407) 277-4903 after Apr. 16**
Host(s): **Victor and Delores Freudenburg**
Location: **½ mi. from E-W Expy., Chickasaw Exit**
No. of Rooms: **3**
No. of Private Baths: **2**
Max. No. Sharing Bath: **4**
Double/pb: **$40**
Single/pb: **$35**
Double/sb: **$30**
Single/sb: **$25**
Suites: **$60 (family)**
Open: **All year**
Breakfast: **Full**
Other Meals: **Available**
Pets: **No**
Children: **Welcome**
Smoking: **No**
Social Drinking: **Permitted**

This spacious home is located in a quiet neighborhood across from the Rio Pinar Golf Course. The rooms are furnished comfortably with both antiques and Americana. Breakfast is served on the porch overlooking a garden and trees. The house is a 30-minute drive from Disney World and nine miles from downtown Orlando. Your hosts recommend an outing to beautiful Rock Springs and they will be glad to pack picnic lunches. They are experienced tour guides who can recommend the sights, including the nearby Church Street Station Complex.

The Spencer Home ✪

313 SPENCER STREET, ORLANDO, FLORIDA 32809

Tel: **(305) 855-5603**
Host(s): **Neal and Eunice Schattauer**
Location: **2 mi. from I-4**
No. of Rooms: **1 suite**
No. of Private Baths: **1**
Suites: **$50 for 2; $60 for 4**

Open: **All year**
Breakfast: **Full**
Other Meals: **Available**
Pets: **No**
Children: **Welcome**
Smoking: **No**
Social Drinking: **Permitted**
Airport/Station Pickup: **Yes**

The guest suite of this neat ranch-style house has a private entrance and consists of a bedroom with a double bed, a living room with a sleeper for two, a full bathroom, and is completely air-conditioned. You are welcome to freshen your traveling duds in the laundry room and yourselves in the swimming pool. Eunice will start your day with breakfast and Neal would be pleased to have you join in harmony singing whenever the mood is right.

Open House Bed & Breakfast Registry

P.O. BOX 3025, PALM BEACH, FLORIDA 33480

Tel: **(305) 842-5190**
Best Time to Call: **Evenings; weekends**
Coordinator(s): **Peggy Maxwell**
States/Regions Covered: **Boca Raton, Boynton Beach, Delray, Jupiter, Lake Worth, Lantana, Palm Beach, Tequesta, West Palm Beach**

Rates (Single/Double):

	Single	Double
Modest:	**$35**	**$45**
Average:	**$45**	**$55**
Luxury:	**$65**	**$75**

Located within the posh Gold Coast of the Palm Beaches, Peggy's roster ranges from a modest twin-bedded room in the home of a retired farmer, to a home in a residential section just off the Intracoastal Waterway in West Palm Beach, to a decorator's waterfront mansion with a private swimming pool and dock on Lake Worth. They are all within easy reach of fine restaurants, shops, galleries, museums, theaters, and sports arenas. The service is closed from July 1 to September 30.

The Homestead Inn ✪

7830 PINE FOREST ROAD, PENSACOLA, FLORIDA 32506

Tel: **(904) 944-4816**
Best Time to Call: **9 AM–5 PM**
Host(s): **Neil and Jeanne Liechty**
Location: **½ mi. from I-10, Exit 2**
No. of Rooms: **6**
No. of Private Baths: **6**
Double/pb: **$59–$69**
Single/pb: **$49–$59**
Open: **All year**
Breakfast: **Full**
Credit Cards: **AMEX, MC, VISA**
Pets: **No**
Children: **Welcome, over 10**
Smoking: **No**
Social Drinking: **Permitted**
Airport/Station Pickup: **Yes**

The inn's architecture and decor are traditional 19th-century Williamsburg, from the spacious veranda and leaded-glass entry to the high ceilings, hardwood floors, and period furnishings. Breakfast features such Southern specialties as grits 'n' eggs, country ham and blueberry pancakes, and endless cups of coffee. After a day at the beach, or a day visiting historic sites, the preservation districts, or the Naval Aviation museum, it's time to select one of the fine restaurants featuring fresh Gulf seafood for dinner. Remember to save some room for the complimentary desserts, such as apple dumplings, strawberry shortcake, or peanut butter pie, that will be waiting when you return "home" to Jeanne and Neil's.

North Hill Inn ✪

422 NORTH BAYLEN STREET, PENSACOLA, FLORIDA 32501

Tel: **(904) 432-9804**
Host(s): **Diane Hinnant**
No. of Rooms: **6**
No. of Private Baths: **4**
Max. No. Sharing Bath: **4**
Double/pb: **$65–$75**
Single/pb: **$60–$70**
Double/sb: **$55**
Single/sb: **$50**
Open: **All year**
Reduced Rates: **10%, off-season**
Breakfast: **Full**
Pets: **No**
Children: **Welcome**
Smoking: **Permitted**
Social Drinking: **Permitted**

The inn, completed in 1904, is part of the North Hill Preservation District, a 60-block area of restored homes dating from the 19th century. Its spacious, high-ceilinged rooms are furnished throughout in the Victorian fashion. You are welcome to relax and enjoy the breezes and views of the historic district from the wicker-filled veranda. The business district, quaint restaurants, Gulf beaches, and the Naval Air Station are within easy reach. Complimentary wine, cheese, and snacks are graciously offered by Diane.

Sunshine Inn ✪

508 DECATUR AVENUE, PENSACOLA, FLORIDA 32507

Tel: **(904) 455-6781**
Best Time to Call: **Evenings**
Host(s): **The Jablonskis**
Location: **8 mi. from I-10**
No. of Rooms: **2**
Max. No. Sharing Bath: **4**
Double/sb: **$30**
Single/sb: **$25**
Open: **All year**
Breakfast: **Full**
Pets: **No**
Children: **Welcome**
Smoking: **No**
Social Drinking: **Permitted**
Airport/Station Pickup: **Yes**
Foreign Languages: **German**

Sun yourself on the whitest sand, swim in the Gulf of Mexico, and return to the Sunshine Inn for a dip in the pool. Or, walk a block to the bayou for fishing. Feel free to relax in the living room and seek touring advice from your knowledgeable hostess Renate. The University of West Florida is nearby.

Carriage Way Bed & Breakfast ✪

70 CUNA STREET, ST. AUGUSTINE, FLORIDA 32084

Tel: **(904) 829-2467**
Best Time to Call: **8:30 AM–4:30 PM**
Host(s): **Karen Burkley**
No. of Rooms: **7**
No. of Private Baths: **7**
Double/pb: **$47–$87**
Single/pb: **$47–$87**
Suites: **$125–$150**
Open: **All year**
Reduced Rates: **10%, seniors; Sun.–Thurs., off-season**
Breakfast: **Continental**
Other Meals: **Available**
Credit Cards: **MC, VISA**
Pets: **Sometimes**
Children: **Sometimes**
Smoking: **Permitted**
Social Drinking: **Permitted**
Airport/Station Pickup: **Yes**

This B&B, located in the heart of the historic district, is a restored Victorian built in 1883. Unique shops, museums, Castillo de San Marcos, fine restaurants, carriage tours, and the waterfront are within an easy walk. The atmosphere is leisurely and casual, in keeping with the feeling of Old St. Augustine. In addition to breakfast, Karen generously includes newspapers, wine, cookies, an open bar, and dessert on Friday and Saturday evenings.

Case de la Paz ✪

22 AVENIDA MENENDEZ, ST. AUGUSTINE, FLORIDA 32084

Tel: **(904) 829-2915**
Best Time to Call: **10 AM–4 PM**
Host(s): **Brenda and Harry Stafford**
Location: **7 mi. from I-95**
No. of Rooms: **4**
No. of Private Baths: **4**
Double/pb: **$65–$89**
Suites: **$89**
Open: **All year**
Breakfast: **Continental**
Credit Cards: **AMEX, MC, VISA**
Pets: **No**
Children: **Welcome, over 9**
Smoking: **No**
Social Drinking: **Permitted**
Airport/Station Pickup: **Yes**
Foreign Languages: **French**

Overlooking historic Matanzas Bay in the heart of old St. Augustine is this three-story Mediterranean-style stucco home. The rooms are comfortably furnished in a pleasant blend of the old and new. Amenities in each room include ceiling fans, central air-conditioning and heat, high-quality linens, cable TV, and complimentary sherry or wine. The veranda rooms have private entrances. Guests are welcome to use the private walled courtyard, well-stocked library, and delightful parlor. It is central to all attractions and convenient to fine restaurants and shops.

Casa de Solana ✪

21 AVILES STREET, ST. AUGUSTINE, FLORIDA 32084

Tel: **(904) 824-3555**
Best Time to Call: **8 AM–9 PM**
Host(s): **Faye and Jim McMurry**
No. of Rooms: **4 Suites**
No. of Private Baths: **4**
Suites: **$100–$125**
Open: **All year**
Reduced Rates: **25% less, weekly**
Breakfast: **Full**
Other Meals: **Lunch available**
Credit Cards: **AMEX, MC, VISA**
Pets: **No**
Children: **Welcome**
Smoking: **No**
Social Drinking: **Permitted**
Airport/Station Pickup: **Yes**

This is a gorgeous Colonial home built in 1763. It is located in the heart of the historic area, within walking distance of restaurants, museums, and quaint shops. Some of the antique-filled suites have fireplaces, while others have balconies that overlook the lovely garden, or a breathtaking view of Matanzas Bay. Jim and Faye include cable TV, chocolates, a decanter of sherry, and the use of their bicycles in the rate.

Kenwood Inn ✪

38 MARINE STREET, ST. AUGUSTINE, FLORIDA 32084

Tel: **(904) 824-2116**
Best Time to Call: **8 AM–8 PM**
Host(s): **Judy and Dick Smith**
Location: **40 mi. S of Jacksonville**
No. of Rooms: **15**
No. of Private Baths: **15**
Double/pb: **$40–$65**
Single/pb: **$40–$65**
Open: **All year**
Breakfast: **Continental**
Credit Cards: **MC, VISA**
Pets: **No**
Children: **Welcome, over 12**
Smoking: **Permitted**
Social Drinking: **Permitted**

If you are to discover a Victorian building in Florida, how appropriate that it should be in the historic section of St. Augustine, the oldest city in the U.S. This New England–style inn is a rarity in the South; this one has old-fashioned beds with color-coordinated touches right down to the sheets and linens. Breakfast may be taken in your room, in the courtyard surrounded by trees, or by the swimming pool. Tour trains, the waterfront shops, restaurants, and museums are within walking distance. Flagler College is three blocks away.

St. Francis Inn ✪

279 ST. GEORGE STREET, ST. AUGUSTINE, FLORIDA 32084

Tel: **(904) 824-6068**
Host(s): **Marie Register**
Location: **2 mi. from US 1**
No. of Rooms: **11**
No. of Private Baths: **11**
Double/pb: **$39–$80**
Guest Cottage: **$80; sleeps 4–6**
Open: **All year**
Breakfast: **Continental**
Credit Cards: **MC, VISA**
Pets: **Sometimes**
Children: **Welcome (crib)**
Smoking: **Permitted**
Social Drinking: **Permitted**
Airport/Station Pickup: **Yes**

Built in 1791, the inn is a Spanish Colonial structure with a private courtyard and garden, located in the center of the restored part of town. Balconies are furnished with rocking chairs, and the swimming pool is a great cooling-off spot. The building is made of coquina, a limestone made of broken shells and coral. Due to its trapezoidal shape, there are no square or rectangular rooms. All of St. Augustine's historic and resort activities are within a three-mile radius.

Victorian House Bed & Breakfast ✪

11 CADIZ STREET, ST. AUGUSTINE, FLORIDA 32084

Tel: **(904) 824-5214**
Host(s): **Daisy Morden**
No. of Rooms: **6**
No. of Private Baths: **6**
Double/pb: **$45**
Suites: **$65**
Separate Guest Cottage: **$75 for 4**
Open: **All year**
Breakfast: **Continental**
Credit Cards: **MC, VISA**
Pets: **No**
Children: **In cottage only**
Smoking: **Permitted**
Social Drinking: **Permitted**

From its location in the heart of the historic district, it's a short walk to fine restaurants, the waterfront, shops, museums, and the plaza. The rooms are charming, with brass and canopy beds, handwoven coverlets, handmade quilts, stenciled walls and floors. The house is comfortably air-conditioned, but the warmth of your hostess is quite special.

Bayboro House on Old Tampa Bay ✪

1719 BEACH DRIVE S.E., ST. PETERSBURG, FLORIDA 33701

Tel: **(813) 823-4955**
Best Time to Call: **After 4 PM**
Host(s): **Gordon and Antonia Powers**
Location: **½ mi. from I-275 (Exit 9)**
No. of Rooms: **3**
No. of Private Baths: **3**
Double/pb: **$50–$55**
Single/pb: **$45–$50**
Open: **All year**
Reduced Rates: **Available**
Breakfast: **Continental**
Credit Cards: **MC, VISA**
Pets: **No**
Children: **No**
Smoking: **No**
Social Drinking: **Permitted**

A unique three-story Queen Anne with airy, high-ceilinged rooms and a wraparound veranda in view of Tampa Bay, it is graced with antique furniture plus tropical plants and flowers. It is the ideal spot for sunning, beachcombing, and fishing. Relax in the hammock or visit unusual shops, fine restaurants, the Sunken Gardens, Salvador Dali museum, or the dog track. The University of South Florida is one mile away.

The Walters House ✪

1115 BOCA CIEGA ISLE, ST. PETERSBURG BEACH, FLORIDA 33706

Tel: **(813) 360-3372**
Host(s): **Karen and Dick Walters**
Location: **4 mi. from I-275**
No. of Rooms: **3**
No. of Private Baths: **1**
Max. No. Sharing Bath: **4**

Double/pb: **$40**
Single/pb: **$35**
Double/sb: **$40**
Single/sb: **$35**
Suite: **$65–$70**
Open: **All year**
Breakfast: **Continental**
Pets: **No**
Children: **Welcome, over 16**
Smoking: **Permitted**
Social Drinking: **Permitted**
Airport/Station Pickup: **Yes**

This spacious, immaculate, air-conditioned house has cathedral ceilings and lots of glass to enhance its tropical setting. Located on a private island, it is a half-mile from the Gulf of Mexico beaches, only 40 minutes to Busch Gardens in Tampa, and 90 minutes to Disney World, Epcot, and Sea World. Karen and Dick offer coffee or popcorn while you relax after a busy day. The University of South Florida and Eckerd College are nearby.

Crescent House

459 BEACH ROAD, SIESTA KEY, SARASOTA, FLORIDA 34242

Tel: **(813) 346-0857**
Host(s): **Patricia and Jean-Marc Murre**
Location: **10 mi. from Sarasota**
No. of Rooms: **4**
No. of Private Baths: **2**
Max. No. Sharing Bath: **4**
Double/pb: **$55**
Double/sb: **$40**
Open: **All year**
Reduced Rates: **Weekly; less, Jun.–Oct.**
Breakfast: **Continental**
Pets: **No**
Children: **Welcome**
Smoking: **No**
Social Drinking: **Permitted**
Airport/Station Pickup: **Yes**
Foreign Languages: **French, Spanish**

This lovely 70-year-old home has been fully restored and furnished with comfortable antiques. Breakfast specialties include freshly squeezed Florida orange juice, homemade muffins, scones, and freshly ground coffee. Relax in the hot tub, sunbathe on a spacious wood deck, or step across the street to a white sandy beach and cool off in the Gulf of Mexico. The house is located within a short walk of Siesta Village and Pavillon, with its many restaurants, quaint shops, tennis courts, and public beach. Your hosts specialize in European service and hospitality, and will gladly guide you to fine dining and sailboat and water sporting gear rentals.

Knightswood ✪

P.O. BOX 151, SUMMERLAND KEY, FLORIDA 33042

Tel: **(305) 872-2246**
Host(s): **Chris and Herb Pontin**
Location: **26 mi. E of Key West**
No. of Rooms: **1**
No. of Private Baths: **1**
Double/pb: **$65**
Single/pb: **$55**
Open: **All year**
Breakfast: **Full**
Pets: **No**
Children: **No**
Smoking: **No**
Social Drinking: **Permitted**

Knightswood overlooks one of the loveliest views in the Keys. Guest accommodations include a bed and bath, kitchenette, rec room, and screened-in porch with barbecue. Snorkeling, fishing, and boating can be enjoyed from a private dock, and guests are welcome to swim in the fresh-water pool. Your hosts will gladly point the way to fine dining and nightlife in Key West.

Cobb's Gulf View Inn ✪

21722 WEST HIGHWAY 98, SUNNYSIDE, FLORIDA 32461

Tel: **(904) 234-6051**
Host(s): **Bill and Tina Cobb**
Location: **2 mi. W of Panama City Beach**
No. of Rooms: **5**
No. of Private Baths: **5**
Double/pb: **$55**
Single/pb: **$50**
Suite: **$75**
Open: **All year**
Reduced Rates: **10%, Sept. 10–Apr. 1**
Breakfast: **Continental**
Pets: **No**
Children: **Welcome (crib)**
Smoking: **Permitted**
Social Drinking: **Permitted**

Cobb's Gulf View Inn is a new two-story beach house painted Cape Cod blue with white lattice trim. The decor is eclectic, with white wicker furnishings on the downstairs porches and modern touches in the bedrooms. Guest quarters have private entrances, TV, carpeting, and ceiling fans. In the morning, dine on the upstairs sun deck overlooking the panoramic Gulf of Mexico. Homemade breads and jellies are specialties of the house. It's just 200 feet across the road to the white, sandy beaches of Sunnyside. Bill and Tina are located convenient to fishing, sailing, golf, tennis, restaurants, and water parks for the children are within easy reach. There's a three-night minimum on holiday weekends.

Fiorito's Bed & Breakfast ✪

421 OLD EAST LAKE ROAD, TARPON SPRINGS, FLORIDA 33589

Tel: **(813) 937-5487**
Best Time to Call: **5–10 PM**
Host(s): **Dick and Marie Fiorito**
Location: **2 mi. from US 19**
No. of Rooms: **1**
No. or Private Baths: **1**
Double/pb: **$35**
Single/pb: **$30**
Open: **All year**
Breakfast: **Full**
Pets: **Sometimes**
Children: **No**
Smoking: **Permitted**
Social Drinking: **Permitted**
Airport/Station Pickup: **Yes**

Just off a quiet road that runs along Lake Tarpon's horse country, this meticulously maintained home offers respite for the visitor. The guest room and bath are decorated in tones of blue, enhanced with beautiful accessories. Fresh fruit, mozzarella cheese omelet, homemade bread and jam, and choice of beverages are the Fiorito's idea of breakfast. It is beautifully served on the tree-shaded, screened terrace. Busch Gardens and Clearwater Beach are 1/2 hour away. It's an hour to Cypress Gardens, 1 1/2 hours to Disney World.

Spring Bayou Inn ✪

32 WEST TARPON AVENUE, TARPON SPRINGS, FLORIDA 33589

Tel: **(813) 938-9333**
Best Time to Call: **11 AM–9 PM**
Host(s): **Ron and Cher Morrick**
Location: **2 mi. W of US 19**
No. of Rooms: **4**
No. of Private Baths: **2**
Max. No. Sharing Bath: **4**
Double/pb: **$55–$60**
Single/pb: **$50–$55**
Double/sb: **$45–$50**
Single/sb: **$40–$45**
Open: **Oct. 1–Aug. 15**
Breakfast: **Continental**
Pets: **No**
Children: **No**
Smoking: **No**
Social Drinking: **Permitted**

This large, comfortable home was built around 1900. It is unique in having architectural details of the past combined with up-to-date conveniences. You will enjoy relaxing on the porch or in the courtyard to take in the sun. The parlor is a favorite gathering place, offering informal atmosphere, complimentary wine, music, books, and games, and the opportunity to make new friends. The fireplace chases the chill on winter evenings. Tarpon Springs is the sponge capital of the world and the nearby sponge docks are interesting to visit. The area is known for its excellent restaurants and variety of shops.

GEORGIA

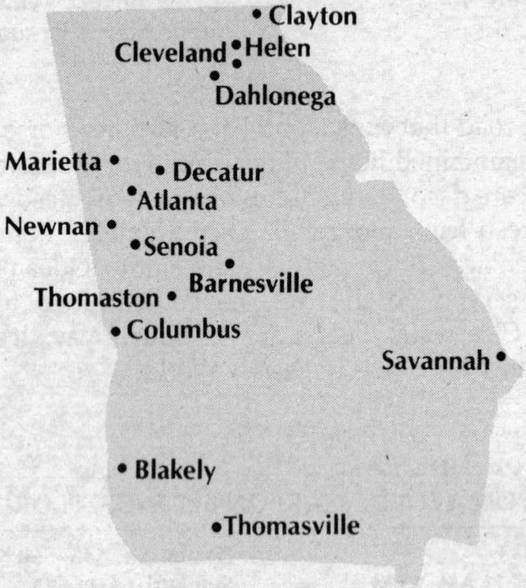

Clayton
Cleveland
Helen
Dahlonega
Marietta
Decatur
Atlanta
Newnan
Senoia
Barnesville
Thomaston
Columbus
Savannah
Blakely
Thomasville

Bed & Breakfast—Atlanta ✪

1801 PIEDMONT AVENUE NE, SUITE 208, ATLANTA, GEORGIA 30324

Tel: **(404) 875-0525**
Best Time to Call: **10 AM–Noon; 2–5 PM**
Coordinator(s): **Madalyne Eplan, Paula Gris**
States/Regions Covered: **Atlanta, Blairsville, Decatur, Dunwoody, Jonesboro, Marietta, Savannah, Smyrna, Stone Mountain**

Rates (Single/Double):

Modest:	**$28–$32**	**$32–$36**
Average:	**$36–$44**	**$40–$48**
Luxury:	**$48–$60**	**$52–$60**

Credit Cards: **AMEX, MC, VISA**

Visit one of America's most gracious cities, with the advantage of being a houseguest. Madalyne and Paula consider transportation and language needs as well as other personal preferences in making your reservation. Locations are offered in the city's most desirable homes, and all offer a private bath. There is an $8 surcharge for a one-night stay. Georgia Tech, Emory University, and Georgia State University are close by.

Quail Country Bed & Breakfast, Ltd. ✪

1104 OLD MONTICELLO ROAD, THOMASVILLE, GEORGIA 31792

Tel: **(912) 226-7218 or 226-6882**
Coordinator(s): **Mercer Watt, Kathy Lanigan**
States/Regions Covered: **Georgia—Thomas County, Thomasville**

Rates (Single/Double):

	Single	Double
Average:	**$30**	**$40**
Luxury:	**$40**	**$50**

Credit Cards: **No**

Mercer and Kathy have a wide selection of homes, several with swimming pools, in lovely residential areas. There's lots to see and do, including touring historic restorations and plantations. Enjoy the Pebble Hill Plantation museum, historic Glen Arven Country Club, and the April Rose Festival. Five-dollar surcharge for one-night stay.

The Bird in the Bush ✪

722 THOMASTON STREET, BARNESVILLE, GEORGIA 30204

Tel: **(404) 358-0050**
Best Time to Call: **After 5:30 PM**
Host(s): **Gyme and Meri Warbrick**
Location: **10 mi. from I-75**
No. of Rooms: **5**
No. of Private Baths: **5**
Double/pb: **$45**
Single/pb: **$35**
Open: **All year**
Reduced Rates: **Weekly**
Breakfast: **Continental**
Other Meals: **Dinner available**
Credit Cards: **MC, VISA**
Pets: **Sometimes**
Children: **Welcome, over 12**
Smoking: **Permitted**
Social Drinking: **Permitted**

Built in 1910 and located in the historic district of Barnesville, this lovely Victorian is tastefully decorated with interesting antiques. Some select pieces are available for purchase. Each of the four guest rooms has a fireplace. For your added comfort and pleasure, the proprietors include a complimentary fruit basket. Madison, Warm Springs, and Callaway Gardens are nearby. Atlanta is only 45 minutes away. Breakfast may be taken in your room or by the pool. Tea is served each afternoon at 4 PM.

Layside ✪

611 RIVER STREET, BLAKELY, GEORGIA 31723

Tel: **(912) 723-8932**
Best Time to Call: **8:30 AM–11 PM**
Host(s): **Ted and Jeanneane Lay**
Location: **1½ mi. from US 27**
No. of Rooms: **3**
Max. No. Sharing Bath: **4**
Double/sb: **$35**
Single/sb: **$25**
Open: **All year**
Reduced Rates: **10%, seniors over 60**
Breakfast: **Continental**
Pets: **No**
Children: **Welcome, over 10**
Smoking: **Permitted**
Social Drinking: **Permitted**

Layside is a southern Colonial, dating back to the turn of the century. Spend the night in a queen-size bed and wake up to homemade bread, jams, and coffee. State parks, Indian burial grounds, good fishing and boating are all nearby attractions. The 60-foot-long front porch is a fine place to relax after a day of touring.

Schlemmer's Bed & Breakfast ✪

ROUTE 4, BOX 4655, CLEVELAND, GEORGIA 30528

Tel: **(404) 865-5897**
Host(s): **John and Karla Schlemmer**
No. of Rooms: **5**
No. of Private Baths: **5**
Double/pb: **$45–60**
Open: **Apr. 15–Nov. 30**
Reduced Rates: **August; after 3 nights**
Breakfast: **Continental**
Pets: **No**
Children: **Sometimes**
Smoking: **No**
Social Drinking: **Permitted**
Airport/Station Pickup: **Yes**
Foreign Languages: **German**

This cozy Bavarian-style home is nestled in the woods on a hillside overlooking the clear water of the Chattahoochee River. The bedrooms are attractively furnished and each has an outside entrance. In summer, a two-bedroom efficiency apartment is available. Surrounded by trees and flowers, there's plenty of room for leisurely strolls, or just relax on the deck with a good book. Alpine Helen, with its quaint shops, restaurants, entertainment, festivals, and friendly people, is just 20 minutes away. Babyland Hospital, home of the Cabbage Patch Kids, is nearby. You have to see it to believe it!

The Mountain Top Lodge ✪

ROUTE 3, BOX 173, DAHLONEGA, GEORGIA 30533

Tel: **(404) 864-5257**
Best Time to Call: **12–6 PM**
Host(s): **David Middleton**
Location: **70 mi. N of Atlanta**

No. of Rooms: **8**
No. of Private Baths: **8**
Double/pb: **$55–$65**
Single/pb: **$45–$55**
Suites: **$65–$75**
Open: **All year**
Reduced Rates: **$10 less, Jan. 1–Apr. 30**
Breakfast: **Full**
Pets: **No**
Children: **Welcome, over 14**
Smoking: **Permitted**
Social Drinking: **Permitted**

Flanked by porches and decks, this gambrel-roofed, rustic cedar lodge is a secluded rural retreat, on 40 acres with a 360° mountain view. Decorated with art and antiques, the pine furniture and accessories made by mountain craftsmen add to the charm. Dahlonega was the site of America's first gold rush, and nature buffs will appreciate the Chattahoochee National Forest and Amicalola Falls State Park. Rafting, hiking, and horseback riding are all nearby. Don't miss the "Alpine village" of Helen, Georgia, only 30 minutes away. The higher rates quoted apply during October for the fall foliage season.

Hilltop Haus

P.O. BOX 154, CHATTAHOOCHEE STREET, HELEN, GEORGIA 30545

Tel: **(404) 878-2388**
Host(s): **Frankie Tysor and Barbara Nichols**
Location: **60 mi. from I-85**
No. of Rooms: **5**
No. of Private Baths: **3**
Max. No. Sharing Bath: **4**
Double/pb: **$40–55**
Single/pb: **$35–45**
Double/sb: **$35–$50**
Single/sb: **$30–$40**
Suite: **$50–65**
Open: **All year**
Breakfast: **Full**
Credit Cards: **MC, VISA**
Reduced Rates: **10%, seniors**
Pets: **No**
Children: **Welcome, over 12**
Smoking: **Permitted**
Social Drinking: **Permitted**

This contemporary split-level overlooks Alpine Helen and the Chattahoochee River. It is near the foothills of the Smoky Mountains, six miles from the Appalachian Trail. Rich wood paneling and fireplaces create a homey atmosphere for the traveler. Guests may choose a private room or the efficiency cottage with separate entrance. Each morning a hearty breakfast includes homemade biscuits and preserves. Your hostess will direct you to many outdoor activities and sights.

Blue and Grey Bed and Breakfast ✪

511 KINGSWOOD AVENUE, MARIETTA, GEORGIA 30066

Tel: **(404) 425-0392**
Best Time to Call: **After 6 PM**
Host(s): **John and Connie Kone**
Location: **25 mi. N of Atlanta**
No. of Rooms: **2**
Max. No. Sharing Bath: **4**
Double/sb: **$35**
Single/sb: **$30**
Open: **All year**
Reduced Rates: **10%, seniors**
Breakfast: **Continental**
Pets: **No**
Children: **Welcome, over 8**
Smoking: **No**
Social Drinking: **Permitted**

This rambling Cape Cod–style home is set in a quiet neighborhood surrounded by trees. The house is warmly decorated, featuring comfortable, extra-large guest quarters. Your hosts are local history buffs, fond of sharing their knowledge of the area. Nearby attractions include Marietta Square, Kennesaw Mountain National Battlefield Park, restaurants, and the new Town Center, one of the largest shopping and entertainment centers in the Southeast.

Parrott-Camp-Soucy House ✪

15 GREENVILLE STREET, NEWNAN, GEORGIA 30263

Tel: **(404) 253-4846**
Host(s): **Chuck and Doris Soucy**
Location: **25 mi. SW of Atlanta**
No. of Rooms: **3**
No. of Private Baths: **1**
Max. No. Sharing Bath: **4**
Double/pb: **$70**
Single/pb: **$60**
Double/sb: **$60**
Single/sb: **$50**
Open: **All year**
Breakfast: **Continental**
Pets: **No**
Children: **No**
Smoking: **No**
Social Drinking: **Permitted**

This extraordinary Second Empire mansion, listed on the National Register of Historic Places, is a brilliant example of Victorian–French Mansard architecture. It took two years to restore it to its original elegance. For example, the fireplace in the front hall is surrounded by tiles that depict characters from the Robin Hood legend, and the magnificent grand staircase is lit by beautiful stained-glass windows. It is no surprise that the house is furnished entirely in antiques. The surprise is that it is so comfortable. You are certain to enjoy the formal gardens, swimming pool and spa, and the game room with its 1851 Brunswick pool table. If you can tear yourself away, Warm Springs, Callaway Gardens, and Atlanta are within each reach.

Savannah Historic Inns and Guest Houses

1900 LINCOLN STREET, SAVANNAH, GEORGIA 31401

Tel: **(912) 233-7666**
Coordinator: **Gloria Hudson**
State/Regions Covered: **Savannah**

Rates (Single/Double):

	Single	Double
Modest:	**$30**	**$38–$48**
Average:	**$55**	**$60–$80**
Luxury:	**$78**	**$108**

Credit Cards: **AMEX, MC, VISA**

Savannah, which dates from 1733, has 2.1 square miles known as the National Landmark Historic District, the largest such designated area in the country. The homes have been restored to their original elegance, and many are near museums, restaurants, and the riverfront. You will be impressed with true Southern hospitality.

Bed & Breakfast Inn ✪

117 WEST GORDON AT CHATHAM SQUARE, SAVANNAH, GEORGIA 31401

Tel: **(912) 238-0518**
Host(s): **Robert McAlister**
No. of Rooms: **11**
No. of Private Baths: **4**
Max. No. Sharing Bath: **4**
Double/pb: **$65**
Single/pb: **$50**
Double/sb: **$38**
Single/sb: **$30**

Open: **All year**
Breakfast: **Full**
Credit Cards: **AMEX, MC, VISA**
Pets: **No**
Children: **Welcome (crib)**
Smoking: **Permitted**
Social Drinking: **Permitted**
Airport/Station Pickup: **Yes**
Foreign Languages: **German, Spanish**

Located in the heart of the historic district, the inn is a Federalist row house built in 1853. It is decorated with a few period pieces and many appropriate reproductions. Some of the bedrooms have poster beds, and all rooms are air-conditioned. The outstanding courtyard, with its profusion of trees and colorful flowers, has twice been photographed by *Southern Living* magazine. Bob is active in a variety of historical organizations and Scottish Heritage groups. He is also the Budget Director of Savannah.

The Culpepper House ✪

P.O. BOX 462, BROAD AT MORGAN, SENOIA, GEORGIA 30276

Tel: **(404) 599-8182**
Best Time to Call: **7 PM–10 PM**
Host(s): **Mary A. Brown**
Location: **37 mi. S of Atlanta**
No. of Rooms: **4**
No. of Private Baths: **1**
Max. No. Sharing Bath: **5**
Double/pb: **$50**
Double/sb: **$45**
Single/sb: **$36–$40**
Open: **All year**
Reduced Rates: **10%, families**
Breakfast: **Full**
Credit Cards: **No**
Pets: **No**
Children: **Welcome, over 10 and infants**
Smoking: **Permitted**
Social Drinking: **Permitted**
Airport/Station Pickup: **Yes**

This Queen Anne Victorian was built in 1871. Gingerbread trim, stained glass, sliding doors, bay windows, and provincial furnishings re-create that turn-of-the-century feeling. Snacks and setups are offered. Your hostess will gladly direct you to surrounding antique and craft shops, state parks, and gardens.

The Guest House ✪

318 WEST MAIN STREET, THOMASTON, GEORGIA 30286

Tel: **(404) 647-1203**
Best Time to Call: **9 AM–5 PM**
Host(s): **Freddie Davis**
Location: **70 mi. S of Atlanta**
No. of Rooms: **5**
No. of Private Baths: **3**
Max. No. Sharing Bath: **4**
Double/pb: **$46**
Single/pb: **$38**
Double/sb: **$36**
Single/sb: **$27**
Open: **All year**
Breakfast: **Continental**
Credit Cards: **MC, VISA**
Pets: **Sometimes**
Children: **Welcome**
Smoking: **Permitted**
Social Drinking: **Permitted**

The Guest House was built in the early 1900s by L. A. Crawford. Your hosts have taken the time to preserve its stately Georgian character. The rooms are filled with all kinds of antiques, and many pieces are available for purchase. The bedrooms all have fireplaces, and modern extras such as TV and phone service are available on request. The warm hospitality includes complimentary fruit, soft drinks, and newspapers daily. Thomaston is a quiet town nestled on the edge of the Pine Mountain Range. It is just a short drive from Callaway Gardens and Warm Springs.

HAWAII

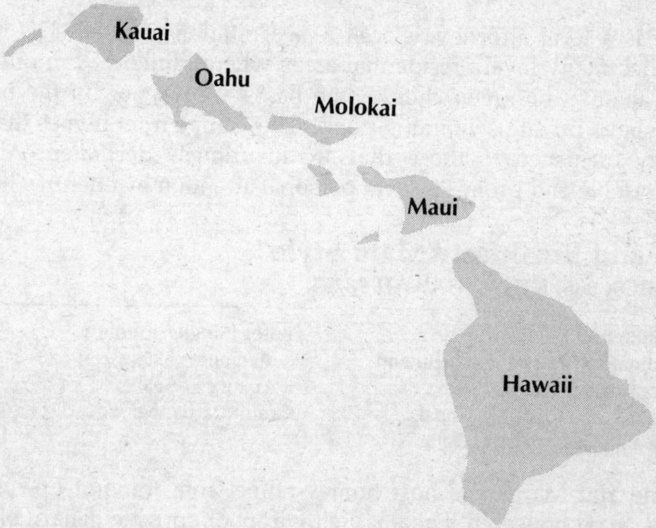

Bed & Breakfast—Hawaii ✪

P.O. BOX 449, KAPAA, HAWAII 96746

Tel: **(808) 822-7771**
Best Time to Call: **8:30 AM–4:30 PM**
Coordinators: **Evie Warner**
States/Regions Covered: **All of the Hawaiian Islands**

Rates (Single/Double):

	Single	Double
Modest:	**$25**	**$35**
Average:	**N/A**	**$45–$50**
Luxury:	**N/A**	**$75**

Credit Cards: **No**

Hawaii is a group of diverse islands, offering traditional warmth and hospitality to the visitor through this membership organization. For a $10 membership fee, you will receive a descriptive directory of accommodations on all five islands. Some are separate units; others are in the main house. Most have private baths. Minimum stay is two nights. The University of Hawaii at Oahu is convenient to many B&Bs.

Honolulu Bed & Breakfast ✪

3242 KAOHINANI DRIVE, HONOLULU, HAWAII 96817

Tel: **(808) 595-6170**
Best Time to Call: **8 AM–10 PM**
Coordinator: **Gene Bridges**
State/Regions Covered: **Island of Oahu: Honolulu, Waikiki, Kailua; Islands of Maui, Molokai, Kauai, Hawaii**

Rates (Single/Double):

	Single	Double
Modest:	**$25**	**$35**
Average:	**$40**	**$50**
Luxury	**$50 up**	**$60 up**

Credit Cards: **No**
Minimum Stay: **2 nights**

Gene is a local attorney as well as a Unitarian minister. His roster includes many lovely residential areas where rainbows can often be seen against the green cliffs. Some B&Bs are near or on the beach; some have private swimming pools. They range from homes that are simply furnished to those that are luxuriously decorated. All are comfortable and promise warm personal attention by attentive hosts.

Bed and Breakfast "Maui Style"

P.O. BOX 886, KIHEI, HAWAII 96753

Tel: **(808) 879-7865 or 2352**
Coordinators: **Jeanne Rominger and Margaret Del Castillo**
States/Regions Covered: **Kauai, Hawaii, Maui, Molokai, Oahu**

Rates (Single/Double):

	Single	Double
Average:	**$25**	**$35–$45**
Luxury	**$65**	**$75**

Credit Cards: **No**

Jeanne and Margaret's host homes range from tranquil up-country spots to a house in Lahaina with a pool, private lanais off the bedroom, car, and three meals included in the price. Another is a quiet studio with a hot tub; another an old plantation home in Haiku. Hosts have a variety of interests and range from an avid chess player to an astrologist to a massage therapist. Although there is no public transportation on Maui, Jeanne will be pleased to arrange a car rental if you wish. A three-day minimum stay is required in most homes.

Haikuleana ✪

69 HAIKU ROAD, HAIKU, HAWAII 96708

Tel: **(808) 575-2890**
Best Time to Call: **8 AM–7 PM**
Host(s): **Clark and Denise Champion**
Location: **12 mi. E of Kahului**
No. of Rooms: **2**
Max. No. Sharing Bath: **4**
Double/sb: **$55**
Single/sb: **$45**

Open: **All year**
Breakfast: **Continental**
Other Meals: **Available**
Pets: **Sometimes**
Children: **Welcome**
Smoking: **Permitted**
Social Drinking: **Permitted**

Experience the real feeling of aloha as a guest in an 1850s Hawaiian plantation home. Haikuleana is set in the agricultural district, close to secluded waterfalls and beautiful beaches. The house is built in the old style, with high ceilings, a porch, and gardens of Hawaiian plants and flowers. The rooms are cool and tropical, with wood motifs, antiques, and quilts. Swimming ponds, fine photographic sites, and the world's foremost windsurfing spot are all nearby.

Bob & Val's Sunset Beach B&B on Oahu ✪

P.O. BOX 487, HALEIWA, HAWAII 96712

Tel: **(804) 638-7258**
Host(s): **Bob and Val Brasch**
Location: **40 mi. N of Honolulu**
No. of Rooms: **3**
No. of Private Baths: **3**
Double/pb: **$45**
Suites: **$55 for 2**
Open: **All year**
Breakfast: **Full**
Pets: **No**
Children: **Welcome, over 16**
Smoking: **Permitted**
Social Drinking: **Permitted**

Just an hour's drive from Honolulu you'll find Bob and Val's beautiful two-story pole house with decks that overlook the North Shore's best wind-surfing beaches. Bob, a retired engineer, and Val, a nurse, have their own dance band in California, but the music you'll hear outside your window is more likely to be the songs of jungle birds greeting the day rather than swing. Val takes great pride in her table settings and the special touches she gives her breakfasts. Bob and Val offer guests a choice of three facilities—the largest with its own full-size kitchen and living room, and the two others, with private entrances and baths, small refrigerators, and television/VCRs.

Armanita's Bed & Breakfast ✪

2703 TERRACE DRIVE, HONOLULU, OAHU, HAWAII 96822

Tel: **(808) 988-6546 or 3046**
Host(s): **Anita Trubitt and Arman Kitapci**
Location: **10 mi. from airport**
No. of Rooms: **2**
Max. No. Sharing Bath: **3**
Double/sb: **$45**
Single/sb: **$40**
Open: **All year**
Reduced Rates: **Weekly**
Breakfast: **Continental**
Pets: **No**
Children: **No**
Smoking: **No**
Social Drinking: **Permitted**
Foreign Languages: **Armenian, French, Spanish, Turkish**

Your hosts live in beautiful Manoa Valley, a quiet residential area a mile from the University of Hawaii. Their two-story home has a panoramic view of the mountains, Diamond Head, the Waikiki skyline, and the ocean. The deck is the site for breakfast, sunning, and relaxing. Anita and Arman will be happy to share their favorite haunts for swimming, hiking, fine dining, shops, music, and theater. Three-day minimum stay.

Bed & Breakfast Waikiki Beach

P.O. BOX 89080, HONOLULU, HAWAII 96830

Tel: **(808) 923-5459**
Host(s): **Carol and Franz Schaier**
No. of Rooms: **1**
No. of Private Baths: **1**
Double/pb: **$45–$55**
Single/pb: **$35–$45**
Open: **All year**
Breakfast: **Continental**
Pets: **No**
Children: **No**
Smoking: **No**
Social Drinking: **Permitted**
Foreign Languages: **French, German, Spanish, Swiss**

The Schaiers' home is a condominium, $1\frac{1}{2}$ blocks from the beach, where their guest bedroom looks exactly like one you'd find in a small country guest house in Switzerland. The reason? Franz is Swiss, a pastry chef by profession. Breakfast is served out on a small terrace overlooking the Waikiki skyline, on a bistro set that the Schaiers brought with them from Switzerland. "We serve cappuccino and espresso with tiny jars of Swiss confitures that our family sends from the Alps, sweet butter, sugar with a vanilla bean in it, and a basket full of croissants, brioches, or some other special Swiss pastry."

Bev & Monty's Bed & Breakfast

4571 UKALI STREET, HONOLULU, HAWAII 96818

Tel: **(808) 422-9873**
Host(s): **Bev and Monty Neese**
Location: **4½ mi. from airport**
No. of Rooms: **2**
Max. No. Sharing Bath: **4**
Double/sb: **$40**
Single/sb: **$25**
Open: **All year**
Reduced Rates: **Weekly**
Breakfast: **Continental**
Pets: **No**
Children: **Welcome**
Smoking: **Permitted**
Social Drinking: **Permitted**
Airport/Station Pickup: **Yes**

This typical Hawaiian home is convenient to many of Hawaii's most popular attractions. Bev and Monty are just a mile above historic Pearl Harbor, and the Arizona Memorial can be seen from their veranda. They enjoy sharing an Hawaiian aloha, for a convenient overnight stay or a long vacation where they can share their favorite places with you. This comfortable home is just off the access road leading east to Honolulu and Waikiki or west to the North Shore beaches, sugar plantations, and pineapple fields. Good hiking country as well as city entertainment and shopping centers are located nearby.

Kay Barker's Bed & Breakfast ✪

P.O. BOX 740, KAPAA, KAUAI, HAWAII 96746

Tel: **(808) 822-3073**
Best Time to Call: **Before noon**
Host(s): **Kay Barker**
No. of Rooms: **4**
No. of Private Baths: **4**
Double/pb: **$30–$40**
Single/pb: **$25–$40**
Open: **All year**
Breakfast: **Full**
Pets: **Sometimes**
Children: **Welcome, over 10**
Smoking: **Permitted**
Social Drinking: **Permitted**

Kauai, the Garden Island, is most beautiful, with its powdery sand beaches and lush waterfalls. Kay, a long-time resident, knows the out-of-the-way places that others dream about. Her home is located on the slopes of the Sleeping Giant, with sweeping views of pastures and mountains. There is a separate TV room, an extensive library, a large lanai, and beautiful gardens. Breakfast often features macadamia nut waffles and pancakes.

Kilohana ✪

212 KAWEHI PLACE, KULA, MAUI, HAWAII 96790

Tel: **(808) 878-6086**
Best Time to Call: **8 AM–6 PM**
Host(s): **Jody Baldwin and Charles Hansen**
Location: **16 mi. NW of Kahului Airport**
No. of Rooms: **1**
No. of Private Baths: **1**
Double/pb: **$55**
Single/pb: **$45**
Open: **All year**
Reduced Rates: **Weekly**
Breakfast: **Full**
Pets: **No**
Children: **No**
Smoking: **No**
Social Drinking: **Permitted**

Drive up, up, up along the slopes of Haleakala, past cabbage and flower fields, and you will come to Jody and Charles's home—a modernized plantation house surrounded by 12 acres of wooded land, with a sweeping view of the islands of Lanai and Molokai. "The quiet and coolness of the countryside bring our visitors back again and again." Must-sees while you're in the "Kula" district are the sunrise from the summit of the crater, the Tedeschi Winery, and exotic Protea Farms. The beach and windsurfing are ½ hour away and restaurants, just 5 to 15 minutes by car. You'll be greeted with refreshments when you arrive and in the morning, after the sun enters your spacious guest room, you'll get up to a breakfast of fresh fruit, homemade pastry, yogurt, sausage, coffee, tea, and "fresh Hawaiian juice."

For key to listings, see inside front or back cover.

✪ This star means that rates are guaranteed through December 31, 1988 to any guest making a reservation as a result of reading about the B&B in *BED & BREAKFAST U.S.A.*—1988 edition.

Please enclose a self-addressed, stamped, business-sized envelope when contacting reservation services.

For more details on what you can expect in a B&B, see Chapter 1.

Always mention *Bed & Breakfast U.S.A.* when making reservations!

If no B&B is listed in the area you'll be visiting, use the form on page 698 to order a copy of our "List of New B&Bs."

We want to hear from you! Use the form on page 697.

IDAHO

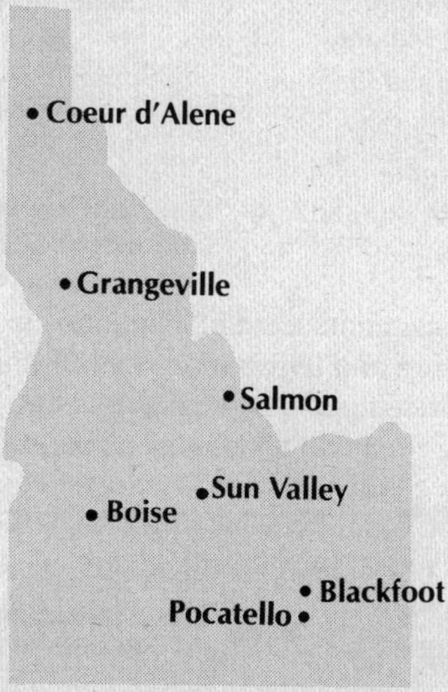

Bed and Breakfast of Idaho ✪

P.O. BOX 7323, BOISE, IDAHO 83702

Tel: **(208) 336-5174**
Best Time to Call: **6–9 PM**
Coordinator: **Lynda Rule**
States/Regions Covered: **Boise, Coeur d'Alene, Kellogg**

Rates (Single/Double):

	Single	Double
Modest:	**$20**	**$25**
Average:	**$30**	**$35**
Luxury:	**$60**	**$65**

Credit Cards: **AMEX, MC, VISA**

Lynda is prepared to arrange a stay to suit your purse and preference. In the "modest" classification, you might stay in a contemporary home with a mountain view; an "average" selection might be an inn located close to a lovely lake; and a "luxury" setting is a large suite with a sunken tub in the bathroom and a fireplace in the sitting area. All the hosts have a genuine desire to share their knowledge of where to eat and what to do in their area. A $5 surcharge is imposed for a one-night stay.

The Blackwell House ✪

820 SHERMAN AVENUE, COEUR d'ALENE, IDAHO 83814

Tel: **(208) 664-0656**
Best Time to Call: **8 AM–8 PM**
Host(s): **Kathleen Sims and Elizabeth Hoy**
Location: **30 mi. E of Spokane, Washington**
No. of Rooms: **8**
No. of Private Baths: **3**
Max. No. Sharing Bath: **4**
Double/pb: **$65**
Single/pb: **$60**
Double/sb: **$50**
Single/sb: **$45**
Suites: **$75**
Open: **All year**
Reduced Rates: **10%, seniors**
Breakfast: **Continental**
Credit Cards: **MC, VISA**
Pets: **No**
Children: **Welcome, over 12**
Smoking: **Permitted**
Social Drinking: **Permitted**

This lovely home is reminiscent of a bygone era. The main floor offers guests a music room and living room with fireplace for relaxation and entertainment. Breakfast is served in the bright and airy morning room overlooking the patio and lawn. A roaring fire takes the chill out of cool mornings. Stroll the World's Largest Floating Boardwalk, hike the nature trails of Tubbs Hill, picnic in the park, or tour the lake in an excursion boat. Canoe, paddleboat, and bicycle rentals are available. Winter sports include snowmobiling and skiing. Kathleen and Elizabeth will be happy to tell you about the best restaurants and shops in town.

Greenbriar Bed and Breakfast Inn ✪

315 WALLACE, COEUR d'ALENE, IDAHO 83814

Tel: **(208) 667-9660**
Best Time to Call: **Before 10 PM**
Host(s): **Kris McIluenna**
Location: **30 mi. E of Spokane, Washington**
No. of Rooms: 7
No. of Private Baths: **3**
Max. No. Sharing Bath: **3**
Double/pb: **$49–$54**
Single/pb: **$44–$49**
Double/sb: **$30–$50**
Single/sb: **$30–$45**
Suites: **$65**
Open: **All year**
Reduced Rates: **10%, seniors**
Breakfast: **Full**
Credit Cards: **MC, VISA**
Pets: **Sometimes**
Children: **Welcome (crib)**
Smoking: **No**
Social Drinking: **Permitted**
Airport/Station Pickup: **Yes**

The Greenbriar is located on the north shore of Lake Coeur d'Alene, four blocks from the beach. The house was built in 1908 and is now listed on the National Register of Historic Places. The interior is unique, with mahogany woodwork, winding staircases, and gracefully arched ceilings. The bedrooms feature gabled ceilings and dormers with mahogany window seats, and are furnished in antiques and genuine linen-covered down comforters, direct from Ireland. Kris's gourmet breakfasts feature eggs in pastry, sourbread French toast, and Swedish pancakes. She will gladly pack picnic lunches and arrange for canoe and bike rentals. An outdoor hot tub invites you to relax after a day of exploring.

Inn The First Place ✪

509 NORTH 15TH STREET, COEUR d'ALENE, IDAHO 83814

Tel: **(208) 667-3346**
Best Time to Call: **7 AM–11:30 PM**
Host(s): **Tom and Lois Knox**
Location: **30 mi. E of Spokane, Washington**
No. of Rooms: **3**
Max. No. Sharing Bath: **4**
Double/sb: **$35**
Single/sb: **$25**
Open: **All year**
Reduced Rates: **Available**
Breakfast: **Full**
Other Meals: **Available**
Credit Cards: **MC, VISA**
Pets: **No**
Children: **Welcome, over 12**
Smoking: **Permitted**
Social Drinking: **Permitted**
Airport/Station Pickup: **Yes**

Tom and Lois welcome you to their unusual home, which was once a grocery store. The guest rooms, located on the second floor, are decorated attractively, with wood paneling or country wallpaper, coordinating quilts, and a smattering of crafts and collectibles. The large living room and fully equipped kitchen are available to guests. In the morning, you can look forward to Lois's specialties, such as stuffed French toast or quiche. The inn is a mile away from beautiful Lake Coeur d'Alene, famous for fishing, swimming, and day cruises.

The Sleeping Place of the Wheels ✪

P.O. BOX 5273, 3308 LODGEPOLE ROAD, COEUR d'ALENE, IDAHO 83814

Tel: **(208) 765-3435**
Host(s): **Donna and Wallace Bedord**
Location: **1 mi. from I-90**
No. of Rooms: **3**
Max. No. Sharing Bath: **2**
Double/sb: **$25–$35**
Single/sb: **$20**
Open: **All year**
Reduced Rates: **10% less, Nov. 1–Mar. 31**
Breakfast: **Full**
Other Meals: **Available**
Pets: **Welcome**
Children: **Welcome**
Smoking: **No**
Social Drinking: **No**
Airport/Station Pickup: **Yes**

Wagon wheels mark the entrance to Donna and Wallace's home, which is surrounded by tall pines and pretty flower gardens. Raspberries, strawberries, plums, and cherries are yours for the picking. Children will delight in the special playhouse with its fireman's slide, swing, and sandbox. Wallace enjoys making burled-wood tables and plant stands made of iron; Donna enjoys quilting and reading. The handstitched quilts and handcrafted wood and iron items are for sale.

Tulip House ✪

BOX L, 403 SOUTH FLORENCE STREET, GRANGEVILLE, IDAHO 83530

Tel: **(208) 983-1034**
Best Time to Call: **9 AM–noon; 5–7 PM**
Host(s): **Doreen Busby**
Location: **72 mi. S of Lewiston**
No. of Rooms: **3**
Max. No. Sharing Bath: **3**
Double/sb: **$40–$55**
Open: **All year**
Breakfast: **Full**
Credit Cards: **MC, VISA**
Pets: **Welcome**
Children: **No**
Smoking: **No**
Social Drinking: **Permitted**
Airport/Station Pickup: **Yes**

Known to Grangeville residents as the town landmark, this two-story farmhouse, built in 1905, is surrounded by stately trees and an acre of lawn and gardens. It is furnished with antiques of the 18th and 19th centuries, accented by bronze statuary and many paintings. One bedroom is dominated by an 1860 American walnut bed with an eight-foot headboard; another has twin beds with European furniture inlaid with marble and linden wood. After a hearty breakfast that often includes Doreen's delicious pecan pancakes, walk two blocks to the park, pool, or nearby golf course. The town is the focal point for river float trips. In January, it is the scene of a sports festival; July 4th it's the site of the Border Days Rodeo and parade. In between it's simply a nice town in which to relax.

Mountain Retreat B&B ✪

4044 MOUNTAIN LOOP, POCATELLO, IDAHO 83204

Tel: **(208) 234-7114**
Host(s): **Keith and Janet Staples**
Location: **2½ mi. from I-15**
No. of Rooms: **3**
No. of Private Baths: **1**
Max. No. Sharing Baths: **4**
Double/pb: **$45–$65**
Single/pb: **$40–$60**
Double/sb: **$35–$50**
Single/sb: **$30–$45**
Open: **All year**
Reduced Rates: **Available**
Breakfast: **Continental**
Pets: **Sometimes**
Children: **No**
Smoking: **Permitted**
Social Drinking: **Permitted**
Airport/Station Pickup: **Yes**

Situated on two wooded acres adjoining the Caribou National Forest is this secluded contemporary designed with wood, glass, and decks. The attractive guest quarters, separate from your hosts, have a private entrance. Janet grinds her own wheat for the delicious raisin-cinnamon bread, served with a generous breakfast of fruit and cereal. The on-premises diversions include a pool table, game table, and horseback riding. A piano is available to serious musicians—no "Chopsticks" please! Hiking and gold-panning are popular pastimes. Chariot horse-racing, the National Dodge Rodeo, and activities at Idaho State University are available nearby.

Heritage Inn

510 LENA STREET, SALMON, IDAHO 83467

Tel: **(208) 756-3174**
Best Time to Call: **6 PM–9 PM**
Host(s): **Audrey Nichols**
Location: **½ mi. from Hwy. 93**
No. of Rooms: **5**
Max. No. Sharing Bath: **3**
Double/sb: **$20**
Single/sb: **$18**
Suites: **$35**
Open: **All year**
Breakfast: **Continental**
Credit Cards: **MC, VISA**
Pets: **No**
Children: **Welcome, over 4**
Smoking: **On porch only**
Social Drinking: **Permitted**

This 100-year-old Victorian farmhouse is set in a valley, surrounded by mountains and pine trees. In the old days, this was a cozy stopover for those traveling by stagecoach. The Heritage has since been lovingly restored and decorated with many antiques. Have a cool drink on the glassed-in sun porch while you enjoy the quiet of this pretty neighborhood. The River of No Return is just half a mile away, and it's just a mile to the city park and swimming pool. Your hostess serves homemade muffins and jams in the sunny dining room or on the porch each morning. She is a native of Salmon and can gladly direct you to restaurants within walking distance, nearby ghost towns, and other places of historic or cultural interest.

ILLINOIS

Bed & Breakfast/Chicago, Inc. ✪

P.O. BOX 14088, CHICAGO, ILLINOIS 60614

Tel: **(312) 951-0085**
Coordinator: **Mary Shaw**
State/Regions Covered: **Arlington Heights, Chicago, Deerfield, Evanston, Glencoe, Northfield, Oak Park, Wilmette**

Rates (Single/Double):

Modest:	**$40**	**$50**
Average:	**$55**	**$65**

Credit Cards: **AMEX, MC, VISA**
Minimum Stay: **2 nights**

Mary welcomes you to midwestern hospitality in the "windy city" and its suburbs. Discover, on foot, Chicago's outdoor sculpture plazas, shop world-famous Marshall Fields, or observe the skyline from the top of the Sears Tower. Follow the happenings on the campuses of Northwestern, University of Chicago, Loyola, and the University of Illinois. There is a three-day minimum stay for apartments without hosts in residence, and a $10 surcharge if you stay only one night in hosted B&Bs.

Curly's Corner ✪

RR #2, BOX 85B, ARCOLA, ILLINOIS 61910

Tel: **(217) 268-3352**
Best Time to Call: **Mornings; after 5 PM**
Hosts: **Warren and Maxine Arthur**
Location: **35 mi. S of Champaign; 5 mi. from I-57**
No. of Rooms: **3**
No. of Private Baths: **2**
Max. No. Sharing Bath: **3**
Double/pb: **$40–$50**
Single/sb: **$30**
Open: **March–Nov.**
Breakfast: **Full**
Pets: **No**
Children: **Welcome, over 10**
Smoking: **No**
Social Drinking: **No**
Airport/Station Pickup: **Yes**

This ranch-style farmhouse is located in a quiet Amish community. Your hosts are dedicated to cordial hospitality and will gladly share information about the area or even take you on a tour. They offer comfortable bedrooms, one with a king-size water bed. In the morning, enjoy a wonderful breakfast of homemade biscuits, apple butter, fresh country bacon, and eggs. Curly's Corner is a half mile from beautiful Rockome Gardens.

Cumberland Trail B&B

201 WEST MAIN STREET, CASEY, ILLINOIS 62420

Tel: **(217) 932-5522 or 5125**
Host(s): **Jack and Brenda; Archie and Judy**
Location: **1 mi. from I-70**
No. of Rooms: **4**
No. of Private Baths: **1**
Max. No. Sharing Bath: **6**
Double/pb: **$40**
Double/sb: **$35**
Single/sb: **$30**
Open: **All year**
Reduced Rates: **Dec.–Mar.; 10%, seniors**
Breakfast: **Continental**
Other Meals: **Available**
Pets: **No**
Children: **Welcome**
Smoking: **Permitted**
Social Drinking: **Permitted**

Just restored, this Victorian home was operated back in the late 1800s, as an inn by a local horseman who owned an adjacent livery stable. Almost 200 years later, the hosts serve breakfast in the same spacious dining room in front of a cozy fireplace. Casey is a small farming town, and one of its nicest features is a nearby park with an Olympic-size swimming pool. The people of Casey love all kinds of sports, and when the weather's nice, there's usually a game of some kind going on. On the Fourth of July, the Shriners go all out with a "bang up" celebration and on Labor Day, hot-air balloon races are the big attraction.

Country House ✪

ROUTE 1, BOX 61, CISCO, ILLINOIS 61830

Tel: **(217) 669-2291**
Host(s): **Carol and Don Padgett**
Location: **17 mi. E of Decatur**
No. of Rooms: **2**
Max. No. Sharing Bath: **2**
Double/sb: **$35**
Single/sb: **$30**
Suites: **$45**
Open: **All year**
Reduced Rates:
Breakfast: **Continental**
Pets: **No**
Children: **No**
Smoking: **Permitted**
Social Drinking: **No**

This 100-year-old country home is located in the heart of prairie farmland. Your hosts, Carol and Don, have decorated the rooms with a blend of traditional, wicker, and antique furnishings. In the warmer weather, a leisurely breakfast may be served on the porch overlooking the flower garden. During cooler months, guests are served in the rustic family room or gracious dining room. Down the road is the private fishing pond with a dock for sunbathing. The city of Monticello is for shopping and dining. The Country House is a short distance from Robert Allerton Park for picnicking, skiing, and biking. Guests are always welcome to relax with a game of pool or a traditional round of horseshoes back at the house.

Hamilton House ✪

500 WEST MAIN STREET, DECATUR, ILLINOIS 62522

Tel: **(217) 429-1669**
Best Time to Call: **After 4 PM**
Hosts: **Nancy and Dave Phillips**
Location: **30 mi. E of Springfield**
No. of Rooms: **5**
Max. No. Sharing Bath: **4**
Double/sb: **$45–$60**
Open: **All year**
Reduced Rates: **10%, seniors**
Breakfast: **Full (except Sunday)**
Credit Cards: **AMEX, MC, VISA**
Pets: **No**
Children: **Welcome (crib)**
Smoking: **Permitted**
Social Drinking: **Permitted**
Airport/Station Pickup: **Yes**

Hamilton House is a brick Victorian mansion located in the Abraham Lincoln historic area. It was built in 1892 and is listed on the National Register of Historic Places. The house has been beautifully maintained and still boasts its original woodwork fireplaces. The guest rooms are decorated with period furnishings and each has a different style antique bed. Breakfasts include quiches, muffins, and coffee cake, served in the formal dining room. Nancy and Dave also specialize in simple, elegant lunches and offer wine and cheese in the living room in late afternoon. Their gift shop specializes in fine treasures of Victorian and American design.

Aldrich Guest House ✪

900 THIRD STREET, GALENA, ILLINOIS 61036

Tel: **(815) 777-3323**
Host(s): **Judy Green**
Location: **1/4 mi. from Rt. 20**
No. of Rooms: **4**
No. of Private Baths: **3**
Max. No. Sharing Bath: **4**
Double/pb: **$60–$65**
Single/pb: **$55–$60**
Double/sb: **$55**
Single/sb: **$50**
Suites: **$110**
Open: **All year**
Breakfast: **Full**
Credit Cards: **MC, VISA**
Pets: **No**
Children: **Welcome, over 6**
Smoking: **Permitted**
Social Drinking: **Permitted**

George Washington didn't sleep here, but Ulysses S. Grant was entertained in the spacious double parlors. Today, guests may have breakfast on the porch overlooking the yard where General Grant's troops drilled. Throughout the house, period decor, antiques, and some reproductions harmonize effectively. Guest rooms are air-conditioned for summer comfort. The house is centrally located in relation to all the historic sites.

Avery Guest House ✪

606 SOUTH PROSPECT STREET, GALENA, ILLINOIS 61036

Tel: **(815) 777-3883**
Best Time to Call: **9 AM–9 PM**
Host(s): **Flo and Roger Jensen**
Location: **15 mi. E of Dubuque**
No. of Rooms: **4**
Max. No. Sharing Bath: **4**
Double/sb: **$40**
Single/sb: **$35**
Open: **All year**
Reduced Rates: **10%, 3-day stays; seniors**
Breakfast: **Continental**
Pets: **Sometimes**
Children: **Welcome (crib, high chair)**
Smoking: **No**
Social Drinking: **Permitted**
Airport/Station Pickup: **Yes**

This spacious 100-year-old home is located two blocks from historic downtown Galena. Enjoy the view of bluffs and Victorian mansions from an old-fashioned porch overlooking the Galena River. Your hosts welcome you to use the piano, or bring your own instrument and join them in chamber music. Enjoy a delicious array of homemade muffins and breads along with cheeses and jams each morning. Breakfast is served in the dining room overlooking the water. Flo and Roger will gladly direct you to Grant's home and other interesting sights in the historic district.

Ahern's Bed & Breakfast ✪

8553 WEST OGDEN AVENUE, LYONS, ILLINOIS 60534

Tel: **(312) 442-1170**
Host(s): **Richard and Brigid Ahern**
Location: **18 mi. W of Chicago**
No. of Rooms: **1**
No. of Private Baths: **1**
Double/pb: **$50**
Single/pb: **$40**
Open: **All year**
Reduced Rates: **10%, seniors**
Breakfast: **Full**
Pets: **No**
Children: **No**
Smoking: **No**
Social Drinking: **Permitted**

A beautiful penthouse apartment is your home base while you are guests of the Aherns. Their apartment has plenty of room—it's 2,000 square feet in all. Your hostess, a native of Ireland, has furnished her home with lovely antiques. The guest room features comfortable furnishings, a walk-in closet, and a television. A whirlpool bath is also available in your hosts' bathroom. Richard and Brigid are very knowledgeable about Chicago and can direct you to many local attractions and restaurants. The Brookfield Zoo is two miles away, and the Chicago loop is just a 20-minute ride. Before a day of touring you'll get a fresh start with a healthy breakfast of eggs, whole wheat toast, and fresh fruit.

Die Blaue Gans (The Blue Goose) ✪

9 S 265 ROUTE 59, NAPERVILLE, ILLINOIS 60565

Tel: **(312) 355-0835**
Best Time to Call: **Early AM**
Host(s): **Molly Konrad**
Location: **35 mi. W of Chicago**
No. of Rooms: **3**
No. of Private Baths: **1**
Max. No. Sharing Bath: **3**
Double/pb: **$50**
Double/sb: **$45**
Single/sb: **$40**
Open: **All year**
Breakfast: **Full**
Pets: **No**
Children: **Welcome (crib)**
Smoking: **Permitted**
Social Drinking: **Permitted**
Airport/Station Pickup: **Yes**
Foreign Languages: **German**

Only 45 minutes from Chicago's Loop is the open prairie with fields of corn and wildflowers. It is in this setting that you will find an Austrian flag marking the spacious yard of this charming home. Painted dressers, ceiling borders, a French brass bed, and Bavarian tea service set the tone. The roof deck, gazebo, and fireplace are perfect spots for relaxing. Visit the Naper Settlement, stroll the Riverwalk where you may picnic and watch the mallard ducks. The band concert is a must on Thursday nights. On a summer's evening you may hear the renowned voices of the Konrad Family Singers practicing for a concert.

The Kaufman House ✪

1641 HAMPSHIRE, QUINCY, ILLINOIS 62301

Tel: **(217) 223-2502**
Best Time to Call: **Noon–9 PM**
Host(s): **Emery and Bettie Kaufmann**
Location: **100 mi. W of Springfield**
No. of Rooms: **3**
No. of Private Baths: **1**
Max. No. Sharing Bath: **4**
Double/pb: **$60**
Single/pb: **$50**
Double/sb: **$40–$50**
Single/sb: **$30**
Open: **All year**
Breakfast: **Continental**
Pets: **No**
Children: **Welcome (crib)**
Smoking: **No**
Social Drinking: **No**
Airport/Station Pickup: **Yes**

History buffs will remember Quincy, set right on the Mississippi River, as the scene of the famous Lincoln-Douglas debates, while architecture buffs will be attracted to the town's feast of Victorian styles—Greek Revival, Gothic Revival, Italianate, and Richardsonian. The Kaufmann house was built 100 years ago, and the owners have been careful to maintain its "country" feeling. Guests may enjoy breakfast in the Ancestor's Room, on a stone patio, or at a picnic table under the trees. They are invited to play the piano, watch television, or enjoy popcorn by the fire. The Kaufmanns describe themselves as "Christians who have a love for God, people, nature, and life."

Top o' the Morning ✪

1505 19TH AVENUE, ROCK ISLAND, ILLINOIS 61201

Tel: **(309) 786-3513**
Best Time to Call: **After 5 PM**
Host(s): **Sam and Peggy Doak**
Location: **1½ mi. from Rte. 92, 18th Ave. Exit**
No. of Rooms: **2**
No. of Private Baths: **2**
Double/pb: **$35–$45**
Open: **All year**
Breakfast: **Full**
Pets: **No**
Children: **Welcome**
Smoking: **Permitted**
Social Drinking: **Permitted**

Sam and Peggy welcome you to their country estate, set on a bluff overlooking the Mississippi River, near the center of the Quad Cities area. The 18-room mansion is situated at the end of a winding drive on three acres of lawn, orchards, and gardens. The guest rooms, graced with lovely chandeliers and Oriental rugs, command a spectacular view of the cities and river. The parlor, with its grand piano and fireplace, is an inviting place to relax. Local attractions are Mississippi River boat rides, harness racing, Rock Island Arsenal, Black Hawk State Park, and Augustine and Marycrest colleges.

Victoria's B&B

201 NORTH 6TH STREET, ROCKFORD, ILLINOIS 61107

Tel: **(815) 963-3232**
Best Time to Call: **10:30 AM–4:30 PM**
Host(s): **Martin Lewis**
Location: **90 mi. W of Chicago**
No. of Rooms: **5**
No. of Private Baths: **5**
Double/pb: **$49–$69**
Single/pb: **$39–$59**
Suites: **$110**
Open: **All year**
Reduced Rates: **Weekly; 10%, seniors**
Breakfast: **Continental**
Other Meals: **Available**
Credit Cards: **MC, VISA**
Pets: **No**
Children: **Welcome, over 12**
Smoking: **Permitted**
Social Drinking: **Permitted**

This is Rockford's first Bed and Breakfast, part of the town's "Victorian Village" area, 20 turn-of-the-century homes that have been restored and converted to boutiques and restaurants. Victoria's features a winding staircase, stained-glass windows, two fireplaces, and the kind of woodwork that you seldom see nowadays. Although the ambiance is Victorian, the comforts are most definitely modern—television, air-conditioning, and refrigerators in each room, and even a Jacuzzi in some. Victoria's restaurant serves breakfast, lunch, and dinner, and on a fall or winter night it's possible to sit in front of the fireplace and enjoy some of the offerings from the kitchen.

The Stagecoach Inn

41 WEST 278 WHITNEY ROAD, ST. CHARLES, ILLINOIS 60174

Tel: **(312) 584-1263**
Host(s): **Pat and Bud Koecher**
Location: **41 mi. W of Chicago**
No. of Rooms: **2**
No. of Private Baths: **2**
Double/pb: **$45**
Single/pb: **$25**
Suites: **$40**
Open: **All year**
Reduced Rates: **Available**
Breakfast: **Continental**
Pets: **No**
Children: **Welcome (high chair)**
Smoking: **No**
Social Drinking: **Permitted**

The Stage Coach Inn is situated on picturesque Lake Campton in a scenic area five miles west of St. Charles. The house is a spacious ranch with a porch for sunning and relaxing. Year-round activities such as ice skating, fishing, and swimming can be enjoyed just steps from your door. Biking, riding, and antiquing are also within easy reach. Your hosts, Pat and Bud, serve assorted muffins, toast, or sweet rolls, with plenty of coffee and tea for breakfast. They also are glad to offer snacks and soft drinks later in the day.

Mischler House

718 SOUTH 8TH STREET, SPRINGFIELD, ILLINOIS 62703

Tel: **(217) 523-3714**
Host(s): **Rhonda Rice**
Location: **¼ mi. from I-55**
No. of Rooms: **2**
Max. No. Sharing Bath: **4**
Double/sb: **$40**
Open: **All year**
Reduced Rates: **After 3 nights; 10%, seniors**
Breakfast: **Continental**
Pets: **Sometimes**
Children: **Welcome**
Smoking: **Permitted**
Social Drinking: **Permitted**
Airport/Station Pickup: **Yes**

Built around 1880, the house is a comfortable blend of old and new. It is located two blocks from the restored Abraham Lincoln Home, and just three blocks from downtown Springfield, where Lincoln's law office and the Old State Capitol are open to visitors. Upon arrival, guests are served coffee or tea, then escorted to one of the comfortable guest rooms. Guests are free to lounge or curl up with a book in one of the parlors after a day of sightseeing. You are welcome to use the TV, laundry facilities, patio barbecue, and the kitchen for light snacks.

Country Charm B&B ✪

ROUTE 2, BOX 154, SYCAMORE, ILLINOIS 60178

Tel: **(815) 895-5386**
Host(s): **Howard and Donna Petersen**
Location: **50 mi. W of Chicago**
No. of Rooms: **3**
No. of Private Baths: **1**
Max. No. Sharing Bath: **4**
Double/pb: **$45**
Double/sb: **$25–$35**
Open: **Mar. 21–Dec. 21**
Breakfast: **Continental**
Pets: **Sometimes**
Children: **Welcome**
Smoking: **No**
Social Drinking: **Permitted**

The Petersens have wanted to have a Bed and Breakfast for years, and now that their kids are grown and gone, they've opened their six-acre "mini-farm" to guests. The Petersens' home was built at the turn of the century, and in the years they've lived there, they've added to and remodeled the original house. There's a living room with a pit fireplace, a television room, and a library with over 2,000 books. Donna loves horses, and one of the nicest features of a stay at Country Charm is the chance to have breakfast overlooking the riding arena. Donna explains the decor this way: "Our house and grounds are fairly plain because we only decorate with things that have meaning to us. Our daughter, an artist, and the many friends we have contribute to our decorating."

INDIANA

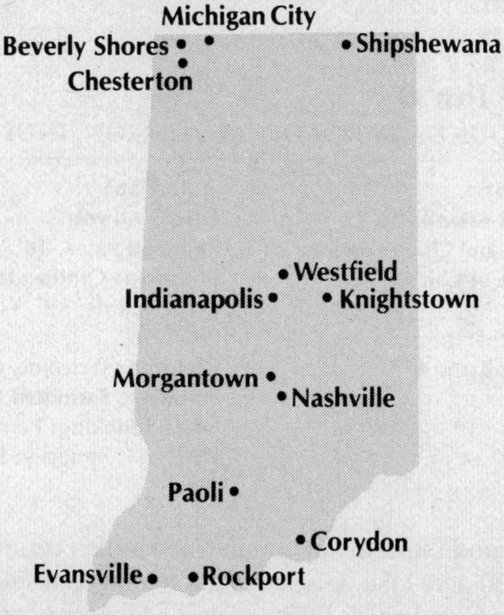

Michigan City
Beverly Shores
Shipshewana
Chesterton
Westfield
Indianapolis
Knightstown
Morgantown
Nashville
Paoli
Corydon
Evansville
Rockport

Dunes Shore Inn

BOX 807, LAKESHORE COUNTY ROAD, BEVERLY SHORES, INDIANA 46301

Tel: **(219) 879-9029**
Best Time to Call: **Evenings**
Host(s): **Fred and Rosemary Braun**
Location: **4 mi. W of Michigan City**
No. of Rooms: **12**
Max. No. Sharing Bath: **5**
Double/sb: **$37**
Single/pb: **$27**
Suite: **$45**
Separate Cottage: **$65; sleeps 5**

Open: **All year except Dec.**
Reduced Rates: **Weekly**
Breakfast: **Continental**
Credit Cards: **MC, VISA**
Pets: **No**
Children: **Welcome**
Smoking: **Permitted**
Social Drinking: **Permitted**
Airport/Station Pickup: **Yes**
Foreign Languages: **German**

This comfortable inn was formerly an old summer hotel that was recently reopened with newly decorated rooms. Many old-fashioned ways remain; the bath is down the hall and there is an absence of phones and TVs in the rooms. Each floor has its own lounge for private reading or relaxing. Your hosts offer juice and snacks daily and a marzipan coffee cake at breakfast. The inn is set in an area of natural wooded dunes, just one block from Lake Michigan. The Michigan City Marina and Indiana Dunes State Park are both close by.

Gray Goose Inn ✪

350 INDIAN BOUNDARY ROAD, CHESTERTON, INDIANA 46304

Tel: **(219) 926-5781**
Best Time to Call: **After 4 PM**
Host(s): **Tim Wilk and Charles Ramsey**
Location: **60 mi. E of Chicago**
No. of Rooms: **5**
No. of Private Baths: **3**
Max. No. Sharing Bath: **4**
Double/pb: **$54**
Single/pb: **$51**
Double/sb: **$48**
Single/sb: **$45**
Suites: **$65**
Open: **All year**
Reduced Rates: **10%, seniors**
Breakfast: **Continental**
Credit Cards: **MC, VISA**
Pets: **No**
Children: **Welcome, over 12**
Smoking: **Permitted**
Social Drinking: **Permitted**
Foreign Languages: **Polish**

Elegant accommodations await you in this English country-style home overlooking a 30-acre lake. Guest rooms feature canopied four-poster beds, fine linens, and thick fluffy towels. All rooms are decorated in Williamsburg style, and some have a fireplace. Enjoy a quiet moment in the common room or relax with a cup of coffee on the screened-in porch. Take long walks beside the shady oaks or feed the Canada geese and wild ducks. The Gray Goose is five minutes from Dunes State and National Lakeshore parks. Swimming, canoeing down the Little Calumet River, hiking, and fishing on Lake Michigan are all within easy reach. Dining, weekend entertainment, and miniature golf are within walking distance.

The Kintner House Inn

CAPITOL AND CHESTNUT, CORYDON, INDIANA 47112

Tel: **(812) 738-2020**
Best Time to Call: **8 AM–9 PM**
Host(s): **Mary Jane Bridgwater**
Location: **1½ mi. from I-64**
No. of Rooms: **14**
No. of Private Baths: **14**
Double/pb: **$40–$65**
Open: **All year**
Breakfast: **Full**
Credit Cards: **AMEX, MC, VISA**
Pets: **No**
Children: **Welcome (crib, high chair)**
Smoking: **No**
Social Drinking: **Permitted**

The elegant experience at this restored 1800s inn begins in the reception area where guests sign in on a unique inlaid registration desk. From there, you'll be shown to your choice of sleeping quarters, ranging in decor from country to formal. A typical bedroom has floral wallpaper, colorful quilt with coordinating curtains, antique wood or poster bed, and a blend of wood tables and love seats. Conversation or cable TV can be enjoyed in the fireplaced parlor, which is decorated with Victorian furnishings. Breakfast is served in a large dining room with antique wood sideboard, sterling silver service, and fine bone china. The inn is located in the center of a small country town and you can watch it all go by from a pillared veranda that runs the length of the Federal-style building. Your hosts will gladly direct you to nearby caves and a wild and scenic river.

Brigadoon Bed & Breakfast Inn ✪

1201 SOUTH EAST 2ND STREET, EVANSVILLE, INDIANA 47713

Tel: **(812) 422-9635**
Host(s): **Kathee Forbes**
Location: **1 mi. from Hwy. 41**
No. of Rooms: **4**
No. of Private Baths: **2**
Max. No. Sharing Bath: **4**
Double/pb: **$40**
Single/pb: **$35**
Double/sb: **$40**
Single/sb: **$35**
Open: **All year**
Reduced Rates: **Families**
Breakfast: **Full**
Other Meals: **Sometimes**
Credit Cards: **MC, VISA**
Pets: **Sometimes**
Children: **Welcome (babysitter)**
Smoking: **Permitted**
Social Drinking: **Permitted**
Airport/Station Pickup: **Yes**

Brigadoon is a white frame Victorian with a gingerbread porch. The inn was built in 1892 and has been thoroughly renovated by the Forbes family. Four fireplaces, original parquet floors, and beautiful stained-glass windows have been lovingly preserved. Modern baths and a country eat-in kitchen have been added. Bedrooms are large and sunny with accents of lace and ruffles, floral wallpapers, and antique furnishings. Guests are welcome to relax in the parlor or library and enjoy complimentary wine and cheese. Breakfast specialties change daily and can include a soufflé or quiche served with lots of homemade breads, jams, and apple butter. This charming Victorian getaway is close to the Historic Preservation area, restaurants, and the riverfront.

Osborne House ✪

1911 N. DELAWARE, INDIANAPOLIS, INDIANA 46202

Tel: **(317) 924-1777**
Host(s): **Iva Osborne**
Location: **1 mi. from I-74**
No. of Rooms: **4**
Max. No. Sharing Bath: **4**
Double/sb: **$35–$40**
Single/sb: **$30–$35**
Open: **All year**
Breakfast: **Continental**
Pets: **Sometimes**
Children: **Welcome, over 12**
Smoking: **Permitted**
Social Drinking: **Permitted**

Built 90 years ago, Iva's Victorian has been beautifully restored and furnished with antiques and collectibles. The guest rooms are comfortable and airy, assuring you of a good night's sleep. The Museum of Art and the Union Station restoration, with its shops and restaurants, are local highlights. If you plan to attend the Indianapolis 500 Race in May, reserve early!

Hollingsworth House Inn

6054 HOLLINGSWORTH ROAD, INDIANAPOLIS, INDIANA 46254

Tel: **(317) 299-6700**
Best Time to Call: **10 AM–5 PM**
Host(s): **Susan Muller and Ann Irvine**
Location: **1 mi. from I-465**
No. of Rooms: **5**
No. of Private Baths: **5**
Double/pb: **$65**
Suites: **$95**
Open: **All year**
Breakfast: **Continental**
Pets: **No**
Children: **No**
Smoking: **Permitted**
Social Drinking: **Permitted**

Built in 1854 and listed on the National Register of Historic Places, this beautifully restored Greek Revival-style farmhouse is set on four acres, adjacent to a 120-acre park. Lovely antiques, fine linens, down comforters, and extra thick towels add to the elegance of your stay. A delicious breakfast of fresh fruit, homemade pecan rolls, and coffee is graciously served on Haviland china with fine silver and crystal accessories.

Old Hoosier House ✪

ROUTE 2, BOX 299-1, KNIGHTSTOWN, INDIANA 46148

Tel: **(317) 345-2969**
Host(s): **Tom and Jean Lewis**
Location: **30 mi. E of Indianapolis**
No. of Rooms: **4**
No. of Private Baths: **1**
Max. No. Sharing Bath: **3**
Double/pb: **$55**
Single/pb: **$45**
Double/sb: **$45**
Single/sb: **$35**

Open: **May 1–Nov. 1**
Reduced Rates: **10%, seniors**
Breakfast: **Full**
Pets: **No**
Children: **Welcome (crib)**
Smoking: **No**
Social Drinking: **No**
Airport/Station Pickup: **Yes**

The Old Hoosier House takes you back more than 100 years, when the livin' was easier. The rooms are large, with high ceilings, arched windows, antiques, and mementos. A library and patio are available for your pleasure. In the morning you'll wake to the aroma of homemade rolls and coffee. Golfers will enjoy the adjoining golf course, while antiques buffs will be glad to know there are hundreds of local dealers in the area. The cities of Anderson and Richmond are close by and the Indianapolis 500 is within an hour's drive.

Plantation Inn ✪

RR 2, BOX 296-S, MICHIGAN CITY, INDIANA 46360

Tel: **(219) 874-2418**
Host(s): **Ann and Robert Stephens**
Location: **60 mi. E of Chicago; 2½ mi. from I-94, Exit 421S**
No. of Rooms: **5**
No. of Private Baths: **5**
Double/pb: **$59–$65**
Single/pb: **$54–$60**
Suites: **$79**
Open: **All year**
Breakfast: **Full**
Credit Cards: **MC, VISA**
Pets: **Sometimes**
Children: **Welcome**
Smoking: **Permitted**
Social Drinking: **Permitted**

The inn is located just minutes away from the Indiana Dunes National Lakeshore. It is situated on two landscaped acres enhanced by patios and a pond; in winter, guests may enjoy winter sports on its 70 acres. Each bedroom is distinctively furnished with king- or queen-size beds, color TVs, and pretty accessories. The living room has a baby grand piano, a selection of books, and some interesting art. Breakfast, served in the dining room, includes fruits of the season, cereal, pastries, preserves, cheese, and beverages. Bikes are available for touring, and there's boat docking in case you wish to tote your own for the great local fishing.

The Rock House ✪

380 WEST WASHINGTON STREET, MORGANTOWN, INDIANA 46160

Tel: **(812) 597-5100**
Host(s): **Marcella and Daniel Braun**
Location: **32 mi. S of Indianapolis**
No. of Rooms: **5**
No. of Private Baths: **2**
Max. No. Sharing Bath: **4**
Double/pb: **$55**
Single/pb: **$45**

Double/sb: **$45**
Single/sb: **$30**
Suites: **$80**
Open: **All year**
Reduced Rates: **10%, seniors**
Breakfast: **Full**
Pets: **No**
Children: **Welcome, over 13**
Smoking: **Permitted**
Social Drinking: **Permitted**
Foreign Languages: **German**

The Rock House was built in the 1890s by James Smith Knight. He used concrete blocks years before they were popular, but it's the way he used them that made him an innovator. Before the concrete dried, Knight embedded in it hundreds of rocks, stones, marbles, and jewelry. The result is spectacular, drawing many sightseers to the house. Inside, guests will find a homey atmosphere and comfortable furnishings. Your hosts will gladly direct you to such local attractions as Lake Monroe, Ski World, and Little Nashville Opry.

Allison House ✪

90 SOUTH JEFFERSON STREET, P.O. BOX 546, NASHVILLE, INDIANA 47448

Tel: **(812) 988-6664**
Best Time to Call: **9 AM–9 PM**
Host(s): **Tammy and Bob Galm**
Location: **50 mi. S of Indianapolis**
No. of Rooms: **5**
No. of Private Baths: **5**
Double/pb: **$65–$75**
Open: **All year**
Reduced Rates: **10%, seniors**
Breakfast: **Continental**
Pets: **No**
Children: **Welcome, over 12**
Smoking: **No**
Social Drinking: **No**

Allison House is a fully restored Victorian located in the heart of Nashville. Tammy and Bob have filled the house with a blend of old mementos and new finds from the local arts and crafts colony. The artisans are quite famous in this area, and they are located within walking distance. Tammy and Bob offer a light breakfast of home-baked goods and will gladly prepare something heartier if you like.

Sunset House ✪

RURAL ROUTE 3, BOX 127, NASHVILLE, INDIANA 47448

Tel: **(812) 988-6118**
Host(s): **Mary Margaret Baird**
Location: **18 mi. from I-65**
No. of Rooms: **3**
No. of Private Baths: **3**
Double/pb: **$50**
Single/pb: **$50**
Suites: **$60**
Open: **Feb.–Nov.**
Breakfast: **Continental**
Pets: **No**
Children: **Welcome (crib)**
Smoking: **Permitted**
Social Drinking: **Permitted**

Mary's home is a magnificent contemporary house with a deck and patio for relaxing. The guest rooms have separate entrances and all are furnished in fine cherry wood. The master suite has a handsome stone fireplace. Although there are many things to keep you busy, the Little Nashville Opry is a major attraction each Saturday, with country-and-western stars entertaining. Indiana University is nearby. Discounts are not in effect in October.

Braxton House Inn B&B

210 NORTH GOSPEL STREET, PAOLI, INDIANA 47454

Tel: **(812) 723-4677**
Best Time to Call: **10 AM–8 PM**
Host(s): **Terry and Brenda Cornwell**
Location: **45 mi. S of Bloomington**
No. of Rooms: **8**
No. of Private Baths: **4**
Max. No. Sharing Bath: **4**
Double/pb: **$40**
Single/pb: **$35**
Double/sb: **$30**
Single/sb: **$25**
Suites: **$60**
Open: **All year**
Reduced Rates: **10%, seniors**
Breakfast: **Continental**
Pets: **Sometimes**
Children: **No**
Smoking: **Permitted**
Social Drinking: **Permitted**

This Queen Anne Victorian was built in 1893. The original cherry, oak, and walnut woodwork is still evident in many of the 21 rooms. Terry and Brenda have carefully refurbished the mansion and decorated with lovely antiques, many of which are for sale. The dining room, with its original wainscoting and wide-pine floors, is where homemade pastries and muffins are on the breakfast menu. Paoli Peaks, a ski resort, is 2 miles away, and it's 15 miles to Patoka, the second largest lake in the state. Coffee, tea, and snacks are graciously offered.

The Rockport Inn ✪

THIRD AT WALNUT, ROCKPORT, INDIANA 47635

Tel: **(812) 649-2664**
Best Time to Call: **8 AM–6 PM**
Host(s): **Emil and Carolyn Ahnell**
Location: **40 mi. E of Evansville**
No. of Rooms: **6**
No. of Private Baths: **6**
Double/pb: **$32–$40**
Single/pb: **$25–$35**
Open: **All year**
Reduced Rates: **30%, weekly**
Breakfast: **Continental**
Other Meals: **Available**
Pets: **Sometimes**
Children: **Welcome (crib)**
Smoking: **Permitted**
Social Drinking: **Permitted**
Foreign Languages: **German, Swedish**

Built in 1855, this white frame two-story residence has a porch and landscaped yard. It's furnished with antiques; plants and flowers add to its cozy atmosphere. Lincoln State Park, Santa Claus Land, and Kentucky Wesleyan College are nearby.

Green Meadow Ranch ✪

R.R. 2, BOX 592, SHIPSHEWANA, INDIANA 46565

Tel: **(219) 768-4221**
Host(s): **Paul and Ruth Miller**
Location: **60 mi. E of South Bend; 9 mi. from I-80**
No. of Rooms: **7**
Max. No. Sharing Bath: **5**
Double/sb: **$40**
Single/sb: **$20**
Open: **Mar. 1–Dec. 31**
Breakfast: **Continental**
Children: **Welcome**
Smoking: **No**
Social Drinking: **No**
Foreign Languages: **Pennsylvania German**

Shipshewana is a large Amish and Mennonite settlement. One of the largest flea markets in the country is held on summer Tuesdays and Wednesdays, and an antique auction every Wednesday, all year long. Ruth and Paul's brick Colonial home, decorated with lovely country antiques, is on their 20-acre ranch. They have miniature horses, donkeys, fancy chickens, and ducks. They offer snacks, fruit, and soft drinks along with information about the Amish way of life. Ruth has a country folk art shop on the grounds.

Country Roads Guesthouse ✪

2731 WEST 146TH STREET, WESTFIELD, INDIANA 46074

Tel: **(317) 846-2376**
Host(s): **Phil Pegram**
Location: **15 mi. N of Indianapolis; 10 mi. from I-465**
No. of Rooms: **2**
Max. No. Sharing Bath: **4**
Double/sb: **$50**
Single/sb: **$36**
Open: **All year**
Breakfast: **Continental**
Pets: **Sometimes**
Children: **Welcome**
Smoking: **Permitted**
Social Drinking: **No**

This 100-year-old farmhouse is situated on four acres, has high ceilings, a kitchen fireplace, and is furnished with antiques. It's air-

conditioned for your summer comfort, and guests are welcome to use the swimming pool and basketball court. The country setting is fine for walking, jogging, or bicycling, and the area is filled with antique shops, historic sites, and fine restaurants. The Herb Barn Country Store and Gardens, and Conner Prairie, a pioneer settlement, are nearby attractions.

IOWA

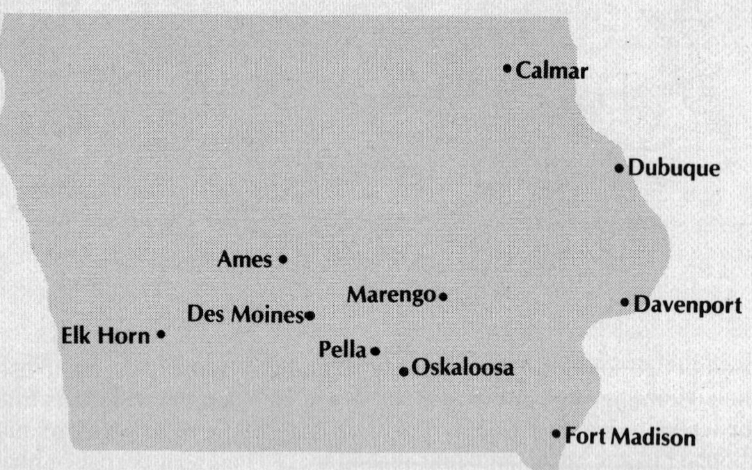

Bed and Breakfast in Iowa, Ltd. ✪

BOX 430, PRESTON, IOWA 52069

Tel: **(319) 689-4222**
Best Time to Call: **Mornings; evenings**
Coordinator: **Wilma Bloom**
States/Regions Covered: **Statewide**

Rates (Single/Double):

Modest:	**$20**	**$35**
Average:	**$25**	**$35–$40**
Luxury:	**$35**	**$65**

Credit Cards: **No**

Wilma has a vast variety of accommodations, ranging from working farms where you can participate in agricultural activities, National Registry homes, mansions overlooking the Mississippi River, and huge ranches overlooking the lakes, bluffs, and cliffs of northeast Iowa. The Iowa State Fair and over 200 statewide festivals will suit all interests, including cultural, historic, sports, and crafts. The University of Iowa, Iowa State, and Drake University are close to several homes. Please send $1 for her directory.

B&B on Ash ✪

517 ASH AVENUE, AMES, IOWA 50010

Tel: **(515) 292-9382**
Host(s): **Helen and Keith McRoberts**
Location: **30 mi. N of Des Moines**
No. of Rooms: **2**
No. of Private Baths: **1½**
Max. No. Sharing Bath: **2**
Double/pb: **$30**
Single/pb: **$25**
Double/sb: **$30**
Single/sb: **$25**
Open: **All year**
Breakfast: **Full**
Pets: **No**
Children: **Welcome**
Smoking: **No**
Social Drinking: **Permitted**

Built in 1913, this beige frame and stucco home is comfortably furnished. Wood beams, a stone fireplace, and the front porch with its wicker furniture spell welcome. The breakfast of omelets, cinnamon rolls, and freshly ground coffee is an instant eye-opener and may be enjoyed on the backyard deck. Iowa State University campus and the Iowa State Center for cultural activities and sports events are nearby.

Calmar Guesthouse ✪

RR 1, BOX 206, CALMAR, IOWA 52132

Tel: **(319) 562-3851**
Best Time to Call: **6–8 AM**
Host(s): **Art and Lucille Kruse**
Location: **10 mi. S of Decorah**
No. of Rooms: **4**
Max. No. Sharing Bath: **4**
Double/sb: **$29**
Single/sb: **$24**
Open: **All year**
Breakfast: **Full**
Pets: **No**
Children: **Welcome**
Smoking: **Permitted**
Social Drinking: **Permitted**
Airport/Station Pickup: **Yes**

A recent guest reports that "The Calmar Guesthouse is a spacious, lovely, newly remodeled Victorian home located on the edge of town. The atmosphere is enhanced by the friendly, charming manner of Lucille, who made us feel right at home. The rooms were comfortable, private, and pretty. After a peaceful night's sleep, we were served a delicious breakfast of fresh farm eggs with ham and cheeses, croissants with butter and jam, homemade cinnamon rolls, and coffee. I would recommend it to anyone visiting the area." Nearby points of interest include Lake Meyer, the world's smallest church, and Spillville, where the hand-carved Billy Bros. Clocks are made.

River Oaks Inn ✪

1234 EAST RIVER DRIVE, DAVENPORT, IOWA 52803

Tel: **(319) 326-2629**
Best Time to Call: **8 AM–8 PM**
Host(s): **Bill and Suzanne Pohl; Ron and Mary Jo Pohl**
Location: **2 mi. from I-80**
No. of Rooms: **4**
No. of Private Baths: **3**
Max. No. Sharing Bath: **4**
Double/pb: **$45**
Double/sb: **$50**
Suites: **$60**
Open: **All year**
Reduced Rates: **Available**
Breakfast: **Continental**
Credit Cards: **MC, VISA**
Pets: **Sometimes**
Children: **Welcome**
Smoking: **In designated areas**
Social Drinking: **Permitted**
Airport/Station Pickup: **Yes**
Foreign Languages: **Spanish**

Abner Davison combined Italianate, Victorian, and Prairie architecture when he built this home back in the 1850s. The house is situated on a rolling lot that still shows evidence of the original carriage drive. Choose from a suite with king-size bed, sun porch, and dressing room; the Ambrose Fulton Room, with double bed and garden view; the Mississippi Room, with queen-size bed and window seat; or the Abner Davison Room, which has twin beds and a bay window. Breakfast is served in the dining room or out on the deck in the warm weather. High tea is served in the afternoon, and guests are welcome to enjoy it outside in the gazebo. The inn is located one block from river boat rides, and is convenient to many area attractions such as Historic Rock Island Arsenal and the village of East Davenport.

Rainbow H Ranch and Campground ✪

ROUTE 1, ELK HORN, IOWA 51531

Tel: **(712) 764-8272**
Best Time to Call: **Mornings; after 6 PM**
Host(s): **Mark and Cherie Hensley**
Location: **60 mi. E of Omaha, Neb.**
No. of Rooms: **2**
No. of Private Baths: **1**
Double/pb: **$32**
Single/pb: **$26**
Open: **All year**
Reduced Rates: **10% after 1 night**
Breakfast: **Full**
Pets: **Sometimes**
Children: **Welcome**
Smoking: **Permitted**
Social Drinking: **No**
Airport/Station Pickup: **Yes**

Enjoy the charm of the Iowa countryside as a guest in this grand brick home. The decor is country French and features a spacious recreation room with fireplace and beamed ceilings. The bedrooms have full or twin-size beds, color TVs; there is a private entrance and outdoor patio for your use. Your hosts raise longhorn cattle and will gladly give you and the kids a tour of the farm. If you prefer, the Hensleys also have a small campground nearby in a parklike setting. The Elk Horn community is home to the largest Danish settlement in the United States. The town has a working windmill and is home to the National Danish Museum and the Tivoli Festival.

The Morton House

#7 HIGHPOINT, FORT MADISON, IOWA 52627

Tel: **(319) 372-9517**
Best Time to Call: **11 AM–9 PM**
Host(s): **Dennis and Carole Morton**
Location: **1 mi. E of Fort Madison**
No. of Rooms: **2**
No. of Private Baths: **2**
Double/pb: **$60**
Single/pb: **$45**
Open: **Apr. 1–Nov. 1**
Reduced Rates: **Available**
Breakfast: **Continental**
Credit Cards: **MC, VISA**
Pets: **Sometimes**
Children: **Welcome, over 16**
Smoking: **In designated areas**
Social Drinking: **Permitted**
Airport/Station Pickup: **Yes**

This 17-room house, perched 120 feet above the Mississippi, was built for the Schaeffer Pen family in the 1920s. The three-story stone and wood-frame home is located off a private road on a two-acre lot surrounded by a variety of trees. The Mortons have decorated the large rooms with antique furniture to complement the rich oak floors and stained glass. Each guest room has a breathtaking view, as does the breakfast room, where you will be served a variety of fresh fruit, pastries, and plenty of hot coffee each morning. Guests may enjoy the river room, screened-in porch, and the outdoor patio, all overlooking the water. The Morton House is five miles from historic Nauvoo and convenient to many Mississippi River regional events and festivals.

Loy's Bed and Breakfast ✪

R.R. 1, MARENGO, IOWA 52301

Tel: **(319) 642-7787**
Best Time to Call: **7 AM, noon, 6 PM**
Host(s): **Loy and Robert Walker**
Location: **3 mi. from I-80**
No. of Rooms: **3**
No. of Private Baths: **3**
Max. No. Sharing Bath: **4**
Double/sb: **$40**
Single/sb: **$25**
Open: **All year**
Breakfast: **Full**
Pets: **If caged**
Children: **Welcome**
Smoking: **No**
Social Drinking: **Permitted**

The Walkers invite you to visit their contemporary farmhouse in the heartland of rural Iowa. Enjoy the peaceful surroundings of a large lawn, gardens, and patio. The rooms are furnished in modern and refinished pieces. Guests are welcome to relax in the family room by the fire or to stop by the rec room for a game of shuffleboard or pool, and a treat from the snack bar. If they are not busy with the harvest, your hosts will gladly take you on day trips. Tours may include Plum Grove, Iowa City, Brucemore Mansion, and Herbert Hoover's birthplace. A visit to the nearby lakes is recommended and a take-along lunch can be arranged. The Amana Colonies is right here and shouldn't be missed.

For key to listings, see inside front or back cover.

✪ This star means that rates are guaranteed through December 31, 1988 to any guest making a reservation as a result of reading about the B&B in *BED & BREAKFAST U.S.A.*—1988 edition.

Please enclose a self-addressed, stamped, business-sized envelope when contacting reservation services.

For more details on what you can expect in a B&B, see Chapter 1.

Always mention *Bed & Breakfast U.S.A.* when making reservations!

If no B&B is listed in the area you'll be visiting, use the form on page 698 to order a copy of our "List of New B&Bs."

We want to hear from you! Use the form on page 697.

KANSAS

Valley Falls
Tonganoxie
Kansas City
Abilene
Overland Park
Prairie Village
Leawood
Modoc
Lawrence
Melvern
Fort Scott

Kansas City Bed & Breakfast—Kansas & Missouri
P.O. BOX 14781, LENEXA, KANSAS 66215

Tel: **(913) 268-4214**

Best Time to Call: **9 AM–10 PM**

Coordinator: **Edwina Monroe**

States/Regions Covered:
Kansas—Leawood, Lenexa, Overland Park; Missouri—Parkville, Kansas City, Independence, St. Joseph

Rates (Single/Double):

Average:	**$35**	**$40**
Luxury:	**$55**	**$60**

Credit Cards: **No**

As the song says, "Everything's up-to-date in Kansas City." You will enjoy visiting such places as Crown Center, Country Club Plaza, Arrowhead Stadium, Royals Stadium, Kemper Arena, and the Missouri Repertory Theatre. A directory fully describing all of the host homes is available. Please send a self-addressed envelope with 39¢ postage. Advise Diane of your selection and she will do the rest. Jewell College, Parkville College, the University of Missouri, and Central Missouri State are close by.

Balfours' House

ROUTE 2, ABILENE, KANSAS 67410

Tel: **(913) 263-4262**
Best Time to Call: **After 5 pm**
Host(s): **Gilbert and Marie Balfour**
Location: **2¼ mi. S of Abilene**
No. of Rooms: **3**
No. of Private Baths: **1**
Max. No. Sharing Bath: **4**
Double/pb: **$35**
Single/pb: **$25**
Double/sb: **$30**
Single/sb: **$20**
Open: **All year**
Breakfast: **Continental**
Credit Cards: **MC, VISA**
Pets: **Sometimes**
Children: **Welcome**
Smoking: **Permitted**
Social Drinking: **Permitted**
Airport/Station Pickup: **Sometimes**

Gilbert and Marie Balfour welcome you to their modern cottage-style home, set on a hillside. The house is located on just over two acres, and has a spacious yard. Guests have their own private entrance into the family room, which includes a fireplace, piano, and TV. The main attraction of the house is a hexagonal recreation room that has a built-in swimming pool, spa, and dressing area with shower. Start your day off with a cup of coffee and Bubble Bread, the specialty of the house. Your hosts will gladly direct you to the Eisenhower Museum, Greyhound Hall of Fame, and many old historic mansions.

Country Quarters ✪

ROUTE 5, BOX 80, FORT SCOTT, KANSAS 66701

Tel: **(316) 223-2889**
Host(s): **Marilyn McQuitty**
Location: **2 mi. S of Fort Scott**
No. of Rooms: **1**
No. of Private Baths: **1**
Double/pb: **$25**
Open: **All year**
Breakfast: **Full**
Pets: **No**
Children: **Welcome**
Smoking: **Permitted**
Social Drinking: **Permitted**

Marilyn McQuitty welcomes you to a real working farm located outside a charming Victorian town. Her 100-year-old farmhouse is furnished with comfortable family pieces. While you're sitting by the fire, ask to hear the story behind the 100-year-old hearth and hand-carved mantelpiece. Guests are welcome to relax on the porch or visit the ceramic shop located on the premises. There is easy access to the Fort Scott Lake, Gunn Park, and the Fort Scott National Historic Site, an authentically restored military fort dating back to 1892. Downtown you can drive past the magnificent old homes, browse through antiques stores, and visit a one-room schoolhouse.

Schoolhouse Inn ✪

106 EAST BECK, BOX 175, MELVERN, KANSAS 66510

Tel: **(913) 549-3473**
Best Time to Call: **After 5 PM**
Host(s): **Bill and Mary Fisher**
Location: **80 mi. SW of Kansas City, Mo.**
No. of Rooms: **4**
No. of Private Baths: **2**
Max. No. Sharing Bath: **4**
Double/pb: **$40**
Single/pb: **$35**
Double/sb: **$37.50**
Single/sb: **$32.50**
Open: **All year**
Credit Cards: **AMEX, MC, VISA**
Reduced Rates: **10%, seniors**
Breakfast: **Full**
Pets: **Sometimes**
Children: **Welcome, over 5**
Smoking: **Permitted**
Social Drinking: **Permitted**

The Schoolhouse was built in 1870 of heavy timbers, and stone from nearby quarries. It was the first schoolhouse in the area and also served as the town meeting place. Today the house has been completely restored to serve as an elegant retreat in a pastoral setting. The second-floor guest rooms are large, with high ceilings and comfortable furnishings. The Schoolhouse is four miles from Melvern Lake and is convenient to state and federal parks and antique shops.

Almeda's Inn ✪

BOX 103, 220 SOUTH MAIN, TONGANOXIE, KANSAS 66086

Tel: **(913) 845-2295**
Best Time to Call: **Before 9 AM; after 6 PM**
Host(s): **Almeda and Richard Tinberg**
Location: **20 mi. W of Kansas City**
No. of Rooms: **7**
No. of Private Baths: **1**
Max. No. Sharing Bath: **4**
Double/pb: **$30**
Double/sb: **$30**
Single/sb: **$25**
Open: **All year**
Breakfast: **Continental**
Pets: **No**
Children: **Welcome, over 4**
Smoking: **Permitted**
Social Drinking: **Permitted**

Located in a picturesque small town, and made a designated Historical Site in 1983, the inn dates back to World War I. You are welcome to sip a cup of coffee at the unique stone bar in the room once used as a bus stop in 1930. In fact, this room was the inspiration for *Bus Stop*. Almeda and Richard will be happy to direct you to the golf course, swimming facilities, the Starlight Theatre, or the University of Kansas at Lawrence.

The Barn Bed and Breakfast Inn ✪

RR #2, BOX 87, VALLEY FALLS, KANSAS 66088

Tel: **(913) 945-3303**
Host(s): **Tom and Marcella Ryan**
Location: **23 mi. NE of Topeka**
No. of Rooms: **8**
No. of Private Baths: **8**
Double/pb: **$44.50**
Single/pb: **$38**
Open: **All year**
Reduced Rates: **Available**
Breakfast: **Full**
Other Meals: **Available**
Pets: **No**
Children: **Welcome**
Smoking: **No**
Social Drinking: **No**
Airport/Station Pickup: **Yes**

The Barn is a real American farm original, dating back over 100 years. It has been converted into a large, gracious home with motifs of wood and plenty of windows. The rooms are decorated with comfortable furnishings, king-size beds, and many antiques. A lovely living room with fireplace takes the chill out of winter nights, and if you like plants, the glassed-in sun deck is the place for you. The Ryans raise their own food and bake their own bread. They offer a farm-style breakfast including pecan rolls, buttermilk pancakes, and bacon and eggs. They love people and would be pleased if your family joined theirs for lunch or dinner. The Barn has its own swimming hole, fishing ponds, and plenty of space for long walks.

KENTUCKY

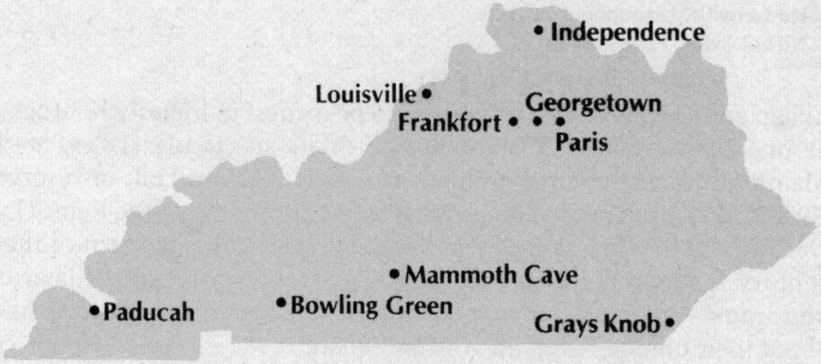

Independence
Louisville
Georgetown
Frankfort
Paris
Mammoth Cave
Paducah
Bowling Green
Grays Knob

Bluegrass Bed & Breakfast ✪

ROUTE 1, BOX 263, VERSAILLES, KENTUCKY 40383

Tel: **(606) 873-3208**
Coordinator: **Betsy Pratt**
States/Regions Covered: **Greensburg, Harrodsburg, Lexington, Midway, Versailles**

Rates (Single/Double):
Modest: **$36**
Average: **$48**
Luxury: **$60**

Most of Betsy's B&Bs are in beautiful old houses that grace the country roads of the area. You may choose among a stone house built in 1796, or a turreted Victorian in downtown Lexington, or a country home where your bedroom windows look out on Thoroughbred horses. Visit Shakertown, where weavers, smiths, and woodworkers display their skills in an 1839 restored village. Take a ride on the winding Kentucky River in a paddlewheel boat. Tour exquisite historic mansions or see the picturesque homes of such Derby winners as Secretariat and Seattle Slew. And don't miss the 1,000-acre Kentucky Horse Park that includes a theater, museum, track, barns, and hundreds of horses. You may even take a horseback ride, because this place will inspire you.

Kentucky Homes Bed & Breakfast, Inc. ✪

1431 ST. JAMES COURT, LOUISVILLE, KENTUCKY 40208

Tel: **(502) 635-7341**
Best Time to Call: **8–11 AM; 4–7 PM**
Coordinator: **Lillian Marshall and John Dillehay**
States/Regions Covered: **Kentucky–Bowling Green, Frankfort, Hodgenville, Lexington, Louisville, Nicholasville, Paducah**

Rates (Single/Double):

	Single	Double
Modest:	**$33–$40**	**$38–$44**
Average:	**$41–$45**	**$46–$50**
Luxury:	**$50 and up**	**$55 and up**

Credit Cards: **MC, VISA (deposit only)**

Lillian and John cordially invite you to be a guest in friendly Kentucky at one of dozens of host homes. Fish in spectacular lakes, visit Mammoth Cave, drop in on Shakertown at Pleasant Hill, or reserve early and assure yourself of a spot at the next running of the Kentucky Derby (held the first Saturday in May). Stay in a gorgeous turn-of-the-century home in restored old Louisville, or a dairy farm that boards and trains racehorses, or many comfortable choices in between. Ask about their unique "prepaid voucher" plan.

Bowling Green Bed & Breakfast ✪

659 EAST 14TH AVENUE, BOWLING GREEN, KENTUCKY 42101

Tel: **(502) 781-3861**
Best Time to Call: **Evenings; Early AM**
Host(s): **Dr. and Mrs. Norman Hunter**
Location: **4 mi. from I-65, Exit 22**
No. of Rooms: **3**
No. of Private Baths: **1**
Max. No. Sharing Bath: **4**
Double/pb: **$40**
Single/pb: **$30**
Double/sb: **$40**
Single/sb: **$30**
Open: **All year**
Breakfast: **Continental**
Pets: **No**
Children: **Welcome, over 14**
Smoking: **No**
Social Drinking: **Permitted**
Airport/Station Pickup: **Yes**

This trim, gray-shingled, comfortably furnished two-story home is situated on a wooded lot. You are welcome to watch TV, select a book from the library, crank out a tune on the old Victrola, or play Ping-Pong in the recreation room. It is an easy drive to state parks, Opryland, and Mammoth Cave. Ronna Lee and Norman teach at nearby Western Kentucky University.

Log Cabin Bed and Breakfast ✪

350 NORTH BROADWAY, GEORGETOWN, KENTUCKY 40324

Tel: **(502) 863-3514**
Host(s): **Clay and Janis McKnight**
Location: **10 mi. N of Lexington**
No. of Rooms: **2**
No. of Private Baths: **1**
Guest Cottage: **$50–$64 (sleeps 4–6)**
Open: **All year**
Breakfast: **Continental**
Pets: **Welcome**
Children: **Welcome**
Smoking: **Permitted**
Social Drinking: **Permitted**

This rustic log cabin was built, circa 1809, with a shake shingle roof and chinked logs. Inside, the living room is dominated by a huge fieldstone fireplace. The master bedroom and bath are on the ground floor, and a loft bedroom will sleep an additional two with ease. The house has been fully restored by the McKnights and is filled with period furnishings. The dining-kitchen wing is equipped with all new appliances and modern amenities. The Log Cabin is located in a quiet neighborhood close to Kentucky Horse Park, Keeneland, and many other historic places. This is the perfect spot to bring the kids and give them a taste of authentic American tradition.

Three Deer Inn ✪

P.O. DRAWER 299, GRAYS KNOB, KENTUCKY 40829

Tel: **(606) 573-6666**
Best Time to Call: **8 AM–6 PM**
Host(s): **C. V. and Blanche Bennet**
Location: **68 mi. from Rte. 175**
No. of Rooms: **5**
No. of Private Baths: **5**
Double/pb: **$49**
Single/pb: **$39**
Suites: **$45**
Open: **All year**
Reduced Rates: **20%, seniors, families**
Breakfast: **Continental**
Credit Cards: **MC, VISA**
Pets: **Sometimes**
Children: **Welcome**
Smoking: **Permitted**
Social Drinking: **Permitted**
Airport/Station Pickup: **Yes**

Three Deer Inn is nestled in the base of Black Mountain and is surrounded by forest. The house is a newly built cedar A-frame with beautiful workmanship that includes a lovely cathedral ceiling. Your hosts want you to learn firsthand about the beauty, splendor, and hospitality found in the mountains of eastern Kentucky. They want to share good food, clean surroundings, and friendliness. Among the local attractions are the Little Shepard trail, a beautiful mountaintop gravel road that offers tremendous views of eastern Kentucky; the Hensley Settlement, a village located on the top of Stone Mountain; Daniel Boone National Forest; and Stone Canyon.

Ehrhardt's B&B ✪

285 SPRINGWELL DRIVE, PADUCAH, KENTUCKY 42001

Tel: **(502) 554-0644**
Best Time to Call: **7–9 AM; 4–6 PM**
Host(s): **Eileen and Phil Ehrhardt**
Location: **1 mi. from I-24**
No. of Rooms: **2**
Max. No. Sharing Bath: **4**
Double/sb: **$30**
Single/sb: **$25**
Open: **All year**
Reduced Rates: **10%, seniors**
Breakfast: **Full**
Other Meals: **Available**
Pets: **No**
Children: **Welcome, over 12**
Smoking: **Permitted**
Social Drinking: **Permitted**
Airport/Station Pickup: **Yes**

This brick Colonial ranch home is just a mile off I-24, which is famous for its beautiful scenery. Your hosts hope to make you feel at home in antique-filled bedrooms and a fireplaced den. Homemade biscuits, jellies, country ham and gravy are breakfast specialties. Enjoy swimming and boating at nearby Lake Barkley, Ky Lake, and Land between the Lakes. Fine dining and Paducah's historic riverfront are nearby.

LOUISIANA

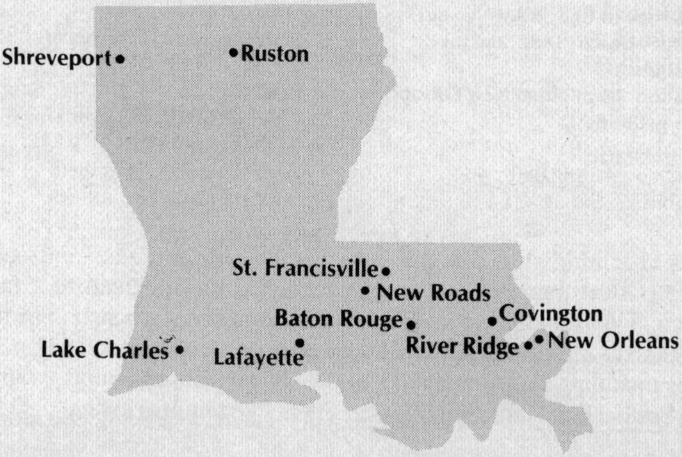

Southern Comfort Bed & Breakfast ✪

2856 HUNDRED OAKS, BATON ROUGE, LOUISIANA 70808

For Information: **(504) 346-1928 or 928-9815**
For Reservation: **800-523-1181, #, Dial Tone, 722**
Best Time to Call: **8 AM–8 PM**
Coordinators: **Susan Morris and Helen Heath**
State/Regions Covered: **Louisiana—Statewide; Mississippi—Natchez, Vicksburg, Port Gibson**

Rates (Single/Double):

Modest:	**\$30–\$40**	**\$35–\$45**
Average:	**\$45–\$55**	**\$50–\$60**
Luxury:	**\$65–\$80**	**\$65–\$150**

Credit Cards: **MC, VISA**

Susan and Helen offer you the best of the old and the new South with hosts in urban and rural areas. The above is only a sample list. Special attractions are Civil War and other historic sites; fabulous New Orleans; Acadian (Cajun) country; sports, deep-sea fishing, and racetracks in Louisiana and New Mexico. Their descriptive directory is $3.

Joy's B & B ✪

4920 PERKINS ROAD, BATON ROUGE, LOUISIANA 70808

Tel: **(504) 766-2291**
Best Time to Call: **6 AM; Noon**
Host(s): **Coach "Dub" and Joy Robinson**
Location: **85 mi. from New Orleans**
No. of Rooms: **2**
No. of Private Baths: **1**
Max. No. Sharing Bath: **4**
Double/sb: **$47.50**
Single/sb: **$37.50**
Open: **All year**
Reduced Rates: **15%, seniors**
Breakfast: **Full**
Pets: **No**
Children: **Welcome, over 12**
Smoking: **Permitted**
Social Drinking: **Permitted**
Airport/Station Pickup: **Yes**

This charming stucco home is furnished with antiques and collectibles. Guest quarters are on the second floor and feature a family room, TV, and kitchen facilities. Your hosts serve a hearty, Southern breakfast with pride. They will gladly direct you to interesting nearby sites including the Atchafalaya basin, the largest hardwood swamp in the South. Louisiana State University is five minutes away.

Plantation Bell Guest House ✪

204 WEST 24th AVENUE, COVINGTON, LOUISIANA 70433

Tel: **(504) 892-1952**
Best Time to Call: **Before 8 AM**
Host(s): **Lila Rapier**
Location: **35 mi. N of New Orleans**
No. of Rooms: **3**
No. of Private Baths: **3**
Double/pb: **$40**
Single/pb: **$35**
Open: **All year**
Reduced Rates: **$5 less on 2nd night**
Breakfast: **Full**
Pets: **Sometimes**
Children: **Welcome**
Smoking: **Permitted**
Social Drinking: **Permitted**

This late Victorian house has an old-fashioned porch with rocking chairs overlooking a quiet street. Inside, the ceilings are 13 feet high, and the old-time fans add to the nostalgic motif. The guest rooms are decorated with cheerful wallpapers and are comfortably air-conditioned. Local possibilities include canoeing, cycling, and shopping in Covington. You are welcome to use the kitchen for light snacks.

Bois des Chenes (Oakwoods) Plantation ✪
538 NORTH STERLING, LAFAYETTE, LOUISIANA 70501

Tel: **(318) 233-7816**
Best Time to Call: **8 AM–5 PM**
Host(s): **Marjorie and Coerte Voorhies**
Location: **140 mi. N of New Orleans**
No. of Rooms: **3**
No. of Private Baths: **3**
Double/pb: **$85**
Single/pb: **$75**
Suite: **$110**
Open: **All year**
Reduced Rates: **10%, seniors**
Breakfast: **Full**
Credit Cards: **AMEX, MC, VISA**
Pets: **Sometimes**
Children: **Welcome (crib)**
Smoking: **No**
Social Drinking: **Permitted**
Airport/Station Pickup: **Yes**

This Victorian carriage house (circa 1825) is furnished with a pleasant blend of Louisiana antiques and French Provincial reproductions. Located on a historic plantation listed on the National Register, it is within an easy drive of many Acadian points of interest, including St. Martinville, the home of Longfellow's Evangeline. Coerte is a petroleum geologist who collects guns and samurai swords. Marjorie weaves, spins cloth, deals in antiques, and is a gourmet cook. Breakfast is certain to be a Cajun feast! In the evening, after-dinner drinks and chocolates are graciously offered. A two-night minimum stay is required.

Bed & Breakfast, Inc. ✪
1360 MOSS STREET, BOX 52257, NEW ORLEANS, LOUISIANA 70152-2257

Tel: **(504) 525-4640 or 800-228-9711/Dial Tone: 184**
Coordinator: **Hazell Boyce**
States/Regions Covered: **New Orleans**

Rates (Single/Double):

	Single	Double
Modest:	**$25–$35**	**$35–$40**
Average:	**$35–$55**	**$40–$50**
Luxury:	**$50 and up**	**$60 and up**

Credit Cards: **No**

New Orleans is called the "City That Care Forgot." You are certain to be carefree, visiting the French Quarter, taking Mississippi riverboat rides, taking plantation tours, as well as dining in fine restaurants or attending jazz concerts. Hazell's hosts will help you get the most out of your stay.

New Orleans Bed & Breakfast ✪

P.O. BOX 8163, NEW ORLEANS, LOUISIANA 70182

Tel: **(504) 822-5038 or 5046**
Best Time to Call: **8 AM–7 PM**
Coordinator: **Sarah-Margaret Brown**
States/Regions Covered:
Louisiana—Covington, Lafayette, Jeanerette, Mendeville, New Iberia, New Orleans

Rates (Single/Double):
Modest: **$25–$35** **$30–$45**
Average: **$35–$55** **$45–$55**
Luxury: **$55 and up** **$55–$150**
Credit Cards: **MC, VISA (for deposits only)**

Sarah-Margaret offers a range from the youth-hostel type for the backpacker crowd, to modest accommodations in all areas of the city, to deluxe B&Bs in lovely and historic locations. If the past intrigues you, treat yourself to an overnight stay in a great Louisiana plantation home.

Jensen's Bed & Breakfast ✪

1631 SEVENTH STREET, NEW ORLEANS, LOUISIANA 70115

Tel: **(504) 897-1895**
Best Time to Call: **7 AM–10 AM; 6 PM–9 PM**
Host(s): **Shirley, Joni, and Bruce Jensen**
No. of Rooms: **3**
Max. No. Sharing Bath: **4**
Double/sb: **$45**

Single/sb: **$35**
Open: **All year**
Breakfast: **Continental**
Pets: **No**
Children: **Welcome**
Smoking: **Permitted**
Social Drinking: **Permitted**

Your hosts have drawn on their backgrounds as an interior decorator, piano teacher, and renovator of vintage homes, to restore this Victorian mansion. Stained glass, 12-foot alcove ceilings, antiques, a grand piano, raised-panel-pocket doors, and carefully chosen furnishings enhance the mansion. Located across the street from the Garden District, an area famed for its lovely homes, it is just a block to the trolley, which will whisk you to the French Quarter, Audubon Park, the zoo, or Tulane University. Breakfast is likely to feature banana cornbread or fried bananas, seasonal fruit, and Louisiana-style coffee. The mansion is air-conditioned for your summer comfort, and you are welcome to use the piano and TV. Rates increase to $65 during Mardi Gras and the Jazz Festival.

Terrell House ✪

1441 MAGAZINE STREET, NEW ORLEANS, LOUISIANA 70130

Tel: **(504) 524-9859**
Host(s): **Stephen and Diana Young**
Location: **½ mi. from I-10**
No. of Rooms: **10**
No. of Private Baths: **10**
Double/pb: **$50–$75**
Single/pb: **$40–$65**
Suites: **$85**
Guest Cottage: **$50, for 2**
Open: **All year**
Breakfast: **Continental**
Credit Cards: **AMEX, MC, VISA**
Pets: **No**
Children: **Welcome, over 13**
Smoking: **Permitted**
Social Drinking: **Permitted**

Built in 1858, this faithfully restored mansion offers antique furnishings with modern conveniences. The twin parlors and the formal dining room, with gas chandeliers, gold mirrors, marble mantels, and period furnishings, capture the grace of yesteryear. All the guest rooms open onto balconies and the landscaped courtyard. They all have telephones, color television, and central air conditioning. Located in the historic Lower Garden District, it's convenient to public transportation that will bring you to the French Quarter. Complimentary cocktails and other refreshments are graciously offered.

Pointe Coupee Bed and Breakfast ✪

605 EAST MAIN STREET, NEW ROADS, LOUISIANA 70760

Tel: **(504) 638-6254**
Host(s): **The Rev. and Mrs. Miller Armstrong**
Location: **35 mi. NW of Baton Rouge**
No. of Rooms: **12**
No. of Private Baths: **9**
Max. No. Sharing Bath: **5**
Double/pb: **$45**
Single/pb: **$40**
Double/sb: **$45**
Single/sb: **$40**
Open: **All year**
Reduced Rates: **Available**
Breakfast: **Full**
Pets: **Sometimes**
Children: **Welcome**
Smoking: **No**
Social Drinking: **Permitted**

Mrs. Miller Armstrong offers accommodations in three restored historic homes. They are: the Bondy House (1902), the Hebert House (1902), and the Claiborne House (1835). All three are modestly furnished and have facilities for parties and socializing. Guests will be treated to a hearty breakfast that includes local honey and cane syrup, dark roast coffee and chicory. Mrs. Miller Armstrong will gladly arrange tours of this historic area, which was settled by followers of La Salle and Iberville. After you tour the historic sights, the recreational ones await you, including False River and the great Mississippi, where the riverboats *Delta Queen* and *Mississippi Queen* dock weekly.

The Levee View ✪

39 HENNESEY COURT, RIVER RIDGE, LOUISIANA 70123

Tel: **(504) 737-5471**
Host(s): **Jack and Clemence Devereux**
Location: **10 mi. E of New Orleans**
No. of Rooms: **2**
No. of Private Baths: **1**
Max. No. Sharing Bath: **4**
Double/pb: **$30**
Single/pb: **$25**
Double/sb: **$25**
Single/sb: **$20**
Suites: **$45**
Open: **All year**
Reduced Rates: **10%, seniors; weekly**
Breakfast: **Continental**
Pets: **No**
Children: **Welcome**
Smoking: **Permitted**
Airport/Station Pickup: **Yes**

The Devereuxs welcome you to their contemporary home, located in a convenient residential suburb of New Orleans. The house is large and attractive, with comfortable family furnishings. Guest quarters are located in a two-story wing with separate entrance, ensuring visitors plenty of privacy and quiet. Breakfast specialties include homemade breads, croissants, and plenty of hot coffee. If you like, you can relax outside on the patio or sip a drink in the gazebo. The levee bordering the Mississippi River is less than 100 feet from the house; many lovely plantation homes are also located nearby. Your hosts will gladly guide you to the best restaurants and shops and will occasionally baby-sit for the kids while you go out on the town.

Twin Gables ✪

711 NORTH VIENNA STREET, RUSTON, LOUISIANA 71270

Tel: **(318) 255-4452**
Host(s): **Carol Hudson**
Location: **2/10 mi. from I-20**
No. of Rooms: **5**
No. of Private Baths: **5**
Double/pb: **$45–$50**
Single/pb: **$40–$45**
Open: **All year**
Reduced Rates: **10%, seniors**
Breakfast: **Continental**
Credit Cards: **MC, VISA**
Pets: **No**
Children: **Welcome, over 12**
Smoking: **No**
Social Drinking: **Permitted**
Airport/Station Pickup: **Yes**

Built in 1882, this refurbished Victorian mansion will please discriminating visitors. Antiques, good paintings, and lots of plants are used in the decor. Teapots and cakes are available for afternoon tea, and the kitchen may be used for snacks. Carol will allow you the use of the washer-dryer to freshen your travel wardrobe. D'Arbonne Lake, Claiborne Lake, and the Sandy Hill Golf Club are close by, as is Louisiana Tech University.

Cottage Plantation ✪

ROUTE 5, BOX 425, ST. FRANCISVILLE, LOUISIANA 70775

Tel: **(504) 635-3674**
Host(s): **Mr. & Mrs. H. M. Brown**
Location: **35 mi. N of Baton Rouge**
No. of Rooms: **6**
No. of Private Baths: **6**
Double/pb: **$70**
Single/pb: **$50**
Open: **All year**
Breakfast: **Full**
Credit Cards: **MC, VISA**
Other Meals: **Available**
Pets: **No**
Children: **Welcome**
Smoking: **Permitted**
Social Drinking: **Permitted**

This sprawling antebellum home is a working plantation listed on the National Register of Historic Places. Andrew Jackson once slept here, and today you can see much of the same furnishings he did. A full Southern-style breakfast is offered. Guests are welcome to tour the original outbuildings built over a century ago. Nearby attractions include Audubon Memorial Park and the historic sites of St. Francisville.

The St. Francisville Inn ✪

118 NORTH COMMERCE, DRAWER 1369, ST. FRANCISVILLE, LOUISIANA 70775

Tel: **(504) 635-6502**
Host(s): **Florence and Dick Fillet**
Location: **24 mi. N of Baton Rouge**
No. of Rooms: **9**
No. of Private Baths: **9**
Double/pb: **$55**

Single/pb: **$45**
Suite: **$55**
Open: **All year**
Reduced Rates: **10%, seniors**
Breakfast: **Continental**
Other Meals: **Available**
Credit Cards: **AMEX, MC, VISA**
Pets: **No**
Children: **Welcome (crib)**
Smoking: **Permitted**
Social Drinking: **Permitted**

The St. Francisville Inn is located in the heart of plantation country in a town that is listed on the National Register of Historic Places. The inn is a Victorian Gothic known as the Wolf-Schlesinger House, built circa 1880. The air-conditioned guest rooms are furnished in lovely antiques and each opens onto a New Orleans–style courtyard out back. Breakfast includes fabulous pastries from a local bakery. Florence is an antique-print dealer, whose specialty is Audubon.

Fairfield Place ✪

2221 FAIRFIELD AVENUE, SHREVEPORT, LOUISIANA 71104

Tel: **(318) 222-0048**
Host(s): **Janie Lipscomb**
Location: **½ mi. from I-20**
No. of Rooms: **6**
No. of Private Baths: **6**
Double/pb: **$65–$80**
Single/pb: **$55–$65**
Open: **All year**
Breakfast: **Continental**
Credit Cards: **AMEX, MC, VISA**
Pets: **No**
Children: **Sometimes**
Smoking: **Permitted**
Social Drinking: **Permitted**
Airport/Station Pickup: **Yes**

You will enjoy this elegant 1900s inn where the legendary hospitality of the Deep South rings true. Begin your day with New Orleans coffee, croissants and strawberry butter, and French pastries. Janie's home features lambskin rugs, king-size beds, 19th-century paintings, Swedish crystal, and designer sheets and linens. It is located in the beautiful Highland Historical Restoration District, convenient to the business district, medical center, and airport. Louisiana Downs Racetrack is minutes away.

The Columns on Jordan ✪

615 JORDAN, SHREVEPORT, LOUISIANA 71101

Tel: **(318) 222-5912**
Best Time to Call: **11 AM; After 5 PM**
Host(s): **Judith and Edwin Simonton**
Location: **½ mi. from I-20**
No. of Rooms: **5**
No. or Private Baths: **3**
Max. No. Sharing Bath: **4**
Double/pb: **$68**

Single/pb: **$64**
Double/sb: **$58**
Single/sb: **$54**
Open: **All year**
Reduced Rates: **10%, clergy; faculty; seniors**
Breakfast: **Full**
Credit Cards: **AMEX, MC, VISA**
Pets: **Sometimes**
Children: **No**
Smoking: **Permitted**
Social Drinking: **Permitted**
Foreign Languages: **Spanish**

At the Columns, you will sleep in the splendor of a spacious room, authentically furnished with period pieces. You'll awaken to enjoy your morning coffee and newspaper on the upstairs porch overlooking the stately magnolias or in the garden at poolside. Breakfast is graciously served in the morning room. Located within the Highland Restoration area, the house is listed on the National Register of Historic Places. The atmosphere is that of Southern charm and thoughtful hospitality as evidenced by the hair dryer, iron, and ironing board in each bedroom.

For key to listings, see inside front or back cover.

✪ This star means that rates are guaranteed through December 31, 1988 to any guest making a reservation as a result of reading about the B&B in *BED & BREAKFAST U.S.A.*—1988 edition.

Please enclose a self-addressed, stamped, business-sized envelope when contacting reservation services.

For more details on what you can expect in a B&B, see Chapter 1.

Always mention *Bed & Breakfast U.S.A.* when making reservations!

If no B&B is listed in the area you'll be visiting, use the form on page 698 to order a copy of our "List of New B&Bs."

We want to hear from you! Use the form on page 697.

MAINE

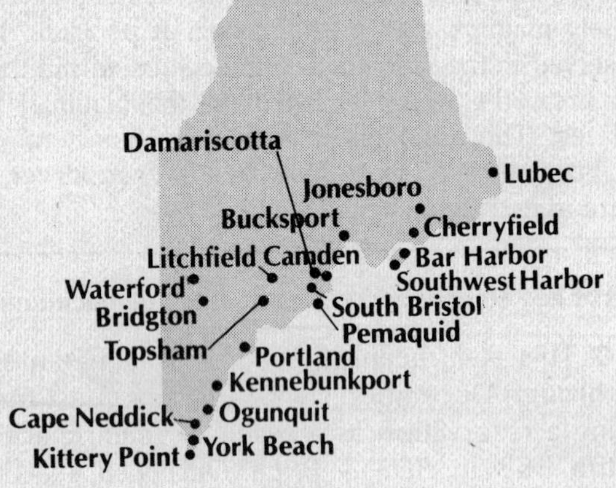

Bed & Breakfast Down East, Ltd.

BOX 547, MACOMBER MILL ROAD, EASTBROOK, MAINE 04634

Tel: **(207) 565-3517**
Coordinator: **Sally B. Godfrey**
States/Regions Covered: **Maine (statewide)**

Rates (Single/Double):

Modest:	**$25**	**$35**
Average:	**$30–$35**	**$40–$50**
Luxury:	**$40–$55**	**$65–$100**

Credit Cards: **AMEX, MC, VISA**

There are delightful accommodations waiting for you, from Kittery Point at the New Hampshire border to "way down East" in Eastport, near F.D.R.'s Campobello Island in New Brunswick, Canada. You are certain to enjoy Bar Harbor, Acadia National Park, the rugged coastline, and inland forests and streams. All of Sally's hosts will make you feel welcome.

Pointy Head Inn

ROUTE 102A, BASS HARBOR, MAINE 04653

Tel: **(207) 244-7261**
Best Time to Call: **9:30 AM–3 PM**
Host(s): **Doris and Warren Townsend**
Location: **18 mi. S of Bar Harbor**
No. of Rooms: **6**
No. of Private Baths: **1**
Max. No. Sharing Bath: **4**
Double/pb: **$55**
Double/sb: **$45**
Single/sb: **$30**
Open: **May 15–Oct.**
Breakfast: **Full**
Pets: **No**
Children: **Welcome, over 10**
Smoking: **No**
Social Drinking: **Permitted**
Airport/Station Pickup: **Yes**

In Colonial times a sea captain made his home here, overlooking beautiful Bass Harbor. Today, this sprawling inn is a haven for artists and photographers who appreciate the quiet side of Mount Desert Island. The house is decorated with nautical accents and homey furnishings. One of its special qualities is the beautiful sunsets that can be enjoyed from your room or the comfortable porch. The inn is set in a quaint fishing village bordering Acadia State Park. Swimming, canoeing, nature trails, fishing, and mountain climbing are just a few of the activities that can be enjoyed locally. A variety of restaurants, shops, and galleries are within walking distance.

"Glad II" ✪

60 PEARL STREET, BATH, MAINE 04530

Tel: **(207) 443-1191**
Host(s): **Gladys Lansky**
Location: **.7 mi. from US 1**
No. of Rooms: **2**
Max. No. Sharing Bath: **4**
Double/sb: **$35–$40**
Single/sb: **$30–$35**
Open: **All year**
Breakfast: **Continental**
Pets: **No**
Children: **Welcome, over 8 (in own room)**
Smoking: **No**
Social Drinking: **Permitted**

This spic-and-span white house with its crisp green trim is comfortable and attractively furnished. Gladys delights in pleasing her guests with breakfasts featuring fresh homemade treats. You are welcome to play the piano, borrow a book from her library, and visit or watch TV in the parlors. It's an easy walk to the Maritime Museum, a short drive to Popham Beach, Reid State Park, Boothbay Harbor, and the Brunswick Naval Air Station. Bowdoin College is eight miles away.

Horatio Johnson House

36 CHURCH STREET, BELFAST, MAINE 04915

Tel: **(207) 338-5153**
Host(s): **Helen and Gene Kirby**
Location: **30 mi. S of Bangor**
No. of Rooms: **3**
No. of Private Baths: **3**
Double/pb: **$40**
Open: **All year**
Breakfast: **Full**
Pets: **No**
Children: **No**
Smoking: **Permitted**
Social Drinking: **Permitted**
Airport/Station Pickup: **Yes**

While the rest of the world is rushing ahead, the small seafaring town of Belfast is rediscovering its past. The waterfront and old town buildings are being refurbished to reflect the way things used to be. Your hosts offer good company and comfortable lodging in a 19th-century home five minutes from the ocean. The Kirbys offer a variety of breakfast specialties such as Belgian waffles and blueberry pancakes. They will gladly recommend flea markets, antique shops, and restaurants galore.

Four Seasons Inn

UPPER MAIN STREET, P.O. BOX 390, BETHEL, MAINE 04217

Tel: **(207) 824-2755**
Host(s): **Sandy and Jack Mahon**
Location: **50 mi. from Augusta**
No. of Rooms: **10**
Max. No. Sharing Bath: **4**
Double/sb: **$50 and up**
Single/sb: **$40 and up**
Open: **All year**
Reduced Rates: **10%, seniors**
Breakfast: **Full**
Minimum stay: **2 days**
Credit Cards: **AMEX, DC, MC, VISA**
Pets: **No**
Children: **Welcome, over 12**
Smoking: **No**
Social Drinking: **Permitted**

Guests are welcomed to this sprawling Victorian mansion with a drink served by the parlor fire. You may choose from ten antique-filled rooms complete with fresh flowers, fruit baskets, and candies on your pillow. In the morning, fresh coffee is available in the privacy of your room. When you're awake, come down to the dining room for flaming fruit compote, eggs Benedict, and ham-and-asparagus-filled crêpes. Rates include guest privileges at the nearby country club, with a regulation nine-hole golf course, tennis courts, swimming pool, sailing, and sauna. The Four Seasons borders on the White Mountain National Forest and is only minutes away from Sunday River and Mt. Abram ski areas. You'll enjoy the many waterfalls, covered bridges, and lakes in the area. After a day of activity, your hosts invite you to an old-fashioned afternoon tea served with petits fours and other goodies.

Kenniston Hill Inn ✪

ROUTE 27, BOOTHBAY, MAINE 04537

Tel: **(207) 633-2159**
Host(s): **Paul and Ellen Morissette**
Location: **50 mi. N of Portland**
No. of Rooms: **8**
No. of Private Baths: **8**
Double/pb: **$55–$75**
Single/pb: **$45–$65**
Open: **Apr.–Dec.**
Breakfast: **Full**
Credit Cards: **MC, VISA**
Pets: **No**
Children: **Welcome, over 12**
Smoking: **Permitted**
Social Drinking: **Permitted**

Kenniston Hill Inn is a white clapboard mansion dating back to 1786. The house is warm and gracious, with a large front porch and open-hearth fireplace. The bedrooms, four with fireplaces, are tastefully decorated with handmade quilts, delicately colored wallpapers, and fresh flowers. Your hosts are former restaurant owners from Vermont. They offer sumptuous breakfast specialties such as zucchini-and-walnut pancakes and a vegetable frittata. The inn is surrounded by woods and gardens, but is within easy reach of shops, restaurants, boat rides, horseback riding, and tennis.

North Woods Bed & Breakfast ✪

55 NORTH HIGH STREET, BRIDGTON, MAINE 04009

Tel: **(207) 647-2100**
Host(s): **Bob and Roxanne Palmer**
Location: **36 mi. W of Portland**
No. of Rooms: **4**
Max. No. Sharing Bath: **4**
Double/sb: **$50**
Single/sb: **$45**
Open: **All year**
Breakfast: **Continental**
Pets: **No**
Children: **Welcome (crib)**
Smoking: **No**
Social Drinking: **Permitted**

An authentic 13-room Victorian dating back to 1874 awaits you in the heart of the Lakes Region. The spacious guest rooms are furnished with lovely antiques, collectibles, and decorative items, all of which are for sale. Enjoy a glass of wine in the old-fashioned parlor, with its cozy armchairs and love seats. A sitting room with TV set is located upstairs for guests. An assortment of fresh fruit, homemade breads, and pastries is served in a sunny dining room with a bay window and period furnishings. North Woods is convenient to Highland Lake and just minutes from tennis and golf at the local country club. Winter guests enjoy alpine and cross-country skiing at Pleasant Mountain.

L'ermitage ✪

219 MAIN STREET, BUCKSPORT, MAINE 04416

Tel: **(207) 469-3361**
Host(s): **Veronique and Richard Melsheimer**
Location: **19 mi. E of Bangor; .8 mi. from US 1**
No. of Rooms: **3**
Max. No. Sharing Bath: **2**
Double/sb: **$40**
Single/sb: **$30**
Open: **All year**
Reduced Rates: **20%, off-season**
Breakfast: **Full**
Other Meals: **Available**
Credit Cards: **MC, VISA**
Pets: **No**
Children: **No**
Smoking: **Permitted**
Social Drinking: **Permitted**
Foreign Languages: **French**

L'ermitage is a 19th-century white Colonial with black shutters, dating back to the 1830s. Your hosts, Veronique and Richard Melsheimer, have patterned their inn after those found in Europe. The spacious rooms are furnished in period antiques, Oriental carpets, and collectibles. A small, reasonably priced restaurant is on the premises and features an extensive wine list. L'ermitage is on Penobscot Bay, near Ft. Knox.

Chestnut House

69 CHESTNUT STREET, CAMDEN, MAINE 04843

Tel: **(207) 236-6137**
Best Time to Call: **Daytime**
Host(s): **June and Chuck Fryer**
No. of Rooms: **3**
Double/pb: **$65**
Single/pb: **$45**
Open: **All year**
Reduced Rates: **Available**
Breakfast: **Full**
Pets: **No**
Children: **Welcome**
Smoking: **Permitted**
Social Drinking: **Permitted**
Airport/Station Pickup: **Yes**

Chestnut House is a lovely old Dutch Colonial, slightly off the beaten path, yet close to Camden's attractions. The rooms have been completely refurbished and guests may choose from comfortable twin or queen-size beds. Breakfast can be a hearty or light meal; either choice includes a variety of home-baked goods. Camden is a strikingly beautiful seacoast village with fine restaurants, historic homes, and a lovely harbor. An indoor pool and squash and racquetball courts are just down the street from Chestnut House; golf, tennis, and boating are also nearby. Your hosts are happy to help plan your day. Join them for afternoon refreshments or an evening by the living room fire.

Hawthorn Inn

9 HIGH STREET, CAMDEN, MAINE 04843

Tel: **(207) 236-8842**
Best Time to Call: **9 AM–8 PM**
Host(s): **Pauline and Brad Staub**
Location: **On Rte. 1, 150 mi. N of Boston**
No. of Rooms: **5**
No. of Private Baths: **2**
Max. No. Sharing Bath: **4**
Double/pb: **$75**
Double/sb: **$60–$65**
Open: **All year**
Reduced Rates: **$10 less daily, Nov. 1–May 25**
Breakfast: **Full**
Credit Cards: **MC, VISA**
Pets: **No**
Children: **Welcome, over 12**
Smoking: **Permitted**
Social Drinking: **Permitted**
Airport/Station Pickup: **Yes**

The airy rooms of this Victorian inn are an elegant mixture of the old and the new. Guests are welcome to wine or coffee while relaxing on the deck or getting warm by the fire. Breakfast is served in a sunny dining room. All rooms overlook either Mt. Battie or Camden Harbor. A score of sports can be enjoyed in the area, and shops and restaurants are a short walk away.

Maine Stay Bed and Breakfast

22 HIGH STREET, CAMDEN, MAINE 04843

Tel: **(207) 236-9636**
Best Time to Call: **After noon**
Host(s): **Sally and Bob Tierney**
Location: **97 mi. NE of Portland**
No. of Rooms: **8**
Max. No. Sharing Bath: **4**
Double/sb: **$40–$60**
Single/sb: **$35**
Open: **All year**
Reduced Rates: **10%, seniors; weekly**
Breakfast: **Full**
Pets: **No**
Children: **Welcome, over 10**
Smoking: **Permitted**
Social Drinking: **Permitted**
Foreign Languages: **French**

This is one of Camden's treasured Colonials, built in 1813. Choose from seven large bedrooms decorated with period pieces. Relax with a cup of coffee or catch up on a book in one of the spacious parlors. Breakfast is served on an attractive deck in warm weather. It's only a five-minute walk to the shops, restaurants and Camden Harbor. Windjammer cruises, a Shakespeare theater, skiing, and Camden Hills State Park are just a few of the local attractions.

Wooden Goose Inn

RTE. 1, BOX 195, CAPE NEDDICK, MAINE 03902

Tel: **(207) 363-5673**
Host(s): **Jerry D. Rippetoe, Anthony V. Sienicki**
Location: **3/4 mi. from I-95, 70 mi. N of Boston**
No. of Rooms: **6**
No. of Private Baths: **6**
Double/pb: **$85**
Suites: **$120**
Open: **Feb. 1–Dec. 31**
Breakfast: **Full**
Pets: **No**
Children: **Welcome, over 12**
Smoking: **Permitted**
Social Drinking: **Permitted**
Airport/Station Pickup: **Yes**

This 19th-century farmhouse was built by a sea captain. It is decorated with porcelain, crystal, and Oriental rugs. Guests are served afternoon tea with croissants and pâté, and the coffeepot is always on. Breakfast might feature either eggs Benedict or Florentine, and sausage. Portsmouth and Ogunquit are nearby.

Ricker House ✪

PARK STREET, P.O. BOX 256, CHERRYFIELD, MAINE 04622

Tel: **(207) 546-2780**
Host(s): **William and Jean Conway**
Location: **32 mi. E of Ellsworth**
No. of Rooms: **3**
Max. No. Sharing Bath: **5**
Double/sb: **$40**
Single/sb: **$35**
Open: **All year**
Reduced Rates: **Available**
Breakfast: **Full**
Pets: **No**
Children: **Welcome (crib)**
Smoking: **No**
Social Drinking: **Permitted**
Airport/Station Pickup: **Yes**

Built in 1803, this comfortable Georgian Colonial has grounds that border the Narraguagus River, one of the best salmon rivers in the States. The village is quaint and historic, and it is fun to tour it on foot or by bike. Reasonable restaurants offer great menus and all feature fabulous local lobster. Your hosts have canoed every river, swum every lake, climbed every mountain, and visited every village in their hometown area, and they will be pleased to help you get the most out of your visit.

Brannon-Bunker Inn

HCR 64, BOX 045L, DAMARISCOTTA, MAINE 04543

Tel: **(207) 563-5941**
Host(s): **Jeanne and Joseph Hovance**
No. of Rooms: **7**
No. of Private Baths: **5**
Max. No. Sharing Bath: **4**
Single/pb: **$45**
Double/sb: **$42**
Single/sb: **$37**
Suites: **$55–$90**
Open: **All year**
Reduced Rates: **Available**
Breakfast: **Continental**
Credit Cards: **MC, VISA**
Pets: **Sometimes**
Children: **Welcome**
Smoking: **Permitted**
Social Drinking: **Permitted**

The Brannon-Bunker Inn is an informal, relaxing inn, ideally situated in rural, coastal Maine. Guests may choose from accommodations in the main 1820 Cape House, the 1900 converted barn, or the carriage house across the stream. Each room is individually decorated in styles ranging from Colonial to Victorian. Hosts Jeanne and Joseph Hovance will help you plan your days over breakfast. Nearby activities include golf, ocean swimming at Pemaquid Beach Park, and fishing on the Damariscotta River.

Isaac Randall House ✪

INDEPENDENCE DRIVE, FREEPORT, MAINE 04032

Tel: **(207) 865-9295**
Best Time to Call: **Noon**
Host(s): **Glynrose and Jim Friedlander**
Location: **16 mi. NE of Portland**
No. of Rooms: **8**
No. of Private Baths: **6**
Max. No. Sharing Bath: **4**
Double/pb: **$55–$75**
Single/pb: **$50–$70**
Double/sb: **$45–$65**
Single/sb: **$40–$60**
Open: **All year**
Breakfast: **Full**
Pets: **Sometimes**
Children: **Welcome (crib)**
Smoking: **Limited**
Social Drinking: **Permitted**
Airport/Station Pickup: **Yes**
Foreign Languages: **Spanish**

One hundred sixty years ago, this Federal-style farmhouse was built as a wedding gift for Isaac Randall, Jr., and his young bride. It later became a stopover on the underground railroad and then a Depression-era dance hall. Today, guests are welcomed to a charming, antiques-filled home set on five wooded acres. The grounds include a spring-fed pond, perfect for ice skating. Hiking and cross-country ski trails start at the front door. Breakfast specialties such as fruit compote, homemade breads, blueberry pancakes, coffee, and assorted teas are served in the country kitchen. Downtown Freeport, home of L. L. Bean, is within walking distance. Maine's beautiful coast, summer theater, Bowdoin College, and Freeport Harbor are just a short drive away. After a day of activity, join your hosts for an evening snack back at the inn.

Chandler River Lodge ✪

ROUTE #1, JONESBORO, MAINE 04648

Tel: **(207) 434-2651; (July and Aug. only); (201) 679-2778; (Sept.–June evenings)**
Host(s): **The Kerr Family**
Location: **50 mi. NE of Ellsworth**
No. of Rooms: **6**
No. of Private Baths: **2**
Max. No. Sharing Bath: **3**
Double/pb: **$35**
Single/pb: **$30**
Open: **July and August**
Breakfast: **Continental**
Pets: **Welcome**
Children: **Welcome**
Smoking: **Permitted**
Social Drinking: **Permitted**

This 18th-century farmhouse is set on 30 acres overlooking the Chandler River. The lodge has comfortable rooms, a cozy den with fireplace, and a sitting porch for enjoying the summer breeze. Your hosts invite you to boat, fish, and swim in the river and will help arrange for tours and deep-sea fishing. The children will want to wander the beautifully landscaped property and will enjoy evenings popping corn by the fire. Homemade breads and muffins are served each morning. The Kerrs will gladly direct you to local craft fairs and the seven wonders of the East Coast.

Arundel Meadows Inn ✪

P.O. BOX 1129, KENNEBUNK, MAINE 04043

Tel: **(207) 985-3770**
Best Time to Call: **Before 5 PM**
Host(s): **Mark Bachelder, Murray Yaeger**
Location: **2 mi. N of Kennebunk**
No. of Rooms: **6**
No. of Private Baths: **6**
Double/pb: **$55–$65**
Suites: **$65–$80**
Open: **All year**
Breakfast: **Full**
Pets: **Sometimes**
Children: **Welcome, over 11**
Smoking: **Permitted**
Social Drinking: **Permitted**

The Arundel Meadows Inn is situated on three and a half acres next to the Kennebunk River. Murray, a professor at Boston University, and Mark, a professional chef, have always loved this area, and it is a dream come true for them to watch others enjoy it. They renovated this 165-year-old house themselves and meticulously planned the decor. Several guest rooms have fireplaces and one suite sleeps four.

Mark's beautifully prepared breakfast specialties, such as brioche, quiche, eggs Benedict, or French toast, are the perfect start for your day. It's just three minutes to the center of town and about ten to Kennebunk Beach. In the afternoon, come back to the inn for tea and enjoy pâtés, homemade sweets, and beverages.

1802 House Bed & Breakfast Inn ✪

LOCKE STREET, P.O. BOX 646-A, KENNEBUNKPORT, MAINE 04046

Tel: **(207) 967-5632**
Best Time to Call: **8 AM–9 PM**
Host(s): **Charlotte Houle**
Location: **22 mi. S of Portland**
No. of Rooms: **8**
No. of Private Baths: **8**
Double/pb: **$69–$84**
Single/pb: **$69–$74**
Open: **All year**
Reduced Rates: **10%, weekly**
Breakfast: **Full**
Credit Cards: **AMEX, MC, VISA**
Pets: **No**
Children: **Welcome, over 12**
Smoking: **Permitted**
Social Drinking: **Permitted**

Tastefully decorated in Colonial style, some of the bedrooms have working fireplaces. The sound of a ship's bell will beckon you to a sumptuous breakfast that might feature sesame French toast or a stack of pancakes with blueberry sauce. In spring, visit the Rachel Carson Wildlife Refuge; in fall, the foliage is glorious; in winter, cross-country ski from the doorstep and return for mulled cider by the fireside; in summer, take in the theater, or swim at the shore. Charlotte will pamper you in all seasons. There is a two-night minimum on weekends.

The Green Heron Inn

DRAWER 151, OCEAN AVENUE, KENNEBUNKPORT, MAINE 04046

Tel: **(207) 967-3315**
Best Time to Call: **Evenings**
Host(s): **Virginia and Wallace Reid**
Location: **4½ mi. from U.S. 1**
No. of Rooms: **10**
No. of Private Baths: **10**
Double/pb: **$36–$44**
Single/pb: **$23.50–$31.50**
Suite: **$52**
Guest Cottage: **$53–$78; sleeps 4 or more**
Open: **June 6–Oct. 12**
Reduced Rates: **15%, weekly**
Breakfast: **Full**
Pets: **Welcome**
Children: **Welcome (crib)**
Smoking: **Permitted**
Social Drinking: **Permitted**
Airport/Station Pickup: **Yes**

This immaculate inn (circa 1908) with its inviting porch and striped awnings, furnished simply and comfortably, is located between the river and the ocean in this Colonial resort village. The full Yankee breakfast is a rib-buster! This is a saltwater fisherman's heaven, with boating, golf, swimming, and tennis all nearby, close to shops and galleries. Virginia and Wallace will be happy to suggest the best place for lobster. Reserve early, because this is a super value in this resort town.

Harbour Watch ✪

FOLLETT LANE, RFD 1, BOX 42, KITTERY POINT, MAINE 03905

Tel: **(207) 439-3242**
Host(s): **Marian and Robert Craig**
Location: **50 mi. S of Portland**
No. of Rooms: **3**
Max. No. Sharing Bath: **3**
Double/pb: **$50**
Open: **Apr.–Oct.**
Breakfast: **Continental**
Pets: **No**
Children: **Welcome, over 14**
Smoking: **Permitted**
Social Drinking: **Permitted**

This beautiful sea captain's house has been in Marian's family since 1797. The harbor views from the property are an ever-changing panorama of lobstermen pulling their traps, sailboat races, the Sunday morning rowing club, and the boat that cruises to the Isle of Shoals. It's a 10-minute drive to Portsmouth, New Hampshire, with historic Strawbery Banke and the Prescott Park summer art and theater series. York Beach is only nine miles away along the coast.

Old Tavern Inn ✪

POST ROAD, P.O. BOX 445, LITCHFIELD, MAINE 04350

Tel: **(207) 268-4965**
Host(s): **Virginia Albert**
Location: **12 mi. SW of Augusta**
No. of Rooms: **6**
Max. No. Sharing Bath: **4**
Double/sb: **$30**
Single/sb: **$27**
Open: **All year**
Breakfast: **Full**
Credit Cards: **MC, VISA**
Pets: **Sometimes**
Children: **Welcome**
Smoking: **Permitted**
Social Drinking: **Permitted**

Virginia's home was built as a tavern in 1808, and the hitching posts that flank it go back to the time when stagecoach horses were tethered there. Furnished with traditional pieces, comfortable antiques, and plants, it is warm and cozy. There's a heated in-ground pool and a pond for fishing; it's an easy walk to Tacoma Lake for boating and fishing. Bates College is nearby.

Breakers-by-the-Bay ✪

37 WASHINGTON, LUBEC, MAINE 04652

Tel: **(207) 733-2487**
Host(s): **E. M. Elg**
Location: **100 mi. E of Bangor**
No. of Rooms: **4**
No. of Private Baths: **1**
Max. No. Sharing Bath: **6**
Double/pb: **$50**
Single/pb: **$40**
Double/sb: **$40**
Single/sb: **$30**
Open: **July 1–Sept. 30**
Reduced Rates: **10%, seniors**
Breakfast: **Full**
Pets: **No**
Children: **No**
Smoking: **Permitted**
Social Drinking: **No**

Breathtaking views of the sea and rocky shores of coastal Maine await you at this 100-year-old blue-and-white New England home. The house is located close to the International Bridge and Campobello, the place F.D.R. used to call his "beloved isle." Today his 34-room summer cottage is the center of the 2,800-acre Roosevelt Campobello International Park. Start your day off with homemade muffins and jellies served on a hand-crocheted tablecloth in the privacy of your room. Then choose from the beautiful vistas of Quoddy Head State Park, Campobello, or just sit back and enjoy the view of the bay. Your hostess will gladly recommend shops, scenic hiking trails, and places to swim and golf.

The Kingsleigh

P.O. BOX 1426, 100 MAIN STREET, SOUTHWEST HARBOR, MT. DESERT ISLAND, MAINE 04679

Tel: **(207) 244-5302**
Host(s): **Jim and Kathy King**
Location: **45 mi. E of Bangor**
No. of Rooms: **6**
No. of Private Baths: **4**
Max. No. Sharing Bath: **4**
Double/pb: **$75–$85**
Double/sb: **$55**
Open: **All year**
Reduced Rates: **$15–$20 less, May 1–June 30, Sept. 8–Oct. 30**
Breakfast: **Full**
Pets: **No**
Children: **Welcome, over 12**
Smoking: **No**
Social Drinking: **Permitted**

Built at the turn of the century, the Kingsleigh is a shingled and pebble-dash Colonial revival. The house is set high on a knoll overlooking magnificent Southwest Harbor, where generations of boatbuilders and fishermen have earned their living. Waverly wall coverings, lace window treatments, plush carpeting, and period furnishings provide a comfortable blend of the old and new. Afternoon tea is served on a wraparound porch overlooking the harbor, while you relax in a white wicker chair. Your hosts serve fresh coffee, imported teas, country omelets, oatmeal pancakes, and other specialties for breakfast. They take pleasure in welcoming you to Mt. Desert Island, and will gladly direct you to swimming, hiking, fishing expeditions, whale-watching, restaurants, and shopping.

Penury Hall ✪

BOX 68, MAIN STREET, SOUTHWEST HARBOR, MT. DESERT ISLAND, MAINE 04679

Tel: **(207) 244-7102**
Host(s): **Gretchen and Toby Strong**
No. of Rooms: **3**
Max. No. Sharing Bath: **3**
Double/sb: **$45**
Single/sb: **$37**
Open: **All year**
Reduced Rates: **Available, Sept. 15–June 30**
Breakfast: **Full**
Pets: **No**
Children: **Welcome, over 16**
Smoking: **Permitted**
Social Drinking: **Permitted**
Airport/Station Pickup: **Yes**

This gray frame house has a red door and a crisp, welcoming air. Built in 1830, it is comfortably furnished with traditional pieces, antiques, and original art. Gretchen and Toby are cosmopolitan and cordial. Their motto is: "Each guest is an honorary member of the family," and you'll soon feel at home. Knowledgeable about the area's highlights, they'll direct you to special shops and restaurants and all the best things to see and do.

Hearthside Inn ✪

7 HIGH STREET, BAR HARBOR, MT. DESERT ISLAND, MAINE 04609

Tel: **(207) 288-4533**
Host(s): **Susan and Barry Schwartz**
No. of Rooms: **9**
No. of Private Baths: **7**
Max. No. Sharing Bath: **4**
Double/pb: **$70–$100**
Double/sb: **$60–$65**
Open: **All year**
Reduced Rates: **No**
Breakfast: **Continental**
Credit Cards: **MC, VISA**
Pets: **No**
Children: **Welcome, over 10**
Smoking: **Permitted**
Social Drinking: **Permitted**

On a quiet street, just a short walk to town, is this gracious home, recently redecorated in the manner of a country cottage. You are invited to share the special ambience of a living room with a cozy fireplace and brimming with books, or the music room with its grand piano and game table. Some rooms have a balcony or a fireplace.

Complimentary iced tea, cheese, crackers, and wine are offered. Two-night minimum stay required during July and August.

Lindenwood Inn ✪

P.O. BOX 1328, SOUTHWEST HARBOR, MT. DESERT ISLAND, MAINE 04679

Tel: **(207) 244-5335**
Host(s): **Gardiner and Marilyn Brower**
No. of Rooms: **7**
No. of Private Baths: **3**
Max. No. Sharing Bath: **4**
Double/pb: **$60–$75**
Double/sb: **$45–$55**
Guest Cottage: **$95; sleeps 4**
Open: **All year**
Reduced Rates: **Nov. 1–June 1**
Breakfast: **Full**
Pets: **No**
Children: **Welcome, over 12 in inn; any age in cottage**
Smoking: **Permitted**
Social Drinking: **Permitted**

Built at the turn of the century as a sea captain's home, the inn derives its name from the stately linden trees that line the front lawn. Most rooms have fine harbor views, and all are comfortably furnished. Cool mornings are warmed by the glowing fireplace in the dining room, where you can enjoy a hearty breakfast. You are welcome to relax on the shaded porch or enjoy the pleasures of a good book or music in the parlor. You can explore the wonders of Acadia National Park, or ask your hosts to arrange for charter sailboat rides or bike rentals.

Oliver Farm Inn ✪

OLD ROUTE 1, BOX 136, NOBLEBORO, MAINE 04555

Tel: **(207) 563-1527**
Host(s): **Joyce, Dick, Karis, and Muffie**
Location: **2 mi. NE of Damariscotta; 1/2 mi. from Coastal Rte. 1**
No. of Rooms: **5**
No. of Private Baths: **1**
Max. No. Sharing Bath: **4**
Double/pb: **$55**
Single/pb: **$40**
Double/sb: **$47**
Single/sb: **$35**
Open: **June 30–Oct. 17**
Breakfast: **Full**
Pets: **No**
Children: **Welcome**
Smoking: **No**
Social Drinking: **Permitted**
Airport/Station Pickup: **Yes**

The inn is set on 20 rural acres overlooking the Great Salt Bay. Partly Victorian, with an older wing built in 1795, it was completely restored in 1983. Large, bright guest rooms are furnished with antiques, handmade quilts, and stenciled walls. Breakfast favorites are Maine blueberry pancakes or quiche. Wandering the fields or woods or exploring nearby lighthouses and quaint fishing harbors are pleasant pastimes. In the evening, wine and snacks are served. There's a two-night minimum on weekends.

The Gazebo ✪

P.O. BOX 668, ROUTE 1, OGUNQUIT, MAINE 03907

Tel: **(207) 646-3733**
Host(s): **Tony Fontes**
Location: **63 mi. N of Boston**
No. of Rooms: **10**
No. of Private Baths: **8**
Max. No. Sharing Bath: **4**
Double/pb: **$75**
Double/sb: **$50–$65**
Suite: **$90**
Open: **Feb. 1–Dec. 31**
Reduced Rates: **Oct. 16–May 16**
Breakfast: **Full**
Credit Cards: **AMEX, MC, VISA**
Pets: **No**
Children: **Welcome, over 12**
Smoking: **Permitted**
Social Drinking: **Permitted**

You'll recognize this 150-year-old farmhouse by its Victorian gazebo on the front lawn. Inside, there are lovely rooms with antique beds and old-fashioned furnishings. Tony loves to cook and offers tea with paté in the afternoon. In the morning, a gourmet breakfast is served by candlelight on fine china and crystal. House specialties include stuffed French toast served with apricot-orange sauce, and ham-and-egg croquettes topped with tomato-basil sauce. The Gazebo is walking distance of the beach and Ogunquit's many recreational activities. There's a swimming pool on the grounds.

Morning Dove Bed and Breakfast ✪

5 BOURNE LANE, OGUNQUIT, MAINE 03907

Tel: **(207) 646-3891**
Host(s): **Peter and Eeta Schon**
Location: **75 mi. N of Boston**
No. of Rooms: **6**
No. of Private Baths: **3**
Max. No. Sharing Bath: **4**
Double/pb: **$55–$65**
Suite: **$60–$70**
Double/sb: **$45–$55**
Open: **All year**
Breakfast: **Continental**
Credit Cards: **AMEX, MC, VISA**
Pets: **No**
Children: **Welcome, over 12**
Smoking: **Permitted**
Social Drinking: **Permitted**

The Morning Dove is a restored farmhouse dating back to the 1860s. The airy rooms feature antiques, luxurious towels, and fresh garden flowers. At night handmade chocolates are placed on the pillows. Breakfast is served on the Victorian porch or in the elegant dining room. The house is within walking distance of beaches, a busy harbor for fishing and boating, and the Marginal Way, a clifftop path along the edge of the ocean. Restaurants, art galleries, and the trolley stop are just a few steps away. A two-night minimum stay is required; three nights on summer holiday weekends.

Little River Inn and Gallery ✪
ROUTE 130, PEMAQUID FALLS, MAINE 04558

Tel: **(207) 677-2845**
Best Time to Call: **Evenings**
Host(s): **Jeffrey and Judith Burke**
Location: **9½ mi. S of Damariscotta**
No. of Rooms: **9**
No. of Private Baths: **2**
Max. No. Sharing Bath: **5**
Double/pb: **$45**
Single/pb: **$40**
Double/sb: **$35–$45**
Single/sb: **$30–$40**
Open: **All year**
Reduced Rates: **Off-season; weekly**
Breakfast: **Full**
Credit Cards: **MC, VISA**
Pets: **Sometimes**
Children: **Welcome**
Smoking: **Permitted**
Social Drinking: **Permitted**
Foreign Languages: **Spanish**

This handsome home is located in a historic area on the bank of the river and above the waterfalls. Jeffrey has painstakingly refurbished each room to reflect its original charm. Judy's breakfast quiche is the best, and her talent for setting a lovely table will be obvious. It's close to the beach, Fort William Henry, Pemaquid Point Lighthouse, and the quaint fishing village of New Harbor.

Captain Purinton House ✪
64 ELM STREET, TOPSHAM, MAINE 04086

Tel: **(207) 729-3603**
Best Time to Call: **Before 9 AM or 4–8 PM**
Host(s): **Gail and John Frothingham**
Location: **2 mi. from I-95, Exit 24**
No. of Rooms: **2**
Max. No. Sharing Bath: **3**
Double/sb: **$40–$50**
Open: **All year**
Breakfast: **Continental**
Pets: **No**
Children: **Welcome, over 10**
Smoking: **No**
Social Drinking: **Permitted**
Airport/Station Pickup: **Yes**

This stately Federal-style country home (circa 1797) retains most of its original features including the wide-pine floors and hand-carved fireplace mantels. One guest room has the original inside shutters. Much of the furnishings were collected by John and Gail during their travels in the Far East. Breakfast, served in the dining room, often features Maine blueberry muffins. The on-premises jogging track will help you keep in shape. Bowdoin College is 1½ miles away.

Broad Bay Inn & Gallery ✪

MAIN STREET, P.O. BOX 607, WALDOBORO, MAINE 04572

Tel: **(207) 832-6668**
Host(s): **Jim and Libby Hopkins**
Location: **80 mi. N of Portland**
No. of Rooms: **5**
No. of Private Baths: **3**
Max. No. Sharing Bath: **4**
Double/sb: **$40–$55**
Single/sb: **$35–$45**
Open: **All year**
Breakfast: **Full**
Other Meals: **Available Fri. & Sat.**
Credit Cards: **MC, VISA**
Pets: **No**
Children: **Welcome, over 12**
Smoking: **Permitted**
Social Drinking: **Permitted**
Foreign Languages: **French**

The inn, located in a charming mid-coast village, is a classic Colonial with light, airy, handsomely decorated rooms. Some of the guest rooms have canopy beds, and all have Victorian furnishings. There's a large deck on which to enjoy afternoon tea or sherry. This is a convenient base from which to enjoy the quaint fishing villages, the Camden Shakespeare Theatre, summer stock theater, and the Maine Seafood Festival. A sumptuous breakfast often includes quiche, crêpes, baked eggs in sausage, or herbed cheese omelets. Guests never go hungry because beverages are served on arrival, wine and cheese are available each afternoon, and snacks are frequently offered. Jim and Libby are retired commercial artists and have a gallery in the barn. They plan art workshops for interested guests.

Tide Watch Inn ✪

P.O. BOX 94, PINE STREET, WALDOBORO, MAINE 04572

Tel: **(207) 832-4987**
Best Time to Call: **Before 10 AM; after 2 PM**
Host(s): **Mel and Cathy Hanson**
Location: **62 mi. N of Portland; 1 7/16 mi. from Rte. 1**
No. of Rooms: **3**
No. of Private Baths: **1**
Max. No. Sharing Bath: **4**
Double/pb: **$45**
Single/pb: **$35**
Double/sb: **$40**
Single/sb: **$30**
Open: **All year**
Breakfast: **Full**
Pets: **No**
Children: **Welcome, over 12**
Smoking: **Permitted**
Social Drinking: **Permitted**
Airport/Station Pickup: **Yes**

Built in 1850, this twin Colonial home is located on the shore of the Medomac River. The first five-masted schooners were crafted right by the inn. You are welcome to bring your boat or canoe, or just watch the

local fishermen sail with the tide. Catherine's forte is keeping the inn "ship-shape," and guests comment on the comfortable ambience she's created. Mel's talent as a retired chef is evident in the ambitious and delicious breakfasts that might include asparagus cordon bleu and a hearty, welcome bowl of clam chowder.

The Wild Rose of York

78 LONG SANDS ROAD, YORK, MAINE 03909

Tel: **(207) 363-2532**
Best Time to Call: **Before 8 AM; afternoons and evenings**
Host(s): **Fran and Frank Sullivan**
Location: **10 mi. N of Portsmouth, N.H.**
No. of Rooms: **4**
No. of Private Baths: **2**
Max. No. Sharing Bath: **4**
Double/pb: **$48**
Single/pb: **$38**
Double/sb: **$45**
Single/sb: **$35**
Suites: **$68, for 3**
Open: **All year**
Reduced Rates: **Nov. 15–May 15**
Breakfast: **Continental**
Pets: **No**
Children: **Welcome**
Smoking: **Permitted**
Social Drinking: **Permitted**
Airport/Station Pickup: **Yes**

This handsome house, built in 1814, sits high on a hill within easy range of the ocean breezes. The bedrooms are cozy, with antique beds, patchwork quilts, fireplaces, and Fran's special artistic touches. Breakfast is special and may feature peach pancakes or nut waffles. In summer, an old-fashioned trolley will take you to the beach. Deep-sea fishing, golf, hiking, shops, galleries, and factory outlets are nearby diversions. Frank, a biology professor, often conducts nature and tidepool walks. In winter, sledding, skating, and cross-country skiing are all fun. An art gallery, featuring works by local artists, is literally on the drawing board for this B&B. Complimentary tea, cookies, and sherry are always offered.

The Jo-Mar B&B on-the-Ocean

41 FREEMAN STREET, BOX 838, YORK BEACH, MAINE 03910

Tel: **(207) 363-4826**
Host(s): **Mary Della Puietra, Joan Curtis**
Location: **5 mi. from I-95**
No. of Rooms: **6**
Max. No. Sharing Bath: **5**
Double/sb: **$40–$47**
Single/sb: **$30**
Guest Cottage: **$300 weekly**
Open: **May 15–Oct. 15**
Reduced Rates: **10% less, May, June, Sept., Oct.; weekly**
Breakfast: **Continental**
Pets: **No**
Children: **Welcome**
Smoking: **Permitted**
Social Drinking: **Permitted**
Foreign Languages: **Italian**

This comfortable home is located on a bluff overlooking Short Sands Beach. Most guest rooms have ocean views and are furnished with antique pieces. The backyard has a barbecue and picnic table, and you can view the mighty Atlantic from a comfortable lawn chair. Store your snacks in the refrigerator and visit in the cozy living room. The amusement park, galleries, and craft shops are just minutes away. It is convenient to Ogunquit's great restaurants and renowned summer theater. Mary and Joan enjoy having visitors and will direct you to discount outlets for Lenox and Royal Doulton china and Waterford crystal. There's a two-night minimum stay on summer weekends.

MARYLAND

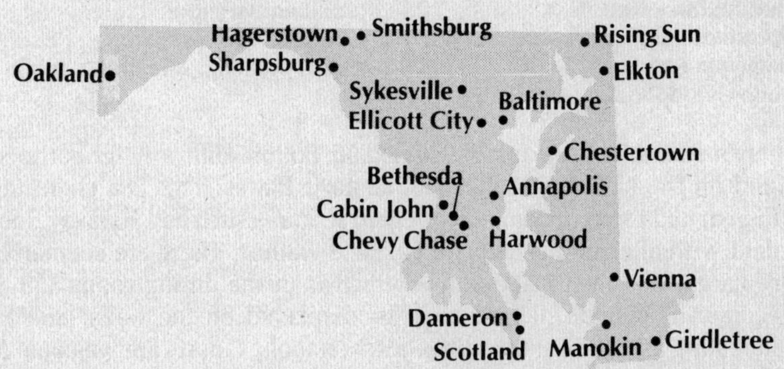

The Traveller in Maryland ✪

P.O. BOX 2277, ANNAPOLIS, MARYLAND 21404

Tel: **(301) 269-6232 or 261-2233**
Best Time to Call: **9 AM–5 PM, Mon.–Thurs.; 9–noon, Fri.**
Coordinator(s): **Cecily Sharp-Whitehill**
States/Regions Covered: **Annapolis, Baltimore, Chestertown, Easton, Hagertown, St. Michaels, Taneytown, Uniontown**

Rates (Single/Double):

Modest:	**$40**	**$45**
Average:	**$45**	**$60**
Luxury:	**$60**	**$120**

Credit Cards: **AMEX, MC, VISA**

Maryland lies between the Atlantic Ocean and the Allegheny Mountains. Chesapeake Bay offers marvelous fishing and boating, and Washington, D.C., is convenient to many of the B&Bs. Many of the B&Bs are located close to Goucher College, Johns Hopkins University, and the U.S. Naval Academy.

Betsy's Bed and Breakfast

1428 PARK AVENUE, BALTIMORE, MARYLAND 21217

Tel: **(301) 383-1274**
Best Time to Call: **8:30 AM–5:30 PM**
Host(s): **Betsy Grater**
Location: **1/2 mi. N of Baltimore**
No. of Rooms: **3**
No. of Private Baths: **2**
Max. No. Sharing Bath: **4**
Double/pb: **$60**
Single/pb: **$55**
Double/sb: **$50**
Single/sb: **$45**
Open: **All year**
Reduced Rates: **10–15%, weekly**
Breakfast: **Continental**
Credit Cards: **AMEX**
Pets: **No**
Children: **Welcome**
Smoking: **No**
Social Drinking: **Permitted**

Betsy's Bed and Breakfast is located in Bolton Hill, a neighborhood listed on the National Register of Historic Places. This is a charming 115-year-old town house, with elegant features such as a hallway floor inlaid with alternating strips of oak and walnut. There are six marble fireplaces, the most elaborate of which is in the dining room. Other decorations include heirloom quilts, displayed on the walls, and an interesting assortment of antique kitchen tools. Guests are welcome to relax in the spacious, high-ceilinged living room with French doors opening out to the garden. Betsy's is convenient to Meyerhoff Symphony Hall, the Lyric Opera House, the Inner Harbor, and some of the city's finest restaurants.

Mulberry House ✪

111 WEST MULBERRY STREET, BALTIMORE, MARYLAND 21201

Tel: **(301) 576-0111**
Host(s): **Charlotte and Curt Jeschke**
No. of Rooms: **4**
Max. No. Sharing Bath: **4**
Double/sb: **$65**
Open: **All year**
Breakfast: **Full**
Pets: **No**
Children: **Welcome, over 16 (in separate room)**
Smoking: **Permitted**
Social Drinking: **Permitted**
Airport/Station Pickup: **Yes**
Foreign Languages: **German**

Mulberry House, in downtown Baltimore, was built circa 1830 as a Federal-period town house. Over the years a fourth floor and a courtyard were added, and a painstaking restoration has now taken place. The owners have added special touches like leaded glass in first-floor transoms, fan windows, and needlepoint cushions from 19th-century wallpaper designs. Guests may choose from the Victorian, Far East, Federal, and Pineapple rooms, all professionally decorated. Guests are treated like old friends and are welcome to relax in the sitting room with its grand piano, sofa, and fireplace. A sumptuous breakfast is served at an 18th-century banquet table each morning. The house is within walking distance of many shops, museums, restaurants, historic sights, and the waterfront area.

The Winslow Home ✪

8217 CARAWAY STREET, CABIN JOHN, BETHESDA, MARYLAND 20818

Tel: **(301) 229-4654**
Best Time to Call: **After 5 PM**
Host(s): **Jane Winslow**
Location: **7 mi. W of D.C.**
No. of Rooms: **2**
Max. No. Sharing Bath: **4**
Double/sb: **$35**
Single/sb: **$25**
Open: **All year**
Reduced Rates: **Seniors; families**
Breakfast: **Full**
Pets: **Welcome**
Children: **Welcome**
Smoking: **No**
Social Drinking: **No**
Airport/Station Pickup: **Yes**

You may enjoy the best of two worlds while staying at Jane's. This comfortable home is located in a lovely residential section of Bethesda, just 20 minutes from downtown Washington, D.C. Imagine touring the capital with some extra pocket money saved on high hotel costs. You are welcome to use the kitchen, laundry facilities, and piano. Georgetown, George Washington, and American universities are close by.

Inn at Mitchell House ✪

BOX 329, R.D. 2, ROUTE 21, CHESTERTOWN, MARYLAND 21620

Tel: **(301) 778-6500**
Best Time to Call: **Evenings**
Host(s): **Dorris and Al Marshall**
Location: **78 mi. E of Washington, D.C.**
No. of Rooms: **6**
No. of Private Baths: **5**
Max. No. Sharing Bath: **2**
Double/pb: **$75–$85**
Single/pb: **$70–$80**
Double/sb: **$75**
Single/sb: **$70**
Suite: **$85**
Open: **All year**
Breakfast: **Full**
Credit Cards: **MC, VISA**
Pets: **No**
Children: **Welcome**
Smoking: **Permitted**
Social Drinking: **Permitted**

This brick Federal-style inn is known as the "Mitchell Mansion," and is listed on the Maryland Register of Historic Homes. The house dates back to 1743 and boasts seven fireplaces, a guest parlor, and a formal dining room with the original beamed ceiling and exposed brick floors. Dorris and Al enjoy providing extra touches like fresh flowers and wine and fruit in the guest rooms. They want you to have a restful night amid period antiques, cozy quilts, designer sheets, and authentic rope beds. Breakfast is always a hearty offering that often includes homemade granola and unusual French toast. Mitchell House is set on ten acres that border a stream. Guests have bathing privileges at a private beach on Chesapeake Bay, just one-half mile from the house. A two-night minimum stay is required.

Radcliffe Cross

QUAKER NECK ROAD, ROUTE 3, BOX 360, CHESTERTOWN, MARYLAND 21620

Tel: **(301) 778-5540**
Host(s): **Dan and Marge Brook**
No. of Rooms: **2**
No. of Private Baths: **2**
Double/pb: **$60**
Open: **All year**
Breakfast: **Full**
Pets: **Sometimes**
Children: **Welcome, infants or over 10**
Smoking: **No**
Social Drinking: **Permitted**

This pre-Revolutionary white brick Colonial, situated on 28 acres, is appropriately furnished with Early American antiques. A unique hanging spiral staircase rises from the center hall to the third floor. Each room boasts its own fireplace. Guests rave about Marge's puff pastries, muffins, and coffee cakes. Coffee, tea, and soft drinks are always available. Reserve well in advance for the popular Chestertown Tea Party Festival in May or the Candlelight Walking Tour of Historic Charleston in September.

Chevy Chase Bed & Breakfast ✪

6815 CONNECTICUT AVENUE, CHEVY CHASE, MARYLAND 20815

Tel: **(301) 656-5867**
Best Time to Call: **Before 9 AM**
Host(s): **S. C. Gotbaum**
Location: **1 mi. N of Washington, D.C.**
No. of Rooms: **2**
No. of Private Baths: **2**
Double/pb: **$45**
Single/pb: **$40**
Single/sb: **$35**
Open: **All year**
Reduced Rates: **5-day stays; families**
Breakfast: **Continental**
Pets: **No**
Children: **Welcome**
Smoking: **Permitted**
Social Drinking: **Permitted**

Enjoy the convenience of being close to the sights of Washington, D.C., while staying at a relaxing country-style house outside the city. Rooms have beamed ceilings and are filled with rare tapestries, Oriental rugs, baskets, copperware, and native crafts from Mexico to the Mideast. Your hostess is a sociologist with a private consulting business. For breakfast she offers homemade muffins, jams, pancakes, French toast, and a special blend of Louisiana coffee. When you want to take a break from touring, a quiet backyard and garden will relax you. Sarah can also guide you to the nearby tennis courts and swimming pool.

Country Hosting

STAR ROUTE, BOX 5, DAMERON, MARYLAND 20628

Tel: **(301) 862-2589**
Coordinator: **Carolyn Lepper**

Rates (Single/Double):
Average: **$35** **$48–$65**

Most of Carolyn's B&Bs are in the historic section of Dameron, within 90 miles of Washington, D.C., and Baltimore. They range from a manor house to a small country inn run by friendly people who are eager to see that you have a pleasant visit. Some hosts are fluent in French, Spanish, or Swedish. Calvert Cliffs, St. Marys City, the Civil War Museum, and the Marine Museum are nearby. The Amish Market, held on Wednesday and Saturday, is particularly interesting. Only children over the age of 12 are accommodated.

The Garden Cottage at Sinking Springs Herb Farm ✪

234 BLAIR SHORE ROAD, ELKTON, MARYLAND 21921

Tel: **(301) 398-5566**
Best Time to Call: **8 AM–8 PM**
Host(s): **Ann and Bill Stubbs**
Location: **4½ mi. from Rte. 40**
No. of Rooms: **2**
Max. No. Sharing Bath: **2**
Double/sb: **$35**
Guest Cottage: **$55; sleeps 3**
Open: **All year**

Reduced Rates: **5%, seniors**
Breakfast: **Continental**
Other Meals: **Available**
Pets: **Sometimes**
Children: **Welcome**
Smoking: **No**
Social Drinking: **Permitted**
Airport/Station Pickup: **Yes**

Guests frequently comment on the peaceful beauty of the farm's setting. You may opt to stay in the main house, furnished with antiques in Early American style, or in the garden cottage, with its sitting room and fireplace adjoining the bedroom. Breakfast features coffee ground from organically grown beans, herbal teas, and homemade buns, fruit, and juice. A full country breakfast prepared with unprocessed food fresh from the farm is available for a nominal charge. Lectures on herbs and craft classes are available, and a gift shop is on the premises. Longwood Gardens and the famed Winterthur Museum are close by.

Hayland Farm ✪

5000 SHEPPARD LANE, ELLICOTT CITY, MARYLAND 21043

Tel: **(301) 531-5593 or (301) 596-9119**
Host(s): **Louis and Dorothy Mobley**
Location: **Bet. Baltimore & D.C.**
No. of Rooms: **3**
No. of Private Baths: **1**
Max. No. Sharing Bath: **4**
Double/pb: **$45**
Single/pb: **$35**
Double/sb: **$35**
Single/sb: **$25**
Open: **All year**
Breakfast: **Full**
Pets: **No**
Children: **Welcome (crib)**
Smoking: **No**
Social Drinking: **Permitted**

When you breathe the country-fresh air, it may surprise you that Baltimore and Washington, D.C., are only a short drive away. At Hayland Farm you will find gracious living in a large manor house furnished in a handsome yet comfortable style. Louis and Dorothy are retired and have traveled extensively. They enjoy sharing conversation with their guests. In warm weather, the 20′ by 50′ swimming pool is a joy.

The Stockmans ✪

P.O. BOX 125, TAYLOR LANDING ROAD, GIRDLETREE, MARYLAND 21829

Tel: **(301) 632-3299**
Best Time to Call: **After 6 PM**
Host(s): **John and Joan Stockman**
Location: **6 mi. S of Snow Hill**
No. of Rooms: **2**
Max. No. Sharing Bath: **4**
Double/sb: **$45**
Single/sb: **$40**
Open: **Mar.–Dec.**
Breakfast: **Continental**
Pets: **Sometimes**
Children: **Welcome, over 4**
Smoking: **No**
Social Drinking: **Permitted**

This large Victorian country house is comfortably furnished with a blend of antiques and charm. Fishing, crabbing, and swimming are nearby, as well as interesting historic sites. The coffeepot is usually full, and you are welcome to enjoy a cup while relaxing on the front porch.

Lewrene Farm B&B ✪

RD 3, BOX 150, HAGERSTOWN, MARYLAND 21740

Tel: **(301) 582-1735**
Host(s): **Lewis and Irene Lehman**
Location: **3½ mi. from I-70 and I-81**
No. of Rooms: **6**
No. of Private Baths: **3**
Max. No. Sharing Bath: **4**
Double/pb: **$55–$65**
Double/sb: **$35**
Single/sb: **$30**
Suites: **$65**

Open: **All year**
Breakfast: **Continental**
Pets: **Sometimes**
Children: **Welcome**
Smoking: **No**
Social Drinking: **No**
Foreign Languages: **Spanish**

Lewis and Irene will help you discover the peaceful beauty of their 125-acre farm located in an historic area near the Antietam Battlefield. Guests are treated like old friends and are welcome to lounge in front of the fireplace or to play the piano in the Colonial-style living room. You're invited to enjoy snacks and a video in the evening. Harpers Ferry, Fort Frederick, the C&O Canal, and Gettysburg are nearby.

Oakwood ✪

4566 SOLOMONS ISLAND ROAD, HARWOOD, MARYLAND 20776

Tel: **(301) 261-5338**
Host(s): **Dennis and Joan Brezina**
Location: **10 mi. S of Annapolis**
No. of Rooms: **2**
Max. No. Sharing Bath: **4**
Double/sb: **$50**
Single/sb: **$45**
Open: **Mar. 1–Nov. 30**
Breakfast: **Full**
Pets: **No**
Children: **Welcome, over 12**
Smoking: **Permitted**
Social Drinking: **Permitted**

This elegant antebellum manor house, featured on Maryland House Tours, has six fireplaces, 11-foot ceilings, and handmade rugs. Guests are welcome to relax on the veranda or stroll in the terraced gardens. Your hosts serve an English-style breakfast in the open-hearthed kitchen. They are happy to advise on day trips to Washington, D.C., or nearby Chesapeake Bay and Annapolis.

Hunters Cove ✪

P.O. BOX 4, MANOKIN, MARYLAND 21836

Tel: **(301) 651-9664**
Best Time to Call: **8–9 AM; 10:30–11:30 PM**
Host(s): **Anne and Bill Wilhelm**
Location: **4 mi. from Rte. 13 S, Exit Rte. 413**
No. of Rooms: **4**
No. of Private Baths: **4**
Double/pb: **$80**
Single/pb: **$40**
Open: **Jan. 1–Feb. 28; May 15–Sept. 1; Sept. 15–Dec. 31**
Reduced Rates: **Weekly**
Breakfast: **Continental**
Pets: **Welcome**
Children: **Welcome (crib)**
Smoking: **Permitted**
Social Drinking: **Permitted**
Airport/Station Pickup: **Yes**

Located in historic Somerset County on the Delmarva Peninsula, this white clapboard farmhouse with its winter and summer porches commands a 1/4-mile waterfront view of the Great Annamessex River. Guests comment upon the spacious rooms, antique wicker, comfortable maple furnishings, and warm family environment. Bike trails, forest trails, fishing, and crabbing are nearby. The ocean beaches are a 45-minute drive. Soft drinks and snacks are always available.

Red Run Inn ✪

ROUTE 5, BOX 268, OAKLAND, MARYLAND 21550

Tel: **(301) 387-6606**
Host(s): **Ruth Umbel**
Location: **180 mi. W of Baltimore**
No. of Rooms: **5**
No. of Private Baths: **5**
Double/pb: **$65**
Single/pb: **$25**
Suites: **$75**
Open: **All year**
Breakfast: **Continental**
Credit Cards: **AMEX, MC, VISA**
Pets: **No**
Children: **Welcome**
Smoking: **Permitted**
Social Drinking: **Permitted**
Airport/Station Pickup: **Yes**

Nestled in a wooded setting on 18 acres, Red Run overlooks the expansive blue waters of Deep Creek Lake. The grounds and structures have been carefully planned to preserve the unspoiled atmosphere. The property includes a swimming pool, tennis courts, horseshoe pits, dock facilities, and a cross-country ski trail.

Chandlee House ✪

168 CHANDLEE ROAD, RISING SUN, MARYLAND 21911

Tel: **(301) 658-6958**
Best Time to Call: **Before 9 AM; 5–9 PM**
Host(s): **Dewey and Renie Newman**
Location: **6 mi. from I-95**
No. of Rooms: **2**
No. of Private Baths: **1**
Max. No. Sharing Bath: **4**
Double/pb: **$55**
Single/pb: **$35**
Double/sb: **$45**
Single/sb: **$35**
Open: **All year**
Reduced Rates: **10%, seniors**
Breakfast: **Continental**
Pets: **Sometimes**
Children: **Welcome**
Smoking: **No**
Social Drinking: **Permitted**

Built of fieldstone in 1712, Chandlee House has been recently embellished with a garden gazebo, in-ground swimming pool, and children's playhouse. It is surrounded by 275-year-old maple trees. The farm buildings, fields, and woods complete the country setting.

Handcrafted furniture and original watercolors by Dewey complement the Early American antiques. Come sit by the fire in winter or enjoy the vista from the old porch swing in summer. Chesapeake Bay is only ten minutes away, while Baltimore, Philadelphia, and Dutch Country are convenient for day trips.

St. Michael's Manor B&B ✪

ST. MICHAEL'S MANOR, SCOTLAND, MARYLAND 20687

Tel: **(301) 872-4025**
Host(s): **Joe and Nancy Dick**
Location: **9 mi. S of St. Mary's City**
No. of Rooms: **2**
Max. No. Sharing Bath: **4**
Double/sb: **$50**
Open: **All year**
Reduced Rates: **10%, after Labor Day**
Breakfast: **Full**
Pets: **No**
Children: **Welcome (crib, high chair)**
Smoking: **Downstairs only**
Social Drinking: **Permitted**

St. Michael's Manor was built in 1805 on land patented to Leonard Calvert during the 17th century. Today, the white stucco manor home on picturesque Long Neck Creek is included on the state's Pilgrimage Tour. The beautifully handcrafted woodwork has been preserved and is complemented with antiques and handcrafts. Guests are sure to enjoy the added touches, such as fresh fruit and flowers in the rooms. For breakfast, choose from a tasty array of homemade muffins, jellies, and farm-fresh fruit in season. Your hosts offer the use of their boat and bicycles for touring this lovely area. The Manor House is near Point Lookout State Park, half a mile from Chesapeake Bay, and close to many historic sites.

Inn at Antietam ✪

220 EAST MAIN STREET, P.O. BOX 119, SHARPSBURG, MARYLAND 21782

Tel: **(301) 432-6601**
Best Time to Call: **Mornings; evenings**
Host(s): **Betty and Cal Fairbourn**
Location: **15 mi. SW of Hagerstown**
No. of Rooms: **5**
No. of Private Baths: **5**
Double/pb: **$55–$65**
Single/pb: **$42.50**
Suites: **$75**
Open: **Jan. 2–Dec. 23**
Reduced Rates: **5%; seniors**
Breakfast: **Continental**
Credit Cards: **AMEX**
Pets: **No**
Children: **Welcome, over 6**
Smoking: **Permitted**
Social Drinking: **Permitted**

This classic Victorian, located next to the historic Antietam Battlefield, was built in 1908. The wraparound porch with its rockers and swing is a great place to relax. The house is decorated in a pleasant mix of styles with Victorian accents. Coffee and cookies are always available. It is close to the C & O Canal and Harpers Ferry, and less than an hour from Gettysburg. Shepherd College in Shepherdstown, West Virginia, is four miles away. Children are not accepted on weekends.

Blue Bear Bed & Breakfast ✪

ROUTE 2, BOX 378, HOLIDAY DRIVE, SMITHSBURG, MARYLAND 21783

Tel: **(301) 824-2292**
Best Time to Call: **After 4 PM**
Host(s): **Ellen Panchula**
Location: **6 mi. from I-70, Exit 35**
No. of Rooms: **2**
Max. No. Sharing Bath: **4**
Double/sb: **$30**
Single/sb: **$22**
Open: **July 1–Aug. 31; weekends, Apr.–June, Sept.–Dec.**
Breakfast: **Continental**
Pets: **No**
Children: **Welcome, over 12**
Smoking: **No**
Social Drinking: **Permitted**

Ellen is a full-time schoolteacher from September through June, so she can entertain guests during the week only in July and August; during the school year it's strictly weekends only. Her home is decorated in an informal country mode, with several antiques complementing the decor. Smithsburg is located in apple and peach country. It is convenient to the Antietam Battlefield in Sharpsburg and to many fine restaurants in Hagerstown. Homemade breads, coffee cakes, quiche, fresh fruit, and beverages comprise the breakfast menu. Snacks, dessert, and wine and cheese are generously offered in the evenings.

Long Way Hill ✪

7406 SPRINGFIELD AVENUE, SYKESVILLE, MARYLAND 21784

Tel: **(301) 795-8129**
Best Time to Call: **6:30–11 AM; 4–10 PM**
Host(s): **Anita-Barbara Huddlestun**
Location: **20 mi. W of Baltimore**
No. of Rooms: **3**
No. of Private Baths: **1**
Max. No. Sharing Bath: **3–4**
Double/pb: **$46**
Single/pb: **$38**
Double/sb: **$46**
Single/sb: **$38**
Open: **All year**
Breakfast: **Full**
Pets: **Sometimes**
Children: **Welcome (high chair)**
Smoking: **Permitted**
Social Drinking: **Permitted**

Anita-Barbara Huddlestun's entire block is listed on the National Register of Historic Places. She welcomes you to her cottage Victorian, set on five and a half landscaped acres. The property includes fruit trees, flowers, woods, and a swimming pool to enjoy in the summer months. The rooms are decorated with charming pieces ranging in period from the 1900s to the 1930s, with lovely wallpapers, wood furnishings, and fine linens. Breakfast specialties such as homemade cinnamon-raisin buns, eggs, and bacon are served in a sunny dining room with floral wallpaper and an old-fashioned curio cabinet. Long Way Hill is located in a rural area, yet is close to fine dining, shopping, and a movie theater. Columbia and Newmarket, the antiques capital of the state, are just a short drive from the house.

The Tavern House ✪

111 WATER STREET, P.O. BOX 98, VIENNA, MARYLAND 21869

Tel: **(301) 376-3347**
Host(s): **Harvey and Elise Altergott**
Location: **15 mi. NW of Salisbury**
No. of Rooms: **3**
Max. No. Sharing Bath: **4**
Double/sb: **$55–$60**
Single/sb: **$45–$55**
Open: **All year**
Reduced Rates: **After 1 night**
Breakfast: **Continental**
Credit Cards: **MC, VISA**
Pets: **No**
Children: **No**
Smoking: **Permitted**
Social Drinking: **Permitted**
Foreign Languages: **German, Spanish**

Vienna is a quiet little town where one can escape the stress of the 20th century. Careful restoration has brought back the simple purity of this Colonial tavern. The stark white "lime, sand, and hair" plaster accents the authentic furnishings. This is a place for those who enjoy looking at the river and marshes, watching an osprey, or taking a leisurely walk. Days begin with fruits of the season and end with complimentary cheese and wine. For the sports minded, there's tennis, boating, and flat roads for bicycling, all within easy reach. This is an excellent base for exploring the Eastern Shore, interesting small towns and antiques shops, and Blackwater National Wildlife Refuge.

Winchester Country Inn ✪

430 SOUTH BISHOP STREET, WESTMINSTER, MARYLAND 21157

Tel: **(301) 876-7373**
Best Time to Call: **7 AM–7 PM**
Host(s): **Vince Fiore**
Location: **35 mi. NW of Baltimore**
No. of Rooms: **5**
No. of Private Baths: **3**

Max. No. Sharing Bath: **4**
Double/pb: **$65**
Single/pb: **$60**
Double/sb: **$60**
Single/sb: **$55**
Open: **All year**
Reduced Rates: **10% weekly; 10% seniors**
Breakfast: **Full**
Credit Cards: **MC, VISA**
Pets: **No**
Children: **Welcome, over 6**
Smoking: **Permitted**
Social Drinking: **Permitted**
Foreign Languages: **Sign, Spanish**

Built in the 1760s, this inn is one of the most historic inns in Maryland. It is furnished with period antiques that enhance the interior. It is only a quarter of a mile to the historic Carroll County Farm Museum, which houses special events such as the Maryland Wine Festival. It is within walking distance to the Farmers Market, where produce, flowers, and crafts may be bought. Breakfast includes farm-fresh eggs and country sausage or ham. In the afternoon, Vince offers complimentary sherry or tea.

For key to listings, see inside front or back cover.

✪ This star means that rates are guaranteed through December 31, 1988 to any guest making a reservation as a result of reading about the B&B in *BED & BREAKFAST U.S.A.*—1988 edition.

Please enclose a self-addressed, stamped, business-sized envelope when contacting reservation services.

For more details on what you can expect in a B&B, see Chapter 1.

Always mention *Bed & Breakfast U.S.A.* when making reservations!

If no B&B is listed in the area you'll be visiting, use the form on page 698 to order a copy of our "List of New B&Bs."

We want to hear from you! Use the form on page 697.

MASSACHUSETTS

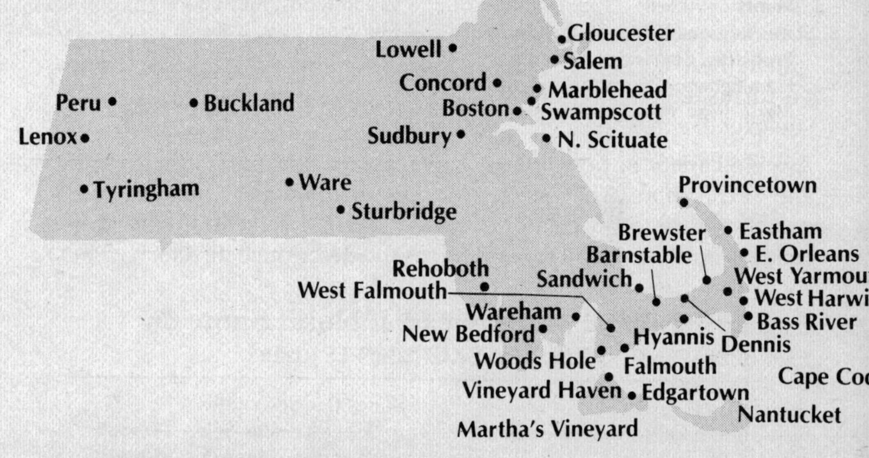

Pineapple Hospitality, Inc. ✪

47 NORTH SECOND STREET, NEW BEDFORD, MASSACHUSETTS 02740

Tel: **(617) 990-1696 or 1798**
Best Time to Call: **9 AM–5 PM Mon.–Sat.**
Coordinator: **Judy Mulford**
States/Regions Covered: **Connecticut, Maine, Massachusetts, New Hampshire, Rhode Island, Vermont**

Rates (Single/Double):

Modest:	**$32–$40**	**$35–$43**
Average:	**$30–$40**	**$45–$59**
Luxury:	**$45–$75**	**$60–$115**

Credit Cards: **MC, VISA**

The pineapple has been the symbol of rare hospitality since early Colonial days, and the host homes on Judy's roster personify this spirit. They are located in cities and in the countryside, at beach resorts and lakeside communities, in historic districts and near hundreds of schools and colleges; you are bound to find just the spot to call home. Send $5.95 for a descriptive directory so that you may make your choices. There's a $3 surcharge for a one-night stay.

Bed & Breakfast Associates—Bay Colony, Ltd. ✪

P.O. BOX 166, BABSON PARK, BOSTON, MASSACHUSETTS 02157

Tel: **(617) 449-5302**
Best Time to Call: **10 AM–12:30 PM; 1:30–5 PM**
Coordinators: **Arline Kardasis, Marilyn Mitchell**
States/Regions Covered: **Boston, Brookline, Cambridge, Concord, Framingham, Gloucester, Lexington, Marblehead, Newton, Wellesley**

Rates (Single/Double):

Modest:	**\$35–\$40**	**\$45–\$50**
Average:	**\$40–\$50**	**\$50–\$55**
Luxury:	**\$55–\$75**	**\$60–\$100**

Credit Cards: **MC, VISA**
Minimum Stay: **2 nights**

A wide variety of host homes is available in the city, in the country, and at the shore. They range from pre-Revolutionary horse farms to contemporary condominiums. Many are convenient to the major colleges and universities. Send $2 for the descriptive directory.

Bed & Breakfast Marblehead & North Shore ✪

P.O. BOX 172, BEVERLY, MASSACHUSETTS 01915

Tel: **(617) 921-1336**
Best Time to Call: **Mon.–Sat. 7:30 AM–8 PM**
Coordinator: **Helena Champion**
States/Regions Covered: **Beverly, Burlington, Danvers, Gloucester, Lynn, Manchester, Marblehead, Peabody, Salem, Swampscott**

Rates (Single/Double):

Modest:	**\$36–\$42**	**\$42–\$50**
Average:	**\$42–\$55**	**\$50–\$70**
Luxury:	**\$55–\$120**	**\$70–\$125**

Credit Cards: **AMEX, MC, VISA**

Ranging from the reasonable to the regal, Helena's B&Bs all assure the warm, friendly atmosphere of a private home. This service has many accommodations within 30 minutes of Boston, yet they are in quaint seaside towns, on the ocean, or in historical areas. Her descriptive directory costs $3.

Bed & Breakfast in Minuteman Country

P.O. BOX 665, CAMBRIDGE, MASSACHUSETTS 02140

Tel: **(617) 576-2112**
Coordinators: **Tally and Pamela Carruthers**
State/Regions Covered: **Massachusetts: Arlington, Bedford, Boston, Brookline, Cambridge, Concord, Lexington, Sudbury, Waltham, Winchester**

Rates (Single/Double):

Average:	**\$35**	**\$60**
Luxury:	**\$50**	**\$80**

Credit Cards: **AMEX, MC, VISA**

Tally and Pamela can place you in host homes convenient to historic Lexington and Concord, downtown Boston, or in selected areas along the scenic North Shore. Many are close to Harvard and MIT, Leahy Clinic, historic Wright Tavern, Emerson's home, Walden Pond, and the Charles River. Unusual restaurants, specialty shops, and cultural happenings abound. Just tell your host about your interests and you will be assured of excellent advice.

Be Our Guest Bed & Breakfast, Ltd. ✪

P.O. BOX 1333, PLYMOUTH, MASSACHUSETTS 02360

Tel: **(617) 837-9867**
Coordinators: **Diane Gillis and Mary Gill**
State/Regions Covered: **Boston, Cohasset, Duxbury, Falmouth, Kingston, Marshfield, Plymouth, Sandwich, Scituate**

Rates (Single/Double):

Modest:	**$28**	**$40**
Average:	**$36**	**$45**
Luxury:	**$75**	**$75**

Credit Cards: **AMEX, MC, VISA**

The homes range from historic to traditional New England style. Some are in private settings; others are surrounded by tourist activities. A few have commanding views of the waterfront. All are hosted by people who are dedicated to making certain that you enjoy your visit. Don't miss Plymouth Rock, the Mayflower, the Wax Museum, and winery tours. If you enjoy the sea, whale watching, deep-sea fishing, and sailing are all available.

BOSTON AREA

Greater Boston Hospitality ✪

P.O. BOX 1142, BROOKLINE, MASSACHUSETTS 02146

Tel: **(617) 277-5430**
Coordinator: **Lauren A. Simonelli**
States/Regions Covered: **Boston, Brookline, Cambridge, Gloucester, Lexington, Marblehead, Needham, Newton, Wellesley, Winchester**

Rates (Single/Double):

Modest:	**$35**	**$45**
Average:	**$45**	**$55**
Luxury:	**$55**	**$100**

Credit Cards: **MC, VISA**

Lauren's homes are convenient to many of the 75 colleges and universities in the greater Boston area. What a boon it is for people applying to school, and to parents visiting undergrads, to have a home-away-from-home nearby. There's a $10 surcharge for one night's stay.

Host Homes of Boston ✪

P.O. BOX 117, NEWTON, MASSACHUSETTS 02168

Tel: **(617) 244-1308 Telex: 136575**
Coordinator: **Marcia Whittington**
State/Regions Covered: **Boston, Brookline, Cambridge, Cape Cod, Framingham, Marblehead, Needham, Newton, Reading, Winchester**

Rates (Single/Double):
Modest: **$36–$40 $46–$48**
Average: **$42–$48 $50–$54**
Luxury: **$50–$75 $56–$80**
Credit Cards: **AMEX, MC, VISA**
Minimum Stay: **2 nights**

Marcia has culled a variety of select private homes in excellent areas convenient to good public transportation. Most hosts prepare a full breakfast, although only Continental breakfast is required. It's their special way of saying welcome to their city of colleges, universities, museums, and cultural life.

Williams Guest House ✪

136 BASS AVENUE, GLOUCESTER, MASSACHUSETTS 01930

Tel: **(617) 283-4931**
Best Time to Call: **8 AM–9 PM**
Host(s): **Betty Williams**
Location: **30 mi. N of Boston**
No. of Rooms: **7**
No. of Private Baths: **5**
Max. No. Sharing Bath: **4**
Double/pb: **$45–$48**
Double/sb: **$38**
Guest Cottage: **$400 (week); sleeps 4**

Open: **May 1–Nov. 1**
Reduced Rates: **Off-season, before June 27, and after Labor Day**
Breakfast: **Continental**
Pets: **No**
Children: **Welcome, over 5**
Smoking: **Permitted**
Social Drinking: **Permitted**
Airport/Station Pickup: **Yes**

Located five miles from Rockport and one and a half miles from Rocky Neck, Gloucester is a quaint fishing village on the North Shore. Betty's Colonial Revival house borders the finest beach, Good Harbor. The guest rooms are furnished with comfort in mind, and her homemade breakfast muffins are delicious. Betty will be happy to suggest many interesting things to do, such as boat tours, sport fishing, whale-watching trips, sightseeing cruises around Cape Ann, the Hammond Castle Museum, and the shops and galleries of the artist colony.

Sherman-Berry House ✪

163 DARTMOUTH STREET, LOWELL, MASSACHUSETTS 01851

Tel: **(617) 459-4760**
Best Time to Call: **Mornings**
Host(s): **David Strohmeyer and Susan Scott**
Location: **23 mi. W of Boston**
No. of Rooms: **2**
Max. No. Sharing Bath: **4**
Double/sb: **$45**
Single/sb: **$40**
Open: **All year**
Reduced Rates: **Available**
Breakfast: **Continental**
Pets: **Sometimes**
Children: **Welcome**
Smoking: **No**
Social Drinking: **Permitted**
Airport/Station Pickup: **Yes**

The Sherman-Berry House is a Queen Anne Victorian dating back to 1893. The queen herself would feel at home here among the fine antiques, stained glass, and shady porches. If you're just a commoner, not to worry; your hosts extend a royal welcome with iced tea or hot cocoa in season and evening sherry in the parlor. This area is filled with historic homes and is just 15 minutes from Concord or Lexington and 30 minutes from Boston. Olmsted enthusiasts will want to stroll down the block to Tyler Park, which was designed by the famous architect.

Rasberry Ink

748 COUNTRY WAY, NORTH SCITUATE, MASSACHUSETTS 02060

Tel: **(617) 545-6629**
Host(s): **Frances Honkonen and Carol Hoban**
Location: **25 mi. SE of Boston**
No. of Rooms: **2**
Max. No. Sharing Bath: **5**
Double/sb: **$50**
Single/sb: **$45**
Open: **All year**
Breakfast: **Full**
Pets: **Sometimes**
Children: **Sometimes**
Smoking: **Permitted**
Social Drinking: **Permitted**
Airport/Station Pickup: **Yes**

This 19th-century farmhouse is set in a small seaside town rich in Colonial and Victorian history. Frances and Carol have restored the house and furnished the rooms with antiques and lace. Guest quarters are located on the second floor and feature a private sitting room. Rasberry Ink is five minutes from the beach and is conveniently located on a bus line, midway between Boston and the Cape Cod Canal. In season, fresh raspberries are offered at breakfast.

Amelia Payson Guest House ✪

16 WINTER STREET, SALEM, MASSACHUSETTS 01970

Tel: **(617) 744-8304**
Host(s): **Ada and Donald Roberts**
Location: **4 mi. from Rte. 128, Exit 25 E**
No. of Rooms: **4**
No. of Private Baths: **1**
Max. No. Sharing Bath: **5**
Double/pb: **$60**
Double/sb: **$50**
Single/sb: **$30**
Open: **All year**
Breakfast: **Continental**
Credit Cards: **AMEX, MC, VISA**
Pets: **No**
Children: **No**
Smoking: **No**
Airport/Station Pickup: **Yes**

Built in 1845, this fine example of Greek Revival architecture is located in the heart of Salem's Historic District. Bedrooms are furnished with canopy or brass beds and antiques. Guests may use the piano or TV; tea and pastries are served in the afternoon. Ada and Don will suggest sightseeing walks or direct you to special shops and waterfront dining on Pickering Wharf. They'll also share information regarding Salem's witchcraft mystique.

Checkerberry Corner

5 CHECKERBERRY CIRCLE, SUDBURY, MASSACHUSETTS 01776

Tel: **(617) 443-8660**
Best Time to Call: **Evenings**
Host(s): **Stuart and Irene MacDonald**
Location: **20 mi. W of Boston**
No. of Rooms: **2**
Max. No. Sharing Bath: **4**
Double/sb: **$50**
Single/sb: **$40**
Open: **All year**
Reduced Rates: **10%, families**
Breakfast: **Full**
Pets: **No**
Children: **Welcome, over 12**
Smoking: **No**
Social Drinking: **Permitted**

Checkerberry Corner is a classic Colonial with stained-glass entry windows, red doors, and a large porch. The rooms are tastefully decorated with traditional mahogany furnishings and comfortable Colonial accents. Guests are greeted with a basket of homemade goodies, and beverages and snacks are always available. Stuart and Irene serve breakfast on fine china in the dining room. Homemade muffins, jams, and coffee cakes are specialties of the house. This charming Colonial is located in a historic district, close to the Lexington Minuteman Statue, the Old North Bridge, the homes of Louisa Mae Alcott, Hawthorne, and Emerson, and Longfellow's Wayside Inn.

Marshall House ✪

11 EASTERN AVENUE, SWAMPSCOTT, MASSACHUSETTS 01907

Tel: **(617) 595-6544**
Host(s): **Pat and Al Marshall**
Location: **10 mi. N of Boston**
No. of Rooms: **2**
Max. No. Sharing Bath: **4**
Double/sb: **$50**
Single/sb: **$40**
Open: **All year**
Reduced Rates: **10%, seniors**
Breakfast: **Continental**
Credit Cards: **AMEX, MC, VISA**
Pets: **No**
Children: **Welcome, over 6**
Smoking: **No**
Social Drinking: **Permitted**
Airport/Station Pickup: **Yes**

Marshall House, built circa 1900, is located just a short walk from the beaches of the North Shore. The many porches of this spacious home offer salty breezes and an ocean view. Inside, the rooms are decorated with country furnishings, some cherished antiques, and accents of wood and stained glass. The bedrooms have modern amenities such as color televisions and refrigerators. Guests are welcome to relax in the common room and warm up beside the wood stove. This B&B is located ten miles from Logan International Airport. Pat and Al will gladly direct you to nearby restaurants, historic seacoast villages, and popular bicycle touring routes.

Oak Shores ✪

64 FULLER AVENUE, SWAMPSCOTT, MASSACHUSETTS 01907

Tel: **(617) 599-7677**
Best Time to Call: **5 PM–8 PM**
Host(s): **Marjorie McClung**
Location: **13 mi. N. of Boston**
No. of Rooms: **2**
Max. No. Sharing Bath: **4**
Double/sb: **$35**
Single/sb: **$30**
Open: **All year**
Breakfast: **Full**
Pets: **No**
Children: **Welcome, over 9**
Smoking: **No**
Social Drinking: **Permitted**

This 55-year-old Dutch Colonial is located on Boston's lovely North Shore. Enjoy rooms filled with fine restored furniture and sleep in the comfort of old brass and iron beds. Relax in the private shady garden, on the deck, or take a two-block stroll to the beach. Swampscott was the summer White House of Calvin Coolidge. It is a convenient place to begin tours of nearby Marblehead, birthplace of the United States Navy, and Salem, famous for its witch trials. Marjorie is glad to help with travel plans, and has an ample supply of maps and brochures.

CAPE COD/MARTHA'S VINEYARD

Bed & Breakfast—Cape Cod

P.O. BOX 341, W. HYANNISPORT, MASSACHUSETTS 02672

Tel: **(617) 775-2772**
Best Time to Call: **9:30 AM–7:30 PM**
Coordinator: **Clark Diehl**
States/Regions Covered: **Cape Cod**

Rates (Single/Double):

Modest:	**$32**	**$42**
Average:	**$40**	**$48**
Luxury:	**$60**	**$105**

Credit Cards: **AMEX, MC, VISA**
Minimum Stay: **2 nights**

It is just a little over an hour's drive from sophisticated Boston to the relaxed, quaint charm of the Cape. Year-round, you can choose from Clark's roster of homes. The house you stay in may be a vine-covered cottage, a Victorian estate, a sea captain's home, or an oceanfront house. Your hosts will direct you to the restaurants and shops off the tourist trail. There is a $5 surcharge for a one-night stay.

House Guests—Cape Cod ✪

BOX 8-AR, DENNIS, MASSACHUSETTS 02638

Tel: **(617) 398-0787**
Coordinator: **Richard Griffin**
States/Regions Covered: **Cape Cod, Martha's Vineyard, Nantucket**

Rates (Single/Double):

Modest:	**$38**	**$45–$50**
Average:	**$40**	**$55–$60**
Luxury:	**$48**	**$70–$110**

Credit Cards: **MC, VISA**
Minimum Stay: **2 nights, June 15–Sept. 15**

Richard's accommodations range from a simple single bedroom with shared bath to historic homes furnished with antiques. Some are on the ocean; others are in wooded country areas. There are even a few self-contained guest cottages on private estates. The area is beautiful in all seasons. His descriptive directory is $3.50.

Orleans Bed & Breakfast Associates ✪

P.O. BOX 1312, ORLEANS, MASSACHUSETTS 02653

Tel: **(617) 255-3824**
Best Time to Call: **8 AM–8 PM**
Coordinator: **Mary Chapman**
States/Regions Covered: **Cape Cod: Brewster, Chatham, Harwich, Orleans, Truro, Wellfleet**

Rates (Single/Double):

Modest:	N/A	$40
Average:	N/A	$50
Luxury:	N/A	$75

Credit Cards: **AMEX, MC, VISA**

Mary offers a variety of accommodations with a diversity of styles, and guests may choose from historic to contemporary houses, all compatible with the atmosphere of the Cape. The fine reputation this service enjoys is largely due to the attitude of the host to the guest. Under Mary's direction, hosts meet regularly to share experiences, role-play B&B situations, and tour member homes. Each host is aware that a guest's experience reflects on the association as a whole. We applaud the professionalism of this organization!

Thomas Huckins House ✪

2701 MAIN STREET (Route 6A), P.O. BOX 515, BARNSTABLE, MASSACHUSETTS 02630

Tel: **(617) 362-6379**
Host(s): **Burt and Eleanor Eddy**
Location: **2 mi. from Rte. 6, Exit 6**
No. of Rooms: **2**
No. of Private Baths: **3**
Double/pb: **$75**
Suites: **$95**
Open: **All year**
Reduced Rates: **Nov. 1–May 15**
Breakfast: **Full**
Credit Cards: **MC, VISA**
Pets: **No**
Children: **Welcome, over 6**
Smoking: **Permitted**
Social Drinking: **Permitted**

Located in the historic district, which is less crowded and less commercial than much of the Cape, the house (circa 1705) has all the privacy and charm of a small country inn. Each bedroom has a small sitting area and a four-poster bed with canopy top. The parlor is comfortably furnished with antiques and handmade reproductions. It's a short walk to a small beach, boat ramp, and the inlet that overlooks the dunes of Sandy Neck. Whale watching, the Nantucket ferry, the Sandwich Glass Museum, and Plimoth Plantation are but 15 minutes away. Eleanor loves to garden, and the jam served at breakfast is literally the fruits of her labor. Breakfast is served in the original keeping room in front of the fireplace. Banana pancakes and Cape Cod cranberry muffins are two favorites.

Old Cape House ✪

108 OLD MAIN STREET, BASS RIVER, MASSACHUSETTS 02664

Tel: **(617) 398-1068**
Host(s): **George and Linda Arthur**
Location: **5 mi. E of Hyannis**
No. of Rooms: **6**
No. of Private Baths: **2**
Max. No. Sharing Bath: **3**
Double/pb: **$48–$60**
Double/sb: **$35–$45**
Single/sb: **$30**
Open: **May–Oct.**
Reduced Rates: **10%, before June 15**
Breakfast: **Continental**
Pets: **No**
Children: **Welcome, over 15**
Smoking: **No**
Social Drinking: **Permitted**
Foreign Languages: **French, Italian**

This fine Greek Revival home was built in 1815 and is convenient to fine beaches, restaurants, and scenic attractions of Cape Cod. You will enjoy home-baked items at breakfast, plus the use of a spacious porch and garden. All the rooms are charmingly decorated in New England style. It's a great place to stay in the fall for visits to antique shops and craft fairs. Linda is from London, and George also lived in Europe for many years, so they know how to bring the bed-and-breakfast tradition here. There is a two-night minimum on holiday weekends and during July and August.

Old Sea Pines Inn ✪

2553 MAIN STREET, BREWSTER, MASSACHUSETTS 02631

Tel: **(617) 896-6114**
Host(s): **Michele and Steve Rowan**
Location: **16 mi. E of Hyannis**
No. of Rooms: **14**
No. of Private Baths: **9**
Max. No. Sharing Bath: **3**
Double/pb: **$40–$65**
Suites: **$70**
Open: **Apr. 1–Nov. 30**
Reduced Rates: **Off-season**
Breakfast: **Continental**
Credit Cards: **AMEX, DC, MC, VISA**
Pets: **No**
Children: **Welcome, over 8**
Smoking: **Permitted**
Social Drinking: **Permitted**
Airport/Station Pickup: **Yes**
Foreign Languages: **German, Italian**

Originally a women's finishing school, this sprawling inn has kept many of its turn-of-the-century features, such as brass and iron beds, plus antique and wicker furniture. A breakfast of homemade specialties is served on the porch or in the sunny dining room. Located on over three acres, the inn is close to beaches, bike paths, shops, and restaurants.

Old Sea Pines Inn

Copper Beech Inn ✪

497 MAIN STREET, CENTERVILLE, MASSACHUSETTS 02632

Tel: **(617) 771-5488**
Best Time to Call: **8:30 AM–5:30 PM**
Host(s): **Joyce Diehl**
Location: **4 mi. W of Hyannis**
No. of Rooms: **3**
No. of Private Baths: **3**
Double/pb: **$65**
Open: **All year**
Breakfast: **Full**
Credit Cards: **AMEX, MC, VISA**
Pets: **No**
Children: **Welcome, over 11**
Smoking: **Permitted**
Social Drinking: **Permitted**
Airport/Station Pickup: **Yes**

Home of the largest copper beech tree in Cape Cod, the inn is set in the heart of historic Centerville amid private estates and vintage homes. It features traditional furnishings, formal parlors, well-kept grounds with sunning areas, and duck pond. Golf, tennis, fishing, sailing, and swimming are available nearby; Craigville Beach is less than a mile away. In summer, the Cape Cod Melody tent features stars of stage and screen on its stage. There's a two-night minimum stay.

Isaiah B. Hall House ✪

152 WHIG STREET, DENNIS, MASSACHUSETTS 02638

Tel: **(617) 385-9928**
Best Time to Call: **8 AM–10 PM**
Host(s): **Marie and Dick Brophy**
Location: **7 mi. E of Hyannis**
No. of Rooms: **11**
No. of Private Baths: **10**
Max. No. Sharing Bath: **4**
Double/pb: **$50–$65**
Single/pb: **$35–$50**
Double/sb: **$40**
Single/sb: **$30**
Open: **Feb.–Dec.**
Breakfast: **Continental**
Credit Cards: **MC, VISA**
Pets: **No**
Children: **Welcome, over 7**
Smoking: **Permitted**
Social Drinking: **Permitted**

This Cape Cod farmhouse built in 1857 offers casual country living on the quiet, historic northside. The house is decorated in true New England style with quilts, antiques, and Oriental rugs. Four rooms have balconies and one has a fireplace. Within walking distance are the beach, good restaurants, the Cape Playhouse, and countless antiques and craft shops. It is also close to freshwater swimming, bike paths, and golf.

The Penny House

P.O. BOX 238, ROUTE 6, EASTHAM, MASSACHUSETTS 02651

Tel: **(617) 255-6632**
Host(s): **Paul and Barbara Landry**
No. of Rooms: **11**
Max. No. Sharing Bath: **4**
Double/sb: **$60–$65**
Open: **All year**
Reduced Rates: **20%, Sept.–June**
Breakfast: **Full**
Credit Cards: **MC, VISA**
Pets: **No**
Children: **No**
Smoking: **Permitted**
Social Drinking: **Permitted**
Foreign Languages: **French**

Back in 1751, Captain Isiah Horton built the Penny House and crowned it with a shipbuilder's bow roof. She has weathered many a storm, but this spacious cape just gets more charming. The rooms have wide-pine floors and are decorated with a blend of antiques and country accents. Your hosts provide special treats in the public room, where beautiful old wooden beams provide a sense of nostalgia. The Penny House is five minutes from National Seashore Park, and just as convenient to the warm waters off Cape Cod Bay.

The Parsonage ✪

P.O. BOX 1016, 202 MAIN STREET, EAST ORLEANS, MASSACHUSETTS 02643

Tel: **(617) 255-8217**
Best Time to Call: **9 AM–9 PM**
Host(s): **Chris and Lloyd Shand**
Location: **90 mi. SE of Boston**
No. of Rooms: **6**
No. of Private Baths: **2**
Max. No. Sharing bath: **4**
Double/pb: **$50**
Single/pb: **$45**
Double/sb: **$45**
Single/sb: **$40**
Suites: **$60**
Open: **All year**
Reduced Rates: **20%, Nov.–Apr.**
Breakfast: **Continental**
Credit Cards: **MC, VISA**
Pets: **No**
Children: **Welcome**
Smoking: **Permitted**
Social Drinking: **Permitted**

The Parsonage is located on the road to Nauset Beach, a street lined with lovely old homes of early settlers and sea captains. This spacious Cape Cod, circa 1770, has old wavy glass windows, low ceilings, and is decorated with antiques. Enjoy a homemade breakfast on a tray in your room or outside in the sunny courtyard. Cranberry muffins are the specialty of the house. The Parsonage is located between the Atlantic Ocean and Cape Cod Bay. Bike trails, restaurants, sailing, fishing, and swimming are minutes away.

The Arbor ✪

222 UPPER MAIN STREET, P.O. BOX 1628, EDGARTOWN, MARTHA'S VINEYARD, MASSACHUSETTS 02539

Tel: **(617) 627-8137**
Best Time to Call: **8 AM–8 PM**
Host(s): **Peggy Hall**
Location: **7 mi. SE of Woods Hole Ferry**
No. of Rooms: **6**
No. of Private Baths: **4**
Max. No. Sharing Bath: **4**
Double/pb: **$85–$90**
Single/pb: **$70**
Double/sb: **$70**
Open: **May 1–Oct. 31**
Reduced Rates: **$25 less, May 1–June 14; Sept. 15–Oct. 30**
Breakfast: **Continental**
Credit Cards: **MC, VISA**
Pets: **No**
Children: **Welcome, over 12**
Smoking: **Permitted**
Social Drinking: **Permitted**

This turn-of-the-century guest house offers island visitors a unique experience in comfort and charm. The house is walking distance from downtown, and at the same time provides the feeling of being away from it all. Relax in a hammock, enjoy tea on the porch, and retire to a cozy room filled with the smell of fresh flowers. Peggy provides setups and mixers at cocktail time, and will gladly direct you to unspoiled beaches, walking trails, sailing, fishing, and the delights of Martha's Vineyard. There's a three-night minimum stay required in season.

Captain Tom Lawrence House

75 LOCUST STREET, FALMOUTH, MASSACHUSETTS 02540

Tel: **(617) 540-1445 or 548-9178**
Best Time to Call: **8 AM till noon**
Host(s): **Barbara Sabo**
Location: **67 mi. S of Boston**
No. of Rooms: **6**
No. of Private Baths: **4**
Max. No. Sharing Bath: **4**
Double/pb: **$58–$75**
Double/sb: **$45–$60**
Open: **All year**
Reduced Rates: **Off-season**
Breakfast: **Full**
Credit Cards: **MC, VISA**
Pets: **No**
Children: **Welcome, over 11**
Smoking: **Permitted**
Social Drinking: **Permitted**
Airport/Station Pickup: **Yes**
Foreign Languages: **German**

Captain Lawrence was a successful whaler in the 1800s. When he retired from the sea, he built himself a town residence on Locust Street. Today, the house remains much as he left it, including the original hardwood floors. In the morning, Barbara serves a hearty breakfast of fruit and specialties such as quiche, crêpes, and eggs Florentine. She grinds her own flour from organically grown grain. She will gladly help you get around town—it's half a mile to the beach, a short walk to downtown Falmouth, and four miles to Woods Hole Seaport.

Palmer House Inn ✪

81 PALMER AVENUE, FALMOUTH, MASSACHUSETTS 02540

Tel: **(617) 548-1230**
Best Time to Call: **After 2 PM**
Host(s): **Phyllis Niemi and Bud Peacock**
Location: **1 block from Rte. 28**
No. of Rooms: **8**
No. of Private Baths: **8**
Double/pb: **$75–$90**
Single/pb: **$60–$65**
Open: **All year**
Reduced Rates: **Off-season**
Breakfast: **Full**
Credit Cards: **MC, VISA**
Pets: **No**
Children: **Welcome, over 14**
Smoking: **Permitted**
Social Drinking: **Permitted**

Warmth and charm are evident in this turn-of-the-century Victorian home, with its stained-glass windows, soft warm wood, antiques, and collectibles. Centrally located within the Historic District, it is convenient to recreational diversions, miles of sandy beaches, ferries, and Woods Hole. Return from your afternoon activities and enjoy a glass of lemonade in a rocker on the front porch. Spend your after-dinner hours relaxing before the fireplace or sampling theater offerings close by.

Village Green Inn ✪

40 WEST MAIN STREET, FALMOUTH, MASSACHUSETTS 02540

Tel: **(617) 548-5621**
Host(s): **Linda and Don Long**
Location: **18 mi. from Rte. 6, Exit 1**
No. of Rooms: **4**
No. of Private Baths: **2**
Max. No. Sharing Bath: **4**
Double/pb: **$80**
Double/sb: **$70**
Suites: **$95**
Open: **All year**
Reduced Rates: **20%, Oct. 15–May 15**
Breakfast: **Full**
Pets: **No**
Children: **No**
Smoking: **No**
Social Drinking: **Permitted**
Airport/Station Pickup: **Yes**

This lovely Victorian is located on Falmouth's village green. Feel free to relax on the outdoor porch, in the parlor, or in the study. Three of the guest rooms have fireplaces to take the chill out of blustery evenings. Breakfast is a gastronomical treat that includes hot, spiced fruit, eggs Mornay, and homemade breads and muffins topped off with freshly ground coffee. Linda and Don look forward to pampering you with such delights as sherry, cordials, lemonade, fresh flowers, and sinfully delicious chocolates.

Wyndemere House ✪

718 PALMER AVENUE, FALMOUTH, MASSACHUSETTS 02540

Tel: **(617) 540-7069**
Best Time to Call: **Mornings; evenings**
Host(s): **Carole Railsback**
Location: **.8 mi. from Rte. 28 South**
No. of Rooms: **6**
No. of Private Baths: **4**
Max. No. Sharing Bath: **4**
Double/pb: **$85**
Single/pb: **$75**
Double/sb: **$75**
Single/sb: **$65**
Suite: **$95**
Open: **May–Oct.**
Reduced Rates: **Weekly**
Breakfast: **Full**
Pets: **No**
Children: **Welcome, over 12**
Smoking: **Permitted**
Social Drinking: **Permitted**
Airport/Station Pickup: **Yes**

This Paul Revere Colonial was built at the end of the 18th century and was completely renovated in 1980. Its bright, airy rooms are filled with

English furnishings, elegant antiques, and chintz accents. Guests are encouraged to make themselves at home in the reading areas and library, TV room, and on the patio. In the afternoon, tea is served on the terrace, along with coffee and sangria. Your hostess also provides setups for cocktails. In the morning such breakfast delights as eggs Benedict or apple Dutch pancakes are offered in the main dining room. Wyndemere House is nestled in a cool, wooded area off the beaten track, yet is close to downtown Falmouth and is a few minutes from two beautiful beaches. A minimum two-night stay is required.

The Coach House ✪

74 SISSON ROAD, HARWICH PORT, MASSACHUSETTS 02646

Tel: **(617) 432-9452**
Host(s): **Sara and Cal Ayer**
Location: **1 mi. from Rtes. 39 and 124**
No. of Rooms: **2**
No. of Private Baths: **2**
Double/pb: **$60**
Single/pb: **$60**
Open: **Apr.–Oct.**
Breakfast: **Continental**
Credit Cards: **AMEX, MC, VISA**
Pets: **No**
Children: **No**
Smoking: **Permitted**
Social Drinking: **Permitted**

Built in 1909, the Coach House was the original barn of one of Cape Cod's old estates. In the mid-1950s the barn was fully converted into a lovely Cape Cod home. The rooms are quiet and elegant, and guests may choose from king- and queen-size beds. A breakfast of fresh fruit compote, home-baked muffins, coffee cake, or croissants is served in the dining room each morning. Enjoy three picturesque harbors, beautiful beaches, sailing, windsurfing, golf, and tennis. A 21-mile hard-surface bike trail will take you through the scenic woods and cranberry bogs to the National Seashore. Your hosts will gladly recommend shops, museums, fine restaurants, and summer theater.

The Inn on Bank Street ✪

88 BANK STREET, HARWICH PORT, MASSACHUSETTS 02646

Tel: **(617) 432-3206**
Best Time to Call: **8 AM–10 PM**
Host(s): **Arky and Janet Silverio**
Location: **85 mi. S of Boston**
No. of Rooms: **6**
No. of Private Baths: **6**
Double/pb: **$50–$60**
Single/pb: **$45–$55**
Suites: **$85–$100**
Open: **Apr. 1–Nov. 30**
Reduced Rates: **Available**
Breakfast: **Continental**
Credit Cards: **MC, VISA**
Pets: **No**
Children: **Welcome, over 7**
Smoking: **Permitted**
Social Drinking: **Permitted**
Airport/Station Pickup: **Yes**
Foreign Languages: **Italian, Spanish**

This contemporary, sprawling Cape is set in a quaint old town named after an English village. The main house has a large living room and library, with a fine selection of vacation reading. Guest rooms are decorated with comfortable country-style modern pieces. In the morning, breakfast is served on the sun porch or outdoors on the shady grounds where the roses grow wild. Specialties of the house include cranberry crisp, French toast, and fresh-baked breads. The ocean is a five-minute walk from the inn, and you can bike the paved trails for a closer look at Harwich Port. Restaurants, art galleries, and a movie theater are also within walking distance.

Hawthorn Hill ✪

P.O. BOX 777, SANDWICH, MASSACHUSETTS 02563

Tel: **(617) 888-3333**
Best Time to Call: **Evenings**
Host(s): **Maxime Caron**
Location: **60 mi. S of Boston**
No. of Rooms: **2**
No. of Private Baths: **2**
Double/pb: **$60**
Open: **May–Nov.**
Breakfast: **Continental**
Pets: **Sometimes**
Children: **Sometimes**
Smoking: **Permitted**
Social Drinking: **Permitted**
Airport/Station Pickup: **Yes**
Foreign Languages: **German**

This rambling English country house, off Grove Street, is set on a hill surrounded by trees, with both the conveniences of an in-town location and the pleasantness of a country setting. The property has a spring-fed pond for boating and swimming, and there is plenty of space for long walks through the woods. Inside, your hostess welcomes you to large, sunny rooms, comfortably furnished. Hawthorn Hill is close to beaches, fishing, museums, and shops, and is adjacent to the Heritage Plantation. Maxime will gladly help plan sightseeing in this historic town or day trips to many nearby points of interest.

The Summer House ✪

P.O. BOX 341, 158 OLD MAIN STREET, SANDWICH, MASSACHUSETTS 02563

Tel: **(617) 888-4991**
Host(s): **Pamela Hunt**
Location: **2 mi. from Rte. 6**
No. of Rooms: **5**
No. of Private Baths: **1**
Max. No. Sharing Bath: **4**
Double/pb: **$60**
Double/sb: **$50**
Single/sb: **$35**
Open: **May 1–Nov. 30**
Breakfast: **Continental**
Credit Cards: **MC, VISA**
Pets: **No**
Children: **Welcome, over 10**
Smoking: **Permitted**
Social Drinking: **Permitted**
Airport/Station Pickup: **Yes**

The Summer House is a Greek Revival dating back to 1835. Antique furniture, fireplaces, original woodwork, and hardwood floors bring back the original aura of this newly restored home. A sunny breakfast room filled with books and the adjoining parlor provide for comfortable relaxation. Your hostess invites you to enjoy the surrounding lawns and gardens. Pamela is happy to direct guests to the famous Sandwich Glass Museum and the beach, a half mile away.

Little Harbor Guest House ✪

20 STOCKTON SHORTCUT, WAREHAM, MASSACHUSETTS 02571

Tel: **(617) 295-6329**
Host(s): **Dennis and Ken**
Location: **15 mi. N of Plymouth**
No. of Rooms: **4**
Max. No. Sharing Bath: **4**
Double/sb: **$47**
Single/sb: **$40**
Suites: **$67**
Open: **All year**
Reduced Rates: **20%, Nov. 1–May 1**
Breakfast: **Continental**
Pets: **Sometimes**
Children: **Welcome**
Smoking: **Permitted**
Social Drinking: **Permitted**
Airport/Station Pickup: **Yes**

The Little Harbor Guest House is set on three acres surrounded by a lovely 18-hole golf course. The house is a rambling Cape Cod, dating back to 1703. The large, sunny rooms are comfortable and quiet, furnished in antiques, wicker, and lots of plants. Dennis and Ken prepare a lovely breakfast, featuring many types of homemade breads. They have bicycles to lend, and will gladly give directions to local attractions. The beach is less than a half mile away, and it's just 20 minutes to Plymouth and Hyannis.

The Manor House

57 MAINE AVENUE, WEST YARMOUTH, MASSACHUSETTS 02673

Tel: **(617) 771-9211**
Host(s): **Sherry Braun**
Location: **1 mi. E of Hyannis**
No. of Rooms: **6**
No. of Private Baths: **6**
Double/pb: **$55–$60**
Single/pb: **$52–$57**
Open: **May 15–Oct. 10**
Reduced Rates: **Off-season**
Breakfast: **Continental**
Pets: **No**
Children: **Welcome, over 6**
Smoking: **Permitted**
Social Drinking: **Permitted**

This large white Dutch Colonial is one block from the beach on Lewis Bay. It is decorated with lovely antiques, handmade quilts, plants, and dried flower arrangements. It is close to golf, tennis, antique shops, fine restaurants, and the ferry dock, although it is in a quiet seaside area.

The Marlborough ✪

320 WOODS HOLE ROAD, WOODS HOLE, MASSACHUSETTS 02543

Tel: **(617) 548-6218**
Best Time to Call: **3–9 PM**
Host(s): **Patricia Morris**
Location: **2½ mi. from Rte. 28**
No. of Rooms: **6**
No. of Private Baths: **5**
Max. No. Sharing Bath: **4**
Double/pb: **$65–$85**
Double/sb: **$60–$80**
Single/pb: **$65–$70**
Single/sb: **$60–$65**
Separate Guest Cottage: **$85, for 2**
Open: **All year**
Reduced Rates: **Available**
Breakfast: **Full**
Pets: **Sometimes**
Children: **Welcome**
Smoking: **Permitted**
Social Drinking: **Permitted**
Foreign Languages: **French**

This faithful reproduction of a Full Cape house is decorated with collectibles, antiques, designer quilts, and handcrafted spreads. It is situated on a shaded half-acre that includes a paddle tennis court, swimming pool, a hammock, croquet, and picnicking facilities. A private beach is nearby with a three-mile bike path running past it. It's a mile from the Martha's Vineyard and Nantucket ferries. Patricia serves a pre-dinner treat of cheese and sherry, and her gourmet breakfast is a celebration. Afternoon tea is a three-course mini-meal. The Oceanographic and Marine Biological laboratories are in town.

CENTRAL/WESTERN/SOUTHERN MASSACHUSETTS

1797 House of Amacord ✪

1797 UPPER STREET, BUCKLAND, MASSACHUSETTS 01338

Tel: **(413) 625-2975, 625-2697**
Best Time to Call: **Evenings; weekends**
Host(s): **Janet Turley**
Location: **13 mi. from Rte. 91, Exit 26**
No. of Rooms: **2**
No. of Private Baths: **2**
Double/pb: **$58**
Single/pb: **$42**
Open: **Jan. 2–Oct. 31**
Breakfast: **Full**
Pets: **No**
Children: **No**
Smoking: **Permitted**
Social Drinking: **Permitted**

This white center-hall Colonial (circa 1797) has a lovely screened-in porch for summer enjoyment and four fireplaces for cozy winter pleasure. Prestigious Deerfield Academy, Old Deerfield, Sturbridge Village, and the historic sights of Pioneer Valley are all close by. The University of Massachusetts, Smith, Amherst, and Williams are convenient to Janet's home. Special French toast served with stuffed baked tomatoes is a sensational breakfast treat.

Chalet d'Alicia

EAST WINDSOR ROAD, PERU, MASSACHUSETTS 01235

Tel: **(413) 655-8292**
Host(s): **Alice and Richard Halvorsen**
Location: **15 mi. E of Pittsfield**
No. of Rooms: **3**
Max. No. Sharing Bath: **4**
Double/sb: **$35**
Single/sb: **$35**
Open: **All year**
Breakfast: **Full**
Pets: **Sometimes**
Children: **Welcome**
Smoking: **Permitted**
Social Drinking: **Permitted**

Chalet d'Alicia is set high in the Berkshire Mountains overlooking the majestic countryside. This Swiss chalet–style home offers a private, casual atmosphere. The large front deck is a perfect spot for reading, sunning, or chatting. Alice and Richard are proud to make everyone feel at home. For breakfast they serve homemade muffins, and jams made from local wild berries. The property has a pond and plenty of places for cross-country skiing. Tanglewood, Jacob's Pillow, and the Williamstown Theatre Festival are all within easy reach.

Perryville Inn ✪

157 PERRYVILLE ROAD, REHOBOTH, MASSACHUSETTS 02769

Tel: **(617) 252-9239**
Best Time to Call: **8 AM–10 PM**
Host(s): **Tom and Betsy Charnecki**
Location: **8 mi. E of Providence, R.I.**
No. of Rooms: **5**
No. of Private Baths: **3**
Max. No. Sharing Bath: **4**
Double/pb: **$55–$75**
Double/sb: **$40**
Open: **All year**
Breakfast: **Continental**
Credit Cards: **AMEX, MC, VISA**
Pets: **Sometimes**
Children: **Welcome**
Smoking: **Permitted**
Social Drinking: **Permitted**

This 19th-century restored farmhouse is located on 4½ acres featuring a quiet brook, stone walls, and shaded paths, with ample spots for a picnic or enjoying nature. You are welcome to use your hosts' bikes for local touring. There's a public golf course across the road, hiking, tennis, hayrides, cross-country skiing, and hot-air balloon rides. It's a short drive to antique shops, museums, a restored one-room schoolhouse, and fine seafood restaurants. Don't miss a traditional New England clambake. All rooms are accented with colorful handmade quilts, and the sitting rooms are well stocked with books, games, and puzzles. Brown University, Wheaton College, and the Rhode Island School of Design are within a 10-mile radius of the inn.

Lakeshore Bed and Breakfast ✪

94 SOUTH SHORE DRIVE, STURBRIDGE, MASSACHUSETTS 01566

Tel: **(617) 347-9495**
Best Time to Call: **9 AM–9 PM**
Host(s): **Paul and Jeannette Baillargeon**
Location: **50 mi. W of Boston**
No. of Rooms: **3**
Max. No. Sharing Bath: **3**
Double/sb: **$50**
Single/sb: **$45**
Open: **May 1–Oct. 31**
Breakfast: **Full**
Pets: **No**
Children: **Welcome**
Smoking: **Permitted**
Social Drinking: **Permitted**
Foreign Languages: **French**

This lakeside contemporary is on one of Massachusetts's cleanest lakes, Quacumquasit. Enjoy fishing, boating, swimming, sunbathing, and beautiful sunsets on a private beach, just steps from your room. A hearty breakfast is served on the terrace each morning. In the evening, you are welcome to use the grill and picnic tables for a barbecue. Lakeshore is four miles from Old Sturbridge Village and shopping areas. Your hosts are happy to help make sightseeing plans for you.

The Golden Goose ✪

MAIN ROAD, BOX 36, TYRINGHAM, MASSACHUSETTS 01264

Tel: **(413) 243-3008**
Best Time to Call: **8 AM–8 PM**
Host(s): **Lilja and Joseph Rizzo**
Location: **4 mi. from Mass. Tpk., Exit 2-Lee**
No. of Rooms: **5**
No. of Private Baths: **3**
Max. No. Sharing Bath: **4**
Double/pb: **$60–$70**
Single/pb: **$55–$65**
Double/sb: **$50–$60**
Single/sb: **$45–$55**
Suites: **$70–$85**
Open: **All year**
Reduced Rates: **Available**
Breakfast: **Continental**
Pets: **No**
Children: **Welcome, in apt. suite**
Smoking: **Permitted**
Social Drinking: **Permitted**

The inn lies between Stockbridge and Lenox in the Berkshires. Antique beds with firm new mattresses, and washstands are in each bedroom. Lilja and Joseph serve hors d'oeuvres and drinks by the fireside in the two common rooms. In warm weather, you may play croquet, volleyball, badminton, hike the Appalachian Trail, or fish for trout in the brook across the street and barbecue it at "home." In summer, the cultural attractions of Tanglewood and Jacob's Pillow are nearby. Skiing is popular in winter. There's a two-night weekend minimum during the Tanglewood season, and a three-night minimum on holidays. A $5 surcharge is added for one-night stays.

The Wildwood Inn ✪

121 CHURCH STREET, WARE, MASSACHUSETTS 01082

Tel: **(413) 967-7798**
Best Time to Call: **5–8 PM**
Host(s): **Margaret and Geoffrey Lobenstine**
Location: **70 mi. W of Boston**
No. of Rooms: **5**
Max. No. Sharing Bath: **3**
Double/sb: **$33–$61**
Open: **All year (Nov.–Apr., weekends only)**
Reduced Rates: **10%, weekly**
Breakfast: **Full**
Pets: **No**
Children: **Welcome, over 6**
Smoking: **No**
Social Drinking: **Permitted**

Everything about this old-fashioned country home with its rambling two acres is designed to help you unwind. There's a swing on the porch, a hammock under the firs, a blazing fire in the winter, a Norman Rockwell-esque brook-fed swimming hole in the summer. Your hosts have furnished their guest rooms with heirloom quilts and American primitive antiques, all of which work to spell welcome. Homemade bread and Margaret's own peach butter and "country yummies" are included with breakfast. Sturbridge Village, Old Deerfield, and Amherst offer recreational activities that are all close by. You can stroll to the tennis court or borrow the canoe, or visit in the parlor for stimulating conversation. Margaret does her best to spoil you.

NANTUCKET

Lynda Watts Bed & Breakfast ✪

10 UPPER VESTAL STREET, NANTUCKET, MASSACHUSETTS 02554

Tel: **(617) 228-3828**
Host(s): **Lynda and David Watts**
No. of Rooms: **2**
Max. No. Sharing Bath: **4**
Double/sb: **$60**
Open: **All year**
Reduced Rates: **20%, Jan. 1–Apr. 15**
Breakfast: **Continental**
Pets: **No**
Children: **Welcome**
Smoking: **Permitted**
Social Drinking: **Permitted**

Lynda and David's 12-year-old saltbox house is located on a quiet street in a residential neighborhood, only a seven-minute walk to town. It is simply furnished, and guest rooms are equipped with TVs. Weather permitting, breakfast is served on the sunny patio. A two-night minimum stay is required.

MICHIGAN

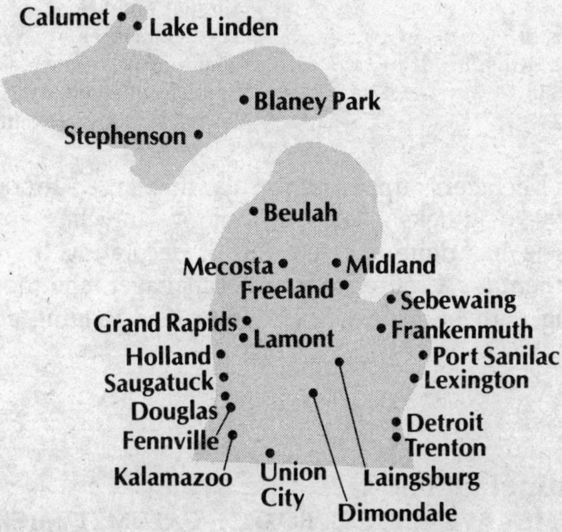

Calumet
Lake Linden
Blaney Park
Stephenson
Beulah
Mecosta
Midland
Freeland
Sebewaing
Grand Rapids
Lamont
Frankenmuth
Holland
Port Sanilac
Saugatuck
Lexington
Douglas
Detroit
Fennville
Trenton
Kalamazoo
Union City
Laingsburg
Dimondale

Windermere Inn ✪

747 CRYSTAL DRIVE, BEULAH, MICHIGAN 49617

Tel: **(616) 882-7264**
Best Time to Call: **1–6 PM**
Host(s): **Loralee and Bill Ludwig**
Location: **200 mi. N of Detroit**
No. of Rooms: **4**
No. of Private Baths: **4**
Double/pb: **$60**
Single/pb: **$60**

Open: **All year**
Reduced Rates: **10%, weekly**
Breakfast: **Continental**
Credit Cards: **MC, VISA**
Pets: **No**
Children: **No**
Smoking: **Permitted**
Social Drinking: **Permitted**

Set among century-old pine trees, this many-gabled white farmhouse is delightfully decorated with antiques. Loralee and Bill put fruit and flowers in each room daily, and coffee and snacks are always available. There's a fine view of Crystal Lake, and you're close to Sleeping Bear National Lakeshore and Interlochen Arts Academy. Recreational activities are plentiful in all seasons.

Celibeth House

ROUTE 1, BOX 58A, M-77 BLANEY PARK ROAD, BLANEY PARK, MICHIGAN 49836

Tel: **(906) 283-3409**
Host(s): **Elsa Strom**
Location: **60 mi. W of Mackinaw Bridge**
No. of Rooms: **8**
No. of Private Baths: **8**
Double/pb: **$30**
Single/pb: **$25**
Open: **May 1–Dec. 1**
Reduced Rates: **10% less on 3rd night**
Breakfast: **Continental**
Credit Cards: **No**
Pets: **Sometimes**
Children: **Welcome (crib)**
Smoking: **Permitted**
Social Drinking: **Permitted**

Located on Michigan's upper peninsula, this large 24-room mansion, built in 1890, overlooks a lake. Elsa enjoys traveling and collecting antiques. She has done a lovely job of decorating the house with special mementos. A retired personnel manager, she thoroughly enjoys visiting with her guests. Gardening and reading are her pleasures.

The Calumet House ✪

1159 CALUMET AVENUE, P.O. BOX 126, CALUMET, MICHIGAN 49913

Tel: **(906) 337-1936**
Host(s): **George and Rose Chivses**
Location: **10 mi. N of Hancock-Houghton**
No. of Rooms: **2**
Max. No. Sharing Bath: **4**
Double/sb: **$22**
Single/sb: **$18**
Open: **May 15–Sept. 15**
Breakfast: **Full**
Pets: **No**
Children: **No**
Smoking: **No**
Social Drinking: **Permitted**
Airport/Station Pickup: **Yes**
Foreign Languages: **Finnish**

The Calumet House is set in a historic old mining town, known for its clean air and scenic vistas. Built in 1895, the house boasts its original woodwork and is filled with local antique furnishings. In the morning, you're in for a treat with Rose's home cooking. Breakfast specialties include English scones, pancakes, local berries in season, and homemade jam. Calumet House is within walking distance of the village, with its opera house, museum, and antique shops. Your hosts will also direct you to local hunting and fishing, as well as to places that any botanist would call paradise. It's 10 miles north of Michigan Technological University and Suomi College.

"Griffin House" ✪

303 NORTHBRIDGE STREET, DEWITT, MICHIGAN 48820

Tel: **(517) 669-9486**
Best Time to Call: **Before noon**
Host(s): **Phyllis and Roger Griffin**
Location: **5 mi. from I-96**
No. of Rooms: **1**
No. of Private Baths: **1**
Double/pb: **$40**
Open: **Sept.–June**
Breakfast: **Full**
Pets: **No**
Children: **No**
Smoking: **No**
Social Drinking: **Permitted**
Foreign Languages: **German**

Built in 1851, this large Colonial is situated on a quiet main street in a small country town. It is only 20 minutes from the campus of Michigan State University, where Roger lectures, or to downtown Lansing and the new Conference Center. The area abounds with golf courses, 17 at last count. Antiquing in Williamstown is a pleasant activity. A mammoth English breakfast, including eggs, meats, mushrooms and tomatoes, cereal, marmalade, and hot rolls, is a good reason to skip lunch!

Bannicks B&B ✪

4608 MICHIGAN ROAD, DIMONDALE, MICHIGAN 48821

Tel: **(517) 646-0224**
Host(s): **Pat and Jim Bannick**
Location: **5 mi. SW of Lansing**
No. of Rooms: **2**
Max. No. Sharing Bath: **3**
Double/sb: **$30**
Single/sb: **$15**
Open: **All year**
Breakfast: **Full**
Pets: **No**
Children: **Welcome**
Smoking: **No**
Social Drinking: **No**

This large ranch-style home features a stained-glass entry, nautical-style basement, and a Mona Lisa bathroom. Guest accommodations consist of comfortable bedrooms and a den-TV room. Your hosts invite you to share a cup of coffee anytime. They will be happy to advise on the sights of Michigan's capital city, just five minutes away. Michigan State University is eight miles away.

Rosemont Inn ✪

83 LAKESHORE DRIVE, P.O. BOX 541, DOUGLAS, MICHIGAN 49406

Tel: **(616) 857-2637**
Best Time to Call: **8 AM–8 PM**
Host(s): **Ric and Cathy Gillette**
Location: **10 mi. S of Holland**
No. of Rooms: **14**
No. of Private Baths: **14**
Double/pb: **$75**
Open: **All year**
Reduced Rates: **Weekly; off-season**
Breakfast: **Continental**

Credit Cards: **MC, VISA**
Pets: **No**
Children: **Welcome**
Smoking: **Permitted**
Social Drinking: **Permitted**

The Rosemont is a Victorian inn with gingerbread trim. It began receiving guests in 1886 and still maintains a tradition of country living and hospitality. The house is furnished in country prints and antiques reproductions, with fireplaces in ten of the guest rooms. On a large porch, enjoy the cool breezes from Lake Michigan, whose beaches are directly across the street. Or swim in the inn's heated pool. Your hosts will gladly supply information on boat trips, golf, and the sights of Saugatuck.

Hidden Pond Farm

5975 128TH AVENUE, FENNVILLE, MICHIGAN 49408

Tel: **(616) 561-2491**
Host(s): **Edward Kennedy**
Location: **40 mi. SW of Grand Rapids**
No. of Rooms: **2**
No. of Private Baths: **2**
Double/pb: **$85**
Open: **All year**
Reduced Rates: **Available**
Breakfast: **Continental**
Credit Cards: **VISA**
Pets: **No**
Children: **Welcome**
Smoking: **Permitted**
Social Drinking: **Permitted**
Airport/Station Pickup: **Yes**

Hidden Pond Farm is set on 28 acres of woods, perfect for bird-watching, hiking, and cross-country skiing. Your host designed the sprawling, 13-room house to provide for the privacy and relaxation of visitors. Seven rooms on the entry level are for the exclusive use of guests and include the bedrooms and baths, a living room with fireplace, dining room, den, kitchen, and breakfast porch. Edward Kennedy is a retired insurance executive who enjoys pleasing guests and creating an atmosphere of quiet elegance. There are no schedules, and breakfast is served when you wake up. Behind the house is a ravine with a pond where you may see a deer or two. An outdoor deck and patio are available for relaxing and taking in the sun. This lovely retreat is near the beaches on Lake Michigan, the boutiques of Saugatuck, and the winery and cider mill in Fennville.

Frankenmuth Bed & Breakfast Reservations ✪

337 TRINKLEIN STREET, FRANKENMUTH, MICHIGAN 48734

Tel: **(517) 652-8897**
Coordinator: **Beverley J. Bender**
State/Regions Covered: **Bay City, Bridgeport, Frankenmuth, Harbor Beach, Sebewaing, Trenton**

Rates (Single/Double):

	Single	Double
Modest:	**N/A**	**$35–$40**
Average:	**N/A**	**$40–$45**
Luxury:	**N/A**	**$45**

Credit Cards: **AMEX**

Dating back to the mid-1800s, this area has a distinctive German flavor. There's a Bavarian Festival in June, Volkslaufe races in July, a Polka Festival in August, an Oktoberfest, and a shopping spree in any season at Bronners Christmas Wonderland. To assure that you feel more like a friend than a paying guest, you will receive the name and address of your host after first meeting Beverley. Instead of paying the host, payment is made directly to the reservation service. She usually escorts you to the B&B personally to make the introductions.

Wellock Inn ✪

404 SOUTH HURON AVENUE, HARBOR BEACH, MICHIGAN 48441

Tel: **(517) 479-3645**
Host(s): **Bill and Lavonne Cloutier**
Location: **125 mi. N of Detroit**
No. of Rooms: **4**
No. of Private Baths: **2**
Max. No. Sharing Bath: **4**
Double/pb: **$40**
Double/sb: **$35**
Open: **All year**
Reduced Rates: **Weekly; seniors**
Credit Cards: **MC, VISA**
Breakfast: **Continental**
Pets: **Welcome**
Children: **Welcome**
Smoking: **Permitted**
Social Drinking: **Permitted**
Airport/Station Pickup: **Local marina**

Beautiful oak woodwork, antique furnishings, and the artful use of beveled glass add to the charm of Lavonne and Bill's gracious home. You may enjoy breakfast in the privacy of your room or with the other guests in the dining room. Afterward, stroll to the nearby beach, browse through local shops or historic sites, fish from the breakwall, launch your boat, or play tennis or have a picnic in the park. Or, just relax at the inn and feel free to use the kitchen, living room, porch, laundry facilities, picnic table, and barbecue.

Dutch Country Bed & Breakfast ✪

339 EAST 16TH STREET, HOLLAND, MICHIGAN 49423

Tel: **(616) 396-3344**
Coordinator: **Shelley Walters**
State/Regions Covered: **Holland, Overisel, Saugatuck, Zeeland**
Rates (Single/Double):
Average: **$35** **$45**

Shelley's host homes reflect a delightful Dutch ambience originating from a proud heritage and tradition. Every effort is made to accommodate children, the handicapped, nonsmokers, and foreign-speaking visitors. Windmill Island, Dutch Village, Holland State Park, theater, beaches, and all sorts of activities will keep you busy. Holland is ablaze with colorful tulips during the month of May. So reserve well in advance if you don't want to miss the tulips in bloom.

Old Wing Inn ✪

5298 EAST 147TH AVENUE, HOLLAND, MICHIGAN 49423

Tel: **(616) 392-7362**
Host(s): **Chuck and Chris Lorenz**
Location: **2 mi. SE of Holland**
No. of Rooms: **5**
Max. No. Sharing Bath: **4**
Double/sb: **$35**
Single/sb: **$35**
Open: **All year**
Breakfast: **Continental**
Pets: **No**
Children: **Welcome, over 8**
Smoking: **Permitted**
Social Drinking: **Permitted**

The Old Wing Inn, on the National Register of Historic Places, is Holland's oldest historic landmark home. It was built as the center of an Ottawa Indian mission 140 years ago. Your hosts are local-history buffs eager to share their knowledge of the area. They have filled the house with lovely antiques and special pieces from their bottle collection. Perhaps you'll want to visit in May when the tulips bloom and the area is alive with color and special events. Local sights include a Dutch village, two wooden shoe factories, Windmill Island, and the Netherlands Museum. Note that the rates as shown are special for our readers, so be certain to say you read about the inn in *Bed & Breakfast U.S.A.* (The usual tariff is $40–$55.)

Hall House

106 THOMPSON STREET, KALAMAZOO, MICHIGAN 49007

Tel: **(616) 343-2500**
Best Time to Call: **Noon–8 PM**
Host(s): **Pamela and Terry O'Connor**
Location: **150 mi. E of Detroit**
No. of Rooms: **5**
No. of Private Baths: **3**
Max. No. Sharing Bath: **4**
Double/pb: **$63**
Single/pb: **$54**
Double/sb: **$44**
Single/sb: **$38**
Open: **All year**
Reduced Rates: **10%, weekly**
Breakfast: **Continental**
Credit Cards: **AMEX, MC, VISA**
Pets: **No**
Children: **Welcome, over 12**
Smoking: **Permitted**
Social Drinking: **Permitted**
Airport/Station Pickup: **Yes**

This stately Georgian Revival Colonial, with its spacious rooms and architecturally significant details, is located midway between Chicago and Detroit. It is less than an hour from winter skiing, the Lake Michigan shore, and the Midwest's largest wine-producing region. Pamela and Terry have tastefully furnished with an artful blend of contemporary and period styles. They will be happy to assist with your plans for theater, music, or sporting events. There are several fine restaurants nearby and they'll reserve a table for you.

Seven Oaks Farm ✪

7891 HOLLISTER ROAD, LAINGSBURG, MICHIGAN 48848

Tel: **(517) 651-5598**
Host(s): **Terry and Mary Brock**
Location: **15 mi. NE of East Lansing**
No. of Rooms: **3**
Max. No. Sharing Bath: **4**
Double/sb: **$40**
Single/sb: **$20**
Open: **All year**
Breakfast: **Full**
Other Meals: **Available**
Pets: **Welcome**
Children: **Welcome (crib)**
Smoking: **Permitted**
Social Drinking: **Permitted**
Airport/Station Pickup: **Yes**

Seven Oaks is a large, comfortable home on a quiet country road. There are 100 acres to roam, a fishing pond, and ample opportunity for bird watching, snowmobiling and cross-country skiing. The house dates back 100 years, with spacious, double-bedded rooms now newly remodeled. Guests are invited to browse in the library or relax on the screened-in porch. Nearby are country auctions, bowling, movies, golf, and museums, as well as Michigan State University.

The Stagecoach Stop ✪

0-4819 LEONARD ROAD WEST, P.O. BOX 18, LAMONT, MICHIGAN 49430

Tel: **(616) 677-3940**
Host(s): **Marcia Ashby**
Location: **3 mi. from I-96**
No. of Rooms: **3**
No. of Private Baths: **1**
Max. No. Sharing Bath: **4**
Double/pb: **$55**
Single/pb: **$50**
Double/sb: **$50**
Single/sb: **$45**
Open: **All year**
Breakfast: **Continental**
Credit Cards: **MC, VISA**
Pets: **Sometimes**
Children: **Welcome (crib)**
Smoking: **Permitted**
Social Drinking: **No**

Built in 1859, this clapboard house was a thriving stagecoach stop for many years. Its location, midway between Grand Rapids and Grand Haven, made it ideal for the weary traveler. While much has been added over time, the original section of the house remains unchanged. The decor is a blend of Early American furnishings and turn-of-the-century antiques. Guest quarters are extra large and located in a separate wing of the house. This picturesque village overlooking the Grand River has much to offer sightseers. After a day of activity, relax on the front-porch swing or inside an enclosed porch furnished in wicker and warmed by a wood stove.

Governor's Inn ✪

LEXINGTON, MICHIGAN 48450

Tel: **(313) 359-5770**
Host(s): **Jane and Bob MacDonald**
Location: **20 mi. N of Port Huron**
No. of Rooms: **3**
No. of Private Baths: **3**
Double/pb: **$35**
Single/pb: **$35**
Open: **May 1–Sept. 30**
Breakfast: **Continental**
Pets: **No**
Children: **Welcome, over 12**
Smoking: **Permitted**
Social Drinking: **Permitted**

A handsome residence built in 1859, it is located near the shore of Lake Huron. It has been refurbished to its original "summer home" style. Wicker furniture, rag rugs, iron beds, and green plants accent the light, airy decor. You can stroll to the nearby beach, browse through interesting shops, fish from the breakwater, or play golf or tennis. Jane and Bob, both educators, look forward to sharing their quaint village surroundings with you.

Vickie Van's Bed and Breakfast

5076 SOUTH LAKESHORE ROAD, LEXINGTON, MICHIGAN 48450

Tel: **(313) 359-5533**
Best Time to Call: **Mornings**
Host(s): **Vickie Van**
Location: **80 mi. N of Detroit**
No. of Rooms: **4**
No. of Private Baths: **2**
Max. No. Sharing Bath: **4**
Double/pb: **$43**
Single/pb: **$38**
Double/sb: **$43**
Single/sb: **$38**
Open: **All year**
Reduced Rates: **Available**
Breakfast: **Continental**
Pets: **No**
Children: **Welcome, over 11**
Smoking: **Permitted**
Social Drinking: **Permitted**

Vickie Van's is a big old white farmhouse with three porches. The house is situated on five acres right across the street from Lake Huron. The comfortable rooms are furnished with antiques, wicker, and canopy beds. Breakfast is served in the bright, colorful dining room, and includes fresh-picked berries, homemade muffins, hot croissants, served on fine linen and silver. Your hostess offers lemonade or iced tea in the afternoon. She will gladly direct you to the nearby marina, flea market, orchards, golf course, and much more.

Blue Lake Lodge ✪

9765 BLUE LAKE LODGE LANE, P.O. BOX 1, MECOSTA, MICHIGAN 49332

Tel: **(616) 972-8391**
Host(s): **Frank and Elaine Huisgen**
Location: **65 mi. NE of Grand Rapids**
No. of Rooms: **6**
Max. No. Sharing Bath: **6**
Double/sb: **$35**
Single/sb: **$30**
Open: **All year**
Reduced Rates: **10%, seniors**
Breakfast: **Continental**
Credit Cards: **MC, VISA**
Pets: **Sometimes**
Children: **Welcome (crib)**
Smoking: **No**
Social Drinking: **Permitted**
Airport/Station Pickup: **Yes**

This is a large, informal home built in 1913 and located on the shore of a beautiful lake. All lakeside activities, such as swimming, boating, and fishing, are available. It's close to restaurants, but cooking grills, guest refrigerator, and picnic tables will help you cut down on dining costs.

Raymond House Inn ✪

111 SOUTH RIDGE STREET, M-25, PORT SANILAC, MICHIGAN 48469

Tel: **(313) 622-8800**
Host(s): **Shirley Denison**
Location: **30 mi. N of Port Huron**
No. of Rooms: **6**
No. of Private Baths: **6**
Double/pb: **$50**
Open: **May 1–Oct. 31**
Reduced Rates: **10%, seniors**
Breakfast: **Continental**
Pets: **No**
Children: **Welcome, over 12**
Smoking: **Permitted**
Social Drinking: **Permitted**

Shirley will put you right at ease in her antique-filled inn with the conveniences of today and the ambience of 1895. Each bedroom is furnished with period furniture, brightly colored spreads, and lace curtains. There's an old-fashioned parlor and a dining room where you are served breakfast. Sport fishermen and sailboat enthusiasts will enjoy this area; cultural activities, quilting bees, and the annual summer festival are longtime traditions here. There is a pottery and sculpture gallery and an antique shop in the inn.

The Park House ✪

888 HOLLAND STREET, SAUGATUCK, MICHIGAN 49453

Tel: **(616) 857-4535**
Best Time to Call: **Evenings**
Host(s): **Lynda and Joe Petty**
Location: **35 mi. SW of Grand Rapids**
No. of Rooms: **7**
No. of Private Baths: **7**
Double/pb: **$55–$75**
Suites: **$100, for 5**
Open: **All year**
Reduced Rates: **Available**
Breakfast: **Continental**
Credit Cards: **MC, VISA**
Pets: **No**
Children: **Welcome, over 12**
Smoking: **Permitted**
Social Drinking: **Permitted**
Airport/Station Pickup: **Yes**

From Susan B. Anthony to the early Oxbow artists, guests have enjoyed the hospitality of Saugatuck's oldest residence. This two-story Greek Revival is located in the historic district, just a mile from Lake Michigan. The rooms have a country style, created with antiques, wide-pine floors, and a cozy fireplace. Spend the night in a queen-size bed and wake up to muffins and homemade jam. Nearby attractions include a boardwalk, dune schooner rides, the winery, and the Holland Tulip Festival.

Twin Gables Country Inn ✪

900 LAKE STREET, P.O. BOX 881, SAUGATUCK, MICHIGAN 49453

Tel: **(616) 857-4346**
Best Time to Call: **Afternoon**
Host(s): **Michael and Denise Simcik**
Location: **9 mi. S of Holland**
No. of Rooms: **10**
No. of Private Baths: **10**
Double/pb: **$50–$78**
Suites: **$67–$84**
Open: **All year**
Reduced Rates: **$34–$58, off-season**
Breakfast: **Continental**
Credit Cards: **MC, VISA**
Pets: **No**
Children: **Welcome, over 12**
Smoking: **Permitted**
Social Drinking: **Permitted**
Airport/Station Pickup: **Yes**
Foreign Languages: **French, Italian, Maltese**

This turn-of-the-century inn, a registered State Historic Site, overlooks Lake Kalamazoo. The guest rooms are attractively furnished with wicker, brass, and antiques. The embossed tin ceilings add to the charm. It's a short walk to the beach, marinas, museum, and theater. There is a two-night weekend minimum, May 1 through Labor Day. Michael and Denise specialize in old-fashioned hospitality.

Wickwood Inn ✪

510 BUTLER STREET, SAUGATUCK, MICHIGAN 49453

Tel: **(616) 857-1097**
Best Time to Call: **8 AM–5 PM**
Host(s): **Sue and Stub Louis**
Location: **8 mi. S of Holland**
No. of Rooms: **11**
No. of Private Baths: **11**
Double/pb: **$80–$115**
Suites: **$85–$110**
Open: **All year**
Reduced Rates: **$65–$100, Jan. 1–Apr. 30**
Breakfast: **Continental**
Credit Cards: **AMEX, MC, VISA**
Pets: **No**
Children: **No**
Smoking: **Permitted**
Social Drinking: **Permitted**
Airport/Station Pickup: **Yes**

The bedrooms of this stately Federal-style inn have pleasant British accents, with Laura Ashley fabrics and wallpapers; in each bath there are fine soaps and shampoos from London. All have fine antiques of pine, walnut, and cherry. Relax in the sunken garden room, screened gazebo, and library-bar, which is designed like an English gentleman's club. Guests will find hospitable touches throughout their stay, such as fresh flowers, afternoon teas, and homemade cakes at breakfast. The beaches at Lake Michigan, golf, tennis, and historic homes are all close by. There's a two-night minimum on weekends.

Rummel's Tree Haven ✪

41 NORTH BECK STREET, M-25, SEBEWAING, MICHIGAN 48759

Tel: **(517) 883-2450**
Best Time to Call: **Afternoons; evenings**
Host(s): **Carl and Erma Rummel**
Location: **28 mi. NE of Bay City**
No. of Rooms: **2**
Max. No. Sharing Bath: **3**
Double/sb: **$40**
Single/sb: **$30**
Open: **All year**
Breakfast: **Continental**
Pets: **Sometimes**
Children: **No**
Smoking: **Permitted**
Social Drinking: **Permitted**
Airport/Station Pickup: **Yes**

A tree grows right through the porch and roof of this charming old home that was built by the Beck family in 1878. Guests can relax in large, airy rooms furnished with twin beds and comfortable family pieces. City dwellers are sure to enjoy the small-town friendliness and the quiet of the countryside. Saginaw Bay offers fine fishing, hunting, boating, bird-watching, or just plain relaxing. Carl and Erma offer color TV, videocassettes, and the use of the barbecue and refrigerator. They love having company and will do all they can to make you feel welcome and relaxed.

Top of the Hill ✪

STAR ROUTE, BOX 1, STEPHENSON, MICHIGAN 49887

Tel: **(906) 753-4757**
Host(s): **Art and Phyllis Strohl**
Best Time to Call: **After 4 PM**
Location: **1 block from US 41**
No. of Rooms: **1**
No. of Private Baths: **1**
Double/pb: **$35**
Single/pb: **$30**
Open: **All year**
Reduced Rates: **10%, seniors**
Breakfast: **Continental**
Pets: **No**
Children: **Welcome, over 11**
Smoking: **No**
Social Drinking: **Permitted**

Top of the Hill is a comfortable bilevel home set in a pretty, small town. Art and Phyllis have been in the dairy business for 40 years and enjoy hosting travelers from all parts of the world. They offer one bedroom upstairs, and one on the lower level adjoining the rec room. Guests will find Stephenson to be a charming example of small-town America—some joke that there are sometimes more deer than people here. This is a wonderful place to take a break from tourist traps and discover nature. The Strohls are close to the shores of Green Bay, cross-country skiing, and a river for swimming. You are welcome to join your hosts for an evening snack.

Bear Haven

2947 FOURTH STREET, TRENTON, MICHIGAN 48183

Tel: **(313) 675-4844**
Best Time to Call: **After 4 PM**
Host(s): **Mike and Mary Passerman**
Location: **20 mi. S of Detroit**
No. of Rooms: **1**
No. of Private Baths: **1**
Double/pb: **$45**
Single/pb: **$35**
Open: **All year**
Breakfast: **Continental**
Pets: **No**
Children: **No**
Smoking: **Permitted**
Social Drinking: **Permitted**

Bear Haven is an 1870s farmhouse located in the Detroit metropolitan area. Mary is a collector of teddy bears, and her acquisitions are displayed throughout the house. The rooms are furnished eclectically, with both Early American and Victorian pieces. Guests are welcomed with tea and cookies, and are shown to comfortable rooms with beamed ceilings, fresh flowers, and fruit bowls. Mike and Mary go out of their way to please guests, and serve afternoon tea and sweets. In the morning, coffee will be brought right to your door. Later, you can come downstairs for fruit-filled croissants or fresh-baked muffins. The Passermans are close to the Henry Ford Museum, the Mazda plant, and near the boat to Bob-Lo Amusement Park.

The Victorian Villa Guesthouse ✪

601 NORTH BROADWAY STREET, UNION CITY, MICHIGAN 49094

Tel: **(517) 741-7383**
Host(s): **Ron Gibson**
Location: **20 mi. S of Battle Creek**
No. of Rooms: **8**
No. of Private Baths: **6**
Max. No. Sharing Bath: **4**
Double/pb: **$65–$70**
Single/pb: **$60–$65**
Double/sb: **$55**
Single/sb: **$50**
Open: **All year**
Breakfast: **Full**
Credit Cards: **MC, VISA**
Pets: **No**
Children: **Welcome**
Smoking: **No**
Social Drinking: **Permitted**
Airport/Station Pickup: **Yes**

The Victorian Villa is a 19th-century estate house furnished with antiques. Guests may choose from eight private chambers, all elegantly appointed. Chilled champagne, wine, cheese, and a private "tea-for-two" can be arranged. Fancy chocolates, a specialty of the house, are placed on the pillows at night. Your host will help make your visit as sparkling as you like, directing you to summer theater, museums, antique shops, and restaurants. Ask Ron about the special "getaway" weekends.

MINNESOTA

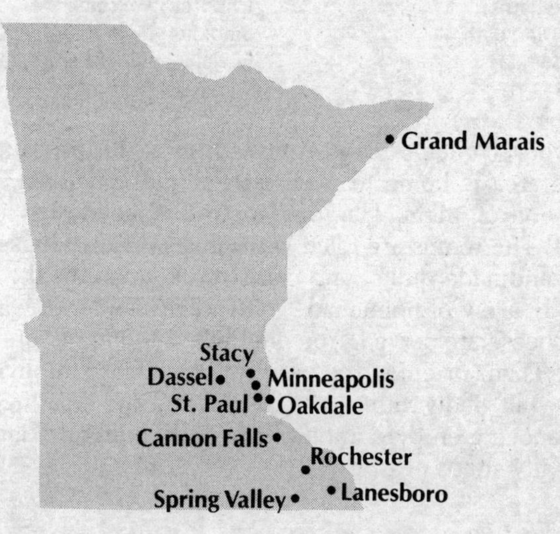

Bed & Breakfast Registry, Ltd.

P.O. BOX 80174, ST. PAUL, MINNESOTA 55108

Tel: **(612) 646-4238**
Best Time to Call: **9 AM–5 PM**
Coordinator: **Gary Winget**
States/Regions Covered: **Statewide and national**

Rates (Single/Double):

Modest:	**$25**	**$30**
Average:	**$40**	**$45**
Luxury:	**$85**	**$155**

Credit Cards: **MC, VISA**

The Twin City attractions of the Guthrie Theater, Walker Art Center, Art Institute, Omni Theater, and Science Center attract visitors from all over the country. There are delightful urban accommodations on Gary's roster, as well as more rural B&Bs for quiet serenity. He will be happy to offer vacation packages for your entire itinerary throughout North America. There is a $6 surcharge for a one-night stay.

Basswood Hills Farm ✪

ROUTE 1, BOX 331, CANNON FALLS, MINNESOTA 55009

Tel: **(507) 778-3259**
Best Time to Call: **Mornings**
Host(s): **Sylvia Pettit**
Location: **35 mi. SE of Minneapolis**
No. of Rooms: **4**
No. of Private Baths: **2**
Max. No. Sharing Bath: **4**
Double/pb: **$59**
Double/sb: **$49**
Suites: **$68**
Open: **All year**
Breakfast: **Full**
Credit Cards: **MC, VISA**
Pets: **No**
Children: **Welcome**
Smoking: **Permitted**
Social Drinking: **Permitted**

This sprawling contemporary is nestled on a hill in beautiful Sogn Valley. The area is home to many artists and craftsmen, and your hostess is one of them. Her flair for color and design is evident throughout. The rooms are filled with English furnishings, Victorian antiques, handmade quilts, and crafts of all kinds. In the morning, you'll find an array of homemade coffee cakes, and in the afternoon, wine and cheese are served. You are invited to lounge on the patio, explore the farm, or enjoy the beautiful view from the living room. Your host will gladly direct you to fishing and boating on Lake Byllesby, canoeing on the Cannon River, golf, riding, hiking, and the many specialty shops nearby.

Gabrielson's B&B

RURAL ROUTE 1, BOX 269, DASSEL, MINNESOTA 55325

Tel: **(612) 275-3609**
Best Time to Call: **Evening**
Host(s): **Elaine and Don Gabrielson**
Location: **65 mi. W of Minneapolis**
No. of Rooms: **1**
Max. No. Sharing Bath: **3**
Double/sb: **$30**
Single/sb: **$25**
Open: **All year**
Breakfast: **Continental**
Pets: **Sometimes**
Children: **Welcome, over 9**
Smoking: **No**
Social Drinking: **Permitted**

Perched on a hilltop, this 1910 white clapboard farmhouse, decorated in Early American style, overlooks a private lake. You are welcome to use the paddleboat for getting to the little island, where you can picnic. Or, try your hand at archery, trap shooting, or pond fishing. Elaine and Don are busy raising corn and beans, but they'll happily arrange a farm tour of Meeker County. Wine, cheese, and rolls are stocked in the guest refrigerator. The University of Minnesota is nearby. A hot tub and central air-conditioning add to your comfort.

Young's Island B&B ✪

GUNFLINT TRAIL 67-I, GRAND MARAIS, MINNESOTA 55604

Tel: **(218) 388-4487, 800-328-3325**
Best Time to Call: **7:30 AM–9:30 PM**
Host(s): **Barbara and Ted Young**
Location: **140 mi. NE of Duluth**
No. of Rooms: **1**
Max. No. Sharing Bath: **5**
Double/sb: **$50**
Single/sb: **$25**
Open: **All year**
Breakfast: **Full**
Other Meals: **Available in winter**
Pets: **No**
Children: **Welcome**
Smoking: **No**
Social Drinking: **Permitted**
Airport/Station Pickup: **Yes**

Young's Island is a secluded getaway overlooking the Boundary Waters wilderness. This 18-acre private island is located on Poplar Lake, a half mile from the Gunflint Trail. In summer, Barbara and Ted's 18-foot boat will transport you here from the mainland, while in winter they'll use their snowmobile for this purpose. Their 50-year-old home is of vertical split-log construction. It is nestled amid towering evergreens. Breakfast is hearty and plentiful, featuring just-collected eggs, and bacon, fried potatoes, fruit and cheese, biscuits with special jams, and lots of coffee. In summer, a canoe is provided for the duration of your stay. In winter, backcountry ski touring can be arranged.

Carrolton Country Inn & Cottage

ROUTE 2, BOX 139, LANESBORO, MINNESOTA 55949

Tel: **(507) 467-2257**
Best Time to Call: **Evenings**
Host(s): **Charles and Gloria Ruen**
Location: **35 mi. SE of Rochester**
No. of Rooms: **4**
Max. No. Sharing Bath: **4**
Double/sb: **$35**
Single/sb: **$20**
Separate Guest Cottage: **$15 per person; sleeps 6**
Suites: **$40**
Open: **All year**
Reduced Rates: **$5 less, Sun.–Thurs.; weekly**
Breakfast: **Full**
Pets: **Sometimes**
Children: **Welcome**
Smoking: **No**
Social Drinking: **Permitted**
Airport/Station Pickup: **Yes**
Foreign Languages: **Scandinavian**

Charles and Gloria Ruen welcome you to their country farmhouse, circa 1882. Nestled among the hills in an open valley, this is the perfect spot to enjoy the fresh air and the changing of the seasons. The house is decorated, country style, with antiques and still boasts the original milk-painted woodwork, dumbwaiter in the butler's pantry, and the old potbelly stove. Homemade muffins, jams, and plenty of hot coffee are served at breakfast, and snacks are offered later in the day.

Antique stores, craft shops, a winery, and the largest state fish hatchery are nearby. Hiking, biking, fishing, canoeing, and cross-country skiing can all be enjoyed here.

Creekside Bed & Breakfast ✪

P.O. BOX 19164, MINNEAPOLIS, MINNESOTA 55419

Tel: **(612) 922-9142**
Host(s): **John and Jeanne Banovetz**
Location: **1½ mi. from I-35W, Diamond Lake Exit**
No. of Rooms: **2**
No. of Private Baths: **1**
Max. No. Sharing Bath: **2**
Double/pb: **$40**
Single/pb: **$30**
Double/sb: **$35**
Single/sb: **$25**
Open: **All year**
Reduced Rates: **Weekly; family**
Breakfast: **Full**
Pets: **No**
Children: **Welcome**
Smoking: **Permitted**
Social Drinking: **Permitted**
Airport/Station Pickup: **Yes**

This Country-French brick and stucco three-story home is located within minutes of the Walker Art Center, Guthrie Theater, antiques shops, lakes, recreational sports, and Minnehaha Falls. You are welcome to relax in the living room, which features a cozy, book-lined window seat, fireplace, piano, and several antique pieces. The French doors lead to a screened porch. Breakfast is served in the formal dining room and features homemade breads, jams, fresh fruit, and granola. You are welcome to use the laundry facilities. John and Jeanne graciously offer afternoon snacks.

Evelo's Bed & Breakfast ✪

2301 BYRANT AVENUE SOUTH, MINNEAPOLIS, MINNESOTA 55405

Tel: **(612) 374-9656**
Best Time to Call: **After 4 PM**
Host(s): **David and Sheryl Evelo**
No. of Rooms: **4**
Max. No. Sharing Bath: **6**
Double/sb: **$30–$35**
Single/sb: **$20–$25**
Open: **All year**
Breakfast: **Full**
Pets: **No**
Children: **Welcome**
Smoking: **Permitted**
Social Drinking: **Permitted**

Located in the historic Lowry Hill East neighborhood, this century-old Victorian has one of the best-preserved interiors in the area and is furnished with fine period pieces. David and Sheryl are both schoolteachers. Breakfast often features quiche or egg casseroles. The house is within walking distance of the Guthrie Theater and the Walker Art Center.

Oakdale Tanners Lake ✪

886 GLENBROOK AVENUE NORTH, OAKDALE, MINNESOTA 55119

Tel: **(612) 739-0193**
Host(s): **Ray and Audrey Furchner**
Location: **10 mi. E of St. Paul**
No. of Rooms: **2**
No. of Private Baths: **1**
Max. No. Sharing Bath: **2**
Double/pb: **$40**
Single/sb: **$30**
Open: **All year**
Breakfast: **Continental**
Pets: **No**
Children: **No**
Smoking: **Permitted**
Social Drinking: **Permitted**

You can take in the excitement of nearby Minneapolis and St. Paul and return "home" to Ray and Audrey's contemporary split-level home to relax. Thoughtful touches such as a phone and TV are part of your accommodations. Their hobby is constructing and furnishing doll houses. You are welcome to use the pool table and the backyard; the coffeepot is always on.

Canterbury Inn Bed & Breakfast ✪

723 SECOND STREET S.W., ROCHESTER, MINNESOTA 55902

Tel: **(507) 289-5553**
Host(s): **Mary Martin and Jeffrey Van Sant**
Location: **90 mi. SE of Minneapolis**
No. of Rooms: **4**
No. of Private Baths: **4**
Double/pb: **$65**
Single/pb: **$55**
Open: **All year**
Breakfast: **Full**
Credit Cards: **MC, VISA**
Pets: **No**
Children: **Sometimes**
Smoking: **Permitted**
Social Drinking: **Permitted**
Airport/Station Pickup: **Yes**
Foreign Languages: **Italian**

This is a Victorian structure, just three blocks from the Mayo Clinic, with polished hardwood floors, stained-glass windows, and a cozy fireplace complete with carved mantel. Lace curtains and eclectic furnishings give it an air in keeping with its age. Enjoy games, music, and conversation in the parlor. Breakfast is served in the formal dining room and may include such delicious fare as eggs Benedict and German apple pancakes. Afternoon tea at 5:30 generally lingers into the evening.

Chase's Bed & Breakfast

508 NORTH HURON, SPRING VALLEY, MINNESOTA 55975

Tel: **(507) 346-2850**
Best Time to Call: **3 PM–9 PM**
Host(s): **Bob and Jeannine Chase**
Location: **26 mi. S of Rochester**
No. of Rooms: **5**
No. of Private Baths: **2**
Max. No. Sharing Bath: **3**
Double/pb: **$50**
Single/pb: **$50**
Double/sb: **$35**
Single/sb: **$30**
Open: **May–Oct.**
Reduced Rates: **15%, weekly**
Breakfast: **Full**
Credit Cards: **MC, VISA**
Pets: **Sometimes**
Children: **Welcome (crib, cots)**
Smoking: **Permitted**
Social Drinking: **Permitted**
Airport/Station Pickup: **Yes**

William H. Strong built this Second Empire–style home in 1879 for $8,000. At the time, it was considered to be the most handsome home in the county. Over the years, the house has been an office, motel, and rest home, but is now listed on the National Register of Historic Places. Guests will find elegant rooms furnished in period antiques, many of which are for sale. Bob and Jeannine serve a hearty breakfast and offer snacks and setups in the evening. Nearby activities include swimming, tennis, golf, trout fishing, and hiking. Chase's is 18 miles from the airport and 28 miles from the Mayo Clinic.

Kings Oakdale Park Guest House ✪

6933 232 AVENUE N.E., STACY, MINNESOTA 55079

Tel: **(612) 462-5598**
Host(s): **Donna and Charles Solem**
Location: **38 mi. N of St. Paul**
No. of Rooms: **3**
No. of Private Baths: **2**
Double/pb: **$28**
Single/pb: **$25**
Double/sb: **$26**
Single/sb: **$23**
Suites: **$28**
Open: **All year**
Breakfast: **Continental**
Pets: **Sometimes**
Children: **No**
Smoking: **Permitted**
Social Drinking: **Permitted**
Foreign Languages: **French**

This comfortable home is situated on four landscaped acres on the banks of Typo Creek. The picnic tables, volleyball net, and horseshoe game are sure signs of a hospitable country place. It is a serene retreat for people on business trips to the Twin Cities. The Wisconsin border and the scenic St. Croix River, where boat trips are offered, are minutes from the house. Charles and Donna will direct you to the most reasonable restaurants in town. For late snacks, refrigerators in the bedrooms are provided.

MISSISSIPPI

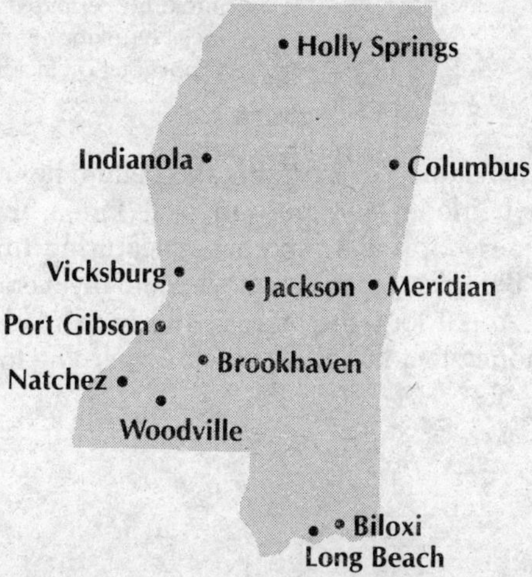

Holly Springs
Indianola
Columbus
Vicksburg
Jackson
Meridian
Port Gibson
Brookhaven
Natchez
Woodville
Biloxi
Long Beach

Lincoln, Ltd. Bed & Breakfast ✪

P.O. BOX 3479, MERIDIAN, MISSISSIPPI 39303

Tel: **(601) 482-5483**
Best Time to Call: **8:30 AM–4:30 PM**
Coordinator: **Barbara Lincoln Hall**
State/Regions Covered: **Aberdeen, Brookhaven, Columbus, Holly Springs, Jackson, Meridian, Natchez, Oxford, Mississippi Gulf Coast, Port Gibson, Vicksburg**

Rates (Single/Double):
Average: **$40–$60** **$45–$65**
Luxury: **$65–$75** **$75–$110**
Credit Cards: **MC, VISA**

For the traveling business person or for the vacationer, a stay with one of Barbara's hosts offers a personal taste of the finest Southern hospitality. All rooms have private baths. Mississippi abounds with historic-house tours, called "pilgrimages," in March and April, and Natchez and Vicksburg have similar pilgrimages in autumn. In May, Meridian is host to the Jimmie Rodgers Festival. There's a $3 charge for her descriptive directory.

Hamilton Place ✪

105 EAST MASON AVENUE, HOLLY SPRINGS, MISSISSIPPI 38635

Tel: **(601) 252-4368**
Host(s): **Linda and Jack Stubbs**
Location: **35 mi. SE of Memphis, TN**
No. of Rooms: **3**
No. of Private Baths: **3**
Double/pb: **$65**
Single/pb: **$50**
Open: **All year**
Breakfast: **Full**
Credit Cards: **MC, VISA**
Pets: **No**
Children: **Welcome**
Smoking: **Permitted**
Social Drinking: **Permitted**
Airport/Station Pickup: **Yes**

On the National Historic Register, this antebellum home, circa 1838, is furnished with heirloom antiques. In fact, Linda and Jack have a delightful antique shop on the premises featuring furniture, china, and cut glass. Breakfast can be enjoyed on the veranda or in the garden gazebo. You'll love the taste of the homemade biscuits with strawberry or honey-lemon butter. You are welcome to use the sauna or swimming pool.

Oak Square

1207 CHURCH STREET, PORT GIBSON, MISSISSIPPI 39150

Tel: **(601) 437-4350 or 437-5771**
Best Time to Call: **Morning; evening**
Host(s): **Mr. and Mrs. William D. Lum**
Location: **On Hwy. 61 between Natchez and Vicksburg**
No. of rooms: **7**
No. of Private Baths: **7**
Double/pb: **$65–$75**
Single/pb: **$50–$60**
Open: **All year**
Breakfast: **Full**
Credit Cards: **AMEX, MC, VISA**
Pets: **No**
Children: **Welcome**
Smoking: **Permitted**
Social Drinking: **Permitted**

Port Gibson is the town that Union General Ulysses S. Grant said was "too beautiful to burn." Oak Square is the largest and most palatial antebellum mansion (circa 1850) in Port Gibson, and is listed on the National Historic Register. The guest rooms are all furnished with family heirlooms, and most have canopied beds. Guests will enjoy the courtyard, gazebo, and beautiful grounds. A chairlift for upstairs rooms is available. You will enjoy the delightful Southern breakfast and tour of the mansion. Your hosts offer complimentary wine, tea, or coffee, and will enlighten you on the many historic attractions in the area.

Square Ten Inn ✪

242 DEPOT STREET, P.O. BOX 371, WOODVILLE, MISSISSIPPI 39669

Tel: **(601) 888-3993**
Host(s): **Elizabeth M. Treppendahl**
Location: **35 mi. S of Natchez**
No. of Rooms: **3**
No. of Private Baths: **3**
Double/pb: **$34**
Suites: **$39.50**
Open: **All year**
Reduced Rates: **25%, 5 day stay**
Breakfast: **Continental**
Pets: **No**
Children: **Welcome, over 6**
Smoking: **Permitted**
Social Drinking: **Permitted**

This inn is an 1830 town house listed on the National Register of Historic Places. It features a New Orleans–style courtyard and antique furnishings. Other amenities include a stocked breakfast pantry, complimentary wine, and fresh fruit. Woodville was chosen by Harvard University as the city best typifying the old South in appearance, customs, and traditions. Rosemont, the boyhood home of Jefferson Davis, is nearby.

For key to listings, see inside front or back cover.

✪ This star means that rates are guaranteed through December 31, 1988 to any guest making a reservation as a result of reading about the B&B in *BED & BREAKFAST U.S.A.*—1988 edition.

Please enclose a self-addressed, stamped, business-sized envelope when contacting reservation services.

For more details on what you can expect in a B&B, see Chapter 1.

Always mention *Bed & Breakfast U.S.A.* when making reservations!

If no B&B is listed in the area you'll be visiting, use the form on page 698 to order a copy of our "List of New B&Bs."

We want to hear from you! Use the form on page 697.

MISSOURI

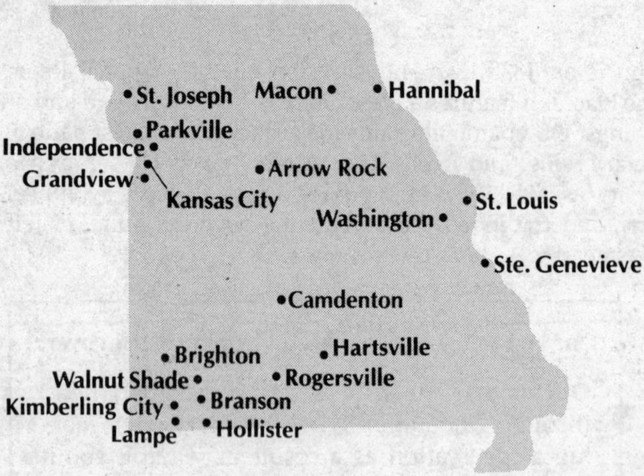

St. Joseph
Macon
Hannibal
Parkville
Independence
Grandview
Kansas City
Arrow Rock
St. Louis
Washington
Ste. Genevieve
Camdenton
Brighton
Hartsville
Walnut Shade
Rogersville
Kimberling City
Branson
Lampe
Hollister

Ozark Mountain Country B&B Service ✪

BOX 295, BRANSON, MISSOURI 65616

Tel: **(417) 334-4720; 5077**
Best Time to Call: **5–10 PM**
Coordinators: **Linda Johnson, Kay Cameron**
States/Regions Covered:
Missouri—Branson, Brighton, Camdenton, Hollister, Kimberling City, Rogersville; Arkansas—Eureka Springs, Pindall

Rates (Single/Double):

	Single	Double
Modest:	**$30–$35**	**$30–$35**
Average:	**$40–$50**	**$40–$50**
Luxury:	**$55**	**$55–$80**

Credit Cards: **No**

Linda and Kay will send you a complimentary copy of their descriptive listing of homes, so you can select the host of your choice; they'll take care of making your reservation.

Borgman's Bed & Breakfast ✪

ARROW ROCK, MISSOURI 65320

Tel: **(816) 837-3350**
Best Time to Call: **7–9 AM**
Host(s): **Helen and Kathy Borgman**
Location: **100 mi. E of Kansas City**
No. of Rooms: **4**
Max. No. Sharing Bath: **4**
Double/sb: **$30–$40**
Single/sb: **$30**
Open: **All year**
Reduced Rates: **10%, 3 nights**
Breakfast: **Continental**
Other Meals: **Dinner (winter only)**
Pets: **Sometimes**
Children: **Welcome**
Smoking: **No**
Social Drinking: **Permitted**

This 1860 home is spacious and comfortable, and it is furnished with cherished family pieces. Helen is a seamstress, artisan, and baker. Wait till you taste her fresh breads! Daughter Kathy is a town tour guide, so you will get firsthand information on this National Historic Landmark town at the beginning of the Santa Fe Trail. A fine repertory theater, the Lyceum, is open in summer. Craft shops, antique stalls, and the old country store are fun places to browse in. Good restaurants are within walking distance.

Lakeside Guest House ✪

R.R. 2, BOX 41, NORMAC, CAMDENTON, MISSOURI 65020

Tel: **(314) 346-3767**
Best Time to Call: **Evenings**
Host(s): **Virginia Dyck**
Location: **180 mi. SE of Kansas City**
No. of Rooms: **2**
No. of Private Baths: **2**
Double/pb: **$35**
Single/pb: **$30**
Open: **May 1–Oct. 31**
Breakfast: **Continental**
Pets: **No**
Children: **No**
Smoking: **No**
Social Drinking: **Permitted**

Virginia's lovely home is a bilevel, modified A-frame just 50 feet from the Lake of the Ozarks, with cathedral ceilings and many glass doors opening onto the patio and deck. You will be lulled to sleep by the sound of lapping water. HaHa Tonka Mansion and Trails, Bridal Cave, country music shows, antique shops and many fine restaurants are all close by.

Ramblewood Bed and Breakfast ✪

402 PANORAMIC DRIVE, CAMDENTON, MISSOURI 65020

Tel: **(314) 346-3410 or 816-479-5698**
Best Time to Call: **After 5 PM**
Host(s): **Mary and Gail Massey**
Location: **90 mi. S of Columbia**
No. of Rooms: **2**
Max. No. Sharing Bath: **4**
Double/sb: **$35**
Single/sb: **$30**

Open: **Apr. 15–Oct. 31**
Breakfast: **Full**
Pets: **Sometimes**
Children: **No**
Smoking: **No**
Social Drinking: **Permitted**

Ramblewood is a pilgrim-red home with white trim. Set on a quiet wooded lot, it has the feel of an English country cottage. Spend the night in an attractive, comfortable room and awaken to breakfast served on a sunny deck. Ham-and-cheese omelets and homemade muffins are specialties of the house. The inn is minutes from Lake of the Ozarks, HaHa Tonka State Park and Castle, and antiques shops and restaurants to suit any taste. After a busy day, enjoy a cool drink on the porch.

The Fountains ✪

12610 BLUE RIDGE, GRANDVIEW, MISSOURI 64030

Tel: **(816) 763-6260**
Best Time to Call: **9 AM–10 PM**
Host(s): **Sally J. Stewart**
Location: **1½ mi. from Rte. 71**
No. of Rooms: **4**
Max. No. Sharing Bath: **4**
Double/sb: **$35**
Single/sb: **$30**
Open: **Jan. 11–Dec. 9**
Reduced Rates: **15%, weekly; 10%, Tues.–Thurs.; 15%, seniors**
Breakfast: **Continental**
Pets: **Sometimes**
Children: **Welcome, over 9**
Smoking: **Permitted**
Social Drinking: **Permitted**

Sally's home is convenient to the Truman Library and home, the Nelson-Atkins Art Gallery, Starlight Theatre, Worlds of Fun park, and the famous plaza of Kansas City. The guest quarters has its own private entrance, dining room with fireplace, and kitchen. You are welcome to use the patio, barbecue, and gazebo. Sally enjoys having guests, and her good humor and warm hospitality will make you feel welcome immediately.

Fifth Street Mansion B&B ✪

213 SOUTH FIFTH STREET, HANNIBAL, MISSOURI 63401

Tel: **(314) 221-0445**
Best Time to Call: **8 AM–noon; after 4 PM**
Host(s): **Marie and Park Urquhart**
Location: **75 mi. N of St. Louis**
No. of Rooms: **7**
No. of Private Baths: **2**
Max. No. Sharing Bath: **5**
Double/pb: **$45**
Single/pb: **$40**
Double/sb: **$45**
Single/sb: **$35**
Suites: **$55–$70**
Open: **Apr.–Oct.**

Breakfast: **Continental**
Pets: **No**
Children: **Welcome**
Smoking: **Permitted**
Foreign Languages: **Ukrainian**
Social Drinking: **Permitted**
Airport/Station Pickup: **Yes**

This three-story home was built in 1865 and designed to resemble an Italian country villa. The brass lighting fixtures, Tiffany stained glass, and unusual fireplaces have been retained to add to the Victorian charm. The library, done in hand-grained walnut paneling, is the perfect spot to curl up in a wingback chair with a copy of *Huckleberry Finn*. This is Mark Twain country, and you will delight in seeing the backgrounds of his famous stories come to life. Marie and Park serve complimentary coffee or wine in the evening.

Frisco House ✪

P.O. BOX 118, CORNER CHURCH AND ROLLA STREETS, HARTVILLE, MISSOURI 65667

Tel: **(417) 741-7304 or 833-0650**
Best Time to Call: **7–9 AM; 6–10 PM**
Host(s): **Betty and Charley Roberts**
Location: **50 mi. E of Springfield**
No. of Rooms: **4**
Max. No. Sharing Bath: **4**
Double/sb: **$35**
Single/sb: **$30**
Open: **All year**
Reduced Rates: **5%, after 3 nights; 5%, seniors**
Breakfast: **Full**
Pets: **Sometimes**
Children: **Infants or over 12 welcome**
Smoking: **Permitted**
Social Drinking: **Permitted**
Airport/Station Pickup: **Yes**

Located in the noncommercial historic area of the Missouri Ozarks, this 1890 Victorian, listed on the National Historic Register, has been completely restored, retaining absolute authenticity while being unobtrusively outfitted with central air-conditioning and up-to-date plumbing and heating systems. Many of the furnishings are third- and fourth-generation family heirlooms, including oil paintings, Oriental rugs, and hanging lamps, as well as china, brass, and wooden artifacts. Most bedrooms have marble-topped sinks. The wainscoted dining room is furnished in oak and decorated with railroad pictures and maps. This is where you'll be served refreshments on arrival, and a bountiful breakfast. The interesting Amish community is close by.

Pridewell ✪

600 WEST 50TH STREET, KANSAS CITY, MISSOURI 64112

Tel: **(816) 931-1642**
Best Time to Call: **4–9 PM**
Host(s): **Edwin and Louann White**
No. of Rooms: **1**
No. of Private Baths: **1**
Double/pb: **$58**
Single/pb: **$52**
Open: **All year**
Breakfast: **Full**
Pets: **No**
Children: **No**
Smoking: **No**
Social Drinking: **Permitted**
Airport/Station Pickup: **Yes**

This fine Tudor residence is situated in a wooded residential area on the battlefield of the Civil War's Battle of Westport. The Nelson Art Gallery, the University of Missouri at Kansas City, and the Missouri Repertory Theatre are close by. It is adjacent to the Country Club Plaza shopping district, which includes several four-star restaurants, tennis courts, and a park.

Wardell Guest House ✪

1 WARDELL ROAD, MACON, MISSOURI 63552

Tel: **(816) 385-4352**
Best Time to Call: **After 5 PM**
Host(s): **Larry and Marie Hyde**
Location: **1 mi. from US 36**
No. of Rooms: **4**
No. of Private Baths: **2**
Max. No. Sharing Bath: **4**
Double/pb: **$55**
Single/pb: **$50**
Double/sb: **$45**
Single/sb: **$40**
Open: **All year**
Reduced Rates: **Sun.–Thurs.**
Breakfast: **Full**
Other Meals: **Available**
Credit Cards: **MC, VISA**
Pets: **No**
Children: **Welcome, over 12**
Smoking: **No**
Social Drinking: **Permitted**
Airport/Station Pickup: **Yes**

Built in 1890, this gracious Victorian is listed on the National Register of Historic Places. It is located on eight acres in the heart of a city that is known for its peace, tranquillity, and natural beauty. Spend the day on one of the many surrounding lakes or visit the boyhood homes of Mark Twain, Walt Disney, or General John Pershing. Closer to "home," you are welcome to play croquet during spring and summer, enjoy the beautiful fall foliage, or share an old-fashioned Christmas in this beautiful old mansion.

Down-to-Earth Lifestyles

ROUTE 22, PARKVILLE, MISSOURI 64152

Tel: **(816) 891-1018**
Host(s): **Lola and Bill Coons**
Location: **15 mi. N of downtown Kansas City**
No. of Rooms: **4**
No. of Private Baths: **4**
Double/pb: **$55**
Single/pb: **$50**
Open: **All year**
Reduced Rates: **$20 less, after 3 nights; families**
Breakfast: **Full**
Other Meals: **Available**
Pets: **Sometimes**
Children: **Welcome**
Smoking: **Permitted**
Social Drinking: **Permitted**
Airport/Station Pickup: **Yes**

This spacious new earth-integrated home, with its picture windows and skylights, emphasizes close contact with nature. It's located on an 85-acre ranch where there are horses and cows, a fishing pond, and lots of space for mind and soul. The furnishings complement the country setting, and the heated indoor pool, exercise room, and jogging and walking trails will keep you in shape. Lola and Bill will be pleased to suggest nearby places of interest if you can bear to tear yourself away from this restorative haven.

Anchor Hill Lodge ✪

ANCHOR HILL RANCH, ROUTE 1, ROGERSVILLE, MISSOURI 65742

Tel: **(417) 753-2930**
Best Time to Call: **After 7 PM**
Host(s): **Mrs. T. E. Atkinson**
Location: **23 mi. SE of Springfield**
No. of Rooms: **2**
No. of Private Baths: **2**
Double/pb: **$40**
Single/pb: **$30**
Open: **All year**
Breakfast: **Continental**
Pets: **Horses only**
Children: **Welcome (crib)**
Smoking: **Permitted**
Social Drinking: **Permitted**
Airport/Station Pickup: **Yes**

If your horse hasn't taken a vacation in a while, he's most welcome to accompany you to this rural ranch in the foothills of the Ozark Mountains. For $5 he will have a box stall and all he can eat, while you enjoy the comfort of an old-fashioned country home. Your hosts breed and ride Arabian horses and there are miles of trails for you to enjoy. In addition, there's lots to do and see, including an exotic animal farm, theater, museums, water sports, hiking, and craft fairs. Enjoy the relaxing hot tub on-premises, as well as the beautiful views.

Memory House

505 ROZIER STREET, SAINTE GENEVIEVE, MISSOURI 63670

Tel: **(314) 883-3939**
Best Time to Call: **9 AM–5 PM; evenings**
Host(s): **Lily and Alvin Donze**
Location: **60 mi. S of St. Louis**
No. of Rooms: **2**
Max. No. Sharing Bath: **4**
Double/sb: **$25**
Single/sb: **$20**
Open: **All year**
Reduced Rates: **Available**
Breakfast: **Continental**
Pets: **No**
Children: **Welcome**
Smoking: **Designated area**
Social Drinking: **Permitted**
Airport/Station Pickup: **Yes**

The name of this comfortable Colonial comes from the many memories Lily and Alvin share, after raising nine children here. Guest rooms are furnished with comfortable beds, fine linens, pretty curtains, and wallpaper. You are welcome to fix a drink in the living room wet bar, or relax on the sunny patio. Your hosts hope you will take in the many interesting sights in Sainte Genevieve. Historic sites include Ribault Living History Museum, where you can catch a glimpse of life as it was in the 18th and 19th centuries; a preserved frontier house, the Guibourd-Valle House, built by a pioneer French settler; and the Green Tree Tavern, where an unusual triangular fireplace opens into three rooms.

Schuster-Rader Mansion

703 HALL STREET, ST. JOSEPH, MISSOURI 64501

Tel: **(816) 279-9464**
Host(s): **Charles and Joetta Rader**
Location: **50 mi. N of Kansas City; 3 mi. from I-29**
No. of Rooms: **4**
No. of Private Baths: **1**
Max. No. Sharing Bath: **4**
Double/pb: **$65**
Single/pb: **$55**
Double/sb: **$65**
Single/sb: **$55**
Open: **All year**
Breakfast: **Full**
Pets: **No**
Children: **No**
Smoking: **No**
Social Drinking: **Permitted**
Airport/Station Pickup: **Yes**

This magnificent Italianate mansion, built in 1881, is a classic example of yesterday's elegance and charm. Located in the Historic Hall Street District overlooking the Missouri River, it is listed on the National Register of Historic Places. It is tastefully furnished with fine antiques and period decor. Joetta's pecan waffles and special crêpes are breakfast treats. In May, the Apple Blossom Festival is a special attraction to visitors. The Pony Express Museum is always an interesting stop.

Bed & Breakfast St. Louis

4418 WEST PINE, ST. LOUIS, MISSOURI 63108

Tel: **(314) 533-9299**
Coordinators: **Marie Holliday**
States/Regions Covered: **St. Louis Metropolitan Area**

Rates (Single/Double):

	Single	Double
Modest:	**N/A**	**$35**
Average:	**$30**	**$40–$43**
Luxury:	**$35**	**$50**

Credit Cards: **MC, VISA**

Marie offers a selection of homes convenient to the Gateway Arch, the Missouri Botanical Garden, the Mississippi River with its cruise boats and the Goldenrod Showboat, Busch Brewery, and Washington University. Services offered include airport pickup and tours of the various attractions for a reasonable fee. There is a $5 surcharge for a one-night stay.

Lafayette House

2156 LAFAYETTE AVENUE, ST. LOUIS, MISSOURI 63104

Tel: **(314) 772-4429**
Best Time to Call: **After 6 PM**
Host(s): **Sarah and Jack Milligan**
No. of Rooms: **3**
No. of Private Baths: **1**
Max. No. Sharing Bath: **3**
Double/pb: **$45**
Double/sb: **$35**
Suite: **$55**
Open: **All year**
Breakfast: **Full**
Pets: **No**
Children: **Welcome (crib)**
Smoking: **Permitted**
Social Drinking: **Permitted**
Airport/Station Pickup: **Yes**

This 1876 Queen Anne mansion is located in the historic district overlooking Lafayette Park. The house is furnished comfortably with several antiques and features a deck overlooking the famous Arch. The suite on the third floor, accommodating six, has a private bath and kitchen. Your hosts serve a special egg dish and homemade breads each morning, and offer wine, cheese, and crackers later. They will gladly take you on tour or can direct you to the Botanical Gardens, Convention Center, and other nearby attractions.

Stelzer Bed & Breakfast

7106 GENERAL SHERMAN LANE, ST. LOUIS, MISSOURI 63123

Tel: **(314) 843-5757**
Best Time to Call: **Mornings; evenings**
Host(s): **Pat and Anita Stelzer**
Location: **10 mi. W of St. Louis**
No. of Rooms: **2**
No. of Private Baths: **1**
Max. No. Sharing Bath: **2**
Double/pb: **$30**
Single/pb: **$20**
Double/sb: **$25**

Single/sb: **$18**
Open: **All year**
Breakfast: **Continental**
Pets: **No**
Children: **Welcome**
Smoking: **No**
Social Drinking: **No**
Airport/Station Pickup: **Yes**

Pat and Anita Stelzer have a corner house with green siding and window awnings. The lot is quite spacious, with lovely trees and flowers. Inside, you'll find a mixture of Windsor chairs, old-fashioned rockers, books, and family treasures such as the old spoon collection mounted on the wall. Breakfast on fresh fruit, biscuits, cereals, eggs, and bacon. The Stelzers are located ten miles from the riverfront and within easy reach of the Botanical Garden, fine dining, and shops.

The Schwegmann House B&B Inn ✪

438 WEST FRONT STREET, WASHINGTON, MISSOURI 63090

Tel: **(314) 239-5025**
Host(s): **George, Barbara, and Cathy**
Location: **50 mi. W of St. Louis**
No. of Rooms: **9**
No. of Private Baths: **7**
Max. No. Sharing Bath: **4**
Double/pb: **$55**
Single/pb: **$45**
Double/sb: **$40**
Single/sb: **$30**
Open: **All year**
Breakfast: **Continental**
Credit Cards: **MC, VISA**
Pets: **No**
Children: **Welcome**
Smoking: **Permitted**
Social Drinking: **Permitted**

A three-story 1861 Georgian brick house included on the National Historic Register, it is located on the Missouri River. It is tastefully furnished with antiques; handmade quilts complement the decor of each guest room. It is close to Daniel Boone's home, Meramec Caverns, Missouri's Rhineland wineries, antiques shops, and fine restaurants. Relax in the graceful parlor by the fireside or stroll the gardens that overlook the river. George, Barbara, and Cathy serve a bountiful breakfast including fresh-ground coffee, imported cheeses, croissants, and grape juice from Missouri's vineyards.

MONTANA

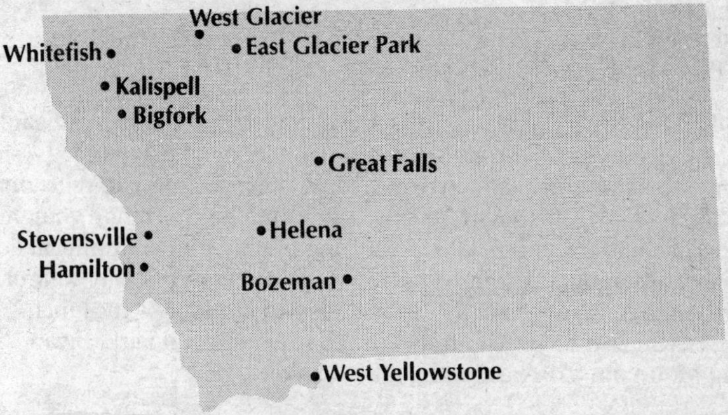

West Glacier
Whitefish
East Glacier Park
Kalispell
Bigfork
Great Falls
Stevensville
Helena
Hamilton
Bozeman
West Yellowstone

Bed & Breakfast Rocky Mountains—Montana ✪

P.O. BOX 804, COLORADO SPRINGS, COLORADO 80901

Tel: **(303) 630-3433**
Best Time to Call: **9 AM–5 PM May 15–Sept. 15; 1–5 PM rest of year**
Coordinator: **Kate Peterson Winters**
States/Regions Covered: **Statewide**

Rates (Single/Double):

Modest:	**$25**	**$35**
Average:	**$30**	**$45**
Luxury:	**$38**	**$55**

Credit Cards: **MC, VISA**

This is Glacier National Park country, and Kate's hosts can give you an insider's view of ranching, calving, branding, and roundups. They can also advise on spots to fish or hike, or on where to find natural hot springs or river rafting. Ranches, homes, and small inns all offer warm Western hospitality. There is a $3 charge for Kate's directory.

O'Duach'Ain Public House ✪

675 FERNDALE DRIVE, BIGFORK, MONTANA 59911

Tel: **(406) 837-6851**
Best Time to Call: **Noon–9 PM**
Host(s): **Margot and Tom Doohan**
Location: **17 mi. S of Kalispell**
No. of Rooms: **5**
Max. No. Sharing Bath: **5**
Double/sb: **$50**
Single/sb: **$42.50**
Separate Guest Cottage: **$70–$75**
Open: **All year**
Breakfast: **Full**
Other Meals: **Available**
Credit Cards: **MC, VISA**
Pets: **Welcome**
Children: **Welcome, over 12**
Smoking: **No**
Social Drinking: **Permitted**
Airport/Station Pickup: **Yes**

O'Duach'Ain is a gracious three-level log home set on five beautiful acres. Inside, you'll find a casual atmosphere of open wood logs, stone fireplaces, antiques, and artwork. Guests are welcome to relax on the deck and take in the spectacular view. In the morning, your hosts provide a gourmet breakfast, featuring freshly prepared international dishes. Margot and Tom will gladly take you on a one-day tour of the area in their luxury van; the fee includes an outdoor picnic lunch. Your hosts will also direct you to nearby Glacier National Park, Swan Lake, Big Mountain Ski Area, and Flatland Lake.

Voss Inn ✪

319 SOUTH WILLSON, BOZEMAN, MONTANA 59715

Tel: **(406) 587-0982**
Best Time to Call: **10 AM–9 PM**
Host(s): **Ken and Ruthmary Tonn**
Location: **3 mi. from I-90**
No. of Rooms: **6**
No. of Private Baths: **6**
Double/pb: **$50-$70**
Single/pb: **$40-$60**
Open: **All year**
Reduced Rates: **Business travelers, Sun.–Thurs.**
Breakfast: **Full**
Credit Cards: **MC, VISA**
Pets: **No**
Children: **Sometimes**
Smoking: **Permitted**
Social Drinking: **Permitted**

This handsome 100-year-old brick mansion flanked by Victorian gingerbread porches is set like a gem on a tree-lined street in historic Bozeman. The bedrooms are elegantly wallpapered and furnished with brass and iron beds, ornate lighting, Oriental throw rugs over polished hardwood floors . . . a perfect spot for a first or second honeymoon. The parlor has a good selection of books, as well as a chess set for your pleasure. It's north of Yellowstone, on the way to Glacier, with trout fishing, mountain lakes, and skiing within easy reach. Don't miss the Museum of the Rockies on the Montana State University campus 10 blocks away.

Park Garden B&B ✪

#3 PARK GARDEN ESTATES, GREAT FALLS, MONTANA 59404

Tel: **(406) 727-8127**
Best Time to Call: **8 AM–9 PM**
Host(s): **Dolores and Bill Harrer**
No. of Rooms: **4**
No. of Private Baths: **1**
Max. No. Sharing Bath: **4**
Double/pb: **$35**
Single/pb: **$30**
Double/sb: **$35**
Single/sb: **$30**
Open: **All year**
Breakfast: **Full**
Pets: **Sometimes**
Children: **Welcome**
Smoking: **No**
Social Drinking: **Permitted**
Airport/Station Pickup: **Yes**

Park Garden is located next to a country club in a restful, relaxing neighborhood. Dolores and Bill invite you to relax in the lovely yard, sun yourself on the patio, or take a dip in the pool. This is the spot for families, as the rooms can also function as two separate suites. The Harrers offer such breakfast specialties as homemade rolls and croissants. They will gladly direct you to Natural Springs, shopping centers, and the famous C. M. Russell Museum.

Bitterroot Valley ✪

1217 SOUTH FIRST STREET, HAMILTON, MONTANA 59840

Tel: **(406) 363-1740**
Best Time to Call: **After 4:30 PM**
Host(s): **Kamie and Jim Jetter**
Location: **45 mi. S of Missoula**
No. of Rooms: **2**
Max. No. Sharing Bath: **4**
Double/sb: **$25**
Single/sb: **$15**
Open: **All year**
Reduced Rates: **50%, children under 16**
Breakfast: **Full**
Pets: **No**
Children: **Welcome, over 3**
Smoking: **Permitted**
Social Drinking: **Permitted**
Airport/Station Pickup: **Yes**

Kamie and Jim Jetter have a neat white bungalow-style home surrounded by a well-manicured lawn and flowers. They are retired teachers interested in sharing their home with a variety of people, glad to help their visitors explore the nearby sights. A full country breakfast including homemade breads and jams awaits you in the morning. Then it's off to any one of a number of regional activities, including hunting, fishing, and climbing in the scenic mountains.

Mission Mountains B&B

RR BOX 183A, ST. IGNATIUS, MONTANA 59865

Tel: **(406) 745-4331**
Best Time to Call: **9 AM–5 PM**
Host(s): **Doris Peterson**
Location: **1/4 mi. W of Hwy. 93**
No. of Rooms: **2**
Max. No. Sharing Bath: **4**
Double/sb: **$33**
Single/sb: **$29**
Open: **All year**
Reduced Rates: **10%, seniors**
Breakfast: **Full**
Other Meals: **Available**
Pets: **No**
Children: **Welcome (crib, high chair)**
Smoking: **No**
Social Drinking: **No**

A casual, comfortable atmosphere awaits you in this quiet rural ranch house. The views are spectacular, with the Mission Mountains 5 miles to the east, the Cabinet Mountains 10 miles to the west, and the National Bison Range to the south. Nine Pipe National Wildlife Refuge is just north of here and the St. Ignatius Church, a National Historic Monument, is located in town, just a short drive away. Your hosts love catering to guests and offer snacks and fresh tea or coffee. In the morning they serve a breakfast of Swedish pancakes, homemade breads, coffee cake, and jams. Activities such as fishing, hiking, boating, white-water rafting, golf, and skiing can all be enjoyed within a 30-mile drive.

Country Caboose ✪

852 WILLOUGHBY ROAD, STEVENSVILLE, MONTANA 59870

Tel: **(406) 777-3145**
Host(s): **Lisa and Kirk Thompson**
Location: **35 mi. S of Missoula**
No. of Rooms: **1**
No. of Private Baths: **1**
Double/pb: **$30**
Single/pb: **$30**
Open: **May–Sept.**
Breakfast: **Full**
Other Meals: **Available**
Pets: **No**
Children: **Welcome**
Smoking: **No**
Social Drinking: **Permitted**

If you enjoy romantic train rides, why not spend the night in an authentic caboose? This one dates back to 1923, is made of wood, and is painted red, of course. It is set on real rails in the middle of the countryside. The caboose sleeps two and offers a spectacular view of the Bitterroot Mountains, right from your pillow. In the morning, breakfast is served at a table for two. Specialties include huckleberry pancakes, quiche, and strawberries in season. Local activities include touring St. Mary's Mission, hiking the mountain trails, fishing, and hunting.

Duck Inn ✪

1305 COLUMBIA AVENUE, WHITEFISH, MONTANA 59937

Tel: **(406) 862-DUCK**
Host(s): **Ken and Phyllis Adler**
Location: **25 mi. from Glacier Nat'l. Park**
No. of Rooms: **10**
No. of Private Baths: **10**
Double/pb: **$48**
Single/pb: **$40**
Open: **All year**
Reduced Rates: **5%, seniors**
Breakfast: **Continental**
Credit Cards: **AMEX, DC, MC, VISA**
Pets: **No**
Children: **Welcome**
Smoking: **Permitted**
Social Drinking: **Permitted**
Airport/Station Pickup: **Yes**

The Duck Inn is on the Whitefish River, eight miles from Big Mountain Ski Area. Each guest room features a brass or white iron bed, cozy fireplace, deep soak tub, and a balcony. A large living room with a view of Big Mountain and the river is a relaxing spot. Your hosts offer a different kind of fresh-baked bread each morning, and can provide information on Glacier National Park, wilderness areas, and spots to swim, sail, and fish. A Jacuzzi is available after a heavy day of touring.

NEBRASKA

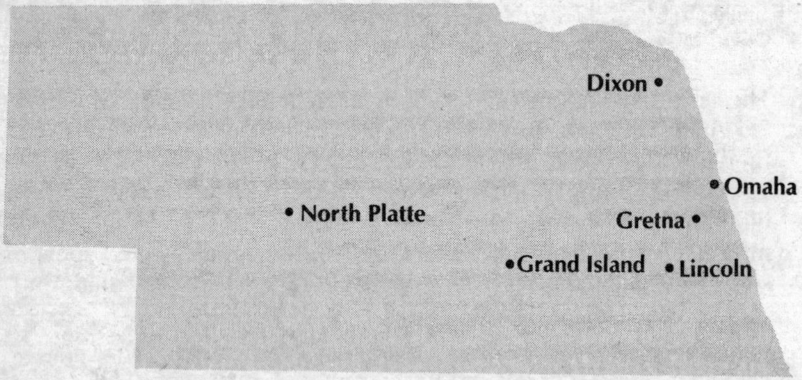

Dixon
Omaha
North Platte
Gretna
Grand Island
Lincoln

The Georges ✪

ROUTE 1, BOX 50, DIXON, NEBRASKA 68732

Tel: **(402) 584-2625**
Best Time to Call: **6:30 AM–6 PM**
Host(s): **Harold and Marie George**
Location: **35 mi. W of Sioux City, Iowa**
No. of Rooms: **3**
Max. No. Sharing Bath: **4**
Double/sb: **$30**
Single/sb: **$20**
Open: **All year**
Breakfast: **Full**
Other Meals: **Available**
Pets: **Sometimes**
Children: **Welcome**
Smoking: **No**
Social Drinking: **Permitted**
Airport/Station Pickup: **Yes**
Foreign Languages: **Swedish**

The Georges have a large remodeled farmhouse with a spacious backyard. They offer the opportunity to see a farming operation at first hand, right down to the roosters crowing and the birds singing in the morning. Harold and Marie are now full-time farmers after careers in social work and engineering. They prepare a hearty country breakfast featuring homemade jellies and jams. The Georges are close to Wayne State College and Ponca State Park.

Bundy's Bed and Breakfast ✪

RR #2, BOX 39, GRETNA, NEBRASKA 68028

Tel: **(402) 332-3616**
Best Time to Call: **7 AM–9 PM**
Host(s): **Bob and Dee Bundy**
Location: **30 mi. S of Omaha**
No. of Rooms: **4**
Max. No. Sharing Bath: **4**
Double/sb: **$25**
Single/sb: **$15**
Open: **All year**
Breakfast: **Full**
Pets: **Sometimes**
Children: **No**
Smoking: **No**
Social Drinking: **No**

The Bundys have a pretty farmhouse painted white with black trim. Here you can enjoy country living just 30 minutes from downtown Lincoln and Omaha. The rooms are decorated with antiques, attractive wallpapers, and collectibles. In the morning, wake up to farm-fresh eggs and homemade breads. The house is just a short walk from a swimming lake and is three miles from a ski lodge.

Rogers House ✪

2145 B STREET, LINCOLN, NEBRASKA 68502

Tel: **(402) 476-6961**
Best Time to Call: **12–4 PM**
Host(s): **Nora Houtsma and James Young**
No. of Rooms: **8**
No. of Private Baths: **8**
Double/pb: **$45–$55**
Single/pb: **$40–$50**
Suites: **$90–$110**
Open: **All year**
Reduced Rates: **10% on 3rd night; 15% thereafter**
Breakfast: **Full**
Credit Cards: **AMEX, MC, VISA**
Pets: **No**
Children: **Welcome, over 12**
Smoking: **Permitted**
Social Drinking: **Permitted**

This Jacobean Revival–style brick mansion was built in 1914 and is a local historic landmark. There are three sun porches, attractively furnished with wicker and plants, and the air-conditioned house is decorated with lovely antiques. James can arrange walking tours in the historic district, and Nora will direct you to the diverse cultural attractions available at the nearby University of Nebraska. Don't miss a visit to the Children's Zoo and the beautiful Sunken Gardens. Breakfast is hearty and delicious and often features a quiche or soufflé. A professional staff of five is eager to serve you.

Watson Manor Inn ✪

410 SOUTH SYCAMORE, P.O. BOX 458, NORTH PLATTE, NEBRASKA 69103

Tel: **(308) 532-1124**
Host(s): **Ron and Patty Watson**
Location: **2 mi. N of I-80**
No. of Rooms: **4**

No. of Private Baths: **1**
Max. No. Sharing Bath: **4**
Double/pb: **$45**
Single/pb: **$40**
Double/sb: **$40**
Single/sb: **$35**
Suites: **$60**
Open: **All year**
Reduced Rates: **10% less after 2 nights**
Breakfast: **Full**
Credit Cards: **AMEX, MC, VISA**
Pets: **No**
Children: **Welcome**
Smoking: **No**
Social Drinking: **Permitted**
Airport/Station Pickup: **Yes**

This is a beautiful two-story brick home with white shutters, stately pillars, and a manicured lawn. Ron and Patty have furnished it with carefully chosen antiques and comfortable decor. Breakfast often features omelets, French toast, or quiche, and is always served with a smile that says, "We're glad you're here!" The area was once the home of Colonel William "Buffalo Bill" Cody. His ranch, Scouts Rest, has been reconstructed as part of an historical park. You're welcome to relax on the deck and refresh yourself in the spa, and have some wine and cheese before going out to dinner and perhaps taking in the local color at the nightly rodeo.

The Offutt House ✪

140 NORTH 39TH STREET, OMAHA, NEBRASKA 68131

Tel: **(402) 553-0951**
Best Time to Call: **Evenings; weekends**
Host(s): **Jeannie K. Swoboda**
Location: **1 mi. from I-80**
No. of Rooms: **5**
No. of Private Baths: **2**
Max. No. Sharing Bath: **5**
Double/pb: **$50**
Single/pb: **$40**
Double/sb: **$50**
Single/sb: **$40**
Suites: **$60**
Open: **All year**
Reduced Rates: **After 5 nights**
Breakfast: **Continental**
Pets: **Sometimes**
Children: **Welcome**
Smoking: **Permitted**
Social Drinking: **Permitted**

This comfortable mansion (c. 1894) is part of the city's Historic Gold Coast, a section of handsome homes built by Omaha's wealthiest residents. Offering peace and quiet, the rooms are air-conditioned, spacious, and furnished with antiques; some have fireplaces. Jeannie will direct you to nearby attractions such as the Joslyn Museum or the Old Market area, which abounds with many beautiful shops and fine restaurants. She graciously offers coffee or wine in late afternoon.

NEVADA

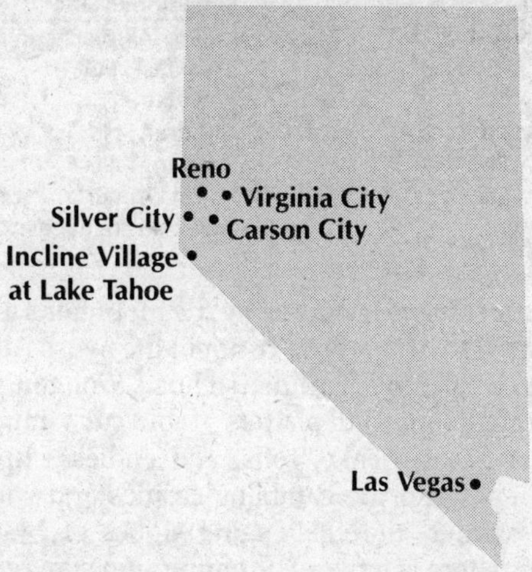

Reno
Virginia City
Silver City
Carson City
Incline Village at Lake Tahoe
Las Vegas

Winters Creek Ranch

1201 U.S. 395 NORTH, CARSON CITY, NEVADA 89701

Tel: **(702) 849-1020**
Best Time to Call: **Mornings**
Host(s): **Myron Sayan and Susan Hannah**
Location: **14 mi. S of Reno**
No. of Rooms: **4**
No. of Private Baths: **4**
Double/pb: **$75**
Single/pb: **$75**
Separate Guest Cottage: **$85, for 4**
Open: **All year**
Breakfast: **Full**
Credit Cards: **MC, VISA**
Pets: **Sometimes**
Children: **Welcome, over 13**
Smoking: **No**
Social Drinking: **Permitted**
Foreign Languages: **Spanish**

Established in 1865, this historic horse ranch is nestled among ponderosa pines and meadows on 50 acres. You may choose Oliver's Nook, a delicate blend of lavender and lace, the Colonial Room with its cozy fireplace, or the Nevada Room with a lovely deck. Enjoy the beautiful countryside from the back of a horse. Other activities include fishing, ice skating, hiking, and picnicking. Your hosts invite you to use the hot tub, and offer complimentary wine and hors d'oeuvres in the afternoon. Carson City, Reno, Virginia City, and Lake Tahoe are minutes away.

Haus Bavaria ✪

P.O. BOX 3308, 593 NORTH DYER CIRCLE, INCLINE VILLAGE, LAKE TAHOE, NEVADA 89450

Tel: **(702) 831-6122**
Best Time to Call: **9 AM–8 PM**
Host(s): **Wolfgang and Anna Zimmermann**
Location: **35 mi. SW of Reno**
No. of Rooms: **5**
No. of Private Baths: **5**
Double/pb: **$70**
Single/pb: **$60**
Open: **All year**
Breakfast: **Full**
Pets: **No**
Children: **No**
Smoking: **No**
Social Drinking: **Permitted**
Foreign Languages: **German**

This immaculate residence is framed by the mountains and convenient to the lake. It's hard to believe you're not in the Swiss Alps! Each guest room opens onto a balcony. Continental hosts Wolfgang and Anna set a breakfast table with bountiful platters of cold cuts, imported cheeses, sliced fruits, boiled eggs, cake, rolls, and endless cups of delicious coffee or tea. It's close to the gambling casinos and shows, all water sports, and, in winter, the challenging slopes of Mount Rose and Heavenly Valley. There is a two-night minimum stay required.

Las Vegas B&B

CONTACT: BED AND BREAKFAST INTERNATIONAL, 151 ARDMORE ROAD, KENSINGTON, CALIFORNIA 94707

Tel: **(415) 525-4569**
Best Time to Call: **8:30 AM–5 PM**
Host(s): **Jean Brown**
No. of Rooms: **2**
No. of Private Baths: **1**
Max. No. Sharing Bath: **3**
Double/pb: **$42–$48**
Single/pb: **$36–$42**
Double/sb: **$42**
Single/sb: **$40**
Open: **All year**
Breakfast: **Full**
Pets: **No**
Children: **Swimmers only**
Smoking: **Permitted**
Social Drinking: **Permitted**

Located a few minutes from the fabled "Strip" of hotels, casinos, and restaurants is this two-story contemporary home. The quiet residential neighborhood is a welcome respite from the 24-hour hoopla available nearby. You are welcome to use your host's swimming pool.

Hardwicke House ✪

P.O. BOX 96, SILVER CITY, NEVADA 89428

Tel: **(702) 847-0215**
Best Time to Call: **Before 7 PM**
Host(s): **Cleo Ross**
Location: **4 mi. S of Virginia City**
No. of Rooms: **3**
Max. No. Sharing Bath: **6**
Double/sb: **$45**
Single/sb: **$30**
Open: **All year**
Breakfast: **Full**
Smoking: **Permitted**
Social Drinking: **Permitted**
Pets: **Welcome**
Children: **Welcome**
Foreign Languages: **French, German, Spanish**

Cleo spent years traveling through Europe, Africa, and Australia. Now she's happy to stay home and have the world visit her. This unique B&B was originally an icehouse constructed of quarried stone with walls that are three feet thick. Decorated simply with lots of plants, you are certain to feel comfortable here. It's only a short drive to Virginia City, Reno, Lake Tahoe, and Carson City.

Edith Palmer's Country Inn ✪

SOUTH "B" STREET, P.O. BOX 756, VIRGINIA CITY, NEVADA 89449

Tel: **(702) 847-0707**
Best Time to Call: **Daytime**
Host(s): **Erlene and Norm Brown**
Location: **23 mi. S of Reno**
No. of Rooms: **5**
No. of Private Baths: **1**
Max. No. Sharing Bath: **4**
Double/pb: **$70**
Single/pb: **$65**
Double/sb: **$70**
Single/sb: **$65**
Open: **All year**
Breakfast: **Full**
Other Meals: **Available**

Credit Cards: **MC, VISA**
Pets: **No**
Children: **No**
Smoking: **No**
Social Drinking: **Permitted**
Airport/Station Pickup: **Yes**

One of Nevada's first wine merchants built this country Victorian over 100 years ago. What was once a stone wine cellar is now a gourmet restaurant with rock walls and a fireplace crafted from local ores and gemstones. Spend the night in a comfortable bedroom and wake up to a breakfast of freshly ground coffee and a variety of hot breads and egg dishes. Outside, the pretty gardens are often used for wedding receptions. Many celebrities find this inn a wonderful escape spot. Even if you're not a star, you'll be treated like one. Edith Palmer's is within walking distance from the historic sights of Virginia City and close to Lake Tahoe and Reno.

For key to listings, see inside front or back cover.

✪ This star means that rates are guaranteed through December 31, 1988 to any guest making a reservation as a result of reading about the B&B in *BED & BREAKFAST U.S.A.*—1988 edition.

Please enclose a self-addressed, stamped, business-sized envelope when contacting reservation services.

For more details on what you can expect in a B&B, see Chapter 1.

Always mention *Bed & Breakfast U.S.A.* when making reservations!

If no B&B is listed in the area you'll be visiting, use the form on page 698 to order a copy of our "List of New B&Bs."

We want to hear from you! Use the form on page 697.

NEW HAMPSHIRE

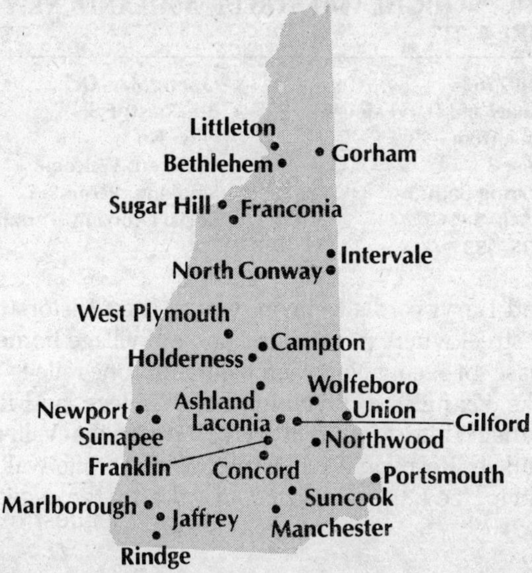

New Hampshire Bed & Breakfast ✪

RFD 3, BOX 53, LACONIA, NEW HAMPSHIRE 03246

Tel: **(603) 279-8348**
Best Time to Call: **10 AM–5 PM**
Coordinator: **Martha W. Dorais**
States/Regions Covered: **Statewide**

Rates (Single/Double):

Modest:	**$25–$30**	**$35–$40**
Average:	**$35–$40**	**$40–$50**
Luxury:	**$50**	**$55–$85**

Credit Cards: **MC, VISA**
Minimum Stay: **2 nights, holidays and fall foliage**

New Hampshire is a haven for the sports-minded, having facilities for every type of recreation. Shoppers will find it a bargain haven since there's no sales tax on merchandise. Martha's roster ranges from an 18th-century Cape house where the hostess makes her own cheese, to a mountainside home overlooking Lake Winnipesaukee with its own pool and tennis court, to a contemporary home convenient to the

Manchester factory outlets. Send $1 for her descriptive directory, make your selection, and she will make the reservation for you.

Cheney House ✪

P.O. BOX 683, 40 HIGHLAND STREET, ASHLAND, NEW HAMPSHIRE 03217

Tel: **(603) 968-7968**
Host(s): **Michael and Daryl Mooney**
Location: **1 mi. from I-93**
No. of Rooms: **3**
Max. No. Sharing Bath: **6**
Double/sb: **$40–$44**
Single/sb: **$35–$39**
Open: **May–Oct.**
Breakfast: **Full**
Pets: **No**
Children: **Welcome**
Smoking: **Permitted**
Social Drinking: **Permitted**

Michael and Daryl cordially invite you to their Victorian home on a residential street where pastureland and old village homes meet. This is a great base for seeing New Hampshire. It's one mile to the beach on Squam Lake, six miles to Plymouth State College, and in 20 minutes you're at the White Mountain parks, Waterville Valley, and Lake Winnipesaukee. Relax on a porch overlooking stone walls and flower gardens, help feed the chickens, or take in the New Hampshire Symphony.

The Mulburn Inn ✪

MAIN STREET, BETHLEHEM, NEW HAMPSHIRE 03574

Tel: **(603) 869-3389**
Best Time to Call: **9 AM–9 PM**
Host(s): **Bob and Cheryl Burns, Moe and Linda Mulkigian**
Location: **20 mi. SE of St. Johnsbury**
No. of Rooms: **7**
No. of Private Baths: **7**
Double/pb: **$50–$60**
Single/pb: **$30**
Open: **All year**
Reduced Rates: **10%, weekly**
Breakfast: **Full**
Other Meals: **Available**
Credit Cards: **MC, VISA**
Pets: **No**
Children: **Welcome (crib)**
Smoking: **No**
Social Drinking: **No**
Airport/Station Pickup: **Yes**

Back in the early 1900s, this sprawling Tudor home was known as the Ivie Estate, a family summer retreat. It boasts original oak staircases, stained-glass windows, rounded-corner architecture, three tile fireplaces, and even has an elevator. There is plenty of room here, with three enclosed wraparound porches for relaxing and a large living room for reading and fireside chats. Breakfast is served by the fire in a sunny dining room. In the afternoon, your hosts offer seasonal snacks such as soup or cider and cheese. If you are visiting in March or April, you'll be treated to fresh syrup right from the family maples. This lively inn is located in the heart of the White Mountains, near Franconia Notch, the Old Man in the Mountain, Mt. Washington, plus places to ski, shop, and dine.

The Campton Inn

RT. 175 NORTH, BOX 282, CAMPTON, NEW HAMPSHIRE 03223

Tel: **(603) 726-4449**
Best Time to Call: **Mornings, evenings**
Host(s): **Doris Thibeault and Ken Martin**
Location: **45 mi. N of Concord**
No. of Rooms: **8**
No. of Private Baths: **1**
Max. No. Sharing Bath: **4**
Double/pb: **$40–$50**
Single/pb: **$30–$35**
Double/sb: **$30–$48**
Single/sb: **$20–$32**
Open: **All year**
Reduced Rates: **Available**
Breakfast: **Full**
Credit Cards: **AMEX, MC, VISA**
Pets: **Sometimes**
Children: **No**
Smoking: **Permitted**
Social Drinking: **Permitted**

This 1835 country home is a friendly place to stay while visiting the lakes, Waterville Valley, and White Mountain region. Awake to the aroma of fresh-brewed coffee and sizzling bacon. After a busy day enjoying the slopes, Polar Caves, the Old Man in the Mountain, The Flume, Franconia Notch, and the delightful shops, come back and relax by the fireplace. Doris and Ken are known for their hearty country meals.

Mountain-Fare Inn

BOX 553, CAMPTON, NEW HAMPSHIRE 03223

Tel: **(603) 726-4283**
Best Time to Call: **After 5 PM**
Host(s): **Susan and Nick Preston**
Location: **40 mi. N of Concord**
No. of Rooms: **9**
No. of Private Baths: **5**
Max. No. Sharing Bath: **4**
Double/pb: **$48**
Single/pb: **$27**
Double/sb: **$40**
Single/sb: **$22**
Open: **All year**
Reduced Rates: **10% less, Apr.–June; families**
Breakfast: **Full**
Other Meals: **Sometimes**
Pets: **Sometimes**
Children: **Welcome**
Smoking: **No**
Social Drinking: **Permitted**

Built in the 1800s, this white clapboard farmhouse is located in the foothills of the White Mountains, just minutes away from Franconia Notch and the Waterville Valley Resort. Susan and Nick are professional skiers and into physical fitness. Their enthusiasm is contagious! Generous seasonal snacks are offered. During the ski season, you are invited to have a family-style dinner for $8.50 per person. Plymouth State College is nearby. There is a two-day minimum stay on weekends.

Maria W. Atwood Inn

R.F.D. #2, ROUTE 3A NORTH, FRANKLIN, NEW HAMPSHIRE 03235

Tel: **(603) 934-3666**
Best Time to Call: **Mornings; afternoons**
Host(s): **Philip and Irene Fournier**
Location: **21 mi. N of Concord**
No. of Rooms: **8**
No. of Private Baths: **8**
Double/pb: **$48**
Single/pb: **$38**
Open: **All year**
Breakfast: **Full**
Credit Cards: **AMEX, MC, VISA**
Pets: **No**
Children: **Welcome, over 11**
Smoking: **Permitted**
Social Drinking: **Permitted**
Airport/Station Pickup: **Yes**

At the turn of the century, Maria Atwood and her husband bought this brick, Federal-style home along with 200 acres. Over the years, the house became known for its quality restorations and impeccable maintenance. The grounds feature formal gardens and acres of fields for walking or cross-country skiing. Today the inn features new plumbing and electrical systems, but restoration has been made according to original designs, and the locks still take an old turnkey. The decor features period antiques, and bedrooms all have old-fashioned beds and fine linens. Your hosts offer complimentary snacks and invite you to BYOB if you like. This lovely inn is within ten minutes of swimming and boating and half an hour from the ski slopes.

Webster Lake Inn ✪

WEBSTER AVENUE, FRANKLIN, NEW HAMPSHIRE 03235

Tel: **(603) 934-4050**
Host(s): **Shirley and Henry McCue and Roland and Sheryl Tyne**
No. of Rooms: **8**
No. of Private Baths: **2**
Max. No. Sharing Bath: **4**
Double/pb: **$60**
Single/pb: **$53**
Double/sb: **$44**
Single/sb: **$35**
Open: **All year**
Breakfast: **Full**
Pets: **No**
Children: **Welcome**
Smoking: **Permitted**
Social Drinking: **Permitted**

This country inn, modeled after a Swiss chalet, is set on picturesque Webster Lake. Enjoy a quiet moment in a lovely waterfront gazebo or by the great fireplace in the sitting room. Bedrooms feature panoramic views and original handcrafted furnishings. Your hosts serve a country-style breakfast in a fireplaced dining room overlooking the water. Nearby activities include swimming, fishing, hiking, golf, skiing, and snowmobiling. There are many regional events throughout the year such as Winter Carnival and an assortment of country fairs. Webster Lake Inn is a short drive from Lake Winnipesaukee and less than an hour from the White Mountains.

Cartway House

OLD LAKE SHORE ROAD, GILFORD, NEW HAMPSHIRE 03246

Tel: **(603) 528-1172**
Host(s): **The Shortway family**
Location: **33 mi. N of Concord**
No. of Rooms: **10**
Max. No. Sharing Bath: **5**
Double/sb: **$52**
Single/sb: **$45**
Open: **All year**
Breakfast: **Full**
Other Meals: **Available**
Credit Cards: **MC, VISA**
Pets: **No**
Children: **Welcome**
Smoking: **Permitted**
Social Drinking: **Permitted**
Airport/Station Pickup: **Yes**
Foreign Languages: **French, Italian**

This clapboard Colonial, built in 1771, is set on a hill overlooking fields and mountains. Recent renovations include a French country kitchen where special desserts are served Saturday nights. Some of the guest rooms have bunk beds, suitable for groups of skiers and hikers. The more private rooms have double beds, and there is a suite with separate entrance. Breakfast specialties include eggs Benedict and French toast. Afternoon tea is served to wind down your busy day. Ski areas, a private beach, and Lake Winnipesaukee are just a few of the area attractions.

The Gables ✪

139 MAIN, GORHAM, NEW HAMPSHIRE 03581

Tel: **(603) 466-2876**
Host(s): **Bill and Dot Dunton**
No. of Rooms: **4**
No. of Private Baths: **2**
Max. No. Sharing Bath: **4**
Double/pb: **$40**
Single/pb: **$25**
Double/sb: **$40**
Single/sb: **$25**
Open: **All year**
Reduced Rates: **10%, seniors**
Breakfast: **Full**
Credit Cards: **AMEX**
Pets: **No**
Children: **Welcome**
Smoking: **Permitted**
Social Drinking: **Permitted**

The Gables is a New England clapboard farmhouse painted antique blue. This village home is decorated in country style, with old family pieces and antique furnishings. Guests are welcome to gather around the living room fireplace to share a cup of coffee and perhaps some conversation. Bill and Dot serve a hearty breakfast featuring homemade bran muffins. They are just a short walk from antique shops, restaurants, and a shopping plaza. Mount Washington is just west of town, in the Presidential Range of the White Mountains. You can reach the summit by foot, auto, or the famous Cog Railway.

Roy Family Bed & Breakfast ✪

473 OCEAN BOULEVARD, HAMPTON BEACH, NEW HAMPSHIRE 03842

Tel: **(603) 926-7893 or 926-5505**
Best Time to Call: **After 1 PM**
Host(s): **Debbie and Richard Roy**
Location: **50 mi. N of Boston**
No. of Rooms: **6**
Max. No. Sharing Bath: **4**
Double/sb: **$45–$60**
Open: **May 15–Sept. 15**
Reduced Rates: **Available**
Breakfast: **Continental**
Credit Cards: **AMEX, MC, VISA**
Pets: **No**
Children: **Welcome, over 12**
Smoking: **Permitted**
Social Drinking: **Permitted**
Foreign Languages: **French**

The Atlantic Ocean is right at your feet when you stay at this comfortable New England-style home. The house is decorated in a mixture of traditional, Victorian, and casual pieces. Bedrooms are immaculate and furnished Colonial-style. Choose from two spacious decks to enjoy the sun and the ocean view. There is a television room furnished in white wicker for rainy days. The beach is one and a half miles long, and includes boardwalk shops, boutiques, and restaurants. A short drive away are many discount shopping areas, Seabrook Raceway, and Portsmouth Harbor.

The Inn on Golden Pond ✪

ROUTE 3, BOX 126, HOLDERNESS, NEW HAMPSHIRE 03245

Tel: **(603) 968-7269**
Best Time to Call: **Evenings**
Host(s): **Bill and Bonnie Webb**
Location: **4 mi. from I-93**
No. of Rooms: **8**
No. of Private Baths: **6**
Max. No. Sharing Bath: **4**
Double/pb: **$70**
Single/pb: **$50**
Double/sb: **$60**
Single/sb: **$40**
Open: **All year**
Breakfast: **Full**
Credit Cards: **MC, VISA**
Pets: **No**
Children: **Welcome, over 12**
Smoking: **No**
Social Drinking: **Permitted**
Airport/Station Pickup: **Yes**

If you saw the film *On Golden Pond,* you are familiar with the beauty of the countryside surrounding this inn. Built in 1879 on 55 acres, the house is across the street from Squam Lake, the setting for the movie. The rooms are bright and airy, decorated in a warm, homey style. Breakfast specialties include apple pancakes with local maple syrup, and a sausage, egg, and cheese casserole. Your hosts will gladly pack a picnic lunch for taking along to the lakes, mountains, and streams. Nearby are two golf courses, Waterville Valley, and Loon Mountain.

The Forest—A Country Inn ✪

ROUTE 16A, P.O. BOX 37, INTERVALE, NEW HAMPSHIRE 03845

Tel: **(603) 356-9772**
Best Time to Call: **After noon**
Host(s): **Rae and Ken Wyman**
Location: **50 mi. from Rte. 93**
No. of Rooms: **13**
No. of Private Baths: **7**
Max. No. Sharing Bath: **4**
Double/pb: **$48–$66**
Single/pb: **$38–$56**
Double/sb: **$44–$62**
Single/sb: **$38–$56**
Guest Cottage: **$72; sleeps 2**
Open: **May 1–Mar. 31**
Reduced Rates: **Oct. 25–Dec. 10; May 1–June 15**
Breakfast: **Full**
Other Meals: **Available**
Credit Cards: **AMEX, MC, VISA**
Pets: **No**
Children: **Welcome**
Smoking: **Permitted**
Social Drinking: **Permitted**
Airport/Station Pickup: **Yes**

Reigning over 25 wooded acres in the White Mountains, this three-story Victorian inn has been in continuous operation since the late 1800s. Inside, the inn has the feel of a big country home—full of braided rugs, comfortable chairs, antiques, crafts, and country collectibles. The stone cottage has a fireplace and is a favorite of honeymooners. Outside, you're close to all of the wonderful recreational possibilities that the valley has to offer—downhill skiing, hiking, biking, canoeing, kayaking, tennis, golf, and more. In back of the inn is a swimming pool and, in winter, all you have to do is go across the street to the Intervale Nordic Learning Center where you can use the cross-country ski trails at no extra cost.

The Galway House

OLD PETERBOROUGH ROAD, JAFFREY, NEW HAMPSHIRE 03452

Tel: **(603) 532-8083**
Host(s): **Joe and Marie Manning**
Location: **1 mi. from US 202**
No. of Rooms: **2**
Max. No. Sharing Bath: **4**
Double/sb: **$40**
Single/sb: **$35**
Open: **Aug. 15–June 30**
Breakfast: **Full**
Pets: **No**

Children: **Welcome (crib)**
Smoking: **Permitted**
Social Drinking: **Permitted**
Airport/Station Pickup: **Yes**

This new, oversize Cape with a spacious yard and sun deck is situated on a rural road surrounded by acres of woodland. It is located in the center of the Monadnock Region, known as the "Currier and Ives" corner of the state. It is at the foot of 3,165-foot Grand Monadnock, second only to Mt. Fuji for its appeal to climbers. Picturesque in every season, the area will make sports enthusiasts revel in the choice of activities. Joe and Marie welcome you to a warm hearth, a suitable beverage, and comfortable accommodations! From July 4 till August 15 they offer B&B on board their sailing sloop for an unusual adventure.

Lilac Hill Farm ✪

5 INGALLS ROAD, JAFFREY, NEW HAMPSHIRE 03452

Tel: **(603) 532-7278**
Best Time to Call: **Before 10 AM**
Host(s): **Frank, Ellen, Jacqulyn McNeill**
Location: **60 mi. NW of Boston**
No. of Rooms: **6**
No. of Private Baths: **1**
Max. No. Sharing Bath: **4**
Double/pb: **$55**
Single/pb: **$45**
Double/sb: **$55**
Single/sb: **$45**
Open: **All year**
Breakfast: **Full**
Pets: **No**
Children: **Welcome, over 12**
Smoking: **No**
Social Drinking: **Permitted**

Lilac Hill is a gentleman's farm set on 50 well-groomed acres at the base of Mount Monadnock. Enjoy superb views, long trails, and friendly farm animals. The house is imaginatively decorated with antiques and collectibles. Each room is noted for its quality furnishings and attention to detail. The same care goes into the homemade meals and snacks served in a welcoming atmosphere.

Ferry Point House ✪

R-1 BOX 335, LACONIA, NEW HAMPSHIRE 03246

Tel: **(603) 524-0087**
Best Time to Call: **After 6 PM**
Host(s): **Diane and Joe Damato**
Location: **90 mi. N of Boston**
No. of Rooms: **4**
No. of Private Baths: **4**
Double/pb: **$55**
Single/pb: **$45**
Open: **Memorial Day—Labor Day; Weekends during fall foliage**
Reduced Rates: **15%, weekly**
Breakfast: **Continental**
Pets: **No**
Children: **Welcome**
Smoking: **Downstairs only**
Social Drinking: **Permitted**
Airport/Station Pickup: **Yes**
Foreign Languages: **French**

New England's past is well preserved in this 150-year-old Victorian located on picturesque Lake Winnisquam. Enjoy breathtaking views of the water and the mountains from a 60-foot veranda. Of course, the view is even more enjoyable when you're sipping lemonade or the house blend of coffee. Guest rooms overlook the lake and are furnished with antiques, collectibles, and fresh flowers. Breakfast is served in a Victorian-style dining room, and your hosts take pride in offering unusual dishes, such as cheese baked apples, crêpes, or Grand Marnier French toast. Ferry Point House is minutes from regional activities such as boating, skiing, dinner cruises, and a large selection of fine restaurants.

The Tin Whistle Inn ✪

1047 UNION AVENUE, LACONIA, NEW HAMPSHIRE 03246

Tel: **(603) 528-4185**
Host(s): **Maureen C. Blazok**
Location: **10 mi. from Rte. 93**
No. of Rooms: **3**
No. of Private Baths: **1**
Max. No. Sharing Bath: **4**
Double/pb: **$55–$65**
Double/sb: **$50–$60**
Single/sb: **$42–$52**
Open: **All year**
Reduced Rates: **20%, Mar.–Apr.**
Breakfast: **Full**
Credit Cards: **AMEX, MC, VISA**
Pets: **Sometimes**
Children: **Welcome**
Smoking: **Permitted**
Social Drinking: **Permitted**
Airport/Station Pickup: **Yes**

Step back to the Victorian age where you can relax in a quiet, homey atmosphere in front of a crackling fire. There's always a steaming cup of coffee waiting for you. It is minutes away from a multitude of activities for the adventurous as well as the more inhibited. Try your hand at para sailing, scuba diving, water slides, hiking, skiing, and snowmobiling. You are welcome to play the piano, watch TV, or just relax on the large veranda overlooking Paugus Bay on Lake Winnipesaukee.

The Beal House Inn

247 WEST MAIN STREET, LITTLETON, NEW HAMPSHIRE 03561

Tel: **(603) 444-2661**
Best Time to Call: **10 AM–10 PM**
Host(s): **Doug and Brenda Clickenger**
Location: **1 mi. I-93**
No. of Rooms: **14**
No. of Private Baths: **10**
Max. No. Sharing Bath: **4**
Double/pb: **$42–$75**
Single/pb: **$38–$45**
Double/sb: **$38–$45**
Single/sb: **$32**
Suites: **$65–$110**
Open: **All year**
Reduced Rates: **Groups**
Breakfast: **Continental**
Credit Cards: **AMEX, DC, MC, VISA**
Pets: **No**
Children: **Welcome (crib)**
Smoking: **Permitted**
Social Drinking: **Permitted**
Airport/Station Pickup: **Yes**

Doug and Brenda have an antiques shop and have furnished their Federal-style home with choice pieces. The decor is constantly changing since so many guests buy these pieces and take them away. Breakfast features hot popovers served by the fireside. The inn is conveniently accessible to six great ski areas, Franconia Notch, and the famed Old Man of the Mountain. Popcorn, cheese, and crackers are complimentary. Tea is always available.

Manor On The Park

503 BEECH STREET, MANCHESTER, NEW HAMPSHIRE 03104

Tel: **(603) 669-8600**
Best Time to Call: **9 AM–5 PM**
Host(s): **Jan Dennis**
Location: **50 mi. N of Boston**
No. of Rooms: **8**
Max. No. Sharing Bath: **4**
Double/sb: **$44**
Single/sb: **$40**
Open: **All year**
Reduced Rates: **10%, seniors**
Breakfast: **Continental**
Credit Cards: **AMEX, MC, VISA**
Pets: **No**
Children: **No**
Smoking: **No**
Social Drinking: **Permitted**

Overlooking a pretty park, the inn is minutes from downtown and is close to restaurants, shops, theaters, and museums. The entire facility is designed with your comfort in mind. The bedrooms are cheerfully decorated. Little extras, such as luxuriously thick towels, fluffy down pillows, cozy bathrobes, and use of the laundry facilities, attest to your host's thoughtfulness. Guests enjoy visiting in the gracious living room with its pleasant decor and gentle stereo sounds serving as background to compatible conversation.

Peep-Willow Farm ✪

BIXBY STREET, MARLBOROUGH, NEW HAMPSHIRE 03455

Tel: **(603) 876-3807**
Best Time to Call: **7:30 PM–7:30 AM**
Host(s): **Noel Aderer**
Location: **7 mi. E of Keene**
No. of Rooms: **3**
Max. No. Sharing Bath: **4**
Double/sb: **$35**
Single/sb: **$20**
Open: **All year**
Breakfast: **Full**
Pets: **No**
Children: **Welcome**
Smoking: **No**
Social Drinking: **Permitted**
Airport/Station Pickup: **Yes**

Noel Aderer has a new Colonial farmhouse on a working Thoroughbred horse farm. She raises and trains horses for competition, and while there is plenty of room for petting and admiring, guests are not permitted to ride. Peep-Willow is named after horses number one and two, respectively. It is a charming place with lots of wood accents and antiques. Breakfast specialties include French toast, with local maple syrup, and bacon and eggs. Guests are welcome to watch farm chores, visit the horses, and enjoy a cup of coffee with Noel, who has done everything from working on a kibbutz to training polo ponies for a maharajah.

The Inn at Coit Mountain

HCR 63, BOX 3, NEWPORT, NEW HAMPSHIRE 03773

Tel: **(603) 863-3583 or 800-367-2364**
Host(s): **Dick and Judi Tatem**
Location: **8 mi. S of Route 89**
No. of Rooms: **5**
Max. No. Sharing Bath: **4**
Double/sb: **$55–$85**
Single/sb: **$45–$75**
Open: **All year**
Reduced Rates: **Weekly**
Breakfast: **Full**
Other Meals: **Available**
Credit Cards: **MC, VISA**
Pets: **No**
Children: **Welcome (crib)**
Smoking: **Permitted**
Social Drinking: **Permitted**
Airport/Station Pickup: **Yes**

This elegant Georgian home was built in 1790. It was later purchased by the Corbins, wealthy entrepreneurs known for developing Coney Island. The romantic history of the inn is well blended with the comforts of today. The library, with its massive granite fireplace, offers year-round warmth. Just off the library is the Stoneagle Frame Studio, whose large arched window is modeled after the one in Independence Hall in Philadelphia. The bedrooms are comfortable and spacious, some with cozy fireplaces. The Lake Sunapee area provides much to see and do, including swimming, boating, cross-country skiing, hiking, and golfing.

Peacock Inn ✪

P.O. BOX 1012, NORTH CONWAY, NEW HAMPSHIRE 03860

Tel: **(603) 356-9041**
Best Time to Call: **8:30 AM–12 PM**
Host(s): **Claire and Larry Jackson**
Location: **1½ mi. from Rte. 16**
No. of Rooms: **18**
No. of Private Baths: **14**
Max. No. Sharing Bath: **4**
Double/pb: **$75**
Single/pb: **$65**
Double/sb: **$70**
Single/sb: **$60**
Suites: **$85**
Open: **All year**
Breakfast: **Full**
Other Meals: **Available**
Credit Cards: **AMEX, MC, VISA**
Pets: **No**
Children: **Welcome (crib)**
Smoking: **Permitted**
Social Drinking: **Permitted**
Airport/Station Pickup: **Yes**

The Jacksons say that their peaceful setting draws people to the Peacock, but it's the personal attention they receive here that brings them back. The guest book of this 32-room Victorian dates back to 1873. The house is one of the most historic in the Mt. Washington Valley, and is soon to be included on the National Register. Each guest room has a special feature such as a brass or canopy bed, skylights, or antique rockers, and all rooms offer fresh fruit and flowers, chocolates, and bath salts. Everyone's favorite is the fireplaced common room where guests can share wine, conversation, and a beautiful mountain view. In the warm weather, the glass doors open out to a comfortable sun deck. Skiing, fishing, mountain climbing, and golf are walking distance from the inn. Your hosts also invite you to the Mt. Cranmore Racquet Club, where you can swim, take a sauna or aerobics class, or relax in the whirlpool.

Meadow Farm ✪

JENNESS POND ROAD, NORTHWOOD, NEW HAMPSHIRE 03261

Tel: **(603) 942-8619**
Host(s): **Douglas and Janet Briggs**
Location: **18 mi. E of Concord**
No. of Rooms: **3**
Max. No. Sharing Bath: **3**
Double/sb: **$40**
Single/sb: **$30**
Open: **All year**
Reduced Rates: **Families**
Breakfast: **Full**
Pets: **Sometimes**
Children: **Welcome**
Smoking: **Permitted**
Social Drinking: **Permitted**

Meadow Farm is set on 50 acres of quiet woods and horse pastures. The house is an authentic New England Colonial dating back to 1770, with wide pine floors, beamed ceilings, and old fireplaces. In the morning, a country breakfast of homemade breads, seasonal fruit, and local syrup is served in the keeping room. Guests are invited to relax on the private beach on an adjacent lake. The property also has plenty of wooded trails for long walks or cross-country skiing. Meadow Farm is an ideal location for those en route to Concord, the seacoast, or the mountains.

Leighton Inn ✪

69 RICHARDS AVENUE, PORTSMOUTH, NEW HAMPSHIRE 03801

Tel: **(603) 433-2188**
Host(s): **Catherine Stone**
Location: **1 mi. from I-95**
No. of Rooms: **5**
No. of Private Baths: **1**
Max. No. Sharing Bath: **4**
Double/pb: **$70**
Single/pb: **$60**
Double/sb: **$60**
Single/sb: **$50**
Open: **All year**
Reduced Rates: **Nov.–Apr.**
Breakfast: **Full**
Credit Cards: **MC, VISA**
Pets: **No**
Children: **Welcome**
Smoking: **Permitted**
Social Drinking: **Permitted**
Airport/Station Pickup: **Yes**
Foreign Languages: **French**

In 1809, cabinetmaker Samuel Wyatt built himself a Federal-style home, sparing no expense. Now named for a prominent Portsmouth family who lived there in the 1800s, the inn is just a short walk from Strawbery Banke, a "living museum" that traces the history of this colorful waterfront city through four centuries. Swimming, boating, and fishing are just a short drive away, and whale-watch cruises can easily be arranged. In summer, guests breakfast on the porch that overlooks the inn's formal gardens; in winter, they sit in front of a fire in the pine-paneled country kitchen. And, if you're musically inclined, Catherine invites you to sit down at the 1913 Steinway concert grand piano in the library and play as long as you'd like.

Grassy Pond House

RINDGE, NEW HAMPSHIRE 03461

Tel: **(603) 899-5166/5167**
Best Time to Call: **Mornings**
Host(s): **Carmen Linares and Robert Multer**
Location: **60 mi. NW of Boston**
No. of Rooms: **3**
No. of Private Baths: **2**
Max. No. Sharing Bath: **4**
Double/pb: **$65**
Double/sb: **$55**
Single/sb: **$40**
Open: **All year**
Breakfast: **Full**
Pets: **No**
Children: **Welcome, over 14**
Smoking: **No**
Social Drinking: **Permitted**
Airport/Station Pickup: **Yes**
Foreign Languages: **Spanish**

This secluded 19th-century farmhouse is set among 130 acres of woods and fields on the west shore of an unspoiled lake. The house has been restored, enlarged, and decorated in period pieces. Guest quarters feature a private entrance and a living room with fireplace. Breakfast specialties include pancakes with local maple syrup, fresh eggs and bacon, and plenty of good Colombian coffee. This setting high in the Monadnock region is perfect for hiking, skiing, boating, fishing, and swimming. Nearby are Cathedral of the Pines, Rhododendron State Reservation, Franklin Pierce College, and a choice of restaurants, summer theaters, and festivals.

Tokfarm Inn ✪

BOX 229, WOOD AVENUE, RINDGE, NEW HAMPSHIRE 03461

Tel: **(603) 899-6646**
Best Time to Call: **Early AM, evenings**
Host(s): **Mrs. W. B. Nottingham**
Location: **50 mi. NW of Boston**
No. of Rooms: **5**
Max. No. Sharing Bath: **4**
Double/sb: **$32–$40**
Single/sb: **$18**
Open: **Apr. 16 to Nov. 14**
Breakfast: **Continental**
Pets: **No**
Children: **No**
Smoking: **No**
Social Drinking: **Permitted**
Airport/Station Pickup: **Yes**
Foreign Languages: **Dutch, French, German**

This 150-year-old farmhouse has a spectacular view of three states from its 1,400-foot hilltop. Mt. Monadnock, the second most climbed peak in the world (Mt. Fuji is first), is practically in its backyard! Mrs. Nottingham raises Christmas trees, is a world traveler, and loves to ski. She'll recommend things to keep you busy. Don't miss the lovely Cathedral of the Pines. Franklin Pierce College is nearby.

The Hilltop Inn ✪

MAIN STREET, P.O. BOX 9, SUGAR HILL, NEW HAMPSHIRE 03585

Tel: **(603) 823-5695**
Host(s): **Mike and Meri Hern**
Location: **4 mi. W of Franconia**
No. of Rooms: **5**
No. of Private Baths: **1**
Max. No. Sharing Bath: **5**
Double/sb: **$45**
Single/sb: **$35**
Suites: **$35–$100**
Open: **All year**
Breakfast: **Full**
Pets: **Welcome**
Children: **Welcome (crib)**
Smoking: **Permitted**
Social Drinking: **Permitted**
Airport/Station Pickup: **Yes**

The Hilltop Inn is a sprawling 19th-century Victorian located in a small, friendly village. Inside, you'll find a warm, cozy atmosphere, comfortable furnishings, and lots of antiques. The kitchen is the heart of the house in more ways than one. In the morning, homemade muffins are served fresh from the old-fashioned Garland stove. In the evening, the sunsets from the deck are breathtaking. Your hosts are professional caterers and are pleased to cater to you. Join them for wine and cheese after a day of activities. Local attractions include Franconia Notch, White Mountain National Forest, North Conway, great skiing, and spectacular foliage.

Times Ten Inn ✪

ROUTE 103B, BOX 572, SUNAPEE, NEW HAMPSHIRE 03782

Tel: **(603) 763-5120**
Host(s): **Audrey and Dick Kelly**
Location: **90 mi. NW of Boston**
No. of Rooms: **3**
Max. No. Sharing Bath: **4**
Double/sb: **$40**
Single/sb: **$35**
Open: **All year**
Reduced Rates: **Families**
Breakfast: **Full**
Pets: **No**
Children: **Welcome**
Smoking: **Permitted**
Social Drinking: **Permitted**
Airport/Station Pickup: **Yes**

An 1820 New England farmhouse, with floor-to-ceiling living room windows overlooking a wildlife preserve, it's 25 miles to Dartmouth College, recreational Lake Sunapee, and skiing. Audrey and Dick offer a huge breakfast of Swedish pancakes, real maple syrup, homemade preserves, bacon, or sausage. Complimentary cheese snacks and good conversation are always on tap.

Suncook House

62 MAIN STREET, SUNCOOK, NEW HAMPSHIRE 03275

Tel: **(603) 485-8141**
Best Time to Call: **Mornings**
Host(s): **Gerry and Evelyn Lavoie**
Location: **6 mi. S of Concord**
No. of Rooms: **4**
No. of Private Baths: **2**
Max. No. Sharing Bath: **3**
Double/pb: **$48**
Single/pb: **$40**
Doubie/sb: **$40**
Single/sb: **$34**
Open: **All year**
Reduced Rates: **10%, seniors**
Breakfast: **Full**
Pets: **No**
Children: **Welcome, over 12**
Smoking: **No**
Social Drinking: **Permitted**
Airport/Station Pickup: **Yes**

Suncook House is a spacious brick Georgian set on three beautifully maintained acres. The house is newly renovated and its comfortable rooms are furnished with period pieces. A formal living room, sun parlor, den, and an excellent organ are available for your relaxation and pleasure. This country home allows one the benefits of feeling away from it all while still being able to enjoy the convenience of a main road that leads to the mountains and lakes. Walk to village churches, restaurants, and tennis courts. New Hampshire College and Bear Brook State Park are both within a five-mile drive.

Thirteen Colonies Farm

R.F.D., ROUTE 16, UNION, NEW HAMPSHIRE 03887

Tel: **(603) 652-4458**
Best Time to Call: **After 6 PM**
Host(s): **Roger and Jeanne Burkhart**
Location: **30 mi. N of Portsmouth**
No. of Rooms: **6**
No. of Private Baths: **4**
Max. No. Sharing Bath: **4**
Doubls/pb: **$45**
Double/sb: **$45**
Single/sb: **$40**
Open: **All year**
Reduced Rates: **Available**
Breakfast: **Full**
Other Meals: **Sometimes**
Pets: **No**
Children: **Welcome (crib, toys)**
Smoking: **Permitted**
Social Drinking: **Permitted**
Airport/Station Pickup: **Yes**

There is something for everybody on this 100-acre working farm with its many animals, fruit trees, and vegetable gardens. The house is an 1841 Colonial with a long "ell" connecting the house and barn. The guest room in the main house has a fireplace and is more traditional than the other rooms. Those in the ell are rustic, with old beams, knotty-pine walls, and a mixture of antique and handcrafted pieces. Roger combines farming with running a church parish. Jeanne is a teacher who will gladly instruct those interested in pottery and weaving. Together they have a great deal of knowledge to share about farming and the outdoors. Start the day with such breakfast specialties as homemade breads, farm-fresh fruit, and blueberry pancakes. Then you can either be part of farm activities or be as private as you like. A lake and river are one mile away through the woods, and other local activities such as skiing, hiking, and mountain climbing can be enjoyed nearby.

Crab Apple Inn ✪

ROUTE 25, WEST PLYMOUTH, NEW HAMPSHIRE 03264

Tel: **(603) 536-4476**
Best Time to Call: **6–10 PM**
Host(s): **Bill and Carolyn Crenson**
Location: **4 mi. from Rte. 93**
No. of Rooms: **4**
No. of Private Baths: **2**
Max. No. Sharing Bath: **4**
Double/pb: **$60–$65**
Double/sb: **$54–$58**
Suites: **$65–$70**
Open: **All year**
Breakfast: **Full**
Pets: **No**
Children: **Welcome, over 8**
Credit Cards: **MC, VISA**
Smoking: **Permitted**
Social Drinking: **Permitted**
Airport/Station Pickup: **Yes**

Located in the beautiful Baker River Valley at the gateway to the White Mountain region, the inn is an 1835 brick building of Federal design situated beside a small brook at the foot of Tenny Mountain. The bedrooms on the second floor have fireplaces; those on the third floor have a panoramic view of the mountains. All are tastefully furnished. There are several fine restaurants nearby, and the inn is within a 10-minute drive of Plymouth State College. Gift studios and handcraft and antique shops in the area provide treasures for both the discerning and casual buyer.

Isaac Springfield House ✪

RFD 1, ROUTE 28 SOUTH, WOLFEBORO, NEW HAMPSHIRE 03894

Tel: **(603) 569-3529**
Best Time to Call: **Mornings, evenings**
Host(s): **Rose LeBlanc and Andrew Terrragni**
Location: **2 mi. S of Wolfeboro**
No. of Rooms: **4**
Max. No. Sharing Bath: **4**
Double/sb: **$60**
Single/sb: **$55**
Open: **All year**
Reduced Rates: **Available**
Breakfast: **Full**
Credit Cards: **MC, VISA**
Pets: **Sometimes**
Children: **Welcome**
Smoking: **Permitted**
Social Drinking: **Permitted**

Isaac Springfield built this spacious Victorian back in 1871. It is painted a warm yellow and has a large, old-fashioned, wraparound porch.

Inside, the rooms are decorated with antique and brass furnishings. There is a cozy parlor with fireplace and piano where guests may want to bring a bottle of wine. Rose and Andrew will gladly provide ice and glasses at any time. Each morning, they serve homemade muffins, fresh fruit, eggs, and pancakes in a spacious dining room. This lovely home is five minutes from beautiful Lake Winnipesaukee and from the quaint shops and attractions in town. Wolfeboro is a center of seasonal activities including boating, hiking, ice sailing, and much more.

Tuc' Me Inn

68 NORTH MAIN STREET, P.O. BOX 657, WOLFEBORO, NEW HAMPSHIRE 03894

Tel: **(603) 569-5702**
Host(s): **Irma and Walter Limberger**
Location: **25 mi. from I-93, Rte. 104 Exit**
No. of Rooms: **7**
No. of Private Baths: **3**
Max. No. Sharing Bath: **4**
Double/pb: **$75**
Single/pb: **$70**
Double/sb: **$70**
Single/sb: **$65**
Open: **All year**
Reduced Rates: **Available**
Breakfast: **Full**
Credit Cards: **MC, VISA**
Pets: **No**
Children: **No**
Smoking: **Permitted**
Social Drinking: **Permitted**
Airport/Station Pickup: **Yes**

This early 1800s Colonial is located in the town that is known as the oldest summer resort in America. Wolfeboro is situated on the eastern shore of Lake Winnipesaukee, a beautiful spot in any season. At the inn, guests will enjoy a homey atmosphere and tastefully furnished rooms. In the morning, wake up to the aroma of freshly brewed coffee and everything that goes with it. You can walk to town or take a cruise on the *Mt. Washington.* After a day of activity, enjoy a cool drink on one of the sun porches back at your home away from home.

NEW JERSEY

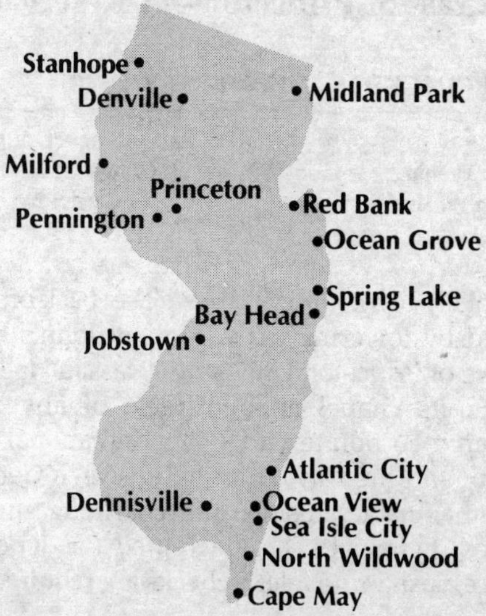

Stanhope
Denville
Midland Park
Milford
Princeton
Pennington
Red Bank
Ocean Grove
Spring Lake
Bay Head
Jobstown
Atlantic City
Dennisville
Ocean View
Sea Isle City
North Wildwood
Cape May

Bed & Breakfast of New Jersey, Inc.

SUITE 132, 103 GODWIN AVENUE, MIDLAND PARK, NEW JERSEY 07432

Tel: **(201) 444-7409**
Best Time to Call: **9 AM–4 PM**
State/Regions Covered: **Delaware River area, Wayne area**

Rates (Single/Double):

	Single	Double
Average:	**$35**	**$55**
Luxury:	**$60**	**$98**

Credit Cards: **MC, VISA**

Whether you crave the sound of lazy waves gently slapping the side of a boat, or the tranquillity of rolling country hills, you'll find it all in New Jersey. Indulge yourself, and take in the lavish elegance of a high-rise condo with a perfect view of the Manhattan skyline. Stay in a restored mountain mansion, in a villa by a great golf course, in an 1889 artist's studio, or in any of hundreds of traditional, well-maintained homes. From the Meadowlands, to Princeton University, to Action

Park, to Edison's home in Menlo Park, to the Pine Barrens, you will find that the Garden State has much to offer. Please send $5 for the descriptive directory.

Bed & Breakfast of Princeton—A Reservation Service ✪

P.O. BOX 571, PRINCETON, NEW JERSEY 08540

Tel: **(609) 924-3189**
Best Time to Call: **Evenings**
Coordinator: **John W. Hurley**
States/Regions Covered: **Princeton**

Rates (Single/Double):
Average: **$30–$55** **$40–$65**
Credit Cards: **No**

Princeton is a lovely town; houses are well set back on carefully tended lawns, screened by towering trees. Most of John's hosts live within walking distance of Princeton University. Nassau Hall (circa 1756) is its oldest building; its chapel is the largest of any at an American university. Nearby corporate parks include national companies such as RCA, Squibb, and the David Sarnoff Research Center. Restaurants feature every imaginable cuisine, and charming shops offer a wide variety of wares. Personal checks accepted for deposit or total payment in advance; cash or traveler's checks are required for any balance due.

Northern New Jersey Bed & Breakfast ✪

11 SUNSET TRAIL, DENVILLE, NEW JERSEY 07834

Tel: **(201) 625-5129**
Best Time to Call: **9 AM–6 PM**
Coordinator: **Al Bergins**
State/Regions Covered: **Northern and Central New Jersey**

Rates (Single/Double):
Modest: **$30** **$40**
Average: **$30–$40** **$40–$50**
Luxury: **$48–$66** **$60–$80**
Credit Cards: **No**

Al has a variety of comfortable suburban homes with all the amenities of country living yet convenient and close to New York City. Some are located near the water, so guests can go swimming and boating in season. Morristown National Park, Waterloo Village, and the Meadowlands Sports Complex are in the vicinity. Corporate transferees may be accommodated for a month or longer at substantially lower rates.

The Abbey

COLUMBIA AVENUE AND GURNEY STREET, CAPE MAY, NEW JERSEY 08204

Tel: **(609) 884-4506**
Host(s): **Jay and Marianne Schatz**
Location: **90 mi. SE of Philadelphia**
No. of Rooms: **14**
No. of Private Baths: **11**
Max. No. Sharing Bath: **5**
Double/pb: **$60–$95**
Single/pb: **$50–$85**
Double/sb: **$72–$76**
Single/sb: **$66**
Suite: **$90**
Open: **Apr.–Nov.**
Breakfast: **Full**
Credit Cards: **AMEX, MC, VISA**
Pets: **No**
Children: **Welcome, over 12**
Smoking: **No**
Social Drinking: **Permitted**

One block from the beach and in the center of the historic district sits this handsome Gothic Revival villa built in 1869 and Victorian cottage (c. 1873). Furnished with museum-quality antiques, the decor is formal but the attitude is warm and casual. Jay and Marianne are former chemists who have passionate interests in antiques and restoration. A full breakfast is served in the spring and fall, often featuring egg casseroles or quiches. Continental buffet is served in summer. Late-afternoon refreshments are always available. A three-night minimum stay is required.

Albert G. Stevens Inn ✪

127 MYRTLE AVENUE, CAPE MAY, NEW JERSEY 08204

Tel: **(609) 884-4717**
Host(s): **Paul and Alice Linden**
Location: **40 mi. S of Atlantic City**
No. of Rooms: **6**
No. of Private Baths: **4**
Max. No. Sharing Bath: **4**
Double/pb: **$85**
Double/sb: **$70**
Suites: **$95**
Open: **Feb. 1–Dec. 31**
Breakfast: **Full**
Credit Cards: **MC, VISA**
Pets: **No**
Children: **No**
Smoking: **No**
Social Drinking: **Permitted**

This 85-year-old Victorian is located next door to historic Wilbrahan Mansion and three blocks from the beach. The antique decor includes mother-of-pearl inlay in the parlor suite, an oak mantel, and other treasures throughout. The wraparound veranda is a wonderful place for sipping your second cup of coffee or for relaxing later in the day. Breakfast often features ham and cheese quiche or waffles with whipped cream. There is a minimum stay of two nights on weekends and three nights for the Fourth of July, Memorial Day, and Labor Day weekends.

Barnard-Good House ✪

238 PERRY STREET, CAPE MAY, NEW JERSEY 08204

Tel: **(609) 884-5381**
Best Time to Call: **8 AM–9 PM**
Host(s): **Nan and Tom Hawkins**
No. of Rooms: **6**
No. of Private Baths: **3**
Max. No. Sharing Bath: **2**
Double/pb: **$85**
Single/pb: **$67.50**
Double/sb: **$65**
Single/sb: **$58.50**
Suites: **$85**
Open: **Apr.–Nov.**
Breakfast: **Full**
Pets: **No**
Children: **No**
Smoking: **No**
Social Drinking: **Permitted**
Airport/Station Pickup: **Yes**

Nan and Tom cordially invite you to their Second Empire Victorian cottage (circa 1869), just two blocks from the "swimming" beach. They love antiques and are continually adding to their collection. They use them generously to create the warm and comfortable atmosphere. Nan's breakfast includes homemade exotic juices, delicious home-baked breads, and unusual preserves. In spring and fall, added gourmet entrées and side dishes make for an epicurean feast. Iced tea and snacks are served evenings. There's a two-night minimum stay in spring and fall; three nights in summer.

The Brass Bed Inn ✪

719 COLUMBIA AVENUE, CAPE MAY, NEW JERSEY 08204

Tel: **(609) 884-8075**
Best Time to Call: **1–3 PM**
Host(s): **John and Donna Dunwoody**
No. of Rooms: **8**
No. of Private Baths: **4**
Max. No. Sharing Bath: **4**
Double/pb: **$85**
Single/pb: **$67.50**
Double/sb: **$65**
Single/sb: **$58.50**
Open: **All year**
Breakfast: **Full**
Pets: **No**
Children: **No**
Smoking: **No**
Social Drinking: **Permitted**
Airport/Station Pickup: **Yes**

This Gothic Revival home was built in 1872. The original furnishings have all been restored, and you are welcome to visit in the sun parlor, handsome parlors, and dining room. It is two blocks to the ocean, shops, and restaurants on the mall. John and Donna suggest that you bring your bikes to truly enjoy this historic town; there's a lock-up area to keep them safe.

The Gingerbread House ✪

28 GURNEY STREET, CAPE MAY, NEW JERSEY 08204

Tel: **(609) 884-0211**
Best Time to Call: **7–10 PM**
Host(s): **Joan and Fred Echevarria**
No. of Rooms: **6**
No. of Private Baths: **3**
Max. No. Sharing Bath: **5**
Double/pb: **$75–$90**
Double/sb: **$68**
Single/sb: **$60**
Open: **All year**
Reduced Rates: **Oct. 1–May 31**
Breakfast: **Continental**
Pets: **No**
Children: **Welcome, over 7**
Smoking: **Permitted**
Social Drinking: **Permitted**

Listed on the National Register of Historic Places, this charming 1869 seaside cottage features cozy guest rooms. The house is cheerfully decorated with plants, lots of fresh flowers, period furniture, and photographs by Fred Echevarria. Located a block from the beach and two blocks from the mall, the house has a comfortable living room and breezy porch that are the gathering places for friendly conversation.

The Mainstay Inn ✪

635 COLUMBIA AVENUE, CAPE MAY, NEW JERSEY 08204

Tel: **(609) 884-8690**
Best Time to Call: **10 AM–4 PM**
Host(s): **Tom and Sue Carroll**
No. of Rooms: **13**
No. of Private Baths: **9**
Max. No. Sharing Bath: **4**
Double/pb: **$75–$98**
Single/pb: **$60–$88**
Double/sb: **$70–$83**
Single/sb: **$60–$73**
Suites: **$75–$98**
Open: **Apr. 1–Dec. 15**
Reduced Rates: **Off-season; weekdays**
Breakfast: **Full**
Pets: **No**
Children: **Welcome, over 12**
Smoking: **No**
Social Drinking: **Permitted**

Located in the heart of the historic district, this 114-year-old mansion was originally built as a private gambling club. Except for a few 20th-century concessions, it still looks much as it did when the gamblers were there, with 14-foot ceilings, elaborate chandeliers, and outstanding Victorian antiques. Tom and Sue serve breakfast either in the formal dining room or on the veranda; afternoon tea and homemade snacks are a ritual. Breakfast often features ham and apple pie, or corn quiche with baked ham. Continental breakfast is served in summer. Rock on the wide veranda; enjoy croquet in the garden; or retreat to the cupola. Minimum stay is three nights in season.

The Henry Ludlam Inn ✪

DENNISVILLE, NEW JERSEY (Mailing address: RD 3, Box 298, Woodbine, New Jersey 08270)

Tel: **(609) 861-5847**
Best Time to Call: **After 5 PM**
Host(s): **Ann and Marty Thurlow**
Location: **25 mi. SW of Atlantic City**
No. of Rooms: **6**
No. of Private Baths: **2**
Max. No. Sharing Bath: **4**
Double/pb: **$65–$75**
Single/pb: **$55**
Double/sb: **$55–$65**
Single/sb: **$45**
Suite: **$75**
Open: **All year**
Reduced Rates: **Weekly**
Breakfast: **Full**
Pets: **No**
Children: **Welcome, over 12**
Smoking: **Permitted**
Social Drinking: **Permitted**
Airport/Station Pickup: **Yes**

Built in 1803, Ann and Marty's home is furnished with antiques, handmade quilts, plants, and other nice touches to complete the decor. It's located in Dennisville, on a 55-acre lake that's 20 minutes from the Stone Harbor beaches. During cold months, breakfast is served in the Keeping Room; in warm months, on the porch overlooking the lake. All the bedrooms have working fireplaces for cozy comfort. Afternoon tea and wine are served.

Daffodil ✪

R.D. 1, BOX 420, JOBSTOWN, NEW JERSEY 08041

Tel: **(609) 723-5364**
Host(s): **Lyd Sudler**
Location: **3 miles from N.J. Tpke. Exit 7**
No. of Rooms: **3**
Max. No. Sharing Bath: **4**
Double/sb: **$40**
Suites: **$65**
Open: **All year**
Breakfast: **Full**

Other Meals: **Available**
Pets: **No**
Children: **Welcome**
Smoking: **Permitted**
Social Drinking: **Permitted**

This spacious contemporary farmhouse was built in 1961 and is attractively furnished with family heirlooms. From the porch, there's a spectacular view of the pastures with the cows grazing and the deer that come out of the woods at dusk. It's situated in the heart of Burlington County, where every little town, including Burlington, Bordentown, and Mt. Holly, is a pre-Revolutionary gem. It is a half hour to Philadelphia or Princeton. Lyd enjoys music, gardening, and pampering her guests.

Chestnut Hill on-the-Delaware ✪

63 CHURCH STREET, MILFORD, NEW JERSEY 08848

Tel: **(201) 995-9761**
Host(s): **Linda and Rob Castagna**
Location: **15 mi. from Rte. 78**
No. of Rooms: **5**
No. of Private Baths: **2**
Max. No. Sharing Bath: **4**
Double/pb: **$70–$75**
Double/sb: **$55**
Single/sb: **$50**
Open: **All year**
Reduced Rates: **Weekly**
Breakfast: **Full**
Pets: **No**
Children: **Welcome**
Smoking: **No**
Social Drinking: **Permitted**

The veranda of this 1860 Neo-Italianate Victorian overlooks the peaceful Delaware River. Linda, Rob, and teenage son Michael have refurbished and restored their home with charm, grace, and beauty. The historic countryside is great for antique hunting, water sports, art shows, and restaurants. It's only minutes to New Hope and Bucks County delights, and to dozens of factory outlets.

Candlelight Inn ✪

2310 CENTRAL AVENUE, NORTH WILDWOOD, NEW JERSEY 08260

Tel: **(609) 522-6200**
Best Time to Call: **8 AM–11 PM**
Host(s): **Paul DiFilippo and Diane Buscham**
Location: **40 mi. S of Atlantic City**
No. of Rooms: **9**
No. of Private Baths: **7**
Max. No. Sharing Bath: **4**
Double/pb: **$60–$80**
Single/pb: **$45–$60**
Single/sb: **$40–$55**
Open: **Feb.–Dec.**
Reduced Rates: **10%, seniors**
Breakfast: **Full**
Credit Cards: **AMEX, MC, VISA**
Pets: **No**
Children: **No**
Smoking: **Permitted**

Social Drinking: **Permitted**
Airport/Station Pickup: **Yes**
Foreign Languages: **French**

Leaming Rice, Sr., built this Queen Anne Victorian at the turn of the century. The house remained in the family until Diane and Paul restored it and created a bed and breakfast. Large oak doors with beveled glass invite you into the main vestibule, which has a fireplace nook. A wide variety of original gas lighting fixtures may be found throughout the house, and each window is adorned with candlelight. Guest rooms have fresh flowers and are furnished with period pieces and antiques. Breakfast is served in the dining room with a built-in oak breakfront, and chestnut picket doors. In the afternoon, enjoy tea and cookies on the wide veranda. This elegant inn is convenient to the beaches, boardwalk, and historic Cape May. There's a three-night minimum during July and August.

Home Suite Home

1410 SURF AVENUE, NORTH WILDWOOD, NEW JERSEY 08260

Tel: **(609) 729-6625**
Best Time to Call: **After 5 PM**
Host(s): **Jim and Connie Costa**
Location: **40 mi. S of Atlantic City**
No. of Rooms: **3**
No. of Private Baths: **1**
Max. No. Sharing Bath: **2**
Double/pb: **$70**
Single/pb: **$60**
Double/sb: **$55–$65**
Single/sb: **$55**
Open: **Mar. 1–Nov. 30**
Reduced Rates: **10%, seniors; weekly**
Breakfast: **Continental**
Pets: **No**
Children: **Welcome, over 12**
Smoking: **Permitted**
Social Drinking: **Permitted**
Foreign Languages: **Italian, Polish**

Jim and Connie Costa welcome you to their white marble executive-style home located one block from the beach. The house is decorated in a Grecian motif with comfortable furnishings and family pieces. There is plenty to do in this resort town, and you're just one and a half blocks from the boardwalk when you stay with the Costas. They can suggest bicycle routes, recommend restaurants, and direct you to even more activities in nearby Atlantic City.

Major Gandy's ✪

180 SHORE ROAD, OCEAN VIEW, NEW JERSEY 08230

Tel: **(609) 624-1080**
Best Time to Call: **Evening**
Host(s): **Roseann and Bernie Keenan**
Location: **20 mi. S of Atlantic City**
No. of Rooms: **4**
No. of Private Baths: **1**
Max. No. Sharing Bath: **5**
Double/pb: **$60**
Double/sb: **$45–$55**
Single/sb: **$40**
Open: **All year**
Reduced Rates: **Weekly**
Breakfast: **Full**
Pets: **No**
Children: **Welcome, over 10**
Smoking: **No**
Social Drinking: **Permitted**

This historic and romantic early Victorian is located in the heart of an antique hunter's paradise. After a good night's sleep in a brass or canopy bed, have your breakfast in the Great Room. Enjoy your second cup of coffee on the porch, while you relax on a wicker rocking chair. The charming village of Cape May and the glitz of Atlantic City are both nearby. The beach is nearby for seasonal pleasures. There is a two-night minimum stay on summer weekends.

Baily Bed & Breakfast ✪

12 LANING AVENUE, PENNINGTON, NEW JERSEY 08534

Tel: **(609) 737-9439**
Best Time to Call: **Early morning or evening**
Host(s): **Carleen and Andy Baily**
Location: **8 mi. W of Princeton 1 mi. from I-95**
No. of Rooms: **1**
Max. No. Sharing Bath: **4**
Double/sb: **$30**
Single/sb: **$28**
Open: **Jan. 2–Dec. 23**
Breakfast: **Continental**
Pets: **No**
Children: **No**
Smoking: **No**
Social Drinking: **Permitted**

Carleen and Andy welcome you to their restored and refurbished home. Sit and relax on the wide front porch, read a favorite book, or take a walk through town. For antiques lovers, New Hope, Pennsylvania, and Lambertville are only 15 minutes away by car, and Princeton University's many attractions are within a short drive.

Cape Associates ✪

340 46TH PLACE, SEA ISLE CITY, NEW JERSEY 08243

Tel: **(609) 263-8700 or 263-4461**
Host(s): **Wish Zurawski, Eileen Rodan**
Location: **3 mi. from Rte. 9**
No. of Rooms: **4**
No. of Private Baths: **1**
Max. No. Sharing Bath: **5**
Double/pb: **$60**
Double/sb: **$50**
Open: **All year**
Reduced Rates: **Available**
Breakfast: **Continental**
Pets: **Sometimes**
Children: **Welcome**
Smoking: **Permitted**
Social Drinking: **Permitted**
Airport/Station Pickup: **Yes**

It's four blocks to the beach from this 1962 brick-and-wood Colonial house on the bay. It's casual and comfortable, with lots of books, records, and artwork, and close to historic Cape May and Atlantic City. Eileen and Wish will arrange to escort you to the casinos. Use the kitchen for light snacks, and the laundry facilities. Cooled by the bay breezes, the deck is a lovely place to relax.

Ashling Cottage ✪

106 SUSSEX AVENUE, SPRING LAKE, NEW JERSEY 07762

Tel: **(201) 449-3553**
Host(s): **Goodi and Jack Stewart**
Location: **8 mi. from Garden State Pky., Exit 98**
No. of Rooms: **10**
No. of Private Baths: **8**
Max. No. Sharing Bath: **4**
Double/pb: **$70–$100**
Single/pb: **$65–$95**
Double/sb: **$55–$78**
Single/sb: **$50–$73**
Open: **Mar.–Dec.**
Reduced Rates: **Sept. 18–May 20**
Breakfast: **Continental**
Pets: **No**
Children: **No**
Smoking: **Permitted**
Social Drinking: **Permitted**
Airport/Station Pickup: **Yes**

The Jersey shore is a block away from this three-story mansard-roofed cottage with bay windows, overhangs, nooks, and a small romantic balcony. Each guest room is different, with such features as dormer windows, wainscoting, and individual porches. A buffet breakfast is served in the glass-enclosed solarium with views of the ocean and boardwalk to the east. To the west is the willow-bordered Spring Lake, popular for boaters, with its wooden foot bridges, ducks, and geese. A two- to three-night minimum stay is required on weekends from May through August.

Whistling Swan Inn ✪

BOX 791, 110 MAIN STREET, STANHOPE, NEW JERSEY 07874

Tel: **(201) 347-6369**
Best Time to Call: **9 AM–6 PM**
Host(s): **Paula Williams and Joe Mulay**
Location: **45 mi. W of New York City**
No. of Rooms: **10**
No. of Private Baths: **10**
Double/pb: **$55–$70**
Open: **All year**
Reduced Rates: **Weekly; 10%, seniors**
Breakfast: **Full**
Credit Cards: **AMEX, MC, VISA**
Pets: **Sometimes**
Children: **Welcome, over 12**
Smoking: **No**
Social Drinking: **Permitted**
Airport/Station Pickup: **Yes**

You'll feel like you're back in grandmother's house when you visit this lovely Queen Anne Victorian located in a small historic village. The massive limestone wraparound porch leads to comfortable rooms filled with family antiques. Your hosts have labored tirelessly to make the ornate woodwork, huge fireplace, old-fashioned fixtures, and even the dumbwaiter look like new. Take a bubble bath in a claw-footed tub and then wrap yourself in a fluffy robe before retiring. Your room will be individually decorated in an Oriental art decor or brass motif. Breakfast includes homemade muffins, breads, and fruit, along with a hot egg, cheese, or fruit dish. Special arrangements are easily made for corporate guests who need to eat early or require the use of a private telephone, copy service, or meeting room. The inn is close to the International Trade Zone, Waterloo Village, Lake Musconetcong, restaurants, and state parks and forests.

NEW MEXICO

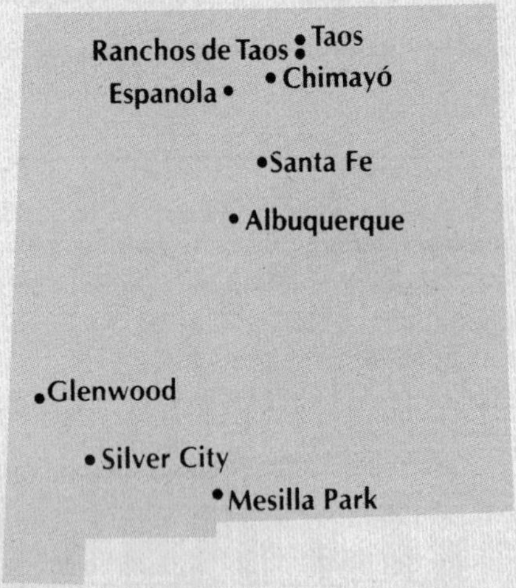

Bed & Breakfast Rocky Mountains—New Mexico ✪

P.O. BOX 804, COLORADO SPRINGS, COLORADO 80901

Tel: **(303) 630-3433**
Best Time to Call: **May 15–Sept. 15, 9 AM–5 PM; 1–5 PM, other times**
Coordinator: **Kate Peterson Winters**
States/Regions Covered: **Albuquerque, Santa Fe, Taos**

Rates (Single/Double):

Modest:	**$35**	**$45**
Average:	**$60**	**$65**
Luxury:	**$60**	**$98**

Credit Cards: **MC, VISA**

The Southwest is a "Land of Enchantment," where folks are able to maintain their bond with a slower, more relaxed pace. Experience Southwestern art galleries, sculptures, ethnic foods, and Indian pueblos. Visit the hot-air balloon festival and the Taos Art Festival; go to the Santa Fe opera; ski in winter. B&Bs are in old thick-walled adobes, lovely suites, modest homes, or unhosted apartments. There is a $3 charge for Kate's directory.

The Corner House

9121 JAMES PLACE NE, ALBUQUERQUE, NEW MEXICO 87111

Tel: **(505) 298-5800**
Host(s): **Jean Thompson**
Location: **8 mi. NE of Albuquerque**
No. of Rooms: **2**
No. of Private Baths: **1**
Max. No. Sharing Bath: **2**
Double/pb: **$40**
Double/sb: **$30**
Open: **All year**
Reduced Rates: **10%, families; seniors**
Breakfast: **Full**
Other Meals: **Available**
Pets: **Sometimes**
Children: **Welcome**
Smoking: **Permitted**
Social Drinking: **Permitted**
Airport/Station Pickup: **Yes**

Jean welcomes you to her handsome Southwestern-style home, decorated in a delightful mix of antiques, handmade collectibles, and family mementos. A complimentary bottle of wine will make you feel right at home. Breakfast specialties include Jean's homemade muffins and Albuquerque's own Monday Goody Company delights. The Corner House is located in a quiet residential neighborhood just minutes from the magnificent Sandia Mountains. It is convenient to Old Town Albuquerque, Santa Fe, and many Indian pueblos.

La Posada de Chimayó ✪

P.O. BOX 463, CHIMAYÓ, NEW MEXICO 87522

Tel: **(505) 351-4605**
Host(s): **Sue Farrington**
Location: **30 mi. N of Santa Fe**
No. of Rooms: **2**
No. of Private Baths: **2**
Double/pb: **$65**
Single/pb: **$55**
Open: **All year**
Reduced Rates: **Weekly, in winter**
Breakfast: **Full**
Credit Cards: **MC, VISA (for deposits)**
Pets: **Sometimes**
Children: **Welcome**
Smoking: **Permitted**
Social Drinking: **Permitted**
Foreign Languages: **Spanish**

Chimayó is known for its historic old church, and its tradition of fine Spanish weaving. This is a typical adobe home with brick floors and *viga* ceilings. The suite is comprised of a small bedroom and sitting room and is made cozy with Mexican rugs, handmade quilts, comfortable furnishings, and traditional corner fireplaces. Sue's breakfasts are not for the fainthearted and often feature stuffed French toast or chilies rellenos. Wine or sun tea are graciously offered after you return from exploring Bandelier National Monument Park, the Indian pueblos, and cliff dwellings on the "High Road" to Taos.

La Puebla House ✪

ROUTE 1, BOX 172A, ESPANOLA, NEW MEXICO 87532

Tel: **(505) 753-3981**
Best Time to Call: **After 6 PM**
Host(s): **Elvira Bain**
Location: **25 mi. N of Santa Fe**
No. of Rooms: **4**
Max. No. Sharing Bath: **6**
Double/sb: **$35**
Single/sb: **$20**
Open: **All year**
Reduced Rates: **Off-season; weekly**
Breakfast: **Continental**
Credit Cards: **MC, VISA**
Pets: **Sometimes**
Children: **Welcome**
Smoking: **No**
Social Drinking: **Permitted**

The house is situated between the famous landscapes of Santa Cruz and Chimayó. Elvira will be happy to direct you to the sights of nearby Santa Fe and Taos. Occasionally Elvira, a gourmet cook, will invite you to be seated at her dinner table for a reasonable price. If you prefer to cook and clean up on your own, a small guest house is often available. Snacks are offered to go along with your self-supplied cocktails.

The Elms ✪

1110 CARVER RD, P.O. BOX 1176, MESILLA PARK, NEW MEXICO 88047

Tel: **(505) 524-1513**
Best Time to Call: **After 5 PM**
Host(s): **Margaret B. Dalton**
Location: **2 mi. from I-10, I-25**
No. of Rooms: **4**
No. of Private Baths: **2**
Max. No. Sharing Bath: **4**
Double/pb: **$50–$75**
Double/sb: **$40**
Single/sb: **$30**
Open: **All year**
Reduced Rates: **10% less, after 5 nights**
Breakfast: **Continental**
Pets: **No**
Children: **Welcome**
Smoking: **No**
Social Drinking: **Permitted**

This large redwood-and-stucco house is set on five acres and shaded by 100-year-old elm trees. Guest rooms are furnished with solid oak antiques and Oriental rugs. Your hosts offer homemade breads and preserves for breakfast. They will gladly direct you to historic sights, White Sands National Monument, Juarez, and the Gila Cliff Dwellings National Monument.

Two Pipe Bed & Breakfast ✪

BOX 52, TALPA ROUTE, RANCHOS DE TAOS, NEW MEXICO 87557

Tel: **(505) 758-4770**
Host(s): **Dusty and Babs Davis**
Location: **4 mi. SE of Taos**
No. of Rooms: **2**
No. of Private Baths: **2**
Double/pb: **$50**

Single/pb: **$40**
Open: **All Year**
Reduced Rates: **10%, 2-day stays May–Aug.**
Breakfast: **Full**
Pets: **No**
Children: **Welcome**
Smoking: **Permitted**
Social Drinking: **Permitted**
Airport/Station Pickup: **Yes**

Beautiful gardens and mountain views surround this 275-year-old adobe hacienda home. The house includes many traditional adobe features such as kiva fireplaces along with many antiques and family furnishings. Guests are welcome to relax in the hot tub or curl up in front of a cozy fire. Your hosts offer complimentary snacks, wine, and beverages, and will do all they can to make you feel welcome. Breakfast specialties include homemade biscuits and gravy, and blueberry pancakes. Five ski areas are located less than an hour from here and a special hearty skiers' breakfast is served in season. Art galleries, museums, Indian pueblos, and Rio Grande Gorge, as well as great hunting and fishing, can all be enjoyed nearby.

Bed & Breakfast of Santa Fe ✪

436 SUNSET STREET, SANTA FE, NEW MEXICO 87501

Tel: **(505) 982-3332**
Best Time to Call: **9 AM–5 PM**
Coordinator: **Gloria Bennett**
State/Regions Covered: **Santa Fe**

Rates (Single/Double):

Modest:	**$25**	**$30**
Average:	**$40**	**$45**
Luxury:	**$50**	**$65**

Credit Cards: **No**

Do come and enjoy the Santa Fe Opera in summer, the vibrant colors of the aspens in autumn, or skiing in winter. Don't miss the nearby Indian pueblos and ancient cliff dwellings, the national forest areas, art colonies, museums, and nearby Taos. Santa Fe still retains the traditions of its early Spanish history, and is blessed with an average of 300 days of sunshine a year. Send for Gloria's free descriptive list of accommodations. There is a two-night minimum stay.

Sunset House ✪

436 SUNSET, SANTA FE, NEW MEXICO 87501

Tel: **(505) 983-3523**
Best Time to Call: **9–11 AM; 5–9 PM**
Host(s): **Jack and Gloria Bennett**
No. of Rooms: **2**
Max. No. Sharing Bath: **4**
Double/sb: **$45**
Single/sb: **$35**
Suites: **$85, for 4–6**
Open: **All year**
Breakfast: **Continental**
Credit Cards: **MC, VISA**
Pets: **No**
Children: **Sometimes**
Smoking: **No**
Social Drinking: **Permitted**
Airport/Station Pickup: **Yes**

Jack and Gloria's home is surrounded by pine trees and glorious views of the mountains. Tastefully furnished, the interior is accented with antiques and art. Museums, shops, galleries, and the state capitol are close by. It is a block away from the public sports complex, which contains a lap pool, jogging course, and tennis and racquetball courts.

American Artists Gallery-House ✪

FRONTIER ROAD, P.O. BOX 584, TAOS, NEW MEXICO 87571

Tel: **(505) 758-4446**
Best Time to Call: **Mornings; evenings**
Host(s): **Benjamin and Myra Carp**
Location: **1/4 mi. from Rt. 68**
No. of Rooms: **3**
No. of Private Baths: **1**
Max. No. Sharing Bath: **4**
Double/pb: **$70**
Single/pb: **$65**
Double/sb: **$60**
Single/sb: **$55**
Separate Guest Cottage: **$40–$45**
Open: **All year**
Breakfast: **Full**
Pets: **No**
Children: **Welcome (crib)**
Smoking: **No**
Social Drinking: **Permitted**
Airport/Station Pickup: **Yes**

This charming adobe-style home is filled with artwork by American artists. A large, comfortable bedroom with a splendid view of Taos Mountain awaits you. Your hosts, gallery owners, will gladly advise on local craft shops and boutiques. Their home is close to Rio Grande Gorge State Park, 900-year-old Taos Pueblo, and places to go fishing and rafting. Complimentary refreshments are served in the evening. Fireplaces, the outdoor hot tub, gardens, and a sculpture courtyard will delight you.

Mountain Light Bed & Breakfast ✪

P.O. BOX 241, TAOS, NEW MEXICO 87571

Tel: **(505) 776-8474**
Best Time to Call: **Early AM or evenings**
Host(s): **Gail Russell**
Location: **12 mi. N of Taos**
No. of Rooms: **3**
No. of Private Baths: **1**
Max. No. Sharing Bath: **4**
Double/pb: **$42**
Single/pb: **$25**
Double/sb: **$37**
Single/sb: **$20**
Open: **All year**
Reduced Rates: **$3 less, 2nd night**
Breakfast: **Continental**
Pets: **Sometimes**
Children: **Welcome**
Smoking: **Permitted**
Social Drinking: **Permitted**
Airport/Station Pickup: **Yes**

This large traditional adobe home is perched on the edge of a mesa and commands a spectacular view. Gail is a professional photographer and the house is her home, studio, and gallery. Her photographs have appeared in many national magazines. There are cozy fireplaces and a wood-burning stove. It is close to the D. H. Lawrence Ranch, the Millicent Rogers Museum, Ski Valley, and the Rio Grande. This is "where the buffalo roam," and good trout fishing is nearby. The coffeepot is always on. Winter rates are slightly higher.

Mountain Vista ✪

P.O. BOX 1303, TAOS, NEW MEXICO 87571

Tel: **(505) 758-4708**
Host(s): **Kathy Kadlec**
Location: **4 mi. N of Taos**
No. of Rooms: **2**
No. of Private Baths: **2**
Double/pb: **$55–$70**
Open: **All year**
Breakfast: **Continental**
Pets: **No**
Children: **Welcome**
Smoking: **No**
Social Drinking: **Permitted**

Mountain Vista is a cream-colored adobe with wonderful views of the magnificent countryside. The house has brick and tile floors and a number of cozy fireplaces. The guest room is furnished with old family pieces and an antique brass bed. Kathy's breakfast specialties include homemade breads and jams. She will gladly direct you to the Rio Grande River and Gorge, Taos Pueblo, Kit Carson Park, and much more. But return in time for the sunset, an unforgettable sight from Mountain Vista, especially when accompanied by a complimentary glass of wine.

NEW YORK

CATSKILLS

Maplewood ✪

PARK ROAD, P.O. BOX 40, CHICHESTER, N.Y. 12416

Tel: **(914) 688-5433**
Best Time to Call: **After 7 PM**
Host(s): **Nancy and Albert Parsons**
Location: **25 mi. NW of Kingston, N.Y.**
No. of Rooms: **4**
Max. No. Sharing Bath: **4**
Double/sb: **$50**
Single/sb: **$40**
Open: **All year**
Reduced Rates: **5%, seniors**
Breakfast: **Full**
Pets: **Sometimes**
Children: **Welcome**
Smoking: **Permitted**
Social Drinking: **Permitted**
Airport/Station Pickup: **Yes**

A Colonial manor on a quiet country lane nestled among stately maples is the site of this charming B&B; each spacious bedroom has a view of the Catskills. In summer, you can swim in the in-ground pool, or play badminton, croquet, or horseshoes. In winter, ski Belleayre, Hunter, and Cortina, all only 12 miles away. In any season, enjoy the art galleries, boutiques, great restaurants, and theater at Woodstock, 20 minutes away. After a great day outdoors, come home to a glass of wine and good conversation. After a good night's sleep, you'll enjoy freshly squeezed orange juice, homemade breads and pastries, and freshly ground coffee.

Scudder Hill House

SCUDDER HILL ROAD, ROXBURY, NEW YORK 12474

Tel: **(607) 326-4215 or 4364**
Host(s): **Carol and Phil O'Beirne**
Location: **50 mi. W of Kingston, N.Y.**
No. of Rooms: **5**
Max. No. Sharing Bath: **5**
Double/sb: **$55–$60**
Single/sb: **$40**
Open: **All year**
Reduced Rates: **Midweek; after 5 days**
Breakfast: **Full**
Credit Cards: **MC, VISA**
Pets: **No**
Children: **Welcome**
Smoking: **Permitted**
Social Drinking: **Permitted**

Within minutes of five major Catskill ski centers, hiking trails, golf courses, and antiques shops, Roxbury is home base for music, art, and country fairs. This 130-year-old Federal-style farmhouse is attractively furnished for comfort, quiet, and relaxation. Carol and Phil enjoy music, books, farming, and cooking. Breakfast breads are homemade; ham, bacon, and eggs are homegrown. You're apt to be spoiled with sherry whenever you wish, and with snacks if you look hungry.

The Lanigan Farmhouse ✪

BOX 399, RD1, STAMFORD, NEW YORK 12167

Tel: **(607) 652-7455**
Host(s): **June and Richard Lanigan**
Location: **23 mi. E of Oneonta**
No. of Rooms: **3**
Max. No. Sharing Bath: **4**
Double/sb: **$50**
Single/sb: **$40**
Open: **All year**
Breakfast: **Continental**
Pets: **Welcome**
Children: **Welcome (crib)**
Smoking: **Permitted**
Social Drinking: **Permitted**

The Lanigan Farmhouse offers the charm of rural life, and is convenient to cultural activities. Guests are welcome to wine and cheese, and are served a breakfast of homemade breads and jams, ham, and omelets. The well-stocked library is a good place for relaxing. Deer Run ski area, golf courses, hiking, tennis, swimming, and antique shops are all nearby.

The Eggery Inn ✪

COUNTY ROAD 16, TANNERSVILLE, NEW YORK 12485

Tel: **(518) 589-5363**
Best Time to Call: **10 AM–8 PM**
Host(s): **Julie and Abe Abramczyk**
Location: **125 mi. N of NYC**
No. of Rooms: **13**
No. of Private Baths: **11**
Max. No. Sharing Bath: **4**
Double/pb: **$65–$70**
Single/pb: **$55**
Double/sb: **$60–$65**
Single/sb: **$50**
Open: **May 16–Sept. 7; Sept. 15–Apr. 1**
Reduced Rates: **Families**
Breakfast: **Full**
Credit Cards: **AMEX, MC, VISA**
Other Meals: **Available**
Pets: **No**
Children: **Welcome**
Smoking: **Permitted**
Social Drinking: **Permitted**

The inn, with its wraparound porch, is nestled amid the majestic ridges of the Catskills at an elevation of 2,200 feet. The sitting room is enhanced by a beautiful oak balustrade leading to cozy guest rooms furnished with antiques, rockers, and warm comforters. The player piano, Mission Oak furnishings, and abundance of plants lend a homey atmosphere. It is in the Catskill Game Preserve, and convenient to Hunter, Cortina, and Windham mountains for skiing, hiking, and seasonal recreational activities. On weekends and holiday periods the above rates change, since dinner is included. There's a two-night minimum on weekends; three nights on holiday weekends.

Sunrise Inn ✪

RD 1, BOX 232B, WALTON, NEW YORK 13856

Tel: **(607) 865-7254**
Best Time to Call: **9 AM–11 PM**
Host(s): **James and Adele Toth**
Location: **135 mi. NW of NYC; 3 mi. from Rte. 17**
No. of Rooms: **2**
Max. No. Sharing Bath: **4**
Double/sb: **$30**
Single/sb: **$27**
Open: **All year**
Reduced Rates: **10%, seniors**
Breakfast: **Continental**
Pets: **No**
Children: **Welcome**
Smoking: **No**
Social Drinking: **Permitted**

Relax and enjoy the sound of the bubbling brook that borders the landscape of this 19th-century farmhouse. You'll awaken to the aroma of Irish sodabread and other homemade goodies, which you are invited to enjoy in the dining area or, weather permitting, on the wraparound porch. Afterward, browse through the antiques shop adjoining the inn. Area activities include fishing, canoeing, golfing, skiing, country fairs, and fine dining. End the day in quiet and homey comfort around the parlor woodstove.

CENTRAL NEW YORK/LEATHERSTOCKING AREA

Bed & Breakfast—Leatherstocking ✪

389 BROCKWAY ROAD, FRANKFORT, NEW YORK 13340

Tel: **(315) 733-0040**
Best Time to Call: **7 AM–10 PM**
Coordinator: **Floranne McCraith**
States/Regions Covered: **Central NY—Booneville, Clinton, Cooperstown, Fort Plain, Hamilton, Oneida, Rome, Utica**

Rates (Single/Double):

	Single	Double
Modest:	**$20**	**$35**
Average:	**$30**	**$45**
Luxury:	**$45**	**$55**

Credit Cards: **MC, VISA**

Leatherstocking Country is an 11-county region of New York that extends from the Catskills across the Mohawk Valley to the Central Adirondacks. It's a region to be visited in all seasons for all reasons, and its residents warmly welcome visitors. Recreational sports and activities, outlet shopping, antiques, fairs, and fine dining are waiting for you, and your B&B host will tell you where to find the best of everything. Send $2 for her descriptive directory.

Bed & Breakfast of the Greater Syracuse Area

143 DIDAMA STREET, SYRACUSE, NEW YORK 13224

Tel: **(315) 446-4199**
Best Time to Call: **10 AM–9 PM**
Coordinator: **Elaine Samuels**
State/Regions Covered: **Auburn, Camillus, Dewitt, Fayetteville, Jamesville, Manilus, Skaneateles, Syracuse, Thousand Islands**

Rates (Single/Double):

	Single	Double
Modest:	**$32**	**$42**
Average:	**$37**	**$47**
Luxury:	**$50**	**$65**

Credit Cards: **No**

Elaine has many host homes in the vicinity of Syracuse University, theaters, ski areas, the Finger Lakes, lovely old villages, excellent discount shopping centers, and exclusive boutiques. This is her hometown and if you tell her your interests, she is certain to find you the perfect home-away-from-home. There's a $6 surcharge for one-night stays on busy university weekends.

Jericho Farm Inn ✪

155 EAST MAIN STREET, AFTON, NEW YORK 13730

Tel: **(607) 639-1842**
Best Time to Call: **8 AM–5 PM**
Host(s): **Patricia and Donald Fabricius**
Location: **25 mi. E of Binghamton**

No. of Rooms: **5**
Max. No. Sharing Bath: **4**
Double/sb: **$40–$45**
Single/sb: **$35**

Suites: **$55**
Open: **All year**
Breakfast: **Full**
Pets: **Sometimes**
Children: **Welcome (crib, stroller)**
Smoking: **Permitted**
Social Drinking: **Permitted**
Airport/Station Pickup: **Yes**

Right out of a Norman Rockwell painting is the way you might describe this 200-year-old Colonial mansion, situated on the Susquehanna River. Step through an entrance graced by four massive pillars and you'll find elegant, comfortable rooms and plenty of hospitality. Breakfast is served in the common room on individual maple tables overlooking the river; a fire is always burning in the winter months. When the sun is shining, take your coffee outside to the courtyard, which has an impressive outdoor fireplace. The six-acre property is great for lawn games, picnicking, and sunning, and offers easy access to water sports on the river.

B&B Adagio ✪

4 CIRCLE DRIVE, BINGHAMTON, NEW YORK 13905

Tel: **(607) 724-5803**
Host(s): **Jean Adagio**
No. of Rooms: **3**
Max. No. Sharing Bath: **4**
Double/sb: **$35**
Single/sb: **$25**
Open: **All year**
Breakfast: **Continental**
Pets: **No**
Children: **Welcome**
Smoking: **No**
Social Drinking: **Permitted**

Located in a quiet residential area, Jean's home has a lovely screened porch for restful relaxation. It's only minutes to the tennis courts at Broome Community College, and SUNY-Binghamton is nearby. Jean loves to quilt, and her bedrooms show samples of her fine handiwork. The bedrooms are air-conditioned for your summer comfort.

Ängelholm ✪

14 ELM STREET, BOX 705, COOPERSTOWN, NEW YORK 13326

Tel: **(607) 547-2483**
Best Time to Call: **4:30 PM–8 PM**
Host(s): **George and Carolin Dempsey**
Location: **65 mi. W of Albany**
No. of Rooms: **4**
Max. No. Sharing Bath: **4**
Double/sb: **$50–$60**
Single/sb: **$30**
Open: **All year**
Breakfast: **Full**
Pets: **No**
Children: **Welcome**
Smoking: **Permitted**
Social Drinking: **Permitted**
Airport/Station Pickup: **Yes**

Ängelholm is one of Cooperstown's historic homes. This 1815 Colonial offers charming rooms furnished with antiques. In the morning, a hearty array of breads, muffins, fresh country eggs, and bacon or sausage is served in the bright formal dining room. You can burn off those calories with a short walk to Main Street and the Baseball Hall of Fame. Your hosts will gladly share with you the delights of Leatherstocking Country, which is rich in history, scenery, recreation, and antique shops.

Creekside Bed & Breakfast

RD 1, BOX 206, COOPERSTOWN, NEW YORK 13326

Tel: **(607) 547-8203**
Host(s): **Fred and Gwen Ermlich**
No. of Rooms: **4**
No. of Private Baths: **4**
Double/pb: **$50–$60**
Suites: **$60**
Guest Cottage: **$80; sleeps 2**
Open: **All year**
Breakfast: **Full**
Pets: **No**
Children: **Welcome**
Smoking: **No**
Social Drinking: **Permitted**
Foreign Languages: **French, German**

This 200-year-old Colonial is perfect for anyone who likes swimming and fishing. Just walk out to the dock for instant pleasure. On nice days, guests can enjoy a full breakfast on the wraparound deck and admire the acres of lawn. At other times of the day, guests are welcome to help themselves to wine, cheese, crackers, coffee, or tea. Just recently the Ermlichs have added a cottage for two to their B&B offering.

The Inn at Brook Willow Farm ✪

R.D. 2, BOX 514, MIDDLEFIELD CENTER ROAD, COOPERSTOWN, NEW YORK 13326

Tel: **(607) 547-9700**
Best Time to Call: **After 6 PM**
Host(s): **Joan and Jack Grimes**
Location: **28 mi. N of Oneonta**
No. of Rooms: **4**
No. of Private Baths: **4**
Double/pb: **$50**
Open: **All year**
Breakfast: **Full**
Pets: **No**
Children: **Welcome (crib)**
Smoking: **Permitted**
Social Drinking: **Permitted**

Located on 14 acres of meadow and woods, nestled among the pines and willows, this charming Victorian cottage with its restored barn is furnished with lovely antiques, wicker, and plants. Enjoy homemade blueberry muffins at breakfast, and wine, fresh fruit, and fresh flowers in your room. The world-famous Baseball Hall of Fame is here, as well as countless historic and cultural sites to visit. Recreational activities abound on unspoiled Lake Otsego.

The Inn at Mill Pond ✪

P.O. BOX 167, COOPERSTOWN, NEW YORK 13326

Tel: **(315) 858-1654 (Nov.–Apr.), or (607) 293-7980**
Best Time to Call: **After 5 PM**
Host(s): **Gail and Ed Newton-Condon**
Location: **½ mi. from Rte. 80**
No. of Rooms: **3**
No. of Private Baths: **1**
Max. No. Sharing Bath: **4**
Double/pb: **$55**
Single/pb: **$50**
Double/sb: **$45**
Single/sb: **$40**
Open: **May 1–Oct. 31**
Breakfast: **Full**
Pets: **No**
Children: **No**
Smoking: **No**
Social Drinking: **Permitted**
Airport/Station Pickup: **Yes**

This inn is perfectly situated for anyone planning their vacation around Cooperstown's many attractions: the Glimmerglass Opera, Cooperstown Theater Festival, the Baseball Hall of Fame, nearby golf courses, museums, and picturesque Otsego Lake. Furnished with local antiques and folk art, the inn reflects Gail and Ed's interests in woodworking, gardening, antiques, herbs, and painting. A nice feature is the late-afternoon tea—just right after a day of sightseeing in the surrounding hills of Central New York State.

Litco Farms Bed and Breakfast ✪

P.O. BOX 148, FLY CREEK, NEW YORK 13337

Tel: **(607) 547-2501**
Host(s): **Margaret and Jim Wolff**
Location: **2 mi. NW of Cooperstown**
No. of Rooms: **2**
Max. No. Sharing Bath: **4**
Double/sb: **$45**
Suites: **$85**
Open: **All year**
Reduced Rates: **Families; off-season**
Breakfast: **Full**
Pets: **No**
Children: **Welcome**
Smoking: **Permitted**
Social Drinking: **Permitted**
Airport/Station Pickup: **Yes**

Seventy acres of unspoiled meadows and woodlands are yours to explore at Litco Farms. The day begins with fresh-baked breads, fresh eggs, milk, and local bacon, served in the dining room-library. Borrow a canoe to fish on Canadarago Lake, which is stocked with freshwater salmon. There are other places to paddle, including Glimmerglass, the lake made famous by James Fenimore Cooper. After spending a day at the Baseball Hall of Fame, guests may relax and unwind around the large in-ground pool. Your hosts recommend a visit to the Cider Mill and the quaint craft and antique shops.

Jonathan House ✪

39 EAST MAIN STREET, P.O. BOX 9, RICHFIELD SPRINGS, NEW YORK 13439

Tel: **(315) 858-2870**
Host(s): **Jonathan and Peter Parker**
Location: **30 mi. S of Utica**
No. of Rooms: **3**
No. of Private Baths: **2**
Max. No. Sharing Bath: **4**
Double/pb: **$55**
Single/pb: **$50**
Double/sb: **$45**
Single/sb: **$40**
Suites: **$65**
Open: **All year**
Reduced Rates: **$10 less, Oct. 20–May 20**
Breakfast: **Full**
Other Meals: **Available**
Credit Cards: **MC, VISA**
Pets: **Sometimes**
Children: **Welcome**
Smoking: **Permitted**
Social Drinking: **Permitted**
Airport/Station Pickup: **Yes**

The Parker brothers enjoy cooking and entertaining, so, when they were both widowed, their friends suggested that they open a B&B in the house they share with their mother. The 1883 house, a hybrid of the Eastlake and Stick styles, has three full floors plus a tower room on a fourth level—a total of 17 rooms in all. The house is elegantly decorated with antiques (some that belonged to the brothers' great-grandparents and grandparents), fine paintings, and Oriental rugs. Breakfast is served in the dining room—with bone china, damask linen, and English silver. The Parkers also serve candlelight dinners, presented just as regally.

Dorchester Farm ✪

P.O. BOX 854, WHITNEY POINT, NEW YORK 13862

Tel: **(607) 692-4511**
Best Time to Call: **8 AM–6 PM**
Host(s): **Katie Brennan and Ted Baer**
Location: **1½ mi. from I-81, Exit 8**
No. of Rooms: **2**
No. of Private Baths: **1**
Max. No. Sharing Bath: **4**
Double/sb: **$45**
Single/sb: **$38**
Suites: **$50**
Open: **All year**
Breakfast: **Full**
Pets: **Sometimes**
Children: **Welcome, over 10**
Smoking: **Permitted**
Social Drinking: **Permitted**
Airport/Station Pickup: **Yes**

Your name will follow President Franklin D. Roosevelt's on the guest list at this 18th-century farmhouse. From the two porches, you can gaze at the adjoining 10,000 acres of woods and a six-mile-long lake with facilities for sailing, canoeing, or windsurfing. Greek Peak Ski Area is 20 minutes away for winter skiing, and the Binghamton campus of SUNY is nearby. Katie is a retired flight attendant; Ted is a radio personality who often entertains in the evening, playing jazz piano, guitar, and singing. They have a beautiful antique clock collection.

CHAUTAUQUA/ALLEGHENY AREA

Rainbow Hospitality—Chautauqua ✪

1149 OVERLOOK TERRACE, BEMUS POINT, NEW YORK 14712

Tel: **(716) 386-3066 or 7361**
Coordinator: **Shirley Ingraham**
States/Regions Covered: **Bemus Point, Chautauqua, Mayville, Westfield**

Rates: (Single/Double):

	Single	Double
Modest:	**$25**	**$35**
Average:	**$30**	**$45**
Luxury:	**$35**	**$50–$65**

Credit Cards: **No**

This area boasts an infinite variety of cities and farm towns, of colleges and commerce, of skiing and sailing, of attractions both natural and man-made. Chautauqua is famous for the cultural, educational, and religious activities of the summer colony on the lake, as well as for its topnotch recreational diversions. Send $1 for Shirley's descriptive directory of accommodations.

Hitchcock House ✪

15 SOUTH MAIN STREET, ALFRED, NEW YORK 14802

Tel: **(607) 587-9102**
Best Time to Call: **8 AM–11 PM**
Host(s): **June and Bob Hitchcock**
Location: **75 mi. S of Rochester**
No. of Rooms: **3**
No. of Private Baths: **1**
Max. No. Sharing Bath: **4**
Double/pb: **$48**
Double/sb: **$35**
Open: **All year**
Reduced Rates: **15%, weekly**
Breakfast: **Full**
Pets: **No**
Children: **Welcome**
Smoking: **Permitted**
Social Drinking: **Permitted**

Bob and June Hitchcock welcome you to the heart of Alfred's Village Historic District. Their house was built in 1932 in the Colonial Revival style by a hometown physician; the small wing of the house that once was the doctor's office has been remodeled for guests. Guest quarters feature a private entrance and bath, queen-size bed, and lace curtains. The kitchen is stocked with eggs, juice, coffee, toast, and muffins for a make-it-yourself breakfast. A large backyard with lounge chairs and a picnic table is available for relaxing. Hitchcock House is located on a quiet, tree-lined street, just a short walk from activities at Alfred University and the state college.

Green Acres ✪

ROUTE 474, ASHVILLE, NEW YORK 14710

Tel: **(716) 782-4254**
Best Time to Call: **Mornings**
Host(s): **Lowell and Mary Ann Green**
Location: **8 mi. W of Jamestown**
No. of Rooms: **2**
Max. No. Sharing Bath: **4**
Double/sb: **$50**
Single/sb: **$30**
Open: **All year**
Breakfast: **Full**
Pets: **No**
Children: **Welcome, over 12**
Smoking: **No**
Social Drinking: **No**

Lowell and Mary Ann once owned an antiques store, and their country Colonial is the perfect setting for their old treasures. The rooms feature hand-hewn beams, paneled walls, and stone fireplaces. Guests are welcome to relax in the comfortable living room or curl up on an old porch rocker. A heated pool is located on the three-acre property, and it is in use from June through September. Just beyond the pool lie the woods, where you can hike, fish in a large stocked pond, and cross-country ski. The breakfast specialty of the house is blueberry pancakes and sausages; the berries are as fresh as you can get, because they grow right out back. Your hosts will gladly direct you to local attractions including skiing, Panama Rocks, and the Chautauqua Institution.

Mansard Inn ✪

RD 1, BOX 633, GERRY LEVANT ROAD, FALCONER, NEW YORK 14733

Tel: **(716) 665-2352 or 4558**
Host(s): **Frank and Debra Viramontes**
Location: **1 mi. from Rte. 17, Exit 13—Falconer**
No. of Rooms: **4**
No. of Private Baths: **2**
Max. No. Sharing Bath: **4**
Double/pb: **$55**
Single/pb: **$50**
Double/sb: $40
Single/sb: **$35**
Suites: **$50**
Open: **All year**
Reduced Rates: **10%, seniors**
Breakfast: **Continental**
Pets: **No**
Children: **Welcome**
Smoking: **Permitted**
Social Drinking: **Permitted**
Airport/Station Pickup: **Yes**

To keep the workers of his brickyard busy during a mid-1800s economic slump, Reuben Neate, an early settler of the area, had them build this villa for his family. The house is surrounded by open pastures, woods, and large flower gardens. The interior of the house re-creates the feel of the Victorian era. Debra loves flowers and, if the season is right, you're bound to find flowers in your room; Frank is an "outdoors type"—just ask him about fishing in the area. Nearby, guests will find horseback riding, hiking, the Chautauqua Institute, and lots of antiques shops.

1870 House ✪

20 CHESTNUT STREET, FRANKLINVILLE, NEW YORK 14737

Tel: **(716) 676-3571**
Best Time to Call: **Before 9 AM; after 6 PM**
Host(s): **Bob and Nancy Kelsey**
Location: **50 mi. S of Buffalo**
No. of Rooms: **3**
Max. No. Sharing Bath: **4**
Double/sb: **$40**
Single/sb: **$35**
Open: **All year**
Breakfast: **Full**
Other Meals: **Available**
Pets: **Sometimes**
Children: **Welcome, over 5**
Smoking: **No**
Social Drinking: **Permitted**

William Ely had this gracious Victorian built circa 1870 on one of Franklinville's original streets. The rooms are decorated in family and period antiques to complement the native cherry wood parquet floors and old-fashioned parlor. Breakfast is served in the dining room or by the family room fireplace and may include freshly ground coffee, homemade breads, local cheeses, seasonal fruits, and specialty egg dishes. The house is in the foothills of the Allegany Mountains in a national historic area, and is near to skiing, state parks, and excellent hunting and fishing. Your hosts offer tours of the local sights, including a cheese factory and antique shops.

The Teepee ✪

RD #1, BOX 543, ROUTE 438, GOWANDA, NEW YORK 14070

Tel: **(716) 532-2168**
Host(s): **Max and Phyllis Lay**
Location: **30 mi. S of Buffalo**
No. of Rooms: **3**
Max. No. Sharing Bath: **3**
Double/sb: **$35**
Single/sb: **$30**
Open: **All year**
Breakfast: **Full**
Pets: **Sometimes**
Children: **Welcome (crib)**
Smoking: **Permitted**
Social Drinking: **Permitted**
Airport/Station Pickup: **Yes**

Max and Phyllis Lay are Seneca Indians living on the Cattaraugus Indian Reservation. Their airy four-bedroom home is clean, modern, and decorated with family Indian articles, many of them crafted by hand. The reservation offers country living and the opportunity of seeing firsthand the customs of a Native American community. A fall festival with arts, crafts, and exhibition dancing is held in September. Canoeing, fishing, rafting, cross-country and downhill skiing, and a javelin sport called snowsnake are among the local activities. Your hosts will gladly arrange tours of the Amish community and hot-air balloon rides over the beautiful rolling hills.

Napoli Stagecoach Inn ✪

NAPOLI CORNERS, LITTLE VALLEY, NEW YORK 14755

Tel: **(716) 938-6735, 358-3928**
Host(s): **Emmett and Marion Waite**
Location: **60 mi. S of Buffalo**
No. of Rooms: **3**
Max. No. Sharing Bath: **4**
Double/sb: **$35**
Single/sb: **$25**
Open: **All year**
Reduced Rates: **Weekly**
Breakfast: **Full**
Credit Cards: **No**
Pets: **No**
Children: **Welcome, over 10**
Smoking: **No**
Social Drinking: **No**
Airport/Station Pickup: **Yes**
Foreign Languages: **Spanish**

Located in the foothills of the Allegany Mountains, this residence was originally built as a stagecoach inn in 1830. It is now part of a seven-acre fruit and vegetable farm where you can enjoy uncrowded comfort and warm hospitality. Emmett and Marion have many hobbies such as antique collecting, building grandfather clocks, china painting, doll making, and quilting. The inn is close to Holiday Valley Ski Area, Kinzua Dam and Reservoir, Chautauqua Institution, and the Seneca-Iroquois National Museum. Their 4,000-volume library is a fine place to browse.

Klartag Farms

P.O. BOX 98, WEST BRANCH ROAD, RUSHFORD, NEW YORK 14777

Tel: **(716) 437-2946**
Host(s): **Jerry and Shirley Thorington**
Location: **50 mi. SE of Buffalo**
No. of Rooms: **2**
Max. No. Sharing Bath: **4**
Double/sb: **$38**
Single/sb: **$30**
Open: **All year**
Reduced Rates: **15%, weekly**
Breakfast: **Full**
Other Meals: **Available**
Pets: **No**
Children: **Welcome (crib)**
Smoking: **No**
Social Drinking: **Permitted**
Airport/Station Pickup: **Yes**

Jerry and Shirley welcome you to their 600-acre working dairy farm in the countryside. Their spacious red farmhouse is trimmed with black shutters and set on a beautifully manicured lawn. Inside, you'll find comfortable rooms with some special antiques such as an old player piano. Your hosts serve a farm-style breakfast including home-cured bacon and sausage, homemade jams, and breads. They invite you for complimentary coffee, tea, or wine in the afternoon. The farm is within 30 minutes of several ski areas and a state park. Farm tours are gladly given, and fishing and hunting can be enjoyed on the premises.

European Yankee ✪

P.O. BOX 1059, 23 JAMESTOWN ROAD, SINCLAIRVILLE, NEW YORK 14782

Tel: **(716) 962-8515**
Best Time to Call: **Evening**
Host(s): **Gerald Nagle**
Location: **12 mi. N of Jamestown**
No. of Rooms: **3**
No. of Private Baths: **1**
Max. No. Sharing Bath: **4**
Double/pb: **$50**
Single/pb: **$35**
Double/sb: **$50**
Single/sb: **$35**
Open: **All year**
Breakfast: **Continental**
Pets: **Sometimes**
Children: **Welcome**
Smoking: **Permitted**
Social Drinking: **Permitted**
Foreign Languages: **German**

European Yankee is a multilevel cottage in the heart of Chautauqua country. The house is decorated "country style" with antiques, artwork, French windows, and wood motifs. Your host stays at bed and breakfasts in Europe, and enjoys serving a large Continental breakfast with fresh-baked goods, fruits, and cheeses. This area of western New York gets an average of 200 inches of snow each season. Cross-country trails are everywhere and the slopes of Cockaigne are six miles away. In the warmer weather enjoy boating at a nearby 21-mile lake. An Amish community, antiques shops, wineries, and Chautauqua Institution are a short drive from the house.

Town & Country Bed & Breakfast ✪

P.O. BOX 208, PINE STREET, SOUTH DAYTON, NEW YORK 14138

Tel: **(716) 988-3340**
Best Time to Call: **After 5 PM**
Host(s): **Rick and Jeanne Easterly**
Location: **12 mi. from NYS Thruway, Exit 58**
No. of Rooms: **2**
Max. No. Sharing Bath: **4**
Double/sb: **$35**
Single/sb: **$25**
Open: **All year**
Breakfast: **Continental**
Pets: **No**
Children: **Welcome**
Smoking: **No**
Social Drinking: **Permitted**

Aptly named because of its location in a small rural village, this restored Victorian is decorated with family treasures and special "finds" that were refinished by Rick and Jeanne. He's a computer engineer; she's a secretary. They offer a simple breakfast weekdays and a full feast on weekends. It is close to the Amish community, 12 miles to Cockaigne Ski Area, 10 miles to local wineries, and 50 miles to Niagara Falls. In fruit-picking season, bring your own baskets and literally go home with the fruits of your labor.

Simpsons ✪

16 BIRD STREET, WESTFIELD, NEW YORK 14787

Tel: **(716) 326-2523**
Best Time to Call: **After 4 PM**
Host(s): **Mildred and James Simpson**
Location: **1 mi. from I-90**
No. of Rooms: **2**
Max. No. Sharing Bath: **4**
Double/sb: **$20**
Open: **All year**
Reduced Rates: **15%, after 5 nights; 20%, families**
Breakfast: **Full**
Other Meals: **Available**
Pets: **Sometimes**
Children: **Welcome (crib)**
Smoking: **Permitted**
Social Drinking: **Permitted**

Westfield is a small rural village located at the hub of I-90 and routes 394, 20, and 5. Primarily an agricultural community specializing in Concord grapes, there are six wineries nearby that you may tour. The famous Chautauqua Institution is 10 miles away, and Westfield is a mecca for collectors of antiques. There are 14 antiques shops right in town. Mrs. Simpson is most cordial and will allow you to use her kitchen for light snacks.

FINGER LAKES/ROCHESTER AREA

Bed & Breakfast—Rochester ✪

P.O. BOX 444, FAIRPORT, N.Y. 14450

Tel: **(716) 223-8510**
Coordinator: **Beth Kinsman**
States/Regions Covered: **Rochester Area**

Rates (Single/Double):

	Single	Double
Modest:	**$30–$35**	**$35–$40**
Average:	**$35–$40**	**$45–$50**
Luxury:	**$55–$65**	**$65**

Credit Cards: **No**

Friendly hosts offer a variety of accommodations ranging from a contemporary on Lake Ontario to a traditional suburban home. All will be happy to advise you on the sights and "doings" in their areas. Don't miss the International Museum of Photography at George

Eastman House, or the Museum of Victorian Memorabilia. The University of Rochester, Colgate, and SUNY-Brockport are three local campuses.

Four Seasons

470 WEST LAKE ROAD, ROUTE 54A, BRANCHPORT, NEW YORK 14418

Tel: **(607) 868-4686; Nov. 2–May 29, (607) 732-5581**
Best Time to Call: **10 AM or 7 PM**
Host(s): **Brent and Martha Olmstead**
Location: **50 mi. SE of Rochester**
No. of Rooms: **4**
No. of Private Baths: **1**
Max. No. Sharing Bath: **6**
Double/pb: **$50**
Single/pb: **$45**
Double/sb: **$45**
Single/sb: **$40**
Open: **June 1–Nov. 1; weekends only Nov. 2–May 29**
Reduced Rates: **No**
Breakfast: **Full**
Pets: **Sometimes**
Children: **Welcome, over 12**
Smoking: **Permitted**
Social Drinking: **Permitted**
Foreign Languages: **Spanish**

This charming white clapboard house with its crisp-looking green shutters and inviting front porch is located on the west side of Keuka Lake, famous for its wineries. The casual country atmosphere is enhanced by chestnut, pine, and oak antiques, handmade quilts, and wicker accents. Breakfast is a feast of apple-puffed-pancakes, eggs Gruyère, or peaches 'n' cream French toast. Brent and Martha's interests are photography, sailing, architectural history, and classical music. There's a two-day minimum stay on holiday weekends.

The Country House ✪

37 MILL STREET, CANASERAGA, NEW YORK 14822

Tel: **(607) 545-6439**
Best Time to Call: **11 AM–1 PM, 5–7 PM**
Host(s): **Robert and Renée Coombs**
Location: **50 mi. S of Rochester**
No. of Rooms: **6**
Max. No. Sharing Bath: **4**
Double/sb: **$35**
Single/sb: **$20**
Open: **All year**
Breakfast: **Full**
Pets: **Welcome**
Children: **Welcome (crib)**
Smoking: **Permitted**
Social Drinking: **Permitted**
Airport/Station Pickup: **Yes**

This 100-year-old Victorian home stands on a quiet street in a charming rural village. Guest rooms are comfortably furnished with antiques and all are for sale. Home-baked pastries and fresh fruit are served each morning in the breakfast room or dining room. Your hosts will happily direct you to the many valleys, forests, and streams nearby for hunting, fishing, hiking, and scenic solitude. Swain Ski Center slopes, Corning Glassworks, and Letchworth State Park are minutes away.

Edge of Thyme ✪

6 MAIN STREET, CANDOR, NEW YORK 13743

Tel: **(607) 659-5155**
Host(s): **Eva Mae and Frank Musgrave**
Location: **29 mi. NW of Binghamton**
No. of Rooms: **6**
No. of Private Baths: **2**
Max. No. Sharing Bath: **5**
Double/pb: **$50**
Single/pb: **$35**
Double/sb: **$45**
Single/sb: **$30**
Suites: **$65**
Open: **All year**
Breakfast: **Full**
Pets: **No**
Children: **Welcome**
Smoking: **No**
Social Drinking: **Permitted**
Airport/Station Pickup: **Yes**

At the turn of the century, Rosa Murphy, John D. Rockefeller's secretary, married Dr. Amos Canfield, and, although they lived in New York City, they decided to spend their summers in Candor. They were determined to do it with style, and built a 22-room Georgian beauty. Now the house belongs to the Musgraves—he's a professor of economics, she's a financial counselor—who offer it to guests visiting this gateway to the Finger Lakes. The Musgraves welcome children—and offer families an entire wing to themselves. Guests "are welcome to anything in the cookie jar or pastry bin." There's a two-night minimum on special Cornell or Ithaca College weekends.

Laurel Hill Bed & Breakfast ✪

2670 POWDERHOUSE ROAD, CORNING, NEW YORK 14830

Tel: **(607) 936-3215**
Host(s): **Dick and Marge Woodbury**
Location: **1.7 mi. from Rte. 17**
No. of Rooms: **2**
Max. No. Sharing Bath: **4**
Double/sb: **$55**
Single/sb: **$45**
Open: **All year**
Breakfast: **Continental**
Pets: **No**
Children: **Welcome**
Smoking: **Permitted**
Social Drinking: **Permitted**
Airport/Station Pickup: **Yes**

This traditional Early American house is nestled on a wooded hillside. The solar greenhouse is perfect for bird watching while breakfasting on homemade muffins, breads, and granola. Spacious guest rooms are furnished with brass beds; both the music room with grand piano, and the breezy screened porch are inviting. Nearby attractions include the Corning Glass Center, Finger Lakes wineries, and Watkins Glen.

Rosewood Inn ✪

134 EAST FIRST STREET, CORNING, NEW YORK 14830

Tel: **(607) 962-3253**
Host(s): **Winnie and Dick Peer**
Location: **1 block off Rte. 17**
No. of Rooms: **6**
No. of Private Baths: **4**
Max. No. Sharing Bath: **4**
Double/pb: **$68**
Single/pb: **$63**
Double/sb: **$58**
Single/sb: **$53**
Suites: **$73**
Open: **All year**
Reduced Rates: **Weekly; families**
Breakfast: **Continental**
Credit Cards: **DC, MC, VISA**
Pets: **Sometimes**
Children: **Welcome (crib)**
Smoking: **Permitted**
Social Drinking: **Permitted**
Airport/Station Pickup: **Yes**

This two-story stucco English Tudor is decorated with both antiques and originality. Each guest room is named for a famous person, and the accessories echo the personality of that individual's era. It's within walking distance of the Corning Glass Museum and the Rockwell-Corning Museum of Western Art. Winnie taught school, and Dick was the editor of the daily newspaper. Retired, they look forward to your arrival and greet you with refreshments.

Victoria House

222 PINE STREET, CORNING, NEW YORK 14830

Tel: **(607) 962-3413**
Best Time to Call: **After 4 PM**
Host(s): **Billie Jean and Ron Housel**
Location: **1/4 mi. S of Rte. 17**
No. of Rooms: **3**
No. of Private Baths: **1**
Max. No. Sharing Bath: **4**
Double/pb: **$55**
Single/pb: **$50**
Double/sb: **$45**
Single/sb: **$40**
Open: **All year**
Reduced Rates: **5%, seniors**
Breakfast: **Continental**
Pets: **No**
Children: **Welcome, over 12**
Smoking: **No**
Social Drinking: **Permitted**

This turn-of-the-century home has been restored to its former charm, and is located in a quiet residential area within walking distance of the Corning Glass Center, Rockwell-Corning Museum, and the unique shops and restaurants of Market Street. The rooms are furnished with antiques. You are invited to relax in the spacious reception rooms and on the portico in summer.

White Birch Bed & Breakfast

69 EAST FIRST STREET, CORNING, NEW YORK 14830

Tel: **(607) 962-6355**
Host(s): **Fran and Lois Gehl**
Location: **Off Rte. 17**
No. of Rooms: **3**
No. of Private Baths: **1**
Max. No. Sharing Bath: **4**
Double/pb: **$50**
Single/pb: **$50**
Double/sb: **$45**
Single/sb: **$40**
Suites: **$55**
Open: **All year**
Breakfast: **Continental**
Credit Cards: **AMEX, MC, VISA**
Pets: **No**
Children: **Welcome**
Smoking: **Downstairs only**
Social Drinking: **Permitted**
Airport/Station Pickup: **Yes**

The red-carpet treatment awaits you at this spacious 1865 Victorian. The house has been restored to show off the beautifully crafted winding staircase and hardwood floors. Guests are welcome to choose a game or enjoy television by the fire in the common room. After a good night's sleep in a comfortable queen-size bed, you'll wake to the smell of homemade breads, muffins, and plenty of hot coffee. The White Birch is located in a residential area just two blocks from restored downtown Corning and near such attractions as the Corning Glass Center, Rockwell Museum, and many fine wineries.

Lakeside Terrace ✪

RD 1, BOX 197, 660 EAST WANETA LAKE ROAD, DUNDEE, NEW YORK 14837

Tel: **(607) 292-6606**
Host(s): **Chris and George Patnoe**
Location: **30 mi. S of Geneva**
No. of Rooms: **2**
Max. No. Sharing Bath: **4**
Double/sb: **$45**
Single/sb: **$32**
Open: **All year**
Breakfast: **Continental**
Credit Cards: **MC, VISA**
Pets: **Sometimes**
Children: **Welcome, over 10**
Smoking: **Permitted**
Social Drinking: **Permitted**

It's only 20 miles to the races at Watkins Glen, 30 miles to the Corning Glass Works, or 10 miles to the Hammondsport wineries, but the comfortable white house is the perfect spot for relaxation. Swim, fish, sunbathe, or just sit by the shore at night and enjoy a fire while the country sounds and silence surround you.

Willow Cove ✪

77 SOUTH GLENORA ROAD, R.D. 1, BOX 87, DUNDEE, NEW YORK 14837

Tel: **(607) 243-8482**
Best Time to Call: **After 4:30 PM**
Host(s): **George and Joan Van Heusen**
Location: **10 mi. N of Watkins Glen**
No. of Rooms: **4**
Max. No. Sharing Bath: **4**
Double/sb: **$35**
Single/sb: **$30**
Guest Cottage: **$200; sleeps 6**
Open: **April–Oct. 31**
Breakfast: **Continental**
Pets: **No**
Children: **Welcome (crib)**
Smoking: **Permitted**
Social Drinking: **Permitted**

Located on the western side of Seneca Lake, this 200-year-old inn is a comfortable home-base for the many activities the area offers. Wineries, auctions, country fairs, antique shops, music festivals, art galleries, and stock-car races are but a few of the diversions. George and Joan offer wine and cheese in the evening as well as the use of their kitchen for light snacks.

American House ✪

39 MAIN STREET, GENESEO, NEW YORK 14454

Tel: **(716) 243-5483**
Host(s): **Harry and Helen Wadsworth**
Location: **30 mi. S of Rochester**
No. of Rooms: **6**
No. of Private Baths: **2**
Max. No. Sharing Bath: **4**
Double/pb: **$55**
Single/pb: **$50**
Double/sb: **$45–$50**
Single/sb: **$40–$45**

Suites: **$60**
Open: **All year**
Reduced Rates: **10%, seniors**
Breakfast: **Continental**
Pets: **No**
Children: **Welcome**
Smoking: **Permitted**
Social Drinking: **Permitted**
Airport/Station Pickup: **Yes**

American House is an 1897 Victorian, painted gray with red trim. It sits on the site of the old American Hotel, known throughout the state for its fine accommodations. The hotel burned down, but Harry and Helen carry on its tradition of warm hospitality. They offer comfortable bedrooms furnished with period pieces. Guests are welcome to relax on the sun porch. Most of the village is listed on the National Register of Historic Places; this B&B is close to a state park and Conesus Lake, and is one block from the State University at Geneseo.

The Cobblestones ✪

1160 ROUTES 5 & 20, GENEVA, NEW YORK 14456

Tel: **(315) 789-1896**
Best Time to Call: **7–9:30 PM**
Host(s): **The Lawrence Graceys**
Location: **3½ mi. W of Geneva on Rts. 5 and 20**
No. of Rooms: **4**
Max. No. Sharing Bath: **6**
Double/sb: **$10 and up**
Single/sb: **$10**
Open: **All year**
Breakfast: **No**
Pets: **Sometimes**
Children: **Welcome (crib)**
Smoking: **Permitted**
Social Drinking: **Permitted**

This inspired example of Greek Revival cobblestone architecture was built in 1848. The four large fluted columns crowned by Ionic capitals at the front entrance add to its beauty. There are precious antiques and Oriental rugs, which reflect the fine taste of your gracious hosts. Located in the heart of the Finger Lakes area, tours are available at nearby wineries. Hobart and William Smith colleges are right in town.

Elmshade Guest House ✪

402 SOUTH ALBANY STREET, ITHACA, NEW YORK 14850

Tel: **(607) 273-1707**
Best Time to Call: **2–3 PM**
Host(s): **Ethel D. Pierce**
Location: **3 blocks from Rte. 13**
No. of Rooms: **9**
Max. No. Sharing Bath: **4**
Double/sb: **$36–$40**
Single/sb: **$18–$20**
Open: **All year**
Breakfast: **No**
Pets: **No**
Children: **Welcome, over 6**
Smoking: **Permitted**
Social Drinking: **Permitted**

Located in a lovely residential area, the house is convenient to shopping and excellent inexpensive restaurants. The guest rooms are large, bright, comfortable, and immaculate. Ethel limits guest occupancy to nine at a time so that she can give personal attention to everyone. Cornell University and Ithaca College are nearby.

Glendale Farm ✪

224 BOSTWICK ROAD, ITHACA, NEW YORK 14850

Tel: **(607) 272-8756**
Best Time to Call: **Evenings**
Host(s): **Jeanne Marie Tomlinson**
Location: **2 mi. S of Ithaca**
No. of Rooms: **6**
No. of Private Baths: **4**
Max. No. Sharing Bath: **4**
Double/pb: **$60**
Single/pb: **$40**
Double/sb: **$50**
Suites: **$100**
Separate Guest Cottage: **$75–$100**
Open: **All year**
Breakfast: **Full**
Credit Cards: **MC, VISA**
Pets: **Sometimes**
Children: **Welcome**
Smoking: **Permitted**
Social Drinking: **Permitted**
Airport/Station Pickup: **Yes**

Glendale Farm is nestled in the heart of the Finger Lakes region on a hundred acres of rolling hills, woods, and meadows. Built in 1865, the house is large and comfortable, filled with antiques and Oriental rugs. In winter, a fire always burns in the wood stove; in warmer weather, the large screened-in porch provides a relaxing spot. Your hosts offer popovers, hot from the oven, croissants, assorted cheeses, and homemade jams in the morning. They will gladly direct you to nearby wineries, ski areas, lakes, and parks.

Peregrine House

140 COLLEGE AVENUE, ITHACA, NEW YORK 14058

Tel: **(607) 277-3862; 272-0919**
Best Time to Call: **Mornings; evenings**
Host(s): **Nancy Falconer**
Location: **1 mi. from Rte. 13**
No. of Rooms: **8**
No. of Private Baths: **9**
Double/pb: **$50–$85**
Open: **All year**
Reduced Rates: **Available**
Breakfast: **Continental**
Credit Cards: **AMEX, MC, VISA**
Pets: **No**
Children: **Welcome, over 12**
Smoking: **Permitted**
Social Drinking: **Permitted**

This three-story home with mansard roof dates back to 1874. Its marble fireplaces and carved-wood ceilings have been beautifully preserved and are accented with Victorian oak furnishings. Pick a good book in the library and relax in a wing chair, or watch some television in your room. At five o'clock your hosts have a sherry hour, and they invite you to plan your evening over a drink. Mexican, Italian, Greek, and Indian food can all be enjoyed with a short walk from here. Peregrine House is two blocks from the Cornell campus and only a few blocks from the Ithaca Commons. Cayuga Lake's wonderful boating and swimming, the wine country, biking, hiking, and cross-country skiing are all close by.

Rose Inn

813 AUBURN ROAD, ROUTE 34, BOX 6576, ITHACA, NEW YORK 14851

Tel: **(607) 533-4202**
Host(s): **Sherry and Charles Rosemann**
Location: **55 mi. SW of Syracuse**
No. of Rooms: **9**
No. of Private Baths: **8**
Max. No. Sharing Bath: **2**
Double/pb: **$65–$85**
Double/sb: **$65–$85**
Guest Cottage: **$160; sleeps 4**
Open: **All year**
Reduced Rates: **$10 less, Dec. 1–Apr. 30**
Breakfast: **Continental**
Other Meals: **Available**
Pets: **No**
Children: **Welcome, over 12**
Smoking: **No**
Social Drinking: **Permitted**
Airport/Station Pickup: **Yes**
Foreign Languages: **German, Spanish**

The showpiece of this 19th-century mansion is a circular staircase of solid Honduras mahogany, stretching three stories to the cupola on the roof. Guest rooms and sitting parlors are furnished in elegant period pieces. Special touches such as fresh apples, local wine, huge bath sheets, soft robes, and baskets filled with toiletries are thoughtfully provided. Fresh croissants and homemade jams are served in the fireplaced country kitchen. On request, a honeymoon breakfast cart can be wheeled into your bedroom. Local attractions of the Finger Lakes region include Watkins Glen, Greek Peak Ski Area, and the wine district.

Merryhart Victorian Inn ✪

12 FRONT STREET, MARATHON, NEW YORK 13803

Tel: **(607) 849-3951**
Host(s): **Lou and Bobbie Sisco**
Location: **30 mi. N of Binghamton**
No. of Rooms: **4**
Max. No. Sharing Bath: **5**
Double/sb: **$30–$37**
Single/sb: **$25–$32**
Open: **All year**
Breakfast: **Full**
Pets: **No**
Children: **Welcome**
Smoking: **No**
Social Drinking: **No**
Airport/Station Pickup: **Yes**

When the Siscos decided it was time to realize their dream, move from a big city, and open a B&B, they chose this Queen Anne Victorian, built in 1895. They took the name of the inn from a quotation from Proverbs: "A merry hart doeth good like medicine." The inn sits right on the banks of the Tioughnioga River, and every room has a river view. Guests may also enjoy the view from the wraparound porch, the second-story porch, or the library loft inside. It's just ten minutes to Greek Peak ski area, and five miles to the Maple Hill Golf Club. Whitney Point Lake is just a 15-minute-ride away for boating and picnicking in summer and ice skating in winter.

The Historic Cook House B&B ✪

167 MAIN STREET, NEWFIELD, NEW YORK 14867

Tel: **(607) 564-9926**
Host(s): **Mildred and Dewitt Zien**
Location: **8 mi. SW of Ithaca**
No. of Rooms: **7**
No. of Private Baths: **4**
Max. No. Sharing Bath: **4**
Double/pb: **$50–$60**
Single/pb: **$50–$60**
Double/sb: **$40–$45**
Single/sb: **$45**
Suites: **$120–$140**
Guest Cottage: **$60–$200; sleeps 2–8**
Open: **All year**
Breakfast: **Full**
Pets: **No**
Children: **Welcome in cottage only**
Smoking: **No**
Social Drinking: **Permitted**

High on a hill above Main Street, overlooking the small village of Newfield, is this brick Victorian built more than 100 years ago. The gracious curved staircase, handsome arched doorways, high ceilings, chestnut cabinetry, and pedestal sinks in all the bedrooms are reminders of its grand past. Although many antiques are used throughout, the atmosphere is friendly and informal. Guests always comment on the marvelous mattresses and bountiful breakfasts. Mildren and Dewitt are retired teachers with interest in flying, cycling, travel, skiing, and reading. A two-night minimum is requested for special college weekends since Cornell University and Ithaca College are close by.

Strawberry Castle Bed & Breakfast ✪

1883 PENFIELD ROAD, PENFIELD, NEW YORK 14526

Tel: **(716) 385-3266**
Best Time to Call: **Evenings**
Host(s): **Charles and Cynthia Whited**
Location: **8 mi. E of Rochester**
No. of Rooms: **3**
Max. No. Sharing Bath: **4**
Double/sb: **$60–$70**
Single/sb: **$50–$60**
Suites: **$70**
Open: **All year**

Reduced Rates: **15%, weekly**
Breakfast: **Continental**
Credit Cards: **AMEX, MC, VISA**
Pets: **No**
Children: **Welcome, over 12**
Smoking: **Permitted**
Social Drinking: **Permitted**
Airport/Station Pickup: **Yes**

An outstanding example of the Italian villa style of architecture, the Whiteds' home (circa 1878) features columned porches, heavy plaster moldings, high sculptured ceilings, and a white marble fireplace, and is appropriately furnished with antiques and brass beds. Wander the lawns and gardens, sun on the patio, or take a dip in the pool. Charles and Cynthia will direct you to fine restaurants, golf courses, and all the nearby Rochester attractions.

The Wagener Estate Bed & Breakfast ✪

351 ELM STREET (ROUTE 54-A), PENN YAN, NEW YORK 14527

Tel: **(315) 536-4591**
Host(s): **Norm and Evie Worth**
Location: **20 mi. from NYS Thruway; Exit 42, Geneva**
No. of Rooms: **5**
No. of Private Baths: **1**
Max. No. Sharing Bath: **4**
Double/pb: **$60**
Single/pb: **$50**
Double/sb: **$45**
Single/sb: **$35**
Open: **All year**
Breakfast: **Full**
Credit Cards: **MC, VISA**
Pets: **No**
Children: **Welcome, over 5**
Smoking: **No**
Social Drinking: **Permitted**

The Worths raised their family in this 16-room historic house located at the edge of the village on four scenic acres with shaded lawns, apple trees, and gentle breeze. The pillared veranda is a perfect spot for quiet reflection, conversation, and refreshments. Once the home of Abraham Wagener, the founder of Penn Yan, this B&B is perfectly situated for visits to wine country, the Corning Glass Museum, Watkins Glen, and beautiful Keuka Lake. The Worths are retired now and "have always loved to travel. Now we feel we are still traveling, because people from other states and countries bring the world to our door."

Lake View Farm Bed & Breakfast ✪

4761 ROUTE 364, RUSHVILLE, NEW YORK 14544

Tel: **(716) 554-6973**
Best Time to Call: **After 4 PM**
Host(s): **Betty and Howard Freese**
Location: **20 mi. from NYS Thruway, Exit 44**
No. of Rooms: **2**

Max. No. Sharing Bath: **4**
Double/sb: **$45**
Single/sb: **$35**
Reduced Rates: **10%, after 2 nights; weekly**
Breakfast: **Full**
Pets: **No**
Children: **Welcome, over 10**
Smoking: **No**
Social Drinking: **Permitted**

Several rooms have a view of Candadaigua Lake, a Seneca Indian word meaning "The Chosen Place." The simple architecture and bright and airy atmosphere create a pleasant background for family antiques and pictures. Stroll the grounds, rest in a hammock, or play horseshoes or badminton. Take the time to explore the 170 acres; in winter, cross-country ski. In summer the marina and public beach are just minutes away.

Locustwood Country Inn ✪

3563 ROUTE 89, SENECA FALLS, NEW YORK 13148

Tel: **(315) 549-7132**
Best Time to Call: **Evenings**
Host(s): **Robert and Nancy Hill**
Location: **30 mi. E of Rochester**
No. of Rooms: **4**
Max. No. Sharing Bath: **4**
Double/sb: **$55**
Single/sb: **$45**
Open: **All year**
Breakfast: **Full**
Pets: **No**
Children: **Welcome**
Smoking: **No**
Social Drinking: **Permitted**

This charming country inn was built of brick in 1820, and still has its original huge beams, wide-plank floors, and five fireplaces. Sonnenberg Gardens, fabulous waterfalls, legendary vineyards and wineries, Corning Glass Center, and the Women's Hall of Fame are all close by. Breakfast includes freshly gathered eggs, cereal, homemade jams, plus fruit juice, coffee, and tea.

Maxwell Creek Inn ✪

7563 LAKE ROAD, SODUS, NEW YORK 14551

Tel: **(315) 483-2222**
Host(s): **Joseph and Edythe Ann Long**
Location: **30 mi. E of Rochester**
No. of Rooms: **6**
No. of Private Baths: **1**
Max. No. Sharing Bath: **4**
Double/sb: **$40–$45**
Single/sb: **$30**
Suites: **$65**
Separate Guest Cottage: **$100 for 4**
Open: **All year**
Reduced Rates: **10%, weekly; off-season**
Breakfast: **Continental**
Pets: **No**
Children: **Welcome, over 12**
Smoking: **Permitted**
Social Drinking: **Permitted**

This delightful old inn overlooks Lake Ontario and Maxwell Bay. It dates back to the 1840s and is known as a fine example of cobblestone architecture. Guests may enjoy a sing-along around the player piano or a quiet moment in the fireplaced parlor. Whatever your pleasure, lounging over breakfast pastries, afternoon fishing in a country creek, a walk in an orchard, or a game of tennis, you will find them all right here.

Sage Cottage ✪

BOX 121, 112 EAST MAIN STREET, TRUMANSBURG, NEW YORK 14886

Tel: **(607) 387-6449**
Host(s): **Dorry Norris**
Location: **10 mi. N of Ithaca**
No. of Rooms: **4**
No. of Private Baths: **2**
Max. No. Sharing Bath: **4**
Double/pb: **$40**
Single/pb: **$37**
Double/sb: **$37**
Single/sb: **$34**
Open: **Feb. 1–Jan. 2**
Reduced Rates: **Mon.–Thurs. during Feb. and Mar.**
Breakfast: **Full**
Pets: **No**
Children: **Welcome**
Smoking: **No**
Social Drinking: **Permitted**

This Gothic Revival home built in 1855 has a graceful circular staircase as its focal point. The spacious guest rooms are furnished with period furniture and adorned with treasured family pieces. Greet the morning with a hearty country breakfast on the cheery sun porch. When winter winds blow, relax in front of a cozy fire with a hot cup of tea. The kitchen garden provides the basis for the herb dishes that are so evident in Dorry's delicious cooking. It is convenient to Watkins Glen, Cayuga and Seneca lakes, and fine wineries. A two-night minimum stay is required on Cornell University and Ithaca College "big" weekends and graduation.

HUDSON VALLEY/ALBANY/KINGSTON AREA

The American Country Collection

984 GLOUCESTER PLACE, SCHENECTADY, NEW YORK 12309

Tel: **(518) 370-4948**
Best Time to Call: **10 AM–6 PM, Tues.–Fri.**
Coordinator: **Beverly K. Walsh**
States/Regions Covered: **New York: Albany, Cooperstown, Saratoga, upper Hudson Valley; Vermont: major ski areas; Massachusetts: Lenox, Stockbridge**

Rates (Single/Double):

	Single	Double
Modest:	**$25**	**$30–$40**
Average:	**$30–$35**	**$40–$50**
Luxury:	**$35–$65**	**$50–$90**

Credit Cards: **AMEX, MC, VISA**

The American Country Collection offers comfortable lodging in private homes and small inns. Accommodations range from a 1798 farmhouse where guests are treated to a pancake breakfast with homegrown maple syrup to a stately Georgian home with canopy beds, fireplaces, and Oriental rugs. Each host offers distinctive touches such as fresh flowers in the room or breakfast in bed. Many homes have lakefront property, swimming pools, and tennis courts. All are in areas of scenic and cultural interest, convenient to such attractions as the Baseball Hall of Fame, Empire State Plaza, Saratoga Racetrack, and ski areas.

Bed & Breakfast, U.S.A., Ltd. ✪

P.O. BOX 606, CROTON-ON-HUDSON, NEW YORK 10520

Tel: **(914) 271-6228**
Best Time to Call: **10 AM–4 PM**
Coordinator: **Barbara Notarius**
States/Regions Covered: **Hudson Valley, Westchester County, Upstate New York, NYC, Long Island, Finger Lakes**

Rates (Single/Double):

	Single	Double
Modest:	**$20–$30**	**$30–$40**
Average:	**$35**	**$45–$55**
Luxury:	**$50**	**$60–$130**

Credit Cards: **MC, VISA**

Barbara's extensive network includes host homes convenient to colleges, corporate headquarters, historic sites, recreational activities, and cultural events. The ambience ranges from a simple cabin to an elegant mansion, with many choices in between. The $25 annual membership fee includes unlimited reservations and the informative newsletter. If you choose not to be a member, there is a $15 processing fee for each booking. Sarah Lawrence, Manhattanville, Russell Sage, Vassar, West Point, and Skidmore are but a few of the major colleges nearby. Send $3 for her descriptive directory.

Riell's Bed and Breakfast ✪

40 LOCUST PARK, ALBANY, NEW YORK 12205

Tel: **(518) 869-5239**
Host(s): **James and Dolores Riell**
Location: **6 mi. W of Albany**
No. of Rooms: **2**
No. of Private Baths: **1**
Max. No. Sharing Bath: **4**
Double/pb: **$30**
Single/pb: **$25**
Double/sb: **$30**
Single/sb: **$25**
Open: **All year**
Breakfast: **Full**
Pets: **No**
Children: **Welcome, over 10**
Smoking: **Permitted**
Social Drinking: **Permitted**
Airport/Station Pickup: **Yes**

The Riells welcome you to a cozy Cape Cod home in the heart of New York state's capital district. Guests have a separate entrance leading to the second-floor bedrooms. One room features a wicker sitting area and the other a small office area with desk and chair. Both have wall-to-wall carpeting and coordinating linens, and you'll always find a bowl of fresh fruit. Your hosts welcome you to relax at the family room bar or in the lovely backyard with patio. Saratoga Racetrack, Empire State Plaza, and numerous shopping centers and colleges are nearby.

Ananas Hus Bed and Breakfast ✪

ROUTE 3, P.O. BOX 301, AVERILL PARK, NEW YORK 12018

Tel: **(518) 766-5035**
Host(s): **Thelma and Clyde Tomlinson**
Location: **14 mi. from I-90, Exit 7**
No. of Rooms: **3**
Max. No. Sharing Bath: **4**
Double/sb: **$50**
Single/sb: **$40**
Open: **All year**
Breakfast: **Full**
Pets: **No**
Children: **No**
Smoking: **No**
Social Drinking: **Permitted**
Foreign Languages: **Norwegian**

The welcome mat is out at this hillside ranch home on 30 acres, with a panoramic view of the Hudson River Valley. It is informally furnished in the Early American style, accented with mementos from your hosts' international travels and Thelma's lovely needlework. Thelma is a former schoolteacher; Clyde was in the food business. They are serious amateur photographers who compete internationally.

The Gregory House Inn

P.O. BOX 401, ROUTE 43, AVERILL PARK, NEW YORK 12018

Tel: **(518) 674-3774**
Best Time to Call: **5 PM**
Host(s): **Bette and Bob Jewell**
Location: **10 mi. E of Albany**
No. of Rooms: **12**
No. of Private Baths: **12**
Double/pb: **$50–$60**
Single/pb: **$45 and up**
Open: **All year**
Reduced Rates: **Weekly**
Breakfast: **Continental**
Other Meals: **Available**
Credit Cards: **AMEX, DC, MC, VISA**
Pets: **No**
Children: **Welcome, over 6**
Smoking: **Permitted**
Social Drinking: **Permitted**

The Gregory House is a clapboard Colonial, dating back to 1830. Your hosts purchased the house in 1964 and opened a small restaurant. Recently, the building was expanded to include beautifully appointed guest rooms and a common room, all in keeping with a relaxed, country style. The house is surrounded by the Catskill, Adirondack, Berkshire, and Green mountains, affording year-round beauty and recreation. The inn is also near the Saratoga Performing Arts Center, Tanglewood, Hancock Shaker Village, and Saratoga Springs. Your hosts invite you to explore their beautifully landscaped property and to join them for fine dining in the restaurant.

Cold Brook Inn ✪

COLDBROOK ROAD AND NISSEN LANE, BOICEVILLE, NEW YORK 12412

Tel: **(914) 657-6619**	Reduced Rates: **Available**
Host(s): **Diane and Walter Viries**	Breakfast: **Full**
Location: **20 mi. W of Kingston**	Other Meals: **Available**
No. of Rooms: **2**	Pets: **Sometimes**
Max. No. Sharing Bath: **5**	Children: **Welcome**
Double/sb: **$40**	Smoking: **Permitted**
Single/sb: **$35**	Social Drinking: **Permitted**
Open: **All year**	Airport/Station Pickup: **Yes**

Located on the scenic Esopus Creek, this 125-year-old farmhouse offers a variety of things to do in all seasons. Guests are welcomed with a glass of wine and shown to spacious bedrooms decorated with antiques, marble-topped dressers, and cozy quilts. A separate kitchen and outdoor grill are available for families who like to do their own cooking. If you like, an epicurean weekend special can be arranged with advance notice, featuring hors d'oeuvres, paella, homemade pasta, and chicken Kiev. The country breakfast includes fresh-ground coffee, homemade breads and cakes, eggs, sausage, and smoked bacon. You can work off breakfast by hiking, fishing, cross-country skiing, or by touring local craft shops and art galleries.

Battenkill Bed and Breakfast ✪

ROUTE 313, R.D. 1, CAMBRIDGE, NEW YORK 12816

Tel: **(518) 677-8868**	Open: **All year**
Host(s): **Veronica and Walter Piekarz**	Breakfast: **Full**
Location: **30 mi. E of Saratoga**	Other Meals: **Available**
No. of Rooms: **2**	Pets: **No**
Max. No. Sharing Bath: **4**	Children: **Welcome**
Double/sb: **$40**	Smoking: **Permitted**
Single/sb: **$30**	Social Drinking: **Permitted**

The post-and-beam structure of this Yankee barn contemporary can be spotted throughout its interior. Guests will enjoy the gourmet meals served by their hosts who are interested in music and a back-to-basics way of life. Bromley Mountain, Saratoga Performing Arts Center, Manchester, Vermont, and Bennington College in Vermont are close by. Canoe and tube rentals are available for use in the Battenkill River.

The Lace House

ROUTE 22 AT TUNNEL HILL ROAD, CANAAN, NEW YORK 12029

Tel: **(518) 781-4669**
Best Time to Call: **After 6 PM**
Host(s): **Barbara and Ed Brutsch**
Location: **1 mi. from I-90**
No. of Rooms: **6**
Max. No. Sharing Bath: **4**
Double/sb: **$60**
Open: **Memorial Day–Oct. 31**
Breakfast: **Full**
Credit Cards: **MC, VISA**
Pets: **No**
Children: **Welcome, over 12**
Smoking: **Permitted**
Social Drinking: **Permitted**
Airport/Station Pickup: **Yes**

The Lace House got its name from the intricately detailed rosettes and oval carvings over the windows and doors. The house was built in 1806 in the Federal style. In 1922, a Victorian section was added. The result is a unique combination of architectural styles that has placed The Lace House in the National Register of Historic Places. Barbara and Ed have completely restored the house, and furnished it with antiques and period pieces. An elegant sitting room with Oriental rug and Victorian furnishings is available for private relaxing. In the morning, fresh-baked muffins and blueberry pancakes are favorites, served in one of three dining areas. The Lace House is minutes from Tanglewood, Jacob's Pillow, Williamstown Theatre Festival, many ski areas, and fine restaurants.

One Market Street

COLD SPRING, NEW YORK 10516

Tel: **(914) 265-3912**
Host(s): **Philip and Esther Baumgarten**
Location: **50 mi. N of NYC**
No. of Rooms: **1 suite**
No. of Private Baths: **1**
Suites: **$65**
Open: **All year**
Reduced Rates: **Weekly**
Breakfast: **Continental**
Credit Cards: **VISA**
Pets: **No**
Children: **Welcome, over 10**
Smoking: **Permitted**
Social Drinking: **Permitted**

This beautiful Federal-style building dates back to the 1800s and looks out on the Hudson, surrounding mountains, and the foliage of the valley. The suite's kitchenette is stocked with rolls, juice, tea, and coffee for a make-it-at-your-leisure breakfast. Don't miss nearby West Point, Vassar College, and the Vanderbilt Mansion. Philip and Esther will direct you to the fine restaurants and antiques shops in their historic town.

The Mill Farm ✪

66 CRICKET HILL ROAD, DOVER PLAINS, NEW YORK 12522

Tel: **(914) 832-9198**
Host(s): **Margery Mill**
Location: **1 mi. from Rte. 22**
No. of Rooms: **4**
No. of Private Baths: **1**
Max. No. Sharing Bath: **5**
Double/pb: **$75**
Single/pb: **$70**
Double/sb: **$55**
Single/sb: **$50**
Open: **All year**
Reduced Rates: **10%, families; 15%, weekly**
Breakfast: **Full**
Pets: **Sometimes**
Children: **Welcome**
Smoking: **No**
Social Drinking: **Permitted**
Airport/Station Pickup: **Yes**

This rambling Colonial with its commodious porch is surrounded by horse farms, open fields, and spectacular mountain views. Guests enjoy the crackling fire in winter and swimming pool in summer. Breakfast is so generous it carries many right through till dinner! The bedrooms are furnished with antiques, vintage linens, pretty quilts, and cozy comforters. Margery will direct you to the area's best restaurants and antiques shops. Vassar College and Bard College are close by. There's a two-night minimum of weekends.

Golden Eagle Inn ✪

GARRISON'S LANDING, GARRISON, NEW YORK 10524

Tel: **(914) 424-3067**
Host(s): **George and Stephanie Templeton**
Location: **50 mi. N of NYC**
No. of Rooms: **4**
No. of Private Baths: **2**
Max. No. Sharing Bath: **4**
Double/pb: **$80**
Double/sb: **$65**
Open: **Apr. 1–Jan. 31**
Breakfast: **Continental**
Credit Cards: **AMEX, MC, VISA**
Pets: **No**
Children: **No**
Smoking: **Permitted**
Social Drinking: **Permitted**

Built on the high banks of the Hudson River, this gracious brick mansion (circa 1848) is listed on the National Register of Historic Places. It's close to West Point, Boscobel, and Hyde Park. The rooms are decorated with antiques and original artwork. The Templetons will direct you to some of the best restaurants in the area. A two-night minimum is required on weekends; three nights on holiday weekends.

House on the Hill ✪

P.O. BOX 86, OLD ROUTE 213, HIGH FALLS, NEW YORK 12440

Tel: **(914) 687-9627**
Best Time to Call: **Before 8 PM**
Host(s): **Shelley and Sharon Glassman**
Location: **10 mi. S of Kingston**
No. of Rooms: **3 suites**
Suites: **$65–$75**
Open: **All year**
Breakfast: **Full**
Pets: **No**
Children: **Welcome**
Smoking: **No**
Social Drinking: **Permitted**
Airport/Station Pickup: **Yes**

A bowl of fruit, a bouquet of flowers, and handmade quilts give the suites in this spacious Colonial a special charm. Breakfast is served by the fireside in the living room, or on the glass porch facing the pond. There are woods to explore, lawns for the children to play on, and ice skating on the pond in winter. Tennis, golf, and fine skiing are all nearby. Lake Mohonk and historic Kingston are minutes away. Complimentary wine and cheese are served, and Shelley and Sharon will direct you to the two four-star restaurants within walking distance of their home. SUNY-New Paltz is nearby.

Elaine's Guest House ✪

P.O. BOX 27, JOHNSON, NEW YORK 10933

Tel: **(914) 355-8811**
Host(s): **Elaine Scott**
Location: **10 mi. from I-84**
No. of Rooms: **2**
No. of Private Baths: **1**
Max. No. Sharing Bath: **2**
Double/pb: **$30**
Single/pb: **$15**
Double/sb: **$30**
Single/sb: **$15**
Open: **All year**
Breakfast: **Full**
Pets: **Welcome**
Children: **Welcome**
Smoking: **No**
Social Drinking: **Permitted**

Located ten minutes from Middletown, between Westtown and Slate Hill, Elaine's home features hospitality and comfort. It is furnished with choice items from her on-premises antiques and collectibles shop. She will be pleased to direct you to the area's points of special interest and will suggest good places to dine, suited to your budget.

Bed-N-Breakfast Reservation Services of Greater New York ✪

P.O. BOX 1015, PEARL RIVER, NEW YORK 10965

Tel: **(914) 735-4857**
Coordinator: **David J. Rosen**
States/Regions Covered: **Clarkstown, Haverstraw, Orangetown, Ramapo, Stony Point**

Rates (Single/Double):

Modest:	**$25–$35**	**$35–$45**
Average:	**$35–$45**	**$45–$55**

Rich in history, opportunities for recreational diversions within the many public parks, and cultural experiences, this area is only 25 miles north of New York City. Most of David's B&Bs are within easy reach of public transportation, large shopping centers, and corporate park areas. Bear Mountain, the Hudson River, and the Palisades are just a few popular points of interest.

Maggie Towne's B&B

PHILLIPS ROAD, PITTSTOWN, NEW YORK (Mailing address: Box 82, RD 2, Valley Falls, New York 12185)

Tel: **(518) 663-8369; 686-7331**
Host(s): **Maggie Towne**
Location: **14 mi. E of Troy**
No. of Rooms: **3**
Max. No. Sharing Bath: **4**
Double/sb: **$35**
Single/sb: **$15**
Open: **All year**
Reduced Rates: **10% seniors; families**
Breakfast: **Full**
Other Meals: **Available**
Pets: **Sometimes**
Children: **Welcome (crib)**
Smoking: **No**
Social Drinking: **Permitted**

This lovely old Colonial is located amid beautiful lawns and trees. Enjoy a cup of tea or glass of wine before the huge fireplace in the family room. Use the music room or curl up with a book on the screened-in porch. Mornings, your hostess serves home-baked goodies. She will gladly prepare a lunch for you to take on tour or enjoy at the house. It's 20 miles to historic Bennington, Vermont, and 30 to Saratoga.

Willow Brook Farm ✪

P.O. BOX 375, WARWICK TURNPIKE, WARWICK, NEW YORK 10990

Tel: **(201) 853-7728**
Host(s): **Frances Jacobsen**
Location: **2 mi. from Rte. 94**
No. of Rooms: **25**
Max. No. Sharing Bath: **6**
Double/sb: **$40**
Single/sb: **$20**
Open: **All year**

Breakfast: **Full**
Pets: **No**
Children: **Welcome**
Smoking: **Permitted**
Social Drinking: **Permitted**

Situated in a lovely setting, the Willow Brook offers recreational activities in all seasons. The fishing pond is big enough for summer rowboating and is well lit in winter for nighttime skating. Located on the New York/New Jersey state line, it's minutes to the Appalachian Trail, Vernon Valley Action Park, and Great Gorge. It is also an easy drive to Sterling Forest, Mt. Peter, Waywayanda State Park, and Hidden Valley. Frances is a cordial hostess and will make you feel at home.

LAKE GEORGE AREA

Hayes's B&B Guest House ✪

P.O. BOX 537, 7161 LAKESHORE DRIVE, BOLTON LANDING, NEW YORK 12814

Tel: **(518) 644-5941**
Best Time to Call: **9 AM–9 PM**
Host(s): **Dick Hayes, Mrs. Martha Hayes**
Location **250 mi. N of NYC**
No. of Rooms: **3**
No. of Private Baths: **3**
Double/pb: **$50**
Single/pb: **$40**
Suites: **$60–$65**
Open: **All year**
Breakfast: **Continental**
Pets: **No**
Children: **Welcome, over 12**
Smoking: **No**
Social Drinking: **Permitted**

Close to the shores of Lake George, this elegantly appointed 1920s Cape Cod estate is located across from the town beach, picnic area, and public docks. A five-minute walk to town brings you to tennis courts, shops, and fine restaurants. The Hayes family will arrange boat tours and a picnic lunch for a nominal fee in summer and fall. Cable TV and HBO are available. It's only 40 minutes to Saratoga and its famous racetrack. There's a private trout stream on the property, so pack your fishing gear.

Hilltop Cottage ✪

P.O. BOX 186, 6883 LAKESHORE DRIVE, BOLTON LANDING, NEW YORK 12814

Tel: **(518) 644-2492**
Host(s): **Anita and Charlie Richards**
Location: **9 mi. from I-87**
No. of Rooms: **3**
Max. No. Sharing Bath: **6**
Double/sb: **$35**

Single/sb: **$25**
Separate Guest Cottage: **$45; sleeps 3**
Open: **All year**
Reduced Rates: **10%, seniors**
Breakfast: **Full**
Pets: **Sometimes**
Children: **Welcome, over 4**
Smoking: **Permitted**
Social Drinking: **Permitted**
Foreign Languages: **German**

Hilltop Cottage is a two-story farmhouse furnished in comfortable traditional style. The newly decorated guest rooms are located on the second floor, apart from the family living quarters. Breakfast usually includes a German dish and is served on the screened porch in the warm weather. Your hosts will gladly help you discover the delights of the Lake George area, including "Millionaires' Row," located along Route 9. Beaches, marinas, museums, restaurants, and shops in the town center of Bolton Landing are just a ten-minute walk from the house.

The Crislip's Bed and Breakfast

BOX 57, RIDGE ROAD, GLENS FALLS, NEW YORK 12801

Tel: **(518) 793-6869**
Best Time to Call: **6 PM**
Host(s): **Ned and Joyce Crislip**
Location: **Off I-87**
No. of Rooms: **4**
No. of Private Baths: **3**
Max. No. Sharing Bath: **2**
Double/pb: **$55**
Single/pb: **$45**
Single/sb: **$45**
Open: **All year**
Reduced Rates: **Weekly**
Breakfast: **Full**
Credit Cards: **MC, VISA**
Pets: **Sometimes**
Children: **Welcome, over 4**
Smoking: **No**
Social Drinking: **Permitted**
Airport/Station Pickup: **Yes**

This restored Federal-style home is set on a parklike lawn surrounded by trees. The house boasts fine woodwork and such collectibles as a grandfather clock, Chippendale desk, and Hepplewhite chest. The spacious bedrooms feature four-poster beds and down comforters. A country breakfast of buttermilk pancakes, scrambled eggs, and sausages is served each morning. Your hosts invite you to relax on the front porch and enjoy the mountain views. Lake George, Saratoga, and Glens Falls are minutes from the house. Winter ski rates are $25 per person.

LAKE PLACID/ADIRONDACKS AREA

North Country B&B Reservation Service ✪

BOX 286, LAKE PLACID, NEW YORK 12946

Tel: **(518) 523-3739**
Best Time to Call: **10 AM–10 PM**
Coordinator: **Lyn Witte**
States/Regions Covered:
Chestertown, Glens Falls, Keene, Keeseville, Lake George, Lake Placid, Malone, North Hudson, Saranac Lake, Tupper Lake

Rates (Single/Double):

Modest:	**$15**	**$30–$40**
Average:	**$20**	**$45–$60**
Luxury:	**$40**	**$65–$100**

Lyn has dozens of hosts waiting to show you Adirondack mountain hospitality. Your choice may be convenient to Champlain Valley, Revolutionary War forts, John Brown's farm, or Camp Sagamore. Lake Placid, the Olympic Village, and Lake George offer an endless choice of sports in all seasons. St. Lawrence University, Clarkson, SUNY-Potsdam, and Plattsburgh are nearby.

The Grant Inn ✪

R.D. 1, COLD BROOK, NEW YORK 13324

Tel: **(315) 826-7677**
Host(s): **Roy and Marian Cooper**
Location: **20 mi. N of Utica**
No. of Rooms: **4**
No. of Private Baths: **2**
Max. No. Sharing Bath: **4**
Double/sb: **$35**
Suites: **$55**

Open: **All year**
Reduced Rates: **Families**
Breakfast: **Full**
Other Meals: **Available**
Pets: **No**
Children: **Welcome**
Smoking: **Permitted**
Social Drinking: **Permitted**

Fine food and lodging are the specialties of the house at this 100-year-old inn set in the foothills of the Adirondacks. Black Creek, once a logging stream and now a nature preserve, surrounds the inn on three sides. Inside, newly appointed bedrooms and suites offer comfort and privacy. The Hinkley State Park, with its popular beaches and picnic areas, is only minutes away. Fall brings a painter's palette of colors to the countryside, and in winter, cross-country skiing and snowmobiling can be enjoyed. The Coopers look forward to serving you a dinner of homemade soups, breads, desserts, and a variety of main dishes when you return from a day of activity.

Highland House ✪

3 HIGHLAND PLACE, LAKE PLACID, NEW YORK 12946

Tel: **(518) 523-2377**
Best Time to Call: **Mornings**
Host(s): **Teddy and Cathy Blazer**
Location: **25 mi. from Rte. 87, Exit 30**
No. of Rooms: **9**
No. of Private Baths: **3**
Max. No. Sharing Bath: **4**
Double/pb: **$42–$50**
Double/sb: **$35–$45**
Single/sb: **$20–$30**
Guest Cottage: **$50–$100; sleeps 4–6**
Open: **All year**
Reduced Rates: **Apr.–June; Nov.**
Breakfast: **Full**
Pets: **No**
Children: **Welcome**
Smoking: **Permitted**
Social Drinking: **Permitted**
Airport/Station Pickup: **Yes**

Located in a lovely section of Lake Placid, Highland House is within walking distance of everything in town. Cathy and Teddy have created a warm and comfortable atmosphere that guests notice upon entering this 1910 house. Every bedroom is furnished with a large wooden bunk bed as well as a double bed, each adorned with a bright, fluffy comforter. After a good night's rest, you may look forward to a breakfast of blueberry pancakes or French toast, plus hot cereals, eggs, and beverages.

Stagecoach Inn ✪

OLD MILITARY ROAD, LAKE PLACID, NEW YORK 12946

Tel: **(518) 523-9474**
Best Time to Call: **Noon–6 PM**
Host(s): **Peter and Sherry Moreau**
Location: **285 mi. N of NYC**
No. of Rooms: **8**
No. of Private Baths: **4**
Max. No. Sharing Bath: **5**
Double/pb: **$55–$65**
Single/pb: **$40–$45**
Double/sb: **$45–$50**
Single/sb: **$30–$35**
Suites: **$90**
Open: **All year**
Breakfast: **Full**
Pets: **Sometimes**
Children: **Welcome**
Smoking: **Permitted**
Social Drinking: **Permitted**

The wainscoted, high-ceilinged common room and five fireplaces will make you feel that you've arrived as the inn's original guests did—by stagecoach. Several thousand lakes and ponds for fishing and canoeing are in nearby Adirondack State Park. Local possibilities include golf, tennis, and the village of Lake Placid.

LONG ISLAND

A Reasonable Alternative ✪

117 SPRING STREET, PORT JEFFERSON, NEW YORK 11777

Tel: **(516) 928-4034**
Best Time to Call: **9 AM–1 PM**
Coordinator: **Kathleen B. Dexter**
States/Regions Covered: **Long Island**

Rates (Single/Double):

Modest	**$28**	**$36**
Average:	**$32**	**$40**
Luxury:	**$40**	**$48–$100**

Credit Cards: **MC, VISA**

Bounded by Long Island Sound and the Atlantic Ocean, from the New York City border to Montauk 100 miles to the east, the cream of host homes has been culled by Kathleen for you. There's much to see and do, including museums, historic homes, theater, horse racing, and the famous beaches, including Jones Beach, Fire Island, Shelter Island, and the exclusive Hamptons. (The Hamptons require a two-day minimum stay in July and August.) Adelphi College, Hofstra University, C. W. Post, Stony Brook, and St. Joseph's are a few of the nearby schools.

Bed & Breakfast of Long Island

P.O. BOX 392, OLD WESTBURY, NEW YORK 11568

Tel: **(516) 334-6231**
Best Time to Call: **9 AM–12:30 PM**
Coordinator: **Naomi Kavee**
States/Regions Covered: **Amagansett, Bridgehampton, Garden City, Glen Cove, Long Beach, Manhasset, Sayville, Southold, Syosset, Westbury**

Rates (Single/Double):

Modest	**$38**	**$52**
Average:	**$45**	**$58–$60**
Luxury:	**$55**	**$65–$75**

Credit Cards: **No**
Minimum Stay: **2 nights in summer (resort areas)**

From the rural farm and fishing communities on the North Fork to the fun-filled, exciting ocean beaches on the eastern tip of Montauk, famous for its lighthouse, Naomi's B&Bs are convenient to everything. Hofstra, Adelphi, the U.S. Merchant Marine Academy at Kings Point, North Shore Hospital, Nassau Coliseum, fishing, boating, fine shopping, and 4-star restaurants are but a few of the attractions of this area.

Hampton-on-the-Water ✪

BOX 106, HAMPTON BAYS, NEW YORK 11946

Tel: **(516) 728-3560**
Best Time to Call: **8–9 AM, 8–9 PM**
Host(s): **Miss Ute**

Location: **100 mi. E of NYC**
No. of Rooms: **3**
No. of Private Baths: **2**

Max. No. Sharing Bath: **3**
Double/pb: **$40–$75**
Single/pb: **$45–$70**
Double/sb: **$40–$55**
Single/sb: **$35–$50**
Open: **May–Nov.**
Reduced Rates: **30%, off-season**
Breakfast: **Full**
Pets: **No**
Children: **No**
Smoking: **Permitted**
Social Drinking: **Permitted**
Foreign Languages: **French, German, Spanish**

A spanking-white ranch-style home right on the water of Shinnecock Bay awaits your visit. There's a terrace and large garden for relaxing when you aren't clamming, fishing, or swimming, and kitchen privileges for light meals. Miss Ute permits you to use her windsurfer, small motorboat, or bicycles when the mood strikes you. It's only seven miles from the shops of Southampton. Minimum stay is three days in July and August; two days the rest of the time. Miss Ute also has a fabulous spot in Acapulco, Mexico, available from January 15 until April 15.

Duvall Bed and Breakfast On-the-Garden City-Line ✪

237 CATHEDRAL AVENUE, HEMPSTEAD, NEW YORK 11550

Tel: **(516) 292-9219**
Best Time to Call: **5–9 PM**
Host(s): **Wendy and Richard Duvall**
Location: **20 mi. E of NYC**
No. of Rooms: **3**
No. of Private Baths: **3**
Double/pb: **$45**
Single/pb: **$35**
Suite: **$80 for 4**
Open: **All year**
Reduced Rates: **10%, weekly; families**
Breakfast: **Continental**
Other Meals: **Available**
Pets: **No**
Children: **Welcome (crib)**
Smoking: **No**
Social Drinking: **Permitted**
Airport/Station Pickup: **Yes**
Foreign Languages: **Spanish, German**

Guests feel right at home in this charming Dutch Colonial with four-poster beds and antique reproductions. Wine or soft drinks are served on arrival and breakfast features homemade breads. Jones Beach, Fire Island, and New York City are nearby. Guests are welcome to use the patio, garden, and barbecue. Adelphi, Hofstra, and C. W. Post colleges are close by.

Goose Creek Guesthouse ✪

1475 WATERVIEW DRIVE, BOX 377, SOUTHOLD, NEW YORK 11971

Tel: **(516) 765-3356**
Best Time to Call: **6–9 PM**
Host(s): **Mary Mooney-Getoff**
Location: **22 mi. from I-495, Exit 73**
No. of Rooms: **3**
No. of Private Baths: **1**
Max. No. Sharing Bath: **5**
Double/pb: **$55**
Single/pb: **$40**
Double/sb: **$35**
Single/sb: **$25**
Open: **All year**
Reduced Rates: **10%, seniors**
Breakfast: **Full**
Pets: **Sometimes**
Children: **Welcome**
Smoking: **No**
Social Drinking: **Permitted**
Foreign Languages: **Spanish**

Located on the south shore of Goose Creek on Long Island's scenic North Fork, this Civil War–era home is surrounded by six acres of woods, yet is close to the beaches, museums, and a variety of shops the area is known for. Mary is a food writer and cooking teacher, so you can bet that her whole wheat pancakes, apple rings, scrapple, and preserves are super delicious. Mary loves children, and they will enjoy using the play equipment in the fenced yard.

Seafield House ✪

2 SEAFIELD LANE, WESTHAMPTON BEACH, NEW YORK 11978

Tel: **(516) 288-1559**
Best Time to Call: **After 4 PM**
Host(s): **Elsie Collins**
Location: **90 mi. E of NYC**
No. of Rooms: **3 suites**
No. of Private Baths: **3**
Suites: **$120**
Open: **All year**
Reduced Rates: **$75 Sept. 6–May 26**
Breakfast: **Full**
Pets: **No**
Children: **No**
Smoking: **No**
Social Drinking: **Permitted**

This 100-year-old home in posh Westhampton is five blocks from the beach but boasts its own pool and tennis court. Victorian lounges, a caned rocker, piano, hurricane lamps, Shaker benches, Chinese porcelain all combine to create the casual, country inn atmosphere. When the sea air chills Westhampton Beach, the parlor fire keeps the house toasty warm. The aromas of freshly brewing coffee and Mrs. Collins' breads and rolls baking in the oven are likely to wake you in time for breakfast. You'll leave this hideaway relaxed, carrying one of Mrs. Collins' homemade goodies.

NEW YORK CITY AREA

Bed & Breakfast (& Books)

35 WEST 92ND STREET, NEW YORK, NEW YORK 10025

Tel: **(212) 865-8740**
Best Time to Call: **Mon.–Fri., 10 AM–3 PM; 7–8 PM**
Coordinator: **Judith Goldberg**
State/Regions Covered: **Manhattan**

Rates (Single/Double):

Average:	**$55**	**$65**
Luxury:	**N/A**	**$90**

Credit Cards: **No**
Minimum Stay: **2 nights**

Accommodations are conveniently located in residential areas near transportation and within walking distance of many cultural attractions. Hosts are photographers, psychologists, lawyers, dancers, teachers, and artists. They are pleased to share their knowledge of fine shops, reasonable restaurants, galleries, theater, and bookstores.

Bed & Breakfast Network of New York ✪

134 WEST 32ND STREET, SUITE 601, NEW YORK, NEW YORK 10001

Tel: **(212) 645-8134**
Best Time to Call: **8–10 AM; 1–6 PM**
Coordinator: **Mr. Leslie Goldberg**
States/Regions Covered: **New York City**

Rates (Single/Double):

Modest:	**$30**	**$50**
Average:	**$40**	**$60**
Luxury:	**$60**	**$80**

Credit Cards: **No**

Accommodations appropriate to your purpose and purse are available, from the chic East Side to the arty West Side; from SoHo to Greenwich Village. They range from an historic brownstone where the host is an artist to a terraced apartment near Lincoln Center. Leslie's hosts are enthusiastic about the Big Apple and happy to share their insider information with you.

City Lights B&B, Ltd.

P.O. BOX 20355, CHEROKEE STATION, NEW YORK, NEW YORK 10028

Tel: **(212) 737-7049**
Coordinators: **Yedida Mielsen and Dee Staff**
States/Regions Covered: **New York City**

Rates (Single/Double):

Modest:	**$30–$40**	**$35–$50**
Average:	**$45–$50**	**$65–$80**
Luxury:	**$45–$50**	**$65–$80**

Credit Cards: **MC, VISA**
Minimum Stay: **2 nights**

From the tony East Side to the yuppie West Side; from the downtown New York University and Greenwich Village areas to uptown neighborhoods near Columbia University and the Museum of Natural History, accommodations range from simple to opulent. Many of the hosts are from the theater and the arts; all of them are anxious to make your stay in their town memorable. Unhosted apartments range from $65 to $180 per night, depending upon the location, ambience, and number of people staying. A $10 surcharge is imposed for a one-night stay.

Hosts & Guests, Inc. ✪

P.O. BOX 6798, NEW YORK, NEW YORK 10023

Tel: **(212) 874-4308**
Best Time to Call: **9–11 AM; 4–7 PM (Mon.–Fri.)**
Coordinator: **David M. Gottlieb**
States/Regions Covered: **Manhattan**

Rates (Single/Double):
Average: **$50–$65** **$65**
Luxury: **$65** **$65–$75**
Credit Cards: **AMEX, MC, VISA**

David has an exclusive roster of hosts who live in fashionable neighborhoods all over town. Most are in high-rise, luxury buildings with the security of 24-hour doormen, and practically all have private baths. Many B&Bs are in the posh area of Lincoln Center, where understanding hosts are willing to accept one-night reservations to accommodate guests from the tri-state area who enjoy attending performances without having to leave before the last act is over in order to catch a commuter train. We applaud them!

Judith Mol Agency ✪

357 WEST 37TH STREET, NEW YORK, NEW YORK 10018

Tel: **(212) 971-9001**
Coordinator: **Judith Bodeutsch**
States/Regions Covered: **Manhattan**

Rates (Single/Double):
Modest: **$45** **$55**
Average: **$65** **$80**
Luxury: **$100** **$120**
Credit Cards: **No**
Minimum Stay: **2 nights**

Judith's listings are as diverse as the city. An apartment in the old-world area of Gramercy Park has a queen-size bed and antique decor; one that's close to Columbia University has a loft bed, suitable for one, with a great view of the Hudson River. Another, on the chic East Side, is decorated in contemporary style accented with beautiful art. It has a Jacuzzi in the bathroom and a color TV and VCR in the bedroom.

New World Bed & Breakfast ✪

150 FIFTH AVENUE, SUITE 711, NEW YORK, NEW YORK 10011

Tel: **(212) 675-5600 or (800) 443-3800**
Coordinator: **Laura Tilden**
States/Regions Covered: **New York City**

Rates (Single/Double):

Modest:	**$40**	**$50**
Average:	**$60–$65**	**$75–$80**
Luxury:	**$70–$75**	**$90–$120**

Credit Cards: **AMEX, MC, VISA**
Minimum Stay: **2 nights**

Offering a unique cross section of accommodations in Manhattan, Laura's specialties are residential sections such as Greenwich Village, Chelsea, Gramercy Park, the Upper East Side, and the Upper West Side. Business visitors who want to be convenient to midtown, culture buffs who are happiest near Museum Mile or Lincoln Center, and those who come for theater or shopping are all accommodated. The toll-free phone allows you the luxury of personally discussing your needs and receiving suggestions and descriptions of places on the phone without waiting to receive a descriptive list.

Urban Ventures ✪

P.O. BOX 426, NEW YORK, NEW YORK 10024

Tel: **(212) 594-5650**
Best Time to Call: **9 AM–5 PM on Sat.**
Coordinator: **Mary McAulay**
State/Regions Covered: **Manhattan, New Jersey**

Rates (Single/Double):

Modest:	**$23–$36**	**$34–$45**
Average:	**$40–$50**	**$46–$58**
Luxury:	**$52–$65**	**$65–$85**

Credit Cards: **AMEX, MC, VISA**
Minimum Stay: **2 nights**

The biggest bargains since the Indians sold Manhattan for $24 are offered by this registry. Mary has bedrooms and complete apartments located throughout the best areas of New York City, including landmarked historic districts. She'll be happy to help with theater tickets, restaurant information, current museum exhibits, as well as special tours. Unhosted apartments range from $65 to $120 for two.

A Bit o' the Apple—New York City ✪

Contact: TRAILS END, RD 2, BOX 355A, GREENTOWN, PENNSYLVANIA 18426

Tel: **(212) 321-2930 or (717) 857-0856**
Best Time to Call: **After 7 PM**
Location: **Manhattan**
No. of Rooms: **2 Suites**
No. of Private Baths: **2**

Suites: **$75–$100 for 2**
Open: **All year**
Reduced Rates: **Weekly**
Breakfast: **Continental**
Pets: **No**

Children: **Welcome, over 5**
Smoking: **No**
Social Drinking: **Permitted**
Minimum Stay: **2 nights**

Situated in a luxury high-rise building on the Hudson River, the suites are within walking distance of the World Trade Center, Trinity Church, the Wall Street Stock Exchanges, the Statue of Liberty ferry, and the South Street Seaport. The accommodations are comfortably furnished with traditional furniture, antiques, and lots of plants. You will enjoy the spectacular city or water views. Your hosts, native New Yorkers, live next door and will be happy to direct you to special restaurants and shops off the tourist trail that will make your visit affordable and memorable. A garage, health club, and delightful promenade are on the premises.

NIAGARA/BUFFALO AREA

Rainbow Hospitality ✪

9348 HENNEPIN AVENUE, NIAGARA FALLS, NEW YORK 14304

Tel: **(716) 754-8877 or 283-4794**
Best Time to Call: **9 AM–7 PM**
Coordinators: **Gretchen Broderick and Marilyn Schoenherr**
State/Regions Covered: **Buffalo, Chautauqua, Lewiston, Niagara Falls, Olcott, Youngstown**

Rates (Single/Double):

Modest:	**$20**	**$35**
Average:	**$25**	**$45**
Luxury:	**$32**	**$55**

Credit Cards: **No**

The scenic splendor of Niagara Falls is only the beginning of the attractions in this area. Marilyn and Gretchen welcome travelers with a wide variety of activities to keep everyone interested and busy. Lewiston is the home of Artpark, a 200-acre park and open-air theater featuring productions from May through September. Fishing and antiquing are popular pastimes too. The best part of the area are their hosts, who open their homes to extend the hand of friendship.

Providence Farm ✪

11572 HILLER ROAD, AKRON, NEW YORK 14001

Tel: **(716) 759-2109**
Host(s): **Dr. and Mrs. C. Alan Riedesel**
Location: **10 mi. from the N.Y. Thruway**
No. of Rooms: **2**
No. of Private Baths: **2**
Double/pb: **$40**
Single/pb: **$35**
Open: **Apr. 1–Oct. 31**
Breakfast: **Full**
Pets: **Sometimes**
Children: **Welcome, over 10**
Smoking: **No**
Social Drinking: **Permitted**
Airport/Station Pickup: **Yes**

Providence Farm stretches over 58 acres of fields, ponds, gardens, and wildlife areas. The Riedesels have a 150-year-old farmhouse furnished with many antiques and handcrafts. In the afternoon join your hosts for tea or sherry. Breakfast is served by the fire, in the bay window, or outside on the porch. Freshly made breads, jams, and special farm-fresh egg dishes are among the specialties of the chef. Myriad activities are within easy driving distance, including antiquing, museum visits, theater, tours of Niagara Falls, and sports of all kinds.

B&B of Niagara Frontier ✪

440 LE BRUN ROAD, BUFFALO, NEW YORK 14226

Tel: **(716) 836-0794**
Best Time to Call: **Evenings**
Host(s): **Virginia Trinidad**
Location: **2½ mi. from I-90**
No. of Rooms: **2**
No. of Private Baths: **2**
Double/pb: **$45**
Single/pb: **$30**
Open: **All year**
Reduced Rates: **Weekly; 15%, families**
Breakfast: **Full**
Pets: **No**
Children: **Welcome, over 6**
Smoking: **No**
Social Drinking: **Permitted**
Airport/Station Pickup: **Yes**
Foreign Languages: **Filipino**

Virginia is a health professional who enjoys traveling, music, and meeting people. You are cordially invited to share her sprawling brick ranch-style home located in a prime suburban section of Buffalo. Elegantly furnished and centrally air-conditioned, it is surrounded by parklike grounds where you can jog, toss a frisbee, play badminton, or cross-country ski, depending upon the season. It is only 16 miles to Niagara Falls; 4 miles to the Albright Knox Gallery; 5 miles to Buffalo's theater district. Don't forget to sample the famous Buffalo chicken wings, which can be delivered from a nearby restaurant, and which you are welcome to enjoy in Virginia's kitchen. You'll enjoy the comfort of this home as you would your own.

The Eastwood House ✪

45 SOUTH MAIN STREET, CASTILE, NEW YORK 14427

Tel: **(716) 493-2335**
Best Time to Call: **After 6 PM**
Host(s): **Joan Ballinger**
Location: **63 mi. SE of Buffalo on Rte. 39**
No. of Rooms: **2**
Max. No. Sharing Bath: **4**
Double/sb: **$25**
Single/sb: **$21**
Open: **All year**
Breakfast: **Continental**
Pets: **Sometimes**
Children: **Welcome, over 5**
Smoking: **No**
Social Drinking: **Permitted**

This comfortable house is a few minutes' drive from Letchworth State Park. Your hostess offers coffee, fresh fruit, and juice on arrival. Hot biscuits, freshly whipped cream, and jam are featured at breakfast each morning. Local sights include the Historical Society and the Indian Museum.

Back of the Beyond ✪

7233 LOWER EAST HILL ROAD, COLDEN, NEW YORK 14033

Tel: **(716) 652-0427**
Best Time to Call: **Early AM**
Host(s): **Bill and Shash Georgi**
Location: **30 mi. S of Buffalo**
No. of Rooms: **3**
Max. No. Sharing Bath: **5**
Double/sb: **$45**
Single/sb: **$40**
Separate Guest Cottage: **$35 for 2**
Open: **All year**
Breakfast: **Full**
Pets: **Sometimes**
Children: **Welcome**
Smoking: **No**
Social Drinking: **Permitted**

Bill and Shash have a small country estate near a ski area and an hour from Niagara Falls. They maintain a greenhouse, and grow their vegetables organically. Breakfast reflects all this "healthiness" with delicious herbal omelets, breads, plus other goodies. The guest quarters are in a separate three-bedroom chalet, fully equipped even to the fireplace.

The Davidson House ✪

2447 BAUER ROAD, EDEN, NEW YORK 14057

Tel: **(716) 627-5543**
Best Time to Call: **After 3 PM**
Host(s): **Jim and Dolores Davidson**
Location: **15 mi. SW of Buffalo**
No. of Rooms: **2**
Max. No. Sharing Bath: **4**
Double/sb: **$30**
Single/sb: **$25**
Open: **All year**
Reduced Rates: **15%, weekly; 10%, seniors, families**
Breakfast: **Continental**
Pets: **No**
Children: **Welcome, over 12**
Smoking: **Permitted**
Social Drinking: **Permitted**
Airport/Station Pickup: **Yes**

Jim and Dolores welcome you to their large Colonial-style home set on three acres. The house is surrounded by a lovely lawn, gardens, and a pond where deer can often be seen. The house is decorated with many homemade accessories and comfortable family furnishings. Guests are welcome to relax on the porch swing or sit by the fireplace and enjoy homemade wine and snacks. Breakfast specialties include home-baked breads, jams, and plenty of hot coffee. This quiet rural setting is close to skiing, Niagara Falls, and Lake Erie. The Davidsons love flying and extend a special welcome to private pilots. They also invite you to take advantage of their beauty shop to freshen up on your arrival or before an evening out.

The Peter House ✪

175 SOUTH FOURTH STREET, LEWISTON, NEW YORK 14092

Tel: **(716) 754-8877**
Host(s): **Peter and Gretchen Broderick**
Location: **7 mi. N of Niagara Falls**
No. of Rooms: **3**
No. of Private Baths: **2**
Max. No. Sharing Bath: **3**
Double/pb: **$50–$55**
Single/pb: **$32–$40**
Single/sb: **$25**
Suites: **$55**
Open: **All year**
Reduced Rates: **20%, weekly**
Breakfast: **Full**
Pets: **Sometimes**
Children: **Welcome**
Smoking: **Permitted**
Social Drinking: **Permitted**
Airport/Station Pickup: **Yes**

The Peter House is a gracious Greek Revival home over 150 years old. It is beautifully furnished with old family collectibles and many fine antiques. Guests are invited to relax with a glass of wine beside the fire, or enjoy an iced tea out on the veranda or on one of the covered porches. Peter and Gretchen have a wonderful old recipe for homemade sausage as well as a variety of other breakfast dishes. Their home is a perfect place to stay while visiting Niagara Falls, just five miles from here. The house is a short stroll from all of historic Lewiston and New York State's Performing Arts Complex.

Chestnut Ridge Inn ✪

7205 CHESTNUT RIDGE, LOCKPORT, NEW YORK 14094

Tel: **(716) 439-9124**
Best Time to Call: **Evenings**
Host(s): **Frank and Lucy Cervoni**
Location: **20 mi. E of Niagara Falls**
No. of Rooms: **5**
No. of Private Baths: **2**
Max. No. Sharing Bath: **4**
Double/pb: **$65**
Single/pb: **$60**
Double/sb: **$40**
Single/sb: **$30**
Open: **Apr. 1–Nov. 1**
Breakfast: **Full**
Pets: **No**
Children: **Welcome, over 12**
Smoking: **No**
Social Drinking: **Permitted**
Foreign Languages: **Italian**

Black shutters accent this handsome white Federal mansion built in 1826. Surrounded by eight acres, it boasts a circular staircase, library,

several fireplaces, and appropriate antique and Chippendale furniture. The bedrooms have queen-size beds and are decorated with Laura Ashley fabrics. Both Lucy and Frank are gourmet cooks and will take pleasure in pampering you with wine, cheese, and special snacks.

THOUSAND ISLANDS AREA

Battle Island Inn ✪

BOX 176, RD #1, FULTON, NEW YORK 13069

Tel: **(315) 598-3985**
Host(s): **Joyce and Richard Rice**
Location: **30 mi. N. of Syracuse**
No. of Rooms: **5**
Max. No. Sharing Bath: **4**
Double/sb: **$45**
Single/sb: **$35**
Open: **All year**
Reduced Rates: **10%, seniors**
Breakfast: **Full**
Pets: **No**
Children: **Welcome**
Smoking: **No**
Social Drinking: **Permitted**

The Rice family welcomes you to their pre–Civil War estate, which they restored themselves with lots of love and hard work. The inn is across the street from a golf course and is surrounded by fields and orchards. The rooms feature Victorian antiques and marble fireplaces. Guest bedrooms are spacious and elegant with imposing high-backed beds. Joyce is a full-time hostess who will tempt your palate with homemade rolls, biscuits, and crêpes. Richard is a systems analyst who oversees the challenges of an 1840s house. Whether you're enjoying the privacy of your room or socializing in the formal front parlor, you are sure to appreciate the friendly family atmosphere.

The Way Inn ✪

7377 SALINA STREET, PULASKI, NEW YORK 13142

Tel: **(315) 298-6073**
Host(s): **Don and Barb White**
Location: **40 mi. N of Syracuse**
No. of Rooms: **4**
Max. No. Sharing Bath: **4**
Double/sb: **$35**
Single/sb: **$25**
Open: **All year**
Reduced Rates: **Summer, winter, families**
Breakfast: **Continental**
Credit Cards: **MC, VISA**
Pets: **No**
Children: **Welcome**
Smoking: **Permitted**
Social Drinking: **No**

Within walking distance of the Salmon River with its excellent salmon and trout fishing, this 1840 country home is conveniently located if you're on the way to Canada or the Adirondacks. Home-baked coffee cake and muffins are served in the bay-windowed dining room at breakfast time. An evening snack is graciously offered before you retire.

Pink House Inn ✪

9125 SOUTH MAIN STREET, P.O. BOX 85, SANDY CREEK, NEW YORK 13145

Tel: **(315) 387-3276**
Host(s): **Evelyn Sadowski**
Location: **45 mi. N of Syracuse**
No. of Rooms: **7**
Max. No. Sharing Bath: **4**
Double/pb: **$52.50**
Single/pb: **$26.25**
Double/sb: **$41.60**
Single/sb: **$20.80**
Reduced Rates: **10%, seniors**
Open: **All year**
Breakfast: **Full**
Pets: **No**
Children: **Welcome, over 12**
Smoking: **Permitted**
Social Drinking: **Permitted**
Airport/Station Pickup: **Yes**

Evelyn owns an antiques shop, and many fine pieces accent her comfortable home. This clapboard house, built in 1872, has an inviting screened-in porch. If you are heading for Canada, this is a fine place to rest up, since the house is located on Route 11. It is only five miles to Lake Ontario. Your hostess truly enjoys people.

NORTH CAROLINA

Charlotte Bed and Breakfast ✪

1700-2 DELANE AVENUE, CHARLOTTE, NORTH CAROLINA 28211

Tel: **(704) 366-0979**
Best Time to Call: **9 AM–5 PM**
Coordinator: **Mrs. Ruth Foell Hill**
State/Regions Covered: **Asheville, Beaufort, Chapel Hill, Charlotte, Elkin, Raleigh, Southern Pines, Winston-Salem**

Rates (Single/Double):

Modest:	**$25**	**$30**
Average:	**$30**	**$40**
Luxury:	**$40**	**$65–$80**

Credit Cards: **No**

Ruth is devoted to giving her personal attention to every B&B guest with a sincere effort to place you in a suitable environment. Charlotte, the state's largest city, is a base for international commerce, and is home to Queens College and the University of North Carolina. The Mint Museum of Art and History, the Charlotte Symphony, and Discovery Place are popular attractions. One of her accommodations is in a decorator's home in the Cotswold area; another is a Victorian that was featured in *Travel/Leisure* magazine. Send for Ruth's free brochure.

Albemarle Inn ✪

86 EDGEMONT ROAD, ASHEVILLE, NORTH CAROLINA 28801

Tel: **(704) 255-0027**
Best Time to Call: **8 AM**
Host(s): **Rosina Mellin**
Location: **½ mi. from Rt. 240**
No. of Rooms: **12**
No. of Private Baths: **12**
Double/pb: **$48–$63**
Single/pb: **$46–$57**
Guest Apt: **$48–$63**
Open: **Apr. 1–Dec. 1**
Reduced Rates: **Weekly**
Breakfast: **Full**
Credit Cards: **AMEX, MC, VISA**
Pets: **No**
Children: **Welcome, over 14**
Smoking: **Permitted**
Social Drinking: **Permitted**
Foreign Languages: **German**

This Victorian mansion is listed on the National Register of Historic Places. Bela Bartok wrote his third piano concerto while residing at the inn. Perhaps you too will be inspired by the 12-foot ceilings, carved oak staircases, balconies and clawfoot bathtubs. Your hosts offer homemade breads and pastries each morning. They will gladly direct you to mountain sights, Asheville's finest eateries and the famous Biltmore House. There's a swimming pool on the premises, and tennis courts are nearby.

Cedar Crest Victorian Inn ✪

674 BILTMORE AVENUE, ASHEVILLE, NORTH CAROLINA 28803

Tel: **(704) 252-1389**
Best Time to Call: **Mornings**
Host(s): **Jack and Barbara McEwan**
Location: **1¼ mi. from I-40**
No. of Rooms: **11**
No. of Private Baths: **4**
Max. No. Sharing Bath: **4**
Double/pb: **$72–$85**
Single/pb: **$72–$79**
Double/sb: **$56–$67**
Single/sb: **$50–$62**
Open: **All year**
Breakfast: **Continental**
Credit Cards: **AMEX, MC, VISA**
Pets: **No**
Children: **Welcome, over 12**
Smoking: **Permitted**
Social Drinking: **Permitted**

Built in 1891 and listed on the National Register of Historic places, Cedar Crest is one of the largest and most opulent residences to survive Asheville's boom period. Enter the grand foyer and you'll find the rich warmth of hardwood paneling, lace window treatments, and an intricately carved fireplace. A massive oak staircase leads to the guest rooms, decorated with Victorian antiques and fine linens. Your hosts serve tea or lemonade on the spacious veranda in the summer months. In the cold weather, enjoy hot drinks by the fire. This lovely Queen Anne is located close to the Blue Ridge Parkway, the Biltmore

House, and downtown Asheville. Your hosts will be glad to recommend local eateries and invite you back to the inn for hot chocolate and cookies in the evening.

Cornerstone Inn ✪

230 PEARSON DRIVE, ASHEVILLE, NORTH CAROLINA 28801

Tel: **(704) 253-5644**
Host(s): **Lonnie and Evelyn Wyatt**
No. of Rooms: **3**
No. of Private Baths: **1**
Max. No. Sharing Bath: **5**
Double/pb: **$65**
Single/pb: **$55**
Double/sb: **$55**
Single/sb: **$50**
Open: **All year**
Breakfast: **Full**
Credit Cards: **MC, VISA**
Pets: **No**
Children: **Welcome, over 10**
Smoking: **No**
Social Drinking: **No**
Airport/Station Pickup: **Yes**

This Dutch Tudor home is surrounded by hemlocks and is located in the heart of the historic area. Lonnie and Evelyn have furnished with family heirlooms, antiques, and treasures collected while living and traveling in Europe. It is a brief walk to the Botanical Garden at the University of North Carolina, and a short distance to shops, restaurants, and cultural events. Depending upon the weather, breakfast may be enjoyed on the covered side porch, in the formal dining room, or in the rock-walled garden amid local wildflowers.

Flint Street Inns ✪

100 & 116 FLINT STREET, ASHEVILLE, NORTH CAROLINA 28801

Tel: **(704) 253-6723**
Host(s): **Rick and Lynne Vogel**
Location: **1/4 mi. from Rte. 240**
No. of Rooms: **8**
No. of Private Baths: **8**
Double/pb: **$60**
Single/pb: **$50**
Open: **All year**
Breakfast: **Full**
Credit Cards: **AMEX, MC, VISA**
Pets: **No**
Children: **Welcome**
Smoking: **Permitted**
Social Drinking: **Permitted**

These turn-of-the-century homes are listed on the National Register of Historic Places. Stained glass, pine floors, and a claw-footed bathtub are part of the Victorian decor. Guests are served wine, coffee, and soft drinks. The Blue Ridge Parkway is close by.

Heritage Hill ✪

64 LINDEN AVENUE, ASHEVILLE, NORTH CAROLINA 28801

Tel: **(704) 254-9336**
Best Time to Call: **Mornings; evenings**
Host(s): **Ross and Linda Willard**
No. of Rooms: **6**
No. of Private Baths: **4**
Max. No. Sharing Bath: **6**
Double/pb: **$50–$55**
Double/sb: **$35–$42**
Open: **All year**
Reduced Rates: **Families; winter rates**
Breakfast: **Continental**
Pets: **No**
Children: **Welcome**
Smoking: **Permitted**
Social Drinking: **Permitted**
Airport/Station Pickup: **Yes**

Built in the early 1900s, this large Colonial is set on parklike grounds, and is surrounded by giant maple, oak, pine, and dogwood trees. The large rooms are decorated with family furnishings, books, and collectibles. The house has three fireplaces and a wraparound veranda with 12 white pillars and old-fashioned rockers. Guests are welcome to a glass of wine and a snack, on the porch or beside a roaring fire. Your hosts serve homemade breads, fresh fruits, and plenty of coffee for breakfast. They also provide a guest kitchen for those who would like to do their own cooking. Heritage Hill is three blocks from downtown, and close to the Blue Ridge Parkway.

The Ray House ✪

83 HILLSIDE STREET, ASHEVILLE, NORTH CAROLINA 28801

Tel: **(704) 252-0106**
Best Time to Call: **10 AM–9 PM**
Host(s): **Will and Alice Curtis**
Location: **5 mi. from I-40**
No. of Rooms: **3**
Max. No. Sharing Bath: **4**
Double/sb: **$37**
Single/sb: **$26**
Suites: **$42**
Open: **All year**
Reduced Rates: **Weekly**
Breakfast: **Continental**
Pets: **Sometimes**
Children: **Welcome**
Smoking: **Permitted**
Social Drinking: **Permitted**
Airport/Station Pickup: **Yes**
Foreign Languages: **French**

This restored 1891 home sits on an acre of towering trees that provide leafy privacy in a parklike setting. Interior features include windows of unusual design, beamed ceilings, and handsome woodwork. A breakfast of homemade breads, sweet cakes, and jellies is served in the formal dining room or on the shaded wraparound porch.

Balsam Lodge ✪

BOX 279, RIVER ROAD, BALSAM, NORTH CAROLINA 28707

Tel: **(704) 456-6528**
Best Time to Call: **9 AM–10 PM**
Host(s): **Marie and Gordon Pike**
Location: **35 mi. W of Asheville**
No. of Rooms: **8**
No. of Private Baths: **4**
Max. No. Sharing Bath: **6**
Double/pb: **$40**
Single/pb: **$32**
Double/sb: **$28**
Single/sb: **$20**
Open: **May–Nov.**
Breakfast: **Continental**
Pets: **Sometimes**
Children: **Welcome**
Smoking: **No**
Social Drinking: **Permitted**

Local crafts, fresh flowers, and period pieces fill the rooms of this turn-of-the-century home. The depot, which once served the town of Balsam, is now divided into private accommodations for guests. At the main house, enjoy an evening on a porch rocker; in the morning, your hosts offer homemade muffins and cakes. They are glad to advise on trips to nearby Great Smoky National Park, Blue Ridge Parkway, and the Cherokee Indian Reservation. Western Carolina University is nearby.

Bath Guest House

SOUTH MAIN STREET, BATH, NORTH CAROLINA 27808

Tel: **(919) 923-6811**
Best Time to Call: **9 AM–9 PM**
Host(s): **Paul and Irene Komarow**
No. of Rooms: **5**
No. of Private Baths: **1**
Max. No. Sharing Bath: **4**
Double/pb: **$48**
Single/pb: **$43**
Double/sb: **$43**
Single/sb: **$38**
Open: **All year**
Breakfast: **Full**
Pets: **No**
Children: **Welcome**
Smoking: **Permitted**
Social Drinking: **Permitted**

This is a fine historic home, on the beautiful Pamlico River. You can absorb the abundant history of the town, join the sailing enthusiasts, enjoy hunting and fishing, or just relax on the back porch rocking chairs and watch the sun set over the river. Everything is within walking distance, but bicycles are available for your use. There's no charge for the use of small boats or for docking your own. Special duck-hunting packages are available in season, including experienced guide service and meals. Paul and Irene's Southern breakfasts are special.

The Blackberry Inn ✪

P.O. BOX 965, BLACK MOUNTAIN, NORTH CAROLINA 28711

Tel: **(704) 669-8303**
Best Time to Call: **10 AM–9 PM**
Host(s): **Roy and Barbara DeHaan Miller**
Location: **15 mi. E of Asheville**
No. of Rooms: **6**
No. of Private Baths: **6**
Double/pb: **$45**
Single/pb: **$35**
Open: **All year**
Reduced Rates: **10%, weekly**
Breakfast: **Continental**
Pets: **No**
Children: **Welcome (crib)**
Smoking: **Permitted**
Social Drinking: **Permitted**
Airport/Station Pickup: **Yes**

The Blackberry Inn is a red brick Colonial set on a secluded hilltop surrounded by oaks and evergreens. The house was built in the 1930s, and though it has been renovated, it retains its original charm, with hardwood floors upstairs and polished brass throughout. The rooms have an American country theme and are furnished with antiques of all kinds. Roy and Barbara have a vast collection of photographs, original artwork, and handcrafts on display for your enjoyment. The inn is a short drive from the Blue Ridge Parkway and the Biltmore House. Rustic mountain trails, brilliant foliage, and relaxed hospitality are sure to lure you back to this charming inn.

The Inn at Brevard

410 EAST MAIN STREET, BREVARD, NORTH CAROLINA 28712

Tel: **(704) 884-2105**
Host(s): **Bertrand and Eileen Bourget**
Location: **25 mi. W of Hendersonville**
No. of Rooms: **13**
No. of Private Baths: **13**
Double/pb: **$46–$55**
Single/pb: **$40–$45**
Open: **Mar. 1–Dec. 31**
Reduced Rates: **Weekly**
Breakfast: **Full**
Other Meals: **Available**
Pets: **No**
Children: **Welcome**
Smoking: **Permitted**
Social Drinking: **Permitted**

This white-columned inn is listed on the National Register of Historic Places and has retained the original brass hardware, carved fireplace mantels, and antique furnishings to recall old-time Southern charm. The bedrooms are comfortable and the clear air and mountain breezes will refresh you. Explore the many splendors of this Land of Waterfalls, and return to spend a peaceful evening with other guests on the porch or sitting room.

Hamrick Inn ✪

7787 HIGHWAY 80, BURNSVILLE, NORTH CAROLINA 28714

Tel: **(704) 675-5251**
Best Time to Call: **Mornings**
Host(s): **Neal and June Jerome**
Location: **55 mi. NE of Asheville; 16 mi. from I-40, Exit 72**
No. of Rooms: **4**
No. of Private Baths: **4**
Double/pb: **$45–$50**
Single/pb: **$35–$45**
Open: **All year**
Reduced Rates: **Weekly**
Breakfast: **Continental**
Pets: **No**
Children: **Welcome**
Smoking: **Permitted**
Social Drinking: **Permitted**

This charming three-story Colonial-style stone inn is nestled at the foot of Mt. Mitchell, the highest mountain east of the Mississippi River. Much of the lovely furniture was built by Neal and June. The den has a fine selection of books as well as a TV set for your enjoyment. There is a private porch off each bedroom where you may take in the view and the cool mountain breezes. Golfing, hiking, fishing, rock hounding, craft shopping, and fall foliage are local activities. Pisgah National Park, Linville Caverns, Crabtree Meadows, and the Parkway Playhouse are area diversions.

The Homeplace ✪

5901 SARDIS ROAD, CHARLOTTE, NORTH CAROLINA 28226

Tel: **(704) 365-1936**
Host(s): **Peggy and Frank Dearien**
Location: **10 mi. from I-77; I-85**
No. of Rooms: **3**

No. of Private Baths: **1**
Max. No. Sharing Bath: **4**
Double/pb: **$60**
Single/pb: **$50**
Double/sb: **$50**
Single/sb: **$40**
Open: **All year**
Reduced Rates: **10%, 4 nights**
Breakfast: **Full**
Credit Cards: **AMEX, MC, VISA**
Pets: **No**
Children: **Welcome, over 10**
Smoking: **No**
Social Drinking: **No**

The warm and friendly atmosphere hasn't changed since 1902. The minute you arrive at this country Victorian and walk up to the wraparound porch with its rockers, you'll feel you've "come home." The handcrafted staircase, ten-foot beaded ceilings, and heart-of-pine floors add to the interior's beauty. Complimentary appetizers or desserts are served evenings in the parlor. It's convenient to malls, furniture and textile outlets, and treasure-filled antiques shops.

The Overcarsh House ✪

326 WEST EIGHTH STREET, CHARLOTTE, NORTH CAROLINA 28202

Tel: **(704) 334-8477**
Host(s): **Dennis Cudd and George Brown**
Location: **1 mi. from I-77**
No. of Rooms: **1 suite**
No. of Private Baths: **1**
Suites: **$65–$80 (2–4)**
Open: **All year**
Reduced Rates: **10%, corporate**
Breakfast: **Continental**
Pets: **No**
Children: **Welcome**
Smoking: **Permitted**
Social Drinking: **Permitted**

The Library Suite is a Victorian-style retreat in the luxurious Overcarsh House. The private entrance into the suite leads to a wraparound gallery overlooking Fourth Ward Park. The adjoining sleeping quarters feature a draped Savannah Plantation bed. Your hosts have stocked the floor-to-ceiling bookcases with plenty of books and periodicals. They also provide wine and a wet bar, fresh flowers, cable TV, and coffeemaker. Overcarsh House is listed on the National Register of Historic Places, and is close to the uptown area, the performing arts center, shopping, and restaurants.

Arrowhead Inn ✪

106 MASON ROAD, DURHAM, NORTH CAROLINA 27712

Tel: **(919) 477-8430**
Host(s): **Jerry and Barbara Ryan**
Location: **6.8 mi. from I-85, Exit Roxboro**

No. of Rooms: **6**
No. of Private Baths: **2**
Max. No. Sharing Bath: **4**
Double/pb: **$65–$90**
Double/sb: **$55**
Open: **Jan. 1–Dec. 22**
Reduced Rates: **10%, after 4 nights**
Breakfast: **Full**
Credit Cards: **AMEX, MC, VISA**
Pets: **No**
Children: **Welcome**
Smoking: **Permitted**
Social Drinking: **Permitted**
Foreign Languages: **French**

Arrowhead Inn is a 200-year-old columned manor house in Durham County's tobacco country. Its rooms reflect various moments in the house's history, from Colonial through Tidewater and Victorian. Stroll the nearly four acres, or visit the historic district, the Museum of Life and Science, Duke University, or famous Research Triangle Park. After dinner at one of the area's fine restaurants, join the other guests for VCR, Scrabble, or conversation.

The Trestle House Inn

ROUTE 4, BOX 370, EDENTON, NORTH CAROLINA 27932

Tel: **(919) 482-2282**
Host(s): **Hal and Louise Worthley**
Location: **5 mi. E of Edenton**
No. of Rooms: **4**
No. of Private Baths: **4**
Double/pb: **$50**
Single/pb: **$50**
Open: **All year**
Reduced Rates: **Available**
Breakfast: **Continental**
Credit Cards: **AMEX, MC, VISA**
Pets: **Sometimes**
Children: **Welcome, over 9**
Smoking: **Permitted**
Social Drinking: **Permitted**
Airport/Station Pickup: **Yes**

A private fishing lake and 70 acres of pastures are the backdrop for this Colonial inn. The house was built from 450-year-old California redwood timbers once part of a railroad trestle. The rooms feature open-beam construction, wood-plank floors, and casual furnishings. Guests can choose from numerous places to relax, including a huge family room with a massive stone fireplace, a sun deck with lounge chairs, and a porch with a panoramic view of the lake and native wildlife of all kinds. If the weather is poor, a health room with exercise equipment and ceramic-tiled steam bath is available. Guest rooms have comfortable beds, fine linens, and cable TV. Hal and Louise serve fresh fruit and croissants or muffins in the morning. They invite you to fish in the lake or the pond, and will gladly direct you to the local sights.

Country Lane ✪

P.O. BOX 627, ELKIN, NORTH CAROLINA 28621

Tel: **(919) 366-2915/4565**
Host(s): **Ron and Nancy Garrett**
Location: **4 mi. from I-77, Exit 85; 40 mi. W of Winston-Salem**
No. of Rooms: **1 suite**
No. of Private Baths: **1**
Suites: **$30–$35**
Open: **All year**
Reduced Rates: **15%, weekly**
Breakfast: **Full**
Pets: **Welcome**
Children: **Welcome (crib)**
Smoking: **Permitted**
Social Drinking: **Permitted**

This modernized farmhouse is set on 15 acres in the foothills of the Blue Ridge Mountains. The rooms are comfortably furnished with special touches like braided rugs and mountain crafts. Guest quarters have warm wooden paneling, single beds with calico spreads, and an adjacent sitting room with a queen-size sofa bed. A Southern breakfast featuring homemade muffins, jams, and cheese soufflé is served by the fireside in the dining room or on the porch in summer. The golf course at the nearby country club is available for guests, and there are many local opportunities for hiking, canoeing, and dining.

Buttonwood Inn ✪

190 GEORGIA ROAD, FRANKLIN, NORTH CAROLINA 28734

Tel: **(704) 369-8985**
Best Time to Call: **After 5 PM**
Host(s): **Liz Oehser**
Location: **75 mi. SW of Asheville**
No. of Rooms: **4**
No. of Private Baths: **2**
Max. No. Sharing Bath: **4**
Double/pb: **$45–$55**
Single/pb: **$36**
Double/sb: **$45**
Single/sb: **$30**
Suites: **$75**
Open: **May 15–Dec.**
Breakfast: **Full**
Pets: **No**
Children: **Welcome, over 10**
Smoking: **Permitted**
Social Drinking: **Permitted**

The Buttonwood is a small country inn surrounded by towering pines, a spacious lawn, and mountain views. The original residence was a small cottage built in the late 1920s adjacent to the greens of the Franklin golf course. Years later, a new wing was added with rustic, charming rooms. Guests may choose from comfortable bedrooms decorated with antiques, cozy quilts, and handcrafts, many of which are offered for sale. Breakfast selections include sausage-apple ring, eggs Benedict, or cheese frittata, with coffee cake and plenty of hot coffee or tea. Golfers will be glad to be so close to the beautiful fairways and Bermuda grass greens right next door. Nearby there are also craft shops, hiking trails, the Blue Ridge Parkway, gem mines, and plenty of places to swim and ride.

The Lake House

P.O. BOX 427, LAKESIDE CIRCLE, GLENVILLE, NORTH CAROLINA 28736

Tel: **(704) 743-3360**
Best Time to Call: **Mornings; evenings**
Host(s): **Carol Mount**
Location: **63 mi. W of Asheville**
No. of Rooms: **5**
No. of Private Baths: **1**
Max. No. Sharing Bath: **4**
Double/pb: **$50**
Single/pb: **$40**
Double/sb: **$50**
Single/sb: **$35**
Suites: **$60**
Open: **All year**
Reduced Rates: **10%, Dec., Jan., Feb.**
Breakfast: **Continental**
Other Meals: **Available**
Pets: **Sometimes**
Children: **Welcome, over 6**
Smoking: **Permitted**
Social Drinking: **Permitted**

An artist could not have painted a prettier backdrop for this rustic cedar home, surrounded by mountains and set on Lake Glenville. The rooms are furnished with antiques and Oriental rugs, and offer fabulous views. Enjoy a glass of wine on the deck overlooking the water. The lake extends over 1,400 acres, and swimming and boating can be enjoyed right off the floating dock. Your hostess enjoys hiking and river rafting, and will be glad to guide you as well. To help you look your swimsuit best, healthy breakfast offerings include bran muffins and natural waffles with fresh fruit. The Lake House is near numerous waterfalls, hiking trails in the Great Smokies, and the Blue Ridge Mountains.

Mountain High ✪

BIG RIDGE ROAD, GLENVILLE, NORTH CAROLINA 28736

Tel: **(704) 743-3094**
Host(s): **Margaret and George Carter**
Location: **2 mi. from Rte. 107**
No. of Rooms: **3**
No. of Private Baths: **1**
Max. No. Sharing Bath: **4**
Double/sb: **$30**
Single/sb: **$15**
Open: **July–Nov.**
Reduced Rates: **Weekly**
Breakfast: **Full**
Pets: **No**
Children: **No**
Smoking: **No**
Social Drinking: **Permitted**

It is located 4,200 feet high in the Smoky Mountains, only a short distance from the Carolina Highlands. Margaret and George offer warm hospitality to their guests. You are invited to join your hosts in a fox hunt (the hounds are trained not to kill the fox—just to chase him). You are welcome to use the kitchen for light snacks, and may freshen your wardrobe in the washer and dryer. Western Carolina University-Cullowhee is nearby.

Leftwich House ✪

215 EAST HARDEN STREET, GRAHAM, NORTH CAROLINA 27253

Tel: **(919) 226-5978**
Host(s): **Carolyn Morrow**
Location: **2 mi. S of Burlington**
No. of Rooms: **3**
Max. No. Sharing Bath: **5**
Double/sb: **$35–$45**
Single/sb: **$25–$35**
Open: **All year**
Breakfast: **Full**
Pets: **No**
Children: **Welcome (crib)**
Smoking: **No**
Social Drinking: **No**

Leftwich House has the high ceilings and crystal chandeliers typical of the 1920s. The rooms are filled with handicrafts, needlework, and antiques. The guest room has a queen-size bed of cherry wood, floral wallpaper, and an old rocker. Enjoy cookies and tea on arrival and a complimentary evening snack. Morning coffee, homemade breads, and omelets are served on the porch in season. Your hostess will gladly point the way to nearby Burlington, with its 200 outlet stores. Historic Alamance Battleground is 10 miles away.

Greenwood ✪

205 NORTH PARK DRIVE, GREENSBORO, NORTH CAROLINA 27401

Tel: **(919) 274-6350**
Best Time to Call: **Mornings**
Host(s): **Jo Anne Green**
No. of Rooms: **5**
No. of Private Baths: **3**
Max. No. Sharing Bath: **4**
Double/pb: **$45–$55**
Single/pb: **$30**
Double/sb: **$35**
Single/sb: **$30**
Open: **All year**
Breakfast: **Continental**
Credit Cards: **AMEX, MC, VISA**
Pets: **No**
Children: **Welcome**
Smoking: **Permitted**
Social Drinking: **Permitted**

This stick-style house has been lovingly restored and air-conditioned for your comfort. Inside the house, the decor includes wood carvings and art from all over the world. Guests are welcome to relax by the fireside and enjoy wine or soft drinks. Breakfast features fresh fruit, cereals, breads, and jam. Golf, tennis, boating, and hiking are nearby, in Bryan Park. UNC-Greensboro is nearby. There's a swimming pool on the premises.

Gingerbread Inn ✪

103 SOUTH CHURCH STREET, HERTFORD, NORTH CAROLINA 27944

Tel: **(919) 426-5809**
Host(s): **Jenny Harnisch**
Location: **68 mi. SW of Norfolk**
No. of Rooms: **3**
No. of Private Baths: **3**
Double/pb: **$40**
Single/pb: **$35**
Open: **All year**
Breakfast: **Full**
Credit Cards: **MC, VISA**
Pets: **No**
Children: **Welcome**
Smoking: **Permitted**
Social Drinking: **Permitted**
Foreign Languages: **German, Russian**

This beautifully restored turn-of-the-century home is on the local historic tour and boasts a wraparound porch with paired columns. The comfortably furnished rooms are spacious, with queen- or king-size beds and plush carpeting. The aroma of freshly baked gingerbread is something you can't miss during your stay. Your hostess even offers a souvenir cookie for the ride home.

The Hickory Bed & Breakfast ✪

464 7TH STREET SOUTH WEST, HICKORY, NORTH CAROLINA 28602

Tel: **(704) 324-0548**
Host(s): **Jane and Bill Mohney**
Location: **36 mi. N of Charlotte**
No. of Rooms: **4**
No. of Private Baths: **1**
Max. No. Sharing Bath: **6**
Double/pb: **$40**
Single/pb: **$30**
Double/sb: **$35**
Single/sb: **$25**
Open: **All year**
Breakfast: **Full**
Pets: **No**
Children: **Welcome (crib)**
Smoking: **Permitted**
Social Drinking: **Permitted**
Airport/Station Pickup: **Yes**

Bill and Jane Mohney invite you to their Georgian-style home, built in 1908. Downstairs there are three large rooms for relaxing. The parlor is a cozy room with comfortable furniture, and there is a library in the living room where you may choose from a variety of books. The dining room has a fireplace and is a lovely spot to enjoy a breakfast of homemade bread, bacon, and eggs. Sleeping quarters have fresh flowers in season and are furnished in a range of styles, from traditional to contemporary. Your hosts invite you to relax on the porches, and in the summer months a swimming pool surrounded by bushes, oaks, and grape vineyards is a fine place to spend the afternoon. The Hickory is near a lake, and is walking distance from downtown shops and restaurants.

Colonial Pines Inn ✪

BOX 2309, HIGHLANDS, NORTH CAROLINA 28741

Tel: **(704) 526-2060**
Best Time to Call: **Afternoons**
Host(s): **Chris and Donna Alley**
Location: **80 mi. SW of Asheville**
No. of Rooms: **7**
No. of Private Baths: **7**
Double/pb: **$58**
Single/pb: **$53**
Suites: **$70**
Guest Cottage: **$75, sleeps 4**
Open: **All year**
Reduced Rates: **Weekly; 15% in winter**
Breakfast: **Full**
Credit Cards: **MC, VISA**
Pets: **No**
Children: **Welcome**
Smoking: **No**
Social Drinking: **Permitted**

Located in a charming, uncommercial mountain resort town, this white Colonial is flanked by tall columns and is surrounded by two acres. The scenic view may be enjoyed from comfortable rocking chairs on the wide veranda. Donna, a former interior decorator, has furnished with antiques, art, and interesting accessories. Chris is a classical guitarist, woodworker, and great cook. The egg-'n'-sausage-'n'-cheese quiche, served at breakfast, is the best. Beverages and homemade breads are always available for snacking.

Marshall House ✪

P.O. BOX 606, HILL STREET, MARSHALL, NORTH CAROLINA 28753

Tel: **(704) 649-2999**
Best Time to Call: **Evenings**
Host(s): **Woody Cunningham**
Location: **18 mi. N of Asheville**
No. of Rooms: **8**
No. of Private Baths: **6**
Max. No. Sharing Bath: **6**
Double/pb: **$30–$35**
Single/pb: **$25–$30**
Double/sb: **$20–$25**
Single/sb: **$15–$20**
Open: **All year**
Reduced Rates: **Groups**
Breakfast: **Full**
Other Meals: **Available**
Pets: **Welcome**
Children: **Welcome**
Smoking: **Permitted**
Social Drinking: **Permitted**

Peace and tranquillity are yours to enjoy at Marshall House. The huge veranda offers an overview of the quaint village of Marshall, which is situated on the shores of the beautiful French Broad River. Built in 1902, the house still retains the grace of a bygone era. It is within a 30-minute drive of skiing, white-water rafting, hiking, fishing, and golf. Equally convenient is a choice of theater, musical events, historic home tours, the Cherokee Indian Reservation, and the Blue Ridge Parkway. Breakfast is a Southern feast of bacon, eggs, grits, muffins, juice, and beverage.

The Inn on Providence

6700 PROVIDENCE ROAD, MATTHEWS, NORTH CAROLINA 28105

Tel: **(704) 366-6700**
Host(s): **Darlene and Dan McNeill**
No. of Rooms: **4**
No. of Private Baths: **2**
Max. No. Sharing Bath: **4**
Double/pb: **$65**
Single/pb: **$65**
Double/sb: **$50**
Single/sb: **$50**
Open: **All year**
Reduced Rates: **Available**
Breakfast: **Full**
Credit Cards: **MC, VISA**
Pets: **No**
Children: **Welcome, over 11**
Smoking: **No**
Social Drinking: **Permitted**
Airport/Station Pickup: **Yes**

The Inn on Providence is a large, three-story Colonial nestled in South Charlotte, close to many amenities of the Queen City. The walnut-paneled library, sitting room with fireplace, and oak-floored dining room will make both vacationers and business executives feel at home.

The bedrooms are decorated with Early American antiques, and each features something special, such as a canopy bed or a sitting room. In warm weather, breakfast is served on the screened veranda, which is decorated with white wicker and paddle fans. The veranda is also a great place to sip afternoon tea while overlooking the gardens and swimming pool.

Woodside Inn

P.O. BOX 197, MILTON, NORTH CAROLINA 28305

Tel: **(919) 234-8646; 694-4450**
Best Time to Call: **Before 8 AM; after 4 PM**
Host(s): **Tom and Lib McPherson**
Location: **12 mi. E of Danville, Va.; 5 mi. from US 58**
No. of Rooms: **4**
No. of Private Baths: **1**
Max. No. Sharing Bath: **2**
Double/pb: **$52**
Single/pb: **$47**
Double/sb: **$52**
Single/sb: **$47**
Open: **All year**
Reduced Rates: **15% less, weekly**
Breakfast: **Full**
Other Meals: **Available**
Credit Cards: **MC, VISA**
Pets: **Small pets welcome**
Children: **Welcome**
Smoking: **Permitted**
Social Drinking: **Permitted**
Airport/Station Pickup: **Yes**

Built on a hill overlooking the rolling countryside, this 1838 Greek Revival manor house is furnished with elegant late Federal and American Empire antiques. The large bedrooms are air-conditioned for summer comfort and have fireplaces for chilly winter nights. Breakfast treats are Southern raised biscuits, quick breads, country ham, and pancakes. Complimentary beverages are offered, and laundry facilities are available. Tom is a County Supervisor; Lib directs a school nutrition program. They share interests in history, music, travel, golf, reading, and bridge. The on-premises restaurant serves lunch and dinner.

Morehead Manor ✪

107 NORTH 10TH STREET, MOREHEAD CITY, NORTH CAROLINA 28557

Tel: **(919) 726-0760**
Best Time to Call: **After 9 AM**
Host(s): **Danny and Judy Pridgen, James and Lisa Daniels**
No. of Rooms: **10**
No. of Private Baths: **1**
Max. No. Sharing Bath: **4**
Double/pb: **$50–$55**
Single/pb: **$45–$50**
Double/sb: **$45–$50**
Single/sb: **$40–$45**
Suites: **$90–$100**
Open: **All year**
Reduced Rates: **Weekly; off-season**

Breakfast: **Continental**
Credit Cards: **MC, VISA**
Pets: **Sometimes**
Children: **Welcome, over 12**
Smoking: **Permitted**
Social Drinking: **Permitted**
Airport/Station Pickup: **Yes**

Morehead Manor was built circa 1909; recently renovated, it is furnished with comfortable furnishings and accents of antique wood and brass. Three porches with white wooden swings, rocking chairs, and tables are perfect for enjoying the cool breezes. A large living room is also available for relaxing. The beach is just five minutes away, and downtown Morehead, the marinas, and many restaurants are within walking distance. Historic Beaufort is just a short drive across the bridge.

Pine Ridge B&B Inn

2893 WEST PINE STREET, MT. AIRY, NORTH CAROLINA 27030

Tel: **(919) 789-5034**
Host(s): **Ellen and Manford Haxton**
Location: **2 mi. from I-77**
No. of Rooms: **7**
No. of Private Baths: **5**
Max. No. Sharing Bath: **4**
Double/pb: **$75**
Double/sb: **$40**
Open: **All year**
Reduced Rates: **10%, Jan.–Mar.**
Breakfast: **Continental**
Other Meals: **Available**
Credit Cards: **MC, VISA**
Pets: **No**
Children: **Welcome (crib)**
Smoking: **Permitted**
Social Drinking: **Permitted**
Airport/Station Pickup: **Yes**

Luxury and elegance await you in this 40-year-old mansion set on eight acres in the shadow of the Blue Ridge Mountains. Each guest room is attractively decorated and has a telephone and cable TV. Read in the wood-paneled library, soak in the hot tub, work out on the Nautilus equipment in the exercise room, or swim in the backyard pool. Golf and tennis are available nearby. A few miles away are outlet stores, the world's largest open-face granite quarry, and the famous frescoes of Ashe County.

The Aerie ✪

509 POLLOCK STREET, NEW BERN, NORTH CAROLINA 28560

Tel: **(919) 636-5553**
Host(s): **Lois and Karl Taylor**
Location: **120 mi. SE of Raleigh**
No. of Rooms: **5**
No. of Private Baths: **5**
Double/pb: **$75**
Single/pb: **$52**
Open: **All year**
Breakfast: **Full**
Credit Cards: **AMEX, MC, VISA**

Pets: **No**
Children: **Welcome, over 6**
Smoking: **No**
Social Drinking: **Permitted**
Airport/Station Pickup: **Yes**

The sitting room of this Victorian mansion has beautiful oak floors accented by Oriental rugs. Furnishings are a blend of antiques and fine reproductions. The old mahogany player piano is a magnet for all to gather 'round and sing along. A sumptuous breakfast is served on a seven-foot harvest table. You can work off the calories by taking a walking tour of the historic district and a visit to famed Tryon Palace. Lois and Karl, innkeepers for years, often run seminars on the subject.

Kings Arms Inn ✪

212 POLLOCK STREET, NEW BERN, NORTH CAROLINA 28560

Tel: **(919) 638-4409**
Best Time to Call: **8 AM–8 PM**
Host(s): **David and Diana Parks**
No. of Rooms: **8**
No. of Private Baths: **8**
Double/pb: **$60–$62**
Single/pb: **$45**
Open: **All year**
Breakfast: **Continental**
Credit Cards: **AMEX, MC, VISA**
Pets: **Only Seeing-Eye dog**
Children: **Welcome (crib)**
Smoking: **Permitted**
Social Drinking: **Permitted**

The Kings Arms is named for an old town tavern said to have hosted members of the First Continental Congress. The inn boasts its own historic significance, as many of its rooms date back to the early 1800s. Today its rooms are available to those seeking superior accommodations in the historic district. The bedrooms have fireplaces, antiques, brass, canopied, or poster beds, plus color TV. Homemade biscuits and banana bread are brought to guests each morning. Your hosts will gladly direct you to the waterfront, Tryon Palace, and fine restaurants.

The Oakwood Inn ✪

411 NORTH BLOODWORTH STREET, RALEIGH, NORTH CAROLINA 27604

Tel: **(919) 832-9712**
Best Time to Call: **8 AM–noon; 3–10 PM**
Host(s): **Diana Newton**
No. of Rooms: **6**
No. of Private Baths: **2**
Max. No. Sharing Bath: **4**
Double/pb: **$70**
Single/pb: **$65**
Double/sb: **$60**
Single/sb: **$55**
Open: **All year**
Breakfast: **Full**
Credit Cards: **AMEX, MC, VISA**
Pets: **No**
Children: **Welcome, over 12**
Smoking: **Permitted**
Social Drinking: **Permitted**
Airport/Station Pickup: **Yes**

Built in 1871, the inn is listed on the National Register of Historic Places. Recently restored to their prior elegance, all the rooms are enhanced by the tasteful use of antique furnishings, appropriate draperies, and accessories. The inn is located within the 20-square-block area of homes built from 1879 to 1920, and visiting it is really like taking a step back in time into an era of horse-drawn carriages and gingerbread architecture. There are six colleges nearby offering cultural opportunities, and a number of museums for history buffs.

Eli Olive's ✪

3719 US 70 WEST, SMITHFIELD, NORTH CAROLINA 27577

Tel: **(919) 934-9823; 934-0246**
Host(s): **Kay and Taylor Jolliff**
Location: **½ mi. W of I-95**
No. of Rooms: **7**
No. of Private Baths: **7**
Double/pb: **$49**
Single/pb: **$42**
Open: **All year**
Reduced Rates: **10%, seniors**
Breakfast: **Full**
Other Meals: **Available**
Credit Cards: **MC, VISA**
Pets: **No**
Children: **Welcome**
Smoking: **Permitted**
Social Drinking: **Permitted**
Airport/Station Pickup: **Yes**

One of Johnston County's most celebrated citizens was Eli Olive, who in his day was famous for riding down the streets scattering silver coins for the children. The inn named in his honor is a restored two-story plantation home with fireplaces, handcrafts, and antebellum charm. Each guest room is named for a celebrated local and features North Carolina furnishings, linens, candles, and soaps. In the dining room, menu selections highlight specialties such as Smithfield ham, corn pudding, beer-battered Vidalia onions, fresh seafood, and peaches-and-cream pie. Your hosts will direct you to local sights such as the Ava Gardner Museum, Southland Winery, and Bentonville Battleground.

The Richmond Inn

101 PINE AVENUE, SPRUCE PINE, NORTH CAROLINA 28777

Tel: **(704) 765-6993**
Best Time to Call: **7 AM–7 PM**
Host(s): **Barbara and Dave Richmond**
Location: **4 mi. from Blue Ridge Pkwy., Exit 331**
No. of Rooms: **7**
No. of Private Baths: **7**
Double/pb: **$50–$60**
Single/pb: **$40–$45**
Open: **All year**
Breakfast: **Full**
Credit Cards: **MC, VISA**
Pets: **No**
Children: **Welcome**
Smoking: **Permitted**
Social Drinking: **Permitted**
Foreign Languages: **French, German**

Surrounded by towering pines, this white wooden house trimmed with black window shutters has a stone terrace and rock walls. It is furnished in a comfortable blend of antiques and family treasures. Dave is originally from England, so it is no surprise that a full British breakfast is often served. Most mornings, Barbara fixes a Southern repast with bacon, eggs, and grits. Spruce Pine is the mineral capital of the world, and panning for gemstones such as garnets and amethysts is a popular pastime. Hiking the Appalachian Trail, playing golf, or working out at your hosts' community spa will keep you in shape. Internationally known artists schedule shows throughout the year.

Little Warren ✪

304 EAST PARK AVENUE, TARBORO, NORTH CAROLINA 27886

Tel: **(919) 823-1314**
Host(s): **Patsy and Tom Miller**
Location: **20 mi. E of Rocky Mount**
No. of Rooms: **3**
No. of Private Baths: **3**
Double/pb: **$45**
Single/pb: **$38**
Open: **All year**
Breakfast: **Full**
Credit Cards: **MC, VISA**
Pets: **No**
Children: **Welcome, over 4**
Smoking: **Permitted**
Social Drinking: **Permitted**
Airport/Station Pickup: **Yes**
Foreign Languages: **Spanish**

Little Warren is actually a large and gracious family home built in 1913. It is located along the Albemarle Trail in Tarboro's Historic District. The deeply set wraparound porch overlooks one of the last originally chartered town commons still in existence. Inside, you'll find rooms of beautiful antiques from England and America, many of which can be purchased. In the morning, choose from a full English, Southern, or Continental breakfast.

Mill Farm Inn ✪

P.O. BOX 1251, TRYON, NORTH CAROLINA 28782

Tel: **(704) 859-6992**
Best Time to Call: **Mornings**
Host(s): **Chip and Penny Kessler**
Location: **45 mi. SE of Asheville**
No. of Rooms: **8**
No. of Private Baths: **8**
Double/pb: **$48**
Single/pb: **$40**
Suites: **$70–$90**
Open: **Mar. 1–Jan. 1**
Reduced Rates: **10%, seniors**
Breakfast: **Continental**
Pets: **No**
Children: **Welcome**
Smoking: **Permitted**
Social Drinking: **Permitted**
Foreign Languages: **French**

The Pacolet River flows past the edge of this three-and-one-half-acre property in the foothills of the Blue Ridge Mountains. Sitting porches and the living room with fireplace are fine spots to relax. A hearty breakfast of fresh fruit, cereal, English muffins, preserves, and coffee is served. Craft shops, galleries, and antiquing will keep you busy.

Anderson Guest House ✪

520 ORANGE STREET, WILMINGTON, NORTH CAROLINA 28401

Tel: **(919) 343-8128**
Best Time to Call: **8 AM–5 PM**
Host(s): **Landon and Connie Anderson**
No. of Rooms: **2**
No. of Private Baths: **2**
Double/pb: **$55**
Single/pb: **$50**
Open: **All year**
Breakfast: **Full**
Pets: **Sometimes**
Children: **Welcome**
Smoking: **Permitted**
Social Drinking: **Permitted**
Airport/Station Pickup: **Yes**

This 19th-century town house has a private guest house overlooking a garden. The bedrooms have ceiling fans, fireplaces, and air-conditioning. Enjoy cool drinks upon arrival and a liqueur before bed. Breakfast specialties are eggs Mornay, blueberry cobbler, and crêpes. Your hostess can point out the sights of this historic town and direct you to the beaches.

Pilgrims Rest ✪

600 WEST NASH STREET, WILSON, NORTH CAROLINA 27893

Tel: **(919) 243-4447**
Host(s): **Doug and June Stewart**
Location: **50 mi. E of Raleigh**
No. of Rooms: **3**
No. of Private Baths: **1**
Max. No. Sharing Bath: **4**
Double/pb: **$49**
Single/pb: **$49**
Double/sb: **$39**
Single/sb: **$39**
Open: **All year**
Breakfast: **Continental**
Credit Cards: **MC, VISA**
Pets: **Sometimes**
Children: **Welcome**
Smoking: **Permitted**
Social Drinking: **Permitted**
Airport/Station Pickup: **Yes**

The Stewarts welcome you to their large Victorian surrounded by flowering shrubs and old trees. The house is in Wilson's historic district and is listed on the National Register of Historic Places. After a day of sightseeing you're welcome to pull up a comfortable chair on the beautiful porch. Your hosts will gladly direct you to a famous tobacco market, museums, and numerous places to find interesting antiques.

NORTH DAKOTA

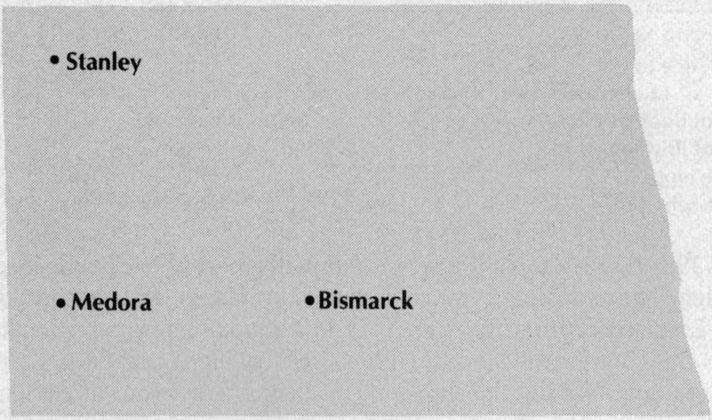

• Stanley

• Medora

• Bismarck

The Rough Riders
MEDORA, NORTH DAKOTA 58645

Tel: **(701) 623-4422**
Host(s): **Sherwin Dockter**
Location: **160 mi. W of Bismarck**
No. of Rooms: **9**
No. of Baths: **9**
Double/pb: **$43–$50**
Single/pb: **$36**

Open: **May 15–Sept. 7**
Other Meals: **Available**
Credit Cards: **AMEX, MC, VISA**
Pets: **No**
Children: **Welcome**
Smoking: **Permitted**
Social Drinking: **Permitted**

Located at the center of town, the hotel is constructed inside and out of rough lumber. The facade bears the many branding marks of cattle barons, including that of Theodore Roosevelt. The "cowtown" atmosphere has been retained, down to the wooden sidewalk. The center staircase leads to the guest quarters, which are furnished with antiques. Don't miss the Outdoor Memorial Musical, an extravaganza complete with horses, stagecoaches, and a rousing tribute to Teddy

Roosevelt. The Museum of Wildlife, the Doll House Museum, and the spectacular beauty of the Badlands will make your visit memorable.

The Triple T. Ranch

ROUTE 1, BOX 93, STANLEY, NORTH DAKOTA 58784

Tel: **(701) 628-2418**
Best Time to Call: **8 AM–noon**
Host(s): **Joyce and Fred Evans**
Location: **60 mi. W of Minot**
No. of Rooms: **2**
Max. No. Sharing Bath: **4**
Double/pb: **$30**
Single/pb: **$25**
Open: **All year**
Reduced Rates: **Available**
Breakfast: **Full**
Pets: **Sometimes**
Children: **Welcome (crib)**
Smoking: **No**
Social Drinking: **No**

You're warmly invited to come to Joyce and Fred's rustic ranch home, where you're welcome to take a seat in front of the stone fireplace, put your feet up, and relax. There's a lovely view of the hills and the valley, and their herd of cattle is an impressive sight. Lake Sakakawea, for seasonal recreation such as fishing and swimming, is 11 miles away. Indian powwows, area rodeos, and hunting for Indian artifacts are fun. The State Fair is held every July.

OHIO

Ohio Valley Bed & Breakfast

6876 TAYLOR MILL ROAD, INDEPENDENCE, KENTUCKY 41051

Tel: **(606) 356-7865**
Coordinators: **Nancy Cully and Sallie Lotz**
States/Regions Covered: **Northern Kentucky; Greater Cincinnati, Ohio, Southeastern Indiana**

Rate (Single/Double):

Modest:	**$25**	**$30**
Average:	**$30**	**$40**
Luxury:	**$40**	**$65**

Credit Cards: **MC, VISA**

Nancy and Sallie have host homes ranging from a restored log cabin (circa 1820) on 95 acres offering country living, horseback riding, bird watching and canoeing to an 18-acre gentleman's farm with fishing lakes and a small game preserve. Others are convenient to the area's attractions, which include professional football and baseball, cultural activities, the University of Cincinnati, Xavier University, and Northern Kentucky University. Regattas and paddleboat cruises are delightful Ohio River attractions. There's a surcharge of up to $10 for one night's stay in some B&Bs.

Helen's Hospitality House ✪

1096 PALMETTO, AKRON, OHIO 44306

Tel: **(216) 724-7151; 3034**
Best Time to Call: **8 AM–8 PM**
Host(s): **Helen Claytor**
No. of Rooms: **2**
No. of Private Baths: **1**
Max. No. Sharing Bath: **4**
Double/pb: **$30**
Single/pb: **$25**
Double/sb: **$30**
Single/sb: **$25**
Open: **All year**
Reduced Rates: **Weekly**
Breakfast: **Full**
Pets: **No**
Children: **No**
Smoking: **No**
Social Drinking: **Permitted**
Airport/Station Pickup: **Yes**

Located in a quiet neighborhood on a dead-end street, Helen's house is a bit of country in the city. It is a renovated old farmhouse furnished with antiques and reproductions. On warm days, breakfast is served on the screened, glass-enclosed porch. Quaker Square, Akron University, the Firestone PGA, and Portage Lakes are just a few of the local attractions.

Portage House ✪

601 COPLEY ROAD, STATE ROUTE 162, AKRON, OHIO 44320

Tel: **(216) 535-1952**
Best Time to Call: **Before 11 PM**
Host(s): **Jeanne and Harry Pinnick**
Location: **2 mi. from I-77**
No. of Rooms: **5**
No. of Private Baths: **1½**
Max. No. Sharing Bath: **7**
Double/pb: **$28**
Single/pb: **$22**
Double/sb: **$28**
Single/sb: **$22**
Open: **Feb. 1–Nov. 30**
Reduced Rates: **$3 off 2nd night**
Breakfast: **Full**
Other Meals: **Available**
Pets: **Yes**
Children: **Welcome (crib)**
Smoking: **Permitted**
Social Drinking: **Permitted**
Foreign Languages: **French, Spanish**

Steeped in history, nestled in a parklike setting, this gracious Tudor home dates back to 1917. There is a stone wall down the street that was the western boundary of the United States in 1785. Harry is a physics professor at the university, and Jeanne is a gracious hostess. The coffeepot is always on, refreshments are available, and if bread is being baked, you'll be given some with butter. It's close to Akron University.

Vickery's Bed & Breakfast ✪

4942 STATE ROUTE 7 NORTH, ANDOVER, OHIO 44003

Tel: **(216) 293-6875**
Host(s): **Robert and Ruth Vickery**
Location: **60 mi. E of Cleveland**
No. of Rooms: **2**
Max. No. Sharing Bath: **4**
Double/sb: **$25**
Single/sb: **$18**
Open: **All year**
Breakfast: **Full**
Pets: **Sometimes**
Children: **Welcome**
Smoking: **Permitted**
Social Drinking: **Permitted**

Painted yellow and trimmed with white shutters, this 100-year-old home is set on 100 acres where there's something for everyone. You may play volleyball or horseshoes or take a ride on the pond in a paddleboat. If you prefer, just walk the land and breathe deeply of fresh air. The bedrooms have floral wallpaper, tie-back curtains, and antique dressers. Breakfast specialties, such as blueberry pancakes and bacon, are served in the cozy dining room. It is five minutes from Pymatuning Lake, where a spectacular spillway of fish and ducks attracts many visitors. You are welcome to use the kitchen for light snacks and the laundry to freshen your travel wardrobe.

Murbach House ✪

504 NORTH DEFIANCE STREET, ARCHBOLD, OHIO 43502

Tel: **(419) 445-5195**
Host(s): **Gary and Judy Sears**
Location: **10 mi. from Ohio Tpk, Exit 3**
No. of Rooms: **5**
No. of Private Baths: **1**
Max. No. Sharing Bath: **4**
Double/pb: **$48**
Single/pb: **$43**
Double/sb: **$45**
Single/sb: **$40**
Open: **All year**
Breakfast: **Full**
Pets: **No**
Children: **Welcome, over 5**
Smoking: **Permitted**
Social Drinking: **Permitted**

Built in the late 1800s, this house, with its large, pillared front porch, has retained its lovely oak woodwork and stained-glass windows. The interior is furnished with antiques and equipped with such modern conveniences as an elevator and air-conditioning. In pleasant weather, wander across the lush lawn to the little path that leads to a fragrant, secluded nook—a special place to daydream. You may make use of the TV, piano, and laundry facilities.

Williams House ✪

249 VINEWOOD, AVON LAKE, OHIO 44012

Tel: **(216) 933-5089**
Best Time to Call: **4–9 PM**
Host(s): **Edred and Margaret Williams**
Location: **20 mi. W of Cleveland**
No. of Rooms: **1**
No. of Private Baths: **1**
Double/pb: **$40**
Single/pb: **$25**
Open: **Closed Christmas, Easter weeks**
Reduced Rates: **20%, seniors**
Breakfast: **Full**
Pets: **No**
Children: **No**
Smoking: **No**
Social Drinking: **Permitted**
Airport/Station Pickup: **Yes**

Located a mile from the Lake Erie public beach, Edred and Margaret live in a quiet residential neighborhood. The house is comfortably decorated in a harmonious blend of styles. They serve beverages and snacks upon your arrival, and will help you plan a pleasant visit. Breakfast is a dandy, from juice to cereal to eggs to bacon to coffee or tea.

The Winkeljohn House ✪

416 EAST ANTHONY, CELINA, OHIO 45822

Tel: **(419) 586-2155**
Best Time to Call: **After 5 PM**
Host(s): **Mary Ellen Winkeljohn**
Location: **70 mi. NW of Dayton**
No. of Rooms: **2**
Max. No. Sharing Bath: **4**
Double/sb: **$35**
Single/sb: **$30**
Open: **All year**
Breakfast: **Continental**
Pets: **No**
Children: **No**
Smoking: **No**
Social Drinking: **Permitted**

Located on a quiet residential street where a leisurely stroll may still be enjoyed, this neat-as-a-pin B&B furnished in Early American style personifies our "4 C's": Comfort, Cleanliness, Cordiality, and Cost-value! Mary Ellen has traveled widely and knows exactly how to please guests. She enjoys crafts, sewing, and baking, and her idea of a pleasant evening is talking with her visitors and serving cold drinks and hot popcorn. She'll be happy to direct you to some exceptional museums in the area as well as a most interesting Amish settlement in nearby Berne, Indiana.

Private Lodgings, Inc.

P.O. BOX 18590, CLEVELAND, OHIO 44118

Tel: **(216) 321-3213**
Best Time to Call: **9 AM–5 PM**
Coordinator: **Jane McCarroll**
States/Regions Covered: **Cleveland**

Rate (Single/Double):
Modest: **$20** **$25**
Average: **$40** **$50**
Luxury: **$60** **$65**
Credit Cards: **No**

This is a city with world-renowned cultural and biomedical resources, as well as major corporations and recreational areas. Special attention is given to the needs of relocating and visiting professionals, outpatients, and relatives of hospital in-patients, as well as vacationers. Every effort is made to accommodate persons with physical handicaps. Discounted rates are provided for extended stays. Case Western Reserve, John Carroll, and Cleveland State universities are convenient to the B&Bs.

The Sarah Frisch House ✪

1564 SOUTH TAYLOR ROAD, CLEVELAND, OHIO 44118

Tel: **(216) 321-5694**
Host(s): **Sarah Frisch**
Location: **4 mi. from I-90**
No. of Rooms: **2**
No. of Private Baths: **1**
Max. No. Sharing Bath: **3**
Double/pb: **$45**
Single/pb: **$35**
Double/sb: **$40**
Single/sb: **$25–$35**

Open: **All year**
Reduced Rates: **Available**
Breakfast: **Continental**
Other Meals: **Available**
Pets: **Sometimes**
Children: **Welcome**
Smoking: **No**
Social Drinking: **Permitted**
Airport/Station Pickup: **Yes**

Sarah's brick-and-shingle, comfortably furnished bungalow has a large yard and pretty garden. Sarah will make you feel at home. It is convenient to good shopping, fine restaurants, sports facilities, and all the cultural activities that Cleveland is famous for. Complimentary fruit and cheese are offered.

Columbus Bed & Breakfast

763 S. THIRD STREET, GERMAN VILLAGE, COLUMBUS, OHIO 43206

Tel: **(614) 443-3680 or 444-8888**
Coordinator(s): **Fred Holdridge, Howard Burns**
States/Regions Covered: **Columbus**

Rates (Single/Double):
Average: **$20** **$40**
Credit Cards: **No**

Historic German Village is a registered National Historic Area. It's close to downtown Columbus but a century away in character. Small brick houses, brick sidewalks and streets, and wrought-iron fences combine to create an Old World atmosphere. Charming shops and restaurants are within easy walking distance.

Slavka's Bed & Breakfast ✪

180 REINHARD AVENUE, COLUMBUS, OHIO 43206

Tel: **(614) 443-6076**
Best Time to Call: **10 AM–10 PM**
Host(s): **Gloria Slavka**
Location: **½ mi. from Rte. 70**
No. of Rooms: **3**
Max. No. Sharing Bath: **5**
Double/sb: **$35**
Single/sb: **$25**
Open: **All year**
Breakfast: **Full**
Pets: **Sometimes**
Children: **Welcome**
Smoking: **Permitted**
Social Drinking: **Permitted**
Airport/Station Pickup: **Yes**
Foreign Languages: **Serbo-Croatian**

This 100-year-old home is located by the park in German Village, a restored historic community. Slavka, a watercolorist, specializes in paintings of florals, cityscapes, and portraits. She still finds time to spoil her guests with delicious Yugoslavian recipes at breakfast. Complimentary snacks and soft drinks may be enjoyed on the lovely garden patio.

Studio 12 Bed and Breakfast ✪

2850 BAILEY ROAD, CUYAHOGA FALLS, OHIO 44221

Tel: **(216) 928-5843**
Host(s): **Edith L. Stinaff**
Location: **6 mi. N of Akron; 7 mi. from I-80**
No. of Rooms: **2**
Max. No. Sharing Bath: **4**
Double/sb: **$30**
Single/sb: **$22**
Open: **All year**
Reduced Rates: **10%, seniors; after 1 night**
Breakfast: **Full**
Pets: **Sometimes**
Children: **Welcome (crib)**
Smoking: **No**
Social Drinking: **Permitted**
Airport/Station Pickup: **Yes**

Edith Stinaff offers attractive accommodations for guests in the new addition to her home, a 1930s brick bungalow. Guest quarters consist of two bedrooms on the second floor with a studio living room and bath. In the morning your hostess serves a hearty breakfast of scrambled eggs, fresh fruit, bacon, and warm muffins or toast. Studio 12 is convenient to the University of Akron, Kent State University, Blossom Music Center, and Hale Farm.

Hill View Acres ✪

7320 OLD TOWN ROAD, EAST FULTONHAM, OHIO 43735

Tel: **(614) 849-2728**
Host(s): **Jim and Dawn Graham**
Location: **10 mi. SW of Zanesville**
No. of Rooms: **2**
Max. No. Sharing Bath: **4**
Double/sb: **$32**
Single/sb: **$25**
Open: **All year**
Reduced Rates: **10% after 2 nights; seniors**
Breakfast: **Full**
Other Meals: **Available**
Pets: **Sometimes**
Children: **Sometimes**
Smoking: **Permitted**
Social Drinking: **Permitted**

Hill View is a comfortable, unpretentious large white house situated on 21 acres with a fishing pond. Homemade breads and specialties such as crispy-apple-sausage bake are breakfast fare. You are welcome to relax on the deck, play the piano, or watch TV. Dawn is a former teacher; Jim is a retired personnel specialist. Their interests are cooking, crafts, and genealogy.

Quiet Country

14758 TR 453, LAKEVILLE, OHIO 44638

Tel: **(216) 378-3882**
Best Time to Call: **Mornings**
Host(s): **Jane Bowman**
Location: **70 mi. SW of Cleveland**
No. of Rooms: **4**
No. of Private Baths: **½**
Max. No. Sharing Bath: **3**
Double/pb: **$65**
Double/sb: **$50**
Single/sb: **$50**
Open: **Spring–fall**
Breakfast: **Full**
Pets: **No**
Children: **No**
Smoking: **No**
Social Drinking: **No**

Located between Millersburg and Loudonville, this lovely restored farmhouse is set among 100 acres of rolling hills and woods. Relax on the patio and watch the swallows over the pond or spend some time on the versatile sport court. Inside you'll find a quiet, comfortable atmosphere that features many of the original floors and windows, Williamsburg wallpapers, and a smattering of antiques. Breakfast is served in the kitchen, complete with fireplace and rocker, or in the dining room overlooking the old barn and grazing horses. Farm-fresh eggs, local meats, and seasonal fruits are usuals on the menu. Two state parks and the Amish area, with its quaint shops and restaurants, are within easy reach.

Grandma Betty's

ROUTE 1, BOX 60A, LEWISVILLE, OHIO 43754

Tel: **(614) 567-3465**
Best Time to Call: **5:30–10:30 PM**
Host(s): **Betty Hogue**
Location: **4 mi. W of Woodsfield; 26 mi. from I-77**
No. of Rooms: **3**
Max. No. Sharing Bath: **5**
Double/sb: **$35**
Single/sb: **$30**
Open: **All year**
Reduced Rates: **10%, seniors**
Breakfast: **Full**
Credit Cards: **MC, VISA**
Pets: **Sometimes**
Children: **Welcome**
Smoking: **No**
Social Drinking: **Permitted**

This two-story, spic-and-span country home is surrounded by the scenic beauty of Monroe County. It is attractively decorated with an artful mix of traditional and Early American furniture, handmade quilts, plants, and dried-flower arrangements. Guests may choose between a conventional bed or a water bed. Betty, who looks too young to be a grandma, provides a game room complete with stereo, exercise equipment, and pool table; treat yourself to a visit to her on-premises beauty salon. In summer, the backyard swimming pool is a popular gathering spot. Nearby attractions include the Parry Museum, Piatt Park, Monroe Lake, and Hannibal Locks and Dam.

Happy Hill ✪

1 LEXINGTON ONTARIO-ROAD, ROUTE 8, MANSFIELD, OHIO 44904

Tel: **(419) 884-3916**
Host(s): **Bill and Sam Masur**
Location: **4 mi. from I-71, Exit Route 13**
No. of Rooms: **3**
No. of Private Baths: **2**
Max. No. Sharing Bath: **4**
Double/pb: **$42**
Single/pb: **$27**
Double/sb: **$40**
Single/sb: **$25**
Open: **All year**
Breakfast: **Continental**
Pets: **Sometimes**
Children: **Welcome (crib)**
Smoking: **No**
Social Drinking: **Permitted**

This sprawling brick ranch home is set on six acres in the picturesque village of Lexington. The rooms are elegantly appointed with antiques. After a day at the local racetrack, come home for a swim in a huge private swimming pool. In winter, enjoy a hot drink in front of the fire after a day on the ski slopes. Your hosts grow berries on the grounds, and you can taste them in the Blueberry Buckel, the breakfast specialty of the house.

Locust Hill ✪

1659 EAST US 22-3, MORROW, OHIO 45152

Tel: **(513) 899-2749**
Best Time to Call: **Evenings**
Host(s): **Gail Istler**
Location: **10 mi. NE of Cincinnati**
No. of Rooms: **3**
No. of Private Baths: **2**
Max. No. Sharing Bath: **2**
Double/pb: **$45**
Single/pb: **$35**
Double/sb: **$45**
Single/sb: **$35**
Open: **All year**
Breakfast: **Full**
Pets: **No**
Children: **Welcome, over 10**
Smoking: **Permitted**
Social Drinking: **Permitted**
Airport/Station Pickup: **Yes**

Locust Hill is a Victorian house and farm, complete with fields, family pets, and barns. Your hostess loves crafts and has decorated the house with stenciling, quilts, wicker, and many antiques. A sailboat is available for your use at Cowan Lake, which is a 20-minute drive from the house. Bicycles are available for exploring the 27 miles of winding trail along the Miami River. Picnic lunches will gladly be provided. Other local activities include antiquing, canoeing, and touring the Fort Ancient Park and Indian Museum. A grill and picnic table are available on the patio, and everyone is welcome to cook out. It is ten minutes to historic Lebanon and the Kings Island Amusement Park.

The Bayberry Inn ✪

25675 STATE ROUTE 41 NORTH, PEEBLES, OHIO 45660

Tel: **(513) 587-2221**
Host(s): **Marilyn and Larry Bagford**
Location: **75 mi. E of Cincinnati**
No. of Rooms: **3**
Max. No. Sharing Bath: **6**
Double/sb: **$35**
Single/sb: **$25**
Open: **May 15–Oct. 15**
Breakfast: **Full**
Pets: **Sometimes**
Children: **Welcome**
Smoking: **No**
Social Drinking: **Permitted**

If you expect to find warm hospitality, cozy accommodations with comfortable appointments, and a front porch on which to relax after a hearty old-fashioned breakfast, you won't be disappointed in Marilyn and Larry's Victorian farmhouse. It's located in Adams County, the hub for those with geological, historical, recreational, and agricultural interests. You are certain to enjoy Serpent Mound, Seven Caves, winery tours, riverboat rides, and outdoor theater productions.

Tudor Country Inn ✪

BOX 113, PETTISVILLE, OHIO 43553

Tel: **(419) 445-2351**
Best Time to Call: **8:30 AM–9 PM**
Host(s): **LeAnna and Dale Gautsche**
Location: **30 mi. W of Toledo; 5 mi. from Ohio Tpk**
No. of Rooms: **2**
Max. No. Sharing Bath: **4**
Double/sb: **$40**
Single/sb: **$35**
Open: **All year**
Breakfast: **Full**
Pets: **Sometimes**
Children: **Welcome**
Smoking: **No**
Social Drinking: **No**

LeAnna and Dale were restaurant owners until they opened this English Tudor inn. It is set on the edge of a small village, surrounded by farmland in the heart of the Mennonite community. Besides soaking in the hot tub, you may lounge in the great room, where snacks are served in the evenings and a fire burns in winter. Breakfast often includes "Belly Stickers," a creamy-bottom tart, and homemade raised donuts. Local attractions include a farm, craft shops, a country store, and an ice-cream parlor, all in the Pennsylvania Dutch style.

Inn at the Green

500 SOUTH MAIN STREET, POLAND, OHIO 44514

Tel: **(216) 757-4688**
Best Time to Call: **After 12 PM**
Host(s): **Ginny and Steve Meloy**
Location: **7 mi. SE of Youngstown**
No. of Rooms: **4**
No. of Private Baths: **2**
Max. No. Sharing Bath: **4**
Double/pb: **$50**
Single/pb: **$45**
Double/sb: **$40**
Single/sb: **$35**
Open: **All year**
Breakfast: **Continental**
Other Meals: **No**
Credit Cards: **MC, VISA**
Pets: **No**
Children: **Welcome, over 10**
Smoking: **Permitted**
Social Drinking: **Permitted**

The Inn at the Green is an 1876 Victorian town house located on the south end of the village green. The rooms have the grandeur of bygone days, with original moldings, 12-foot ceilings, and original poplar floors. There are five Italian marble fireplaces and extensive public rooms furnished with gracious antiques. Guests are welcome to relax in the parlor, sitting room, and library. Sleeping quarters are furnished with poster beds, Sealy Posturepedic mattresses, and antiques. Coffee, croissants, muffins, and French jam are served in the greeting room in winter and on the wicker-furnished porch during moderate weather. Enjoy a glass of sherry on the porch overlooking the garden before dinner. Your hosts will gladly direct you to gourmet dining as well as cross-country ski trails, golf, tennis, and the Butler Institute, home of one of the nation's finest American art collections.

The Vineyard ✪

BOX 283, PUT-IN-BAY, OHIO 43456

Tel: **(419) 285-6181**
Host(s): **Barbi and Mark Barnhill**
Location: **An island 35 mi. E of Toledo**
No. of Rooms: **3**
No. of Private Baths: **2**
Max. No. Sharing Bath: **4**
Double/pb: **$65**
Double/sb: **$50**
Single/sb: **$50**
Open: **Mid-Apr.–Oct.**
Reduced Rates: **10%, seniors**
Breakfast: **Full**
Pets: **Sometimes**
Children: **No**
Smoking: **No**
Social Drinking: **Permitted**
Airport/Station Pickup: **Yes**

This 130-year-old woodframe house is set on 20 acres of island seclusion. Your hosts grow Catawba grapes for the local winery, which is part of the region's famous wine industry. Guests are greeted with wine and cheese and shown to newly renovated bedrooms furnished with family antiques. You are invited to sun and swim on a private beach after a day of touring. Local attractions include a picturesque harbor and a monument offering a view of Lake Erie's islands.

Pipe Creek ✪

2719 COLUMBUS AVENUE, SANDUSKY, OHIO 44870

Tel: **(419) 626-2067**
Best Time to Call: **Before 5 PM**
Host(s): **Beryl and Carl Dureck**
Location: **55 mi. W of Cleveland**
No. of Rooms: **3**
Max. No. Sharing Bath: **6**
Double/sb: **$40**
Open: **May–Oct.**
Breakfast: **Full**
Pets: **No**
Children: **Welcome, over 11**
Smoking: **Permitted**
Social Drinking: **Permitted**

Pipe Creek is a Queen Anne Victorian set on a quiet acre of land, surrounded by large trees and a gentle creek. The rooms are large and airy, furnished in fine antiques. Little extras, such as fresh flowers and candy, make you feel like an honored guest. Beryl and Carl invite you to share a glass of wine on the patio or to bask in the afternoon sun out in the backyard. They prepare a hearty breakfast from scratch, and you are sure to taste the care and patience in the cooking. Situated at the gateway to the Lake Erie islands, you'll find Put-in-Bay, Cedar Point Amusement Park, and Edison's birthplace all nearby.

Colonial Manor ✪

6075 BUFFHAM ROAD, SEVILLE, OHIO 44273

Tel: **(216) 769-3464**
Best Time to Call: **8 AM; after 5 PM**
Host(s): **Jane and Herman Perry**
Location: **15 mi. W of Akron**
No. of Rooms: **2**
Max. No. Sharing Bath: **4**
Double/sb: **$35**
Single/sb: **$30**
Open: **May–Nov. 1**
Breakfast: **Full**
Pets: **Welcome**
Children: **Welcome**
Smoking: **Permitted**
Social Drinking: **Permitted**

Spend the night in a comfortable room away from noisy highways. There are 63 acres of farmland to wander and an endless amount of fresh air to breathe. Your hosts enjoy entertaining in their 100-year-old Colonial, and serve specialties of the house for breakfast each morning. The manor is close to the Amish country, several historical sights, and small towns.

3 B's Bed 'n' Breakfast ✪

103 RACE STREET, SPRING VALLEY, OHIO 45370

Tel: **(513) 862-4241 or 878-9944**
Best Time to Call: **After 5 PM**
Host(s): **Pat and Herb Boettcher**
Location: **16 mi. SE of Dayton**
No. of Rooms: **3**
Max. No. Sharing Bath: **4**
Double/sb: **$35–$40**
Single/sb: **$28–$33**
Open: **All year**
Reduced Rates: **15% weekly**
Breakfast: **Full**
Other Meals: **Available**
Pets: **Sometimes**
Children: **Welcome, over 4**
Smoking: **Permitted**
Social Drinking: **Permitted**
Airport/Station Pickup: **Yes**

This restored 19th-century farmhouse is a great place to unwind. The rooms are spacious and airy, and abound with family heirlooms and homemade crafts. The quilts on the beds are handmade. Nearby attractions include historic Lebanon, Kings Island, Dayton's Air Force Museum, and the antique shops at Waynesville. Pat and Herb are retired from the Air Force and look forward to visiting with you. Wright State University is nearby.

Shirlee's Chambers ✪

535 ADELAIDE NORTH EAST, WARREN, OHIO 44483

Tel: **(216) 372-1118**
Host(s): **Shirlee and Wayne Chambers**
Location: **7 mi. from I-80**
No. of Rooms: **3**
Max. No. Sharing Bath: **3**
Double/sb: **$35**
Single/sb: **$29**
Open: **All year**
Reduced Rates: **10%, seniors**
Breakfast: **Full**
Pets: **No**
Children: **Welcome, over 12**
Smoking: **Permitted**
Social Drinking: **Permitted**
Airport/Station Pickup: **Yes**

Shirlee welcomes you to her Colonial home with wine, cheese, or tea and cookies. Her guest rooms are comfortably furnished. Start the day with a French mushroom omelet, the specialty of the house. Your hosts can direct you to the many nearby antique shops. Local attractions include summer theater and fine dining.

Locust Lane Farm ✪

5590 KESSLER COWLESVILLE ROAD, WEST MILTON, OHIO 45383

Tel: **(513) 698-4743**
Best Time to Call: **Early morning; late evening**
Host(s): **Ruth Shoup**
Location: **7 mi. SW of Troy**
No. of Rooms: **3**
No. of Private Baths: **1**
Max. No. Sharing Bath: **4**
Double/pb: **$30**
Single/pb: **$25**
Double/sb: **$25**
Single/sb: **$20**
Open: **All year**
Breakfast: **Full**
Pets: **No**
Children: **Welcome (high chair)**
Smoking: **No**
Social Drinking: **Permitted**

Enjoy a peaceful night in a big old farmhouse, tucked away in a locust grove, set on 58 acres in the country. This air-conditioned house is tastefully decorated with family antiques. Your host offers fluffy bath towels, extra pillows, and goodies such as hot spiced cider, quick breads, and iced tea in the afternoon. Ruth loves entertaining and serves a farm-style breakfast of fresh fruit, muffins, eggs, homemade breads, and sweet rolls. In the warmer weather, breakfast is served on a lovely screened porch. Locust Lane is convenient to Milton and Troy, and four restaurants are located within two miles.

Priscilla's Bed & Breakfast ✪

5 SOUTH WEST STREET, WESTERVILLE, OHIO 43081

Tel: **(614) 882-3910**
Best Time to Call: **10 AM–5 PM**
Host(s): **Priscilla H. Curtis**
Location: **10 mi. N of Columbus**
No. of Rooms: **2**
Max. No. Sharing Bath: **3**
Double/sb: **$35**
Single/sb: **$25**
Guest Cottage: **$35; sleeps 2**
Open: **All year**
Reduced Rates: **15%, weekly**
Breakfast: **Continental**
Pets: **Sometimes**
Children: **Welcome**
Smoking: **Permitted**
Social Drinking: **Permitted**
Airport/Station Pickup: **Yes**

Located in a historic area adjacent to Otterbein Campus, this 1854 home, surrounded by a white picket fence, abounds with antiques and collectibles. Guests are welcome to borrow bicycles, use the patio, enjoy concerts in the adjoining park, walk to the Benjamin Hanby Museum or the quaint shops, or just stay "home" and relax. Priscilla is an authority on miniatures and dollhouse construction. Everyone enjoys browsing through her on-premises shop.

The Howey House

340 NORTH BEVER STREET, WOOSTER, OHIO 44691

Tel: **(216) 264-8231**
Host(s): **James and Joe Howey**
Location: **60 mi. S of Cleveland**
No. of Rooms: **4**
No. of Private Baths: **1**
Max. No. Sharing Bath: **6**
Double/sb: **$34**
Single/sb: **$24**
Suites: **$45**
Open: **All year**
Breakfast: **Continental**
Pets: **No**
Children: **Welcome, over 12**
Smoking: **No**
Social Drinking: **No**

This 137-year-old Victorian Gothic Revival home is located on Route 30 between Canton and Mansfield. The house has been recently restored, and each room is furnished with comfortable family pieces. Your hosts offer an assortment of pastries, fruit juice, fresh fruit, and freshly brewed coffee for breakfast. Howey House is located near the College of Wooster, the Ohio Agricultural Research and Development Center, and the Amish Country. Several fine restaurants and downtown Wooster are within walking distance.

Hattle House ✪

502 NORTH KING STREET, XENIA, OHIO 45385

Tel: **(513) 372-2315**
Host(s): **Mary and Bill Hattle**
No. of Rooms: **3**
No. of Private Baths: **3**
Double/pb: **$40**
Single/pb: **$35**
Open: **All year**
Breakfast: **Continental**
Pets: **No**
Children: **Welcome (crib)**
Smoking: **Permitted**
Social Drinking: **Permitted**

This 100-year-old Victorian home is furnished with fine period antiques. Bedroom accommodations are large and comfortable. Xenia is the home of the epic outdoor drama *Blue Jacket,* shown June through September. Other attractions include Dayton Air Force Museum, Kings Island, Cincinnati Riverfront Stadium and Zoo, and numerous state parks. A treat for history buffs is a visit to Lebanon or Waynesville, the antiques capitals of the Midwest.

For key to listings, see inside front or back cover.

✪ This star means that rates are guaranteed through December 31, 1988 to any guest making a reservation as a result of reading about the B&B in *BED & BREAKFAST U.S.A.*—1988 edition.

Please enclose a self-addressed, stamped, business-sized envelope when contacting reservation services.

For more details on what you can expect in a B&B, see Chapter 1.

Always mention *Bed & Breakfast U.S.A.* when making reservations!

If no B&B is listed in the area you'll be visiting, use the form on page 698 to order a copy of our "List of New B&Bs."

We want to hear from you! Use the form on page 697.

OKLAHOMA

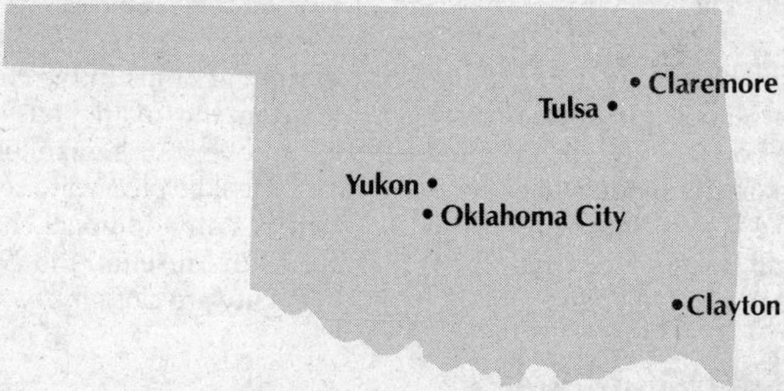

Claremore
Tulsa
Yukon
Oklahoma City
Clayton

Bed & Breakfast—Oklahoma City

11621 HASTINGS AVENUE, YUKON, OKLAHOMA 73099

Tel: **(405) 373-2733**
Coordinator: **Esther Pahlka**
States/Regions Covered: **Greater Oklahoma City**

Rates (Single/Double):
Average: **$38** **$42**

Most of Esther's hosts are located in the lovely suburban, country club area. All are warm, hospitable people who will help you plan a delightful stay. The homes are all air-conditioned, have private bath accommodations, and TVs in the guest rooms. Many have swimming pools and hot tubs. Beef is king in Oklahoma City, and there are dozens of great restaurants that serve excellent steak dinners. Don't miss the Cowboy Hall of Fame, Indian City (site of the Artifacts of the Five Civilized Tribes), and a tour of the Oklahoma State Capitol and Pioneer Museum.

Country Inn

ROUTE 3, BOX 1925, CLAREMORE, OKLAHOMA 74017

Tel: **(918) 342-1894**
Best Time to Call: **2–10 PM**
Host(s): **Leland Jenkins**
Location: **25 mi. NE of Tulsa**
No. of Rooms: **2**
No. of Private Baths: **2**
Double/pb: **$35**
Single/pb: **$30**
Open: **All year**
Reduced Rates: **15%, seniors**
Breakfast: **Continental**
Other Meals: **Available**
Pets: **Sometimes**
Children: **No**
Smoking: **No**
Social Drinking: **Permitted**

Leland looks forward to making you feel right at home in the charming barn-style guest quarters, separate from the main house. He invites you to enjoy the swimming pool, improve your suntan, or just sit back in the shade and enjoy a cool drink. He'll be pleased to serve a charcoal steak dinner and a bottle of wine for an additional charge. The Will Rogers Memorial, the J. M. Davis Gun Museum, the 29,500-acre Oologah Lake, and Oral Roberts University are close by.

Clayton Country Inn

ROUTE 1, BOX 8, HIGHWAY 271, CLAYTON, OKLAHOMA 74536

Tel: **(918) 569-4165 or 627-1956**
Best Time to Call: **7 AM–10 PM**
Host(s): **Clint and Shirley Brewster**
Location: **140 mi. SE of Tulsa**
No. of Rooms: **11**
No. of Private Baths: **11**
Double/pb: **$30**
Single/pb: **$24**
Guest Cottage: **$32–$50; sleeps 5**
Open: **All year**
Breakfast: **Continental**
Other Meals: **Available**
Credit Cards: **MC, VISA**
Pets: **No**
Children: **Welcome**
Smoking: **Permitted**
Social Drinking: **Permitted**

Perched on a hill amid 135 acres and surrounded by the Kiamichi Mountains is this 40-year-old two-story stone and wood inn. It's furnished in a simple traditional style with a beamed ceiling and fireplace. The restaurant on-premises is noted for its fine cooking. Bass fishing at Lake Sardis is two miles away, and an 18,000-acre game preserve is just across the highway. Feel free to bring your horse and enjoy trail rides under the vast western skies.

Sunrise Bed and Breakfast ✪

4510 EAST 32ND PLACE, TULSA, OKLAHOMA 74135

Tel: **(918) 743-4234**
Best Time to Call: **Before 8 AM; after 5 PM**
Host(s): **Sue Sark**
Location: **4 mi. from I-244**
No. of Rooms: **1**
No. of Private Baths: **1**
Double/pb: **$35**
Single/pb: **$20**
Open: **Jan. 15–Nov. 15**
Breakfast: **Continental**
Pets: **No**
Children: **No**
Smoking: **Permitted**
Social Drinking: **Permitted**

Sunrise Bed and Breakfast is a comfortable ranch-style home, minutes from downtown Tulsa. The atmosphere is clean and homey and relaxed. In the morning, enjoy Sue's coffee and homemade cinnamon rolls. The Sarks will gladly direct you to the nearby Philbrook and Gilcrease museums and Oral Roberts University, as well as places to shop and dine.

OREGON

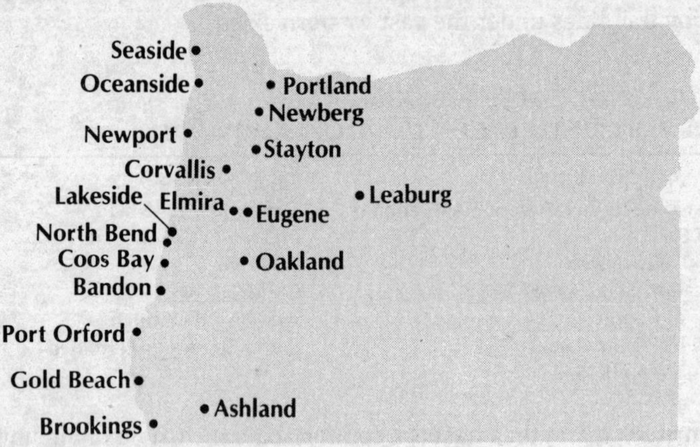

Seaside
Oceanside
Portland
Newberg
Newport
Stayton
Corvallis
Lakeside
Elmira
Eugene
Leaburg
North Bend
Coos Bay
Oakland
Bandon
Port Orford
Gold Beach
Ashland
Brookings

Bed & Breakfast Accommodations—Oregon Plus

5733 SW DICKINSON STREET, PORTLAND, OREGON 97219

Tel: **(503) 245-0642**
Best Time to Call: **10 AM–4 PM**
Coordinator: **Marcelle Tebo**
State/Regions Covered:
Oregon—statewide; Washington; California

Rates (Single/Double):

	Single	Double
Modest:	**$20**	**$30**
Average:	**$35**	**$45**
Luxury:	**$75**	**$150**

Credit Cards: **MC, VISA**

Marcelle's roster of helpful hosts will happily direct you to a variety of activities to suit your pleasure and purse. Suggestions might include the Japanese Gardens, the elephant herd at the zoo, fishing in the sea, lake, or streams, the Pendleton Woolen Mills, winter or summer sporting pleasures, whale watching, or a visit to Mt. Hood National Forest. A descriptive brochure of accommodations is available for $4 and includes listings in Vancouver and Victoria as well as the San Juan Islands.

Northwest Bed and Breakfast Travel Unlimited

610 SW BROADWAY, SUITE 609, PORTLAND, OREGON 97205

Tel: **(503) 246-8366**
Coordinators: **Laine Friedman, Gloria Shaich, and Sarah Stadler**
States/Regions Covered: **Washington, Oregon, California, Hawaii, Idaho, Canada—British Columbia**

Rates (Single/Double):

Modest:	**$22**	**$30**
Average:	**$30**	**$40**
Luxury:	**$40**	**$75**

Credit Cards: **No**

Laine, Gloria, and Sarah have a network of hundreds of host homes throughout the Pacific Northwest and Canada. They charge an annual membership fee of $15 (individual) or $20 (two or more in the same family). Upon joining, you will receive a directory of all the lodgings, which range from city to suburban to rural to coast, mountains, and desert. There is just a $5 processing fee for those that will only use the service once. The directory charge is $7.50. A variety of package tours, complete with car rental if required, can be arranged with stops at suitable B&Bs along the way.

Chanticleer ✪

120 GRESHAM STREET, ASHLAND, OREGON 97520

Tel: **(503) 482-1919**
Best Time to Call: **9 AM–5 PM**
Host(s): **Jim and Nancy Beaver**
Location: **2 mi. from I-5, Exit 14**
No. of Rooms: **7**
No. of Private Baths: **7**
Double/pb: **$69–$89**
Suites: **$99–$109**
Open: **All year**
Breakfast: **Full**
Pets: **No**
Children: **Welcome**
Smoking: **No**
Social Drinking: **Permitted**
Airport/Station Pickup: **Yes**

The Chanticleer overlooks Bear Creek Valley and the Cascade foothills. A large living room with a stone fireplace, a sunny patio, and French country furnishings create a comfortable atmosphere. Guests are welcome to juices, coffee, and sherry. Some of the specialty breakfast items include Italian roast coffee, blintzes, and cheese-baked eggs. Shops, restaurants, and the site of the Shakespeare Festival are a short walk away. Mount Ashland ski area and the Rogue River are a 30-minute drive from the house. Southern Oregon State College is nearby.

The Coach House Inn ✪

70 COOLIDGE STREET, ASHLAND, OREGON 97520

Tel: **(503) 482-2257**
Best Time to Call: **Evenings**
Host(s): **Pamela and Jack Evans**
No. of Rooms: **3**
Max. No. Sharing Bath: **3**
Double/sb: **$48**
Open: **Mar. 1–Oct. 31**
Breakfast: **Continental**
Pets: **No**
Children: **Welcome, over 12**
Smoking: **No**
Social Drinking: **Permitted**
Airport/Station Pickup: **Yes**
Foreign Languages: **German**

The guest rooms at this Victorian inn are decorated with antiques and offer mountain views. Enjoy soaking in the claw-foot bathtub, or a game of croquet on the spacious lawn. Breakfast features fresh fruit cobblers and homemade jams. Guests are welcome to join daily picnic tours of the local creamery and vineyards. The Shakespeare Theatre, historic homes, and antique shops are all nearby. A two-night minimum stay is requested.

Neil Creek House ✪

341 MOWETZA DRIVE, ASHLAND, OREGON 97520

Tel: **(503) 482-1334**
Best Time to Call: **After 10 AM**
Host(s): **Edith and Thomas Heumann**
No. of Rooms: **2**
No. of Private Baths: **2**
Double/pb: **$75**
Single/pb: **$70**
Open: **All year**
Reduced Rates: **10%, weekly; $10 less Nov.–Feb.**
Breakfast: **Full**
Pets: **No**
Children: **No**
Smoking: **Permitted**
Social Drinking: **Permitted**
Foreign Languages: **French, German**

This country house is set on five wooded acres with a duck pond and creek for boating. Guests are welcome to relax by the swimming pool or on the decks. Afternoon tea and coffee are served. Breakfast treats may include homemade jams and syrups, ranch eggs, sausage, bacon, or ebelskivers. The guest rooms overlook the creek or mountains, and are furnished with antiques and 19th-century art. Skiing, sailing, river rafting, and Shakespeare performances are nearby.

Royal Carter House ✪

514 SISKIYOU BOULEVARD, ASHLAND, OREGON 97520

Tel: **(503) 482-5623**
Best Time to Call: **Mornings**
Host(s): **Alyce and Roy Levy**
No. of Rooms: **4**
No. of Private Baths: **4**
Double/pb: **$44–$55**
Suites: **$60**
Open: **Feb. 1–Nov. 1**

Breakfast: **Full**
Pets: **No**
Children: **Welcome, over 7**
Smoking: **No**
Social Drinking: **Permitted**
Airport/Station Pickup: **Yes**

This beautiful 1909 home is listed on the National Historic Register. Located four blocks from Ashland's famous Shakespeare Theatre, it is surrounded by lovely old trees in a parklike setting. It is suitably modernized but retains the original room structure. Alyce has added decorator touches of vintage hats and old periodicals to the antique furnishings. The Levys have traveled extensively abroad and will share stories of their experiences with you. Southern Oregon State College is four blocks away.

Cliff Harbor ✪

P.O. BOX 769, BANDON, OREGON 97411

Tel: **(503) 347-3956**
Host(s): **Bill and Doris Duncan**
Location: **1 mi. from Hwy. 101**
No. of Rooms: **2**
No. of Private Baths: **2**
Suites: **$52–$85**
Open: **All year**
Reduced Rates: **10%, Nov. 1–May 1**
Pets: **No**
Children: **Welcome (crib)**
Smoking: **No**
Social Drinking: **Permitted**

You'll fall in love with this oceanfront cottage perched on a bluff above pounding surf and sandy beaches strewn with driftwood. Both guest rooms have private entrances, phones, and cable TV. The Harbor Suite is wheelchair accessible and has a queen-size bed, bay windows, and enclosed patio, garden, and deck. Bill and Doris serve a full breakfast including fruit, home-baked breads, bacon and eggs, and beverages. The Cliffside Studio has a kitchen, fireplace, two double beds, and panoramic ocean and river views. Continental breakfast is provided, and a two-night minimum is required in this accommodation. Cliff Harbor is featured on our cover.

Spindrift Bed & Breakfast ✪

2990 BEACH LOOP ROAD, BANDON, OREGON 97411

Tel: **(503) 347-2275**
Host(s): **Don and Robbie Smith**
Location: **½ mi. from Hwy. 101**
No. of Rooms: **2**
No. of Private Baths: **1**
Max. No. Sharing Bath: **2**
Double/pb: **$62**
Single/pb: **$57**
Double/sb: **$53**
Single/sb: **$48**
Open: **All year**
Breakfast: **Full**
Credit Cards: **MC, VISA**
Pets: **No**
Children: **Welcome, over 8 (if both rooms are taken by same family)**
Smoking: **No**
Social Drinking: **Permitted**
Airport/Station Pickup: **Yes**

Enjoy the breathtaking beauty of the Oregon coast from this lovely home, perched on a bluff just 40 feet above a long, sandy beach and framed by massive offshore rock formations. Uninterrupted vistas are yours from floor-to-ceiling windows, or from the deck with its direct beach access. Relax in the sunken living room with its vaulted beamed ceiling and inviting fireplace. Breakfast is a real feast, and afternoon refreshments are offered by Don and Robbie.

Sea Dreamer Inn ✪

P.O. BOX 1840, 15167 McVAY LANE, BROOKINGS, OREGON 97415

Tel: **(503) 469-6629**
Host(s): **Bob and Judy Blair**
Location: **On US Hwy. 101**
No. of Rooms: **4**
No. of Private Baths: **2**
Max. No. Sharing Bath: **4**
Double/pb: **$55–$60**
Single/pb: **$50–$55**
Double/sb: **$45–$50**
Single/sb: **$40–$45**
Open: **All year**
Breakfast: **Full**
Credit Cards: **MC, VISA**
Pets: **No**
Children: **No**
Smoking: **No**
Social Drinking: **Permitted**
Airport/Station Pickup: **Yes**

Situated midway between Portland and San Francisco, this vintage 1912 Colonial is set amid pine trees, fruit trees, and flowers that bloom all year long. It has a view of the famous lily fields that slope gently to the Pacific. Refreshments are served each evening to supplement the magnificent sunsets or by the cozy fire on chilly nights. Judy's breakfast specialties are apple pfannkuchen, French toast stuffed with ricotta cheese, and a variety of soufflés. Whale watching, sport fishing, jet-boat trips, and beachcombing are a few diversions. The climate is springlike in all seasons.

Wheeler's Bed & Breakfast ✪

BOX 8201, COBURG, OREGON 97401

Tel: **(503) 344-1366**
Host(s): **Joe and Isabel Wheeler**
Location: **7 mi. N of Eugene; 1/2 mi. from I-5, Exit 199**
No. of Rooms: **3**
Max. No. Sharing Bath: **4**
Double/sb: **$35**
Single/sb: **$30**
Open: **Mar. 1–Dec. 1**
Breakfast: **Full**
Pets: **Sometimes**
Children: **Welcome, over 10**
Smoking: **Permitted**
Social Drinking: **Permitted**
Airport/Station Pickup: **Yes**
Foreign Languages: **Spanish**

Joe and Isabel welcome you to their historic town, which offers a unique atmosphere of antiques shops and century-old homes. Whether you stroll the few blocks to the world-renowned Coburg Inn (circa 1857), which boasts its own ghost, or bicycle down the country lanes, your stay will be rewarding. The guest quarters are separate from the rest of the house, offering complete privacy. Visit in the living room, use the washer-dryer, and make yourselves "at home."

Captain's Quarters Bed & Breakfast ✪

P.O. BOX 3231, 265 SOUTH EMPIRE BOULEVARD, COOS BAY, OREGON 97420

Tel: **(503) 888-6895**
Best Time to Call: **8 AM–8 PM**
Host(s): **John and Jean Griswold**
Location: **3 mi. W of Coos Bay**
No. of Rooms: **3**
Max. No. Sharing Bath: **3**
Double/sb: **$45**
Open: **All year**
Breakfast: **Full**
Pets: **Sometimes**
Children: **Welcome, over 10**
Smoking: **No**
Social Drinking: **Permitted**
Airport/Station Pickup: **Yes**

Captain's Quarters is an 1890 Victorian painted gray with white trim. It was the home of Captain Thomas McGenn, chief of the steamship *Breakwater.* John and Jean have lovingly restored the house to its original beauty and created a homey atmosphere with antiques and even some of the old captain's memorabilia. Bedrooms face the beautiful bay and the North Spit, where you can watch the ships come in. Homemade hotcakes with berries, fresh-baked breads, and local cheeses are just some of the breakfast treats served in the dining room or sun parlor. Later, your hosts invite you to have a snack or a cup of coffee in the parlor. A vast selection of activities can be enjoyed nearby, including beachcombing, boat charters, crabbing, and clamming. You can take a trip to the botanical gardens, or just take a break at one of the restaurants tucked along the shores.

This Olde House B&B ✪

202 ALDER STREET, CORNER 2ND AVENUE, COOS BAY, OREGON 97420

Tel: **(503) 267-5224**
Host(s): **Ed and Jean Mosieur**
Location: **½ block from Hwy. 101**
No. of Rooms: **4**
No. of Private Baths: **1**
Max. No. Sharing Bath: **4**
Double/pb: **$55**
Single/pb: **$48**
Double/sb: **$48**
Open: **All year**
Reduced Rates: **10%, seniors**
Breakfast: **Full**
Pets: **No**
Children: **Welcome, over 12**
Smoking: **Permitted**
Social Drinking: **Permitted**
Airport/Station Pickup: **Yes**

Situated with a view of the bay, this stately Victorian beauty is located only one half block from Highway 101. Guests can catch a glimpse of ships on the bay just before they head downstairs to a breakfast of fresh fruit, eggs, muffins, and coffee or tea, served in the dining room. Downtown Coos Bay is only two blocks away from the house, and after a short drive, guests will find a lovely state park, a small boat basin, beaches, South Slough Sanctuary, and the beautiful gardens of Shore Acres.

Huntington Manor

3555 N.W. HARRISON BOULEVARD, CORVALLIS, OREGON 97330

Tel: **(503) 753-3735**
Best Time to Call: **8 AM–8 PM**
Host(s): **Ann Sink**
Location: **84 mi. S of Portland**
No. of Rooms: **2**
No. of Private Baths: **2**
Double/pb: **$45**
Open: **All year**
Reduced Rates: **20%, weekly**
Breakfast: **Full**
Credit Cards: **MC, VISA**
Pets: **No**
Children: **Welcome, over 12**
Smoking: **Permitted**
Social Drinking: **Permitted**
Airport/Station Pickup: **Yes**

Huntington Manor is a 62-year-old Williamsburg Colonial, set beneath towering trees and surrounded by flowering gardens. The house has been completely refurbished and furnished with a mixture of American and European antiques. Guest rooms feature queen or double beds, color TV, down comforters, fine imported linens, and special touches such as a decanter of wine and fresh fruit. Your hostess has 20 years of experience in interior design, and she loves caring for her home and catering to guests. Breakfast specialties include ham-and-cheese-filled crêpes, egg strata, and homemade muffins; tea and scones are served in the afternoon. Huntington Manor is four blocks from Oregon State University and within walking distance of parks, churches, and the countryside.

McGillivray's Log Home and Bed and Breakfast ✪

88680 EVERS ROAD, ELMIRA, OREGON 97437

Tel: **(503) 935-3564**
Best Time to Call: **8 AM–8 PM**
Host(s): **Dick and Evelyn McGillivray**
Location: **14 mi. W of Eugene**
No. of Rooms: **2**
No. of Private Baths: **2**
Double/pb: **$40–$50**
Single/pb: **$35–$45**
Open: **All year**
Breakfast: **Full**
Credit Cards: **MC, VISA**
Pets: **No**
Children: **Welcome**
Smoking: **No**
Social Drinking: **Permitted**
Airport/Station Pickup: **Yes**

Dick and Evelyn dreamed of owning their own log cabin for more than 30 years. Their massive home is situated on five acres covered with pines and firs. The structure is designed with six kinds of wood and features a split-log staircase, wooden door latches, and hollow log lamps, all handcrafted. Guests may choose from a spacious, wheelchair-accessible bedroom or an upstairs room that can accommodate a family. All are beautifully decorated in a classic Americana motif. Evelyn prepares buttermilk pancakes on a 1920s wood stove that her mother used to use. She also offers fresh-squeezed juice from farm-grown apples and grapes, fresh bread, eggs, and all the trimmings. It's just three miles to a local vineyard; country roads for bicycling and a reservoir for fishing and boating are close by.

Backroads Bed and Breakfast

85269 LORANE HIGHWAY, EUGENE, OREGON 97405

Tel: **(503) 485-0464**
Best Time to Call: **Afternoons**
Host(s): **Janet and Frank Arundel**
Location: **12 mi. SW of Eugene**
No. of Rooms: **2**
Max. No. Sharing Bath: **2–4**
Double/sb: **$45–$50**
Single/sb: **$40–$45**
Open: **May–Sept.**
Reduced Rates: **Families**
Breakfast: **Full**
Pets: **No**
Children: **Welcome, over 2**
Smoking: **No**
Social Drinking: **Permitted**
Airport/Station Pickup: **Yes**

On a wooded hillside overlooking a peaceful valley sits this contemporary passive solar home. Six acres of oak, pine, and fir trees provide beautiful views from every window. Open beams, brick floors, sunny rooms, and wood furnishings provide an informal and comfortable atmosphere. Relax on the sun deck with a book from the library or do a little stargazing from the telescope. Guest quarters, located on the ground floor, consist of a sitting room, a sunroom, two bedrooms, a bath, and a deck. The full or Continental breakfast features homemade breads and sweet rolls. The scenic Willamette and Mckenzie rivers, several lakes for boating and fishing, wineries, and biking trails are all close at hand; Oregon's famous coastline is just 60 minutes west.

Griswold's Bed and Breakfast ✪

552 WEST BROADWAY, EUGENE, OREGON 97401

Tel: **(503) 683-6294**
Host(s): **Phyllis Griswold**
Location: **Off Rte. 105**
No. of Rooms: **2**
Max. No. Sharing Bath: **4**
Double/sb: **$35–$39**
Single/sb: **$30–$34**
Open: **All year**

Reduced Rates: **Available**
Breakfast: **Full**
Pets: **No**
Children: **Welcome**
Smoking: **Permitted**
Social Drinking: **Permitted**
Airport/Station Pickup: **Yes**

The Griswold home is ideally located in an older, quiet part of Eugene, less than six blocks from downtown. Guests may choose the Blue Room, with its brass bed and antique maple dresser, or the Peach Room, a special blend of maple and oak pieces. The house is near the jogging and biking trails, which run parallel to the Willamette River, the Public Market, and Hult's Performing Arts Center. A short drive from Eugene takes you into the Cascade Mountains for fishing, hiking, rafting, or skiing. Before you set off for a day of activity, a fine breakfast of homemade breads and jams, omelets, fresh fruit, and plenty of coffee will be served.

The House in the Woods ✪

814 LORANE HIGHWAY, EUGENE, OREGON 97405

Tel: **(503) 343-3234**
Best Time to Call: **Mornings; evenings**
Host(s): **Eunice and George Kjaer**
Location: **3 mi. from I-5**
No. of Rooms: **2**
No. of Private Baths: **1**
Max. No. Sharing Bath: **2**
Double/pb: **$55**
Single/pb: **$40**
Double/sb: **$50**
Single/sb: **$38**
Open: **All year**
Reduced Rates: **Available**
Breakfast: **Full**
Pets: **No**
Children: **Welcome, under 1 or over 14**
Smoking: **No**
Social Drinking: **Permitted**
Airport/Station Pickup: **Yes**
Foreign Languages: **German**

This turn-of-the-century home is situated in a wooded glen surrounded by fir trees, rhododendrons, and azaleas. Inside, you'll find Oriental rugs on the original hardwood floors, a cozy fireplace, antiques, and a square grand piano. Guest rooms always have fresh flowers. Breakfast is served on the porch or beside the warmth of the Franklin stove. Specialties of the house include homemade jams and breads, fruit soups, and a variety of egg dishes. The neighborhood is full of wildlife and bicycle and jogging trails, yet is close to shops, art galleries, museums, wineries, and restaurants.

Shelley's Guest House

1546 CHARNELTON STREET, EUGENE, OREGON 97401

Tel: **(503) 683-2062**
Host(s): **Bill and Lois Shelley**
Location: **100 mi. S of Portland**
No. of Rooms: **2**
No. of Private Baths: **1**
Max. of Sharing Bath: **4**
Double/sb: **$40–$45**
Suite: **$60**
Single/sb: **$30–$35**
Open: **All year**
Reduced Rates: **Weekly**
Breakfast: **Full**
Pets: **No**
Children: **Sometimes**
Smoking: **No**
Social Drinking: **No**
Airport/Station Pickup: **Yes**

The Shelley's Guest House is a cottage-style retreat dating back to the 1920s. Traditional wallcoverings, restored brass accents, turn-of-the-century furnishings, and antiques are in keeping with the architectural style of the house. Choose from the master bedroom with queen-size brass and iron bed, plush carpet, and floral wallpaper, or the "Guest Room" with iron bed, homespun spread, and cozy rocker. Breakfast specialties like eggs Benedict and waffles with strawberries are served in an elegant dining room with oak parquet floors. After a day in Eugene or at the fairgrounds, enjoy fresh fruit and cheese or a cool lemonade, compliments of the Shelleys. You are welcome to soothe your weary bones in the gazebo's hot tub.

Endicott Gardens ✪

95768 JERRY'S FLAT ROAD, GOLD BEACH, OREGON 97444

Tel: **(503) 247-6513**
Host(s): **Mary Endicott**
No. of Rooms: **4**
No. of Private Baths: **4**
Double/pb: **$45**
Single/pb: **$35**
Open: **All year**
Breakfast: **Full**
Pets: **Sometimes**
Children: **Welcome**
Smoking: **Permitted**
Social Drinking: **Permitted**
Airport/Station Pickup: **Yes**

This classic contemporary B&B is across the road from Rogue River, famous for fishing and riverboat trips to white water. The guest rooms are located in a private wing of the house with decks overlooking the forest, mountains, and beautiful grounds. Homegrown strawberries, blueberries, apples, and plums are often featured in delicious breakfast treats served on the deck or in the dining room. In cool weather, the living room with its cozy fireplace is a favorite gathering spot. Mary will be happy to share her collection of restaurant menus from nearby eating establishments with you.

Fair Winds Bed and Breakfast

P.O. BOX 1274, GOLD BEACH, OREGON 97444

Tel: **(503) 247-6753**
Best Time to Call: **10 AM or 6 PM**
Host(s): **Marion "Butch" Jarman**
Location: **3 mi. S of Gold Beach**
No. of Rooms: **2**
Max. No. Sharing Bath: **3**
Double/sb: **$40**
Single/sb: **$30**

Open: **All year**
Reduced Rates: **20%, weekly**
Breakfast: **Full**
Pets: **No**
Children: **Welcome**
Smoking: **No**
Social Drinking: **Permitted**
Airport/Station Pickup: **Yes**

Fair Winds is a small cedar-clad country home situated high in the foothills of the Siskiyou Mountains. Five acres of wooded, rolling hills create a parklike, private setting. Guests are invited to sun on the deck or stroll down the walkway to the gazebo, where a hot tub/Jacuzzi beckons in the shade of the myrtlewood trees. Marion enjoys gardening, reading, and making guests feel welcome. She has created a homespun look with a unique blend of Americana and finds from around the world. Her breakfast specialties include homemade breads, jams, cheeses, and a variety of hams. She will also be glad to offer a glass of sherry and nibbles or a light supper. This charming country retreat is in the middle of some of the most beautiful coastline anywhere. It is also five miles from the Rogue River, one of the first wilderness waterways in the country.

Ahif House Bed & Breakfast ✪

762 N.W. 6TH STREET, GRANTS PASS, OREGON 97526

Tel: **(503) 474-1374**
Host(s): **Herbert and Betty Buskirk; Rosemary Althaus**
Location: **.6 mi. N of Grants Pass**
No. of Rooms: **2**
Max. No. Sharing Bath: **4**
Double/sb: **$60**
Single/sb: **$50**

Open: **All year**
Breakfast: **Full**
Pets: **No**
Children: **No**
Smoking: **No**
Social Drinking: **Permitted**
Airport/Station Pickup: **Yes**

Ahif House is located on a main street on a hill overlooking the surrounding mountains. The house dates back to 1902 and is listed on the National Register of Historic Places. The rooms are beautifully appointed and furnished in fine antiques. Guest rooms feature fluffy comforters, down pillows, fresh flowers, and candles. Enjoy a cup of fresh coffee first thing in the morning in the quiet of your room or on the sunny front porch. Your coffee is followed by a full gourmet breakfast including fruit, fresh-baked muffins, and homemade jams and jellies. There is much to explore in Grants Pass, which is set on the Rogue River and is surrounded by the beautiful Cascade Mountains. Your hosts can direct you to guided fishing, raft trips, and jet boats. In the evening, return to this lovely Victorian for parlor music, complimentary wine, and a light snack.

The Handmaiden's Inn ✪

230 RED SPUR DRIVE, GRANTS PASS, OREGON 97527

Tel: **(503) 476-2932**
Host(s): **Bette and Jody Hammer**
Location: **3 mi. S of Grants Pass**
No. of Rooms: **3**
No. of Private Baths: **1**
Max. No. Sharing Bath: **4**
Double/pb: **$65**
Double/sb: **$50**
Single/sb: **$45**
Open: **All year**
Reduced Rates: **15%, families**
Breakfast: **Full**
Other Meals: **Available**
Credit Cards: **MC, VISA**
Pets: **No**
Children: **Welcome, over 11**
Smoking: **No**
Social Drinking: **No**
Airport/Station Pickup: **Yes**

The Handmaiden's Inn is a newly built three-story cedar home. The house is surrounded by beautifully landscaped greenery and gardens. The inside is filled with elegant country oak furnishings. Guests are welcome to sun themselves on the spacious deck furnished with comfortable chairs and lounges. Bette and Jody are professional cooks who used to have a catering business in Southern California. They lovingly prepare hearty breakfasts featuring sausage and egg dishes, homemade breads and jams, fresh fruit, and plenty of coffee. They also invite you to join them for complimentary wine and cheese. The inn is located five minutes from white-water rafting and salmon fishing, and is 45 minutes from the Ashland Shakespeare Festival.

Mt. Baldy Bed & Breakfast ✪

678 TROLL VIEW ROAD, GRANTS PASS, OREGON 97527

Tel: **(503) 479-7998**
Best Time to Call: **Before 10 AM; after 4 PM**
Host(s): **John and June Gustafson**
No. of Rooms: **2**
No. of Private Baths: **2**
Double/pb: **$45**
Single/pb: **$35**
Open: **All year**
Reduced Rates: **10%, seniors**
Breakfast: **Full**
Pets: **No**
Children: **Welcome, over 7**
Smoking: **No**
Social Drinking: **Permitted**
Airport/Station Pickup: **Yes**

Relax and enjoy the fresh air and beautiful sunsets from high on the slope of Mt. Baldy overlooking Grants Pass and the Rogue River Valley. Each guest room has a queen-size bed and private entrance. John and June will spoil you with farm-fresh products at breakfast. Fishing, rafting, visiting caves, Crater Lake National Park, historic Jacksonville, and the Shakespeare Festival in Ashland are a few activities to keep you busy.

The Washington Inn Bed & Breakfast ✪

1002 N.W. WASHINGTON BOULEVARD, GRANTS PASS, OREGON 97526

Tel: **(503) 476-1131**
Host(s): **Maryan and Bill Thompson**
Location: **½ mi. from I-5**
No. of Rooms: **3**
No. of Private Baths: **2**
Max. No. Sharing Bath: **2**
Double/pb: **$50–$65**
Single/pb: **$40–$55**
Double/sb: **$40–$55**
Single/sb: **$30–$45**
Open: **All year**
Reduced Rates: **Available**
Breakfast: **Continental**
Credit Cards: **MC, VISA**
Pets: **No**
Children: **Welcome, over 14**
Smoking: **No**
Social Drinking: **Permitted**
Airport/Station Pickup: **Yes**

The Washington Inn is a charming Victorian listed on the National Register of Historic Places. Each guest room is named for one of the Thompsons' three children, and offers individual charms. Linda's is a large suite with fireplace, queen-size bed, private bath, and balcony overlooking the mountains; Pattie's Parlor is a spacious red room with fireplace and large private bath with claw-footed tub; Sally's Sunny View overlooks the mountains, has a canopied bed, and is decorated in delicate pink. Your hosts offer bicycles for exploring the area, and many interesting shops and restaurants are within easy walking distance. Fishing, rafting, and jet-boat rides can be enjoyed on the Rogue River. If you prefer, spend the afternoon relaxing on the porch swing, taking in the view.

Country Lane Bed & Breakfast ✪

P.O. BOX Y, 777 COUNTRY LANE, LAKESIDE, OREGON 97449

Tel: **(503) 759-3869**
Best Time to Call: **8 AM–12 PM**
Host(s): **Roy and Carolyn Sindell**
Location: **8 mi. from Hwy. 101**
No. of Rooms: **2**
Max. No. Sharing Bath: **4**
Double/sb: **$45**
Single/sb: **$40**
Open: **All year**
Breakfast: **Full**
Pets: **No**
Children: **Welcome, over 12**
Smoking: **No**
Social Drinking: **No**
Airport/Station Pickup: **Yes**

Nestled in a wooded cul-de-sac of Sunlake Park, this owner-built chalet is at the end of a scenic drive with picture postcard views. You are sure to feel right at home in the great room, which features exposed post-and-beam construction, oak floors, a fireplace, and a wood stove. Choose from the Garden View Room, with twin beds, or the Country Room, with queen-size bed. Both have electric blankets and comfortable furnishings. The Sindells invite you to explore the forest trails and country lanes, relax in a hammock near the creek, play badminton, or barbecue on the grill. Start your day off with a hearty breakfast of juice, homemade breads, honey, and special egg dishes, followed by homemade pie and lots of coffee. Lakeside, where you can walk for miles on an unspoiled driftwood-strewn beach, watch the dune buggies, or stretch out on the sand, is seven miles away.

Marjon Bed and Breakfast Inn ✪

44975 LEABURG DAM ROAD, LEABURG, OREGON 97489

Tel: **(503) 896-3145**
Host(s): **Margie Haas**
Location: **24 mi. E of Eugene**
No. of Rooms: **2**
No. of Private Baths: **2**
Double/pb: **$60**
Suites: **$80**
Open: **All year**
Reduced Rates: **10% Sun.–Thurs.; weekly**
Breakfast: **Full**
Pets: **No**
Children: **No**
Smoking: **Permitted**
Social Drinking: **Permitted**
Airport/Station Pickup: **Yes**

This cedar chalet is located on the banks of the McKenzie River. The suite overlooks the river and a secluded Japanese garden, and features a sunken bath. The other has a fish bowl shower and a view of a 100-year-old apple tree. Relax in the living room with its wraparound seating and massive stone fireplace. One of the walls is made entirely of glass with sliding doors that lead to a terrace that faces the river. A multicourse breakfast is served there on balmy days. Waterfalls, trout fishing, white-water rafting, and skiing are all nearby.

The Owl's View B&B ✪

P.O. BOX 732, NEWBERG, OREGON 97132

Tel: **(503) 538-6498**
Best Time to Call: **8 AM–7 PM**
Host(s): **Chuck and Jean Carr**
Location: **25 mi. SW of Portland**
No. of Rooms: **2**
No. of Private Baths: **2**
Double/pb: **$55**
Single/pb: **$55**
Suites: **$85**
Open: **All year**
Breakfast: **Full**
Pets: **No**
Children: **No**
Smoking: **No**
Social Drinking: **Permitted**

Chuck and Jean welcome you to their large contemporary home set on two and a half acres. The house overlooks the beautiful Willamette Valley and is surrounded by lush greenery and a flower garden with gazebo. The guest rooms share a mezzanine sitting room for relaxing. One room has a Jacuzzi and a small balcony. The other has a private bath and a view of the valley. In the morning, quiches and special egg dishes are served along with locally made honey, nut butter, and jams. The Owl's View is convenient to Yamhill County wineries and is 45 minutes from Portland.

Ocean House B&B

4920 NORTH WEST WOODY WAY, NEWPORT, OREGON 97365

Tel: **(503) 265-6158**
Best Time to Call: **8 AM–6 PM**
Host(s): **Bob and Bette Garrard**
Location: **120 mi. SW of Portland**
No. of Rooms: **4**
No. of Private Baths: **2**
Max. No. Sharing Bath: **4**
Double/pb: **$70**
Single/pb: **$55–$65**
Double/sb: **$40–$50**
Single/sb: **$35–$45**
Suites: **$70–$115**
Open: **Jan. 11–Dec. 14**
Reduced Rates: **Available**
Breakfast: **Full**
Credit Cards: **MC, VISA**
Pets: **No**
Children: **Welcome, over 12**
Smoking: **No**
Social Drinking: **Permitted**

Ocean House is a lovely old home surrounded by a beautiful coastal garden of flowers and native shrubs. The rooms are decorated comfortably and are enhanced by a beautiful art collection. The windows of the cozy bedrooms open toward the sea and overlook the surf at Agate Beach. Early risers will find coffee or tea waiting downstairs with the morning paper. Some take a mug and walk down the private trail to the beach and tidal pools. Those so inclined take an early jog to the lighthouse. Afterward, a hearty breakfast is served in the sun room, on the patio, or on one of the porches. Special attention is given to table settings, and the meal always includes fresh fruit and a hot entrée. Bob and Bette can easily accommodate special diets and needs. Ocean House is near to golf, fishing, and clamming. It is also the place to relax by an open fire and do nothing at all.

Baywood Bed and Breakfast ✪

P.O. BOX 1044, NORTH BEND, OREGON 97459

Tel: **(503) 756-6348**
Best Time to Call: **Evenings**
Host(s): **Vern and Caroline Stevens**
Location: **4 mi. E of US 101**
No. of Rooms: **3**
No. of Private Baths: **2½**
Double/pb: **$35**
Single/pb: **$30**
Suites: **$40**
Open: **All year**
Breakfast: **Full**
Credit Cards: **MC, VISA**
Pets: **Sometimes**
Children: **Welcome**
Smoking: **Permitted**
Social Drinking: **Permitted**
Airport/Station Pickup: **Yes**

This lovely shoreline home is set on Coos Bay, overlooking the McCullough Bridge. Many windows overlook the water, where ships pass on their way to the world's largest lumber port. The rooms are furnished traditionally, with many antiques and elegant touches. One features a private deck overlooking the bay. Located at the heart of the Oregon coast, Baywood is close to state parks and miles of sand dunes offering excellent opportunities for birdwatchers and photographers. Many restaurants, movies, the Little Theatre in the Bay, and a golf course are all nearby.

The Highlands Bed and Breakfast ✪

608 RIDGE ROAD, NORTH BEND, OREGON 97459

Tel: **(503) 756-0300**
Best Time to Call: **After 5 PM**
Host(s): **Jim and Marilyn Dow**
Location: **4 mi. from Hwy. 101**
No. of Rooms: **2**
No. of Private Baths: **1**
Max. No. Sharing Bath: **1**
Double/pb: **$55**
Single/pb: **$45**
Single/sb: **$35**

Open: **All year**
Breakfast: **Full**
Pets: **No**
Children: **No**
Smoking: **No**
Social Drinking: **Permitted**
Airport/Station Pickup: **Yes**

This uniquely designed contemporary cedar home, with its wide expanses of glass and wraparound deck, has a spectacular view of the valley, inlet, and bay. From the floor-to-ceiling windows of the family room, you'll be able to watch unforgettable sunrises and sunsets. Dark oak-pegged flooring, beamed vaulted ceilings, and cedar paneling make a perfect setting for the Dows' antiques. A separate entrance for guests assures privacy, and separate heat controls assure comfort. Breakfast includes fresh-squeezed juice, fruit compote with special sauce, baked eggs on rice with cheese, ham or bacon, and freshly baked muffins or popovers. A short drive away are Oregon's beaches, sand dunes, and many fine restaurants. The Dows are retired and like to fly, sail, and garden.

The Pringle House ✪

P.O. BOX 578, OAKLAND, OREGON 97462

Tel: **(503) 459-5038**
Best Time to Call: **9 AM–10 PM**
Host(s): **Jim and Demay Pringle**
Location: **1½ mi. from I-5, Exit 138**
No. of Rooms: **2**
Max. No. Sharing Bath: **4**
Double/sb: **$40**
Single/sb: **$30**
Open: **All year**
Breakfast: **Full**
Pets: **No**
Children: **Welcome, over 12**
Smoking: **No**
Social Drinking: **Permitted**

Built in 1893, Pringle House stands on a rise overlooking historic downtown Oakland. Returned to its original Victorian beauty by Jim and Demay, it is listed on the National Register of Historic Places. Breakfast of fresh juice, compote, cheese, freshly baked croissants, and often a house specialty is served in the dining room. You will enjoy seeing Demay's doll collection.

Three Capes Bed & Breakfast

1685 MAXWELL MOUNTAIN ROAD, P.O. BOX 138, OCEANSIDE, OREGON 97134

Tel: **(503) 842-6126**
Host(s): **Ross and Kathy Holloway**
Location: **75 mi. W of Portland**
No. of Rooms: **2**
No. of Private Baths: **2**
Double/pb: **$45**

Single/pb: **$35**
Open: **All year**
Reduced Rates: **Available**
Breakfast: **Continental; full weekends**
Pets: **Yes**
Children: **Welcome (playpen, high chair)**
Smoking: **No**
Social Drinking: **Permitted**

Ross and Kathy welcome you to their large contemporary overlooking the Pacific Ocean. Here you'll be welcomed like family but treated like a special guest. Bedrooms are newly remodeled in French country wallpapers and woodwork. Each room offers ocean views, and those staying in the Cape Lookout Room will enjoy a private deck. Fresh flowers, afternoon tea, and goodies are just a few of the special touches. Pamper yourself with leisurely baths in a claw-footed tub and wake up to coffee brought to your room in the morning. Breakfast specialties include fresh fruit with whipped cream, local cheeses, and homemade pastries, with crêpes and soufflés on the weekends. Enjoy easy access to miles of sandy, uncrowded beaches and breathtaking views of the rocks and the water. A protected wildlife refuge is located just offshore and is home to a colony of sea lions as well as hundreds of shore birds. Clamming, fishing, biking, boating, and surfing can also be enjoyed nearby.

Corbett House B & B ✪

7533 SOUTH WEST CORBETT AVENUE, PORTLAND, OREGON 97219

Tel: **(503) 245-2580**
Host(s): **Sylvia Malagamba**
Location: **3½ mi. S of Portland**
No. of Rooms: **4**
No. of Private Baths: **1**
Max. No. Sharing Bath: **3**
Double/pb: **$60**
Single/pb: **$55**
Double/sb: **$50**
Single/sb: **$35–$45**
Open: **All year**
Reduced Rates: **Available**
Breakfast: **Continental**
Credit Cards: **AMEX, MC, VISA**
Pets: **No**
Children: **Welcome, over 10**
Smoking: **No**
Social Drinking: **Permitted**
Minimum Stay: **2 days on summer weekends**

This 1920s Art Deco residence is located in a gracious neighborhood, five minutes from downtown. The inn has views of Mount St. Helens, the Willamette River, and Mount Hood. Hardwood floors, artwork, antiques, and contemporary pieces create a look of casual elegance. King, queen, or twin beds are available. Your hosts provide robes and hair dryers for your convenience. Riverfront Park and interesting restaurants are minutes from the inn.

Home by the Sea ✪

444 JACKSON STREET, PORT ORFORD, OREGON 97465

Tel: **(503) 332-2855**
Best Time to Call: **9 AM–6 PM**
Host(s): **Brenda and Alan Mitchell**
Location: **54 mi. S of Coos Bay**
No. of Rooms: **2**
No. of Private Baths: **2**
Double/pb: **$45**
Single/pb: **$40**
Open: **All year**
Reduced Rates: **Available**
Breakfast: **Full**
Credit Cards: **MC, VISA**
Pets: **No**
Children: **Sometimes**
Smoking: **No**
Social Drinking: **Permitted**
Airport/Station Pickup: **Yes**

This two-story contemporary was built by the Mitchells, long-time residents of Port Orford. The house offers a dramatic view of the ocean and is just a block from an extraordinary harbor, with easy access to miles of agate- and driftwood-festooned beaches. Storm-watchers love to observe the exciting winter storms; this part of the coast is also a favorite of scuba divers and surfers. Whale-watching season runs from October to May, and the Oregon National Wildlife Refuge is just offshore.

The Boarding House Bed & Breakfast

208 NORTH HOLLADAY DRIVE, SEASIDE, OREGON 97138

Tel: **(503) 738-9055**
Host(s): **Dick and Carole Rees**
Location: **1/2 mi. from Rte. 101**
No. of Rooms: **6**
No. of Private Baths: **6**
Double/pb: **$40–$54**
Single/pb: **$35–$49**
Separate Guest Cottage: **$65; sleeps 4**
Open: **All year**
Reduced Rates: **Available**
Breakfast: **Full**
Credit Cards: **MC, VISA**
Pets: **Sometimes**
Children: **No**
Smoking: **No**
Social Drinking: **Permitted**
Airport/Station Pickup: **Yes**

Located on the banks of the Necanicum River, this rustic Victorian was built as a private residence in 1898. During World War I, the house became a boarding home. After an extensive renovation, the wood walls and beamed ceilings have been restored to their original charm. Guest rooms feature brass or white iron beds, down quilts, family heirlooms, wicker, and wood. Claw-footed tubs, window seats, antiques, and a picture of grandma make you feel as if this house is your own. A fire is often burning in the fir-paneled parlor, and an old melody sounds just right on the old-fashioned organ. A 100-year-old guest cottage with wood paneling, country furnishings, bedroom, loft, and lake view is also available. Breakfast specialties such as cheese-and-egg strata, oven-baked French toast, and caramel sticky buns are served in the dining room or outside on the wraparound porch. The house is just four blocks from the ocean and two blocks from downtown.

Horncroft ✪

42156 KINGSTON LYONS DRIVE, STAYTON, OREGON 97383

Tel: **(503) 769-6287**
Host(s): **Dorothea and Kenneth Horn**
Location: **17 mi. E of Salem**
No. of Rooms: **3**
No. of Private Baths: **1**
Max. No. Sharing Bath: **4**
Double/pb: **$35**
Single/pb: **$30**
Double/sb: **$30**
Single/sb: **$25**
Open: **All year**
Breakfast: **Full**
Pets: **No**
Children: **Welcome (crib)**
Smoking: **No**
Social Drinking: **Permitted**

This lovely home is situated in the foothills of the Cascade Mountains on the edge of Willamette Valley. In summer, swim in the heated pool or hike on one of the scenic nature paths. The area is dotted with farms, and the valley is abundant in fruits, berries, and vegetables. Willamette and Oregon State universities are nearby. The Mount Jefferson Wilderness hiking area is an hour away. A guest comments, "The hospitality and breakfasts were topnotch!"

PENNSYLVANIA

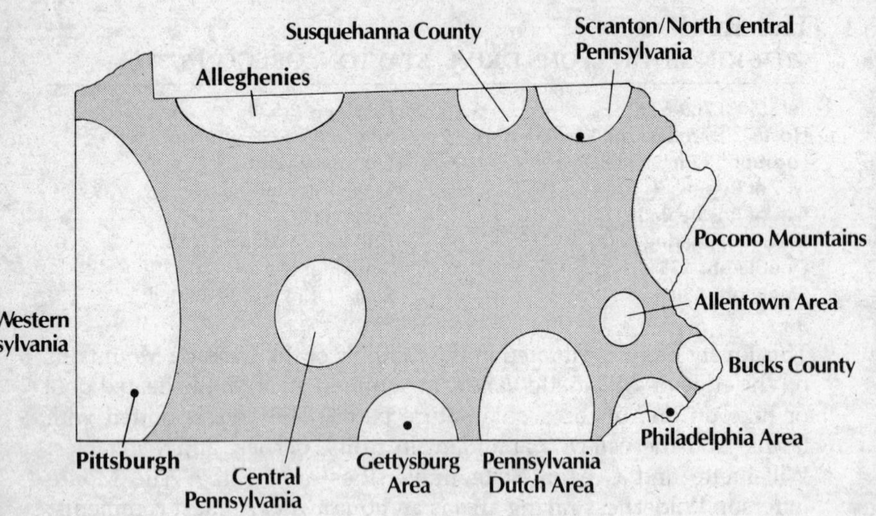

ALLEGHENIES

Bed & Breakfast in Pennsylvania—A Referral Service ✪

P.O. BOX 194, WORCESTER, PENNSYLVANIA 19490

Tel: **(215) 885-0991**
Best Time to Call: **1:30–5:30 PM (Mon.–Fri.)**
Coordinator: **Janet Mochel**
States/Regions Covered: **Statewide**
Rates (Single/Double):
Average: **$10–$60** **$20–$100**
Credit Cards: **Varies with each B&B**

Call Janet for the name and phone number of a B&B in the area you want to visit anywhere in the state. You can then call the host directly. Accommodations range from a clean but simple mountain lodge, to a comfortable suburban split-level, to a pre-Revolutionary manor house. There is no charge for this service. If you haven't decided where in the state you'd like to go, Janet sells a loose-leaf directory that includes all her inspected member homes for $7.50, post-paid.

Allegheny Bed & Breakfast Association ✪

BOX 95, TURTLE POINT, PENNSYLVANIA 16750

Tel: **(814) 642-2334**
Coordinator: **Peter Meissner**
States/Regions Covered:
Allegheniesc—Potter County, McKean County, Warren County
Rates (Single/Double):
Average: **$30–$35 $40–$50**
Credit Cards: **MC, VISA**

One can find peace and tranquility at an unrushed pace in this rural pocket in the mountains. Horseback riding, hiking on mountain trails, cross-country skiing, the Kinzua Reservoir for boating and swimming, the Allegheny National Forest, summer fairs, and year-round antiquing are some of the local diversions. Truly off the beaten path, the area hosts genuinely appreciate the "excitement" of having visitors and go out of their way to please them.

BUCKS COUNTY

Ash Mill Farm

P.O. BOX 202, HOLICONG, PENNSYLVANIA 18928

Tel: **(215) 794-5373**
Host(s): **Caroline and Jeff Rawes**
Location: **30 mi. N of Philadelphia**
No. of Rooms: **4**
No. of Private Baths: **2**
Max. No. Sharing Bath: **4**
Double/pb: **$65**
Single/pb: **$65**
Double/sb: **$55–$65**
Single/sb: **$55–$65**
Open: **All year**
Reduced Rates: **Mon.–Thurs., all rooms $55**
Breakfast: **Continental**
Credit Cards: **MC, VISA**
Pets: **No**
Children: **Sometimes**
Smoking: **Permitted**
Social Drinking: **Permitted**

This 18th-century farmhouse is set on ten wooded acres in the rolling hills of Bucks County. The Rawes' home has high ceilings, bright rooms, and a central stairway. The comfortably furnished bedrooms are accented with handcrafted quilts and family antiques. Mornings begin with homemade breads, fresh fruit with honey 'n' yogurt dressing, or quiche, served before an open fire in winter, and on the stone porch in warm weather. The farm is located adjacent to Peddlers' Village and nearby state parks, the Bucks County Playhouse, the outlets of Flemington, New Jersey, and many fine restaurants. There is a two-night minimum on weekends from April through November.

Pineapple Hill ✪

1324 RIVER ROAD, NEW HOPE, PENNSYLVANIA 18938

Tel: **(215) 862-9608**
Host(s): **Suzie and Randy Leslie**
Location: **40 mi. N of Philadelphia**
No. of Rooms: **5**
No. of Private Baths: **3**
Max. No. Sharing Bath: **4**
Double/pb: **$60–$70**
Double/sb: **$50–$60**
Suites: **$70–$80**
Open: **All year**
Reduced Rates: **5 nights**
Breakfast: **Continental**
Credit Cards: **AMEX**
Pets: **No**
Children: **Sometimes**
Smoking: **No**
Social Drinking: **Permitted**
Minimum Stay: **2 nights weekends**

The 18-inch walls, fireplace, and traditional woodwork attest to the 18th-century origin of this charming farmhouse. Suzie and Randy have furnished it with spool and brass beds, antique furniture, folk art, Persian carpets, pewter, and stoneware. When you return from the dozens of activities the area offers, relax in front of the fire, read, play backgammon, and visit.

Plumsteadville Inn

ROUTE 611 AND STUMP ROAD, P.O. BOX 40, PLUMSTEADVILLE, PENNSYLVANIA 18949

Tel: **(215) 766-7500**
Host(s): **Deborah and John Nyari**
Location: **4 mi. N of Doylestown**
No. of Rooms: **16**
No. of Private Baths: **16**
Double/pb: **$75**
Suites: **$125**
Open: **All year**
Reduced Rates: **20% less, Mon.–Thurs.**
Breakfast: **Full**
Credit Cards: **MC, VISA**
Pets: **No**
Children: **Welcome**
Smoking: **Permitted**
Social Drinking: **Permitted**
Airport/Station Pickup: **Yes**

This three-story Colonial stone house was built before the American Revolution. The guest rooms are individually decorated with antique furniture, custom drapery, and plush carpeting. One room has a canopy bed with a handmade crewel canopy, a crocheted-lace bedspread, and soft white carpeting. Bathrooms feature marble sinks and brass fixtures. Deborah and John will prepare gourmet omelets, apple pancakes, and muffins for breakfast. Just 45 minutes from Princeton, local attractions include the Pearl S. Buck home, Mercer Museum, and the artsy town of New Hope.

CENTRAL PENNSYLVANIA

Rest & Repast Bed & Breakfast Service ✪

P.O. BOX 126, PINE GROVE MILLS, PENNSYLVANIA 16868

Tel: **(814) 238-1484**
Coordinators: **Linda Feltman, Brent Peters**
States/Regions Covered: **State College, Bellefonte, Lemont, Potters Mills, Spruce Creek**

Rates (Single/Double):

Modest:	**$25–$27**	**$30–$34**
Average:	**$28–$29**	**$35–$37**
Luxury:	**N/A**	**$38–$55**

Credit Cards: **No**

You will enjoy touring historic mansions, Penns Cave, Woodward Cave, and several Civil War museums in this lovely area. A two-day minimum stay is required for the second week in July, the time of the annual Central Pennsylvania Festival of the Arts, and for the Penn State University Homecoming Football game in autumn. Rates are increased during football weekends to a maximum of $55 per night double. (No single rates on football weekends.) Pennsylvania State University is close by.

The Garmanhaus ✪

BOX 307, BOILING SPRINGS, PENNSYLVANIA 17009

Tel: **(717) 258-3980**
Host(s): **John and Molly Garman**
Location: **5 mi. from Rts. 76 & 81**
No. of Rooms: 4
Max. No. Sharing Bath: **4**
Double/sb: **$47**

Open: **Apr.–Dec.**
Breakfast: **Continental**
Pets: **No**
Children: **Welcome, over 12**
Smoking: **Permitted**
Social Drinking: **Permitted**

The Garmans' elegant Victorian is on Front Street, by the lake. John, an insurance agent, and Molly, a realtor, will help you feel at home. Snacks, beverages, wine, and beer are always on hand for your enjoyment. Feel free to use the grill, TV, laundry facilities, and tennis court. Bicycles and a canoe may be rented. Fairleigh Dickinson University is in the vicinity.

Yoders ✪

R.D. 1, BOX 312, HUNTINGDON, PENNSYLVANIA 16652

Tel: **(814) 643-3221**
Best Time to Call: **After 4 PM**
Host(s): **Randy and Peggy Yoder**
Location: **On Rte. 22**

No. of Rooms: **3**
No. of Private Baths: **2**
Double/pb: **$35**
Single/pb: **$28**

Open: **All year**
Reduced Rates: **10%, seniors**
Breakfast: **Continental**
Other Meals: **Available**
Pets: **Sometimes**
Children: **No**
Smoking: **No**
Social Drinking: **No**
Airport/Station Pickup: **Yes**

After you've visited the Swigart Museum of antique American automobiles, explored the caves or Lincoln Caverns, or taken advantage of Lake Raystown with its recreational diversions, come home to Randy and Peggy's. The house, fronted with a huge picture window and native stone, is located at the edge of a 200-acre forest where you may feel free to hike. Breakfast often features croissants, waffles, pancakes, or special omelets. Fresh fruit and cheese snacks are complimentary.

GETTYSBURG AREA

Historic Paul Sourss Plantation House

P.O. BOX 238, BENDERSVILLE, PENNSYLVANIA 17306

Tel: **(717) 677-6688**
Best Time to Call: **After 6 PM**
Host(s): **Mrs. Viola Earnst**
Location: **17 mi. N of Gettysburg**
No. of Rooms: **3**
No. of Private Baths: **3**
Double/pb: **$55**
Suites: **$55**
Open: **All year**
Breakfast: **Full**
Other Meals: **Available**
Pets: **No**
Children: **No**
Smoking: **Permitted**
Social Drinking: **Permitted**
Airport/Station Pickup: **Yes**

This stone plantation house was built by G. C. Mason in 1802, and is located in a quiet orchard setting. The decor features Victorian furnishings, herbal showpieces, Oriental rugs, and handmade baskets. In warm weather, morning coffee is served on the veranda with a French country breakfast of homemade bread, fruit and crêpes. In the evening, enjoy a snack of homegrown roasted chestnuts before dinner. Your hosts will gladly direct you to the many nearby antiques shops and markets. Hershey and Gettysburg National Park are also within an easy drive from the house.

The Leas-Bechtel Mansion Inn ✪

400 WEST KING STREET, EAST BERLIN, PENNSYLVANIA 17316

Tel: **(717) 259-7760**
Host(s): **Charles Bechtel**
Location: **18 mi. E of Gettysburg**
No. of Rooms: **7**
No. of Private Baths: **7**
Double/pb: **$60–$85**
Single/pb: **$45–$70**
Suites: **$95**

Open: **All year**
Reduced Rates: **10%, seniors**
Breakfast: **Continental**
Credit Cards: **AMEX, MC, VISA**
Pets: **No**
Children: **Welcome**
Smoking: **No**
Social Drinking: **Permitted**

This sprawling mansion was designed for the William Leas family in 1897. The rooms have been beautifully restored and feature original brass chandeliers, stained glass, and oak sliding doors. Sleeping quarters are elegantly appointed with handmade quilts and antique furnishings. Choose from the Balcony Room, with its turret-shaped bay window, or the Downstairs Suite, with its handmade walnut furniture and folding oak interior shutters. Guests are welcome to relax in the living room with an oak-and-mahogany secretary and a red Bokhara rug. Fresh muffins and coffee are served in the dining room, which has a large window seat, etched-glass windows, and antique rug. There is a large front-and-side porch for sipping a glass of wine or just relaxing and watching the village activity.

The Herb Cottage

LINCOLN WAY EAST, RTE. 30, FAYETTEVILLE, PENNSYLVANIA 17222

Tel: **(717) 352-7733**
Best Time to Call: **8 AM–9 PM**
Host(s): **Jim and Lois Stewart**
Location: **14 mi. W of Gettysburg**
No. of Rooms: **6**
No. of Private Baths: **6**
Double/pb: **$65**
Separate Guest Cottage: **$85; sleeps 4**
Open: **All year**
Reduced Rates: **10%, Jan.–Mar.**
Breakfast: **Full**
Credit Cards: **MC, VISA**
Pets: **No**
Children: **No**
Smoking: **No**
Social Drinking: **No**
Airport/Station Pickup: **Yes**

Beautiful greenery and gardens surround this old-fashioned lodge, set on 20 acres. The inn is a rustic log retreat built with American chestnut wood and natural stone. Rooms are carefully decorated with primitive country antiques, handmade quilts, fresh flowers, and homespuns. Your hosts offer a country breakfast, including gourmet coffees, homemade breads, herb butters, and cheeses. They invite you to visit their gift shop, where you can find unusual handcrafts and collectibles. There are endless activities and attractions nearby, including Gettysburg Battlefield, ski resorts, Caledonia and Michaux State parks, fine dining, and brilliant fall foliage.

The Brafferton Inn ✪

44-46 YORK STREET, GETTYSBURG, PENNSYLVANIA 17325

Tel: **(717) 337-3423**
Host(s): **Mimi and Jim Agard**
Location: **90 mi. N of D.C.; 2 mi. from Rte. 15, York Exit**
No. of Rooms: **8**
No. of Private Baths: **2**
Max. No. Sharing Bath: **5**
Double/pb: **$65**
Double/sb: **$60**
Open: **All year**
Reduced Rates: **10%, seniors**
Breakfast: **Full**
Credit Cards: **MC, VISA**
Pets: **No**
Children: **Welcome, over 7**
Smoking: **No**
Social Drinking: **Permitted**

This Early American stone structure is listed on the National Register of Historic Places. The clapboard addition dates back to pre-Civil War days. Four of the guest rooms, decorated with hand-painted stencils, are separated from the main house by an atrium where one may sit and enjoy the pretty plantings during the warm months. The sumptuous breakfast is served in the dining room on antique tables. There are hosts of activities to whet the appetite of the history buff, sportsman, antique collector, or nature lover.

The Old Appleford Inn

218 CARLISLE STREET, GETTYSBURG, PENNSYLVANIA 1732

Tel: **(717) 337-1711**
Host(s): **Del and Nancie Gudmestad**
Location: **3 mi. from US 15**
No. of Rooms: **10**
No. of Private Baths: **1**
Max. No. Sharing Bath: **3**
Double/pb: **$69**
Double/sb: **$59**
Single/sb: **$49**
Suites: **$79**
Open: **All year**
Reduced Rates: **10% less Dec.–Mar.**
Breakfast: **Full**
Credit Cards: **MC, VISA**
Pets: **No**
Children: **Welcome, over 12**
Smoking: **Permitted**
Social Drinking: **Permitted**

This is a beautiful brick mansion built in 1867 and decorated with country antique furnishings dating back to the Civil War. After your tour of the battlefield, Del and Nancie invite you to enjoy the warmth of several fireplaces, sip a complimentary sherry, and bask in the mellifluous strains of the baby grand piano in the parlor. There are ski slopes nearby for winter sports enthusiasts, spring apple blossoms, and fall foliage to enjoy. You are certain to awaken each morning to the scent of homemade breads, muffins, or to the house specialty, Appleford pancakes.

Twin Elms ✪

228 BUFORD AVENUE, GETTYSBURG, PENNSYLVANIA 17325

Tel: **(717) 334-4520**
Best Time to Call: **9 AM–9 PM**
Host(s): **Estella Williams**
No. of Rooms: **3**
Max. No. Sharing Bath: **6**
Double/sb: **$20**
Open: **All year**
Breakfast: **No**
Pets: **No**
Children: **Welcome, over 4**
Smoking: **Permitted**
Social Drinking: **No**

Estella's comfortable brick home is surrounded by the historic Gettysburg Battlefield. It is within walking distance of museums, the National Cemetery, swimming, golfing; the Eisenhower farm is close by, as well as diverse eating places. Your hostess is a former teacher and history buff who enjoys having guests.

The Doubleday Inn ✪

104 DOUBLEDAY AVENUE, GETTYSBURG BATTLEFIELD, PENNSYLVANIA 17325

Tel: **(717) 334-9119**
Host(s): **Joan and Sal Chandon, Olga Krossick**
Location: **3 mi. from US 15**
No. of Rooms: **11**
No. of Private Baths: **6**
Max. No. Sharing Bath: **4**
Double/pb: **$70–$80**
Double/sb: **$60**
Open: **All year**
Breakfast: **Full**
Credit Cards: **MC, VISA**
Pets: **No**
Children: **Welcome, over 7**
Smoking: **No**
Social Drinking: **Permitted**

Located on the Gettysburg Battlefield, this beautifully restored Colonial recalls past-century charms with Civil War furnishings and antique accessories. Afternoon tea is served with country-style drinks and hors d'oeuvres on the outdoor patio, or by the fireplace in the main parlor. One of the largest known library collections devoted exclusively to the Battle of Gettysburg is available to you. On selected evenings, you are welcome to participate in a discussion with a Civil War historian who brings the battle alive with accurate accounts and displays of authentic memoribilia and weaponry.

Beechmont Inn ✪

315 BROADWAY, HANOVER, PENNSYLVANIA 17331

Tel: **(717) 632-3013**
Best Time to Call: **9 AM–9 PM**
Host(s): **The Hormel family**
Location: **13 mi. E of Gettysburg**
No. of Rooms: **7**
No. of Private Baths: **3**

Max. No. Sharing Bath: **4**
Double/sb: **$55–$65**
Single/sb: **$49–$59**
Suites: **$70–$85**
Open: **All year**
Breakfast: **Full**
Credit Cards: **AMEX, MC, VISA**
Pets: **No**
Children: **Welcome, over 12**
Smoking: **Permitted**
Social Drinking: **Permitted**

This Georgian house, restored to its Federal-period elegance, offers the visitor a bridge across time. Climb the winding staircase to freshly decorated rooms named in honor of the gallant heroes of the Civil War. At breakfast time, enjoy homemade granola, baked goods, a hot entrée, and fruit. Join the other guests in the dining room, or take a tray to your room for breakfast in bed. Visit nearby Gettysburg, the Eisenhower Farm, Hanover Shoe Farms, Codorus State Park for boating and fishing or go antique hunting in New Oxford. Upon your return, you may take tea in the quiet comfort of the parlor. The Hormels look forward to pampering you.

Country View Acres ✪

676 BEAVER CREEK ROAD,
HANOVER, PENNSYLVANIA 17331

Tel: **(717) 637-8992**
Best Time to Call: **Evenings**
Host(s): **Alan and Teena Smith**
Location: **13 mi. E of Gettysburg**
No. of Rooms: **2**
No. of Private Baths: **1**
Max. No. Sharing Bath: **4**
Double/pb: **$38**
Single/pb: **$30**
Double/sb: **$34**
Single/sb: **$27**
Open: **All year**
Reduced Rates: **10%, seniors**
Breakfast: **Full**
Pets: **Sometimes**
Children: **Welcome**
Smoking: **No**
Social Drinking: **Permitted**

This spacious Colonial-style home is on several acres within view of the mountains and valley. The interior features Early American furnishings and a player piano in the living room. Guests may stroll the grounds and use the outdoor whirlpool spa. Attractions such as the Hanover and Lana Lobell Standardbred horse farms and Gettysburg National Military Park are nearby. Boating and sailing are minutes away.

New Salem House ✪

BOX 24, 275 OLD ROUTE 30, McKNIGHTSTOWN, PENNSYLVANIA 17343

Tel: **(717) 337-3520**
Best Time to Call: **Evenings**
Host(s): **Gretchen and Alan Mead**
Location: **5 mi. W of Gettysburg**
No. of Rooms: **4**
No. of Private Baths: **2**
Max. No. Sharing Bath: **4**
Double/pb: **$50**
Single/pb: **$45**
Double/sb: **$45**
Single/sb: **$35**
Open: **All year**
Breakfast: **Full**
Credit Cards: **MC, VISA**
Pets: **Sometimes**
Children: **Welcome, over 12**
Smoking: **Permitted**
Social Drinking: **Permitted**
Airport/Station Pickup: **Yes**

New Salem House is one of the oldest homes in McKnightstown. It is surrounded by flower gardens, a shade and rock garden, and a pond. Gretchen and Alan have a specialty perennial nursery on the property, and guests are invited to walk through and observe the plants. Inside, antiques, a cozy fire, and plenty of hospitality can be found. A hearty breakfast featuring homemade breads and jams is served in the dining room or on the screened porch. Your hosts are well traveled and invite you to join them for wine, cheese, and conversation. This lovely Colonial is five miles from the Gettysburg Battlefields and minutes from skiing, hiking on the Appalachian Trail, excellent antiquing, and miles of apple orchards.

Red Lion B&B ✪

101 SOUTH FRANKLIN STREET, RED LION, PENNSYLVANIA 17356

Tel: **(717) 244-4739**
Best Time to Call: **After 4 PM**
Host(s): **Harry and Marilyn Brown**
Location: **9 mi. SE of York**
No. of Rooms: **2**
Max. No. Sharing Bath: **4**
Double/sb: **$50**
Open: **May 1–Oct. 31; weekends only, May, Sept., Oct.**
Breakfast: **Full**
Pets: **No**
Children: **Welcome, over 5**
Smoking: **No**
Social Drinking: **No**

Sixty-foot pines surround this large red-brick home dating back to the 1920s. Guests are welcomed with afternoon tea and shown to comfortable rooms decorated with an eclectic blend of attic treasures. Enjoy a country breakfast in the dining room, outside on the balcony, or in the privacy of your bedroom. Marilyn and Harry have raised eight children of their own and enjoy meeting new people and entertaining. They will gladly direct you to many fine shops, restaurants, and outlets. York was a meeting place of the Continental Congress and has many interesting and historic places to visit.

PENNSYLVANIA DUTCH AREA

Bed & Breakfast of Lancaster County ✪

P.O. BOX 19, MOUNTVILLE, PENNSYLVANIA 17554

Tel: **(717) 285-7200 or 5956**
Coordinator: **Pat Reno**
States/Regions Covered: **Gettysburg, Harrisburg, Hershey, Lancaster, Reading, York**

Rates (Single/Double):

	Single	Double
Modest:	**$35**	**$45**
Average:	**$45**	**$55–$75**
Luxury:	**$70**	**$90**

Credit Cards: **MC, VISA**

There are gracious homes, hospitable farms, and quaint inns to accommodate you in the heart of Pennsylvania Dutch country. The area offers something for everyone. Take in history at Gettysburg, bargain shop at the Reading factory outlets; kids of all ages will enjoy Hershey Park. Restaurants featuring good food and plenty of it abound. Craft shops, antiques stores, and flea markets are havens for the discerning shopper.

Umble Rest ✪

R.D. #1, BOX 79, ATGLEN, PENNSYLVANIA 19310

Tel: **(215) 593-2274**
Host(s): **Ken and Marilyn Umble**
Location: **15 mi. E of Lancaster**
No. of Rooms: **2**
Max. No. Sharing Bath: **4**
Double/sb: **$20–$22**
Open: **April 15–Oct. 15**
Breakfast: **No**
Pets: **Sometimes**
Children: **Welcome**
Smoking: **No**
Social Drinking: **No**
Minimum Stay: **Holiday weekends**

Ken and Marilyn are busy Mennonite farmers with interests in crafts, quilting, and restoring their 1700 farmhouse. You are invited to watch the milking of their 50 cows, stroll a country lane to their pond, and to participate in the simple life-style. Bring your children to play with their boys, ages four and seven. All the popular tourist attractions are nearby.

Greystone Motor Lodge ✪

2658 OLD PHILADELPHIA PIKE, P.O. BOX 270, BIRD-IN-HAND, PENNSYLVANIA 17505

Tel: **(717) 393-4233**
Best Time to Call: **Weekdays AM**
Host(s): **Jim and Phyllis Reed**
No. of Rooms: **12**
No. of Private Baths: **12**
Double/pb: **$48**
Single/pb: **$44**
Suites: **$58**
Open: **Mar. 15–Nov. 15**
Reduced Rates: **Available**
Breakfast: **Continental—coffee and donuts**
Credit Cards: **AMEX, MC, VISA**
Pets: **No**
Children: **Welcome (crib)**
Smoking: **Permitted**
Social Drinking: **Permitted**

Situated on two acres of lush lawn and trees, the lodge was built in 1883. Back then, this French Victorian mansion and carriage house did not boast of air-conditioning, TV, and suites with kitchens, as it does today. Though a great deal of renovation has taken place, the antique features and charm of the mansion are intact. Good restaurants are nearby.

Winding Glen Farm Tourist Home

BOX 160, RD 2, CHRISTIANA, PENNSYLVANIA 17509

Tel: **(215) 593-5535**
Host(s): **Minnie Metzler**
Location: **19 mi. E of Lancaster**
No. of Rooms: **5**
Max. No. Sharing Bath: **5**
Double/sb: **$30**
Single/sb: **$25**
Open: **Apr. 1–Nov. 19**
Reduced Rates: **Families**
Breakfast: **Full**
Pets: **No**
Children: **Welcome**
Smoking: **No**
Social Drinking: **No**
Airport/Station Pickup: **Yes**

Watching 40 cows being milked on this dairy farm is a sight to behold, especially if your calcium usually comes from a container. You will also be impressed to learn that the walls in this 250-year-old stone farmhouse are 16 inches thick. It is air-conditioned for your summer comfort. Minnie's home cooking and baking are the focus of the family-style meals; breakfast and dinner are included in the rate. The Metzlers will be happy to share their slide show, "Our Way of Life," with you. If you're interested in taking home a handmade quilt or handcrafted souvenirs, there are many Amish shops nearby.

Rocky-Side Farm ✪
R.D. 1, ELVERSON, PENNSYLVANIA 19520

Tel: **(215) 286-5362**
Best Time to Call: **Before 5 PM**
Host(s): **Reba Yoder**
Location: **18 mi. S of Reading**
No. of Rooms: **2**
Max. No. Sharing Bath: **4**
Double/sb: **$20**
Single/sb: **$10**
Open: **All year**
Breakfast: **Full**
Other Meals: **Available**
Pets: **No**
Children: **Welcome (crib)**
Smoking: **No**
Social Drinking: **No**

You will be warmly welcomed by the Yoders to their farm, where they raise dairy cows, corn, wheat, soybeans, and hay. The stone-and-stucco farmhouse dates back to 1919 and has a wraparound columned porch for lazing away an afternoon. The rooms are furnished country style, complemented by handmade braided-wool rugs and pretty quilts. Bountiful breakfasts are Reba's style, so you're certain to be off your diet during your stay. Hopewell Village and the Amish countryside are pleasant destinations.

Covered Bridge Inn ✪
990 RETTEW MILL ROAD, EPHRATA, PENNSYLVANIA 17522

Tel: **(717) 733-1592**
Best Time to Call: **After 11 AM**
Host(s): **Betty Lee Maxey**
Location: **10 mi. from Lancaster**
No. of Rooms: **4**
Max. No. Sharing Bath: **4**
Double/sb: **$45–$50**
Single/sb: **$40**
Open: **All year**
Reduced Rates: **Available**
Breakfast: **Full**
Pets: **No**
Children: **Welcome, over 10**
Smoking: **No**
Social Drinking: **Permitted**
Airport/Station Pickup: **Yes**

Beautiful shade trees, an old stone mill, and a rustic covered bridge surround this limestone farmhouse. The inn was built 170 years ago on land purchased from William Penn's family. Guest rooms are large, sunny, and filled with fresh flower and herb bouquets from the garden. Air-conditioned, each is decorated with antiques, including the linens. One features a pencil-post bed with canopy and Laura Ashley linens. Another has a red-rope bed with an Amish star quilt. Breakfast specialties include hot breads, homemade jams, quiche, and cinnamon pancakes. Later, enjoy lemonade and cookies served on the porch or a cup of coffee by the living room hearth. Nearby sights include the Amish country, Ephrata Cloister, and antiques markets.

Gerhart House B&B

287 DUKE STREET, EPHRATA, PENNSYLVANIA 17522

Tel: **(717) 733-0263**
Best Time to Call: **9 AM–10 PM**
Host(s): **Shirley and Ray Smith**
Location: **13 mi. N of Lancaster**
No. of Rooms: **4**
No. of Private Baths: **3**
Max. No. Sharing Bath: **4**
Double/pb: **$55–$75**
Single/pb: **$45–$60**
Double/sb: **$45–$50**
Single/sb: **$40**
Open: **All year**
Reduced Rates: **10%, weekly**
Breakfast: **Full**
Pets: **No**
Children: **Sometimes**
Smoking: **Permitted**
Social Drinking: **Permitted**

Gerhart House was built in 1926 by one of Ephrata's most prominent designers. Alexander Gerhart saw to it that his spacious brick home reflected the rich woods and elegant fixtures of the period. The front parlor has oak flooring with walnut inlays, chestnut woodwork, and comfortable furnishings. Bedrooms are decorated in warm Williamsburg colors and have large, sunny windows, fresh flowers, and vintage carpets. In summer, enjoy a glass of lemonade on the porch or large veranda; in winter, afternoon tea is served. House specialties such as exra-thick French toast and quiche are served in a quiet breakfast room with small tables. Gerhart House is a short walk from the Ephrata Cloister, close to the Amish coutry, outlet shopping, and antiques markets.

Hershey Bed & Breakfast Reservation Service

P.O. BOX 208, HERSHEY, PENNSYLVANIA 17033

Tel: **(717) 533-2928**
Best Time to Call: **10 AM–4 PM**
Coordinator: **Renee Deutel**
States/Regions Covered: **Harrisburg, Hershey, Lancaster, Palmyra**

Rates (Single/Double):

	Single	Double
Modest:	**$30**	**$39**
Average:	**$45**	**$55**
Luxury:	**$55**	**$60 and up**

Credit Cards: **MC, VISA**

Renee has a small roster of lovely homes close to main thoroughfares. Hosts come from a variety of interesting backgrounds, and all share a common enthusiasm to share their homes and communities. You may choose a cozy farmhouse with separate apartment perfect for a family; there's even a fishing pond for the kids. A large older home with beautiful furnishings may be more what you're looking for. Whatever your wishes, the town that chocolate made famous will welcome you.

Gibson's Bed & Breakfast ✪

141 WEST CARACAS AVENUE, HERSHEY, PENNSYLVANIA 17033

Tel: **(717) 534-1035**
Host(s): **Frances and Bob Gibson**
Location: **One block off Rte. 422**
No. of Rooms: **3**
Max. No. Sharing Bath: **3**
Double/sb: **$45**
Single/sb: **$35**
Open: **All year**
Breakfast: **Full**
Pets: **No**
Children: **Welcome, over 5**
Smoking: **Permitted**
Social Drinking: **Permitted**
Airport/Station Pickup: **Yes**
Foreign Languages: **Italian**

Bob and Frances Gibson have a 50-year-old Cape Cod, located in the center of Hershey, walking distance from many local attractions. The house has been recently renovated to enhance the charm of the hardwood floors, wood trim, and original windows. The atmosphere is friendly and informal, and your hosts are glad to offer complimentary nibbles such as wine and cheese. Gourmet specialties such as Scotch eggs, scones, homemade breads, jams, and cinnamon buns are served each morning in a cozy breakfast room. The Gibsons will gladly help you find local sights such as Hershey Park, Chocolate World, Founders Hall, and the Amish country.

Groff Tourist Farm Home ✪

**766 BRACKBILL ROAD,
KINZERS, PENNSYLVANIA 17535**

Tel: **(717) 442-8223**
Best Time to Call: **7–8 AM, 5–7 PM**
Host(s): **Harold and Mary Ellen Groff**
Location: **12 mi. E of Lancaster**
No. of Rooms: **5**
No. of Private Baths: **1**
Max. No. Sharing Bath: **5**
Double/pb: **$42**
Double/sb: **$28**
Single/sb: **$26**
Reduced Rates: **Available**
Open: **All year**
Breakfast: **Continental**
Pets: **No**
Children: **Welcome**
Smoking: **No**
Social Drinking: **No**

This old-fashioned stone farmhouse, recently redecorated, has a porch on which to relax; each comfortable bedroom is cross-ventilated, so you can enjoy the crisp country air. In her spare time, hostess Mary enjoys visiting with her guests, while stitching the gorgeous quilts her grandmother taught her to make. Nearby restaurants serve good food. A two-night minimum stay is required.

Sycamore Haven Farm Guest House ✪

35 SOUTH KINZER ROAD, KINZERS, PENNSYLVANIA 17535

Tel: **(717) 442-4901**
Best Time to Call: **9 AM–9 PM**
Host(s): **Charles and Janet Groff**
No. of Rooms: **3**
Max. No. Sharing Bath: **8**
Double/sb: **$20**
Single/sb: **$20**
Open: **Mar.–Oct.**
Breakfast: **Continental, 75¢**
Pets: **Sometimes**
Children: **Welcome**
Smoking: **No**
Social Drinking: **No**

This spacious home is a dairy farm where 40 cows are milked each day. You are welcome to watch the process. The children will be kept busy enjoying the swing, kittens, sheep, and games. You may use the Groff kitchen to fix light snacks and the guest refrigerator for storing them.

Buona Notte Bed & Breakfast ✪

2020 MARIETTA AVENUE, LANCASTER, PENNSYLVANIA 17603

Tel: **(717) 295-2597**
Best Time to Call: **Mornings**
Host(s): **Joe and Anna Kuhns Predoti**
Location: **1 mi. from Rte. 30, Rohrerstown Exit**
No. of Rooms: **4**
No. of Private Baths: **1**
Max. No. Sharing Bath: **6**
Double/pb: **$50**
Double/sb: **$30**
Single/sb: **$30**
Open: **All year**
Breakfast: **Continental**
Pets: **No**
Children: **Welcome, over 2**
Smoking: **No**
Social Drinking: **No**
Foreign Languages: **French, Italian**

Anna, a former nurse, and Joe, a schoolteacher, invite you to their home with its comfortable rooms and commodious porch. Enjoy homemade breads, granola, and jams for breakfast. Hershey Park, outlet shopping, local antique and craft shops, and ethnic restaurants are some of the nearby diversions. When you come home, coffee and tea are always available.

Hollinger House ✪

2336 HOLLINGER ROAD, LANCASTER, PENNSYLVANIA 17602

Tel: **(717) 464-3050**
Host(s): **Jean and Leon Thomas**
No. of Rooms: **5**
Max. No. Sharing Bath: **4**
Double/sb: **$45–$50**
Single/sb: **$35–$40**
Open: **All year**
Reduced Rates: **Dec.–May**
Breakfast: **Full**
Pets: **No**

Children: **Welcome (crib)**
Smoking: **No**
Social Drinking: **Permitted**
Airport/Station Pickup: **Yes**
Foreign Languages: **German**

While this house, built in 1870, is undeniably grand in its style, it is also homey. Leon and Jean invite you to relax on the wide porch, or stroll about the five acres of land crossed by a woodland stream. Although it is convenient to all the area's attractions, it is peacefully away from the tourist traffic. Jean has led tours throughout the Lancaster area and will be happy to answer your questions and give expert advice.

Meadowview Guest House ✪

2169 NEW HOLLAND PIKE, LANCASTER, PENNSYLVANIA 17601

Tel: **(717) 299-4017**
Best Time to Call: **Before 10:30 PM**
Host(s): **Edward and Sheila Christie**
No. of Rooms: **4**
No. of Private Baths: **1**
Max. No. Sharing Bath: **6**
Double/pb: **$30**
Single/pb: **$29**
Double/sb: **$21–$24**
Single/sb: **$20–$23**
Reduced Rates: **$3 less on 3rd night**
Open: **Mar. 1–Nov. 30**
Breakfast: **Continental**
Pets: **No**
Children: **Welcome, over 7**
Smoking: **No**
Social Drinking: **Permitted**
Airport/Station Pickup: **Yes**

Situated in the heart of Pennsylvania Dutch country, the house has a pleasant blend of modern and traditional furnishings. Your hosts offer a fully equipped guest kitchen where you can store and prepare your own light meals. Ed and Sheila supply coffee and tea. The area is known for great farmers' markets, antiques shops, craft shops, country auctions, and wonderful restaurants.

The Loom Room

R.D. 1, BOX 1420, LEESPORT, PENNSYLVANIA 19533

Tel: **(215) 926-3217**
Host(s): **Mary and Gene Smith**
Location: **4 mi. N of Reading**
No. of Rooms: **2**
No. of Private Baths: **2**
Double/pb: **$45**
Single/pb: **$45**
Open: **All year**
Breakfast: **Full**
Reduced Rates: **Weekly**
Pets: **No**
Children: **Welcome (crib)**
Smoking: **Permitted**
Social Drinking: **Permitted**
Airport/Station Pickup: **Yes**

The Loom Room is a stucco-covered stone farmhouse dating back more than 175 years. It is located in the countryside surrounded by shade trees, flowers, and herb gardens. Inside, the spacious rooms feature country antiques, open beams, fireplaces, and handwoven accessories. Mary invites you to her studio, where her work is on display. Her talents also extend to the kitchen, where she helps Gene cook up eggnog French toast, homemade jams, muffins, and chipped beef. Breakfast may be served in the sunny kitchen or outside in the gazebo. This lovely farm is near major outlet complexes, Blue Marsh Recreation Area, Crystal Cave, and many historic sights.

Dot's Bed & Breakfast ✪

525 WEST MARION STREET, LITITZ, PENNSYLVANIA 17543

Tel: **(717) 627-0483**
Best Time to Call: **7–9 AM; 6–11 PM**
Host(s): **Dorothy and Erwin Boettcher**
Location: **7 mi. N of Lancaster**
No. of Rooms: **1**
Max. No. Sharing Bath: **4**
Double/sb: **$30**
Single/sb: **$25**
Open: **All year**
Breakfast: **Continental**
Pets: **Sometimes**
Children: **Welcome (crib)**
Smoking: **No**
Social Drinking: **Permitted**
Foreign Languages: **German**

Dot's is located in a quiet residential suburb of Lititz, home of the country's first pretzel bakery. Much of this quaint little town has stayed the way it was in 1756, the year it was founded. You are sure to enjoy an easy stroll past Lititz Springs Park, the historic buildings on Main Street, and the Linden Hall Girl's School. After a busy day, you'll be glad to return to Dot's, where you'll find a quiet guest room furnished with a cozy bed, lounge chair, rocker, and plenty of books. Awake to the birds singing and come downstairs for some of Dot's homemade muffins or shoofly pie. Your hosts will gladly direct you to the nearby sights, including the Wilbur Chocolate Factory.

Herr Farmhouse Inn

ROUTE 7, BOX 310, MANHEIM, PENNSYLVANIA 17545

Tel: **(717) 653-9852**
Best Time to Call: **After 4 PM**
Host(s): **Barry A. Herr**
Location: **9 mi. W of Lancaster; 1/4 mi. from Rte. 283**
No. of Rooms: **4**
No. of Private Baths: **2**
Max. No. Sharing Bath: **4**
Double/pb: **$75**
Double/sb: **$65**
Suites: **$85**
Open: **All year**
Breakfast: **Continental**
Pets: **No**
Children: **Welcome, over 6**
Smoking: **Permitted**
Social Drinking: **Permitted**

Nestled on more than 11 acres of rolling farmland, this farmhouse, dating back to 1738, has been restored with the greatest of care and attention to detail. Fanlights adorn the main entrance, there are six working fireplaces, and it has the original pine floors. Whether spending a winter's night by a cozy fire, or a bright summer morning sipping tea in the sun room, it is the perfect retreat. It is less than 20 minutes to the sights, shops, and restaurants of Amish country.

Maple Lane Guest House ✪

505 PARADISE LANE, PARADISE, PENNSYLVANIA 17562

Tel: **(717) 687-7479**
Host(s): **Marion and Edwin Rohrer**
Location: **60 mi. W of Philadelphia**
No. of Rooms: **4**
No. of Private Baths: **1**
Max. No. Sharing Bath: **4**
Double/pb: **$35–$45**
Single/pb: **$32–$35**
Double/sb: **$35–$40**
Single/sb: **$32–$38**
Open: **All year**
Breakfast: **Continental**
Pets: **No**
Children: **Welcome (crib)**
Smoking: **No**
Social Drinking: **No**

From the hill nearby you can see for 40 miles. Stroll the 200 acres of this working farm, with its stream and woodland. Your hosts welcome you to rooms decorated with homemade quilts, needlework, and antiques. The sights of the Amish country, such as the farmers' market, antiques shops, flea markets, and restaurants, are within easy reach. A two-night minimum stay is required on weekends.

The Rose and Crown

44 FROGTOWN ROAD, PARADISE, PENNSYLVANIA 17562

Tel: **(717) 768-7684**
Host(s): **Allan and Linda Helmbrecht**
Location: **10 mi. E of Lancaster**
No. of Rooms: **4**
Max. No. Sharing Bath: **4**
Double/sb: **$45**
Single/sb: **$35**
Open: **All year**
Reduced Rates: **15%, Nov.–Mar.**
Breakfast: **Full**
Pets: **No**
Children: **Welcome (crib, high chair)**
Smoking: **No**
Social Drinking: **Permitted**

Set amid the rolling pastures of the Pennsylvania Dutch farmlands, this was once the home of a country squire. The house was built circa 1760, and its large rooms have been fully restored and decorated with comfortable, informal furnishings. Each bedroom features a queen-size bed and can accommodate a family of four. Breakfast specialties such as French toast and Pennsylvania scrapple are served outside in the gazebo or on the sun porch. The Rose and Crown is near canoeing and hiking at Pinnacle Point, Lake Eldred Recreational Area, and the attractions of the Pennsylvania Dutch countryside.

Lofty Acres ✪

R.D. 1, BOX 331, PEACH BOTTOM, PENNSYLVANIA 17563

Tel: **(717) 548-3052**
Host(s): **Gary Hufford**
Location: **20 mi. S of Lancaster; 1 mi. from 272**
No. of Rooms: **3**
No. of Private Baths: **1**
Max. No. Sharing Bath: **4**
Double/sb: **$55**
Single/sb: **$35**
Suites: **$65**
Open: **Feb. 1–Jan. 2**
Breakfast: **Full**
Pets: **Sometimes**
Children: **Welcome, over 12**
Smoking: **Permitted**
Social Drinking: **Permitted**
Airport/Station Pickup: **Yes**

This charming 200-year-old farmhouse is as rich in history as it is in charm. The quiet setting offers a relaxing environment. Take a stroll by the pond or watch the farmers at work from the porch. Inside, the antiques and collectibles are enhanced by a working fireplace in every room. The house is centrally located, and the nearby attractions of Strasburg and Paradise are yours to enjoy. It is also convenient to the lush country estates of Chester County where the local gentry still ride to the hunt. Longwood Gardens and Chadds Ford are close by. Gary is an excellent cook who enjoys serving a variety of Pennsylvania Dutch breakfast treats.

Pennsylvania Hosts Bed & Breakfast ✪

819 MADISON AVENUE, READING, PENNSYLVANIA 19601

Tel: **(215) 372-3346**
Best Time to Call: **Evenings**
Coordinator: **Amy Nawa**
States/Regions Covered: **Berks County, Reading**

Rates (Single/Double):

	Single	Double
Modest:	**$28**	**$35**
Average:	**$38**	**$50**

Credit Cards: **No**

Amy Nawa has been in the Bed and Breakfast business for a few years, and she enjoys it so much that she likes to teach others the business. Amy teaches a college class on how to start your own Bed and Breakfast. Her roster includes 48 lovely homes close to the many attractions of Berks County. Explore the restored homes of Daniel Boone and Conrad Weiser, tour the Appalachian foothills, or shop the famous outlets. Whatever your pleasure, you'll enjoy it that much more as a guest in a friendly, relaxing host home. Almost all homes are located near the Penn State University campus in Wyomissing.

El Shaddai ✪

229 MADISON AVENUE, HYDE VILLA, READING, PENNSYLVANIA 19605

Tel: **(215) 929-1341 or 373-6639**
Host(s): **Dale and Joan Gaul**
No. of Rooms: **3**
No. of Private Baths: **1**
Max. No. Sharing Bath: **4**
Double/pb: **$36**
Single/pb: **$26**
Double/sb: **$36**
Single/sb: **$26**
Open: **All year**
Breakfast: **Full**
Pets: **No**
Children: **No**
Smoking: **No**
Social Drinking: **No**
Airport/Station Pickup: **Yes**

El Shaddai is a stone farmhouse over 100 years old. Guests will enjoy relaxing in the sitting room with cooking hearth and spacious outdoor side porch. Each morning a hearty breakfast featuring homemade jam is prepared by your hostess. Nearby places of interest include the factory outlet in Reading, the historical sites of Berks County, and the Pennsylvania Dutch country. Albright College and Kutztown University are nearby.

Fairhaven ✪

RD 12, BOX 445, KELLER ROAD, YORK, PENNSYLVANIA 17406

Tel: **(717) 252-3726**
Best Time to Call: **Early AM**
Host(s): **Adelaide Price**
Location: **8 mi. from I-83**
No. of Rooms: **3**
Max. No. Sharing Bath: **4**
Double/sb: **$35**
Single/sb: **$25**
Open: **Mar. 15–Nov. 30**
Breakfast: **Full**
Pets: **No**
Children: **Welcome, over 3**
Smoking: **No**
Social Drinking: **No**

Relax in an old German farmhouse furnished with treasures handed down for generations. Take a dip in the pool or visit where history was made in Gettysburg or York. Visit Lancaster for museums and local attractions, Hershey's Chocolate World, and numerous outlet shops. Penn State and York College are close by.

The Inn at Mundis Mills ✪

586 MUNDIS RACE ROAD, YORK, PENNSYLVANIA 17402

Tel: **(717) 755-2002**
Best Time to Call: **Afternoons**
Host(s): **Joseph and Marilyn Korsak**
Location: **2½ mi. from Rte. 30**
No. of Rooms: **2**
No. of Private Baths: **2**
Double/pb: **$50**
Single/pb: **$40**
Open: **All year**
Breakfast: **Full**
Pets: **No**
Children: **Welcome**
Smoking: **No**
Social Drinking: **Permitted**

This quiet country inn is surrounded by York County farmland. The wide front porch welcomes guests to sit and spend some time listening to the chatter of the birds. The pre–Civil War Dutch farmhouse is restored and warmly furnished with antiques. Homemade muffins and jams, fruits, cereals, eggs, and meats will start your day. And, you can walk off the calories as you tour the nearby museums, battlegrounds, and wineries.

PHILADELPHIA AREA

Bed & Breakfast—The Manor ✪

P.O. BOX 656, HAVERTON, PENNSYLVANIA 19083

Tel: **(215) 642-1323**
Coordinators: **Jackie Curtis and Mary Lou Paolini**
States/Regions Covered: **Ardmore, Bryn Mawr, Havertown, Merion, Narberth, Philadelphia, Phoenixville, Springfield, Wynnewood**

Rates (Single/Double):

	Single	Double
Modest:	**$30**	**$40**
Average:	**$35**	**$45**
Luxury:	**$45**	**$65**

Credit Cards: **MC, VISA**

Mary Lou and Jackie can place you in a variety of B&Bs in the Philadelphia area ranging from a cozy bedroom with a double bed, to a Main Line manor house where the guest room has a comfortable rocker from which you may watch TV, to a historic house built in 1790 that's furnished with antiques and has a canopy bed, afternoon tea, and a swimming pool as part of the package. Many are convenient to the University of Pennsylvania, Bryn Mawr, and Haverford and Villanova colleges.

Bed & Breakfast of Chester County

P.O. BOX 825,
KENNETT SQUARE, PENNSYLVANIA 19348

Tel: **(215) 444-1367**
Coordinator: **Doris Passante**
States/Regions Covered: **Chester County, Chadds Ford, Valley Forge**

Rates (Single/Double):

	Single	Double
Modest:	**$30**	**$40**
Average:	**$35**	**$60**
Luxury:	**$50**	**$60 and up**

Credit Cards: **No**

Doris has a wide selection of homes located in the beautiful and historic Brandywine Valley, which is known for the River Museum, Longwood Gardens, Winterthur, Brandywine Battlefield, and Valley Forge. The area is convenient to the Pennsylvania Dutch country. Send for her brochure, which fully describes each B&B. The University of Delaware, Lincoln University, and West Chester University are close by. There's a $5 surcharge for one-night stays.

Bed & Breakfast of Philadelphia ✪

P.O. BOX 680, DEVON, PENNSYLVANIA 19333

Tel: **(215) 688-1633**
Coordinator: **Betsy Augustine**
State/Regions Covered: **Philadelphia and suburbs**

Rates (Single/Double):

	Single	Double
Modest:	**$30**	**$40**
Average:	**$40**	**$55**
Luxury:	**$60**	**$70 and up**

Credit Cards: **MC, VISA**

Philadelphia is the "City of Brotherly Love," and you'll be made to feel like family in the B&Bs. Selections include luxury town houses in the heart of Society Hill, refurbished Victorians, suburban manor homes, country guest cottages, apartments near the museums, and places that are convenient to all the universities. There's a $5 surcharge for one night's lodging.

Bed & Breakfast of Valley Forge

P.O. BOX 562, VALLEY FORGE, PENNSYLVANIA 19481-0562

Tel: **(215) 783-7838**
Coordinator: **Carolyn J. Williams**
States/Regions Covered: **Valley Forge and Philadelphia suburbs**

Rates (Single/Double):

	Single	Double
Average:	**$25–$50**	**$35–$75**

Credit Cards: **MC, VISA**

George Washington would applaud the manner in which Carolyn has brought the British tradition of Bed and Breakfast to the area of his headquarters. Her roster includes charming private homes surrounded by nature yet convenient to major highways. Most are within 25 miles of such attractions as the Audubon Wildlife Sanctuary, Chadds Ford, the Devon Horse Show, King of Prussia, Longwood Gardens and Winterthur, Philadelphia, the Valley Forge Convention Center, and the Valley Forge Music Fair. The Valley Forge National Historic Park has wonderful hiking trails, bridle paths, and cross-country skiing within its 3,000 acres. There's a $5 surcharge for one-night lodging.

The Bed & Breakfast Traveler ✪

P.O. BOX 21, DEVON, PENNSYLVANIA 19333

Tel: **(215) 687-3565**
Coordinators: **Ann Goodman and Margaret Gregg**
States/Regions Covered: **Philadelphia and suburbs**

Rates (Single/Double):
Modest: **$25** **$35**
Average: **$40** **$50**
Luxury: **$60** **$65**
Credit Cards: **AMEX, MC, VISA**

You may choose from a select group of B&Bs including a secluded contemporary home with a ground-floor guest room. The adjoining den has a fireplace and TV just for you. There's a 1770 fieldstone farmhouse in the picturesque "hunt country" where your bedroom is appointed with antiques and a fireplace. Or luxuriate in a Tudor mansion with its billiard room, library, conservatory, and bedroom decorated in Dutch decor. Add a $5 surcharge for one-night stays plus a $5 handling fee for all reservations. A descriptive directory is free for the asking.

Guesthouses

R.D. 9, WEST CHESTER, PENNSYLVANIA 19380

Tel: **(215) 692-4575**
Best Time to Call: **Noon–4 PM**
Coordinator: **Joyce K. Archbold**
States/Regions Covered: **Main Line Philadelphia, Brandywine Valley, Chesapeake Bay**

Rates (Single/Double):
Modest: **$40–$45**
Average: **$50–$55**
Luxury: **$70–$75 and up**
Credit Cards: **AMEX, MC, VISA**

Most of the homes on Joyce's roster are architecturally or historically significant. Choose from an 18th-century home with a swimming pool and surrounded by gardens, or an authentic log house on a large estate adjacent to the Brandywine River. Some hosts are professional chefs, interior designers, or teachers who enjoy sharing cultural and scenic surroundings. Many homes are listed on the National Register of Historic Places. All are comfortable and friendly, serving the high-tech corridor, local prep schools and universities, and much more.

Philadelphia B&B Service

P.O. BOX 4755, PHILADELPHIA, PENNSYLVANIA 19134

Tel: **(215) 634-4444**
Best Time to Call: **Evenings, 9–11 PM**
Coordinator: **Gary Bruner**
States/Regions Covered: **Philadelphia and suburbs; New Jersey—Atlantic City, Cape May**

Rates (Single/Double):

Modest:	**$8**	**$25**
Average:	**$20**	**$28–$40**
Luxury:	**$28**	**$50–$65**

Credit Cards: **No**

Gary Bruner has a diverse listing of lodgings ranging from luxury town houses, high-rise apartments, and Victorian homes, to student dormitories. Most are located within easy reach of transportation, theaters, museums, fine restaurants, shops, and universities. Extras, such as free use of a health club, tours of historic sights, and visits with Pennsylvania Dutch families in the Amish country, may be arranged.

Buttonwood Farm ✪

231 PEMBERTON ROAD, KENNETT SQUARE, PENNSYLVANIA 19348

Tel: **(215) 444-0278**
Host(s): **Loes and Ray Hutmacher**
Location: **45 mi. S of Philadelphia**
No. of Rooms: **3**
Max. No. Sharing Bath: **3**
Double/sb: **$45**
Separate Guest Cottage: **$45; sleeps 2**
Open: **All year**
Breakfast: **Full**
Other Meals: **Available**
Pets: **Sometimes**
Children: **Welcome**
Smoking: **Permitted**
Social Drinking: **Permitted**
Airport/Station Pickup: **Yes**
Foreign Languages: **Dutch, French, German**

Ray and Loes Hutmacher have 20 years of experience as captain and chef aboard private luxury yachts throughout the world, and have recently dropped anchor in the rolling hills of Chester County. Their charming stone farmhouse is furnished in antiques and is situated on a lovely property with woods, pastures, a barn, and clay tennis courts. Relax with complimentary wine and cheese before dinner. The Hutmachers serve dinner by prior arrangement, and their own home-raised veal is the specialty of the house. There are also many fine restaurants in the area. Loes serves homemade French bread, blueberry muffins, jams, and fresh-squeezed orange juice as part of a hearty farm breakfast. This lovely home is within a 15-minute drive of Longwood Gardens and Brandywine River Museum, housing the Wyeth Family art collections. Trail riding, golf, canoeing, gliding, and Brandywine Polo can also be enjoyed nearby.

Le Clos Normand ✪

773 MARLBORO SPRING ROAD, KENNETT SQUARE, PENNSYLVANIA 19348

Tel: **(215) 347-2123**
Best Time to Call: **Before 11 AM; after 4 PM**
Host(s): **Marie-Anne Eidman**
No. of Rooms: **3**
No. of Private Baths: **1**
Max. No. Sharing Bath: **4**
Double/pb: **$60**
Single/pb: **$50**
Double/sb: **$50**
Single/sb: **$40**
Open: **All year**
Breakfast: **Full**
Pets: **No**
Children: **Welcome, over 10**
Smoking: **No**
Social Drinking: **Permitted**
Airport/Station Pickup: **Yes**
Foreign Languages: **French**

Marie-Anne has brought the ambience of her native Paris and Normandy to her two-story, red-brick B&B. Situated on two acres off a quiet country road, it is the perfect spot to unwind after touring nearby Winterthur and Longwood Gardens. A woman of refined taste, she has melded the style of 18th-century French furniture with Philadelphia antiques and a touch of the contemporary. Beautiful art, statuary, and fresh flowers complement the decor. The dining room is the setting for breakfast where the delectable entrées are served on Limoges china. You haven't eaten French toast until you've had Marie-Anne's, made with French croissants. Her clafouti, a mouthwatering fruit-and-custard treat, is included in our recipe section. Wine, tea, and coffee are always available.

Meadow Spring Farm ✪

201 EAST STREET ROAD, KENNETT SQUARE, PENNSYLVANIA 19348

Tel: **(215) 444-3903**
Host(s): **Anne and John Hicks**
Location: **2 mi. from Rte. 1**
No. of Rooms: **4**
No. of Private Baths: **1**
Max. No. Sharing Bath: **4**
Double/pb: **$45**
Single/pb: **$35**
Double/sb: **$45**
Single/sb: **$35**

Open: **All year**
Reduced Rates: **10%, families**
Breakfast: **Full**
Other Meals: **Available**
Pets: **No**
Children: **Welcome (crib)**
Smoking: **Permitted**
Social Drinking: **Permitted**
Airport/Station Pickup: **Yes**

This large stone house dates back to the 1830s. A hot tub and screened-in porch are two of the recent additions. The rooms are decorated with family antiques and Victorian whimsy. Your hostess welcomes you with tea, wine, and goodies. In season, she serves corn fritters, mushroom omelets, and homemade breads on the porch. Local attractions include Longwood Gardens, Brandywine River Museum, Winterthur, and downtown Philadelphia. Anne's collection of dolls and teddy bears delights children of all ages.

Mrs. K's ✪

404 RIDGE AVENUE, KENNETT SQUARE, PENNSYLVANIA 19348

Tel: **(215) 444-5559**
Best Time to Call: **7 AM–10 PM**
Host(s): **Charlotte Kanofsky**
Location: **30 mi. S of Philadelphia**
No. of Rooms: **3**
Max. No. Sharing Bath: **4**
Double/sb: **$40–$45**
Single/sb: **$35–$40**
Open: **All year**
Breakfast: **Full**
Pets: **No**
Children: **Welcome, over 3**
Smoking: **No**
Social Drinking: **Permitted**

Arriving guests are greeted with cheese, crackers, and appropriate beverages. Charlotte has made her guest-house business a labor of love. Her lovely air-conditioned home is on a quiet residential street but close to many attractions. This is Andrew Wyeth's territory (Chadds Ford). Longwood Gardens, Brandywine Battlefield, and Brandywine River Museum are all worthwhile stops to make. It's less than a half hour from Wilmington, Delaware, home of Winterthur, the Hagley and the Natural History museums. You are welcome to use the kitchen for snacks. West Chester University and the University of Delaware are close by. Lancaster is an hour away.

The Waln House ✪

1242 BROWNSVILLE ROAD, LANGHORNE, PENNSYLVANIA 19047

Tel: **(215) 757-2921**
Best Time to Call: **9 AM–9 PM**
Host(s): **Terence and Virginia McGee**
Location: **25 mi. NE of Philadelphia**
No. of Rooms: **2**
Max. No Sharing Bath: **4**

Double/sb: **$55**
Single/sb: **$50**
Open: **All year**
Reduced Rates: **10%, seniors; 3rd night**
Breakfast: **Full**
Pets: **No**
Children: **Welcome**
Smoking: **Permitted**
Social Drinking: **Permitted**
Airport/Station Pickup: **Yes**
Foreign Languages: **German**

At the end of a long driveway, bordered by ageless trees, is this fieldstone farmhouse built in 1682. Random-width pine floors and beamed ceilings are hallmarks of this historic home. Much of the furnishings have been handcrafted by Terence and Virginia and beautiful quilts grace the canopied beds. The 10-foot hearth of the walk-in fireplace is the setting for the bountiful breakfast. Breakfast features seasonal fruit such as raspberries, blueberries, or strawberries from the garden. Washington Crossing, New Hope, the shops of Peddlers' Village, the discount stores of Flemington, Sesame Place, and Princeton University are minutes away.

Blackberry Hill ✪

295 BOOT ROAD, MALVERN, PENNSYLVANIA 19355

Tel: **(215) 647-0554**
Best Time to Call: **After 3:30 PM**
Host(s): **Barton and Jacqueline Davis**
Location: **20 mi. from Philadelphia**
No. of Rooms: **2**
No. of Private Baths: **2**
Double/pb: **$50**
Open: **All year**
Breakfast: **Full**
Pets: **No**
Children: **Welcome, over 12**
Smoking: **No**
Social Drinking: **Permitted**

This sprawling contemporary is located high on a knoll overlooking several horse farms. The house is furnished country style, and guest quarters have their own private entrance. Bedrooms have twin beds, 19-inch TVs, private phone, and ample sitting space. A secluded patio and large pool are available in summer time. The day begins with the newspaper, fresh coffee, and a country meal of fresh breads, bacon or sausage, eggs, jams, and marmalades; the dining room table is always set with fine crystal and silver. In the evening, a glass of port or sherry is just the right thing before retiring to your room. Your hosts will gladly arrange riding lessons, and will direct you to nearby attractions such as Valley Forge National Park and Tyler Arboretum.

The Barn ✪

1131 GROVE ROAD, WEST CHESTER, PENNSYLVANIA 19380

Tel: **(215) 436-4544**
Host(s): **Susan Hager and son, Ted**
Location: **30 mi. SW of Philadelphia; 16 mi from Pa. Turnpike**
No. of Rooms: **2**
No. of Private Baths: **1**
Max. No. Sharing Bath: **4**
Double/pb: **$55**
Double/sb: **$55**
Suites: **$90 (2 bedrooms)**
Open: **All year**
Reduced Rates: **$10 less after 1st night**
Breakfast: **Full**
Pets: **Welcome**
Children: **Welcome**
Smoking: **Permitted**
Social Drinking: **Permitted**
Airport/Station Pickup: **Train**

Dating back to the 1800s, the Barn has been beautifully restored without sacrificing its original identity. Old beams, random-width pine floors, and stone walls are enhanced by simple furnishings and special antiques. Susan's pewter collection, old earthenware, and dried flowers are artfully arranged to add a nice touch. Children love the third-floor "open room," with its double bed, cots, and TV. It's 15 minutes away from Longwood Gardens, Winterthur, and Brandywine Valley attractions. Breakfast often features scrambled eggs in crêpes with Hollandaise sauce, Philadelphia scrapple, popovers, and fresh fruit. Wine and cheese are graciously served in the evening.

Quarry House ✪

R.D. 5, STREET ROAD, WEST CHESTER, PENNSYLVANIA 19382

Tel: **(215) 793-1725**
Host(s): **Marc and Diane Norton**
Location: **1 mi. from Rte. 202**
No. of Rooms: **2**
Max. No. Sharing Bath: **4**
Double/sb: **$60**
Single/sb: **$55**
Open: **All year**
Reduced Rates: **Weekly**
Breakfast: **Continental**
Children: **Welcome**
Smoking: **No**
Social Drinking: **Permitted**

Listed on the State Historic Register, Quarry House was built in 1884 with local green serpentine stone. Accommodations include a library for your reading pleasure and a sunny social room with a refrigerator. The bedrooms are attractively furnished with handmade quilts, antique dressers, and appropriate collectibles. Breakfast features homemade sticky buns and muffins. Marc and Diane will direct you to Longwood Gardens and the Brandywine River Museum as well as a nearby Victorian village. In late afternoon, you're welcome to join them for wine and cheese.

POCONO MOUNTAINS

Toby Valley Lodge

P.O. BOX 431, ROUTE 940, BLAKESLEE, PENNSYLVANIA 18610

Tel: **(717) 646-4893**
Best Time to Call: **Weekends**
Host(s): **Marion and George Whitner**
Location: **1½ mi. from Rte. 80**
No. of Rooms: **7**
No. of Private Baths: **7**
Double/pb: **$40–$50**
Open: **All year**
Reduced Rates: **Weekly**
Breakfast: **Continental**
Pets: **Sometimes**
Children: **Welcome**
Smoking: **Permitted**
Social Drinking: **Permitted**

If you've ever longed for your own mountain retreat, you'll feel as if your dream came true at this B&B. It faces the woods and Tobyhanna Creek, an excellent trout stream. In chilly weather, the huge fireplace serves as a cheery backdrop to the breakfast area. The comfortable furnishings are accented with antiques, good prints, and western art. Marion and George provide a guest refrigerator, and you may stock it with drinks and snacks. Activities for the sportsminded abound in the area. Jack Frost Ski Area and Pocono International Raceway are nearby attractions. There's a two-night minimum stay on weekends.

Dreamy Acres ✪

**P.O. BOX 7, SEESE HILL ROAD AND RTE. 447,
CANADENSIS, PENNSYLVANIA 18325**

Tel: **(717) 595-7115**
Best Time to Call: **8 AM–10 PM**
Host(s): **Esther and Bill Pickett**
Location: **16 mi. N of Stroudsburg**
No. of Rooms: **6**
No. of Private Baths: **4**
Max. No. Sharing Bath: **4**
Double/pb: **$38–$45**
Double/sb: **$30**
Open: **All year**
Breakfast: **Continental—May–Oct.**
Pets: **No**
Children: **Welcome, over 6**
Smoking: **Permitted**
Social Drinking: **Permitted**
Minimum Stay: **3 nights holiday weekends**

Situated in the heart of the Pocono Mountains, this comfortably furnished 100-year-old lodge is on over three acres, with a stream and a pond. Year-round recreation includes fishing, tennis, state parks, golf, horseback riding, skiing, and skating. There are many fine restaurants, boutiques, and churches in the area. Esther and Bill have been entertaining guests for over 25 years; their motto is: "You are a stranger here but once."

Nearbrook ✪

ROUTE 447, CANADENSIS, PENNSYLVANIA 18325

Tel: **(717) 595-3152**
Best Time to Call: **Mornings; evenings**
Location: **Bet. I-80 and I-84**
Host(s): **Barb and Dick Robinson**
No. of Rooms: **2**
No. of Private Baths: **1**
Max. No. Sharing Bath: **4**
Double/pb: **$40**
Single/pb: **$20**
Double/sb: **$30–$35**
Open: **All year**
Breakfast: **Full**
Pets: **Welcome**
Children: **Welcome**
Smoking: **No**
Social Drinking: **Permitted**

Enjoy the Poconos while making Barb and Dick's charming, informal home your base. Meander through rock gardens and down a woodland path to a clear mountain stream. Nearby are well-marked hiking trails and vacation activities in all seasons. The rooms are adorned with artistic touches. Each bedroom has its own sink. A two-night minimum is required on weekends.

La Anna Guest House ✪

R.D. 2, BOX 1051, CRESCO, PENNSYLVANIA 18326

Tel: **(717) 676-4225**
Best Time to Call: **After 6 PM**
Host(s): **Kay and Julie Swingle**
Location: **9 mi. from I-80**
No. of Rooms: **4**
Max. No. Sharing Bath: **4**
Double/sb: **$25**
Single/sb: **$20**
Open: **All year**
Breakfast: **Continental**
Pets: **Welcome**
Children: **Welcome (crib)**
Smoking: **Permitted**
Social Drinking: **Permitted**

This Victorian home has large rooms furnished with antiques; it is nestled on 25 acres of lush, wooded land, and has its own pond. Kay will happily direct you to fine dining spots that are kind to your wallet. Enjoy scenic walks, waterfalls, mountain vistas, Tobyhanna and Promised Land state parks; there's cross-country skiing right on the property. Lake Wallenpaupack is only 15 minutes away.

Hemlock Grove Bed and Breakfast ✪

R.D. 1, BOX 12-A, GREENTOWN, PENNSYLVANIA 18426

Tel: **(717) 676-4511**
Host(s): **Peggy and Mike Ackerman**
Location: **2 mi. from I-84**
No. of Rooms: **2**
No. of Private Baths: **1**
Max. No. Sharing Bath: **4**
Double/pb: **$40**
Single/pb: **$35**
Double/sb: **$40**
Single/sb: **$35**
Open: **All year**
Reduced Rates: **Available**

Breakfast: **Full**
Credit Cards: **MC, VISA**
Pets: **No**
Children: **Welcome, over 6**
Smoking: **Permitted**
Social Drinking: **Permitted**

This light and airy tri-level country home is surrounded by one and a half acres of groomed lawns, is edged by a stream, and is bordered by shade trees. It is attractively furnished in a comfortable mix of Laura Ashley and "Nana's treasures," and there's a pastoral view through every window. A wholesome breakfast with farm-fresh ingredients is served in the spacious, bright kitchen. Guests return in all seasons to this special area, unspoiled by the wheels of progress. Lake Wallenpaupack is only three miles away for boating, fishing, swimming, and snowmobiling. Golfing, riding, antiques shops, country fairs, restaurants, Bushkill Falls, and skiing are nearby. Best of all is returning "home," where Peggy and Mike will treat you to a snack, drinks, and a movie on the VCR. Justin and Travis will be happy to share their games and outdoor equipment with your children.

Academy Street Bed & Breakfast ✪

528 ACADEMY STREET, HAWLEY, PENNSYLVANIA 18428

Tel: **(717) 226-3430**
Host(s): **Judith and Sheldon Lazan**
Location: **100 mi. NW of New York City**
No. of Rooms: **7**
No. of Private Baths: **2**
Max. No. Sharing Bath: **5**
Double/pb: **$55**
Single/pb: **$35**
Double/sb: **$50**
Single/sb: **$30**
Open: **May–Oct.**
Breakfast: **Full**
Credit Cards: **MC, VISA**
Pets: **No**
Children: **Welcome, over 12**
Smoking: **Permitted**
Social Drinking: **Permitted**

This Italian-style Victorian (circa 1865) is situated on a rise near the Lackawaxen River. Judith and Sheldon have done a marvelous job of restoring the rare and beautiful woodwork, paneling, and inlay to make a fitting background for their lovely antiques and furnishings. You'd better diet before you arrive because you won't be able to resist the culinary delights at breakfast or the complimentary high tea. It's only minutes away from famed Lake Wallenpaupack.

The Harry Packer Mansion

PACKER HILL, ROUTE 209, JIM THORPE, PENNSYLVANIA 18229

Tel: **(717) 325-8566**
Host(s): **Bob and Pat Handwerk**
Location: **On Rte. 209**
No. of Rooms: **7**
No. of Private Baths: **3**
Max. No. Sharing Bath: **4**
Double/pb: **$75**
Double/sb: **$65**
Suites: **$110**
Open: **All year**
Breakfast: **Full**
Credit Cards: **MC, VISA**
Pets: **No**
Children: **Welcome, over 6**
Smoking: **Permitted**
Social Drinking: **Permitted**

The town, named for the Olympic legend, is a mecca of Victorian preservation and restoration. The mansion has been faithfully restored to recall an era of timeless ease featuring original Tiffany windows, English Minton tiles, exquisite chandeliers, and unique fireplace mantels. Pat and Bob have created fun themes including an Adventure Package for the sportsminded, a Romantic Getaway for a first or second honeymoon, and a Mystery Weekend with murder and mayhem to be solved. In addition, they plan guided tours, Victorian fetes, and fancy balls.

The Vines ✪

107 EAST ANN STREET, MILFORD, PENNSYLVANIA 18337

Tel: **(717) 296-6775**
Host(s): **Joan and Don Voce**
Location: **1 mi. from I-84**
No. of Rooms: **4**
Max. No. Sharing Bath: **3**
Double/sb: **$40–$50**
Single/sb: **$20–$40**
Open: **All year**
Reduced Rates: **20%, seniors**
Breakfast: **Full**
Credit Cards: **MC, VISA**
Pets: **No**
Children: **Welcome**
Smoking: **No**
Social Drinking: **Permitted**

The Vines is a Queen Anne Victorian, built in 1864, and has been completely restored. There are parks, flea markets, canoeing, antiquing, historical sites, skiing, fishing, and many charming restaurants within a short distance. Coffee and tea are available upon request; Saturday nights often have the added attraction of wine and cheese. It is a mile from Grey Towers, Apple Valley with its quaint little shops, and the Milford Theatre.

Bonny Bank ✪

P.O. BOX 481, MILLRIFT, PENNSYLVANIA 18340

Tel: **(717) 491-2250**
Best Time to Call: **9 AM–10 PM**
Host(s): **Doug and Linda Hay**
Location: **5 mi. from I-84**
No. of Rooms: **1**
No. of Private Baths: **1**
Double/sb: **$35**
Single/sb: **$25**
Open: **May 1–Oct. 31**
Reduced Rates: **15% weekly; seniors**
Breakfast: **Full**
Pets: **No**
Children: **No**
Smoking: **No**
Social Drinking: **Permitted**

Stay in a picture-book small town on a dead-end road. The sound of the rapids will lull you to sleep in this charming bungalow perched on the banks of the Delaware River. Doug and Linda invite you to use their private swimming area and will lend you inner-tubes for float trips. Nearby attractions include the Zane Grey house, Minisink Battlefield, Grey Towers Historical Site, the Victorian village of Milford, and all the sports and variety of restaurants the Poconos are known for.

Elvern Country Lodge ✪

P.O. BOX 177, STONE CHURCH-FIVE POINTS ROAD, MOUNT BETHEL, PENNSYLVANIA 18343

Tel: **(215) 588-7922**
Best Time to Call: **After 4 PM**
Host(s): **Dos and Herb Deen**
Location: **16 mi. N of Easton; 6 mi. from I-80**
No. of Rooms: **4**
No. of Private Baths: **2**
Max. No. Sharing Bath: **5**
Double/pb: **$60**
Single/pb: **$35**
Double/sb: **$50**
Single/sb: **$30**
Suite: **$70**
Open: **All year**
Reduced Rates: **10%, seniors; weekly; former guests**
Breakfast: **Full**
Other Meals: **Available**
Pets: **Sometimes**
Children: **Welcome (crib)**
Smoking: **Permitted**
Social Drinking: **Permitted**
Airport/Station Pickup: **Yes**

This is a working farm in the foothills of the Pocono Mountains. The house dates back to the Victorian period and includes a sun deck and patio. Guest quarters have cool summer breezes, individual thermostats, and wall-to-wall carpeting. Your hosts raise their own beef, vegetables, and fruit. They prepare a breakfast of country bacon, fresh eggs, and homemade jams. Fishing, boating, and swimming can be enjoyed in the two-acre lake on the farm. The Delaware Water Gap Recreation Area, Appalachian Trail, and Pocono Recreation Area are nearby.

The Redwood House ✪

BOX 9B, EAST SIDE BORO, WHITE HAVEN, PENNSYLVANIA 18661

Tel: **(717) 443-7186; (215) 355-1754**
Host(s): **John and Emma Moore**
No. of Rooms: **4**
No. of Private Baths: **2**
Max. No. Sharing Bath: **4**
Double/pb: **$35**
Single/pb: **$25**
Double/sb: **$30**
Single/sb: **$20**
Suites: **$60**
Open: **All year**
Reduced Rates: **5%, seniors**
Breakfast: **Continental**
Pets: **No**
Children: **Welcome**
Smoking: **Permitted**
Social Drinking: **Permitted**

This frame chalet is minutes from the slopes at Big Boulder and Jack Frost. In summer enjoy sunning and swimming at Hickory Run State Park. Nearby Lehigh River offers fishing and rafting. Your hosts recommend a visit to Eckley, where the movie *The Molly Maguires* was filmed—a true example of what life was like in a 19th-century mining community. After a day of touring, come and relax on the large, comfortable porch.

SCRANTON/NORTH-CENTRAL PENNSYLVANIA

Sommerville Farms

RD 2, BOX 33, JERSEY SHORE, PENNSYLVANIA 17740

Tel: **(717) 398-2368**
Host(s): **Bill and Jane Williams**
Location: **12 mi. W of Williamsport**
No. of Rooms: **6**
Max. No. Sharing Bath: **4**
Double/sb: **$35**
Single/sb: **$25**
Open: **All year**
Breakfast: **Continental**
Pets: **No**
Children: **Welcome**
Smoking: **Permitted**
Social Drinking: **Permitted**
Airport/Station Pickup: **Yes**

This beautiful white farmhouse, situated on a 200-acre working farm, consists of the original 125-year-old plank home with a Victorian addition built by the Williams family in 1880. A pre–Revolutionary

War cemetery is located on the property. One living room is graced with a massive, hand-rubbed cherry mantel and original wallpaper, and hand-painted scenes decorate the ceiling. Jane is a former antiques dealer; Bill is a bank executive. Bucknell, Lock Haven, and Penn State universities are within an hour's drive. Early spring is calving season and is an especially exciting time to visit.

Ye Olde Library B&B Home ✪

310 SOUTH MAIN STREET, JERSEY SHORE, PENNSYLVANIA 17740

Tel: **(717) 398-4880**
Best Time to Call: **9 AM–9 PM**
Host(s): **Helen and Bill Goodbrod**
Location: **16 mi. from I-80**
No. of Rooms: **4**
Max. No. Sharing Bath: **6**
Double/sb: **$35**
Single/sb: **$30**
Open: **All year**
Breakfast: **Full**
Pets: **No**
Children: **Welcome**
Smoking: **No**
Social Drinking: **No**
Airport/Station Pickup: **Yes**

Set in a scenic valley, this neat red-brick Colonial house once served as the town's public library. The 85-year-old building is furnished in Early American decor with a fine private library of Civil War books. Comfortable chairs on the commodious porch are a perfect spot to relax. Helen loves to show off her pretty flower gardens; Bill has an unusual collection of metal pencil sharpeners. It's not unusual to enjoy a sing-along around the living room piano.

Hill Top Haven

RD #1, BOX 5C, LIBERTY, PENNSYLVANIA 16930

Tel: **(717) 324-2608**
Host(s): **Richard and Betty Landis**
Location: **29 mi. N of Williamsport**
No. of Rooms: **3**
No. of Private Baths: **1**
Max. No. Sharing Bath: **4**
Double/pb: **$35**
Single/pb: **$30**
Double/sb: **$30**
Single/sb: **$25**
Open: **All year**
Reduced Rates: **10%**
Breakfast: **Full**
Pets: **No**
Children: **Welcome**
Smoking: **No**
Social Drinking: **No**

This sprawling ranch home is in a rural mountain area surrounded by fields, flower beds, and woods. The house is furnished with many antiques and offers beautiful views of the surrounding countryside. A 10-acre lake is available for fishing and snowmobiling, and biking trails abound. The kids will want to visit the ducks, geese, and dairy cows, and the pony is sure to bring out the child in you. State parks and a ski resort are close by, but if all you desire is fresh air and quiet, you'll find plenty of both at Hill Top Haven.

The Carriage House at Stonegate

RD #1, BOX 23, MONTOURSVILLE, PENNSYLVANIA 17754

Tel: **(717) 433-4340**
Best Time to Call: **5:30 PM–9:30 PM**
Host(s): **Harold and Dena Mesaris**
Location: **6 mi. E of Williamsport**
No. of Rooms: **2**
No. of Private Baths: **1**
Guest Cottage: **$45 for 2; $55 for 4**
Open: **All year**
Breakfast: **Continental**
Pets: **Welcome**
Children: **Welcome**
Smoking: **Permitted**
Social Drinking: **Permitted**
Airport/Station Pickup: **Yes**

This self-contained facility was converted from the original carriage house of an 1830 farmhouse. Perfect for a family, there are two bedrooms, a bathroom, a living room with cable television, a dining area, and a kitchen stocked with all your breakfast needs. Decorated in country fashion, with some antiques, it offers complete privacy just 30 yards from your host's home. You'll have access to a creek, a barn complete with a variety of animals, and 30 acres on which to roam. It's close to the Little League Museum and Loyalsock Creek for swimming, canoeing, tubing, and fishing. Bucknell University is less than an hour away.

The Bodine House ✪

307 SOUTH MAIN STREET, MUNCY, PENNSYLVANIA 17756

Tel: **(717) 546-8949**
Best Time to Call: **Evenings**
Host(s): **David and Marie Louise Smith**
Location: **15 mi. S of Williamsport; 10 mi. from I-80, Exit 31B**
No. of Rooms: **4**
No. of Private Baths: **2**
Max. No. Sharing Bath: **3**
Double/pb: **$40–$45**
Single/pb: **$35–$40**
Double/sb: **$35**
Single/sb: **$30**
Open: **All year**
Credit Cards: **MC, VISA**
Breakfast: **Full**
Pets: **No**
Children: **Welcome, over 6**
Smoking: **Permitted**
Social Drinking: **Permitted**

This restored town house dates back to 1805. A baby grand piano, four fireplaces, and a candlelit living room add to its old-fashioned appeal. A full country breakfast and wine and cheese are on the house. Local attractions include the Susquehanna River, the Endless Mountains, and the fall foliage.

SOUTHEASTERN PENNSYLVANIA

Bed & Breakfast of Southeast Pennsylvania

RD 1, BARTO, PENNSYLVANIA 19504

Tel: **(215) 845-3526**
Coordinator: **Joyce Stevenson**
States/Regions Covered: **Allentown, Bernville, Bethlehem, East Greenville, Ephrata, Oley, Plumsteadville, Pottstown, Reading, Robesonia**

Rates (Single/Double):

	Single	Double
Modest:	**$20**	**$30**
Average:	**$35**	**$45**
Luxury:	**$55**	**$70**

Credit Cards: **MC, VISA**

Joyce's territory can easily suit your mood, taste, purse, and palate in all seasons. The historic sights of Bethlehem, artsy Bucks County, Reading bargain factory outlets, county fairs, music festivals, antiques shops, craft boutiques, and wonderful restaurants are among your choices. Your "home base" can range from a suburban farmhouse to an elegant country inn. A two-night minimum is required on holiday weekends. Send $2 for her directory.

Brennans B&B

3827 LINDEN STREET, ALLENTOWN, PENNSYLVANIA 18104

Tel: **(215) 395-0869**
Best Time to Call: **7 AM–7 PM**
Host(s): **Lois and Edward Brennan**
Location: **1 mi. from 78 & 22**
No. of Rooms: **2**
No. of Private Baths: **1**
Max. No. Sharing Bath: **2**
Double/pb: **$40**
Single/pb: **$35**
Double/sb: **$30**
Single/sb: **$25**
Open: **Apr.–Dec.**
Breakfast: **Full**
Pets: **Sometimes**
Children: **Welcome**
Smoking: **Permitted**
Social Drinking: **Permitted**
Airport/Station Pickup: **Yes**

Furnished in Early American fashion, accented with lush plants and family treasures, this comfortable brick ranch-style house can be your home away from home. The Brennans are history buffs who, now that they're retired, enjoy traveling and entertaining travelers. Breakfast features bacon and eggs with home fries, or sausages and pancakes, or delicious muffins to go with the homemade jam. You can walk off the calories on your way to the Haines Mill, Dorney Park, or one of the area's many museums.

Longswamp Bed and Breakfast ✪

RD 2, BOX 26, MERTZTOWN, PENNSYLVANIA 19539

Tel: **(215) 682-6197**
Host(s): **Elsa Dimick and Dr. Dean Dimick**
Location: **12 mi. SW of Allenton**
No. of Rooms: **7**
No. of Private Baths: **3**
Max. No. Sharing Bath: **4**
Double/pb: **$60**
Single/pb: **$50**
Double/sb: **$60**
Single/sb: **$50**
Open: **All year**
Breakfast: **Full**
Credit Cards: **MC, VISA**
Pets: **No**
Children: **Welcome, over 8**
Smoking: **Permitted**
Social Drinking: **Permitted**
Airport/Station Pickup: **Yes**
Foreign Languages: **French**

This guest house was originally built around 1750 and served as the first post office in town. The main house, completed in 1863, was a stop on the underground railroad. Today, Longswamp is a comfortable place with high ceilings, antiques, large fireplaces, plants, and bookcases full of reading pleasure. Breakfast specialties include home-dried fruits, *pain perdu,* quiche, and homemade breads. Your hostess offers wine, cheese, and coffee anytime. She will gladly direct you to antiques shops, auction houses, Reading, and the Amish country.

SUSQUEHANNA COUNTY

Log Cabin B&B ✪

BOX 393, HALLSTEAD, PENNSYLVANIA 18822

Tel: **(717) 879-4167**
Host(s): **Bob and Ruth Leonard**
Location: **1 mi. from Rte. 81, Exit 68**
No. of Rooms: **1**
No. of Private Baths: **1**
Double/pb: **$35**
Single/pb: **$30**
Guest Cottage: **$35–$55; sleeps 2–4**
Open: **All year**
Reduced Rates: **Weekly**
Breakfast: **Continental**
Pets: **Sometimes**
Children: **Welcome**
Smoking: **Permitted**
Social Drinking: **No**
Airport/Station Pickup: **Yes**

Fish the waters of the nearby Susquehanna River, shop the local antiques shops, take in the Friday night country auction, or browse in Ruth's antique doll shop on the premises. In spring, you are welcome to watch the making of maple syrup and enjoy its sweet taste on your breakfast pancakes. The accommodations are most comfortable and your hosts are most cordial. If you miss city life, Binghamton, New York, is only 20 minutes away.

WESTERN PENNSYLVANIA

Pittsburgh Bed & Breakfast ✪

2190 BEN FRANKLIN DRIVE, PITTSBURGH, PENNSYLVANIA 15237

Tel: **(412) 367-8080**
Coordinator: **Judy Antico**
States/Regions Covered: **Pittsburgh and western Pennsylvania**

Rates (Single/Double):

Modest:	**$25**	**$35**
Average:	**$30**	**$40**
Luxury:	**$45**	**$65**

Credit Cards: **MC, VISA**

Judy has many comfortable accommodations in the historic Northside, South Hills, Shadyside, Squirrel Hill, and Mount Washington areas. Many homes are convenient to Carnegie-Mellon University, Duquesne, and the University of Pittsburgh. This is a great place to stop off en route to Cleveland (80 miles), Chicago (400 miles), and West Virginia (60 miles).

Garrott's Bed & Breakfast ✪

RD 1, BOX 73, COWANSVILLE, PENNSYLVANIA 16218

Tel: **(412) 545-2432**
Host(s): **John and Denise Garrott**
Location: **50 mi. NE of Pittsburgh**
No. of Rooms: **3**
Max. No. Sharing Bath: **3**
Double/sb: **$50**
Single/sb: **$40**
Open: **All year**
Reduced Rates: **50%, children under 12**
Breakfast: **Full**
Other Meals: **Available**
Pets: **Sometimes**
Children: **Welcome**
Smoking: **Downstairs only**
Social Drinking: **Permitted**

Experience year-round country living in this 100-year-old restored farmhouse set on 40 acres. This is a nature lover's paradise, with rolling fields, groves of trees, and a fishing pond. Sled riding, ice skating, or cross-country skiing can be enjoyed on the grounds, followed by hot drinks around the wood stove. If you're an amateur astronomer, Garrott's is an ideal spot for serious star watching because of the altitude and absence of pollution. John and Denise offer comfortable rooms decorated in antiques, collectibles, and colorful rugs. A cozy TV room and a sunny sitting area are available for relaxing. Breakfast includes farm-fresh eggs, preserves, and freshly baked muffins. Special arrangements can be made for basket lunches and home-cooked dinners.

Royal Acre Retreat

5131 LANCASTER ROAD, ERIE, PENNSYLVANIA 16506

Tel: **(814) 838-7928**
Best Time to Call: **7 PM–9 PM**
Host(s): **Betty Pelletier**
Location: **4 mi. S of Erie**
No. of Rooms: **2**
Max. No. Sharing Bath: **3**
Double/sb: **$30**
Single/sb: **$15**
Open: **All year**
Reduced Rates: **10%, seniors**
Breakfast: **Continental**
Pets: **No**
Children: **Welcome (crib, high chair)**
Smoking: **Permitted**
Social Drinking: **Permitted**
Airport/Station Pickup: **Yes**

The deed to this Victorian farmhouse describes it as a "royal acre," and that description still applies. The house dates back to the early 1900s, and is situated on a quiet property that includes a split-rail corral. Your hostess has decorated the bright, airy rooms with Early American and contemporary furnishings. She will gladly help you plan your visit over a glass of wine and cheese. Start the day with breakfast served in the oversize kitchen, dining room, or outside on the porch. There is something for everyone nearby—golf, skiing, several wineries and universities, and a state park with boating, swimming, and seven miles of beaches.

Das Tannen-Lied (The Singing Pines) ✪

1195 EAST LAKE ROAD, JAMESTOWN, PENNSYLVANIA 16134

Tel: **(412) 932-5029**
Best Time to Call: **8 AM–9 PM**
Host(s): **Marian Duecker**
Location: **85 mi. N of Pittsburgh**
No. of Rooms: **2**
Max. No. Sharing Bath: **4**
Double/sb: **$35**
Single/sb: **$30**
Open: **Apr. 2–Oct. 31**
Breakfast: **Full**
Pets: **No**
Children: **Welcome, over 10**
Smoking: **Permitted**
Social Drinking: **Permitted**

This Victorian home, built in 1872, is set on the shore of Pymatuning Lake, which offers many recreational activities. Or, you may simply sit on the big front porch and watch the boats go by. Marian is a retired home economics teacher and dietitian, and on advance notice she will prepare picnic baskets, lunch, or dinner at reasonable prices. You are welcome to play the piano, browse in her library, and enjoy a cool beverage whenever you wish. Thiel College is close by.

Villa Mayer ✪

1027 EAST LAKE ROAD, JAMESTOWN, PENNSYLVANIA 16134

Tel: **(412) 932-5194**
Host(s): **Walt and Ann Mayer**
Location: **21 mi. W of I-79**
No. of Rooms: **2**
Max. No. Sharing Bath: **4**
Double/sb: **$30**
Single/sb: **$25**
Open: **Apr. 1–Nov. 1**
Breakfast: **Full**
Other Meals: **Available**
Pets: **No**
Children: **Welcome, over 12**
Smoking: **Permitted**
Social Drinking: **Permitted**

This country villa is situated at the East Lake Road entrance to beautiful Pymatuning Lake State Park. The lake is a fine spot for boating, swimming, and fishing. Closer to home, a pond is located on the side of the house and a patio and swimming pool are right out back. Wake up to a country breakfast including homemade jams, jellies, and sweet rolls. Then go out and enjoy the nature trails, tennis courts, or golf course, all located within half a mile. Your hosts will gladly prepare picnic lunches and dinners with advance notice.

Magoffin Guest House ✪

129 SOUTH PITT STREET, MERCER, PENNSYLVANIA 16137

Tel: **(412) 662-4611**
Host(s): **Janet McClelland**
Location: **60 mi. N of Pittsburgh; 2 mi. from I-80, Exit 2**
No. of Rooms: **6**
No. of Private Baths: **4**
Max. No. Sharing Bath: **4**
Double/pb: **$50**
Single/pb: **$45**
Double/sb: **$40**
Single/sb: **$35**
Suites: **$65**
Open: **All year**
Reduced Rates: **Available**
Breakfast: **Continental**
Credit Cards: **MC, VISA**
Pets: **No**
Children: **Welcome**
Smoking: **Permitted**
Social Drinking: **Permitted**

The Magoffin Guest House is a large Queen Anne Victorian dating back to the turn of the century. It is situated on a tree-lined street next to a museum and opposite one of the country's most impressive courthouses. The rooms are furnished with antiques and handcrafted items from local dealers, including some from the Old Order Amish, who live in the countryside. If you like, items in the comfortable rooms and those in the "Spareroom" gift shop may be purchased. A public swimming pool, many lakes for boating and fishing, and the Amish country are all nearby.

The Stranahan House ✪

117 EAST MARKET STREET, MERCER, PENNSYLVANIA 16137

Tel: **(412) 662-4516**
Host(s): **Jim and Ann Stranahan**
Location: **60 mi. N of Pittsburgh**
No. of Rooms: **2**
Max. No. Sharing Bath: **4**
Double/sb: **$50**
Single/sb: **$45**
Open: **All year**
Reduced Rates: **15%, weekly**
Breakfast: **Full**
Pets: **No**
Children: **Welcome**
Smoking: **No**
Social Drinking: **Permitted**

Jim and Ann welcome you to share their 150-year-old Colonial Empire decorated with local antiques and cherished family heirlooms. After a delicious breakfast of quiche Lorraine, German apple pancakes, or ham and country eggs, Ann will be pleased to arrange a tour of the area based upon your interests. It may include Indian artifacts, a pioneer display, the historical museum, observing the Old Order Amish, visiting local artisans, with a stop at the corner drugstore with its old-fashioned soda fountain. Wine and snacks are offered while you sit around the fireplace or on the back porch.

Windward Inn ✪

51 FREEPORT ROAD, NORTH EAST, PENNSYLVANIA 16428

Tel: **(814) 725-5336**
Best Time to Call: **9–10 AM**
Host(s): **Bill and Ruth Brown**
Location: **15 mi. E of Erie**
No. of Rooms: **4**
No. of Private Baths: **2**
Max. No. Sharing Bath: **4**
Double/pb: **$45**
Single/pb: **$40**
Double/sb: **$40**
Single/sb: **$35**
Open: **All year**
Breakfast: **Full**
Pets: **Sometimes**
Children: **Welcome, over 11**
Smoking: **Permitted**
Social Drinking: **Permitted**

This large Colonial Revival home is set among vineyards, a salmon and trout stream, and the beaches of Lake Erie. It is furnished with antiques and treasures collected from the Browns' seven years spent abroad. Bill is an educator; Ruth cooks, weaves, and attends country auctions whenever possible. They will happily assist you with dining reservations, visits to local wineries, shopping, or directions to the famous Chautauqua Institute.

Oakwood ✪

235 JOHNSTON ROAD, PITTSBURGH, PENNSYLVANIA 15241

Tel: **(412) 835-9565**
Best Time to Call: **8 AM–8 PM**
Host(s): **Cynthia Wagar**
Location: **5 mi. from Rte. 79, Bridgeville Exit**
No. of Rooms: **2**
No. of Private Baths: **2**
Double/pb: **$45**
Open: **All year**
Breakfast: **Full**
Pets: **No**
Children: **No**
Smoking: **Permitted**
Social Drinking: **Permitted**

Tea, complete with small sandwiches and sweets, is served at 4 PM at this Colonial home set on two acres of oaks, lawns, and gardens. You are welcome to enjoy the Scandinavian spa, pool, track, exercise equipment, and raquetball facility. Breakfast often features special omelets and home-baked banana bread. It is always served on fine Limoges or Spode china, with lovely silver and linen napery. This is a charming home furnished with fine antiques of the 18th and 19th centuries. Area attractions include the Frick Museum, Trolley Museum, Buhl Planetarium, plus Carnegie-Mellon, Duquesne, and Pittsburgh universities.

Millstone Inn ✪

BOX 279, SCHELLSBURG, PENNSYLVANIA 15559

Tel: **(814) 733-4864**
Host(s): **Mike and Patti Murphy**
Location: **10 mi. from Pa. Tpk., Exit 11**
No. of Rooms: **2**
No. of Private Baths: **2**
Max. No. Sharing Bath: **4**
Double/pb: **$65**
Single/pb: **$60**
Double/sb: **$45–$60**
Single/sb: **$40–$55**
Open: **All year**
Reduced Rates: **Mon.–Thurs.**
Breakfast: **Continental**
Pets: **No**
Children: **Welcome**
Smoking: **Permitted**
Social Drinking: **Permitted**

This Georgian-style stone house has porches off the first and second floors. In the evening, guests often roast marshmallows in the outdoor fireplace. A player piano keeps everyone entertained. Breakfast features home-baked breads and pastries, and occasionally, Patti's apple dumplings. Bedford County is noted for its gorgeous mountain scenery and 15 covered bridges. The Blue Knob Ski Resort is a short drive from the inn; in summer, swimming, boating, and fishing are within easy reach.

Bennett's Bed & Breakfast

1700 PENNSYLVANIA AVENUE EAST, WARREN, PENNSYLVANIA 16365

Tel: **(814) 723-7358**
Best Time to Call: **9 AM–9 PM**
Host(s): **Charles and Dorothy Bennett**
Location: **70 mi. SW of Buffalo**
No. of Rooms: **3**
No. of Private Baths: **1**
Max. No. Sharing Bath: **4**
Double/pb: **$45**
Single/pb: **$40**
Double/sb: **$35**
Open: **All year**
Breakfast: **Full**
Pets: **No**
Children: **Welcome, over 10**
Smoking: **Permitted**
Social Drinking: **Permitted**
Airport/Station Pickup: **Yes**

Several large maple trees surround this remodeled Victorian with charming greenhouse. The house features rooms with warm paneling furnished in Americana and a few antiques. Guest rooms have twin beds, television, and air-conditioning. Charles and Dorothy serve a full English breakfast in a sunny garden room. Specialties of the house include French toast, quiche, and bran muffins. Bennett's is close to a variety of recreational activities, including hiking, fishing, hunting, golf, and swimming. The Kinzua Dam and the Chautauqua Institute are both nearby.

Bird Garden B&B

1415 MAPLEVIEW DRIVE, WASHINGTON, PENNSYLVANIA 15301

Tel: **(412) 745-8381**
Host(s): **Gene and Janet Shaw**
Location: **25 mi. S of Pittsburgh; 3½ mi. from I-70 and I-79**
No. of Rooms: **1 suite**
No. of Private Baths: **1**
Suites: **$50**

Open: **All year**
Breakfast: **Continental**
Other Meals: **Available**
Pets: **Welcome**
Children: **Welcome**
Smoking: **Permitted**
Social Drinking: **Permitted**

Bird Garden is situated on a high hill overlooking a cattle farm, yet it is only 30 minutes from downtown Pittsburgh. Both Gene and Janet are semiretired newspaper publishers. They offer a private guest studio suite, featuring a Franklin fireplace and picture window overlooking the bird garden. The suite sleeps two and includes a kitchenette, TV, and bath. Gene bakes bread and is happy to serve you some at breakfast. Guests are welcome to sit in the garden near the fountain, or walk the bluebird trail. Good restaurants are nearby, and the Meadows Harness Race Track is a mile away.

For key to listings, see inside front or back cover.

✪ This star means that rates are guaranteed through December 31, 1988 to any guest making a reservation as a result of reading about the B&B in *BED & BREAKFAST U.S.A.*—1988 edition.

Please enclose a self-addressed, stamped, business-sized envelope when contacting reservation services.

For more details on what you can expect in a B&B, see Chapter 1.

Always mention *Bed & Breakfast U.S.A.* when making reservations!

If no B&B is listed in the area you'll be visiting, use the form on page 698 to order a copy of our "List of New B&Bs."

We want to hear from you! Use the form on page 697.

RHODE ISLAND

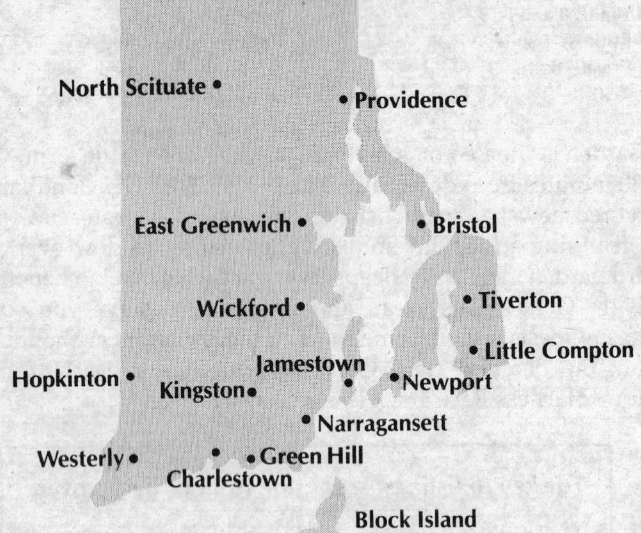

Bed & Breakfast of Rhode Island ✪

P.O. BOX 3291, NEWPORT, RHODE ISLAND 02840

Tel: **(401) 849-1298**
Best Time to Call: **9 AM–5:30 PM**
Coordinator: **Joy Meiser**
State/Regions Covered: **Rhode Island statewide; Massachusetts; Connecticut—Mystic**

Rates (Single/Double)

Modest:	**\$30–\$35**	**\$38–\$45**
Average:	**\$40–\$50**	**\$50–\$70**
Luxury:	**\$55–\$80**	**\$75–\$120**

Credit Cards: **MC, VISA**
Minimum stay: **3 nights, holiday weekends; 2 nights, summer weekends**

Joy will share her interest in local history with you from the time she confirms your reservation. Many B&Bs are listed on the National Register of Historic Places; some are near the shore, and several are located in or near Newport. Send $2 for a descriptive host directory or phone with details of your needs and she will place you in a comfortable lodging that suits your taste and purse. There's a surcharge for one-night stays.

Fairfield-By-The-Sea ✪

527 GREEN HILL BEACH ROAD, GREEN HILL, RHODE ISLAND 02879

Tel: **(401) 789-4717**
Host(s): **Jeanne Ayers Lewis**
Location: **15 mi. from I-95**
No. of Rooms: **2**
Max. No. Sharing Bath: **4**
Double/sb: **$56**
Single/sb: **$52**
Open: **All year**
Reduced Rates: **Oct. 12–Apr. 1**
Breakfast: **Continental**
Pets: **No**
Children: **Welcome**
Smoking: **Permitted**
Social Drinking: **Permitted**

"Stress reduction is the order of the day here," says Jeanne. She's a home economist who has taught school and worked as a consultant for McCalls. Her house, designed and built by her artist-husband, is a contemporary gem graced with balconies, a sunning deck, and a spiral staircase that leads to the guest rooms. The walls are a gallery of art by her talented family. Seafood feasts are sometimes organized as a cooperative venture among guests, who may try their luck at catching blue crabs or harvesting mussels in the waters nearby. It is convenient to all sorts of sporting activities, the Mystic Seaport, and the University of Rhode Island.

Hedgerow Bed & Breakfast ✪

11 MOORESFIELD ROAD (RTE. 138), P.O. BOX 1586, KINGSTON, RHODE ISLAND 02881

Tel: **(401) 783-2671**
Host(s): **Ann and Jim Ross**
Location: **11 mi. from I-95, Exit 3A**
No. of Rooms: **2**
Max. No. Sharing Bath: **4**
Double/sb: **$50**
Single/sb: **$45**
Open: **All year**
Breakfast: **Full**
Pets: **No**
Children: **Welcome (crib)**
Smoking: **Permitted**
Social Drinking: **Permitted**
Airport/Station Pickup: **Yes**

Built in 1933, this white shingled Colonial with its Wedgewood blue shutters is just half a mile from the University of Rhode Island. The grounds are maintained in accordance with the original horticultural blueprints and include hedgerows, gardens, a fish pond, and a gazebo. The tennis court in no way distracts from the landscaping. The dining room, with its pink marble fireplace and corner cabinets housing a lovely china collection, is the setting for a bountiful breakfast. Providence, Newport, and Block Island are nearby, but be sure to return at 5 PM for the wine-and-cheese hour.

The House of Snee ✪

191 OCEAN ROAD, NARRAGANSETT, RHODE ISLAND 02882

Tel: **(401) 783-9494**
Best Time to Call: **After 6 PM**
Host(s): **Mildred Snee**
Location: **15 mi. SW of Newport**
No. of Rooms: **3**
Max. No. Sharing Bath: **4**
Double/sb: **$40–$45**
Single/sb: **$30**
Open: **All year**
Reduced Rates: **10%, seniors**
Breakfast: **Full**
Pets: **No**
Children: **Welcome over 2**
Smoking: **Permitted**
Social Drinking: **Permitted**
Airport/Station Pickup: **Yes**

This century-old Dutch Colonial overlooks the waters of Rhode Island Sound. It's just across the street from the fishing pier where you can buy tackle and everything you need to hook a big one. It's a mile to the beach and just minutes from the Block Island ferry. Mildred's kitchen is her kingdom and her breakfast often features delicious specialties such as crêpes, egg and meat combinations, homemade scones, and plenty of freshly brewed coffee. Winery tours are a fun diversion in the area. The University of Rhode Island is nearby.

Ilverthorpe Cottage ✪

41 ROBINSON STREET, NARRAGANSETT, RHODE ISLAND 02882

Tel: **(401) 789-2392**
Best Time to Call: **Before 10 AM; after 5 PM**
Host(s): **Chris and Jill Raggio**
Location: **15 mi. SW of Newport**
No. of Rooms: **4**
No. of Private Baths: **2**
Max. No. Sharing Bath: **4**
Double/pb: **$55–$65**
Double/sb: **$45–$55**
Single/pb: **$40–$45**
Open: **All year**
Reduced Rates: **Weekly**
Breakfast: **Full**
Pets: **No**
Children: **Welcome**
Smoking: **Permitted**
Social Drinking: **Permitted**
Airport/Station Pickup: **Yes**

Located in the heart of the historic district, three blocks from the town's pier beach, is this charming hip-roofed Victorian built in 1896. The rooms are tastefully decorated with family antiques, providing a perfect background for relaxing. The wicker rockers on the veranda are a favorite with the guests. Fine restaurants, shops, and the summer band concerts in town are close by, and Newport's mansions, the Block Island ferry, and the fishing village of Galilee are just a short drive. Breakfast often features Belgian waffles or soufflés. Complimentary wine, coffee, and tea are offered in the evening. Two-night minimum on weekends from June through September is requested.

Ellery Park House ✪

44 FAREWELL STREET, NEWPORT, RHODE ISLAND 02840

Tel: **(401) 847-6320**
Best Time to Call: **After 5 PM**
Host(s): **Margo Waite**
Location: **25 mi. from I-95**
No. of Rooms: **2**
Max. No. Sharing Bath: **4**
Double/sb: **$50**
Single/sb: **$50**
Open: **All year**
Breakfast: **Continental**
Pets: **No**
Children: **No**
Smoking: **Permitted**
Social Drinking: **Permitted**
Airport/Station Pickup: **Yes**

Enjoy European hospitality in a turn-of-the-century home, just four blocks from the waterfront. Guest rooms are small and cozy, featuring fluffy towels and lots of reading material. Fresh juice, homemade jam, muffins, and freshly ground coffee are served mornings. You may like a peek at the kitchen with its restaurant stove and array of copper cookware. Margo will gladly direct you to the beach, waterfront restaurants, and historic homes.

The Pilgrim House

123 SPRING STREET, NEWPORT, RHODE ISLAND 02846

Tel: **(401) 846-0040**
Best Time to Call: **Early mornings; evenings**
Host(s): **Bruce and Pam Bayuk**
Location: **10 mi. from I-95, Exit 3**
No. of Rooms: **10**
No. of Private Baths: **8**
Max. No. Sharing Bath: **4**
Double/pb: **$85**
Double/sb: **$75**
Open: **All year**
Breakfast: **Continental**
Credit Cards: **MC, VISA**
Pets: **No**
Children: **Welcome, over 14**
Smoking: **Permitted**
Social Drinking: **Permitted**
Airport/Station Pickup: **Yes**

Centrally located, Pilgrim House sits on a historic hill next to Trinity Church. It is an easy walk to shops, restaurants, the wharf area, the spectacular mansions, and the beaches. The third-floor deck is often the site for breakfast when one may enjoy gourmet coffee and fresh fruit while watching the boats in the harbor. The inn is a turn-of-the-century gray Victorian surrounded by bright flowers. The rooms are decorated with period furnishings and appropriate wallpapers.

Woody Hill Guest House ✪

RR3, BOX 676E, WOODY HILL ROAD, WESTERLY, RHODE ISLAND 02891

Tel: **(401) 322-0452**
Best Time to Call: **After 5 PM, during school year**
Host(s): **Ellen L. Madison**
Location: **3/4 mi. from Rt 1**
No. of Rooms: **4**
Max. No. Sharing Bath: **4**
Double/sb: **$52**
Single/sb: **$46**
Open: **All year**
Reduced Rates: **Off-season**
Breakfast: **Full**
Pets: **No**
Children: **Welcome**
Smoking: **No**
Social Drinking: **Permitted**

This Colonial reproduction is set on a hilltop among informal gardens and fields. Antiques, wide-board floors, and handmade quilts create an Early American atmosphere. Your hostess serves homemade jams, muffins, and fresh raspberries in the morning. She can direct you to Mystic Seaport, Block Island, and historic areas. Watch Hill and Westerly beaches are two miles away.

SOUTH CAROLINA

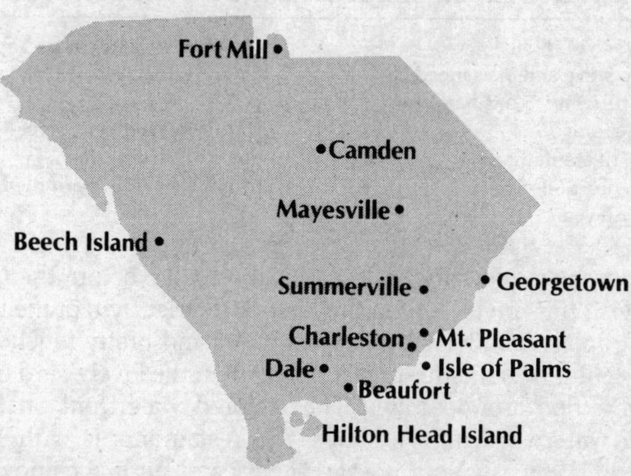

Old Point Inn

212 NEW STREET, BEAUFORT, SOUTH CAROLINA 29902

Tel: **(803) 524-3177**
Best Time to Call: **After 5 PM**
Host(s): **Sandra and Charlie Williams**
Location: **69 mi. S of Charleston**
No. of Rooms: **3**
No. of Private Baths: **3**
Double/pb: **$50–$60**
Single/pb: **$45**
Open: **All year**
Breakfast: **Continental**
Credit Cards: **MC, VISA**
Pets: **No**
Children: **Welcome**
Smoking: **No**
Social Drinking: **Permitted**

Located in the historic district with views of the river, this Queen Anne Victorian was built in 1898 in the Beaufort style. The rooms are furnished in antiques, reproductions, and fine Southern crafts from your hosts' gift shop. Breakfast specialties include homemade cranberry and blueberry muffins, fresh fruit, yogurt, and granola. Guests are welcome to watch the boats go by on the Intracoastal Waterway from one of two porches. A comfortable hammock also awaits those who want to put up their feet. The inn is close to downtown shops, the marina, and Waterfront Park. Your hosts are happy to help you discover the delights of their town, which has been the backdrop for such films as *The Big Chill* and *The Great Santini*.

The Rhett House Inn

1009 CRAVEN STREET, BEAUFORT, SOUTH CAROLINA 29902

Tel: **(803) 524-9030**
Host(s): **Steve and Marianne Harrison**
Location: **69 mi. S of Charleston**
No. of Rooms: **5**
No. of Private Baths: **5**
Double/pb: **$60–$75**
Open: **All year**
Breakfast: **Continental**
Credit Cards: **MC, VISA**
Pets: **No**
Children: **Welcome, over 12**
Smoking: **Permitted**
Social Drinking: **Permitted**

If you ever wondered what the South was like before the Civil War, come visit this inn located in the historic district. Two of the bedrooms have fireplaces; all have homespun quilts and pretty touches such as freshly cut flowers. After breakfast, stroll in the lovely gardens or take a bicycle ride around town. The restored waterfront on the Intracoastal waterway with its shops and restaurants is within walking distance. If you ask, your hosts will pack a picnic lunch and direct you to the beach. Hilton Head Island is 35 miles away.

The Cedars

1325 WILLISTON ROAD, P.O. BOX 117, BEECH ISLAND, SOUTH CAROLINA 29841

Tel: **(803) 827-0248**
Host(s): **Ralph and Maggie Zieger**
Location: **6 mi. E of Augusta, Ga.**
No. of Rooms: **4**
No. of Private Baths: **3**
Max. No. Sharing Bath: **4**
Double/pb: **$48**
Single/pb: **$42**
Double/sb: **$40**
Single/sb: **$35**
Suites: **$65**
Open: **All year**
Reduced Rates: **15%, weekly; 10%, seniors**
Breakfast: **Continental**
Other Meals: **Available**
Credit Cards: **MC, VISA**
Pets: **No**
Children: **Welcome, over 12**
Smoking: **Permitted**
Social Drinking: **Permitted**
Airport/Station Pickup: **Yes**
Foreign Languages: **German**

Beautifully set in 12 parklike acres, surrounded by dogwood and wisteria, this elegant manor (circa 1835) has been completely renovated. The gracious guest rooms feature queen-size poster beds, ceiling fans, fireplaces, and traditional furniture with antique accents.

It is easily accessible to the Masters Golf Tournament, fine restaurants, antique shops, and Aiken, South Carolina, famed for its Thoroughbred horse farms. Maggie and Ralph will be pleased to extend their country club privileges of golf, tennis, and swimming to you. A gift shop is on the premises.

The Carriage House ✪

1413 LYTTLETON STREET, CAMDEN, SOUTH CAROLINA 29020

Tel: **(803) 432-2430**
Best Time to Call: **After 10 AM**
Host(s): **Dr. and Mrs. Robert Watkins**
Location: **30 mi. N of Columbia**
No. of Rooms: **2**
No. of Private Baths: **1½**
Double/pb: **$45**
Single/pb: **$45**
Open: **All year**
Breakfast: **Full**
Pets: **No**
Children: **Welcome, over 6**
Smoking: **Permitted**
Social Drinking: **Permitted**
Airport/Station Pickup: **Yes**

The Carriage House is an antebellum cottage with window boxes and a picket fence. Located in the center of historic Camden, it is within walking distance of tennis, parks, and shops. The guest rooms have twin or double beds and are decorated with colorful fabrics and lovely antiques. Visitors are welcomed to their quarters with complimentary sherry, fruit, and cheese. Your hosts serve a Southern-style breakfast featuring grits, eggs, and fresh-squeezed juices.

Charleston East Bed & Breakfast ✪

1031 TALL PINE ROAD,
MOUNT PLEASANT, SOUTH CAROLINA 29464

Tel: **(803) 884-8208**
Best Time to Call: **4 PM–9 PM**
Coordinator: **Bobbie Auld**
State/Regions Covered: **East Cooper, Sullivans Island, Isle of Palms, Mt. Pleasant, McClellanville**

Rates (Single/Double):

	Single	Double
Modest:	**$20**	**$30**
Average:	**$30**	**$35**
Luxury:	**$35**	**$55**

Bobbie has lovely homes in the geographic area known as East Cooper, three miles from downtown historic Charleston. Several are furnished in antiques; others are contemporary. One is in the small fishing village north of Charleston, where the host offers cruises in the evening on his houseboat. One is accessible for the handicapped in wheelchairs. The noncommercial beaches of Sullivans Island and the

Isle of Palms are close by. There is a $5 surcharge for one night's lodging in the spring.

Historic Charleston Bed & Breakfast ✪

43 LEGARE STREET, CHARLESTON, SOUTH CAROLINA 29401

Tel: **(803) 722-6606**
Best Time to Call: **1–6 PM**
Coordinator: **Charlotte Fairey**
State/Regions Covered: **Charleston**

Rates (Single/Double):

	Single	Double
Modest:	**$40**	**$55**
Average	**$60**	**$75**
Luxury:	**$80**	**$100**

Credit Cards: **AMEX, MC, VISA**

This port city is one of the most historic in the U.S. Through the auspices of Charlotte, you will enjoy your stay in a private home, carriage house, or mansion in a neighborhood of enchanting walled gardens, cobblestoned streets, and moss-draped oak trees. Each home is unique, yet each has a warm and friendly atmosphere provided by a host who sincerely enjoys making guests welcome. All are historic properties dating from 1720 to 1890, yet all are up to date, with air-conditioning, phones, and television. Reduced rates are available for weekly stays, but there is a $5 surcharge for one-night visits.

Ann Harper's Bed & Breakfast

56 SMITH STREET, CHARLESTON, SOUTH CAROLINA 29401

Tel: **(803) 723-3947**
Host(s): **Ann D. Harper**
Location: **½ mi. from I-26**
No. of Rooms: **2**
Max. No. Sharing Bath: **3**
Double/sb: **$50**
Single/sb: **$35**

Open: **All year**
Breakfast: **Full**
Pets: **No**
Children: **Welcome, over 10**
Smoking: **Permitted**
Social Drinking: **Permitted**
Foreign Languages: **Gullah**

This attractive home (circa 1870) is located in Charleston's historic district. The rooms, ideally suited for two friends traveling together, are decorated with wicker pieces and family treasures. Take a moment to relax on the porch or in the intimate walled garden out back. Ann serves a hot Southern-style breakfast each morning featuring home-made bread and hominy grits. She will gladly direct you to the interesting sights of this historic area. There is a $5 surcharge for one night's stay.

1837 Bed & Breakfast & Tea Room ✪

126 WENTWORTH STREET, CHARLESTON, SOUTH CAROLINA 29401

Tel: **(803) 723-7166**
Best Time to Call: **9 AM–7 PM**
Host(s): **Sherri Weaver and Richard Dunn**
Location: **60 mi. from I-95**
No. of Rooms: **7**
No. of Private Baths: **7**
Double/pb: **$39–$69**
Suites: **$65–$85**
Guest Cottage: **$85–$125; sleeps 4**
Open: **All year**
Reduced Rates: **Nov. and Feb.**
Breakfast: **Continental**
Pets: **No**
Children: **Welcome**
Smoking: **Permitted**
Social Drinking: **Permitted**

Located in the center of the historic district, the original slave quarters of this pre–Civil War home are still intact, as are the original brick walls and wooden beams. Each guest room has a private entrance. Most days in Charleston are fair, so rocking chairs on the three levels of porches provide excellent places to lounge. The rooms are decorated with antiques and interesting embellishments by Sherri and Richard, talented artists. High tea is served, and during the high season, the general public is invited to sip and snack, too.

Coosaw Plantation ✪

DALE, SOUTH CAROLINA 29914

Tel: **(803) 846-8225**
Best Time to Call: **After 6 PM**
Host(s): **Peggy Sanford**
Location: **50 mi. S of Charleston; 15 mi. from I-95**
Guest Cottage: **$45 (for 2); $55 (for 4)**
Open: **Mar.–Dec.**
Breakfast: **Continental**
Pets: **Welcome**
Children: **Welcome**
Smoking: **Permitted**
Social Drinking: **Permitted**
Foreign Languages: **Spanish, French**

This sprawling plantation offers a relaxed setting on the Coosaw River. The guest cottage has a living room with fireplace, a full kitchen, and a bath. Your hosts will prepare a breakfast of muffins or casseroles, or will leave the fixings for you. Boating, fishing, or a visit to Beaufort and Savannah are just a few of the local possibilities. Or, stay "home" and use the pool and tennis court on-premises.

Pleasant Valley Bed & Breakfast Inn ✪

160 EAST AT BLACKWEIDER, P.O. BOX 446, FORT MILL, SOUTH CAROLINA 29715

Tel: **(803) 548-5671**
Best Time to Call: **8 AM–8 PM**
Host(s): **Mr. and Mrs. Bob Lawrence**
Location: **5½ mi. from I-77, Exit 85**
No. of Rooms: **9**
No. of Private Baths: **9**
Double/pb: **$45**
Open: **All year**
Reduced Rates: **10%, seniors**
Breakfast: **Continental**
Pets: **No**
Children: **Welcome**
Smoking: **No**
Social Drinking: **No**
Airport/Station Pickup: **Yes**

Nestled in the beautiful Olde English District, the inn is located on five wooded acres in the peaceful countryside. Built in 1874, it has been restored and furnished with antiques. Each of the bedrooms has a telephone and television. After breakfast in the spacious country kitchen, take a stroll in the shade of 100-year-old oaks. Equipped with facilities for the disabled, it is convenient to Carowinds Theme Park, Heritage USA, and Lancaster.

Shaw House ✪

8 CYPRESS COURT, GEORGETOWN, SOUTH CAROLINA 29440

Tel: **(803) 546-9663**
Best Time to Call: **Early AM**
Host(s): **Mary Shaw**
Location: **1 block off Hwy. 17**
No. of Rooms: **3**
No. of Private Baths: **3**
Double/pb: **$40**
Single/pb: **$40**
Open: **All year**
Reduced Rates: **10% after 4 nights**
Breakfast: **Full**
Pets: **No**
Children: **Welcome**
Smoking: **Permitted**
Social Drinking: **Permitted**
Airport/Station Pickup: **Yes**

Shaw House is a two-story Colonial with a beautiful view of the Willowbank Marsh. Your hostess is knowledgeable about antiques and has filled the rooms with them. The rocking chairs and cool breeze will tempt you to the porch. Each morning a pot of coffee and Southern-style casserole await you. Fresh fruit and homemade snacks are available all day. The house is within walking distance of the historic district and is near Myrtle Beach, Pawleys Island, golf, tennis, and restaurants.

Ambiance Bed & Breakfast ✪

8 WREN DRIVE, HILTON HEAD ISLAND, SOUTH CAROLINA 29928

Tel: **(803) 671-4981**
Best Time to Call: **Evenings**
Host(s): **Marny Kridel Daubenspeck**
Location: **40 mi. from I-95, Exit 28**
No. of Rooms: **2**
No. of Private Baths: **2**
Double/pb: **$55–$65**
Single/pb: **$50–$60**
Open: **All year**
Breakfast: **Continental**
Pets: **No**
Children: **Welcome, over 12**
Smoking: **Permitted**
Social Drinking: **Permitted**

This contemporary cypress home is located in the area of Sea Pines Plantation. Floor-length windows afford beautiful views of the subtropical surroundings. Marny runs an interior decorating firm, so it's no surprise that everything is in excellent taste. You are welcome to use the TV, laundry facilities, pool, and nearby tennis court.

Windsong ✪

ROUTE 1, BOX 300, MAYESVILLE, SOUTH CAROLINA 29104

Tel: **(803) 453-5004**
Host(s): **Billy and Lynda Dabbs**
Location: **15 mi. NE of Sumter; 3 mi. from Hwy. 401, Exit 154**
No. of Rooms: **2**
No. of Private Baths: **2**
Double/pb: **$45**
Single/pb: **$35**
Open: **All year**
Breakfast: **Full**
Other Meals: **Available**
Pets: **No**
Children: **Welcome (crib)**
Smoking: **Permitted**
Social Drinking: **Permitted**
Airport/Station Pickup: **Yes**

Situated in open farmland, surrounded by miles of private country trails, this large, comfortable house with its balconies and porches is a great place to relax. You are welcome to make yourself at home in the large den with its open fireplace or use the barbecue grill and picnic table for a do-it-yourself meal. The Windsong is an excellent stopover for travelers driving the north-south route.

Gadsden Manor Inn ✪

P.O. BOX 1710, OLD POSTERN ROAD, SUMMERVILLE, SOUTH CAROLINA 29483

Tel: **(803) 875-1710**
Best Time to Call: **8 AM–6 PM**
Host(s): **Antonio and Deborah Diz**
Location: **20 mi. NW of Charleston; 2 mi. from I-26, Exit 199**
No. of Rooms: **14**
No. of Private Baths: **14**
Double/pb: **$85**
Single/pb: **$75**
Suites: **$95**

Open: **All year**
Reduced Rates: **Available**
Breakfast: **Continental**
Credit Cards: **AMEX, DC, MC, VISA**
Pets: **No**
Children: **Welcome**
Smoking: **Permitted**
Social Drinking: **Permitted**
Airport/Station Pickup: **Yes**
Foreign Languages: **Spanish**

Gadsden Manor Inn is a Georgian Revival surrounded by lush foliage and gardens. The house dates back to 1906, and is furnished with four-poster beds and claw-footed tubs. Traditions such as live parlor music, bedtime turndown service, and leisurely afternoon refreshments also recall a more elegant past. Guests are given the royal treatment here with complimentary brandy and truffles, newspaper delivery, and even shoe shines. Breakfast specialties include blueberry muffins, currant scones, and croissants. Lunch is available Monday through Fridays for $4.

SOUTH DAKOTA

Buffalo
Webster
Watertown
Volga
Brookings
Deadwood
Milesville
Rapid City
Wall
Philip
Canova
Salem
Mitchell
Sioux Falls
Academy
Armour
Beresford
Yankton

South Dakota Bed and Breakfast ✪

P.O. BOX 80137, SIOUX FALLS, SOUTH DAKOTA 57116

Tel: **(605) 528-6571 or 339-0759**
Best Time to Call: **After 6 PM**
Coordinators: **Kathy Hales and Karen Olson**
State/Regions Covered: **Buffalo, Canton, Deadwood, Hill City, Mitchell, Platte, Rapid City, Salem, Sioux Falls, Volga**

Rates (Single/Double):

Average:	**$20**	**$30**
Luxury:	**$45**	**$65**

Credit Cards: **No**

From the majestic Black Hills across rolling prairie to the city and to awesome Mt. Rushmore, you will be treated to midwestern hospitality at its best. Whether traveling through the state, skiing, hunting, or on business, you will enjoy staying in a private home of one of Kathy and Karen's hosts.

Old West and Badlands B&B Association ✪

BOX 728, PHILIP, SOUTH DAKOTA 57567

Tel: **(605) 859-2040**
Best Time to Call: **Early AM or late PM**
Coordinator: **Phillis Thorson**
State/Regions Covered: **Philip, Wall**

Rates (Single/Double):

	Single	Double
Modest:	**$20**	**$30**
Average:	**$30**	**$50**

Credit Cards: **No**
Minimum Stay: **No**

You are warmly invited to bring your family to explore the natural beauty of the land that stretches from the Missouri River to the famous Black Hills. You'll all enjoy the historic sites, plains, Indian settlements, stagecoach trails, and being part of rural America. Bring your camera!

Skoglund Farm ✪

CANOVA, SOUTH DAKOTA 57321

Tel: **(605) 247-3445**
Best Time to Call: **Early AM, evenings**
Host(s): **Alden and Delores Skoglund**
Location: **12 miles from I-90**
No. of Rooms: **5**
Max. No. Sharing Bath: **3**
Double/sb: **$50**
Single/sb: **$25**
Open: **All year**
Reduced Rates: **Under 18**
Breakfast: **Full**
Other Meals: **Dinner included**
Pets: **Welcome**
Children: **Welcome (crib)**
Smoking: **Permitted**
Social Drinking: **Permitted**
Airport/Station Pickup: **Yes**

This is a working farm where the emphasis is on the simple good life. It is a welcome escape from urban living. You may, if you wish, help with the farm chores, or just watch everyone else work; the family raises cattle, fowl, and peacocks. You may ride the horses over the wide open spaces. You are welcome to use the laundry facilities or play the piano. The coffeepot is always on.

Fitch Farms

BOX 8, MILESVILLE, SOUTH DAKOTA 57553

Tel: **(605) 544-3227**
Best Time to Call: **Evenings**
Host(s): **Ed and Frances Fitch**
Location: **2 mi. off Hwy. 34**
No. of Rooms: **2**
No. of Private Baths: **1**
Max. No. Sharing Bath: **4**
Double/pb: **$40**
Single/pb: **$25**
Double/sb: **$35**
Single/sb: **$25**
Open: **All year**
Reduced Rates: **Available**
Breakfast: **Full**

Pets: **Yes**
Children: **Welcome**
Smoking: **Permitted**
Social Drinking: **Permitted**
Airport/Station Pickup: **Yes**

Ed and Frances Fitch welcome you to their Western-style ranch home set on a working farm. The rooms are decorated country-style, with hand-woven rugs, patchwork quilts, and many handcrafts. Make yourself at home beside the fireplace or ask for a tour of the ranch. Your hosts serve a hearty breakfast, including fresh fruit, bacon, eggs, and homemade cakes. This comfortable farm home is close to the Cheyenne Indian Reservation and the unique Badlands area.

Audrie's Cranbury Corner B&B ✪

RR 8, BOX 2400, RAPID CITY, SOUTH DAKOTA 57702

Tel: **(605) 342-7788**
Host(s): **Audry Kuhnhauser**
Location: **1/4 mi. from Hwy. 44**
No. of Rooms: **2**
No. of Private Baths: **2**
Double/pb: **$55**
Single/pb: **$50**
Open: **All year**
Breakfast: **Full**
Pets: **No**
Children: **No**
Smoking: **No**
Social Drinking: **Permitted**
Airport/Station Pickup: **Yes**

Located in the beautiful Black Hills, just 30 miles from Mt. Rushmore, Audrie's country home is the epitome of Old World hospitality. The fireplaced guest rooms have private entrances, private patios, hot tubs, and are furnished with lovely antiques. She will be happy to lend you a fishing pole so you can try your hand at trout fishing at nearby Rapid Creek. Complimentary wine, assorted beverages, and tempting appetizers are offered. The Old Powerhouse Antique and Gift Shop is on the premises and makes for fun browsing and gift buying.

Bed and Breakfast Domivara ✪

KEYSTONE ROUTE, BOX 3004, RAPID CITY, SOUTH DAKOTA 57702

Tel: **(605) 574-4207**
Best Time to Call: **Mornings, evenings**
Host(s): **Betty Blount**
Location: **21 mi. SW of Rapid City**
No. of Rooms: **2**
No. of Private Baths: **2**
Double/pb: **$65**
Single/pb: **$50**
Open: **All year**
Breakfast: **Full**
Other Meals: **Available**
Pets: **Sometimes**
Children: **Welcome**
Smoking: **Permitted**
Social Drinking: **Permitted**
Airport/Station Pickup: **Yes**

Enjoy Western hospitality in a unique log home located in the picturesque Black Hills of South Dakota. The homey wood interior is decorated with comfortable antiques and accents of stained glass. A large picture window overlooks the counryside where you may see an occasional wild turkey or deer. Betty Blount offers complimentary snacks served with wine or coffee. She prepares a variety of special breakfast dishes including sourdough pancakes, egg soufflés, fresh trout, and homemade blueberry muffins. There are good restaurants nearby, or if you prefer home cooking, your hostess will be glad to prepare dinner for you. Domivara is conveniently located just 20 minutes from Mr. Rushmore and the Crazy Horse Memorial.

Lakeside Farm

RR 2, BOX 52, WEBSTER, SOUTH DAKOTA 57274

Tel: **(605) 486-4430**
Host(s): **Joy and Glenn Hagen**
Location: **60 mi. E of Aberdeen on Hwy. 12**
No. of Rooms: **2**
Double/sb: **$30**
Single/sb: **$20**
Open: **All year**
Breakfast: **Full**
Pets: **No**
Children: **Welcome**
Smoking: **No**
Social Drinking: **No**

This 750-acre farm where Joy and Glenn raise oats, corn, and a herd of 50 Holstein dairy cows, is located in the Lake Region where recreational activities abound. You are certain to be comfortable in their farmhouse, built in 1970 and furnished in a simple, informal style. You will awaken to the delicious aroma of Joy's heavenly cinnamon rolls or bread and enjoy breakfast served on the enclosed porch in view of the pretty garden. Nearby attractions include Fort Sisseton and the June festival that recounts Sam Browne's historic ride. You will also enjoy the Blue Dog fish hatchery, and the Game Reserve. Don't leave till you've watched the cows being milked and had a dish of home-churned ice cream!

The Mulberry Inn ✪

512 MULBERRY STREET, YANKTON, SOUTH DAKOTA 57078

Tel: **(605) 665-7116**
Best Time to Call: **9 AM–9 PM**
Host(s): **Linda Cameron**
Location: **90 mi. SW of Sioux Falls**
No. of Rooms: **5**
No. of Private Baths: **1**
Max. No. Sharing Bath: **4**
Double/pb: **$57**
Single/pb: **$50**
Double/sb: **$45**
Single/sb: **$40**
Open: **Apr. 1–Dec. 15**

Charge Cards: **MC, VISA**
Reduced Rates: **10%, seniors; families**
Breakfast: **Full**
Pets: **Sometimes**
Children: **Welcome**
Smoking: **Permitted**
Social Drinking: **Permitted**
Airport/Station Pickup: **Yes**

The Mulberry Inn is an 18-room red-brick house built in 1873. It is listed on the National Register of Historic Places, a distinction it shares with many of its neighbors. Open the massive hand-carved front door and enter a setting of parquet floors, high ceilings, and marble fireplaces. Guest rooms are beautifully decorated with pastel colors, pine antiques, and Laura Ashley prints. Breakfast is served in the beautiful country kitchen beside a wood-burning fireplace. Linda prepares gourmet coffee, lemon bread, omelets, or quiches. She also invites you for an afternoon glass of wine in one of the parlors or out on the covered porch. This lovely inn is minutes away from the Missouri River for fishing and boating, and just as close to the Lewis and Clark Lake.

For key to listings, see inside front or back cover.

✪ This star means that rates are guaranteed through December 31, 1988 to any guest making a reservation as a result of reading about the B&B in *BED & BREAKFAST U.S.A.*—1988 edition.

Please enclose a self-addressed, stamped, business-sized envelope when contacting reservation services.

For more details on what you can expect in a B&B, see Chapter 1.

Always mention *Bed & Breakfast U.S.A.* when making reservations!

If no B&B is listed in the area you'll be visiting, use the form on page 698 to order a copy of our "List of New B&Bs."

We want to hear from you! Use the form on page 697.

TENNESSEE

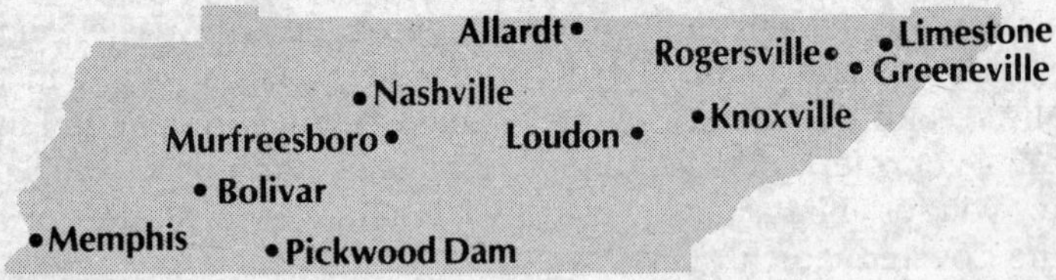

Allardt
Limestone
Rogersville
Greeneville
Nashville
Knoxville
Murfreesboro
Loudon
Bolivar
Memphis
Pickwood Dam

Bed & Breakfast Host Homes of Tennessee ✪

P.O. BOX 110227, NASHVILLE, TENNESSEE 37222

Tel: **(615) 331-5244**
Coordinator: **Fredda Odom**
States/Regions Covered:
Chattanooga, Columbia, Franklin, Gatlinburg, Greeneville, Knoxville, Memphis, Nashville, Shelbyville

Rates (Single/Double):

Modest:	**$28**	**$38**
Average:	**$30**	**$40**
Luxury:	**$80–$100**	**$80–$120**

Credit Cards: **AMEX, MC, VISA**

From the Great Smoky Mountains to the Mississippi, here is a diversity of attractions that includes fabulous scenery, Tennessee's Grand Ole Opry and Opryland, universities, Civil War sites, horse farms, and much more. Fredda will arrange sightseeing tours, car rentals, tickets to events, and everything she can to assure you a pleasant stay.

Charlo ✪

P.O. BOX 69, TAYLOR PLACE ROAD, ALLARDT, TENNESSEE 38504

Tel: **(615) 879-8056**
Best Time to Call: **After 5 PM**
Host(s): **Charles and Lowanda Gernt**
Location: **3 mi. from Hwy. 127**
No. of Rooms: **3**
No. of Private Baths: **3**
Double/pb: **$50**
Single/pb: **$40**
Open: **All year**
Breakfast: **Full**
Pets: **No**
Children: **Welcome, over 12**
Smoking: **No**
Social Drinking: **Permitted**

This handsome two-story center-hall home, with its white pillars and shutters, is located in a quaint German community settled in 1880 by Charles's grandfather. The area abounds in history, from the English colony of Rugby to Jamestown, home to the World War I hero, Sgt. Alvin York, as well as Mark Twain's parents. Big South Fork National Park and Picket State Park are a scenic 30-minute drive away. Lowanda and Charles want you to feel perfectly at home, and offer the use of their TV, piano, and laundry facilities. Join them for a glass of Highland Manor wine from Tennessee's first licensed winery.

Big Spring Inn

315 NORTH MAIN STREET, GREENEVILLE, TENNESSEE 37743

Tel: **(615) 638-2917**
Host(s): **Jeanne Driese and Cheryl Van Dyck**
Location: **70 mi. NE of Knoxville**
No. of Rooms: **5**
No. of Private Baths: **4**
Max. No. Sharing Bath: **2**
Double/pb: **$60–$70**
Single/pb: **$55–$65**
Double/sb: **$50**
Single/sb: **$45**
Open: **All year**
Reduced Rates: **Available**
Breakfast: **Full**
Other Meals: **Available**
Credit Cards: **AMEX, MC, VISA**
Pets: **Sometimes**
Children: **Welcome, over 12**
Smoking: **Permitted**
Social Drinking: **Permitted**
Airport/Station Pickup: **Yes**

Big Spring Inn is a three-story manor house located in Greeneville's historic district, an area that includes Davy Crockett's birthplace. The inn has a grand entrance hall, leaded and stained-glass windows, and many fireplaces. The rooms are spacious, with high ceilings, and are decorated with a comfortable mix of antiques and reproductions. The bedrooms have special touches, such as fresh flowers, snacks, baskets of toiletries, and even terry-cloth robes. Jeanne and Cheryl serve homemade breads and pastries, with a variety of egg dishes for breakfast; gourmet dinners are also available. Big Spring is within an hour of Smoky Mountain National Park and the Blue Ridge Parkway.

Mountain Breeze Bed & Breakfast ✪

501 MOUNTAIN BREEZE LANE, KNOXVILLE, TENNESSEE 37922

Tel: **(615) 966-3917**
Best Time to Call: **9 AM–9 PM**
Host(s): **Brad and Cindy Rogers**
Location: **2½ mi. from I-40, Exit 373**
No. of Rooms: **2**
No. of Private Baths: **2**
Double/pb: **$35–$45**
Open: **All year**
Breakfast: **Full**
Other Meals: **Available**
Pets: **No**
Children: **Welcome, over 12**
Smoking: **Permitted**
Social Drinking: **Permitted**

This two-story brick and clapboard Cape Cod is located on a quiet cul-de-sac in a wooded country setting. It is warmly furnished with antiques and country accents, and the den has a nautical theme and stained glass. Cindy loves to cook and serves a bountiful breakfast in the cozy nook or on the deck overlooking the wooded backyard. It is 15 minutes from the University of Tennessee; 20 minutes from the Blount Mansion, White Fort, and other historic sites. Recreational activities on TVA lakes abound in all seasons.

Windy Hill B&B ✪

1031 WEST PARK DRIVE, KNOXVILLE, TENNESSEE 37909

Tel: **(615) 690-1488**
Host(s): **Mary M. Mitchell**
Location: **1.6 mi. from I-75-40, Exit 380**
No. of Rooms: **1**
No. of Private Baths: **1**
Double/pb: **$40**
Single/pb: **$35**

Open: **All year**
Breakfast: **Continental**
Pets: **Sometimes**
Children: **Welcome**
Smoking: **Permitted**
Social Drinking: **Permitted**
Airport/Station Pickup: **Yes**

Located in a pleasant, quiet neighborhood with numerous shade trees, Mary's B&B is air-conditioned and has a private entrance with no steps to climb. There's a double bed and a rollaway is available. Breakfast features homemade muffins or cinnamon rolls with coffee. Windy Hill is convenient to the University of Tennessee; Oakridge is only a 15-minute drive, while Smoky Mountain National Park is an hour away.

Snapp Inn B&B

ROUTE 3, BOX 102, LIMESTONE, TENNESSEE 37681

Tel: **(615) 257-2482**
Best Time to Call: **Before 10 AM; after 7 PM**
Host(s): **Dan and Ruth Dorgan**
Location: **4 mi. from Rte. 11 E**
No. of Rooms: **2**
Max. No. Sharing Bath: **4**
Double/sb: **$40**
Single/sb: **$35**
Open: **All year**
Breakfast: **Continental**
Pets: **No**
Children: **Welcome (one at a time)**
Smoking: **No**
Social Drinking: **Permitted**
Airport/Station Pickup: **Yes**

Built in 1815 and situated in farm country, this Federal brick home has lovely mountain views. The house is decorated with antiques, including a Victorian reed organ. Now retired, Ruth and Dan have the time to pursue their interests in antiques restoration, history, needlework, and bluegrass music. It is an easy walk to Davy Crockett Birthplace State Park, and 15 minutes to Historic Jonesboro or the Andrew Johnson Home in Greeneville. A swimming pool, golf, and fishing are close by. You are welcome to use the laundry facilities, television, and pool table.

River Road Inn ✪

ROUTE 1, BOX 372, RIVER ROAD, LOUDON, TENNESSEE 37774

Tel: **(615) 458-4861**
Best Time to Call: **Before 8 PM**
Host(s): **Dave, Dan, and Kaky Smith**
Location: **30 mi. SW of Knoxville; 1½ mi. from I-75, Exit 72**
No. of Rooms: **7**
No. of Private Baths: **4**
Max. No. Sharing Bath: **3**
Double/pb: **$50**
Double/sb: **$50**
Open: **All year**
Breakfast: **Full**
Other Meals: **Available**
Credit Cards: **MC, VISA**
Pets: **Sometimes**
Children: **Welcome**
Smoking: **Permitted**
Social Drinking: **Permitted**
Airport/Station Pickup: **Yes**

Nestled in the foothills of the Smoky Mountains stands the home, built in 1857, of the late Albert Lenoir. The inn is an antebellum mansion that was the site of General Sherman's encampment during the Civil War. It is newly restored and has earned a place on the National Register of Historic Places. Bedrooms are furnished with beautiful antiques and other period pieces. Three rooms have their own fireplaces and Oriental rugs on the hardwood floors. Three of the bedrooms have private half-baths, but share a tub and shower. Guests are invited to unwind in the parlor or relax by the pool. Kaky enjoys cooking and serves a country breakfast featuring ham, biscuits, and all the trimmings. You will want to take the time to have an elegant dinner here, too, served in the formal dining room.

Lowenstein-Long House ✪

217 NORTH WALDRAN–1084 POPLAR, MEMPHIS, TENNESSEE 38105

Tel: **(901) 527-7174 or 274-0509**
Host(s): **Martha and Charles Long**
No. of Rooms: **7**
No. of Private Baths: **4**
Max. No. Sharing Bath: **3**
Double/pb: **$50**
Double/sb: **$50**
Suites: **$75**
Open: **All year**
Breakfast: **Continental**
Credit Cards: **MC, VISA**
Pets: **No**
Children: **Welcome**
Smoking: **Permitted**
Social Drinking: **Permitted**

Listed on the National Register of Historic Places, Lowenstein-Long House has been fully restored to its original grandeur. It is located half a mile from a Victorian village, and close to Mud Island, the DeSoto Bridge, and Beale Street. Elvis fans will note that the route to Graceland is nearby.

Clardy's Guest House ✪

435 EAST MAIN STREET, MURFREESBORO, TENNESSEE 37130

Tel: **(615) 893-6030**
Best Time to Call: **After 3 PM**
Host(s): **Frank Clardy and Barbara Deaton**
Location: **2 mi. from I-24**
No. of Rooms: **6**
No. of Private Baths: **4**
Max. No. Sharing Bath: **4**
Double/pb: **$25**
Single/pb: **$20**
Double/sb: **$20**
Single/sb: **$17.50**
Open: **All year**
Breakfast: **Continental**
Pets: **Sometimes**
Children: **Welcome (crib)**
Smoking: **Permitted**
Social Drinking: **Permitted**

This Romanesque-style Victorian dates back to 1898. The 20 rooms are filled with antiques; with 40 antiques dealers in town, you can guess what Murfreesboro is best known for. The world championship horse show at Shelbyville is 30 minutes away. Your hosts will be glad to advise on local tours and can direct you to the home of Grand Ole Opry, one hour away in Nashville, and fine eating places. Middle Tennessee State University is close by.

Miss Anne's Bed & Breakfast ✪

3033 WINDEMERE CIRCLE, NASHVILLE, TENNESSEE 37214

Tel: **(615) 885-1899**
Best Time to Call: **After 4 PM**
Host(s): **Anne Cowell**
Location: **2 mi. from I-40**
No. of Rooms: **4**
No. of Private Baths: **1**
Max. No. Sharing Bath: **4**
Double/pb: **$30**
Single/pb: **$27**
Double/sb: **$27**
Single/sb: **$24**
Open: **All year**
Breakfast: **Full**
Pets: **No**
Children: **Welcome**
Smoking: **Permitted**
Social Drinking: **Permitted**
Airport/Station Pickup: **Yes**

Visiting Anne is easy and pleasant in her comfortable home furnished with a cozy blend of antiques and lots of wood and glass. Her collection of doll dishes is quite special. Breakfast features such delectables as French toast, German pancakes, and homemade raspberry preserves. Opryland, the Hermitage, and the Parthenon are all nearby, as is Vanderbilt University.

The Oaks ✪

1001 MEMORIAL DRIVE, PARIS, TENNESSEE 38242

Tel: **(901) 642-4231**
Best Time to Call: **After 4 PM**
Host(s): **Mike and Joan Mills**
Location: **100 mi. NW of Nashville**
No. of Rooms: **1**
No. of Private Baths: **1**
Double/pb: **$30**
Single/pb: **$25**
Open: **All year**
Reduced Rates: **10%, seniors**
Breakfast: **Full**
Other Meals: **Available**
Pets: **No**
Children: **Welcome**
Smoking: **Permitted**
Social Drinking: **Permitted**

This immaculate brick Colonial with its inviting front porch is furnished with country antiques. Paris Landing State Park, Land Between the Lakes, and the Tennessee River are just 10 miles away, with some of the best fishing in the nation. In fact, the World's Biggest Fishfry is held here in April every year. Your hosts are retired and interested in gardening and handicrafts. Breakfast is a hearty meal of country sausage and eggs, homemade biscuits, and lots of delicious coffee.

The Homestead House Inn ✪

P.O. BOX 76, PICKWICK DAM, TENNESSEE 38365

Tel: **(901) 689-5500**
Best Time to Call: **9 AM–9 PM**
Host(s): **Gladys Youngblood**
Location: **100 mi. E of Memphis**
No. of Rooms: **5**
No. of Private Baths: **2**
Max. No. Sharing Bath: **4**
Double/pb: **$50**
Single/pb: **$40**
Double/sb: **$45**
Single/sb: **$40**
Suites: **$85; sleeps 4**
Open: **Apr. 1–Oct. 31**
Breakfast: **Continental**
Credit Cards: **AMEX, MC, VISA**
Pets: **No**
Children: **Welcome, over 12**
Smoking: **Permitted**
Social Drinking: **Permitted**

The Homestead House Inn was built in 1843 as the Red Sulphur Springs Hotel. In its glory days, people came to soak in the sulphur springs and attend annual fox hunts. Today the house sits on 14 wooded acres and offers beautifully restored rooms decorated with antiques. Your hostess loves catering to her guests and serves a selection of Danish pastries, seasonal fruit, and the house special strawberry bread for breakfast. You are sure to enjoy the colorful past of the inn, where it is said Jesse and Frank James hid out between raids. Your hosts will do all they can to ensure you a pleasant stay and will direct you to such historic sights as Shiloh National Park and Battlefield.

Hale Springs Inn ✪
ROGERSVILLE, TENNESSEE 37857

Tel: **(615) 272-5171**
Host(s): **Stan and Kim Pace**
Location: **60 mi. NE of Knoxville**
No. of Rooms: **10**
No. of Private Baths: **10**
Double/pb: **$40**
Single/pb: **$35**
Suites: **$55**

Open: **All year**
Breakfast: **Continental**
Other Meals: **Available**
Credit Cards: **AMEX, MC, VISA**
Pets: **Sometimes**
Children: **Welcome**
Smoking: **Permitted**
Social Drinking: **Permitted**

This three-story Federal inn dates from 1824. George Washington did not sleep here, but Andrew Jackson and James Polk did. Large, high-ceilinged rooms with fireplaces, antiques, and four-poster beds continue the hosting tradition. Guests will enjoy touring the rest of the historic district. Davy Crockett's home, Lake Cherokee, and the Smoky Mountains are nearby. Rogersville is one of Tennessee's oldest towns. Candlelight dinners are served in the Colonial-style dining room.

TEXAS

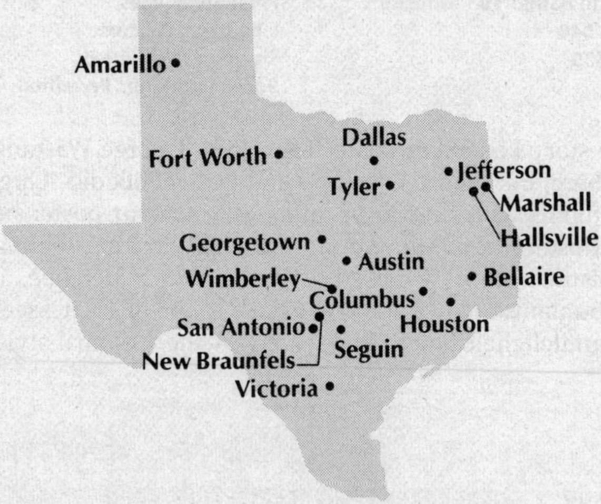

The Bed & Breakfast Society of Texas ✪

921 HEIGHTS BOULEVARD, HOUSTON, TEXAS 77008

Tel: **(713) 868-4654**
Best Time to Call: **9 AM–5 PM**
Coordinator: **Marguerite Swanson**
States/Regions Covered: **Texas: Statewide**

Rates (Single/Double):

Modest:	**$25**	**$35**
Average:	**$30**	**$40**
Luxury:	**$50**	**$75**

Credit Cards: **MC, VISA**

Whether you're traveling for business or pleasure, Marguerite's hosts offer the kind of friendliness and individualized care that will make your stay pleasant. The area is known for the Astrodome, Galveston Bay, NASA, and the Texas Medical Center. There are wonderful restaurants, shops, museums, and historic sights, and Baylor, Rice, and the University of Houston are nearby. Many are conveniently located urban homes, serene country houses, historic inns, and waterfront cottages.

Bed & Breakfast Texas Style ✪

4224 W. RED BIRD LANE, DALLAS, TEXAS 75237

Tel: **(214) 298-8586**
Best Time to Call: **9 AM–6 PM**
Coordinator: **Ruth Wilson**
States/Regions Covered: **Arlington, Austin, Corsicana, Dallas, Fort Stockton, Fort Worth, Houston, San Antonio, Waco**

Rates (Single/Double):

	Single	Double
Modest:	**$25**	**$39**
Average:	**$30**	**$45**
Luxury:	**$40**	**$70**

Credit Cards: **MC, VISA**

The above cities are only a small sample of the locations of hosts waiting to give you plenty of warm hospitality. Ruth's register includes comfortable accommodations in condos, restored Victorians, lakeside cottages, and ranches. To make your choice, please send $3 for her descriptive directory. Texas University, Southern Methodist University, Baylor University, Rice University, and Texas Christian University are convenient to many B&Bs.

Parkview House ✪

1311 SOUTH JEFFERSON, AMARILLO, TEXAS 79101

Tel: **(806) 373-9464**
Best Time to Call: **Before 10 AM; after 5 PM**
Host(s): **Nabil and Carol Dia**
Location: **½ mi. from I-40**
No. of Rooms: **4**
No. of Private Baths: **1**
Max. No. Sharing Bath: **4**
Double/pb: **$55**
Double/sb: **$45**
Single/sb: **$40**
Open: **All year**
Breakfast: **Continental**
Credit Cards: **MC, VISA**
Pets: **No**
Children: **No**
Smoking: **No**
Social Drinking: **Permitted**
Foreign Languages: **Arabic**

Carol is a full-time hostess; Nabil a civil engineer. Both share interests in restoration and stained glass, which is evident in their charming Victorian located in the historic district. The guest rooms are furnished with selected antiques, lace, and luxurious linens. The large columned porch is a fine place to start the day with breakfast or to relax. Palo Duro Canyon State Park, Lake Meredith, and West Texas State University are nearby. They enjoy having guests join them for a "social hour" before dinner.

Southard House ✪

908 BLANCO, AUSTIN, TEXAS 78703

Tel: **(512) 474-4731**
Host(s): **Jerry, Rejina, Kara Southard**
No. of Rooms: **5**
No. of Private Baths: **5**
Double/pb: **$45**
Single/pb: **$35**
Suites: **$100**
Open: **All year**

Reduced Rates: **15%, after 2 nights**
Breakfast: **Continental (weekdays)**
Credit Cards: **AMEX, MC, VISA**
Pets: **No**
Children: **Welcome, over 12**
Smoking: **Permitted**
Social Drinking: **Permitted**
Airport/Station Pickup: **Yes**

Conveniently located in downtown Austin, this 1900 manor house is furnished with antiques and original art. White cutwork lace coverlets are on the queen-size beds, and breakfast is served on a 19th-century English refectory table. On weekends, the breakfast is expanded to include such delicious fare as apple pancakes, eggs-and-cheese casserole, and a variety of meats and berries. Complimentary drinks and snacks are always offered. You are welcome to use their extensive library and to relax on the deck, porch, or in the gazebo.

Lain's Bed and Breakfast

1118 PRAIRIE STREET, COLUMBUS, TEXAS 78934

Tel: **(409) 732-8373**
Host(s): **Ernie and Dorothy Lain**
Location: **60 mi. W of Houston**
No. of Rooms: **2**
No. of Private Baths: **1**
Max. No. Sharing Bath: **4**
Double/pb: **$35**
Double/sb: **$25**
Open: **All year**

Reduced Rates: **10%, seniors**
Breakfast: **Full**
Pets: **Sometimes**
Children: **Welcome**
Smoking: **No**
Social Drinking: **Permitted**
Airport/Station Pickup: **Yes**
Foreign Languages: **Spanish**

Ernie and Dorothy Lain have a Southern-style home decorated with antiques and family pieces. The rooms are large, with high ceilings and plenty of windows. The Lains love entertaining and making new friends. Breakfast features homemade bread and jam and wrap-arounds, sausages in flour tortillas. Columbus has all the advantages of a small town, yet is only one hour from Houston. Guests will want to tour the historic domed courthouse and the many old, elegant homes. There are also plenty of recreational activities to be enjoyed on the Colorado River, which borders the northern and eastern parts of town.

Medford House ✪

2344 MEDFORD COURT EAST, FORT WORTH, TEXAS 76109

Tel: **(817) 924-2765**
Best Time to Call: **After 6 PM**
Host(s): **Maribeth Ashley**
Location: **1 mi. S of I-30**
No. of Rooms: **1**
No. of Private Baths: **1**
Double/pb: **$50**
Single/pb: **$45**
Guest Cottage: **$50–$60**
Open: **All year**
Reduced Rates: **5%, seniors**
Breakfast: **Continental**
Other Meals: **Available**
Pets: **No**
Children: **Welcome**
Smoking: **No**
Social Drinking: **Permitted**
Airport/Station Pickup: **Yes**

Medford House is located in a historic neighborhood with lovely sidewalks and old-fashioned street lamps. The house is an English Tudor with stately oak woodwork, vaulted ceilings, and antique furnishings. Your host offers complimentary wine and cheese, as well as milk and cookies for the children. Guests are welcome to enjoy the swimming pool, gas grill, and patio house. Medford House is within walking distance of the historic Log Cabin Village and Texas Christian University.

Lone Star Inn ✪

ROUTE 3, BOX 1895, GEORGETOWN, TEXAS 78664

Tel: **(512) 863-7527**
Best Time to Call: **Mornings**
Host(s): **Patty Thomas and Carol Gafford**
Location: **30 mi. N of Austin**
No. of Rooms: **4**
No. of Private Baths: **2**
Max. No. Sharing Bath: **4**
Double/pb: **$68**
Double/sb: **$52**
Open: **All year**
Breakfast: **Full**

Pets: **No**
Children: **Welcome, over 12**
Smoking: **No**
Social Drinking: **Permitted**
Airport/Station Pickup: **Yes**

Surrounded by three acres of trees, the inn is located in historic Georgetown, just east of Southwestern University. It's a restored 1910 farmhouse complete with a wraparound porch and a porch swing. The extraordinary Texas breakfasts include orange muffins and ham with red-eye gravy. An outstanding collection of antiques furnishes each room, creating an ambience that preserves a time now past. The LBJ Library and Highland Lakes are nearby. Patty and Carol will be pleased to recommend good dinner spots, but be sure to save room for their complimentary evening dessert buffet.

Bluebonnet B&B ✪

ROUTE 3, BOX 135, HALLSVILLE, TEXAS 75650

Tel: **(214) 668-4554**
Best Time to Call: **Before 9 AM or after 6 PM**
Host(s): **Jane Walley**
Location: **3 mi. from I-20, Exit 60S**
No. of Rooms: **3**
Max. No. Sharing Bath: **3**
Double/sb: **$45**
Guest Cottage: **$50–$60; sleeps 2–3**
Open: **All year**
Breakfast: **Full**
Pets: **Sometimes**
Children: **Welcome, over 3**
Smoking: **No**
Social Drinking: **Permitted**

The driveway leads to a landscaped yard of lovely trees and shrubs, past the herb garden, the Lincolnesque log cabin, and brings you to a two-story cedar-and-stone prairie-style house. Mexican tile floors, stained glass, and a stone fireplace serve as background for the carefully chosen antique furnishings. Depending upon the weather, breakfast may be enjoyed on the porch, at poolside, or in the dining room. Treat yourself to a walk on the nine acres and enjoy the various gardens and a visit to the hen pen, with its resident peacock. The Michaelson Reeves Art Gallery in Marshall, Stroh's Brewery, and tours of historic homes are pleasant diversions nearby.

Sara's Bed & Breakfast Inn ✪

941 HEIGHTS BOULEVARD, HOUSTON, TEXAS 77008

Tel: **(713) 868-1130**
Best Time to Call: **After 11 AM**
Host(s): **Donna and Tillman Arledge**
Location: **1/4 mi. from I-40**
No. of Rooms: **12**
No. of Private Baths: **3**
Max. No. Sharing Bath: **4**
Double/pb: **$50**

Double/sb: **$46–$58**
Suites: **$96 for 4**
Open: **All year**
Breakfast: **Continental**
Credit Cards: **AMEX, MC, VISA**
Pets: **No**
Children: **Welcome, over 10**
Smoking: **No**
Social Drinking: **Permitted**

This Queen Anne Victorian, with its turret and widow's walk, is located in Houston Heights, a neighborhood of 90 historic homes, many of which are on the National Historic Register. Each bedroom is uniquely furnished, having either single, double, queen-size, or king-size beds. The Balcony Suite consists of two bedrooms, two baths, full kitchen, living area, and a fine view overlooking the deck and spa. Cool drinks or hot coffee are graciously offered in the afternoon. The sights and sounds of downtown Houston are four miles away.

Woodlake House

2100 TANGLEWILDE, #371, HOUSTON, TEXAS 77063

Tel: **(713) 972-1979**
Best Time to Call: **After 6 PM**
Host(s): **Marilynn Wrigley**
Location: **3 mi. from Hwy. 10**
No. of Rooms: **2**
No. of Private Baths: **1**
Max. No. Sharing Bath: **3**
Double/pb: **$40**
Single/pb: **$35**
Double/sb: **$35**
Single/sb: **$30**
Open: **All year**
Reduced Rates: **5%, seniors**
Breakfast: **Continental**
Pets: **No**
Children: **Welcome**
Smoking: **Permitted**
Social Drinking: **Permitted**
Airport/Station Pickup: **Yes**

This charming town house, part of a condominium complex, is set in a lovely wooded area complete with a park, walking trails, tennis and racquetball courts, swimming pools, and a health club. It is beautifully furnished in lovely pastels with antique accents. A full English breakfast is offered on weekends, and includes eggs, meats, grilled mushrooms and tomatoes, and, of course, English muffins. Marilynn used to run a B&B in England, so she is an expert in such matters. The AstroDome, AstroWorld, NASA, and Galleria are within easy reach.

Hale House

702 LINE STREET, JEFFERSON, TEXAS 75657

Tel: **(214) 665-8877**
Best Time to Call: **8 AM–10 PM**
Host(s): **Mark and Linda Leonard**
Location: **175 mi. E of Dallas**
No. of Rooms: **6**
No. of Private Baths: 2

Max. No. Sharing Bath: **4**
Double/pb: **$65**
Double/sb: **$45–$55**
Open: **All year**
Reduced Rates: **Weekdays**
Breakfast: **Full**
Credit Cards: **MC, VISA**
Pets: **No**
Children: **Welcome**
Smoking: **No**
Social Drinking: **Permitted**
Airport/Station Pickup: **Yes**

Built in 1865, this gracious white-frame home is surrounded by magnolias and crepe myrtle trees. The large, airy guest rooms are comfortably furnished in turn-of-the-century oak and pine. Jefferson, the second oldest city in Texas, was a Civil War river port. Relax on the sun porch or in the comfortable parlor after a busy day of touring historic homes, museums, shopping in the 23 antiques shops, or enjoying a cruise in a handcrafted boat on Big Cypress Bayou. You are sure to enjoy Mark and Linda's bountiful breakfast.

McKay House ✪

306 EAST DELTA, JEFFERSON, TEXAS 75657

Tel: **(214) 665-7322**
Host(s): **Peggy Taylor and Nobie West**
Location: **150 mi. E of Dallas**
No. of Rooms: **4**
No. of Private Baths: **2**
Max. No. Sharing Bath: **4**
Double/pb: **$70**
Single/pb: **$65**
Double/sb: **$60**
Single/sb: **$50**
Separate Cottage: **$65**
Open: **All year**
Reduced Rates: **Weekly**
Breakfast: **Full**
Credit Cards: **MC, VISA**
Pets: **No**
Children: **Welcome**
Smoking: **No**
Social Drinking: **Permitted**

The McKay House is listed on the National Register of Historic Places. It dates back to 1851 and is within walking distance of more than 200 homes and commercial buildings in the historic district. This Greek Revival house has 14-foot ceilings and 9-foot windows. Each room has been restored and features a fireplace and antique furnishings. Your hostess wears a long period dress when she serves breakfast. Enjoy country ham and biscuits with the sun streaming through the lace curtains of the morning room. After you've had a gentleman's breakfast, you're ready to explore the delights of this riverboat town.

Three Oaks

609 NORTH WASHINGTON AVENUE, MARSHALL, TEXAS 75670

Tel: **(214) 938-6123**
Host(s): **Sandra and Bob McCoy**
Location: **30 mi. W of Shreveport, La.**
No. of Rooms: **2**
No. of Private Baths: **2**
Double/pb: **$65**

Suites: **$90**
Open: **All year**
Reduced Rates: **Available**
Breakfast: **Full**
Pets: **No**
Children: **Welcome, over 9**
Smoking: **No**
Social Drinking: **Permitted**
Airport/Station Pickup: **Yes**

Towering oak trees shelter this lovely Victorian home, located in a National Historic District. The house was constructed in 1835 and was later rebuilt after a fire destroyed a corner section. Original leaded-glass transoms, seven hand-carved fireplaces, beamed ceilings, and polished oak floors will take you back to an earlier era. If you like, breakfast is wheeled into your bedroom on a tea cart adorned with antique linens, silver, and fine china. Your hosts invite you to browse through their vintage magazine collection, watch a video movie, or join them for an evening cordial and dessert. They will gladly direct you to the many interesting sights of the Ginocchio Historic District.

The White House

217 MITTMAN CIRCLE, NEW BRAUNFELS, TEXAS 78130

Tel: **(512) 629-9354**
Best Time to Call: **9 AM–9 PM**
Host(s): **Bevery and Jerry White**
Location: **35 mi. N of San Antonio**
No. of Rooms: **3**
Max. No. Sharing Bath: **4**
Double/sb: **$30–$35**
Single/sb: **$25–$30**
Open: **All year**
Breakfast: **Full**
Other Meals: **Available**
Pets: **Sometimes**
Children: **Welcome (crib)**
Smoking: **No**
Social Drinking: **Permitted**
Airport/Station Pickup: **Yes**

This Spanish-style white-brick ranch is nested among the cedar and oaks in the Texas hill country. Guests are welcomed here with tea and pastries and shown to comfortable rooms with antique iron beds and cozy quilts. A large fishing pond is located on the premises, and a few miles away you may enjoy a refreshing tube or raft ride down the Guadalupe River. Your hosts have giant inner tubes to lend, as well as bicycles for exploring the countryside. In the fall, visitors flock to the New Braunfels famous Wurstfest, the largest held outside Germany. Other attractions include the Alamo, the River Walk, and the many old missions located in nearby San Antonio.

Bed & Breakfast Hosts of San Antonio ✪

166 ROCKHILL, SAN ANTONIO, TEXAS 78209

Tel: **(512) 824-8036**
Best Time to Call: **9 AM–5 PM**
Coordinator: **Lavern Campbell**
States/Regions Covered: **San Antonio**

Rates (Single/Double):
Modest: **$29** **$42.50**
Average: **$40.50** **$59**
Luxury: **$51.50** **$80**

Credit Cards: **MC, VISA**

You'll find hospitable hosts waiting to welcome you and to suggest how best to enjoy this beautiful and historic city. Don't miss the Paseo del Rio (a bustling river walk), the Alamo, the Arneson River Theatre showplace, El Mercado (which is a restored Mexican and Farmers Market), the Southwest Craft Center, wonderful restaurants, marvelous shops, and delightful, friendly folks. The University of Texas, Trinity University, and St. Mary's University are nearby.

Cardinal Cliff ✪

3806 HIGHCLIFF, SAN ANTONIO, TEXAS 78218

Tel: **(512) 655-2939**
Host(s): **Roger and Alice Sackett**
No. of Rooms: **3**
Max. No. Sharing Bath: **4**
Double/sb: **$25**
Single/sb: **$18**
Open: **All year**
Breakfast: **Full**
Pets: **No**
Children: **Welcome (crib)**
Smoking: **No**
Social Drinking: **Permitted**

This comfortable home in a quiet residential area overlooks a wooded river valley. It is a 20-minute drive on an expressway from the house to all the downtown San Antonio attractions, and museums and universities are close by. Homemade breads and preserves are a breakfast feature.

International House ✪

4910 NEWCOME DRIVE, SAN ANTONIO, TEXAS 78229

Tel: **(512) 647-3547**
Best Time to Call: **5 PM–10 PM**
Host(s): **Virginia Y. Wong**
No. of Rooms: **2**
No. of Private Baths: **2**
Double/pb: **$45**
Single/pb: **$30**
Open: **All year**
Reduced Rates: **10%, seniors**
Breakfast: **Continental**
Other Meals: **Available**
Pets: **No**
Children: **No**
Smoking: **Permitted**
Social Drinking: **Permitted**
Airport/Station Pickup: **Yes**

Here is your chance to experience both Eastern and Western cultures in the south of Texas. This split-level home is beautifully decorated with Oriental art and furniture. Your hostess, a global education consultant, welcomes you to her eclectic home with Chinese tea and cookies. She offers a choice of Continental or Oriental-style breakfast in the morning. Dinners are prepared on request, featuring Oriental, Mexican, or downhome Texas cooking. Ginny is a native of this exciting city and will gladly make suggestions to enhance your visit. The Alamo, Paseo del Rio, South Texas Medical Center, and Lackland and Ft. Sam Houston military bases are all nearby.

Lake Placid Guest House ✪

945 REILEY ROAD, SEGUIN, TEXAS 78155

Tel: **(512) 379-7830**
Best Time to Call: **Evenings**
Host(s): **Joyce V. Lawrence**
Location: **25 mi. E of San Antonio**
Guest Cottage: **$50; sleeps 4**
Open: **Mar. 1–Dec. 31**
Breakfast: **Full**
Pets: **No**
Children: **Welcome**
Smoking: **Permitted**
Social Drinking: **Permitted**

This private cottage with white wood siding and yellow shutters is set apart from the main house. Accommodations include two bedrooms, living room, kitchen, and a comfortable deck overlooking the water. Joyce recommends the fine local fishing and water skiing. She is an artist who finds many of her subjects in this picturesque boating retreat.

Rosevine Inn ✪

415 SOUTH VINE AVENUE, TYLER, TEXAS 75702

Tel: **(214) 592-2221**
Host(s): **Bert and Rebecca Powell**
Location: **10 mi. from I-20**
No. of Rooms: **5**
No. of Private Baths: **5**
Double/pb: **$50–$75**
Open: **All year**
Breakfast: **Full**
Pets: **No**
Children: **Welcome, over 12**
Smoking: **No**
Social Drinking: **Permitted**
Airport/Station Pickup: **Yes**

Dr. Irwin Pope, Jr., made his home here on a quaint brick street back in the 1930s. Years later a devastating fire burned all but the foundation and beautiful grounds. Your hosts bought the property in 1986 and built the Rosevine Inn, a Federal-style red-brick home. They have furnished the house with antiques and country collectibles, many of which are for sale. In the morning, wake-up coffee is provided in the central hallway. When you come downstairs, hot muffins, baked breads, fresh fruit, and quiches are served. Your hosts will help you discover the charms of Tyler, known as the "Rose Capital of the

World." Antiques shops are nearby, and the Rosevine makes an excellent base for discovering the many parks and lakes in the area. After a busy day, return to the inn, where you can sip a hot chocolate by the fire or relax in a quiet courtyard.

Country Cousins Bed and Breakfast ✪

ROUTE 7, BOX 344-A, VICTORIA, TEXAS 77901

Tel: **(512) 578-5336**
Host(s): **Glen and Rita Dyer**
No. of Rooms: **1**
No. of Private Baths: **1**
Double/pb: **$35**

Open: **All year**
Breakfast: **Full**
Pets: **No**
Children: **Welcome**
Smoking: **No**

Glen and Rita Dyer have a 32-acre farm, 15 miles from Victoria, Texas. A comfortable guest cottage provides complete privacy. Visit the animals, tour the garden, rock in the porch swing, and just watch the birds. It's like visiting your own country cousins. Your hosts provide a delicious country breakfast including fresh eggs, homemade bread, jams, and jellies. Nearby attractions include Riverside Park, Texas Zoo, Lake Texana, and the Gulf of Mexico.

The Guest House ✪

2209 MIRAMAR, WICHITA FALLS, TEXAS 76308

Tel: **(817) 322-7252**
Host(s): **Mr. and Mrs. Robert Vinson**
Location: **130 mi. NW of Dallas**
No. of Rooms: **1**
No. of Private Baths: **1**
Double/pb: **$55**
Single/pb: **$35**

Open: **All year**
Breakfast: **Continental**
Pets: **Sometimes**
Children: **Welcome**
Smoking: **No**
Social Drinking: **Permitted**

The Vinsons invite you to a separate three-room guest house located on the grounds of their Colonial mansion. Decorated in Early American and Victorian antiques, the rooms feature unusual touches such as antique doll furniture, oil paintings, and Oriental rugs. Your hosts welcome you here with afternoon refreshments such as hot tea or white wine. They will be glad to direct you to the 12 public tennis courts, located three blocks away, and a local golf course, just one mile from the house.

UTAH

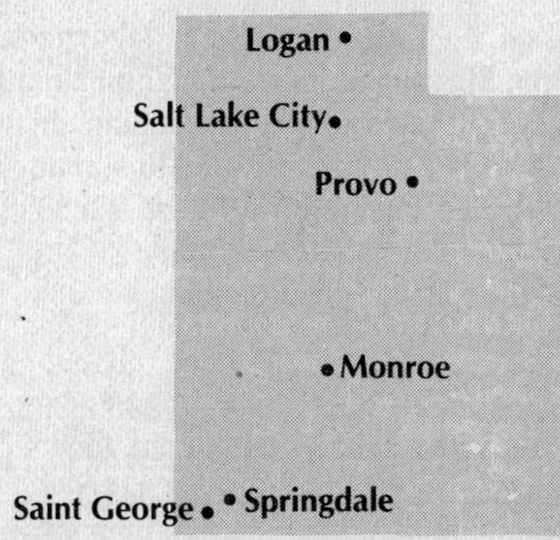

Bed 'n' Breakfast Homestay of Utah ✪

P.O. BOX 365, SALT LAKE CITY, UTAH 84110-0355

Tel: **(801) 532-7076**
Best Time to Call: **9 AM–5 PM**
Coordinators: **Barbara Baker, Nadine Smith**
States/Regions Covered: **Statewide**

Rates (Single/Double):
Average: **$25–$40** **$35–$50**
Luxury: **$55** **$65–$125**
Credit Cards: **No**
Minimum Stay: **2 nights in Salt Lake City**

Utah has something for everyone, and Barbara and Nadine have a roster of hosts who delight in making you feel at home. A full breakfast is included with most of the accommodations. Location and season are taken into consideration in the rate, and discounts are offered to families, and for extended stays. Brigham Young University, University of Utah, Southern Utah State College (site of the Utah Shakespeare Festival in summer) are near many B&Bs.

Bed and Breakfast Rocky Mountains—Utah ✪

P.O. BOX 804, COLORADO SPRINGS, COLORADO 80901

Tel: **(303) 630-3433**
Best Time to Call: **9 AM–5 PM, May–Sept.; in winter, 12–5 PM**
Coordinator: **Kate Peterson Winters**
States/Regions Covered: **Statewide**

Rates (Single/Double):

	Single	Double
Modest:	**$25**	**$35**
Average:	**$30**	**$45**
Luxury:	**$65**	**$95–$140**

Credit Cards: **MC, VISA**

Don't miss Salt Lake City and the Mormon Tabernacle, especially the Sunday morning Free Mormon Tabernacle Choir Broadcast. The B&Bs range from a modest inn to an elegant mansion. In winter, ski Park City, Alta, Snowbird, Brighton, or Solitude! Reservations for any other cities or areas are two-night minimum. There is a $3 charge for Kate's directory.

Center Street Bed and Breakfast Inn ✪

169 EAST CENTER STREET, LOGAN, UTAH 84321

Tel: **(801) 752-3443**
Host(s): **Clyne and Ann Long**
Location: **84 mi. N of Salt Lake City**
No. of Rooms: **10**
No. of Private Baths: **8**
Max. No. Sharing Bath: **4**
Double/pb: **$25–$35**
Single/pb: **$20**
Double/sb: **$20–$25**
Suites: **$50–$70**
Open: **All year**
Breakfast: **Continental**
Pets: **No**
Children: **Welcome, over 12**
Smoking: **No**
Social Drinking: **Permitted**

Relax in a spacious Victorian in the center of Logan's historic district. Nineteenth-century charm fills the house, and each room offers something special. One large and airy room features lace curtains, an antique doll collection, and a view of a waterfall from the east window. The Blue Room has a king-size four-poster canopy bed and large bathroom with antique fixtures. The Garden Suite has a canopied water bed, marble Jacuzzi, crystal chandelier hanging from a vaulted ceiling, and a massage unit in the bath. Your hosts will gladly direct you to a nearby Mormon temple, the ski slopes, and Utah State University.

Peterson's Bed and Breakfast

95 NORTH 300 WEST, MONROE, UTAH 84754

Tel: **(801) 527-4830**
Best Time to Call: **After 6 PM**
Host(s): **Mary Ann & Howard Peterson**
Location: **8 mi. SW of Richfield**
No. of Rooms: **2**
No. of Private Baths: **1**
Double/pb: **$35**
Single/pb: **$25**
Suite: **$55**
Open: **All year**
Reduced Rates: **10%, families**
Breakfast: **Full**
Other Meals: **Available**
Pets: **No**
Children: **Welcome**
Smoking: **No**
Social Drinking: **No**

This immaculate farmhouse, casual and comfortable, is surrounded by 10,000-foot mountains in the heart of hunting and fishing country. The Petersons have traveled extensively, and Mary Ann has written a marvelous cookbook called *Country Cooking.* Hot Springs is seven blocks away. It's a 2½-hours drive to Provo, Salt Lake City, or St. George. The Petersons accommodate just one couple or family at a time to ensure privacy.

The Pullman Bed and Breakfast ✪

415 SOUTH UNIVERSITY AVENUE, PROVO, UTAH 84601

Tel: **(801) 374-8141**
Best Time to Call: **After 8 AM**
Host(s): **The Morganson Family**
Location: **1 mi. from I-15**
No. of Rooms: **6**
No. of Private Baths: **4**
Max. No. Sharing Bath: **4**
Double/pb: **$47.50–$49.50**
Single/pb: **$40–$42**
Double/sb: **$35.50–$39.50**
Single/sb: **$28–$32**
Open: **All year**
Reduced Rates: **10%, families; 3 nights or more**
Breakfast: **Full**
Other Meals: **Available**
Credit Cards: **AMEX, MC, VISA**
Pets: **No**
Children: **Welcome**
Smoking: **No**
Social Drinking: **Permitted**

The Pullman is a magnificent Victorian built in 1898 by a railroad magnate. It has been beautifully restored and is listed on the National Register of Historic Places. The house has an old-fashioned character with its winding staircase, handcarved woodwork, stained glass, and wide porch. In the guest rooms you'll find a hand-stitched quilt on the bed, and a tray of hand-dipped chocolates on the bed table. In the morning, enjoy homemade breads, jams, and fluffy omelets in the sunny dining room. The house is within walking distance of the sights of Provo, including the historic town square. Your hosts also specialize in luncheons, receptions, and meetings.

Seven Wives Inn ✪

217 NORTH 100 WEST, ST. GEORGE, UTAH 84770

Tel: **(801) 628-3737**
Best Time to Call: **After 9 AM**
Host(s): **Jay and Donna Curtis and Alison and Jon Bowcutt**
Location: **125 mi. NE of Las Vegas**
No. of Rooms: **9**
No. of Private Baths: **9**
Double/pb: **$25–$65**
Open: **All year**
Breakfast: **Full**
Credit Cards: **MC, VISA**
Pets: **Welcome**
Children: **Welcome (crib)**
Smoking: **No**
Social Drinking: **Permitted**
Airport/Station Pickup: **Yes**

This delightful inn is featured on the walking tour of St. George; it is just across from the Brigham Young home and two blocks from the historic Washington County Court House. Your hosts offer traditional Western hospitality. Their home is decorated with antiques collected

in America and Europe. Each bedroom is named after one of the seven wives of Donna's polygamous great-grandfather. A gourmet breakfast is served in the elegant dining room that will give you a hint of the past. St. George is located near Zion and Bryce National Parks, boasts six golf courses, and is noted for its mild winters. Dixie College is nearby. There's a swimming pool and hot tub for your pleasure.

The National Historic Bed & Breakfast ✪

936 EAST 1700 SOUTH, SALT LAKE CITY, UTAH 84105

Tel: **(801) 885-3535**
Best Time to Call: **7–11 AM; 7–11 PM**
Host(s): **Katie and Mike Bartholome**
Location: **6 blocks from I-80**
No. of Rooms: **5**
No. of Private Baths: **3**
Max. No. Sharing Bath: **4**
Double/pb: **$67**
Single/pb: **$57**
Double/sb: **$57**
Single/sb: **$47**
Suites: **$97**
Open: **All year**
Reduced Rates: **Weekly**
Breakfast: **Full**
Credit Cards: **AMEX, MC, VISA**
Pets: **No**
Children: **Welcome, over 3**
Smoking: **No**
Social Drinking: **Permitted**
Airport/Station Pickup: **Yes**

The ornate façade of this house combines brick, wood, and stained glass to achieve its handsome Victorian style. Located in the historic Sugarhouse section, its 19th-century pieces meld attractively with Art Deco and contemporary furnishings. The pretty floral designs created by Katie enhance the decor. Mike is justifiably proud of their antique radios, a victrola, and jukebox. Conveniently located, it's just 2 blocks from Westminster College, 5 minutes to the Mormon Temple and downtown, and only 20 minutes away from the famed ski slopes of Snowbird, Alta, and Solitude.

Under the Eaves Guest House ✪

P.O. BOX 29, 980 ZION PARK BOULEVARD, SPRINGDALE, UTAH 84767

Tel: **(801) 772-3457**
Host(s): **Marcus Thomson and Nicole Grayson**
Location: **45 mi. E of St. George**
No. of Rooms: **3**
No. of Private Baths: **2**
Max. No. Sharing Bath: **4**
Double/pb: **$65**
Single/pb: **$55**
Double/sb: **$35–$45**
Single/sb: **$25–$35**
Suites: **$65**
Open: **All year**
Reduced Rates: **Available**

Breakfast: **Full**
Other Meals: **Available**
Credit Cards: **AMEX, MC, VISA**
Pets: **Sometimes**
Children: **Welcome**
Smoking: **Permitted**
Social Drinking: **Permitted**
Airport/Station Pickup: **Yes**
Foreign Languages: **German, Spanish**

Under the Eaves is a historic stone-and-stucco cottage located at the gate of Zion National Park. Constructed of massive sandstone blocks from the canyon, the guest house has served as a landmark for visitors to Zion for more than 50 years. Choose from two antique-filled bedrooms or a luxurious suite. The size of this house allows your hosts to provide extras like complimentary cocktails and a turndown service at night. Served by advance request, dinners feature grilled halibut, lamb with rosemary, barbecued chicken, and garden-fresh vegetables.

Zion House ✪

801 ZION PARK BOULEVARD, P.O. BOX 323, SPRINGDALE, UTAH 84767

Tel: **(801) 772-3281**
Best Time to Call: **Mornings; evenings**
Host(s): **Lillian Baiardi**
Location: **At Zion National Park**
No. of Rooms: **3**
No. of Private Baths: **1**
Max. No. Sharing Bath: **4**
Double/pb: **$46**
Single/pb: **$40**
Double/sb: **$39**
Single/sb: **$33**
Open: **All year**
Breakfast: **Full**
Pets: **No**
Children: **Welcome, over 12**
Smoking: **No**
Social Drinking: **Permitted**

Surrounded by beautiful mountain peaks, within a mile of Zion National Park, Zion House offers comfort, hospitality, and spectacular views of the Watchman and Eagle Crags. You are welcome to relax in the living room, choose a book from the library, or watch a variety of birds seen from the rec room. A typical breakfast often consists of fresh fruit salad, German ham pancakes, and bran muffins. Horseback riding, river tubing, and the Shakespearean Festival are just a few of the local attractions.

VERMONT

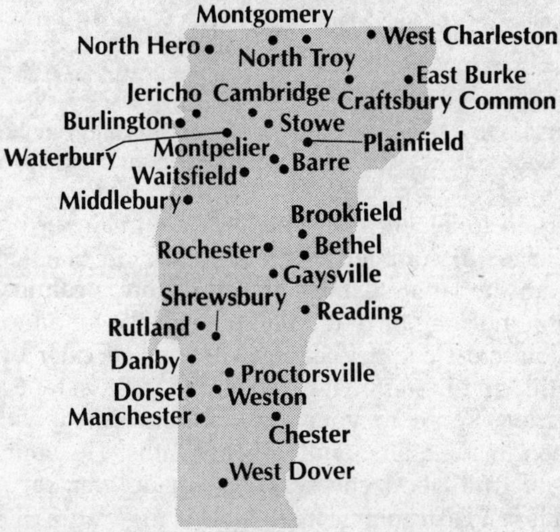

Woodruff House ✪

13 EAST STREET, BARRE, VERMONT 05641

Tel: **(802) 476-7745**
Best Time to Call: **evenings**
Host(s): **Robert and Terry Somaini**
Location: **60 mi. S of Montreal**
No. of Rooms: **2**
Max. No. Sharing Bath: **4**
Double/sb: **$45**
Single/sb: **$35**
Reduced Rates: **Weekly**
Open: **All year**
Breakfast: **Full**
Pets: **No**
Children: **Welcome**
Smoking: **No**
Social Drinking: **No**

Woodruff House is located in a quiet park in the heart of town. The house is painted Victorian style, using three colors: blue with white trim and cranberry shutters. Guest rooms are furnished in antiques and decorated with flair. Guests are welcome to relax in the two living rooms and use the TV and piano. Breakfast specialties include homemade breads and eggs prepared with Vermont cheddar. Your host will point the way to the state capital, five ski areas, museums, and some of the greatest fall foliage in the state.

The Parmenter House ✪

BOX 106, BELMONT, VERMONT 05730

Tel: **(802) 259-2009**
Best Time to Call: **8–10 AM; evenings**
Host(s): **Lester and Cynthia Firschein**
Location: **25 mi. SE of Rutland; 2 mi. from Rte. 155**
No. of Rooms: **5**
No. of Private Baths: **5**
Double/pb: **$50–$70**
Single/pb: **$45–$65**
Open: **May 27–Apr. 3**
Reduced Rates: **Available**
Breakfast: **Continental**
Credit Cards: **MC, VISA**
Pets: **No**
Children: **Welcome, over 7**
Smoking: **No**
Social Drinking: **Permitted**
Airport/Station Pickup: **Yes**

You are certain to benefit from the clear mountain air of this idyllic lakeside village. In summer, swim or canoe on Star Lake by day, stargaze from the large deck by night. Explore a country lane on a crisp autumn morning or rent an all-terrain bike for an excursion. In winter, follow cross-country skiing with mulled cider by the wood stove. Cynthia and Lester invite you to relax in the serene atmosphere of their parlor. Retire to your bedroom furnished with Victorian antiques, handmade quilts, and herbal wreaths. The bountiful breakfast buffet of fruit, local cheeses, homemade granola, and freshly baked breads is a gastronomic treat.

Greenhurst Inn

RIVER STREET, BETHEL, VERMONT 05032

Tel: **(802) 234-9474**
Host(s): **Lyle and Barbara Wolf**
Location: **30 mi. E of Rutland**
No. of Rooms: **13**
No. of Private Baths: **7**
Max. No. Sharing Bath: **5**
Double/pb: **$60–$80**
Single/pb: **$50–$70**
Double/sb: **$40–$45**
Single/sb: **$30–$35**
Open: **All year**
Breakfast: **Continental**
Credit Cards: **MC, VISA**
Pets: **Welcome (no cats)**
Children: **Welcome (crib)**
Smoking: **Permitted**
Social Drinking: **Permitted**

Located 100 yards from the White River, this elegant Queen Anne mansion is listed on the National Register of Historic Places. Built in 1890, the heavy brass hinges, embossed floral brass doorknobs, and etched windows at the entry have withstood the test of time. The cut-crystal collection is magnificent, and the stereoscope and old Victrola add to the old-fashioned atmosphere. It's close to many points of historic interest, and seasonal recreational activities are abundant. There's tennis and croquet on the premises. Vermont Law School is close by.

Poplar Manor

RD 2, ROUTES 12 and 107, BETHEL, VERMONT 05032

Tel: **(802) 234-5426**
Host(s): **Carmen and Bob Jaynes**
Location: **16 mi. N of Woodstock**
No. of Rooms: **4**
Max. No. Sharing Bath: **4**
Double/sb: **$29**
Single/sb: **$20**
Suites: **$32**
Open: **All year**
Reduced Rates: **10%, weekly**
Breakfast: **Continental**
Pets: **Sometimes**
Children: **Welcome**
Smoking: **Permitted**
Social Drinking: **Permitted**
Foreign Languages: **Spanish**

This early 19th-century Colonial is surrounded by green meadows and cornfields. The rooms are large and bright, with exposed-beam ceilings, collectibles, and plants. Your hosts offer wine and mulled cider, served "spiked," if you wish. The fields back up to the White River and a swimming hole. Other area attractions include the National Fish Hatchery, Silver Lake, seasonal sports, and the shops of Woodstock. Vermont Law School is nearby. There's a two-night minimum stay during foliage and holiday weekends.

Green Trails Country Inn ✪

POND VILLAGE, BROOKFIELD, VERMONT 05036

Tel: **(802) 276-3412**
Host(s): **Betty and Jack Russell**
Location: **8 mi. from I-89, Exit 4**
No. of Rooms: **12**
No. of Private Baths: **10**
Max. No. Sharing Bath: **4**
Double/pb: **$62**
Single/pb: **$45**
Double/sb: **$56**
Single/sb: **$42**
Open: **All year**
Reduced Rates: **10%, seniors**
Breakfast: **Full**
Other Meals: **Available**
Pets: **No**
Children: **Welcome (crib)**
Smoking: **No**
Social Drinking: **Permitted**
Airport/Station Pickup: **Yes**

The inn consists of two buildings. One is an 1840 farmhouse; the other was built in the late 1700s and has pumpkin pine floorboards. They are located across from the famous Floating Bridge and Sunset Lake. Furnished in antiques and "early nostalgia," the rooms have stenciling (circa 1800), handmade quilts, and fresh flowers. The historic village is a perfect base for seasonal excursions to the Shelburne Museum or Woodstock. Cross-country skiers can start at the doorstep, while downhill enthusiasts can try Sugarbush and Killington.

Stone Hearth Inn ✪

ROUTE 11, CHESTER, VERMONT 05143

Tel: **(802) 875-2525**
Host(s): **Janet and Don Strohmeyer**
Location: **10 mi. from I-91, Exit 6**
No. of Rooms: **10**
No. of Private Baths: **8**
Max. No. Sharing Bath: **4**
Double/pb: **$48–$70**
Single/pb: **$34–$48**
Double/sb: **$40–$62**
Single/sb: **$30–$44**
Open: **All year**
Reduced Rates: **Available**
Breakfast: **Full**
Pets: **Sometimes**
Children: **Welcome (crib)**
Smoking: **Permitted**
Social Drinking: **Permitted**
Airport/Station Pickup: **Yes**
Foreign Languages: **Dutch, French, German**

This white 19th-century Colonial is set on seven acres of fields and wooded land. The rooms have been lovingly restored and feature wide-board pine floors and open beams, floral wallpapers, antiques, quilts, and a player piano. A fireplaced living room and library are available. After a busy day, relax in the licensed pub and recreation room. Horseback riding, downhill and cross-country skiing, and swimming in the river across the road are but a handful of the local pleasures. Your hosts offer fresh-baked breads, pancakes, and French toast for breakfast. The dining room is open to the public for lunch and dinner.

Craftsbury Bed & Breakfast on Wylie Hill ✪

CRAFTSBURY COMMON, VERMONT 05827

Tel: **(802) 586-2206**
Best Time to Call: **Morning or evening**
Host(s): **Margaret Ramsdell**
Location: **40 mi. N of Montpelier**
No. of Rooms: **4**
Max. No. Sharing Bath: **4**
Double/sb: **$45–$55**
Single/sb: **$30–$40**
Open: **All year**
Breakfast: **Full**
Other Meals: **Available**
Pets: **No**
Children: **Welcome (crib)**
Smoking: **No**
Social Drinking: **Permitted**
Foreign Languages: **French**

This 1860 Georgian hilltop farmhouse has beautiful views. The homey guest rooms adjoin the living room with its wood stove, where you are welcome to relax and visit. You may use Margaret's kitchen, barbecue, and picnic table should the crisp mountain air stoke your appetite. You're sure to enjoy the bountiful breakfast that often features apple pancakes with fresh maple syrup. Other meals are served only by prior arrangement. The ski slopes of Stowe are 30 miles away, and cross-country skiing, lakes, and rivers are within a two-mile radius.

The Quail's Nest Bed and Breakfast ✪

P.O. BOX 221, MAIN STREET, DANBY, VERMONT 05739

Tel: **(802) 293-5099**
Host(s): **Chip and Anharad Edson**
Location: **13 mi. N of Manchester**
No. of Rooms: **5**
No. or Private Baths: **1**
Max. No. Sharing Bath: **4**
Double/pb: **$50-$55**
Single/pb: **$40-$45**
Double/sb: **$45-$50**
Single/sb: **$35-$40**
Open: **All year**
Breakfast: **Full**
Credit Cards: **MC, VISA**
Pets: **No**
Children: **Welcome, over 10**
Smoking: **Permitted**
Social Drinking: **Permitted**

The Quail's Nest is a Federal-style inn circa 1835. The guest rooms are furnished with antiques and handmade country quilts. Your hostess loves entertaining and offers such homemade breakfast specialties as apple-puff pancakes, muffins, and quiches. Danby is a quiet village close to five major ski areas. The Green Mountains are just east of here, offering some of the finest swimming, fishing, hiking, and downhill and cross-country skiing in the state.

The Little Lodge at Dorset ✪

ROUTE 30, BOX 673, DORSET, VERMONT 05251

Tel: **(802) 867-4040**
Host(s): **Allan and Nancy Norris**
Location: **6 mi. N of Manchester**
No. of Rooms: **5**
No. of Private Baths: **5**
Double/pb: **$70–$85**
Single/pb: **$60–$70**
Open: **All year**
Breakfast: **Continental**
Credit Cards: **AMEX**
Pets: **No**
Children: **Welcome (crib)**
Smoking: **Permitted**
Social Drinking: **Permitted**

Situated in one of the prettiest little towns in Vermont, this delightful 1820 Colonial house, on the Historic Register, is perched on a hillside overlooking the mountains and its own trout pond that's used for skating in winter or canoeing in summer. The original paneling and wide floorboards set off the splendid antiques. After skiing at nearby Stratton or Bromley, toast your feet by the fireplace while sipping hot chocolate. If you prefer, bring your own liquor, and Nancy and Allan will provide Vermont cheese and crackers.

Maplewood Colonial House ✪

BOX 1019, ROUTE 30, DORSET, VERMONT 05251

Tel: **(802) 867-4470**
Best Time to Call: **After 5 PM**
Host(s): **Marge and Leon Edgerton**
No. of Rooms: **5**
No. of Private Baths: **3**
Max. No. Sharing Bath: **4**
Double/pb: **$60**
Single/pb: **$45**
Double/sb: **$55**
Single/sb: **$40**
Open: **All year**
Breakfast: **Continental**
Pets: **Sometimes**
Children: **Welcome**
Smoking: **No**
Social Drinking: **Permitted**

This large, 20-room white Colonial with green shutters is in a lovely setting. The five corner bedrooms are airy, comfortably furnished with antiques; the dining table is pre–Civil War vintage. You are welcome to wander the acreage, canoe on the pond, bicycle, or browse in Marge and Leon's library. In winter, skiing at Bromley or Stratton is convenient. The fall foliage is fabulous. Credit cards may be used to secure a reservation. A three-night minimum is required on holiday weekends.

Blue Wax Farm

PINKHAM ROAD, EAST BURKE, VERMONT 05832

Tel: **(802) 626-5542**
Host(s): **Kenneth and Ingrid Parr**
Location: **45 mi. N of White River Junction**
No. of Rooms: **4**
No. of Private Baths: **2**
Max. No. Sharing Bath: **3**
Double/pb: **$26**
Single/pb: **$15**
Double/sb: **$26**
Single/sb: **$15**
Open: **All year**
Breakfast: **Continental**
Credit Cards: **MC, VISA**
Pets: **No**
Children: **Welcome**
Smoking: **Permitted**
Social Drinking: **Permitted**
Foreign Languages: **Finnish, Spanish**

If you want to ski Vermont without bedding down at resorts with bars and discos, reserve a room here. Kenneth and Ingrid have a quiet retreat adjoining the Burke Mountain ski resort. There is cross-country skiing on the property, in addition to the downhill trails on Burke. Both casual and serious hikers will find this an ideal spot, and bikers originate tours here. The cordiality of your hosts and the view of the countryside, especially the fall foliage, are well worth the trip in all seasons. Lyndon State College is nearby.

Burke Green Guest House ✪

RURAL ROUTE 1, EAST BURKE, VERMONT 05832

Tel: **(802) 467-3472**
Best Time to Call: **10 AM–9 PM**
Host(s): **Harland and Beverly Lewin**
Location: **15 mi. N of St. Johnsbury**
No. of Rooms: **3**
No. of Private Baths: **2**
Max. No. Sharing Bath: **5**
Double/pb: **$32–$38**
Single/pb: **$28–$30**
Double/sb: **$32–$35**
Single/sb: **$28–$30**
Open: **All year**
Reduced Rates: **Weekly**
Breakfast: **Full**
Pets: **No**
Children: **Welcome**
Smoking: **Permitted**
Social Drinking: **Permitted**

You will enjoy the quiet 25-acre country setting and spacious 1840 farmhouse, remodeled with modern conveniences but retaining the original wooden beams. The view of Burke Mountain is spectacular. Sit in the family room and enjoy the warmth of the cozy fireplace. It is 10 minutes from skiing and snow sports; summertime fun includes swimming, fishing, and hiking. The kitchen is always open for cookies and beverages, and you are welcome to use the laundry facilities, guest refrigerator, and picnic table. Lyndon State College is nearby.

The Kiln Guest House ✪

BENEDICT ROAD, EAST DORSET, VERMONT 05253

Tel: **(802) 362-4889**
Host(s): **Dennis and Catherine Conroy**
Location: **4.5 mi. N of Manchester**
No. of Rooms: **4**
Max. No. Sharing Bath: **4**
Double/sb: **$42.40**
Single/sb: **$21.20**
Open: **All year**
Reduced Rates: **10%, seniors; 15% weekly, families**
Breakfast: **Full**
Pets: **Sometimes**
Children: **Welcome**
Smoking: **Permitted**
Social Drinking: **Permitted**
Airport/Station Pickup: **Yes**

Dennis and Catherine invite you to share their contemporary wood-paneled home where you are welcome to relax on the deck or in front of the wood stove, depending upon the season. There's a pond and a stream for fishing, and it is located close to Emerald Lake State Park. It is 15 minutes from the slopes at Bromley; 30 minutes to Stratton. The coffeepot is always on, and pretzels and chips are complimentary.

Cobble House Inn ✪

P.O. BOX 49, GAYSVILLE, VERMONT 05746

Tel: **(802) 234-5458**
Best Time to Call: **8 AM–9 PM**
Host(s): **Philip and Beau Benson**
Location: **Off Rte. 107**
No. of Rooms: **6**
No. of Private Baths: **6**
Double/pb: **$84.70**
Single/pb: **$72.60**
Open: **All year**
Breakfast: **Full**
Other Meals: **Available**
Credit Cards: **MC, VISA**
Pets: **No**
Children: **Welcome (crib)**
Smoking: **No**
Social Drinking: **Permitted**

A grand 1860s mansion awaits you on a hilltop overlooking the beautiful Green Mountains. Each guest room is decorated with antiques and accented with country furnishings. Ornate carved beds, colorful quilts, and flannel sheets are sure to offer a peaceful night's rest. Breakfast specialties such as French apple pancakes, homemade coffee cakes, peach fritters, or eggs Benedict are served each morning. Just outside the door is the White River, with its clear waters for fishing, canoeing, tubing, and swimming. Skiing, golf, tennis, and horseback riding are all within easy reach. In the evening, the inn offers Italian and French cuisine served in the country dining room.

Milliken's ✪

R.D. 2, BOX 397, JERICHO, VERMONT 05465

Tel: **(802) 899-3993**
Best Time to Call: **Mornings; evenings**
Host(s): **Rick and Jean Milliken**
Location: **12 mi. E of Burlington**
No. of Rooms: **3**
Max. No. Sharing Bath: **4**
Double/sb: **$35**
Single/sb: **$25**
Suites: **$55**
Open: **All year**
Breakfast: **Full**
Pets: **No**
Children: **Welcome**
Smoking: **No**
Social Drinking: **Permitted**
Airport/Station Pickup: **Yes**

This Second Empire early Victorian was built in 1867 by a lumber magnate. The house has a graceful mansard roof, original woodwork, and floors of alternating cherry and white maple. The spaciousness of the rooms is enhanced by high ceilings, large windows, and gracious decor. Rick is a hotel manager and Jean is a choreographer and hostess. She prepares such breakfast specialties as French toast with maple syrup and hot mulled cider. In the evening, a good-night brandy and snack awaits in your guest room. Your family is sure to enjoy its stay with the Millikens, their two children, and a friendly dog named Bailey. Nearby attractions are hiking trails on Mt. Mansfield, skiing, and fabulous fall foliage.

Saxon Inn

SOUTH ORR ROAD, P.O. BOX 337, JERICHO, VERMONT 05465

Tel: **(802) 899-3015**
Best Time to Call: **10 AM–4 PM**
Host(s): **Howard and Anne Reeves**
Location: **12 mi. E of Burlington**
No. of Rooms: **5**
No. of Private Baths: **5**
Double/pb: **$55–$65**
Single/pb: **$50–$60**
Open: **All year**
Reduced Rates: **25%, Jan., Feb., Mar.**
Breakfast: **Continental**
Other Meals: **Available**
Credit Cards: **AMEX, MC, VISA**
Pets: **Sometimes**
Children: **Welcome**
Smoking: **Permitted**
Social Drinking: **Permitted**
Airport/Station Pickup: **Yes**

The Saxon Inn is an 11-year-old barnboard country home set on 28 acres in the Green Mountains. Spectacular views of the magnificent surroundings are enhanced by the large windows throughout the house. Anne enjoys interior decorating, and each room is furnished comfortably with her special touch. Breakfast specialties include French toast with local syrup and sour cream coffee cake. You can swim, fish, chip and putt, hike, ice skate, or cross-country ski without ever stepping past the front gate. After a day of activity, join the Reeves for family-style country dinners. In the evening, they invite you to relax in the fireplace room, choose a book from the library, or retire to the privacy of your cozy room.

Brook 'n' Hearth ✪

STATE ROAD 11/30, BOX 508, MANCHESTER CENTER, VERMONT 05255

Tel: **(802) 362-3604**
Best Time to Call: **2 PM–10 PM**
Host(s): **Larry and Terry Greene**
Location: **1 mi. E of U.S. 7**
No. of Rooms: **3**
No. of Private Baths: **3**
Max. No. Sharing Bath: **4**
Double/pb: **$46**
Single/pb: **$32**
Suites: **$55**
Open: **May 20–Oct. 31; Nov. 18–Apr. 16**
Reduced Rates: **Available**
Breakfast: **Full**
Credit Cards: **AMEX, MC, VISA**
Pets: **No**
Children: **Welcome (crib)**
Smoking: **Permitted**
Social Drinking: **Permitted**

True to its name, a brook runs through the property and a fire warms the living room of this country home. Terry and Larry offer setups and happy-hour snacks for your self-supplied cocktails. You're within five miles of the ski slopes at Bromley and Stratton; it is also convenient to art centers, summer theater, restaurants, and a score of sports that include hiking on the Long Trail. In summer, enjoy the heated pool, lawn games, and barbecue. The game room, with its VCR, pocket billiards, and Ping-Pong, is always available.

Brookside Meadows ✪

RD 3, BOX 2460, MIDDLEBURY, VERMONT 05753

Tel: **(802) 388-6429**
Location: **2½ mi. from Rte. 7**
Host(s): **The Cole Family**
No. of Rooms: **4**
No. of Private Baths: **4**
Double/pb: **$50–$60**
Suites: **$75–$100**
Open: **All year**
Breakfast: **Full**
Pets: **No**
Children: **Welcome, over 5**
Smoking: **Permitted**
Social Drinking: **Permitted**
Airport/Station Pickup: **Yes**

This attractive farmhouse was built in 1979, based on a 19th-century design. The house is on a country road, on 20 acres of meadowland. The property borders on a brook. It is also home to geese, goats, two dogs, and a cat. The two-bedroom suite has a wood stove in the living room as well as a private entrance. Relax on cedar lawn chairs and enjoy a view of the Green Mountains. Area attractions include downhill and cross-country skiing, hiking, maple syrup operations, Middlebury College, and the University of Vermont Morgan Horse Farm. Two-night stays are required in the suite during summer and fall.

Charlie's Northland Lodge ✪

BOX 88, NORTH HERO, VERMONT 05474

Tel: **(802) 372-8822**
Best Time to Call: **Before 8 PM**
Host(s): **Charles and Dorice Clark**
Location: **60 mi. S of Montreal, Canada**
No. of Rooms: **3**
Max. No. Sharing Bath: **5**
Double/sb: **$40**
Single/sb: **$30**
Guest Cottage: **$425; sleeps 6**
Open: **All year**
Reduced Rates: **Sept. 2–Oct. 15**
Breakfast: **Continental**
Pets: **No**
Children: **Welcome, over 5**
Smoking: **Permitted**
Social Drinking: **Permitted**

The lodge is a restored Colonial (circa 1850) located on Lake Champlain, where bass and walleye abound. A sport and tackle shop is on the premises. Fall and winter fishing should appeal to all anglers. In summer, tennis, hiking, or relaxing in the reading room are pleasant activities.

Rose Apple Acres Farm ✪

RFD 1, BOX 300, EAST HILL ROAD, NORTH TROY, VERMONT 05859

Tel: **(802) 988-4300**
Best Time to Call: **Evening**
Host(s): **Jay and Camilla Mead**
Location: **60 mi. N of St. Johnsbury**
No. of Rooms: **3**
No. of Private Baths: **1**
Max. No. Sharing Bath: **4**
Double/pb: **$38**
Double/sb: **$32**
Single/sb: **$20**
Open: **All year**
Breakfast: **Full**
Pets: **No**
Children: **Welcome, over 6**
Smoking: **No**
Social Drinking: **Permitted**
Airport/Station Pickup: **Yes**

Located two miles from the Canadian border, the farm is situated on 52 acres of fields, woods, and streams. The farmhouse has a bright and friendly atmosphere, enhanced by panoramic mountain views. Hiking, cross-country skiing, snowshoeing, and horseback riding may be enjoyed on-premises. It is only 10 miles to Jay Peak for skiing. Camilla and Jay are interested in classical music, gardening, horses, and electric trains.

Yankees' Northview Bed & Breakfast ✪

R.D. #2, PLAINFIELD, VERMONT 05667

Tel: **(802)-454-7191**
Best Time to Call: **Evenings**
Host(s): **Joani and Glenn Yankee**
Location: **9 mi. NE of Montpelier**
No. of Rooms: **3**
Max. No. Sharing Bath: **6**
Double/sb: **$35**
Single/sb: **$30**
Open: **All year**
Reduced Rates: **Available**
Breakfast: **Full**
Pets: **Sometimes**
Children: **Welcome**
Smoking: **No**
Social Drinking: **Permitted**

Although it has a Plainfield mailing address, this roomy Colonial is located on a quiet country lane in the picturesque town of Calais. The house is surrounded by stone walls and white fences. Fresh flowers and after-dinner mints are just a few of the special touches you will find in your antique-filled bedroom. A delightful breakfast is served on the garden patio overlooking the mountains and the meadows. (The kitchen is shown on our back cover.) In cold weather, specialties such as homemade Swedish coffee ring, French toast, pancakes, and eggs are offered in the stenciled dining room or beside the pot-belly stove in the country kitchen. Your hosts invite you to relax with a cup of coffee by the fire, or stroll down to the unique quaking bog, just a five-minute walk from the house. Yankee's Northview is minutes from swimming, boating, horseback riding, and historic Kent's Corner.

The Peeping Cow Bed & Breakfast

P.O. BOX 47, ROUTE 106, READING, VERMONT 05062

Tel: **(802) 484-5036**
Best Time to Call: **7:30–9:45 AM; 5:30–7 PM**
Host(s): **Nancy and Frank Lynch**
Location: **14 mi. from I-91, Exit 9**
No. of Rooms: **2**
No. of Private Baths: **1**
Max. No. Sharing Bath: **4**
Double/pb: **$45**
Double/sb: **$40**
Single/sb: **$20**
Open: **All year**
Breakfast: **Continental**
Pets: **No**
Children: **Welcome, over 16**
Smoking: **No**
Social Drinking: **Permitted**
Airport/Station Pickup: **Yes**
Foreign Languages: **French, Spanish**

The "peeping bovines" are 50 Jerseys in the meadows surrounding Nancy and Frank's circa-1800 white farmhouse. It is attractively furnished with fine English antiques and family heirlooms. Outdoor mountain recreation abounds in all seasons. Mt. Ascutney is five minutes away, convenient to many downhill ski areas, and cross-country skiing starts outside the door. Fishing, horseback riding, tennis, golf, bicycling, swimming, fun summer festivals, hot-air ballooning, steamboat rides on Lake Sunapee are just a few things to do. Dartmouth College is a short drive. There's a two-night minimum during fall foliage.

Harvey Farm Country Inn

ROCHESTER, VERMONT 05767

Tel: **(802) 767-4273**
Host(s): **Don and Maggie Harvey**
Location: **3 mi. from Rte. 100**
No. of Rooms: **9**
Max. No. Sharing Bath: **4**
Double/sb: **$76**
Single/sb: **$42**
Suites: **$84 for 2**
Guest Cottage: **$350/wk, sleeps 4**
Open: **All year**
Reduced Rates: **Families**
Breakfast: **Full**
Other Meals: **Dinner included**
Pets: **Yes—Guest cottage only**
Children: **Welcome, over 3**
Smoking: **Permitted**
Social Drinking: **Permitted**

You can find serenity in this inn that combines modern country living with the beauty of mountains, open meadows, woods, and farmland. After a hearty breakfast, children are invited to help feed the small animals and ride the pony. Everyone is welcome to swim in the pool or go fishing. Picnic lunches are available and delectable dinners are served in the antique-filled dining room. Your last cup of coffee can be enjoyed on the porch or in front of the TV. In winter, the ski slopes of Sugarbush, Middlebury Snowbowl, and Killington are close by.

Hillcrest Guest House ✪

RR 1, BOX 4459, RUTLAND, VERMONT 05701

Tel: **(802) 775-1670**
Host(s): **Bob and Peg Dombro**
Location: **3/10 mi. from Rte. 7**
No. of Rooms: **3**
Max. No. Sharing Bath: **5**
Double/sb: **$35**
Single/sb: **$25**
Open: **All year**
Breakfast: **Continental**
Pets: **No**
Children: **Welcome (crib)**
Smoking: **No**
Social Drinking: **Permitted**
Airport/Station Pickup: **Yes**

This 150-year-old farmhouse, with a comfortable screened porch for warm-weather relaxing, is furnished with country antiques. Pico and Killington ski areas are 7 and 16 miles away. Summer brings the opportunity to explore charming villages, covered bridges, and antiques and craft centers. Country auctions, marble quarries, trout streams, and Sunday-evening band concerts are pleasant pastimes. Bob and Peg always offer something in the way of between-meal refreshments.

Buckmaster Inn ✪

LINCOLN HILL ROAD, SHREWSBURY, VERMONT 05738

Tel: **(802) 492-3485**
Best Time to Call: **8–10 AM; 5–9 PM**
Host(s): **Grace Husselman**
Location: **8 mi. SE of Rutland**
No. of Rooms: **4**
No. of Private Baths: **1**
Max. No. Sharing Bath: **4**
Double/pb: **$50–$65**
Single/pb: **$50–$65**
Double/sb: **$40–$50**
Single/sb: **$35–$50**
Open: **All year**
Reduced Rates: **Weekly**
Breakfast: **Full**
Pets: **No**
Children: **Welcome, over 8**
Smoking: **No**
Social Drinking: **Permitted**
Airport/Station Pickup: **Yes**
Foreign Languages: **Dutch**

The Buckmaster Inn, located near Cuttingsville in the Green Mountains, is a Federal clapboard Colonial overlooking a picturesque valley. Its center hall, grand staircase, and wide pine floors are typical of 19th-century style. This is New England relaxation at its best: fireplaces, woodburning stove, library, and two porches. Homemade muffins, casseroles, and jams are among the specialties served in the country kitchen each morning. A pond for skating and fishing is within walking distance, and ski slopes, hiking trails, and craft shops are nearby.

Watercourse Way ✪

ROUTE 132, SOUTH STRAFFORD, VERMONT 05070

Tel: **(802) 765-4314**
Host(s): **Lincoln and Anna Alden**
Location: **10 mi. from I-91**
No. of Rooms: **3**
Max. No. Sharing Bath: **6**
Double/sb: **$40**
Single/sb: **$20**
Open: **All year**
Breakfast: **Full**
Pets: **Sometimes**
Children: **Welcome**
Smoking: **Permitted**
Social Drinking: **Permitted**

Watercourse Way is situated on the Ompompanoosuc River, surrounded by towering evergreens and fragrant herb gardens. It is an 1850 farmhouse cape with wide pine floors and original Shaker-style doors. Guests will find all the small touches to make them feel at home, such as fresh flowers, cozy quilts, braided rugs, and interesting pictures on the walls. There's a place for everyone beside the giant fieldstone fireplace, and plenty of books to borrow. Freshly ground gourmet coffee and herbal teas from the garden are part of a large country breakfast. Specialties include home-baked muffins, jellies and jams, and French toast or pancakes with fresh local syrup. Skiing, biking, museums, and Lake Fairlee are nearby, and fishing, kayaking, and wading can be enjoyed a few steps from the front door. Dartmouth College in Hanover, New Hampshire, is close by.

Bittersweet Inn

RR #2, BOX, 2900, ROUTE 100, STOWE, VERMONT 05672

Tel: **(802) 253-7787**
Best Time to Call: **7 AM–11 PM**
Host(s): **Barbara and Paul Hansel**
Location: **36 mi. W of Burlington**
No. of Rooms: **8**
No. of Private Baths: **5**
Max. No. Sharing Bath: **2**
Double/pb: **$48**
Single/pb: **$48**
Double/sb: **$46**
Single/sb: **$46**
Suites: **$98**
Open: **All year**
Reduced Rates: **5-day stays**
Breakfast: **Continental**
Credit Cards: **AMEX, MC, VISA**
Pets: **Yes, small ones**
Children: **Welcome (play area)**
Smoking: **Permitted**
Social Drinking: **Permitted**
Airport/Station Pickup: **Yes**
Foreign Languages: **German**

Bittersweet Inn is a brick cape with converted clapboard carriage house, dating back to 1835. The house is set on nine and a half acres, overlooking Camel's Hump Mountain. Inside you'll find comfortable rooms decorated with a combination of antiques and family pieces. It's just a half mile to the center of town and minutes to ski lifts and a cross-country touring center. A good-sized swimming pool is located out back with plenty of room for laps or just taking it easy. In the warmer weather, afternoon tea and pastries are served, and in the winter season hot soup will be waiting after your last ski run. Your hosts Barbara and Paul invite you to relax in the game room with BYOB bar and will help you plan your evening.

Ski Inn ✪

ROUTE 108, STOWE, VERMONT 05672

Tel: **(802) 253-4050**
Best Time to Call: **9–11 AM; evenings**
Host(s): **Larry and Harriet Heyer**
Location: **47 mi. NE of Burlington**
No. of Rooms: **10**
No. of Private Baths: **5**
Max. No. Sharing Bath: **5**
Double/pb: **$37.50–$80**
Single/pb: **$30–$70**
Double/sb: **$25–$55**
Single/sb: **$25–$45**
Open: **All year**
Reduced Rates: **Off-season**
Breakfast: **Continental**
Other Meals: **Included, in winter**
Pets: **Sometimes**
Children: **Welcome**
Smoking: **Permitted**
Social Drinking: **Permitted**

This traditional New England inn is set back from the highway among evergreens on a gentle sloping hillside. This is a quiet place to relax and sleep soundly. In winter, it's a skier's delight, close to Mt. Mansfield's downhill and cross-country trails. A full breakfast and delicious dinner are included in winter rates of $45 to $80. In summer, the rates drop and include just Continental breakfast. Larry and Harriet offer warm hospitality in all seasons.

Blush Hill House ✪

BLUSH HILL ROAD, WATERBURY, VERMONT 05676

Tel: **(802) 244-7529**
Host(s): **Tom and Bobbi O'Connor**
Location: **22 mi. E. of Burlington**
No. of Rooms: **6**
No. of Private Baths: **4**
Max. No. Sharing Bath: **4**
Double/pb: **$50–$55**
Double/sb: **$45–$50**
Open: **All year**
Reduced Rates: **Available**
Breakfast: **Continental**
Credit Cards: **MC, VISA**
Pets: **No**
Children: **Welcome, over 10**
Smoking: **Permitted**
Social Drinking: **Permitted**
Airport/Station Pickup: **Yes**

This 170-year-old brick farmhouse is located halfway between the Stowe and Sugarbush ski areas. The atmosphere is warm and homey, with antiques, old-time rockers, books, and lots of fireplaces. Your hostess is a gourmet cook and enjoys making her own bread and muffins each morning. Cheese, crackers, and setups are offered in the evening to go along with cocktails. A huge lake with boating, swimming, and fishing is located just one and a half miles from the house, and a nine-hole golf course is located directly across the street. At the end of the day, sit back and enjoy the surroundings, relaxing on the large, old-fashioned porch.

The Captain Henry Chase House ✪

RFD 4, BOX 788, WEST BRATTLEBORO, VERMONT 05301

Tel: **(802) 254-4114**
Best Time to Call: **5:30 PM**
Host(s): **Patrick and Lorraine Ryan**
Location: **6½ mi. W of Brattleboro**
No. of Rooms: **2**
Max. No. Sharing Bath: **4**
Double/sb: **$40**
Single/sb: **$30**
Open: **All year**
Breakfast: **Full**
Pets: **No**
Children: **Welcome**
Smoking: **Permitted**
Social Drinking: **Permitted**
Airport/Station Pickup: **Yes**

The Captain Henry Chase House is set in one of the state's prettiest valleys, yet is only 15 minutes from Brattleboro. The farmhouse is an American classic dating back to 1798. It features beautiful wainscoting, a classic walk-in fireplace with hanging pots, and cozy bedrooms. Lorraine prepares huge stacks of pancakes for breakfast, served with the best local syrup. Also from her kitchen come an array of home-baked afternoon snacks, served with fresh coffee. It's just a short walk down a country road to an old-fashioned covered bridge and the summer swimming hole. After a day of riding, hiking, or skiing, come back to the Ryans' warm hospitality and a place by the fire.

Hunt's Hideaway ✪

RFD MORGAN ROAD, WEST CHARLESTON, VERMONT 05872

Tel: **(802) 895-4432 or 334-8322**
Best Time to Call: **7 AM–11 PM**
Host(s): **Pat and Paul Hunt**
Location: **6 mi. from I-91**
No. of Rooms: **3**
Max. No. Sharing Bath: **4**
Double/sb: **$30**
Single/sb: **$20**
Open: **All year**
Reduced Rates: **Available**
Breakfast: **Full**
Pets: **Sometimes**
Children: **Welcome**
Smoking: **Permitted**
Social Drinking: **Permitted**

This modern split-level home is located on 100 acres of woods and fields, with a brook, pond, and large swimming pool. Pancakes with Vermont maple syrup are featured at breakfast. Ski Jay Peak and Burke, or fish and boat on Lake Seymour, two miles away. Visiting antique shops or taking a trip to nearby Canada are other local possibilities.

The Weathervane ✪

DORR FITCH ROAD, BOX 57, WEST DOVER, VERMONT 05356

Tel: **(802) 464-5426**
Host(s): **Liz and Ernie Chabot**
Location: **1 mi. from Rte. 100**
No. of Rooms: **10**
No. of Private Baths: **2**
Max. No. Sharing Bath: **5**
Double/pb: **$64–$72**
Double/sb: **$42–$56**
Single/sb: **$39–$42**
Suites: **$88**
Open: **All year**
Reduced Rates: **Ski weeks; off-season**
Breakfast: **Full**
Pets: **No**
Children: **Welcome (crib)**
Smoking: **Permitted**
Social Drinking: **Permitted**

Only four miles from Haystack, Mount Snow, and Corinthia, this Tyrolean-style ski lodge is decorated with authentic antiques and Colonial charm. The lounge and recreation room have fireplaces and a bring-your-own bar. Winter rates include cross-country ski equipment, sleds, and snowshoes, so that you may explore the lovely marked trails. Summer brings lakeshore swimming, boating, fishing, tennis, riding, museums, and the Marlboro Music Festival.

The Colonial House

ROUTE 100, BOX 138, WESTON, VERMONT 05161

Tel: **(802) 824-6286**
Best Time to Call: **8 AM–10 PM**
Host(s): **Betty and John Nunnikhoven**
Location: **35 mi. SE of Rutland; 24 mi. from I-91, Exit 6**
No. of Rooms: **15**
No. of Private Baths: **9**
Max. No. Sharing Bath: **6**
Double/pb: **$50–$70**
Single/pb: **$40**
Double/sb: **$46–$54**
Single/sb: **$32**
Open: **All year**
Reduced Rates: **Available**
Breakfast: **Full**
Other Meals: **Available**
Credit Cards: **MC, VISA**
Pets: **Sometimes**
Children: **Welcome (crib)**
Smoking: **Permitted**
Social Drinking: **Permitted**

Built in 1790, this cozy farmhouse offers you a country-living experience. Four of the shared-bath bedrooms have lavatories. Enjoy leisurely farm breakfasts, with snacks in the afternoon. There's a guest living room, a solarium, a fireplace, and warm hospitality. Cross-country skiing starts at the doorstep and seasonal activities are all nearby.

VIRGINIA

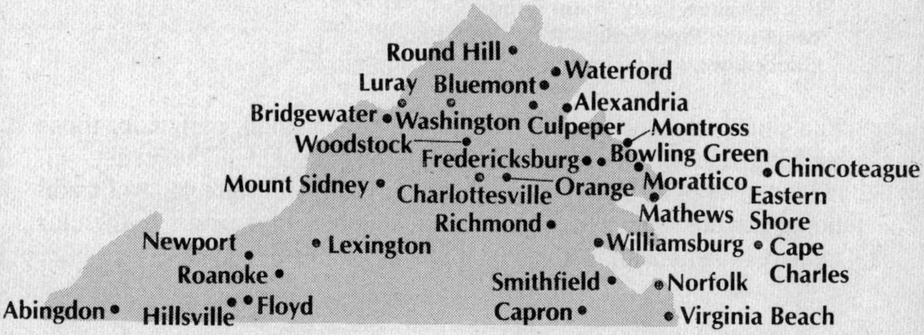

Round Hill
Waterford
Luray
Bluemont
Alexandria
Bridgewater
Washington
Culpeper
Montross
Woodstock
Fredericksburg
Bowling Green
Chincoteague
Mount Sidney
Charlottesville
Orange
Morattico
Eastern Shore
Mathews
Richmond
Newport
Lexington
Williamsburg
Cape Charles
Roanoke
Smithfield
Norfolk
Abingdon
Hillsville
Floyd
Capron
Virginia Beach

Princely/Bed & Breakfast, Ltd. ✪

819 PRINCE STREET, ALEXANDRIA, VIRGINIA 22314

Tel: **(703) 683-2159**
Best Time to Call: **10 AM–6 PM, Mon.-Fri.**
Coordinator: **E. J. Mansmann**
States/Regions Covered: **Alexandria**

Rates (Single/Double):
Luxury: **$65–$75**
Credit Cards: **No**
Minimum Stay: **2 nights**

Alexandria is eight miles from Washington, D.C., and nine miles from Mount Vernon. An immaculate subway transports you to the White House in 20 minutes. Mr. Mansmann, a former State Department official, has an exclusive roster of deluxe accommodations ready for you; they include an 18th-century Federal-style mansion in historic Old Town Alexandria, as well as other historic houses (circa 1751 to 1838) filled with museum-quality antiques. You will be made to feel like visiting royalty, whichever place you choose.

Blue Ridge Bed & Breakfast ✪

ROUTE 2, ROCKS & RILLS, BOX 3895, BERRYVILLE, VIRGINIA 22611

Tel: **(703) 955-2410**
Best Time to Call: **9 AM–2 PM**
Coordinator: **Rita Z. Duncan**
States/Regions Covered: **Virginia—Amissville, Berryville, Flint Hill, Hamilton, Luray, Warm Springs, Winchester; West Virginia—Charkestown, Middleway**

Rates (Single/Double):
Modest: **$35**
Average: **$50**
Luxury: **$135**
Credit Cards: **MC, VISA**

Rita's hosts are within 50 to 200 miles of the Capitol, perfect for those wishing to visit rural areas near Washington, D.C. The variety includes houses on the Historic Register, mountain retreats, and traditional private homes in small towns. This beautiful area is known for its part in American history, horses, and farming.

Shenandoah Valley Bed & Breakfast Reservations ✪

PO BOX 305, BROADWAY, VIRGINIA 22815

Tel: **(703) 896-9702**
Best Time to Call: **After 5 PM**
Coordinators: **Nancy and John Stewart**
States/Regions Covered: **I-81, Exit 66; Amissville, Front Royal, Harrisonburg, Maurertown, McGaheysville, Middletown, Mt. Jackson, Rawley Springs, Staunton, Woodstock**

Rates (Single/Double):

Modest:	**$30**	**$40**
Average:	**$40**	**$45–$56**
Luxury:	**$45**	**$85**

Credit Cards: **MC, VISA (for deposit only)**
Minimum Stay: **2 nights (on weekends)**

Since the 1700s, travelers have raved about the magnificent scenery of the Shenandoah Valley. Nancy and John have a roster of historic homes, farmhouses, and contemporary residences that share the rolling hills between the Alleghenies and Blue Ridge Mountains. The valley is alive with artists, theater, heritage days, fairs, golf courses, ski resorts, and colleges. You are bound to be warmly welcomed and advised on the best restaurants and activities by an interested host. Please send $1 for the descriptive directory. There is a $10 surcharge for one night's stay.

Summerfield Inn ✪

101 WEST VALLEY STREET, ABINGDON, VIRGINIA 24210

Tel: **(703) 628-5905**
Best Time to Call: **Mornings; after 3 PM**
Host(s): **Champe and Don Hyatt**
Location: **15 mi. NE of Bristol**
No. of Rooms: **3**
No. of Private Baths: **1**
Max. No. Sharing Bath: **5**
Double/pb: **$60**
Single/pb: **$50**
Double/sb: **$50**
Single/sb: **$40**
Suites: **$100**
Open: **Apr. 1–Nov. 1**
Reduced Rates: **15%, 3-day stays**
Breakfast: **Continental**
Credit Cards: **MC, VISA**
Pets: **No**
Children: **Welcome, over 12**
Smoking: **Permitted**
Social Drinking: **Permitted**
Airport/Station Pickup: **Yes**

A large covered porch with comfortable rockers graces the front and side of this meticulously restored Victorian residence. Guests are welcome to share the large living room, handsomely appointed morning room, and a sunroom. Your hosts will gladly pack picnic lunches for trips to the mountain trails or for a fishing trip to one of the nearby lakes or rivers. A guests' pantry is also available for preparing light snacks. Summerfield Inn is a short walk from Barter Theatre, Old Abingdon, and fine dining. Set at 2,300 feet and surrounded by mountains, this was one of the first communities formed in western Virginia.

Meadowood ✪

P.O. BOX 29, BOSTON, VIRGINIA 22713

Tel: **(703) 547-3851**
Host(s): **Lorraine Robson**
Location: **80 mi. SW of Washington, D.C.**
No. of Rooms: **4**
No. of Private Baths: **2**
Max. No. Sharing Bath: **4**
Double/pb: **$90**
Single/pb: **$80**
Double/sb: **$75**
Single/sb: **$60**
Open: **All year**
Reduced Rates: **10%, weekly**
Breakfast: **Full**
Other Meals: **Available**
Pets: **Sometimes**
Children: **Welcome, over 12**
Smoking: **No**
Social Drinking: **Permitted**
Airport/Station Pickup: **Yes**

Located in beautiful and historic Rappahannock County between Sperryville and Culpeper, this contemporary house is filled with old-fashioned hospitality. Surrounded by 26 rustic acres for hiking and exploring, there's a stream for fishing, and archery and croquet on-premises. A bountiful breakfast will get you ready to take in nearby

Luray Caverns, Monticello, or the Appalachian Trail. Lorraine will steer you to antiques shops or craft shops as well as local happenings of interest. Dessert is always available when you return from an evening out.

The Old Mansion ✪

BOX 835, BOWLING GREEN, VIRGINIA 22427

Tel: **(804) 633-5781**
Host(s): **Ruth Curlee and Peter Larson**
Location: **70 mi. S of Washington, D.C.**
No. of Rooms: **3**
Max. No. Sharing Bath: **2**
Double/sb: **$55**
Single/sb: **$45**
Suites: **$70 (family of 4)**
Open: **All year**
Reduced Rates: **Available**
Breakfast: **Full**
Pets: **Sometimes**
Children: **Welcome (crib)**
Smoking: **No**
Social Drinking: **Permitted**
Airport/Station Pickup: **Yes**

The Old Mansion was built in 1669 by Thomas Hoomes. Although George Washington never slept inside the house, the general and his troops did camp on the grounds on their way to Yorktown in 1781. Today, guests play croquet on the same grassy lawn surrounded by 126 acres of ancient cedars, boxwood, and gardens. Inside, every room is furnished with antiques of all kinds, some as old as the house. Breakfast specialties include fresh eggs, country sausages, and homemade breads and pastries. Ruth and Peter invite you for a glass of sherry in the afternoon. They will gladly direct you to such attractions as Stratford Hall, Washington's Birthplace, Fredericksburg Historic District, and much more. Picnic lunches are available.

Bear and Dragon Bed & Breakfast ✪

401 NORTH MAIN STREET, BRIDGEWATER, VIRGINIA 22812

Tel: **(703) 828-2807**
Host(s): **Carol and William Gardner**
Location: **5 mi. S of Harrisonburg, 3 mi. from I-81, Exit 61**
No. of Rooms: **4**
Max. No. Sharing Bath: **4**
Double/pb: **$40**
Single/pb: **$35**
Double/sb: **$35**
Single/sb: **$30**
Open: **All year**
Reduced Rates: **Weekly; 10%, seniors**
Breakfast: **Full**
Credit Cards: **MC, VISA**
Pets: **Welcome**
Children: **Welcome (crib)**
Smoking: **Permitted**
Social Drinking: **Permitted**

Built before the Civil War, this two-story brick home has been renovated and decorated with comfort in mind. No pun meant, but the

Gardners love to garden! Their landscaped grounds have a variety of perennials, a Japanese garden, and a stocked fish pond. If you're watching cholesterol, sodium, or calories, Carol will cleverly cater to your dietary needs at breakfast. Some of the diverse points of interest include the Massanutten Ski Resort, New Market Battlefield Park, George Washington National Forest, and the Skyline Drive. If you care to bring your racket, there's a public tennis court just a block away.

Nottingham Ridge ✪

P.O. BOX 97-B, CAPE CHARLES, VIRGINIA 23310

Tel: **(804) 331-1010**
Best Time to Call: **Evenings**
Host(s): **Bonnie Nottingham**
Location: **20 mi. N of Norfolk**
No. of Rooms: **3**
Max. No. Sharing Bath: **4**
Double/sb: **$50**
Single/sb: **$45**
Open: **All year**
Breakfast: **Full**
Other Meals: **Available**
Pets: **Sometimes**
Children: **Welcome**
Smoking: **Permitted**
Social Drinking: **Permitted**
Airport/Station Pickup: **Available**

Nottingham Ridge is a picturesque country retreat high atop the sand dunes of Virginia's eastern shore. Guests can spend hours on a private beach, or charter a fishing boat for the day. Bonnie offers comfortable rooms furnished with antiques and reproductions. She loves entertaining and offers homemade biscuits, Virginia ham, and quiche for breakfast. Later in the day, enjoy wine, cheese, and a breathtaking view of the sun setting over the water. This lovely home is just three and a half miles north of the Chesapeake Bay Bridge Tunnel, and 25 minutes from the Norfolk and Virginia Beach areas. Bonnie will gladly direct you to historic sights, the Nature Conservancy, and the U.S. Fish and Wildlife Refuge.

Picketts Harbor

CAPE CHARLES, VIRGINIA 23310

Tel: **(804) 331-2212**
Best Time to Call: **After 5 PM**
Host(s): **Sara and Cooke Goffigon**
Location: **21 mi. E of Norfolk**
No. of Rooms: **6**
Max. No. Sharing Bath: **4**
Double/sb: **$50**
Single/sb: **$40**
Open: **Alll year**
Breakfast: **Full**
Other Meals: **Available**
Pets: **No**
Children: **Welcome**
Smoking: **No**
Social Drinking: **Permitted**
Airport/Station Pickup: **Yes**

Picketts Harbor is set in a rural, wooded section of Virginia's Eastern Shore. The house is decorated "country-style," with antiques, reproductions, plants, and collectibles. Outside, the property spans 17 acres including a large private beach. Breakfast is served overlooking Chesapeake Bay. There many local opportunities for fishermen and hunters, and your hosts will gladly provide a picnic lunch. Williamsburg, Yorktown, and many historic sights are within an hour's drive.

Sandy Hill Farm B&B ✪

ROUTE 1, BOX 55, CAPRON, VIRGINIA 23829

Tel: **(804) 658-4381**
Host(s): **Anne Kitchen**
Location: **11 mi. from I-95**
No. of Rooms: **2**
Max. No. Sharing Bath: **4**
Double/sb: **$27**
Single/sb: **$22**
Open: **All year**

Reduced Rates: **Families; 5 nights**
Breakfast: **Continental**
Other Meals: **Available**
Pets: **Welcome**
Children: **Welcome**
Smoking: **Permitted**
Social Drinking: **Permitted**

Experience the pleasures of an unspoiled rural setting at this ranch-style farmhouse. There are animals to visit, quiet places to stroll, and a lighted tennis court on the grounds. This is an ideal hub from which to tour southeastern and central Virginia . . . day trips to Williamsburg, Norfolk, or Richmond. Fresh fruits and homemade breads are served at breakfast.

Guesthouses Reservation Service ✪

P.O. BOX 5753, CHARLOTTESVILLE, VIRGINIA 22905

Tel: **(804) 979-7264**
Best Time to Call: **12–5, Mon.–Fri.**
Coordinator: **Mary Hill Caperton**
States/Regions Covered:
Charlottesville, Luray, Albemarle County

Rates (Single/Double):

Modest:	**$36**	**$48**
Average:	**$56**	**$60**
Luxury:	**n/a**	**$160**

Estate cottages: **$72 up**
Credit Cards: **AMEX, MC, VISA**

Charlottesville is a gracious town. The hosts in Mary's hospitality file offer you a genuine taste of Southern hospitality. All places are close to Thomas Jefferson's Monticello and James Madison's Ash Lawn, as well as the University of Virginia. Unusual local activities include ballooning, steeplechasing, and wine festivals. Please note that the office is closed from Christmas through New Year's Day. Reduced rates are available for extended stays, and most hosts offer a full breakfast. Please send $1 for her directory.

Oxbridge Inn Guest House ✪

316 14TH STREET NORTHWEST, CHARLOTTESVILLE, VIRGINIA 22903

Tel: **(804) 295-7707**
Host(s): **George Kollaros and Gray Lee**
No. of Rooms: **8**
No. of Private Baths: **6**
Max. No. Sharing Bath: **4**
Double/pb: **$48**
Double/sb: **$43**
Single/sb: **$35**
Suites: **$75**
Open: **All year**
Reduced Rates: **Families; Nov.–Mar.**
Breakfast: **Full**
Credit Cards: **MC, VISA**
Pets: **Sometimes**
Children: **Welcome**
Smoking: **No**
Social Drinking: **Permitted**
Airport/Station Pickup: **Yes**

This brick Colonial is located in the historic district; it is close to shops, restaurants, and two blocks from the University of Virginia. For relaxing, there are a porch and a garden, and a sitting room with fireplace. Continental breakfast includes homemade breads. Area attractions include the home of Thomas Jefferson, plus Ash Lawn, Castle Hill, and Swannanoa mansions.

Fountain Hall ✪

609 SOUTH EAST STREET, CULPEPER, VIRGINIA 22701-3222

Tel: **(703) 825-6708**
Best Time to Call: **8 AM–8 PM**
Host(s): **Steve and Kathi Walker**
Location: **1 mi. from Va. Rte. 29/522**
No. of Rooms: **6**
No. of Private Baths: **4**
Max. No. Sharing Bath: **4**
Double/pb: **$65**
Single/pb: **$55**
Double/sb: **$55**
Single/sb: **$50**
Suites: **$75**
Open: **All year**
Reduced Rates: **Dec.–Mar.; 10%, seniors; after 3 nights; business travelers**
Breakfast: **Continental**
Credit Cards: **MC, VISA**
Pets: **No**
Children: **Welcome (crib)**
Smoking: **Permitted**
Social Drinking: **Permitted**
Airport/Station Pickup: **Yes**

The first county surveyor of Culpeper was a teenaged George Washington, who called it "a high and pleasant situation." Indeed it still is, with many unspoiled historic and natural treasures for you to enjoy. Fountain Hall is furnished with antiques, comfortable beds, and an old-fashioned flavor. It is a fine home base from which to explore north-central Virginia. Some local points of interest include the Cavalry Museum, the Civil War reenactment of the Battle of Cedar Mountain, Little Fork Church, Commonwealth Park horse shows, wineries, antiquing, and some fine restaurants. Steve and Kathi serve tea, coffee, or lemonade upon your return from touring.

Caledonia Farm

ROUTE 1, BOX 2080, FLINT HILL, VIRGINIA 22627

Tel: **(703) 675-3693**
Host(s): **Phil Irwin**
Location: **68 mi. SW of Washington, D.C.**
No. of Rooms: **2**
Max. No. Sharing Bath: **4**
Double/pb: **$100**
Double/sb: **$70**
Open: **All year**
Reduced Rates: **20% after 3 nights**
Breakfast: **Full**
Pets: **No**
Children: **Welcome**
Smoking: **No**
Social Drinking: **Permitted**

This lovely stone country home dates back to 1812; its grounds border the Shenandoah National Park. Riding, hiking, canoeing, and the Skyline Drive are just a few of the attractions within easy reach. Phil invites you to join him for a welcome beverage and social hour with hors d'oeuvres. He'll help you choose from one of the fine restaurants nearby for dinner.

Brookfield Inn

P.O. BOX 341, FLOYD, VIRGINIA 24091

Tel: **(703) 763-3363**
Best Time to Call: **Before 8 AM; after 5 PM**
Hosts: **Gaynell Thompson**
Location: **12 mi. S of I-81**
No. of Rooms: **2**
Max. No. Sharing Bath: **4**
Double/sb: **$30 and up**
Single/sb: **$25**
Open: **All year**
Breakfast: **Full**
Credit Cards: **MC, VISA**
Pets: **No**
Children: **No**
Smoking: **No**
Social Drinking: **Permitted**

A private road lined with native plants and wildflowers leads to this spacious country home, located on a mountaintop in the heart of the Blue Ridge. The relaxing setting includes several acres of greenery and native woods, a trout pond, and nature trails. Inside, you'll find beautifully furnished bedrooms and a comfortable living area for reading or conversation. The Southern-style breakfast of ham, eggs, and biscuits is served on the patio in warm weather. Your hosts will gladly help you discover the pleasures of rural Floyd County and the beautiful Blue Ridge Mountains.

La Vista Plantation ✪

ROUTE 3, BOX 1255, FREDERICKSBURG, VIRGINIA 22401

Tel: **(703) 898-8444**
Host(s): **Michele and Edward Schiesser**
Location: **60 mi. S of D.C.; 4.5 mi. from I-95**
No. of Rooms: **1 suite**
No. of Private Baths: **1**
Double/pb: **$60**
Single/pb: **$45**
Suites: **$60, can sleep 6**
Open: **All year**
Reduced Rates: **7th night free; families**
Breakfast: **Full**
Credit Cards: **MC, VISA**
Pets: **Sometimes**
Children: **Welcome**
Smoking: **Permitted**
Social Drinking: **Permitted**
Airport/Station Pickup: **Yes**

Guest lodgings at La Vista are located in an English basement blessed with a sunny exposure and featuring a private entrance. The spacious, air-conditioned suite has a large living room with fireplace, full kitchen, sitting room, and bath. Ten acres surround the manor house (circa 1838), and you are welcome to stroll, birdwatch, or fish in a pond stocked with bass and sunfish.

The McGrath House ✪

225 PRINCESS ANNE STREET, FREDERICKSBURG, VIRGINIA 22401

Tel: **(703) 371-4363**
Best Time to Call: **Mornings**
Host(s): **Sylvia McGrath**
Location: **50 mi. S of Washington, D.C.**
No. of Rooms: **3**
Max. No. Sharing Bath: **6**
Double/sb: **$35**
Single/sb: **$30**
Open: **All year**
Reduced Rates: **Weekly**
Breakfast: **Continental**
Pets: **Sometimes**
Children: **Welcome**
Smoking: **No**
Social Drinking: **Permitted**

This carefully restored house, featured on walking tours, dates back to the early 19th century and is located in the oldest part of Fredericksburg on a quiet, tree-lined street. You'll enjoy breakfast in the country kitchen that overlooks a small Colonial herb garden. In the evening, you are welcome to a drink and snacks with Sylvia before retiring. Don't miss seeing the President James Monroe Law Offices, Rising Sun Tavern, the Battlefield, and Kenmore. Mary Washington College is nearby.

Rainbow's End B&B

ROUTE 1, BOX 335, GORE, VIRGINIA 22637

Tel: **(703) 858-2808**
Best Time to Call: **10 AM–8 PM**
Host(s): **Eleanor and Thom McKay**
Location: **20 mi. W of Winchester**
No. of Rooms: **2**
Max. No. Sharing Bath: **3**
Double/sb: **$32**
Single/sb: **$28**
Open: **All year**
Reduced Rates: **10%, seniors**
Breakfast: **Continental**
Pets: **No**
Children: **Welcome, over 10**
Smoking: **No**
Social Drinking: **Permitted**

Rainbow's End is a brick and wood ranch situated on Timber Ridge in the Blue Ridge Mountains. The McKays offer cozy rooms filled with comfortable family furnishings. Eleanor serves a tasty breakfast of homemade breads, muffins, cakes, and coffee. Later in the day, join your hosts for wine and cheese. Guests can experience rural life in the heart of apple country. You may see a deer, a fox, or any one of a number of colorful birds that frequent the pond nestled among the pines. Nearby attractions include George Washington's Office, Ole Towne Winchester with its quaint stores, several famous caverns, and Civil War battlefields.

Tipton House

1043 NORTH MAIN STREET, P.O. BOX 753, HILLSVILLE, VIRGINIA 24343

Tel: **(703) 728-2351**
Best Time to Call: **Late afternoons**
Host(s): **Mary Ann Cameron**
Location: **2.5 mi. from I-77**
No. of Rooms: **4**
No. of Private Baths: **2**
Max. No. Sharing Bath: **4**
Double/pb: **$45–$55**
Double/sb: **$35**
Open: **Apr.–Dec.**
Breakfast: **Full**
Credit Cards: **MC, VISA**
Pets: **No**
Children: **No**
Smoking: **No**
Social Drinking: **Permitted**
Airport/Station Pickup: **Yes**

Guests enjoy the relaxed, friendly atmosphere of this two-story brick home. It has Victorian furnishings, lace curtains, beautifully restored woodwork, and a fireplace in each room. Mary's wholesome breakfast has an ever-changing menu. Because of its Main Street location, you will be within strolling distance of restaurants and shops. Feel free to lounge on the rocking chairs on the large porch, or use the TV, piano, or library.

Fassifern Bed & Breakfast ✪

ROUTE 5, BOX 87, LEXINGTON, VIRGINIA 24450

Tel: **(703) 463-1013**
Best Time to Call: **After 1 PM**
Host(s): **Pat and Jim Tichenor**
Location: **50 mi. N of Roanoke**
No. of Rooms: **6**
No. of Private Baths: **4**
Max. No. Sharing Bath: **4**
Double/pb: **$50–$65**
Single/pb: **$45–$60**
Double/sb: **$40–$45**
Single/sb: **$35–$40**
Suites: **$80**
Open: **All year**
Breakfast: **Continental**
Credit Cards: **MC, VISA**
Pets: **No**
Children: **Welcome, over 16**
Smoking: **Downstairs only**
Social Drinking: **Permitted**
Airport/Station Pickup: **Yes**

Fassifern is a 19th-century manor home, located on three and a half acres with a pond and stately trees. Over the years, the house has been rebuilt and authentically restored. Rooms are furnished with antiques and souvenirs collected during 26 years of worldwide military service. When you relax on the porch, patio, or in the conservatory, your hosts will gladly supply reading or writing materials. They offer such breakfast specialties as homemade breads and pastries, seasonal fruit, freshly ground coffee, and gourmet teas; evening snacks are also offered. Fassifern is two miles from Virginia Military Institute, Marshall Museum, and Washington and Lee University. Virginia Horse Center and downtown are also very close by.

Llewellyn Lodge at Lexington ✪

603 SOUTH MAIN STREET, LEXINGTON, VIRGINIA 24445

Tel: **(703) 463-3235**
Best Time to Call: **8 AM–1 PM**
Host(s): **John Roberts and Ellen Thornber**
Location: **50 mi. N of Roanoke**
No. of Rooms: **5**
No. of Private Baths: **5**
Double/pb: **$55**
Single/pb: **$45**
Suite: **$65**
Open: **All year**
Reduced Rates: **Available**
Breakfast: **Full**
Other Meals: **Available**
Credit Cards: **MC, VISA**
Pets: **No**
Children: **Welcome, over 5**
Smoking: **Permitted**
Social Drinking: **Permitted**
Airport/Station Pickup: **Yes**

Guests are welcomed to this lovely brick Colonial with seasonal refreshments. Your hostess has 20 years of experience in the travel and hospitality business, and guarantees to make you feel at home. The decor combines traditional and antique furnishings. Homemade coffee cake, biscuits, and omelets are favorites at the breakfast table. With advance notice, Ellen will put her gourmet expertise to work and serve a family-style dinner including soup, salad, entree, and dessert. If you don't get a chance to sample some of the garden produce at dinner, you can take some home with you when you leave. Llewellyn is close to local attractions such as the homes of Robert E. Lee and Stonewall Jackson, and the Natural Bridge.

Shenandoah Countryside ✪

ROUTE 2, BOX 377, LURAY, VIRGINIA 22835

Tel: **(703) 743-6434**
Best Time to Call: **Mornings**
Host(s): **Phel and Bob Jacobsen**
No. of Rooms: **3**
No. of Private Baths: **1**
Max. No. Sharing Bath: **4**
Double/pb: **$55**
Single/pb: **$45**
Double/sb: **$55**
Single/sb: **$45**
Open: **All year**
Breakfast: **Full**
Pets: **Sometimes**
Children: **Welcome, over 10, on weekdays**
Smoking: **Permitted**
Social Drinking: **Permitted**
Airport/Station Pickup: **Yes**

Shenandoah Countryside is a new custom brick farmhouse overlooking magnificent pastoral and mountain scenes. The house is set on 45 acres, including a Christmas tree farm, and is surrounded by an English garden filled with fresh herbs. One guest room features a brass bed and private balcony, another has walnut twin beds and a small dressing room. Guests are welcome to unwind in the Finnish sauna or outside on one of the three porches overlooking the Shenandoah Valley. Breakfast is served outdoors in season, and at the harvest table in winter. The Jacobsens offer homemade breads and jams, eggs Benedict, goldenrod French toast, pancakes, and more. Later, they invite you for tea, wine, cookies, and Virginia peanuts. Enjoy sightseeing in Shenandoah National Park, canoeing on the river, touring the Luray Caverns, or borrow a bicycle and explore the country roads.

Riverfront House ✪

ROUTE 14 EAST, PO BOX 310, MATHEWS, VIRGINIA 23109

Tel: **(804) 725-9975**
Host(s): **Annette Goldreyer**
Location: **30 mi. from U.S. 17**
No. of Rooms: **6**
Max. No. Sharing Bath: **4**
Double/sb: **$38–$60**
Open: **Apr.–Dec.**
Reduced Rates: **Available**
Breakfast: **Continental**
Pets: **No**
Children: **Welcome, over 7**
Smoking: **Permitted**
Social Drinking: **Permitted**

This clapboard farmhouse is set on seven acres near the mouth of the East River. The 19th-century design features a gracious front hall and mahogany mantelpieces. The bedrooms blend contemporary with antique furnishings. A buffet of fruit, cheese, and muffins is offered each morning. Breakfast can be enjoyed inside or on the wraparound porch. Sunbathe right on the dock, or drop a crab line and try your luck. Your hosts invite you to share a glass of wine in the parlor. It is within an hour of Williamsburg. There are excellent flat roads for hiking and biking that lead to Chesapeake Bay.

The Inn at Montross ✪

COURTHOUSE SQUARE, MONTROSS, VIRGINIA 22520

Tel: **(804) 493-9097**
Host(s): **Ellen and Michael Longman**
Location: **46 mi. E. of Fredericksburg**
No. of Rooms: **6**
No. of Private Baths: **6**
Double/pb: **$65**
Single/pb: **$55**
Open: **All year**
Reduced Rates: **10%, seniors**
Breakfast: **Continental**
Other Meals: **Available**
Credit Cards: **AMEX, Diners, MC, VISA**
Pets: **Sometimes**
Children: **Welcome**
Smoking: **Permitted**
Social Drinking: **Permitted**

The original sections of the Inn at Montross date back over 300 years. Your hosts have decorated the rooms with a mixture of primitive and modern art, porcelains, antiques, and reproductions. Each guest room is furnished with four-poster beds, with extras such as bedside brandy and chocolates. The main floor boasts a magnificent grand piano, which guests are welcome to use. A small lounge with television and a spacious living room are available for relaxing. Your hosts serve home-baked croissants, fresh fruit, muffins, or danish for breakfast. Bountiful meals at affordable prices are served in the Colonial dining rooms, which are open to the public. The Longmans will be glad to direct you to Stratford Hall, Ingleside Winery, and Westmoreland State Park. Golf and fishing can be enjoyed nearby, and there are tennis courts on the grounds.

Holley Point ✪

P.O. BOX 64, MORATTICO, VIRGINIA 22523

Tel: **(804) 462-7759**
Host(s): **Mary Chilton Graham**
Location: **6 mi. from Rte. 3**
No. of Rooms: **4**
No. of Private Baths: **1**
Max. No. Sharing Bath: **5**
Double/pb: **$30**
Single/pb: **$25**
Double/sb: **$25**
Single/sb: **$20**
Open: **May 1–Nov. 1**
Breakfast: **Continental**
Pets: **Welcome**
Children: **Welcome**
Smoking: **Permitted**
Social Drinking: **Permitted**
Airport/Station Pickup: **Yes**

Your hostess at this stately home claims to be related to George Washington and will be happy to direct you to the local historic sites. You will enjoy the 120 acres of pine forest and views of the scenic Rappahannock River. There are plenty of opportunities for land and water sports, including hunting, hiking, bicycling, swimming, and water skiing. Breakfast, served on the wraparound screened porch, includes fruit from the trees on the property.

The Widow Kip's ✪

ROUTE 1, BOX 117, MT. JACKSON, VIRGINIA 22842

Tel: **(703) 477-2400**
Best Time to Call: **Before noon; after 3 PM**
Host(s): **Rosemary Kip**
Location: **1 mi. from I-81, Exit 69**
No. of Rooms: **7**
No. of Private Baths: **5**
Max. No. Sharing Bath: **4**
Double/pb: **$55**
Single/pb: **$40**
Double/sb: **$50**
Single/sb: **$35**
Suites: **$65**
Open: **All year**
Reduced Rates: **10%, seniors**
Breakfast: **Full**
Other Meals: **Available**
Pets: **Sometimes**
Children: **Welcome**
Smoking: **Permitted**
Social Drinking: **Permitted**

This Colonial homestead, built in 1830, is nestled on seven acres in the Shenandoah Valley. After a breakfast of sausage patties, biscuits with homemade apple butter, and plum gumbo (or other specialities), you may hike, canoe, play tennis, fish, or visit a cavern. Bikes are provided, and Rosemary will pack a picnic lunch for your day's jaunt. If you'd rather "stay home," you may enjoy a dip in the 32-foot pool on warm days, sip sherry or tea in front of your bedroom's fireplace in cool weather, or wander through the rooms where all the furnishings are priced for sale.

The Pittance Inn

ROUTE 11, P.O. BOX 165, MOUNT SIDNEY, VIRGINIA 24467

Tel: **(703) 248-2710**
Host(s): **Minni Olsen**
Location: **9 mi. N of Staunton**
No. of Rooms: **4**
No. of Private Baths: **2**
Max. No. Sharing Bath: **3**
Double/pb: **$35**
Double/sb: **$30**
Single/sb: **$25**
Open: **All year**
Breakfast: **Continental**
Pets: **Sometimes**
Children: **Welcome, over 12**
Smoking: **Permitted**
Social Drinking: **Permitted**

The Pittance Inn is a white-brick Georgian manor, close to the Staunton Historic District. The house is decorated with a mixture of antique and contemporary furnishings, and Minni Olsen enjoys sharing her home and its history. It served as the Sue Hyde Tavern from 1860 to 1875. In 1910, a southern addition was built. Today, this lovely home is surrounded by beautifully landscaped grounds, and is close to many fine restaurants. Nearby attractions include golf, auctions, New Market Battlefield, the birthplace of Woodrow Wilson, and the Blue Ridge Parkway.

The Newport House ✪

ROUTE 2, BOX 10, NEWPORT, VIRGINIA 24128

Tel: **(703) 961-2480**
Host(s): **Harold and Pamela Kurstedt**
Location: **15 mi. from I-81**
No. of Rooms: **3**
No. of Private Baths: **3**
Double/pb: **$55**
Open: **All year**
Breakfast: **Full**
Other Meals: **Available**
Credit Cards: **MC, VISA**
Pets: **No**
Children: **Welcome, over 12**
Smoking: **No**
Social Drinking: **Permitted**
Airport/Station Pickup: **Yes**

Built in 1840, the farmhouse has been enlarged and enhanced by a two-story addition, a sun porch, and commodious bathrooms, including one equipped for the handicapped. Decorated with family furnishings, the beds are covered with Amish quilts; Harold's mother created the needlepoint wall hangings. The cook, Doris Lind, prepares such delights as fluffy ham biscuits, stewed apples, sausage gravy, and a variety of omelets. Complimentary coffee, tea, and cake are served each afternoon. The well-tended grounds, patios, and porches are perfect for relaxing. Virginia Tech, New River canoeing, the Appalachian Trail, and several covered bridges are nearby.

Bed & Breakfast of Tidewater Virginia ✪

P.O. BOX 3343, NORFOLK, VIRGINIA 23514

Tel: **(804) 627-1983 or 627-9409**
Coordinators: **Ashby Willcox and Susan Hubbard**
States/Regions Covered: **Chesapeake, Chincoteague, Eastern Shore of Virginia, Norfolk, Virginia Beach**

Rates (Single/Double):

Modest:	**$30**	**$35**
Average:	**$35**	**$45**
Luxury:	**$55**	**$75**

Credit Cards: **No**

The world's largest naval base is in Norfolk, as are the famed Chrysler Museum and MacArthur Memorial. It is also a cultural hub in which top-rated opera, symphony, and stage productions abound. There are miles of scenic beaches to explore on Chesapeake Bay and the Atlantic Ocean. Old Dominion University, Eastern Virginia Medical School, and Virginia Wesleyan College are conveniently located.

Bed & Breakfast Larchmont

1112 BUCKINGHAM AVENUE, NORFOLK, VIRGINIA 23508

Tel: **(804) 489-8449**
Best Time to Call: **8 AM–8 PM**
Host(s): **Lorna Bowen St. George**
Location: **5 mi. from Rte. 64**
No. of Rooms: **2**
Max. No. Sharing Bath: **3**
Double/sb: **$55**
Single/sb: **$45**
Open: **All year**
Breakfast: **Continental**
Other Meals: **Available**
Pets: **No**
Children: **Welcome**
Smoking: **No**
Social Drinking: **Permitted**
Airport/Station Pickup: **Yes**

Lorna is charm personified, and her two-story white clapboard home, set in an early-20th-century neighborhood, reflects her warmth and good taste. The accommodations are spotless and luxurious, furnished with fine American antiques. The breakfast is deluxe, with all ingredients fresh, homemade, and seasonal. Don't miss the historic district of Ghent with its unusual shops and fine restaurants; or take a ferry ride to nearby Portsmouth. Virginia Beach is less than a half hour car ride from the front porch. Old Dominion University is two blocks away.

Mayhurst Inn ✪

ROUTE 15 SOUTH, P.O. BOX 707, ORANGE, VIRGINIA 22960

Tel: **(703) 672-5597**
Best Time to Call: **9 AM–9 PM**
Host(s): **Stephen and Shirley Ramsey**
Location: **27 mi. N of Charlottesville**
No. of Rooms: **7**
No. of Private Baths: **7**
Double/pb: **$45–$85**
Single/pb: **$45**
Guest Cottage: **$95**

Open: **All year**
Reduced Rates: **Available**
Breakfast: **Full**
Pets: **Sometimes**
Children: **Welcome**
Smoking: **No**
Social Drinking: **Permitted**
Airport/Station Pickup: **Yes**

The Mayhurst is an early Victorian mansion noted for its fanciful architecture and oval spiral staircase ascending four stories to the rooftop gazebo. The rooms are large and sunny, with original floor-to-ceiling windows made of handblown glass. Bedrooms are elegantly furnished with 18th- and 19th-century beds, chests, and tables. Each room is named for someone who spent the night at the inn or is associated with it in some way. The Stonewall Jackson Room was offered to the Confederate general the night before the Battle of Cedar Mountain. Four rooms in the main house have working fireplaces, and the guest cottage features a fireplace, exposed beams, and pine floors. Guests are welcome to congregate in the main hall for afternoon tea or port. In the dining room, the full country breakfast includes Virginia ham or sausage, eggs, baked apples, pumpkin muffins, and homemade marmalade. The Mayhurst is situated on 36 acres with a swimming pond, fields, and magnolias, and is listed on the National Register of Historic Places.

Bensonhouse ✪

2036 MONUMENT AVENUE, RICHMOND, VIRGINIA 23220

Tel: **(804) 648-7560**
Best Time to Call: **10 AM–4 PM**
Coordinator: **Lyn Benson**
States/Regions Covered: **Bowling Green, Gwynn's Island, Petersburg, Richmond, Waynesboro, Williamsburg**

Rates (Single/Double):

Modest:	**$40**	**$45**
Average:	**$46–$50**	**$55–$60**
Luxury:	**$56–$94**	**$65–$100**

Credit Cards: **MC, VISA**

Houses on Lyn's list are of architectural or historic interest, offering charm in the relaxed comfort of a home. The hosts delight in guiding you to the best sights, and advising you on how to get the most out of your visit.

Hanover Hosts

P.O. BOX 25145, RICHMOND, VIRGINIA 23260

Tel: **(804) 355-5855**
Best Time to Call: **Before 9 AM; after 6 PM**
Host(s): **Barbara and Bill Fleming**
Location: **2½ mi. from I-95**
No. of Rooms: **3**
No. of Private Baths: **2**
Max. No. Sharing Bath: **3**
Double/pb: **$55**
Single/pb: **$40**
Double/sb: **$50**
Single/sb: **$35**
Suites: **$125**
Open: **All year**
Reduced Rates: **Weekly**
Breakfast: **Continental**
Pets: **No**
Children: **Welcome, over 12**
Smoking: **Permitted**
Social Drinking: **Permitted**
Airport/Station Pickup: **Yes**

This Victorian town house is located in a turn-of-the-century neighborhood, close to museums, restaurants, and galleries. The house features awnings and a sunny wraparound deck secluded from the street. The rooms are decorated with many antiques, quilts, handcrafts, and stenciling. Guests are welcome to use the wet bar. Nearby sights include Virginia's Capitol Building and St. John's Church. Homemade jams and special bran muffins are served for breakfast.

The Leonine Experience ✪

P.O. BOX 4772, RICHMOND, VIRGINIA 23220

Tel: **(804) 349-1952**
Best Time to Call: **Before 9 AM; after 5 PM**
Host(s): **J. P. Blankenship**
Location: **2½ mi. from I-95**
Suite: **$50 for 2; $40 for 1**
Open: **All year**
Breakfast: **Continental**
Pets: **No**
Children: **Welcome, over 12**
Smoking: **Permitted**
Social Drinking: **Permitted**
Airport/Station Pickup: **Yes**

Complete privacy awaits you on the lower level of a restored Greek Revival town house located in Richmond's historic Fan District. Guest quarters feature an entrance foyer, living room with sleeper sofa, bedroom with TV, and a complete kitchenette and refreshment bar. The suite has its own garden gate entrance and opens onto a charming New Orleans–style brick courtyard. Choose from a light breakfast of fresh muffins, cereal, homemade jellies, and hot coffee, or enjoy a heartier meal served in the formal dining room. Your host invites you to relax on the patio or have a picnic lunch in the rear garden. This is the ideal location for exploring Richmond, and is within walking distance of the Virginia Museum, Monument Boulevard, Virginia Commonwealth University, and the delightful shops of Carytown.

The Mary Bladon House ✪

381 WASHINGTON AVENUE SOUTH WEST, ROANOKE, VIRGINIA 24016

Tel: **(703) 344-5361**
Host(s): **Sally D. Pfister**
Location: **220 mi. S of Washington, D.C.**
No. of Rooms: **4**
No. of Private Baths: **4**
Double/pb: **$55–$65**
Single/pb: **$45–$52**
Suites: **$65**
Open: **All year**
Reduced Rates: **Available**
Breakfast: **Full**
Credit Cards: **MC, VISA**
Pets: **No**
Children: **Welcome, over 12**
Smoking: **No**
Social Drinking: **Permitted**
Airport/Station Pickup: **Yes**
Foreign Languages: **Spanish**

The Mary Bladon House is located in the old southwest neighborhood, just five minutes away from the Blue Ridge Parkway. This Victorian dates back to 1892 and has four porches. Although the original brass light fixtures are still in place, the decor in the public rooms is constantly changing, with works by local artists and craftsmen. All the rooms are elegantly appointed with antiques, and guest rooms feature fresh flowers in season. Breakfast is served by candlelight in the dining room or on the porch in summer months.

Isle of Wight Inn

1607 SOUTH CHURCH STREET, SMITHFIELD, VIRGINIA 23430

Tel: **(804) 357-3176**
Best Time to Call: **9 AM–5 PM**
Host(s): **Bob, Sam, and Marcella**
Location: **27 mi. N of Norfolk**
No. of Rooms: **10**
No. of Private Baths: **10**
Double/pb: **$54**
Single/pb: **$49**
Suites: **$78**
Open: **All year**
Breakfast: **Continental**
Credit Cards: **AMEX, MC, VISA**
Pets: **Sometimes**
Children: **Welcome**
Smoking: **Permitted**
Social Drinking: **Permitted**

The Isle of Wight Inn is a sprawling brick Colonial, one mile from downtown Smithfield. Inside you will find antiques, reproductions, motifs of glass, wood, and wicker, and an old player piano. Wake up to fresh coffee and Smithfield's own ham rolls. This riverport town has numerous historic homes that will surely delight you. Williamsburg, Norfolk, and Virginia Beach are less than an hour's drive from the house.

Thornrose House at Gypsy Hill ✪

531 THORNROSE AVENUE, STAUNTON, VIRGINIA 24401

Tel: **(703) 885-7026**
Best Time to Call: **8 AM–10 PM**
Host(s): **Carolyn and Ray Hoaster**
Location: **34 mi. W of Charlottesville**
No. of Rooms: **3**
No. of Private Baths: **3**
Double/pb: **$45**
Single/pb: **$35**
Open: **All year**
Reduced Rates: **$5 less, Jan.–Mar.**
Breakfast: **Full**
Pets: **Sometimes**
Children: **Welcome**
Smoking: **No**
Social Drinking: **Permitted**
Airport/Station Pickup: **Yes**

A wraparound veranda and Greek colonnades distinguish the entrance of this turn-of-the-century Georgian residence. Inside, family antiques, a grand piano, and fireplaces create a formal but comfortable atmosphere. An unusual winding staircase leads to restful, attractive rooms. The house specialty, "Birchermuesli," a Swiss concoction made from oats, fresh fruits, nuts, and whipped cream, is served at breakfast. Your hosts also offer afternoon tea and evening sherry. They are located adjacent to a 300-acre city park with tennis, golf, walks, and ponds. Other nearby attractions include Blue Ridge National Park, Natural Chimneys, Skyline Drive, and the birthplace of Woodrow Wilson.

Lambsgate Bed and Breakfast ✪

ROUTE 1, BOX 63, SWOOPE, VIRGINIA 24479

Tel: **(703) 337-6929**
Host(s): **Daniel and Elizabeth Fannon**
Location: **6 mi. W of Staunton; 10 mi. from I-81**
No. of Rooms: **3**
Max. No. Sharing Bath: **6**
Double/sb: **$36–$58**
Single/sb: **$31–$35**
Open: **All year**
Reduced Rates: **10%, weekly**
Breakfast: **Full**
Pets: **No**
Children: **Welcome**
Smoking: **No**
Social Drinking: **Permitted**
Airport/Station Pickup: **Yes**

Lambsgate is a restored vernacular farmhouse on seven acres in the Shenandoah Valley. The house dates back to 1816 and though it has been added to and modernized, the bedrooms have retained their original woodwork and floors. The Fannons offer a breakfast of homemade muffins, bacon, eggs, grits, and jellies each morning. They will provide information on such local sights as George Washington National Forest, Shenandoah National Park, and Luray Caverns. There is also plenty to see on the farm. Guests are invited to visit the lambs or relax and enjoy the view from the wraparound veranda.

Bluebird Haven ✪

8691 BARHAMSVILLE ROAD, TOANO, VIRGINIA 23168

Tel: **(804) 566-0177**
Best Time to Call: **Mornings**
Host(s): **June and Ed Cottle**
Location: **10 mi. N of Williamsburg**
No. of Rooms: **3**
No. of Private Baths: **1**
Max. No. Sharing Bath: **4**
Double/pb: **$48**
Single/pb: **$48**
Double/sb: **$38**
Single/sb: **$38**
Open: **All year**
Breakfast: **Full**
Pets: **Sometimes**
Children: **Welcome**
Smoking: **Permitted**
Social Drinking: **Permitted**
Airport/Station Pickup: **Yes**

June and Ed Cottle welcome you to their ranch-style home, located 20 minutes from Colonial Williamsburg. June is interested in many kinds of handcrafts and has decorated the rooms with handmade quilts, spreads, and pictures. Guest rooms are located in a private wing of the house and feature comfortable furnishings and handmade linens. Breakfast includes a Southern-style assortment of homemade breads, jams, country ham, red-eye gravy, and omelets. June also offers gourmet hors d'oeuvres to accompany your evening cocktail. Bluebird Haven is close to Busch Gardens and 35 miles outside of Richmond.

Angie's Guest Cottage ✪

302 24TH STREET, VIRGINIA BEACH, VIRGINIA 23451

Tel: **(804) 428-4690**
Best Time to Call: **10 AM–10 PM**
Host(s): **Donna and Paul Lacy**
Location: **20 mi. E of Norfolk**
No. of Rooms: **6**
No. of Private Baths: **1**
Max. No. Sharing Bath: **4**
Double/pb: **$55**
Single/pb: **$44**
Double/sb: **$36–$50**
Single/sb: **$32–$42**
Guest Cottage: **$310–$360 weekly; sleeps 2 to 5**
Open: **Apr. 1 to Oct. 15**
Reduced Rates: **30%–50%, off-season**
Breakfast: **Continental**
Credit Cards: **MC, VISA**
Pets: **Sometimes**
Children: **Welcome (crib)**
Smoking: **No**
Social Drinking: **Permitted**
Minimum Stay: **2 days**

Just a block from the beach, shops, and restaurants is this bright and comfortable beach house. Former guests describe it as: "cozy, cute, and clean." Deep-sea fishing, nature trails, and harbor tours are but a few things to keep you busy. Freshly baked croissants in various flavors are a breakfast delight.

The Picket Fence ✪

209 43RD STREET, VIRGINIA BEACH, VIRGINIA 23451

Tel: **(804) 428-8861**
Host(s): **Kathleen Hall**
Location: **20 mi. E of Norfolk**
No. of Rooms: **2**
No. of Private Baths: **2**
Double/pb: **$50–$65**
Single/pb: **$50–$65**
Open: **All year**
Breakfast: **Full**
Pets: **No**
Children: **No**
Smoking: **No**
Social Drinking: **Permitted**
Airport/Station Pickup: **Yes**

The furnishings in Kathy's comfortable Colonial home glow with the patina of loving care. She thoroughly enjoys her hobbies of fishing and cooking and often incorporates the two into special breakfasts for her guests. The beach is just a block away and beach chairs and umbrellas are provided for your comfort. Complimentary wine and cheese are graciously served before you go out to dinner. Don't leave the area without visiting the new Marine Science Museum. A two-night minimum stay is required.

The Foster-Harris House

P.O. BOX 333, WASHINGTON, VIRGINIA 22747

Tel: **(703) 675-3757**
Host(s): **Patrick Foster and Camille Harris**
Location: **65 mi. W of Washington, D.C.**
No. of Rooms: **3**
No. of Private Baths: **1**
Max. No. Sharing Bath: **4**
Double/sb: **$55**
Single/sb: **$45**
Suites: **$75**
Open: **All year**
Reduced Rates: **3 nights or more**
Breakfast: **Continental**
Pets: **Sometimes**
Children: **Welcome**
Smoking: **Permitted**
Social Drinking: **Permitted**

This pastoral Victorian is surrounded by the Blue Ridge Mountains. The rooms are furnished with many antiques and the guest quarters are newly renovated. There is much to see in this historic village, which was surveyed by George Washington and was the first place in the country to be named for him. Your hosts serve freshly baked treats each morning and offer wine and cheese or coffee and cookies in the afternoon. They recommend four-star dining at a nearby inn and will gladly direct you to Skyline Drive.

The Pink House ✪

WATERFORD, VIRGINIA 22190

Tel: **(703) 882-3453**
Host(s): **Charles and Marie Anderson**
Location: **38 mi. W of D.C.**
No. of Rooms: **2 three-room suites**
No. of Private Baths: **2**
Suites: **$90**
Open: **All year**
Reduced Rates: **$10 less after 2 nights**
Breakfast: **Full**
Pets: **Sometimes**
Children: **Welcome, over 12**
Smoking: **Permitted**
Social Drinking: **Permitted**

Pink House is in the center of Waterford, one of the few villages entirely designated as a national landmark. Through the years, the house has been a Civil War officers' billet and an apothecary shop. Today, two three-room suites overlook a formal garden, with private entrance, terrace, color TV, and whirlpool among the luxurious features. A breakfast of homemade breads, grits, and sausage is served each morning. Nearby sights include plantations, museums, and the equestrian center at Morvan Park.

The Travel Tree ✪
P. O. BOX 838, WILLIAMSBURG, VIRGINIA 23187

Tel: **(804) 253-1571**
Best Time to Call: **5–9 PM only**
Coordinator(s): **Joann Proper and Sheila Zubkoff**
States/Regions Covered: **Williamsburg, Jamestown, Yorktown**

Rates (Single/Double):

	Single	Double
Average:	**$44**	**$55**
Luxury:	**$60**	**$75**

Credit Cards: **No**
Minimum Stay: **2 nights**

You will thoroughly enjoy Colonial Williamsburg, historic Jamestown and Yorktown, Busch Gardens, and Carter's Grove Plantation. Your bedroom might be furnished with four-poster beds and antiques, or be tucked under the eaves in a wooded setting, or be a two-room suite with a private entrance.

Fox Grape of Williamsburg ✪
701 MONUMENTAL AVENUE, WILLIAMSBURG, VIRGINIA 23185

Tel: **(804) 229-6914**
Host(s): **Pat and Bob Orendorff**
Location: **2 mi. from I-64, Exit 56**
No. of Rooms: **4**
No. of Private Baths: **1**
Max. No. Sharing Bath: **4**
Double/pb: **$50**
Single/pb: **$45**
Double/sb: **$45**
Single/sb: **$40**
Open: **All year**
Reduced Rates: **10%, seniors**
Breakfast: **Continental**
Pets: **No**
Children: **Welcome**
Smoking: **Permitted**
Social Drinking: **Permitted**
Airport/Station Pickup: **Yes**

This brick Cape Cod is within walking distance of the restored area. The rooms have a Colonial decor, with poster beds, stenciled walls, and folk art. Guests are welcomed with a generous fruit basket, and a cup of coffee is always available. The Orendorffs offer fresh muffins, fruit, and cereal in the morning. They will advise on nearby tourist attractions and restaurants. William and Mary College is nearby. On Thanksgiving and Christmas you may join the family for dinner at a nominal cost.

For Cant Hill Guest Home
4 CANTERBURY LANE, WILLIAMSBURG, VIRGINIA 23185

Tel: **(804) 229-6623**
Host(s): **Martha and Hugh Easler**
No. of Rooms: **2**
No. of Private Baths: **2**
Double/pb: **$48.50**
Open: **All year**
Breakfast: **Continental**
Pets: **No**
Children: **Welcome, over 8**
Smoking: **No**
Social Drinking: **Permitted**
Airport/Station Pickup: **Yes**

Martha and Hugh's home is set in a secluded, wooded area overlooking a lake. Their property adjoins the campus of William and Mary, and it is a short walk to the historic district. The guest rooms are comfortably decorated, accented with antiques and pretty glass pieces. Restaurants to suit every budget are nearby.

Himmelbed Guesthouse ✪

706 RICHMOND ROAD, WILLIAMSBURG, VIRGINIA 23185

Tel: **(804) 229-6421**
Host(s): **Bernie and Mary Peters**
Location: **45 mi. E of Richmond**
No. of Rooms: **2**
No. of Private Baths: **2**
Double/pb: **$55**
Single/pb: **$40**
Open: **All year**
Breakfast: **Continental**
Pets: **No**
Children: **Welcome, over 6**
Smoking: **No**
Social Drinking: **Permitted**
Airport/Station Pickup: **Yes**

This air-conditioned Cape Cod–style house is attractively furnished in country antiques. The bedrooms have either spool or canopy beds. It is within walking distance of the historic area and William and Mary College. The coffeepot is always on.

War Hill ✪

4560 LONG HILL ROAD, WILLIAMSBURG, VIRGINIA 23185

Tel: **(804) 565-0248**
Best Time to Call: **Mornings; evenings**
Host(s): **Shirley and Bill Lee**
Location: **2 mi. from Rte. 60**
No. of Rooms: **5**
No. of Private Baths: **5**
Double/pb: **$45–$55**
Suite: **$75**
Open: **All year**
Breakfast: **Continental**
Credit Cards: **AMEX, MC, VISA**
Pets: **No**
Children: **Welcome**
Smoking: **No**
Social Drinking: **Permitted**

War Hill is situated in the center of a 32-acre working farm, just three miles from the tourist attractions. Built in 1968, this Colonial replica couples the charm of yesteryear with today's contemporary conveniences. The suite is comprised of two bedrooms and a bath. The wide heart-pine floors came from an old school, the stairs from a church, the overhead beams from a barn; the oak mantel is over 200 years old. Fruits from a variety of trees in the orchard are yours to pick in season. In autumn, Shirley and Bill serve delicious homemade applesauce and cider. Angus show cattle graze in the pasture, and the sounds you'll hear are crickets, frogs, owls, and the morning crowing of the rooster.

Wood's Guest Home ✪

1208 STEWART DRIVE, WILLIAMSBURG, VIRGINIA 23185

Tel: **(804) 229-3376**
Host(s): **Lonnie and Betty Wood**
No. of Rooms: **3**
Max. No. Sharing Bath: **5**
Double/sb: **$30**
Open: **All year**
Breakfast: **Continental**
Pets: **No**
Children: **Welcome, over 5**
Smoking: **Permitted**
Social Drinking: **Permitted**

This comfortable, rambling house is filled with handmade crafts, antiques, and modern pieces. Relax on the screened-in porch or in the living room with a fresh cup of coffee and a cookie. Colonial Williamsburg, Busch Gardens, Jamestown, Yorktown, and Carter's Grove Plantation are just a few of the local sights.

The Candlewick Inn ✪

127 NORTH CHURCH STREET, WOODSTOCK, VIRGINIA 22664

Tel: **(703) 459-8008**
Best Time to Call: **9 AM–6 PM**
Host(s): **Susan Rapalus and Susan Anderson**
Location: **90 mi. SW of Washington, D.C.**
No. of Rooms: **6**
No. of Private Baths: **2**
Max. No. Sharing Bath: **4**
Double/pb: **$55**
Single/pb: **$50**
Double/sb: **$50**
Single/sb: **$45**
Open: **All year**
Reduced Rates: **10%, weekly**
Breakfast: **Continental**
Pets: **No**
Children: **Welcome, over 11**
Smoking: **Permitted**
Social Drinking: **Permitted**
Airport/Station Pickup: **Yes**
Foreign Languages: **French**

The Candlewick Inn is located on a quiet street facing the Massanutten Mountains. The house is a white frame Victorian with gingerbread trim and a front porch. The rooms are decorated with country antiques and handicrafts, ruffled curtains, delicate wallpapers, fresh flowers, and some family heirlooms. Breakfast specialties include delicious homemade breads, muffins, assorted fruits topped with the house special sauce, jams, jellies, and marmalade butter. Your hostesses also offer a social hour for guests where they serve homemade almond tarts or cheese crisps. Fine dining is just a short stroll away. The Shenandoah River is nearby for fishing, canoeing, and swimming. Antiques shops, national forests, Skyline Drive, and many historic sites are all within easy reach.

The Country Fare ✪

402 NORTH MAIN STREET, WOODSTOCK, VIRGINIA 22664

Tel: **(703) 459-4828**
Best Time to Call: **7–11 AM; 6–10 PM**
Host(s): **Elizabeth Hallgren**
Location: **35 mi. S of Winchester**
No. of Rooms: **3**
No. of Private Baths: **1**
Max. No. Sharing Bath: **3**
Double/pb: **$50**
Double/sb: **$40**
Single/sb: **$35**
Open: **All year**
Reduced Rates: **10%, families**
Breakfast: **Continental**
Pets: **No**
Children: **Welcome, by arrangement**
Smoking: **No**
Social Drinking: **Permitted**

Magnolias, cherry trees, and boxwoods surround this 150-year-old log home, which is painted a bright yellow. The rooms are decorated with hand stenciling and a mixture of grandmother's antiques and country collectibles. Choose from the master bedroom with private shower, an ample guest room with twin beds, and a single room with a fireplace all its own. Guests may enjoy homemade breads and biscuits on the enclosed sun porch, or by the common room fire when the air turns colder. An inviting brick patio overlooks the grounds, and the den includes a television. Your hostess will gladly help you get to know this historic Shenandoah Valley town, and can suggest many restaurants, shops, and interesting sights.

WASHINGTON

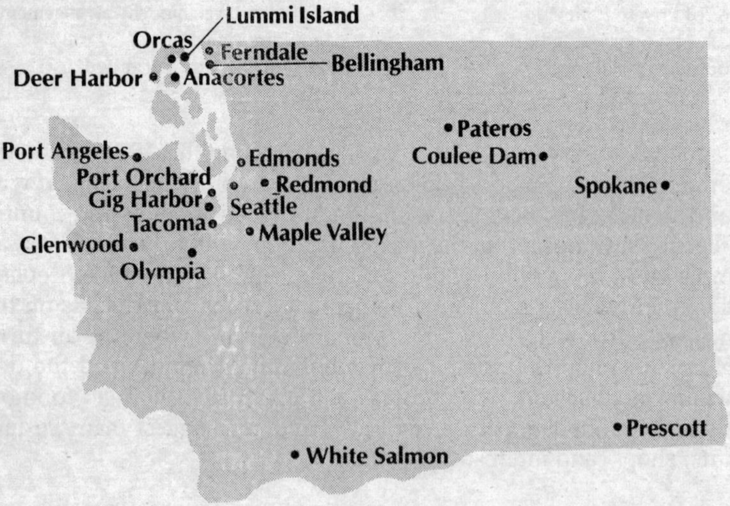

Lummi Island
Orcas
Ferndale
Bellingham
Deer Harbor
Anacortes
Pateros
Port Angeles
Edmonds
Coulee Dam
Port Orchard
Redmond
Spokane
Gig Harbor
Seattle
Tacoma
Maple Valley
Glenwood
Olympia
Prescott
White Salmon

Pacific Bed & Breakfast Agency ✪

701 N.W. 60TH STREET, SEATTLE, WASHINGTON 98107

Tel: **(206) 784-0539**
Best Time to Call: **9 AM–5 PM**
TELEX: **329473 ATT PBB 580**
Coordinator: **Irmgard Castleberry**
States/Regions Covered: **Statewide; Canada—Vancouver, Victoria, British Columbia**

Rates (Single/Double):

Modest:	**$30**	**$35**
Average:	**$35**	**$45**
Luxury:	**$50**	**$145**

Credit Cards: **AMEX, MC, VISA**

Victorians, contemporaries, island cottages, waterfront houses, and private suites with full kitchens are available. Most are close to downtown areas, near bus lines, in fine residential neighborhoods, or within walking distance of a beach. Many extras are included, such as pickup service, free use of laundry facilities, guided tours and more. The University of Washington and the University of Puget Sound are nearby. There is a $5 surcharge for one-night stays in Seattle.

Burrow's Bay B&B ✪

4911 MACBETH DRIVE, ANACORTES, WASHINGTON 98221

Tel: **(206) 293-4792**
Best Time to Call: **Mornings; evenings**
Host(s): **Beverly and Winfred Stocker**
Location: **92 mi. N of Seattle**
Suites: **$55; sleeps 2–6**
Open: **All year**
Breakfast: **Continental**
Credit Cards: **MC, VISA**
Pets: **Sometimes**
Children: **Welcome**
Smoking: **No**
Social Drinking: **Permitted**
Airport/Station Pickup: **Yes**

Enjoy sweeping views of the Skyline Marina and the San Juan Islands from this lovely contemporary Northwest home. The guest suite consists of a large sitting room with a view and a comfortable bedroom with a blue-and-tan motif and wall-to-wall carpeting. You are sure to enjoy the privacy and relaxation of having your own private deck, fireplace, TV, and a separate entrance. Beverly and Winfred Stocker serve two kinds of fresh-baked rolls for breakfast, along with homemade granola, a fruit platter, a meat-and-cheese tray, and plenty of hot coffee and tea. They are located within walking distance of Washington Park, restaurants, and ferry rides to the nearby islands. Your hosts will be glad to provide touring advice for day trips to Victoria, B.C., Deception Pass, and Port Townsend.

The Channel House ✪

2902 OAKES AVENUE, ANACORTES, WASHINGTON 98221

Tel: **(206) 293-9382**
Host(s): **Dennis and Patricia McIntyre**
Location: **65 mi. N of Seattle; 18 mi. W of I-5, Exit 230**
No. of Rooms: **4**
Max. No. Sharing Bath: **4**
Double/sb: **$55–$65**
Single/sb: **$45–$55**
Open: **All year**
Reduced Rates: **$10 less, Oct. 1–Apr. 30**
Breakfast: **Continental**
Credit Cards: **MC, VISA**
Pets: **No**
Children: **Welcome, over 12**
Smoking: **Permitted**
Social Drinking: **Permitted**
Airport/Station Pickup: **Yes**

Built in 1902 by an Italian count, this three-story Victorian house has stained-glass windows, rare antiques, gracious ambience, and is in mint condition. The guest rooms have beautiful views of Puget Sound and the San Juan Islands. It's an ideal getaway for relaxing in the "cleanest corner of the country." Patricia serves gourmet breakfasts in front of the fireplace. The communal hot tub is a treat after salmon fishing, tennis, or golf. And it's only minutes from the ferry for visiting Victoria, British Columbia.

Dutch Treat House ✪

1220 31ST STREET, ANACORTES, WASHINGTON 98221

Tel: **(206) 293-8154**	Open: **Feb. 1–Dec. 31**
Best Time to Call: **10 AM–1 PM**	Breakfast: **Full**
Host(s): **Bill and Mary O'Connor**	Credit Cards: **MC, VISA**
Location: **8 mi. from I-5, Exit 230**	Pets: **No**
No. of Rooms: **3**	Children: **Welcome, over 8**
Max. No. Sharing Bath: **3**	Smoking: **Permitted**
Double/sb: **$50**	Social Drinking: **Permitted**

The large, comfortable rooms have views of Mt. Baker and the marina and are decorated in a casual country theme, enhanced by calico cats, pretty pillows, and other items crafted by Bill and Mary. Breakfast is tastefully prepared with fresh fruits in season, homemade biscuits, eggs, hotcakes, or waffles. In the evening, enjoy the never-empty coffeepot while using the library to read, play cards, or exchange travel experiences with your hosts, who are world travelers. Visit the tidal rapids at Deception Pass, the Naval Air Station, and in spring, the tulip fields at Skagit Valley.

North Garden Inn ✪

1014 NORTH GARDEN STREET, BELLINGHAM, WASHINGTON 98225

Tel: **(206) 671-7828**	Open: **All year**
Host(s): **Frank and Barbara DeFreytas**	Reduced Rates: **10%, weekly**
Location: **90 mi. N of Seattle**	Breakfast: **Continental**
No. of Rooms: **10**	Credit Cards: **MC, VISA**
No. of Private Baths: **2**	Pets: **No**
Max. No. Sharing Bath: **5**	Children: **Welcome, over 9**
Double/pb: **$50**	Smoking: **Designated area**
Double/sb: **$40**	Social Drinking: **Permitted**
Single/sb: **$30**	Airport/Station Pickup: **Yes**

Built in 1896, this turn-of-the-century Victorian is listed on the National Register of Historic Places. A grand staircase leads to comfortable bedrooms, many with a splendid view of the bay and surrounding islands. Guests are welcome to relax in one of two common rooms and the living room. Your host teaches music and is pleased to offer two grand pianos in mint condition for the use of performers or those who love to listen. Breakfast specialties feature homemade muffins and pastries made from flour ground in Barbara's kitchen. The inn is located in a residential neighborhood close to Western Washington University, shopping, and fine dining. It is convenient to skiing at Mt.

Baker, fishing, wine tasting at local vineyards, and touring the San Juan Islands.

Palmer's Chart House ✪

P.O. BOX 51, ORCAS ISLAND, DEER HARBOR, WASHINGTON 98243

Tel: **(206) 376-4231**
Host(s): **Majean and Don Palmer**
Location: **50 mi. N of Seattle**
No. of Rooms: **2**
No. of Private Baths: **2**
Double/pb: **$60–$70**
Single/pb: **$60**
Open: **All year**
Breakfast: **Continental**
Other Meals: **Dinner: $7.50**
Pets: **No**
Children: **No**
Smoking: **No**
Social Drinking: **Permitted**
Foreign Languages: **Spanish**

It's just an hour's ride on the Washington State ferry from Anacortes to Orcas Island. This is an adult private paradise—quiet and informal. Seasoned travelers, Majean and Don know how to make your stay special. The guest rooms are carpeted, spacious, spic-and-span. Each has a private deck from which you may survey the harbor scene. Local seafood often provides the basis for Majean's special dinners. *Amante,* the 33-foot sloop, is available for sailing when Don, the skipper, is free.

Turtleback Farm Inn

ROUTE 1, BOX 650, EASTSOUND, WASHINGTON 98245

Tel: **(206) 376-4914**
Best Time to Call: **9 AM–9 PM**
Host(s): **William and Susan Fletcher**
Location: **60 mi. NW of Seattle**
No. of Rooms: **7**
No. of Private Baths: **7**
Double/pb: **$50–$90**
Single/pb: **$40–$80**
Open: **All year**
Reduced Rates: **Available**
Breakfast: **Full**
Other Meals: **Available**
Credit Cards: **MC, VISA**
Pets: **No**
Children: **Welcome, over 8**
Smoking: **No**
Social Drinking: **Permitted**
Airport/Station Pickup: **Yes**

This peaceful retreat is situated on 80 acres of meadow, pasture, ponds, and woods overlooking lovely Crow Valley. The farmhouse dates back to the early 1900s. Each bedroom is furnished with antiques and each bed boasts an unusual cotton-covered wool comforter. Breakfast might consist of strawberry crêpes, corn waffles, or a delectable quiche, served on Aynsley china with pretty crystal. Guests enjoy leisurely walks, bird watching, the music of Mozart, relaxing on the expansive deck, and the pleasant peace of being pampered.

The Harrison House ✪

210 SUNSET AVENUE, EDMONDS, WASHINGTON 98020

Tel: **(206) 776-4748**
Host(s): **Jody and Harve Harrison**
Location: **15 mi. N of Seattle**
No. of Rooms: **1**
No. of Private Baths: **1**
Double/pb: **$35–$45**
Single/pb: **$25–$35**
Open: **All year**
Breakfast: **Full**
Pets: **No**
Children: **No**
Smoking: **No**
Social Drinking: **Permitted**

This new, informal waterfront home has a sweeping view of Puget Sound and the Olympic Mountains. It is a block north of the ferry dock and two blocks from the center of this historic town. Many fine restaurants are within walking distance. Your spacious room has a private deck, TV, wet bar, telephone, and king-size bed. The University of Washington is nearby.

Heather House ✪

1011 "B" AVENUE, EDMONDS, WASHINGTON 98020

Tel: **(206) 778-7233**
Best Time to Call: **5–6:30 PM**
Host(s): **Harry and Joy Whitcutt**
Location: **15 mi. N of Seattle**
No. of Rooms: **1**
No. of Private Baths: **1**
Double/pb: **$35**
Single/pb: **$30**
Open: **All year**
Breakfast: **Continental—$3**
Pets: **No**
Children: **No**
Smoking: **Permitted**
Social Drinking: **Permitted**

This contemporary home has a spectacular view of Puget Sound and the Olympic Mountains. The guest room has a comfortable king-size bed and opens onto a private deck. Joy and Harry are world travelers and enjoy their guests. The homemade jams, jellies, and marmalades are delicious. You can work off breakfast by walking a mile to the shops, beaches, and fishing pier.

Hudgens Haven

9313 190 SOUTH WEST, EDMONDS, WASHINGTON 98020

Tel: **(206) 776-2202**
Best Time to Call: **4–8 PM**
Host(s): **Lorna and Edward Hudgens**
No. of Rooms: **1**
No. of Private Baths: **1**
Double/pb: **$35**
Single/pb: **$30**
Open: **Jan. 1–Nov. 30**
Breakfast: **Continental**
Pets: **Sometimes**
Children: **Sometimes**
Smoking: **No**
Social Drinking: **Permitted**

Hudgens Haven is located in a picture postcard town on the shores of Puget Sound. The house overlooks the water as well as the Olympic Mountain Range. The rooms are decorated with antiques and the guest room has a queen-size bed, a desk, an easy chair, and plenty of drawer space. Your hostess offers a full or Continental breakfast each morning, depending on the needs of her guest. She will gladly help plan day trips and can suggest waterfront restaurants, fine shopping, and a score of recreational activities.

Anderson House ✪

P.O. BOX 1547, 2140 MAIN STREET, FERNDALE, WASHINGTON 98248

Tel: **(206) 384-3450**
Host(s): **Dave and Kelly Anderson**
Location: **8 mi. N of Bellingham**
No. of Rooms: **5**
No. of Private Baths: **2**
Max. No. Sharing Bath: **4**
Double/pb: **$45**
Double/sb: **$35–$40**
Single/sb: **$28–$30**
Suites: **$65**
Open: **All year**
Breakfast: **Continental**
Credit Cards: **MC, VISA**
Pets: **No**
Children: **Welcome, over 8**
Smoking: **No**
Social Drinking: **Permitted**

Anderson House is a slice of America as it was a hundred years ago. The authenticity of the period is evident in the carefully selected furnishings; the Bavarian crystal swan chandelier is frequently photographed by guests. It hangs over the dining room table, where freshly baked scones and muffins are served with homemade jams, fruit, and freshly ground Kona coffee. It is minutes away from the Straits of Georgia waterfront, 16 miles to Canada, and a one-hour drive to Mt. Baker. There's a two-night minimum on holiday weekends.

Hill Top Bed and Breakfast ✪

5832 CHURCH STREET, FERNDALE, WASHINGTON 98248

Tel: **(206) 384-3619**
Best Time to Call: **Mornings; evenings**
Host(s): **Paul and Doris Matz**
Location: **100 mi. N of Seattle**
No. of Rooms: **2**
No. of Private Baths: **2**
Double/pb: **$34**
Single/pb: **$29**
Suites: **$39**
Open: **All year**
Reduced Rates: **Available**
Breakfast: **Continental**
Pets: **No**
Children: **Welcome (crib)**
Smoking: **No**
Social Drinking: **Permitted**
Airport/Station Pickup: **Yes**

Hill Top Bed and Breakfast is located in the Puget Sound area close to several beautiful state and local parks. The house overlooks Mt. Baker and the Cascade Mountain Range, and the view is especially nice from the patio. The house is decorated with Early American charm and the rooms have four-poster beds and homemade quilts to snuggle up in. The suite has a fireplace. Homemade breakfast specialties include coffee cakes, muffins, jams, and applesauce. This is a perfect spot for families and is convenient to Birch Bay, local islands, and Vancouver, Canada.

No Cabbages B&B ✪

7712 GOODMAN DRIVE NW, GIG HARBOR, WASHINGTON 98335

Tel: **(206) 858-7797**
Host(s): **Jamee and Dale Holder**
Location: **10 mi. from I-5**
No. of Rooms: **2**
Max. No. Sharing Bath: **4**
Double/sb: **$35**
Open: **All year**
Breakfast: **Full**
Pets: **Sometimes**
Children: **No**
Smoking: **Permitted**
Social Drinking: **Permitted**
Airport/Station Pickup: **Yes**

Dwarfed by huge evergreens on the shore of the harbor, this remodeled knotty pine beach house is a peaceful place with easy access to windsurfing, boating, and fishing. It is built into a hill, with windows and a porch facing the water. Jamee, a former restaurant owner, and Dale, an avid fisherman, will direct you to local art galleries, beaches, and the University of Puget Sound.

The Parsonage ✪

4107 BURNHAM DRIVE, GIG HARBOR, WASHINGTON 98335

Tel: **(206) 851-8654**
Best Time to Call: **11 AM–10 PM**
Host(s): **Edward and Sheila Koscik**
Location: **9 mi. W of Tacoma**
No. of Rooms: **2**
Max. No. Sharing Bath: **4**
Double/sb: **$45**
Single/sb: **$35**
Open: **All year**
Breakfast: **Full**
Pets: **Sometimes**
Children: **Sometimes**
Smoking: **Permitted**
Social Drinking: **Permitted**

The Parsonage is a 1901 Victorian surrounded by towering pines and strawberry fields. This was Gig Harbor's first Methodist parsonage, until 1984 when the Kosciks purchased the house. They added modern touches, such as a new guest bath, but were careful to retain the old-fashioned charm of the rooms. Breakfast features fresh seasonal berries, homemade muffins, and applesauce. A glass of wine or cup of coffee is available anytime. The Parsonage is just a short walk from the picturesque harbor, with a variety of restaurants, shops, galleries, and marinas. Rental bicycles are available, and sightseeing and charter boats offer hours of fun and relaxation.

Log Castle Bed & Breakfast ✪

3273 EAST SARATOGA ROAD, LANGLEY, WASHINGTON 98260

Tel: **(206) 321-5483**
Best Time to Call: **8 AM–9 PM**
Host(s): **Jack and Norma Metcalf**
Location: **40 mi. N of Seattle**
No. of Rooms: **3**
No. of Private Baths: **3**
Double/pb: **$60–$75**
Open: **All year**
Minimum Stay: **2 days**
Breakfast: **Full**
Credit Cards: **MC, VISA**
Pets: **No**
Children: **Welcome, over 6**
Smoking: **No**
Social Drinking: **No**
Airport/Station Pickup: **Yes**

You don't have to build your castle on the sand on Whidbey Island, because one already awaits you. The imaginative design of this log lodge includes an eight-sided tower where any modern-day princess would feel at home. Taredo wood stairways, leaded and stained-glass motifs, and comfortable furnishings create a rustic yet sophisticated atmosphere. The three guest rooms all offer beautiful views of the surrounding mountains and water. Relax beside a large stone fireplace or take a rowboat ride or a long walk on the beach. Your hostess offers breads and cinnamon rolls right from the oven as part of a hearty breakfast served on a big, round log table. Host Jack Metcalf is a state senator and also loves to entertain when he is not working at the legislature.

West Shore Farm B&B ✪

2781 WEST SHORE DRIVE, LUMMI ISLAND, WASHINGTON 98262

Tel: **(206) 758-2600**
Best Time to Call: **8 AM–9 PM**
Host(s): **Polly and Carl Hanson**
Location: **10 mi. from I-5, Exit 260**
No. of Rooms: **2**
Max. No. Sharing Bath: **4**
Double/sb: **$40**
Single/sb: **$30**
Open: **All year**
Breakfast: **Full**
Other Meals: **Available**
Credit Cards: **MC, VISA**
Pets: **No**
Children: **Welcome (crib)**
Smoking: **No**
Social Drinking: **Permitted**
Airport/Station Pickup: **Yes**

Architects are intrigued by the Hansons' self-built home, marveling at the design and innovative solution to common storage problems. Large windows overlook the Puget Sound islands and Canadian mountains. Sunsets are stunning. You can sit on the beach and watch bald eagles fly by, seals sunning on the offshore rocks, and boats on course to Alaska and Canada. Polly is a librarian and Carl is an aeronautical engineer who built and flies his own plane. They both enjoy having guests and often treat them to homemade ice cream topped with just-picked local fruit.

Maple Valley Bed & Breakfast ✪

20020 SE 228, MAPLE VALLEY, WASHINGTON 98038

Tel: **(206) 432-1409**
Host(s): **Clarke and Jayne Hurlbut**
Location: **26 mi. SE of Seattle**
No. of Rooms: **2**
Max. No. Sharing Bath: **4**
Double/sb: **$40**
Single/sb: **$35**
Open: **All year**

Reduced Rates: **10%, seniors**
Breakfast: **Full**
Pets: **No**
Children: **Welcome**
Smoking: **No**
Social Drinking: **Permitted**
Airport/Station Pickup: **Yes**

After a good night's sleep in either of the B&B's guest rooms—one with a four-poster log bed and the other complete with a pink rosebud tea set, you'll come down to breakfast at a table that overlooks the lawn, the Hurlbuts' resident peacocks, and a wildlife pond teeming with a variety of northwestern birds. If the morning is cool, you'll be warmed by a stone fireplace and you won't go away hungry after orange juice, lemon-blueberry muffins, a plate-sized hootenanny pancake (served with whipped cream, strawberries, slivered almonds, and syrup), ham, sausage or bacon, fresh-ground coffee, tea, or hot chocolate.

Puget View Guesthouse ✪

7924 61ST NORTHEAST, OLYMPIA, WASHINGTON 98506

Tel: **(206) 459-1676**
Best Time to Call: **Evenings**
Host(s): **Dick and Barbara Yunker**
Location: **4½ mi. from I-5, Exit 111**
No. of Rooms: **2**
No. of Private Baths: **1**
Guest Cottage: **$49–$90; sleeps 2–4**
Open: **All year**
Reduced Rates: **10%, seniors; families**
Breakfast: **Continental**
Credit Cards: **MC, VISA**
Pets: **Sometimes**
Children: **Welcome**
Smoking: **Permitted**
Social Drinking: **Permitted**

This charming waterfront guest cottage is located next to Tolmie State Park and adjacent to Dick and Barbara's log home. The panoramic Puget Sound setting makes it a popular romantic getaway. You are apt to discover simple pleasures such as beachcombing or bird-watching and activities such as kayaking or scuba diving. Barbara and Dick are likely to invite you on a boat picnic or an oystering excursion. Your breakfast tray, a lavish and elegant repast, is brought to the cottage. You are welcome to use the beachside campfire for an evening cookout or to barbecue on your deck.

Sylvester House B&B

1803 CAPITOL WAY, OLYMPIA, WASHINGTON 98501

Tel: **(206) 786-8582**
Best Time to Call: **9 AM–9 PM**
Host(s): **Art and Jane Van Allen**
Location: **½ mi. from I-5**
No. of Rooms: **3**
Max. No. Sharing Bath: **3**
Double/sb: **$45**
Single/sb: **$39**
Open: **All year**
Breakfast: **Full**
Credit Cards: **MC, VISA**
Pets: **No**
Children: **Welcome**
Smoking: **No**
Social Drinking: **Permitted**
Airport/Station Pickup: **Yes**

Listed on the Olympia Historical Register, the house is within walking distance of the State Capitol Campus with its rotunda, gardens, lawns, legislative offices, and governor's mansion. Art and Jane provide thoughtful touches such as fresh flowers in the bedrooms or a candlelit bath for romantics. If you're in town on business, use of their copy machine, personal computer, and phone services can be arranged.

Orcas Hotel

P.O. BOX 155, ORCAS, WASHINGTON 98280

Tel: **(206) 376-4300**
Host(s): **Barbara and John Jamieson**
Location: **90 mi. NW of Seattle**
No. of Rooms: **12**
No. of Private Baths: **3**
Max. No. Sharing Bath: **4**
Double/pb: **$75**
Single/pb: **$65**
Double/sb: **$48–$62**
Single/sb: **$38–$52**
Open: **All year**
Reduced Rates: **Available**
Breakfast: **Continental**
Other Meals: **Available**
Credit Cards: **AMEX, MC, VISA**
Pets: **No**
Children: **Welcome**
Smoking: **Permitted**
Social Drinking: **Permitted**
Airport/Station Pickup: **Yes**
Foreign Languages: **French, Spanish**

The Orcas Hotel is a Victorian seaside inn overlooking Harney Channel and the ferry landing. The hotel has been lovingly restored and is listed on the National Register of Historic Places. The rooms feature antiques and modern queen-size beds, with quilts custom-stitched by island quilters. A fully stocked cocktail lounge with a bar menu and fine wine list is available for your relaxing pleasure. A wide range of homemade pastries, fruit-filled pancakes, sticky buns, omelets, and meats are served for breakfast. Your hosts will gladly direct you to Moran State Park, Cascade Lake, hiking and mo-ped trails, and a score of other activities available in the San Juan Islands.

French House at Lake Pateros ✪

206 WEST WARREN, BOX 595, PATEROS, WASHINGTON 98846

Tel: **(509) 923-2626**
Host(s): **Bob and Charlene Knoop**
Location: **19 mi. N of Chelan**
No. of Rooms: **2**
Max. No. Sharing Bath: **4**
Double/sb: **$45**
Single/sb: **$32**
Open: **All year**
Reduced Rates: **20% off-season; seniors**
Breakfast: **Full**
Pets: **No**
Children: **Welcome**
Smoking: **No**
Social Drinking: **Permitted**

This white Dutch Colonial has a red roof, red shutters, and is furnished with oak, wicker, and plants. The beds have handmade quilts and fluffy down pillows. It is located in the north-central part of the state, the heart of Apple Country. Columbia River provides fabulous year-round fishing and water sports. Bob and Charlene invite you to use the kitchen for light snacks. They will arrange river-raft trips, horseback riding, and llama pack trips if you are enthusiastic outdoorsmen, as they are.

Tudor Inn

1108 SOUTH OAK, PORT ANGELES, WASHINGTON 98362

Tel: **(206) 452-3138**
Host(s): **Jane and Jerry Glass**
No. of Rooms: **5**
No. of Private Baths: **1**
Max. No. Sharing Bath: **4**
Double/pb: **$70**
Single/pb: **$65**
Double/sb: **$48**
Single/sb: **$43**
Open: **All year**
Reduced Rates: **10%, Oct.–Apr.**
Breakfast: **Full**
Other Meals: **Available**
Credit Cards: **MC, VISA**
Pets: **No**
Children: **Welcome, over 10**
Smoking: **No**
Social Drinking: **Permitted**
Airport/Station Pickup: **Yes**

Jane and Jerry Glass welcome you to their English Tudor home located on the Olympic Peninsula. The rooms have been fully restored to their turn-of-the-century elegance and furnished with period antiques. Each bedroom offers a view of the Olympic Mountains or the Strait of Juan de Fuca, and is furnished with queen- or king-size beds. In the morning, a pot of tea or coffee can be placed outside your door upon request. Farm-fresh eggs, homemade jams, French toast, and homemade syrups are just a few of the specialties that will await you in the formal dining room. Guests are invited to relax in the lounge or library, each with its own fireplace. Alpine and cross-country skiing can be enjoyed at Hurricane Ridge, 18 miles away. During the summer season, ferry service connects Port Angeles and Victoria, B.C., less than 20 miles to the north. Your hosts are glad to make arrangements for salmon charters, guided hiking, backpacking, and bicycle rentals.

Ogle's Bed and Breakfast ✪

1307 DOGWOOD HILL SOUTH WEST, PORT ORCHARD, WASHINGTON 98366

Tel: **(206) 876-9170**
Host(s): **Quentin and Louise Ogle**
Location: **12 mi. W of Seattle**
No. of Rooms: **2**
Max. No. Sharing Bath: **3**
Double/sb: **$35**

Single/sb: **$25**
Open: **All year**
Breakfast: **Full**
Pets: **No**
Children: **Welcome, over 10**
Smoking: **No**
Social Drinking: **Permitted**

This single-level contemporary is located on a quiet private road in the hills of Port Orchard. The house is surrounded by fruit trees and blackberry bushes, and overlooks Puget Sound. The rooms are comfortably furnished with special touches like hand-braided wool rugs, Korean brass-bound chests, and nautical memorabilia. Guest rooms have beautiful views of the surrounding hills. Each morning an elegant breakfast is served with fine linen, china, and sterling. Port Orchard is known for its marinas, covered sidewalks, specialty shops and restaurants. It's a good jumping-off point for exploring Seattle and the historic towns of the Olympic Peninsula.

Country Living B&B

ROUTE 1, BOX 87, PRESCOTT, WASHINGTON 99348

Tel: **(509) 849-2819**
Best Time to Call: **Evenings**
Host(s): **Bill and Carol Dicus**
Location: **1 mi. E of Prescott**
No. of Rooms: **1 suite**
No. of Private Baths: **1**
Suites: **$40**
Open: **All year**
Breakfast: **Continental**
Pets: **Sometimes**
Children: **Welcome (crib)**
Smoking: **No**
Social Drinking: **No**

Country Living is a newly remodeled farmhouse set alone in the great dryland wheat country. Bill and Carol offer a comfortable suite with a cozy fireplace and private deck. Blueberry muffins are served outdoors on the deck in the warm weather. In winter, the snow forms a blanket on the fields and the wood stove offers a nice place to warm up, and guests are invited to play the piano or antique organ. The open land and pastures provide excellent hunting and the Snake and Columbia rivers are an hour away, with excellent camping, boating and fishing.

Cedarym ✪

1011 240TH AVENUE NORTHEAST, REDMOND, WASHINGTON 98053

Tel: **(206) 868-4159**
Host(s): **Mary Ellen and Walt Brown**
Location: **15 mi. E of Seattle**
No. of Rooms: **2**
Max. No. Sharing Bath: **4**
Double/sb: **$40**

Open: **All year**
Breakfast: **Full**
Credit Cards: **MC, VISA**
Pets: **No**
Children: **Welcome, over 12**
Smoking: **No**
Social Drinking: **Permitted**
Airport/Station Pickup: **Yes**

Cedarym is a spacious Colonial reproduction located on the Sammamish Plateau. The house has Cape Cod–style pine floors, wrought-iron door latches, and a large cooking-style fireplace in the keeping room. Guest rooms feature antique brass beds and comfortable sitting areas for reading or watching television, and each has old-fashioned wall stenciling. The breakfast table glows with hand-dipped candles and is covered with specialties such as Dutch Babies, muffins, and a variety of egg dishes. Guests are welcome to stroll the spacious grounds and visit the rose garden and the cottage garden, with its flowers and herbs. A gazebo-sheltered spa is guaranteed to relax you. This lovely Colonial is a short drive from historic Marymoor Park, Ste. Michelle Winery, and the sights of Seattle.

Summer Song ✪

P.O. BOX 82, SEABECK, WASHINGTON 98380

Tel: **(206) 830-5089**
Host(s): **Ron and Sharon Barney**
Location: **9 mi. SW of Silverdale**
No. of Rooms: **1**
No. of Private Baths: **1**
Double/pb: **$50**
Open: **All year**
Reduced Rates: **20%, Oct.–Mar.; seniors**
Breakfast: **Full**
Pets: **Sometimes**
Children: **Welcome, over 8**
Smoking: **Permitted**
Social Drinking: **Permitted**

Enjoy your own private cottage on the shores of Hood Canal when you visit Summer Song. The cabin sleeps four, and features a bedroom, living and dining room, full kitchen, and bath. A cozy fireplace, old-fashioned wainscoting, and private decks with fire pit, barbecue, and mountain view complete this cozy retreat. Your hosts serve breakfast at the cottage or on the beach. Huckleberry muffins made from freshly picked fruit are the house specialty. Ron and Sharon provide all the comforts of home, such as beach towels and robes. Their beach is perfect for swimming and a public boat launch is just one mile away. Beautiful nature trails at Scenic Beach State Park are just a short walk away, and many stores and restaurants are also located close by.

Beech Tree Manor ✪

1405 QUEEN ANNE AVENUE NORTH, SEATTLE, WASHINGTON 98109

Tel: **(206) 281-7037**
Best Time to Call: **After 10 AM**
Host(s): **Virginia Lucero**
Location: **2 mi. from I-5, Exit 166**
No. of Rooms: **4**
Max. No. Sharing Bath: **4**
Double/sb: **$55**
Single/sb: **$50**
Open: **All year**
Reduced Rates: **Weekly, Jan.–Apr.**
Breakfast: **Continental**
Credit Cards: **MC, VISA**
Pets: **Sometimes**
Children: **Welcome**
Smoking: **No**
Social Drinking: **Permitted**

The manor's name is derived from the massive copper beech tree in the front yard. The English-style interior, accented by open-beam ceilings and antiques, has been artistically decorated by Virginia. Special touches, such as pure cotton bed linens, oversized, plush bath towels, a shady porch with wicker rockers, and a pleasant parlor reading room, add to your comfort. Breakfast often features Dutch Babies with blackberries, freshly baked scones or popovers, and fresh fruits of the season. Electric trolleys link the manor to downtown Seattle.

Chambered Nautilus Bed and Breakfast Inn ✪

5005 22ND AVENUE NORTH EAST, SEATTLE, WASHINGTON 98105

Tel: **(206) 522-2536**
Host(s): **Kate McDill and Deborah Sweet**
Location: **4 mi. NE of downtown**
No. of Rooms: **6**
Max. No. Sharing Bath: **4**
Double/sb: **$46–$72**
Single/sb: **$42–$68**
Open: **All year**
Reduced Rates: **10% on 5th night**
Breakfast: **Continental**
Credit Cards: **AMEX, DC, MC, VISA**
Pets: **No**
Children: **Welcome, over 12**
Smoking: **No**
Social Drinking: **Permitted**
Foreign Languages: **American sign language**

This 1915 Georgian mansion faces the Cascade Mountains and Lake Washington. One bedroom is romantic, with lots of oak; another is sunny, with inlaid mahogany pieces; several have balconies. Breakfast is served in the fireplaced dining room. Your hosts will be happy to direct you to local theaters, restaurants, and sports activities. The University of Washington is nearby.

Galer Place B&B Guest House ✪

318 WEST GALER, SEATTLE, WASHINGTON 98119

Tel: **(206) 282-5339**
Host(s): **Chris Chamberlain**
Location: **2 mi. from I-5, Mercer St. Exit**
No. of Rooms: **3**
No. of Private Baths: **1**
Max. No. Sharing Bath: **4**
Double/pb: **$60**
Single/pb: **$55**
Double/sb: **$50–$55**
Single/sb: **$45–$50**
Open: **All year**
Breakfast: **Continental**
Credit Cards: **AMEX, DC, MC, VISA**
Pets: **Sometimes**
Children: **Welcome, over 12**
Smoking: **Permitted**
Social Drinking: **No**

A south Queen Anne Hill location sets this early-1900s home within walking distance of Seattle Center. A trolley line provides front-door service to the downtown area. The hallmarks of the generous breakfast are its fresh-baked breads, homemade preserves, and just-ground coffee. Several parks and scenic viewpoints are within strolling distance, as are an indoor swimming pool and running track. A hot tub, on the backyard deck, is a delightful place to unwind. You are invited to join your British hostess for afternoon tea and homemade Scottish shortbread, served each day from 4 to 5 PM.

Hainsworth House ✪

2657 37TH SOUTH WEST, P.O. BOX 16438, SEATTLE, WASHINGTON 98126

Tel: **(206) 938-1020 or 932-0654**
Host(s): **Carl and Charlotte Muia**
Location: **3 mi. W of Seattle**
No. of Rooms: **2**
Max. No. Sharing Bath: **4**
Double/sb: **$55–$65**
Single/sb: **$40–$50**
Suites: **$90 for 4**
Open: **All year**
Reduced Rates: **Weekly**
Breakfast: **Full**
Pets: **No**
Children: **Welcome**
Smoking: **No**
Social Drinking: **Permitted**
Airport/Station Pickup: **Yes**

The Hainsworth House is an English Tudor mansion overlooking Seattle. It is surrounded by beautiful lawns and is across the street from a park donated to the city by the Hainsworth family. The present owners, Carl and Charlotte Muia, have done extensive restoration work to the interior, following the original drawings down to the last ceiling beam. Guests will find the antique-filled rooms and gourmet breakfasts in keeping with the elegant traditions of the house. Eggs

Benedict, salmon strata, German pancakes, and omelets are a few of the favorites.

Hanson House B&B

1526 PALM AVENUE SW, SEATTLE, WASHINGTON 98116

Tel: **(206) 937-4157**
Host(s): **Jody and F. Ken Weaver**
Location: **3 mi. from I-5**
No. of Rooms: **2**
No. of Private Baths: **2**
Double/pb: **$65**
Single/pb: **$55**
Open: **All year**
Reduced Rates: **Nov.–Mar.**
Breakfast: **Continental**
Pets: **Welcome**
Children: **No**
Smoking: **No**
Social Drinking: **Permitted**
Airport/Station Pickup: **Yes**
Foreign Languages: **Spanish**

Hanson House guests are always awed by the spectacular view of Elliott Bay and the Seattle skyline, from Mt. Rainier to Mt. Baker. Ferries slide by every 20 to 30 minutes, the *Princess Marguerite* leaves her berth every day during the summer, and the *Catamaran Clipper* makes its round-trips from Seattle to Victoria and Vancouver and back. Originally built as a summer home, Hanson House was extensively remodeled in 1984. Breakfasts feature the specialty of the house, Dutch Babies pancakes; after an invigorating day of sightseeing, complimentary wine and cheese are served.

Marit's Bed and Breakfast ✪

6208 PALATINE AVENUE, SEATTLE, WASHINGTON 98103

Tel: **(206) 782-7900**
Best Time to Call: **Mornings; evenings**
Host(s): **Marit Nelson**
Location: **5 mi. N of Seattle**
No. of Rooms: **3**
Max. No. Sharing Bath: **4**
Double/sb: **$45**
Single/sb: **$35**
Open: **All year**
Reduced Rates: **10%, weekly; seniors**
Breakfast: **Full**
Pets: **No**
Children: **Welcome (crib)**
Smoking: **No**
Social Drinking: **Permitted**
Airport/Station Pickup: **Yes**
Foreign Languages: **Norwegian**

This ivy-covered brick Tudor home is just ten minutes from downtown Seattle. Guests can enjoy the convenience of being close to the city while staying in comfortable rooms overlooking the mountains and the water. Marit Nelson specializes in Scandinavian hospitality. She prepares Norwegian specialties for breakfast along with homemade bread and jam, juice, fruit, freshly ground coffee, and assorted teas. The house is close to the University of Washington and is within walking distance of the Woodland Park Zoo and Green Lake.

Roberta's Bed and Breakfast

1147 SIXTEENTH AVENUE EAST, SEATTLE, WASHINGTON 98112

Tel: **(206) 329-3326**
Host(s): **Roberta Mar**
No. of Rooms: **4**
Max. No. Sharing Bath: **3**
Double/sb: **$55**
Single/sb: **$50**
Open: **All year**
Breakfast: **Full**
Credit Cards: **AMEX, DC, MC, VISA**
Pets: **No**
Children: **Sometimes**
Smoking: **No**
Social Drinking: **Permitted**

Roberta's is a 1904 frame Victorian with a large, old-fashioned front porch. The house is located in a quiet historic neighborhood near the heart of the city. Cheerful rooms filled with antiques await you: the Peach Room has a brass bed, bay windows, and a cozy Franklin stove; the Plum Room has twin beds and a loft that can sleep an extra person. In the morning you'll smell a pot of coffee right beside your door. That's just a warmup for the large breakfast to come. The specialty of the house is Dutch Babies, a local dish, served with powdered sugar or fresh berries. Guests are welcome to relax in the living room and join Roberta for a glass of sherry.

Salisbury House ✪

750 16TH AVENUE EAST, SEATTLE, WASHINGTON 98112

Tel: **(206) 328-8682**
Best Time to Call: **10 AM–1 PM; 5 PM–8 PM**
Host(s): **Mary and Catherine Wiese**
Location: **1 mi. from I-5**
No. of Rooms: **4**
Max. No. Sharing Bath: **4**
Double/sb: **$50–$55**

Single/sb: **$45–$50**
Open: **All year**
Reduced Rates: **10%, weekly**
Breakfast: **Continental**
Credit Cards: **AMEX, MC, VISA**
Pets: **No**
Children: **Welcome, over 12**
Smoking: **No**
Social Drinking: **Permitted**
Foreign Languages: **Spanish**

This elegant family home, built in 1904, has been lovingly restored by your hostesses, a mother-daughter team. It is located in a quiet neighborhood within walking distance of parks, restaurants, shops, and the Seattle Art Museum. Two of the guest rooms are small and cozy; the other two face the front of the house with window seats providing an attractive accent. A renovated Victorian-style bathroom features a six-foot clawfoot tub. You are invited to enjoy your morning coffee on the sun porch and an evening glass of sherry in the library.

Seattle Bed & Breakfast ✪

2442 N.W. MARKET #300, SEATTLE, WASHINGTON 98107

Tel: **(206) 783-2169**
Host(s): **Inge Pokrandt**
Location: **1 mi. from I-5**
No. of Rooms: **4**
No. of Private Baths: **2**
Suites: **$35–$45**
Guest Cottage: **$55 for 2**
Open: **All year**
Breakfast: **Continental**
Credit Cards: **AMEX, MC, VISA**
Pets: **No**
Children: **Welcome, over 8**
Smoking: **No**
Social Drinking: **Permitted**
Foreign Languages: **German**

The charming two-bedroom cottage is close to downtown, the University of Washington, the zoo, and all sightseeing. Enjoy the privacy, the fine oak furniture, the fireplace, and all the little touches that make you feel welcome. The private suite in Inge's home has a full kitchen, and breakfast food is provided. Fresh flowers, fruits, and candy all spell out a warm welcome.

William House Bed & Breakfast ✪

1505 FOURTH AVENUE NORTH, SEATTLE, WASHINGTON 98109

Tel: **(206) 285-0810**
Best Time to Call: **Mornings**
Host(s): **Susan and Doug Williams**
Location: **½ mi. from I-5**
No. of Rooms: **5**
No. of Private Baths: **1½**
Max. No. Sharing Bath: **4**
Double/pb: **$70**
Single/pb: **$60**
Double/sb: **$45–$55**
Single/sb: **$39–$45**
Open: **All year**
Reduced Rates: **Available**
Breakfast: **Full**
Credit Cards: **AMEX, DC, MC, VISA**
Pets: **No**
Children: **Welcome (crib)**
Smoking: **Permitted**
Social Drinking: **Permitted**

This large family home is located in a quiet neighborhood on top of Queen Anne Hill. It combines easy city access with commanding views of the Cascade Mountains, Mount Rainier, the downtown skyline, and Puget Sound. Built in 1900, the original woodwork and sculptured tin wallcovering give warmth, charm, and character to the living room and dining area. Your hosts feel their primary job is to make your stay the right mix of personal contact and personal privacy.

Fotheringham House ✪

2128 WEST SECOND, SPOKANE, WASHINGTON 99204

Tel: **(509) 838-4363**
Best Time to Call: **7 AM–10 PM**
Host(s): **Sue and Jay Moynahan**
Location: **½ mi. from Route I-90**
No. of Rooms: **7**
No. of Private Baths: **3**
Max. No. Sharing Bath: **4**
Double/pb: **$45–$55**
Single/pb: **$40–$45**
Double/sb: **$37–$42**
Single/sb: **$32**
Open: **All year**
Reduced Rates: **15%, seniors**
Breakfast: **Continental**
Credit Cards: **AMEX, MC, VISA**
Pets: **No**
Children: **Welcome, over 12**
Smoking: **No**
Social Drinking: **Permitted**
Airport/Station Pickup: **Yes**

Jay and Sue have furnished their house (circa 1891), which is located in a National Historic area, in a pleasant blend of Victorian and country French decor. A curved glass window adorning the entry hall, the intricate ball-and-spindle fretwork, tin ceilings, and the open staircase are all original. The house is across the street from Spokane's first park and just next door to the historic Patsy Clark mansion, which has been converted to an outstanding restaurant. Sue spoils her guests with delicious homemade croissants filled with apples, raisins, and honey, or spiced plums in port. In summer, you are welcome to enjoy a glass of wine on the porch; in winter, it is served by a crackling fire.

Luckey's Residence

WEST 828 28TH AVENUE, SPOKANE, WASHINGTON 99203

Tel: **(509) 624-3627**
Host(s): **Robert, Patricia, and Royden Luckey**
Location: **2 mi. from I-90**
No. of Rooms: **4**
No. of Private Baths: **2**
Max. No. Sharing Bath: **4**
Double/sb: **$35**
Single/sb: **$25**
Open: **All year**
Breakfast: **Continental**
Pets: **No**
Children: **Welcome**
Smoking: **No**
Social Drinking: **No**

Luckey's has been described as a "Hansel and Gretel" house. It was built in the 1930s to look like an English cottage. The house is set in the

South Hill section, a neighborhood set on a hillside covered with pine trees and volcanic rock. Your hosts offer a choice of twin- or queen-size beds. They serve a breakfast of homemade breads, cheeses, fruits, assorted juices, and plenty of coffee or tea. Luckey's is two blocks from High Drive, a scenic parkway along the hillside overlooking the canyon. A park with a large public swimming pool, children's wading pool, tennis court, and play area is a short walk from the house.

Inge's Place ✪

6809 LAKE GROVE S.W., TACOMA, WASHINGTON 98499

Tel: **(206) 584-4514**
Host(s): **Ingeborg Deatherage**
Location: **3 mi. from I-5**
No. of Rooms: **3**
No. of Private Baths: **1**
Max. No. Sharing Bath: **4**
Double/pb: **$40**
Single/pb: **$30**
Double/sb: **$40**
Single/sb: **$30**
Suites: **$60**
Open: **All year**
Reduced Rates: **Available**
Breakfast: **Full**
Pets: **No**
Children: **Welcome**
Smoking: **Permitted**
Social Drinking: **Permitted**
Airport/Station Pickup: **Yes**
Foreign Languages: **German**

This spic-and-span home is in a lovely Tacoma suburb called Lakewood. Feel welcome to use the hot tub, large backyard, and patio. There are many restaurants and shopping centers within walking distance, and several nearby lakes where fishing is excellent. Tacoma is the gateway to Mount Rainier. Inge is a world traveler, teacher, and enthusiast about B&Bs.

Keenan House ✪

2610 NORTH WARNER, TACOMA, WASHINGTON 98407

Tel: **(206) 752-0702**
Host(s): **Lenore Keenan**
Location: **2½ mi. from I-5**
No. of Rooms: **8**
No. of Private Baths: **1**
Max. No. Sharing Bath: **4**
Double/pb: **$45**
Single/pb: **$40**
Double/sb: **$40**
Single/sb: **$30**
Open: **All year**
Reduced Rates: **Weekly, 15%; families**
Breakfast: **Full**
Pets: **No**
Children: **Welcome**
Smoking: **No**
Social Drinking: **Permitted**

This spacious Victorian house is located in the historic district near Puget Sound. It is furnished in antiques and period pieces. Afternoon tea is served, and ice is available for cocktails; fruit and croissants are served with breakfast. Local possibilities include Puget Sound, Vashon

Island, the state park, zoo, and ferry. It's only five blocks to the University of Puget Sound.

Traudel's Haus ✪

15313 17TH AVENUE COURT EAST, TACOMA, WASHINGTON 98445

Tel: **(206) 535-4422**
Host(s): **Gertraude M. Taut**
Location: **5 mi. from I-5 & 525**
No. of Rooms: **3**
Max. No. Sharing Bath: **4**
Double/sb: **$35**
Suites: **$55**
Open: **All year**
Reduced Rates: **Weekly, families, seniors**
Breakfast: **Continental**
Pets: **No**
Children: **Welcome, over 12**
Smoking: **Permitted**
Social Drinking: **Permitted**
Airport Pickup: **Yes**
Foreign Languages: **German**

A former guest has written the following recommendation of Gertraude's B&B: "Located in a lovely, quiet neighborhood only minutes from Pacific Lutheran University and Sprinkler Recreation Park, it is an easy springboard for other explorations in and around Tacoma, notably the Northwest Trek and Mt. Rainier National Park. Ms. Taut offers a clean and safe environment, reflecting her experience in health-care facilities. She provides a well-organized, guest-oriented haven for the traveler." Need we say more?

Guest House Bed & Breakfast ✪

835 EAST CHRISTENSON ROAD, GREENBANK, WHIDBEY ISLAND, WASHINGTON 98253

Tel: **(206) 678-3115**
Host(s): **Don and Mary Jane Creger**
Location: **49 mi. NW of Seattle**
Suites: **$60**
Guest Cottage: **$55–$90**
Open: **All year**
Reduced Rates: **Available**
Breakfast: **Continental**
Credit Cards: **AMEX, MC, VISA**
Pets: **Sometimes**
Children: **Welcome, over 14**
Smoking: **No**
Social Drinking: **Permitted**

It is a delightful 15-minute ferry ride from Mukilteo to this lovely island. A variety of accommodations is offered, including a charming suite in the 1920 farmhouse. There are three self-contained private guest cottages cozily furnished with antiques, fireplaces, and minikitchens, as well as a log lodge that sleeps as many as five. Breakfast is included with farmhouse accommodations; a $2.50 charge per person is the tariff in the cottages for a full breakfast setup that can be enjoyed at one's leisure. A swimming pool and spa are on the premises.

WEST VIRGINIA

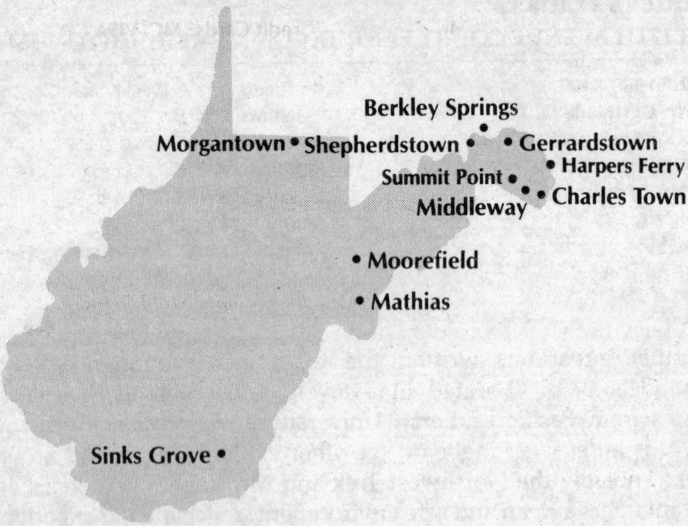

Berkley Springs
Morgantown
Shepherdstown
Gerrardstown
Harpers Ferry
Summit Point
Middleway
Charles Town
Moorefield
Mathias
Sinks Grove

Maria's Garden & Inn

201 INDEPENDENCE STREET, BERKELEY SPRINGS, WEST VIRGINIA 25411

Tel: **(304) 258-2021**
Best Time to Call: **9 AM–9 PM**
Host(s): **Peg Perry and Curtis Perry**
Location: **6 mi. from I-70**
No. of Rooms: **8**
No. of Private Baths: **2**
Max. No. Sharing Bath: **4**
Double/pb: **$55**
Single/pb: **$45**
Double/sb: **$45**
Single/sb: **$35**
Suites: **$55**
Open: **All year**
Breakfast: **Full**
Other meals: **Available**
Credit Cards: **AMEX, DC, MC, VISA**
Pets: **No**
Children: **Welcome (crib)**
Smoking: **Permitted**
Social Drinking: **Permitted**
Airport/Station Pickup: **Yes**

Conveniently located, this B&B is a block away from the Roman Baths, mineral springs, and Berkeley Castle, the only English Norman castle in America. Built in 1929, this brick Colonial has spacious rooms comfortably furnished and accented with antiques. There's a corner porch, perfect for watching the street scene. Curtis and his mother, Peg, have a restaurant on the premises that features an Italian menu. Breakfast often includes waffles or French toast.

The Carriage Inn ✪

417 EAST WASHINGTON STREET, CHARLES TOWN, WEST VIRGINIA 25414

Tel: **(304) 728-8003**
Best Time to Call: **9 AM–3 PM**
Host(s): **Robert and Virginia Kaetzel**
Location: **75 mi. NW of Baltimore**
No. of Rooms: **5**
No. of Private Baths: **5**
Double/pb: **$60–$75**
Open: **All year**
Breakfast: **Full**
Credit Cards: **MC, VISA**
Pets: **No**
Children: **Welcome**
Smoking: **No**
Social Drinking: **Permitted**
Airport/Station Pickup: **Yes**

Built in 1836, this grand white Colonial with its burgundy shutters and columned porch is aptly named because Robert and Virginia provide carriage rides through the historic neighborhoods. It is furnished with antiques and fine reproductions that include walnut canopy beds. Breakfast often features buttermilk pancakes, country eggs, and homemade jams. It is close to Harpers Ferry, Antietam Battlefield, and within walking distance of the Charles Town Races. Tennis, rafting, and golf are minutes away.

The Gilbert House ✪

BOX 1104, CHARLES TOWN, WEST VIRGINIA 25415

Tel: **(304) 725-0637**
Host(s): **Jean and Bernie Heiler**
Location: **5 mi. W of Charles Town**
No. of Rooms: **3**
No. of Private Baths: **3**
Double/pb: **$75–$85**
Open: **All year**
Reduced Rates: **Weekly; families; seniors**
Breakfast: **Full**
Credit Cards: **MC, VISA**
Pets: **No**
Children: **No**
Smoking: **Permitted**
Social Drinking: **Permitted**
Airport/Station Pickup: **Yes**
Foreign Languages: **German, Spanish**

Located in the heart of the historic district, this stone house is listed on the National Register of Historic Places. Built in 1800, it is elegantly appointed with antiques, Oriental rugs, and artwork collected from around the world by Jean and Bernie. Breakfast is a taste treat with its freshly squeezed orange juice, special quiche, and fresh-ground coffee. Afterward, explore the beautiful Shenandoah Valley. You may canoe or hike; shop in antique, craft, or factory outlet stores; or take in a history lecture instead. Your hosts' special thoughtfulness includes complimentary champagne, fruits, and candy in your room; snacks at any time; and a gift of Jean's artwork designed especially for you.

Prospect Hill

BOX 135, GERRARDSTOWN, WEST VIRGINIA 25420

Tel: **(304) 229-3346**
Best Time to Call: **Evening**
Host(s): **Hazel and Charles Hudock**
Location: **4 mi. from Rte. 81**
No. of Rooms: **3**
No. of Private Baths: **3**
Double/pb: **$65–$85**
Single/pb: **$65–$75**
Separate Guest Cottage: **$75 for 2; $100 for 4**
Open: **All year**
Reduced Rates: **Weekdays**
Breakfast: **Full**
Pets: **Sometimes**
Children: **Welcome (in cottage)**
Smoking: **Permitted**
Social Drinking: **Permitted**

Prospect Hill is a Georgian mansion set on 225 acres. The house dates back to the 1790s and is listed on the National Register of Historic Places. One can see that this was a well-to-do gentleman's home, with permanent Franklin fireplaces, antiques, and a hall mural depicting life in the days of the early Republic. Guests may choose one of the beautifully appointed rooms in the main house or the former servants' quarters, complete with country kitchen and a fireplace in the living room. There is much to do on this working farm, including visiting the antebellum outbuildings, fishing, biking, and exploring the vast grounds. Near historic Harpers Ferry, Martinsburg, and Winchester, the area offers fine sightseeing and splendid restaurants.

Valley View Farm ✪

RT. 1, BOX 467, MATHIAS, WEST VIRGINIA 26812

Tel: **(304) 897-5229**
Best Time to Call: **Evenings after 7 PM**
Host(s): **Ernest and Edna Shipe**
Location: **130 mi. SW of D.C.**
No. of Rooms: **4**
Max. No. Sharing Bath: **7**
Double/sb: **$30**
Single/sb: **$15**
Open: **All year**
Reduced Rates: **Weekly**
Breakfast: **Full**
Other Meals: **Available**
Pets: **Welcome**
Children: **Welcome (crib)**
Smoking: **Permitted**
Social Drinking: **Permitted**
Airport/Station Pickup: **Yes**

Edna and Ernest raise cattle and sheep on their 250-acre farm. The 1920s farmhouse is decorated with comfortable Early American–style furniture and family mementos, and there's a nice porch for relaxed visiting. This is no place to diet, because Edna is a good cook. Seasonal recreational activities are available in nearby Lost River State Park and on Rock Cliff Lake. You are certain to enjoy the local festivals, house tours, and interesting craft shops.

Maxwell Bed and Breakfast ✪

ROUTE 12, BOX 197, MORGANTOWN, WEST VIRGINIA 26506

Tel: **(304) 594-3041**
Best Time to Call: **6–9 PM**
Host(s): **Emma B. Maxwell**
Location: **2 mi. from US 48, Exit 10**
No. of Rooms: **2**
Max. No. Sharing Bath: **5**
Double/sb: **$40**
Single/sb: **$30**
Suites: **$70–$80**
Open: **All year**
Breakfast: **Full**
Pets: **No**
Children: **Sometimes**
Smoking: **Permitted**
Social Drinking: **Permitted**
Airport/Station Pickup: **Yes**
Foreign Languages: **Spanish**

Emma faithfully carries out the motto on the Maxwell coat of arms: "I bide ye fair." It means "You'll be cared for well," and she makes certain you will be! This B&B is located on Ridge Way Farm, an organic homestead that raises Scotch Highland cattle, fruits, and vegetables, overlooks Cheat Lake. Guests are polled for preference of the breakfast menu and may select from French toast, waffles, eggs, or pancakes, plus hash browns or French fries, bacon or ham, or hot or cold cereal. It can be served in the dining room, on the deck, or in the suite's sitting room. Within driving distance are fine white-water or skiing opportunities, historic sites, mountain festivals, ethnic celebrations, and athletic activities. Best of all is just watching the wildlife and birds at the homestead.

McMechen House Inn ✪

109 N. MAIN STREET, MOOREFIELD, WEST VIRGINIA 26836

Tel: **(304) 538-2417**
Host(s): **Art and Evelyn Valotto**
Location: **At junction of Rtes. 55 and 220**
No. of Rooms: **11**
No. of Private Baths: **6**
Double/pb: **$35–$40**
Single/pb: **$28**
Suites: **$45–$65**
Open: **Jan. 16–Dec. 31**
Breakfast: **Full**
Credit Cards: **MC, VISA**
Pets: **No**
Children: **Welcome**
Smoking: **Permitted**
Social Drinking: **Permitted**

Cradled in the historic South Branch Valley and surrounded by the majestic mountains of the Potomac Highlands, the inn, built in 1853, is a three-story brick Federal-style house. During the Civil War it served as headquarters for both North and South as the region changed hands. It is furnished in antiques of the period. Breakfast is served family-style in the dining room.

Thomas Shepherd Inn

300 WEST GERMAN STREET, P.O. BOX 1162, SHEPHERDSTOWN, WEST VIRGINIA 25443

Tel: **(304) 876-3715**
Host(s): **Ed and Carol Ringoot**
Location: **70 mi. W of Baltimore, Md.**
No. of Rooms: **6**
No. of Private Baths: **4**
Max. No. Sharing Bath: **4**
Double/pb: **$60**
Double/sb: **$55**
Open: **All year**
Reduced Rates: **Available**
Breakfast: **Full**
Credit Cards: **MC, VISA**
Pets: **No**
Children: **Welcome, over 12**
Smoking: **Permitted**
Social Drinking: **Permitted**
Airport/Station Pickup: **No**
Foreign Languages: **Flemish, French**

Located in the beautiful Eastern Panhandle, this brick Federal-style house, built in 1868, is furnished with period antiques, with an emphasis on comfort and quality. All the guest rooms have antique beds, wing chairs, and Oriental rugs. It is within minutes of the Potomac River and the C&O Canal for hiking and biking, the Shenandoah River for whitewater rafting, and an excellent selection of restaurants and shops. Breakfast favorites of puffed apple pancakes, Belgian waffles, or ham and cheese soufflé are often featured. Complimentary beverages are always generously offered. Washington, D.C., is 65 miles away.

Countryside ✪

BOX 57, SUMMIT POINT, WEST VIRGINIA 25446

Tel: **(304) 725-2614**
Best Time to Call: **8–10 AM; 4–10 PM**
Host(s): **Lisa and Daniel Hileman**
Location: **6 mi. from Rtes. 7, 340**
No. of Rooms: **2**
No. of Private Baths: 2
Double/pb: **$40–$50**
Single/pb: **$40–$50**
Open: **All year**
Breakfast: **Continental**
Pets: **No**
Children: **No**
Smoking: **No**
Social Drinking: **Permitted**
Airport/Station Pickup: **Yes**

In the Shenandoah Valley of the Eastern Panhandle, only 20 minutes from Harpers Ferry, this country home with white shutters, large yard, and patio is on a quiet street in a charming old village. It is furnished with country oak furniture, antique quilts, and original art. Lisa and Daniel offer hospitable touches of fruit and candy, placed in each guest room. Afternoon tea is served; snacks and beverages are always available.

WISCONSIN

Bed & Breakfast Guest-Homes

ROUTE 2, ALGOMA, WISCONSIN 54201

Tel: **(414) 743-9742**
Best Time to Call: **7 AM–9 PM**
Coordinator: **Eileen Wood**
State/Regions Covered: **Statewide**

Rates (Single/Double):

Modest:	$28	$35
Average:	$35	$50
Luxury:	$45	$55

Credit Cards: **MC, VISA**

This reservation service offers you local color and relaxing surroundings. Eileen carefully selects the accommodations to assure each guest of a hospitable host in clean, comfortable homes. All serve full breakfasts. Homes on the waterfront are slightly more expensive from July to early September. There is a 10% discount for week-long stays.

Bed & Breakfast Information Service—Wisconsin

458 GLENWAY STREET, MADISON, WISCONSIN 53711

Tel: **(608) 238-6776**
Best Time to Call: **8–12 AM**
Coordinator: **Carol Jean Buelow**
State/Regions Covered: **Statewide**

Rates (Single/Double):

Modest:	**$20–$30**	**$35–$40**
Average:	**$30–$40**	**$40–$55**
Luxury:	**N/A**	**$40–$105**

Credit Cards: **Some hosts do**

Many of Wisconsin's bed and breakfasts are in historic homes or in areas listed on the National Register of Historic Places, some are near ski hills or popular canoeing spots, and some are in Door County, a midwestern Cape Cod. Send $4 for a descriptive brochure, and make your reservation directly with the host of your choice.

The Parkside ✪

402 E NORTH STREET, APPLETON, WISCONSIN 54911

Tel: **(414) 733-0200**
Best Time to Call: **After 6 PM**
Host(s): **Bonnie Riley**
Location: **100 mi. NNW of Milwaukee**
No. of Rooms: **1 suite**
No. of Private Baths: **1**
Suites: **$50–$60**
Open: **All year**
Breakfast: **Full**
Pets: **No**
Children: **Welcome, over 8**
Smoking: **Permitted**
Social Drinking: **Permitted**
Airport/Station Pickup: **Yes**

Appleton's historic City Park area, once the neighborhood of magician Harry Houdini and author Edna Ferber, is the setting for this 1906 Richardson Romanesque-style home. It's located a short walk from the campus of Lawrence University, and downtown shops and restaurants. Decorative leaded glass is prominent throughout the home. You are invited to enjoy breakfast featuring seasonal fruits, warm breads, and Wisconsin cheese beside the dining room's curved glass window. The bright and airy third-floor suite has a treetop view of City Park.

The Barrister's House ✪

226 9TH AVENUE, BOX 166, BARABOO, WISCONSIN 53913

Tel: **(608) 356-3344**
Host(s): **Glen and Mary Schulz**
Location: **45 mi. NW of Madison**
No. of Rooms: **4**
No. of Private Baths: **4**
Double/pb: **$45–$55**
Single/pb: **$40–$50**
Open: **Daily, June–Aug.; Weekends only, Sept.–May**
Breakfast: **Continental**
Pets: **No**
Children: **Welcome, over 6**
Smoking: **No**
Social Drinking: **Permitted**

This elegant Colonial is named for the prominent town attorney who once lived here. Guests are welcome to settle down with a book in the library or relax around the fireplace in the living room. In summer, enjoy a glass of lemonade on the screened porch, veranda, or terrace. Sleeping quarters include the Garden Room, furnished in wicker and wrought iron, and the Colonial Room, appointed in 18th-century pieces. The Barrister's Room is a favorite for special occasions because of its canopy bed and natural cherry wood and cranberry-glass appointments. Juice, sweet rolls, fresh fruit, and cheese are served beside the black marble fireplace in the dining room, or outside, if you prefer. Glen and Mary will gladly direct you to such nearby sights as Devil's Lake State Park and the Wisconsin Dells.

Frantiques Showplace ✪

704 ASH STREET, BARABOO, WISCONSIN 53913

Tel: **(608) 356-5273**
Host(s): **Fran and Bud Kelly**
Location: **13 mi. from I-90**
No. of Rooms: **1 suite**
No. of Private Baths: **1**
Suites: **$50**
Open: **All year**
Reduced Rates: **10%, seniors**
Breakfast: **Full**
Pets: **No**
Children: **Welcome**
Smoking: **No**
Social Drinking: **Permitted**
Airport/Station Pickup: **Yes**

Fran Kelly has turned her three-story 125-year-old house into a Baraboo tourist attraction. She conducts tours through her house, showing off her antique dishes, children's toys, turn-of-the-century clothing, cameras, 1918 fireless cook stove, and more. The Cinema Suite has movie posters on the walls and comes with an antique brass bed, a refrigerator, stove, microwave oven, private bath, and private entrance. Baraboo is the "Circus City of the World," and Fran seems to have more than just a bit of the showman in her, too. Nearby you'll find the Circus World Museum, the Al Ringling Theater, Devil's Lake State Park, the International Crane Foundation, and, 10 miles away, Wisconsin Dells.

The House of Seven Gables ✪

215 6TH STREET, BARABOO, WISCONSIN 53913

Tel: **(608) 356-8387**
Best Time to Call: **8 AM–10 PM**
Host(s): **Ralph and Pamela W. Krainik**
Location: **13 mi. from I-90**
No. of Rooms: **2**
No. of Private Baths: **2**
Double/pb: **$55**
Single/pb: **$45**

Open: **All year**
Breakfast: **Full**
Credit Cards: **MC, VISA**
Pets: **No**
Children: **Welcome**
Smoking: **No**
Social Drinking: **Permitted**

Seven Gables is a restored 1860 Gothic Revival home. It is on the National Register of Historic Places as one of the best examples of this architecture. The 17 rooms are furnished entirely in the Civil War period. Circus World Museum, Wisconsin Dells, and Devils Head and Cascade ski resorts are close by.

Abendruh Bed and Breakfast Swiss Style

7019 GEHIN ROAD, BELLEVILLE, WISCONSIN 53508

Tel: **(608) 424-3808**
Best Time to Call: **7 AM–9 PM**
Host(s): **Mathilde and Franz Jaggi**
Location: **18 mi. SW of Madison**
No. of Rooms: **2**
No. of Private Baths: **1**
Max. No. Sharing Bath: **4**
Double/pb: **$50**
Single/pb: **$40**
Double/sb: **$45**
Single/sb: **$35**
Open: **All year**
Reduced Rates: **Available**
Breakfast: **Full**
Pets: **No**
Children: **No**
Smoking: **No**
Social Drinking: **No**
Foreign Languages: **French, German, Swiss**

Abendruh is a stucco and stone ranch designed and built by the Jaggi family. The house is filled with homemade items ranging from the furniture to the afghans. Your host, Franz, is a master brick and stone mason. Mathilde is certified as a French Chef, and in hotel and restaurant management. Together they provide a Swiss atmosphere and the utmost in international service. The breakfast menu changes daily according to guest preference. Specialties include homemade muffins, croissants, and a variety of egg dishes. Guests are welcome to explore the spacious grounds or relax in front of a crackling fire at one of the four fireplaces. Abendruh is 30 minutes from downtown Madison and is close to such attractions as New Glarus, America's Little Switzerland, Mt. Horeb, Cave of the Mounds, skiing, and biking.

Ty-Bach B&B ✪

2817 HART COURT, BELOIT, WISCONSIN 54538 (mailing address)

Tel: **(608) 365-1039**
Best Time to Call: **8 AM–10 PM**
Host(s): **Janet and Kermit Bekkum**
Location: **70 mi. N of Wausau**
No. of Rooms: **2**
Max. No. Sharing Bath: **4**

Double/sb: **$40**
Single/sb: **$35**
Open: **All year**
Breakfast: **Full**
Pets: **Welcome**
Children: **No**
Smoking: **No**
Social Drinking: **Permitted**

In Welsh, *ty-bach* means "little house." Located on an Indian Reservation in Lac du Flambeau, this modern little house overlooks a small, picturesque Northwoods lake. Sit back on the deck and enjoy the beautiful fall colors, the call of the loons, and the tranquillity of this out-of-the-way spot. Choose from two comfortable rooms, each furnished with antique brass beds. Your hosts offer oven-fresh coffee cakes, homemade jams, and plenty of fresh coffee along with hearty main entrées.

Stagecoach Inn Bed & Breakfast ✪

W61 N520 WASHINGTON AVENUE, CEDARBURG, WISCONSIN 53012

Tel: **(414) 375-0208**
Host(s): **Brook and Liz Brown**
Location: **17 mi. N of Milwaukee**
No. of Rooms: **9**
No. of Private Baths: **9**
Double/pb: **$55**
Single/pb: **$40**
Suites: **$85**
Open: **All year**
Breakfast: **Continental**
Credit Cards: **AMEX, Discover, MC, VISA**
Pets: **No**
Children: **Welcome**
Smoking: **No**
Social Drinking: **Permitted**

The inn, listed on the National Register of Historic Places, is housed in a completely restored 1853 stone building in downtown, historic Cedarburg. The rooms, air-conditioned for summer comfort, combine antique charm with modern conveniences. Each bedroom is decorated with Laura Ashley linens and trimmed with wall stenciling. A bookstore, candy shop, and a pub that is a popular gathering place for guests, occupy the first floor. Specialty stores, antique shops, a winery, a woolen mill, and a variety of fine restaurants are within walking distance.

Willson House

320 SUPERIOR STREET, CHIPPEWA FALLS, WISCONSIN 54729

Tel: **(715) 723-0055**
Best Time to Call: **Morning; after 6 PM**
Host(s): **Thomas and Barbara Knowlton**
Location: **7 mi. N of Eau Claire**

No. of Rooms: **4**
No. of Private Baths: **1**
Max. No. Sharing Bath: **5**
Double/pb: **$55**
Single/pb: **$45**
Double/sb: **$32**
Single/sb: **$28**
Open: **All year**
Breakfast: **Continental**
Credit Cards: **MC, VISA**
Pets: **No**
Children: **Welcome, over 12**
Smoking: **No**
Social Drinking: **Permitted**
Airport/Station Pickup: **Yes**

Willson House is a spacious Victorian located four blocks from downtown. The house dates back to 1887 and has a distinctive turret and lovely wraparound porch. Inside, the rooms feature stained-glass windows, five fireplaces, and homey furnishings. Your hosts serve pastries from an excellent local bakery for breakfast. They have bicycles to lend for exploring the area, which is known as the gateway to Wisconsin's Indianhead Country. Later, join Thomas and Barbara for wine, cheese, and conversation by the fire.

The Allyn House ✪

511 E. WALWORTH, DELAVAN, WISCONSIN 53115

Tel: **(414) 728-9090**
Best Time to Call: **Weekends**
Host(s): **Joe Johnson and Ron Markwell**
Location: **2 mi. from Rte. 15**
No. of Rooms: **4**
Max. No. Sharing Bath: **4**
Double/sb: **$45–$55**
Single/sb: **$35–$45**
Open: **All year**
Breakfast: **Continental**
Pets: **No**
Children: **Welcome, over 12**
Smoking: **No**
Social Drinking: **Permitted**
Airport/Station Pickup: **Yes**
Foreign Languages: **French**

This 22-room Victorian mansion will transport you to an era of elegant marble fireplaces, gleaming chandeliers, stained glass, and parquet floors. The rooms are furnished with Oriental rugs, antiques, and period pieces, some of which are for sale. Enjoy wine and Wisconsin cheese in front of the parlor fireplace. The hearty breakfast includes home-baked breads, rolls, and preserves in the oak-paneled dining room. In the 19th century, Delavan was home to many circus shows and many of the past entertainers are buried in nearby Oakwood Cemetery. Only five minutes away is Delavan Lake, where you may go horseback riding, play golf, or enjoy many water sports. Some of the best skiing in the state is just ten miles from the house.

La Baye House ✪

803 OREGON, GREEN BAY, WISCONSIN 54303

Tel: **(414) 437-5081**
Best Time to Call: **Mornings; evenings**
Host(s): **Kate Helms and Gene Lundergan**
Location: **1 mi. from I-43**
No. of Rooms: **1**
Max. No. Sharing Bath: **3**
Double/sb: **$50**
Single/sb: **$45**
Open: **All year**
Breakfast: **Continental**
Pets: **No**
Children: **Welcome**
Smoking: **No**
Social Drinking: **Permitted**
Airport/Station Pickup: **Yes**
Foreign Languages: **French**

For a taste of Paris without leaving the states, visit this turn-of-the-century Victorian, located in the historic Old Fort Settlement. Your hosts have worked and lived in Europe and are eager to share experiences. Guest rooms are decorated with many antiques, plants, and special touches such as oak paneling and beveled-glass windows. Afternoon wine and cheese are served by the fire, or when the weather permits, outside on the wraparound porch. Kate and Gene hope you will have the time to take a walking tour that highlights the early French history of this area. La Baye House is near the Fox River and five blocks from the Neville Public Museum.

Jackson Street Inn ✪

210 SOUTH JACKSON STREET, JANESVILLE, WISCONSIN 53545

Tel: **(608) 754-7250**
Host(s): **Ilah and Bob Sessler**
Location: **1.9 mi. from I-90, Exit 11**
No. of Rooms: **4**
No. of Private Baths: **2**
Max. No. Sharing Bath: **4**
Double/pb: **$55**
Single/pb: **$45**
Double/sb: **$45**
Single/sb: **$30**
Suites: **$55**
Open: **All year**
Reduced Rates: **Available**
Breakfast: **Full**
Credit Cards: **MC, VISA**
Pets: **No**
Children: **Welcome**
Smoking: **Permitted**
Social Drinking: **Permitted**
Airport/Station Pickup: **Yes**

This turn-of-the-century home is finely appointed, with brass fixtures, leaded beveled-glass windows, and Italian fireplace mantels. The guest rooms are in soft colors with Colonial-period English wallpaper, fancy pillows, dust ruffles, and cozy quilts. The guest sitting room has books and a refrigerator with ice. Your hosts serve breakfast on the screened-in porch or in the fireplaced dining room, overlooking the grounds. Local attractions include the beach, Old Town restorations, hiking trails, golf, and museums.

Trillium ✪

ROUTE 2, BOX 121, LA FARGE, WISCONSIN 54639

Tel: **(608) 625-4492**
Best Time to Call: **Mornings; evenings**
Host(s): **Joe Swanson and Rosanne Boyett**
Location: **40 mi. SE of LaCrosse**
Guest Cottage: **$45–$55 for 2**
Open: **All year**
Breakfast: **Full**
Pets: **No**
Children: **Welcome (crib)**
Smoking: **Permitted**
Social Drinking: **Permitted**
Airport/Station Pickup: **Yes**

This private cottage is on a working farm located in the heart of a thriving Amish community. It is surrounded by an orchard, garden, and a lovely tree-shaded yard. There's a path beside the stream that winds through woods and fields. The cottage is light and airy, with comfortable wicker furniture. Rosanne and Joe stock your kitchen with homemade breads, jams, cheese, farm-fresh eggs, coffee, tea, and even goat's milk if you wish. Recreational activities abound in the area: art studios, craft shops, and Amish woodworking shops are fun to visit.

O. J.'s Victorian Village Guest House ✪

P.O. BOX 98, LAKE DELTON, WISCONSIN 53940

Tel: **(608) 254-6568**
Best Time to Call: **Evening**
Host(s): **O. J. and Lois Thompto**
Location: **50 mi. N of Madison; 1 mi. from I-94, Exit 92**
No. of Rooms: **4**
No. of Private Baths: **4**
Double/pb: **$40–$55**
Single/pb: **$30**
Guest Cottage: **$55 for 4**
Open: **All year**
Reduced Rates: **10%, Nov. 1–May 31**
Breakfast: **Continental**
Pets: **Sometimes**
Children: **Sometimes**
Smoking: **No**
Social Drinking: **Permitted**
Airport/Station Pickup: **Yes**

Located at Wisconsin Dells, midway between Chicago and the Twin Cities, this brand-new house was built especially for B&B. It is situated on a major waterway; there's access to an enchanting creek and lake for fishing, swimming, and boating. It's five miles from the International Crane Foundation where you can watch cranes from Africa, Asia, and America. O. J. and Lois look forward to greeting you, and will arrange for discounts in many restaurants and shops. The University of Wisconsin at Baraboo is nearby.

Hill House Bed & Breakfast ✪

2117 SHERIDAN DRIVE, MADISON, WISCONSIN 53704

Tel: **(608) 244-2224**
Host(s): **Anne and John Hobbins**
No. of Rooms: **4**
Max. No. Sharing Bath: **4**
Double/sb: **$50**
Single/sb: **$45**
Suite: **$65**
Open: **All year**
Reduced Rates: **After 1st night**
Breakfast: **Full**
Pets: **Sometimes**
Children: **Welcome, over 12**
Smoking: **Permitted**
Social Drinking: **Permitted**
Airport/Station Pickup: **Yes**

This hand-cut cedar shake and stucco home overlooks a large park and is half a block from Lake Mendota's eastern shore. It's 10 minutes from the Capitol and the university campus, and one minute from a lovely natural setting of prairie meadows, wetland lagoons, and oak woods. Tennis courts and an exercise course, swimming beach, and boat launch are available nearby for summer fun; cross-country skiing, skating, and a sledding hill will add to your winter enjoyment. Anne and John are long-time Madison residents who look forward to sharing their knowledge with you.

Bed & Breakfast of Milwaukee, Inc. ✪

320 EAST BUFFALO STREET, MILWAUKEE, WISCONSIN 53202

Tel: **(414) 271-2337**
Best Time to Call: **9 AM–6 PM**
Coordinator: **Barbara Gardner**
State/Regions Covered: **Milwaukee and southeastern Wisconsin**

Rates (Single/Double):

	Single	Double
Modest:	**$25–$30**	**$30–$35**
Average:	**$35–$40**	**$35–$50**
Luxury:	**$55–$70**	**$75–$90**

Credit Cards: **No**

A city of great ethnic diversity, Milwaukee is the site of many festivals and cultural celebrations. There is no shortage of fine restaurants; your host will be happy to make suitable recommendations to suit your taste and purse. There is a fine zoo, museums, and renowned cultural attractions. Major league sports and miles of Lake Michigan offer diversion and fun. The University of Wisconsin and Marquette University are convenient to many B&Bs.

Ogden House ✪

2237 NORTH LAKE DRIVE, MILWAUKEE, WISCONSIN 53202

Tel: **(414) 272-2740**
Host(s): **Mary Jane and John Moss**
No. of Rooms: **2**
No. of Private Baths: **2**
Double/pb: **$55**
Single/pb: **$55**

Suites: **$65**
Open: **All year**
Breakfast: **Continental**
Pets: **No**
Children: **Welcome**
Smoking: **Permitted**
Social Drinking: **Permitted**

The Ogden House is a white-brick Federal-style home listed on the National Register of Historic Places. It is located in the North Point-South district, a neighborhood shared by historic mansions overlooking Lake Michigan. Miss Ogden herself would feel at home here having homemade butterhorns for breakfast in the sun room overlooking the garden. You are sure to feel at home, too, whether you're relaxing on the sun deck, sitting by the fire, or retiring to your four-poster bed. Ogden House is convenient to theaters, the botanical garden, the Brewers' Stadium, the breweries, and many fine restaurants.

The Duke House ✪

618 MAIDEN STREET, HIGHWAY 151, MINERAL POINT, WISCONSIN 53565

Tel: **(608) 987-2821**
Host(s): **Tom and Darlene Duke**
Location: **48 mi. SW of Madison**
No. of Rooms: **3**
Max. No. Sharing Bath: **6**
Double/sb: **$40**
Single/sb: **$30**
Open: **All year**
Breakfast: **Full**
Pets: **Sometimes**
Children: **No**
Smoking: **No**
Social Drinking: **Permitted**

This Colonial corner house is furnished with antique beds and hardwood floors. Tea and pastries or wine and cheese are served in the afternoon. Breakfast features homemade breads and coffee cakes. Local possibilities include House-on-the-Rock, Frank Lloyd Wright's Taliesin, Dubuque Dog Racing Track, and the Artists Colony.

The Wilson House Inn ✪

110 DODGE STREET, HIGHWAY 151, MINERAL POINT, WISCONSIN 53565

Tel: **(608) 987-3600**
Best Time to Call: **Mornings**
Host(s): **Bev and Jim Harris**
Location: **50 mi. SW of Madison**
No. of Rooms: **4**
No. of Private Baths: **2**
Max. No. Sharing Bath: **4**
Double/pb: **$45**
Single/pb: **$40**
Double/sb: **$40**
Single/sb: **$35**
Open: **All year**

Breakfast: **Full**
Credit Cards: **MC, VISA**
Pets: **Welcome**
Children: **Welcome (crib)**
Smoking: **Permitted**
Social Drinking: **Permitted**

The Wilson House Inn is located in the heart of the beautiful uplands area. This red-brick Federal mansion was built in 1853 by Alexander Wilson, who became one of the state's first attorneys general. A veranda was added later, and it is where guests are welcomed with lemonade. The rooms are airy, comfortable, and furnished in antiques. Mineral Point was a mining and political center in the 1880s, and it is filled with many historic sites. Fishing, golfing, swimming, and skiing, and the House on the Rock are all nearby.

Rambling Hills Tree Farm ✪

8825 WILLEVER LANE, NEWTON, WISCONSIN 53063

Tel: **(414) 726-4388**
Best Time to Call: **Evenings**
Host(s): **Pete and Judie Stuntz**
Location: **18 mi. N of Sheboygan**
No. of Rooms: **4**
No. of Private Baths: **2**
Max. No. Sharing Bath: **5**
Double/pb: **$35**
Single/pb: **$25**
Double/sb: **$35**
Single/sb: **$25**
Open: **All year**
Breakfast: **Full**
Pets: **Sometimes**
Children: **Welcome**
Smoking: **Permitted**
Social Drinking: **Permitted**
Airport/Station Pickup: **Yes**

Enjoy the serenity of country living in a comfortable new home, set on 50 acres. The house overlooks the beautiful hills and a private lake. Guests are welcome to make themselves at home, enjoy a cup of coffee on the screened-in porch, or curl up with a book before the fire. Outside there are hiking trails, boats, swimming, and a play area for the children. When the snow falls, the trails are suitable for cross-country skiing and the lake freezes for skating. Your hosts recommend several nearby supper clubs, and can direct you to the attractions of Lake Michigan and the city of Manitowoc.

The Limberlost Inn ✪

HIGHWAY 17, #2483, PHELPS, WISCONSIN 54554

Tel: **(715) 545-2685**
Host(s): **Bill and Phoebe McElroy**
No. of Rooms: **3**
Max. No. Sharing Bath: **4**
Double/sb: **$42**
Single/sb: **$32**
Open: **All year**
Reduced Rates: **10%, weekly**
Breakfast: **Continental**
Other Meals: **Available**
Pets: **No**
Children: **Welcome, over 10**
Smoking: **No**
Social Drinking: **Permitted**
Airport/Station Pickup: **Yes**

The inn was designed and constructed by Bill and Phoebe McElroy. They picked a fine spot for their log home, just a minute from one of the best fishing lakes and largest national forests in the state. Each guest room is decorated with antiques, and the beds all have cozy down pillows and hand-stitched coverlets. Breakfast is served on the screened porch, by the fieldstone fireplace, in the dining room, or in your room. Stroll through the garden, rock on the porch swing, or take a picnic lunch and explore the streams and hiking trails. When you return, a Finnish sauna and a glass of wine or a mug of beer awaits.

Breese Waye Bed & Breakfast ✪

816 MacFARLANE ROAD, PORTAGE, WISCONSIN 53901

Tel: **(608) 742-5281**
Host(s): **Keith and Gretchen Sprecher**
Location: **35 mi. N of Madison**
No. of Rooms: **2**
No. of Private Baths: **1**
Max. No. Sharing Bath: **4**
Double/pb: **$55**
Single/pb: **$45**
Open: **All year**
Breakfast: **Full**
Pets: **Welcome**
Children: **Welcome (crib)**
Smoking: **Permitted**
Social Drinking: **Permitted**
Airport/Station Pickup: **Yes**

This century-old Victorian mansion has three original fireplaces. It is comfortably furnished in "early attic" with lovely wood, glass, and antique accents. Portage is a historic city, so don't miss the Old Indian Agency House and the famed Portage Canal. Bikes are available for leisurely touring. In the immediate area are Cascade Mountain and Devil's Head for downhill skiing; there's also cross-country skiing and snowmobile trails as well as seasonal recreation on nearby lakes. (One room is accessible to the handicapped.)

Country Aire ✪

ROUTE 2, BOX 175, PORTAGE, WISCONSIN 53901

Tel: **(608) 742-5716**
Best Time to Call: **Evenings**
Host(s): **Bob and Rita Reif**
Location: **37 mi. N of Madison**
No. of Rooms: **3**
No. of Private Baths: **2**
Double/pb: **$40**
Single/pb: **$30**
Suites: **$55**
Open: **All year**
Breakfast: **Continental**
Pets: **No**
Children: **Welcome (crib, high chair)**
Smoking: **No**
Social Drinking: **Permitted**

Forty acres of woods and meadows surround this spacious country home, built into a hillside overlooking the Wisconsin River. The house has open cathedral ceilings and a beautiful view from every room. Choose from comfortable bedrooms with queen-size or twin beds; the kids will enjoy the room with bunk beds. Guests are welcome to use the tennis court and go swimming and canoeing in the river. In the winter, great skating can be enjoyed on the pond, and the area is perfect for cross-country skiing. Bob and Rita are minutes away from the Wisconsin Dells, Baraboo, and Devil's Lake State Park. At the end of the day, relax with wine and cheese, and enjoy a beautiful sunset.

Inn at Cedar Crossing ✪

336 LOUISIANA STREET, STURGEON BAY, WISCONSIN 54235

Tel: **(414) 743-4200**
Host(s): **Terry Wulf**
Location: **45 mi. N of Green Bay**
No. of Rooms: **9**
No. of Private Baths: **9**
Double/pb: **$54–$84**
Single/pb: **$49–$79**
Suites: **$74–$84**
Open: **All year**
Reduced Rates: **Available**
Breakfast: **Continental**
Other Meals: **Lunch available**
Credit Cards: **MC, VISA**
Pets: **Sometimes**
Children: **Welcome, over 5**
Smoking: **Permitted**
Social Drinking: **Permitted**
Airport/Station Pickup: **Yes**

The Inn, located in Door County, was built in 1884 as a two-story hotel and enjoys a place on the National Register of Historic Places. The interior features the original 13-foot ceilings and a sweeping banistered staircase. The rooms are decorated in country antiques and primitives, with handwoven rag rugs, fine wallpapers, and beautiful knotty pine woodwork. Double whirlpools are featured in two. Enjoy a restful night in a canopy bed and wake up to homemade breakfast cakes, juice, and coffee. Moravian Sugar Cake, a traditional breakfast bread handed down by the area's original settlers, is the house specialty. Terry invites you for evening popcorn by the fire, or you may retire to the privacy of your room, where hand-dipped chocolates are left on the pillow. The inn is within walking distance of fine restaurants, shops, and the waterfront.

White Lace Inn—A Victorian Guest House

16 NORTH FIFTH AVENUE, STURGEON BAY, WISCONSIN 54235

Tel: **(414) 743-1105**
Host(s): **Dennis and Bonnie Statz**
Location: **150 mi. N of Milwaukee**
No. of Rooms: **15**
No. of Private Baths: **15**
Double/pb: **$65–$95**
Single/pb: **$48–$88**
Suites: **$125**
Open: **All year**
Reduced Rates: **Nov.–May**

Breakfast: **Continental**
Credit Cards: **MC, VISA**
Pets: **No**
Children: **Welcome, over 6**
Smoking: **Permitted**
Social Drinking: **Permitted**
Airport/Station Pickup: **Yes**

This elegant Victorian guest house is beautifully furnished with quality antiques, down pillows, cozy comforters, brass canopy beds, lace curtains, and fine rugs. Six rooms have fireplaces. Located in a residential area close to the bay, it is near shops and historic sites. Winter Lace features great cross-country skiing, snow sports, and hot chocolate in front of the fireplace. Summer offers boating, tennis, and swimming, with iced tea served on the front porch. One of the bedrooms of this inn is pictured on our back cover.

Rosenberry Inn ✪

511 FRANKLIN STREET, WAUSAU, WISCONSIN 54401

Tel: **(715) 842-5733**
Host(s): **Jerry and Pat Artz, son Doug**
Location: **2 mi. from Rtes. 51 & 29**
No. of Rooms: **8**
No. of Private Baths: **8**
Double/pb: **$45**
Single/pb: **$40**
Open: **All year**
Breakfast: **Continental**
Credit Cards: **MC, VISA**
Pets: **No**
Children: **Welcome (crib)**
Smoking: **Permitted**
Social Drinking: **Permitted**
Airport/Station Pickup: **Yes**

Located on a beautiful residential street of fine old mansions, the inn is listed on the National Register of Historic Places. Jerry and Pat have used a rich array of fine Victorian antiques in some rooms, and in others, a primitive country style. The effect is warm, colorful, and unpredictable. Four of the eight rooms have fireplaces, and all have a kitchenette. Rib Mountain ski area is five miles away, and the picturesque Dells of Eau Claire affords a scenic pleasure outing with its nature trails, rock climbing, fishing, picnicking, and canoeing. Antiques shops, boutiques, and restaurants are within walking distance.

WYOMING

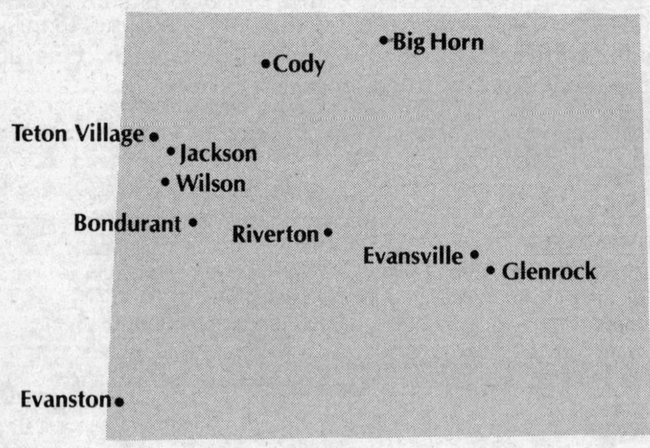

Bed and Breakfast Rocky Mountains—Wyoming ✪

P.O. BOX 804, COLORADO SPRINGS, COLORADO 80901

Tel: **(303) 630-3433**	Rates (Single/Double):
Best Time to Call: **May 15–Sept. 15, 9 AM–5 PM; winter, 1–5 PM**	Modest: **$28** **$35**
Coordinator: **Kate Peterson Winters**	Average: **$40** **$65**
States/Regions Covered: **Statewide**	Luxury: **$48** **$95**

Yellowstone National Park and the spectacular Tetons are within easy reach of Kate's B&Bs, and some hosts can expertly advise you on hiking trails, equipment rentals, and photography excursions. Home-baked goods are the staple for breakfast. You can drive an hour in any direction and see herds of antelope and deer at play. There is a $3 charge for Kate's directory.

Range Rider Reservations ✪

951 MISSOURI VALLEY ROAD, RIVERTON, WYOMING 82501

Tel: **(307) 856-3064; 332-9838**
Coordinators: **Judie Anglen and Pat McPhee**
States/Regions Covered: **Statewide**

Rates (Single/Double):

Modest:	**$25**	**$30**
Average:	**$35**	**$50**
Luxury:	**$50**	**$75**

Credit Cards: **MC, VISA**

Judy and Pat's roster focuses on ranch recreation and provides informal Western hospitality in a variety of settings. They will be happy to cater to your interests and match you to a compatible host. This is the place to bring your hunting gear, your fishing rod, and your camera.

Spahn's Big Horn Mountain Bed and Breakfast

P.O. BOX 579, BIG HORN, WYOMING 82833

Tel: **(307) 674-8150**
Host(s): **Ron and Bobbie Spahn**
Location: **15 mi. SW of Sheridan**
No. of Rooms: **3**
No. of Private Baths: **3**
Double/pb: **$45**
Single/pb: **$35**
Open: **All year**
Reduced Rates: **Families**
Breakfast: **Continental**
Pets: **Sometimes**
Children: **Welcome (baby-sitting)**
Smoking: **No**
Social Drinking: **Permitted**
Airport/Station Pickup: **Yes**

Ron and Bobbie Spahn and their two children built their home and this authentic log cabin. The house is set on 40 acres of whispering pines and borders the Big Horn Mountain forestland, which stretches for over a million acres. The main house has two guest bedrooms with private baths, a three-story living room, and an outside deck. The cabin is secluded from the main house and features a bedroom, large sleeping loft, bath, kitchen facilities, and front porch. You are invited to relax in the hot tub, sip a drink beside the wood stove, or take in the 100-mile view from an old porch rocker. Ron Spahn is a geologist and former Yellowstone Ranger. He can direct you to nearby fishing and hunting and can also tell you where to find the best walking and cross-country skiing trails.

Spring Creek Ranch ✪

P.O. BOX 1033, BONDURANT, WYOMING 82922

Tel: **(307) 733-3974**
Best Time to Call: **Evenings**
Host(s): **Steve and Dallas Robertson**
Location: **41 mi. S of Jackson Hole**

No. of Rooms: **4**
Max. No. Sharing Bath: **4**
Double/pb: **$35**
Single/pb: **$25**
Suites: **$60**
Open: **June 15–Sept. 1**
Reduced Rates: **10%, weekly**
Breakfast: **Full**
Other Meals: **Available**
Pets: **No**
Children: **Welcome**
Smoking: **Permitted**
Social Drinking: **Permitted**
Airport/Station Pickup: **Yes**

Steve and Dallas have a working horse ranch in what is primarily a cattle ranch community. The ranch is quiet, and is surrounded by the beautiful Bridger-Teton National Forest and the Hoback River. The trout fishing is excellent. Accommodations consist of a guest cottage and two cabins, all built of native log in keeping with the style of the Old West. Families are especially welcome, and special activities are often planned for them. The Robertsons take pride in offering good food and good riding. They will gladly direct you to nearby Jackson, where people come from all over to hunt, fish, mountain climb, and ski.

The Lockhart Inn ✪

109 WEST YELLOWSTONE AVENUE, CODY, WYOMING 82414

Tel: **(307) 587-6074**
Best Time to Call: **After noon**
Host(s): **Mark and Cindy Baldwin**
No. of Rooms: **6**
No. of Baths: **6**
Double/pb: **$35–$60**
Guest Cottage: **$75 (2–4)**
Months of operation: **All year**
Breakfast: **Full**
Other Meals: **Available**
Credit Cards: **MC, Discover, VISA**
Pets: **No**
Children: **Welcome**
Smoking: **Permitted**
Social Drinking: **Permitted**
Airport/Station Pickup: **Yes**

Once the home of Cody's famous turn-of-the-century novelist, Caroline Lockhart, Mark and Cindy's historic frontier home has been beautifully restored while retaining the flavor of the old West. The old-fashioned decor is combined with such modern amenities as cable TV, phones, and individually controlled heat. Breakfast is graciously served on fine china in the dining room. Located 50 miles from the eastern entrance to Yellowstone National Park, there's plenty to do in addition to relaxing on the front porch. The Trail Town Museum, Buffalo Bill Historical Center, and the Cody Nightly Rodeo are just some of the attractions.

Pine Gables Bed and Breakfast Inn ✪

1049 CENTER STREET, EVANSTON, WYOMING 82930

Tel: **(307) 789-2069**
Best Time to Call: **7 AM–10 PM**
Host(s): **Jessie and Arthur Monroe**
Location: **83 mi. E of Salt Lake City; 1/2 mi. from I-80**
No. of Rooms: **5**
No. of Private Baths: **5**
Double/pb: **$34.50**
Single/pb: **$28.50**
Suites: **$65**
Open: **All year**
Reduced Rates: **15%, seniors**
Breakfast: **Continental**
Credit Cards: **AMEX, DC, MC, VISA**
Pets: **Sometimes**
Children: **Welcome (crib)**
Smoking: **Permitted**
Social Drinking: **Permitted**
Airport/Station Pickup: **Yes**

This antiques-filled inn is a site on the tour of Evanston's historic district. Each bedroom is furnished with collectibles and decorated using different woods—oak, cherry, mahogany, and walnut. Your hosts operate an antiques shop on-premises. They prepare a breakfast of homemade breads and pastries. Hiking, fishing, skiing, and hunting are nearby.

Hotel Higgins ✪

416 WEST BIRCH, GLENROCK, WYOMING 82637

Tel: **(307) 436-9212**
Best Time to Call: **3 PM**
Host(s): **Jack and Margaret Doll**
Location: **18 mi. E of Casper**
No. of Rooms: **10**
No. of Private Baths: **7**
Max. No. Sharing Bath: **3**
Double/pb: **$46**
Single/sb: **$34**
Double/sb: **$36**
Single/sb: **$29**
Open: **All year**
Reduced Rates: **10% less, Oct.–Apr.**
Breakfast: **Full**
Other Meals: **Available**
Credit Cards: **AMEX, MC, VISA**
Pets: **No**
Children: **Welcome**
Smoking: **Permitted**
Social Drinking: **Permitted**
Airport/Station Pickup: **No**
Foreign Languages: **No**

This fascinating hotel was built in the early 1900s and is today a Designated Historic Site. Filled with many of the original furnishings, beveled-glass doors, and terrazzo tile floors, it currently boasts the award-winning Paisley Shawl restaurant. Located on the historic Oregon Trail, it is minutes from Deer Creek, the home station of the Pony Express. An exquisite variety of quiches or omelets, champagne and orange juice, fresh fruits, and breakfast meats are offered at breakfast. Complimentary hors d'oeuvres are served in the lounge from 4 to 6 PM.

Blue Spruce Lodge ✪

11125 HIGHWAY 789 (U.S. 26), ROUTE 1, BOX 413, RIVERTON, WYOMING 82501

Tel: **(307) 856-5784**
Best Time to Call: **Evenings**
Host(s): **Bonnie Manchak**
No. of Rooms: **2 suites**
No. of Private Baths: **2**
Suites: **$35**
Open: **May–Oct.**
Breakfast: **Full**
Pets: **Sometimes**
Children: **Welcome, over 12**
Smoking: **No**
Social Drinking: **Permitted**
Airport/Station Pickup: **Yes**

Does the idea of clear waters full of walleye and trout appeal to you? If the answer is yes, this B&B, open from May to October, is perfect for you. Surrounded by blue spruce trees, this country lodge sits on three acres with a breathtaking view of the Wind River Mountain Range. During the summer, the Shoshoni and Arapahoe Indians have a colorful powwow nearby, and Indians from all over the country gather to participate. Guests may stay in either of two suites with kitchen, living room, bedroom, bath, and private entrance. Bonnie's husband, an avid hunter and fisherman, will be happy to take you out to hunt, pan for gold, or fish.

Teton Tree House

P.O. BOX 550, WILSON, WYOMING 83014

Tel: **(307) 733-3233**
Host(s): **Chris and Denny Becker**
Location: **8 mi. W of Jackson**
No. of Rooms: **6**
No. of Private Baths: **6**
Double/pb: **$50–$75**
Single/pb: **$40–$65**
Open: **All year**
Reduced Rates: **5%, after 2 nights; 10%, weekly; 25%, families**
Breakfast: **Full**
Credit Cards: **MC, VISA**
Pets: **No**
Children: **Welcome**
Smoking: **No**
Social Drinking: **Permitted**

This is an impressive house of rustic open-beam construction, where guests are entertained in the large living room. The bedroom windows and decks overlook a private, forested mountainside. Wildflowers and berry bushes cover the land in summer; in winter it's a pristine, snowy wonderland. Breakfast is a low-cholesterol feast featuring huckleberry pancakes, zucchini breads, and other homemade treats. It is only eight miles from Grand Teton National Park, ski areas, a mountain climbing school, and a rodeo.

6

CANADA

ALBERTA

Note: All prices listed in this section are quoted in Canadian dollars.

Alberta Bed & Breakfast ✪

P.O. BOX 15477, M.P.O., VANCOUVER, BRITISH COLUMBIA V6B-5B2

Tel: **(604) 682-4610**
Best Time to Call: **8 AM–5 PM**
Coordinator: **June Brown**
States/Regions Covered:
Alberta—Banff, Calgary, Canmore, Hinton, Jasper; British Columbia—Ft. Steele, Kamloos, North Vancouver

Rates (Single/Double):

Modest:	**$25–$30**	**$35–$40**
Average:	**N/A**	**$45–$55**
Luxury:	**$50**	**$60–$95**

Credit Cards: **No**

Try a bit of Canadian western hospitality by choosing from June's variety of lovely homes in the majestic Rocky Mountains. Make a circle tour of Calgary, Banff, Lake Louise, the Columbia Icefields, Jasper, and Edmonton and stay in B&Bs all the way. Send one dollar for a descriptive list of the cordial hosts on her roster, make your selections, and June will do the rest.

BRITISH COLUMBIA

Note: All prices listed in this section are quoted in Canadian dollars.

Canada-West Accommodations ✪

1383 MILL STREET, NORTH VANCOUVER, BRITISH COLUMBIA V7K 1V5

Tel: **(604) 987-1088**
Best Time to Call: **Evenings; weekends**
Coordinator: **Ellison Massey**
States/Regions Covered: **Greater Vancouver**

Rates (Single/Double):

	Single	Double
Modest:	**N/A**	**$40**
Average:	**$35**	**$50**
Luxury:	**N/A**	**$75**

Credit Cards: **VISA**

This registry has over 30 homes, offering suites, or simple bed-and-breakfast rooms in a comfortable host home. Some are near the international airport, all are near fast, efficient public transportation. Canada-West features friendly host families eager to share their knowledge of cultural and scenic attractions.

"Meckies" Bed and Breakfast ✪

3234 SALTSPRING AVENUE, COQUITLAM, BRITISH COLUMBIA V3E 1E9

Tel: **(604) 464-4239**
Best Time to Call: **Tues., Fri.; evenings**
Host(s): **Gabrielle Butz**
Location: **20 mi. E of Vancouver**
No. of Rooms: **1**
No. of Private Baths: **1**
Double/pb: **$45**
Single/pb: **$40**
Open: **Apr.–Oct.**
Breakfast: **Full**
Pets: **No**
Children: **Welcome (crib)**
Smoking: **No**
Social Drinking: **Permitted**
Airport/Station Pickup: **Yes**
Foreign Languages: **German**

Located in a residential neighborhood with a park adjoining the backyard, this white house is accented with flower boxes and dark wood trim. The guest room has a queen-size bed, convertible sofa bed, and color TV. Breakfast features homemade jams, German buns, fresh fruit, breakfast meats, and eggs. You are welcome to relax in the living room or on the garden patio. Tennis, fishing, dining, and shopping are a short walk from the house. Swimming, hiking, Simon Fraser University, and all the attractions of Vancouver are within driving distance. If you're coming without a car, a camper is available for rent.

Grouse Mountain Bed and Breakfast ✪

900 CLEMENTS AVENUE, NORTH VANCOUVER, BRITISH COLUMBIA, CANADA V7R 2K7

Tel: **(604) 986-9630**
Best Time to Call: **Early morning; evening**
Host(s): **Lyne and John Armstrong**
Location: **10 min. from city core**
No. of Rooms: **2**
No. of Private Baths: **1**
Max. No. Sharing Bath: **2**
Double/pb: **$60**
Double/sb: **$60**
Open: **All year**
Reduced Rates: **10%, weekly**
Breakfast: **Full**
Pets: **Welcome**
Children: **Welcome (crib)**
Smoking: **No**
Social Drinking: **Permitted**
Airport/Station Pickup: **Yes**

Your hosts welcome you to a comfortable modern home in the foothills of Grouse Mountain. Enjoy views of Vancouver Island from two sun decks overlooking the secluded grounds, with close proximity to Stanley Park, the beaches, and downtown. Large rooms await you, one with cedar-paneled bath, the other with flagstone fireplace. Both have ample sitting room. Breakfast features something different each day, such as French toast or omelets with homemade jam. Skiing is only five minutes away. (Rates are quoted here in U.S. funds.)

West End Guest House ✪

1362 HARO STREET, VANCOUVER, BRITISH COLUMBIA V6E 1G2

Tel: **(604) 681-2889 or 5979**
Host(s): **Charles Weigum and George Christie**
No. of Rooms: **6**
Max. No. Sharing Bath: **3**
Double/sb: **$49–$59**
Single/sb: **$39–$49**
Open: **All year**
Breakfast: **Full**
Credit Cards: **AMEX, MC, VISA**
Pets: **No**
Children: **Welcome, over 6**
Smoking: **No**
Social Drinking: **Permitted**

The West End Guest House is only six blocks from the town center in one direction, and six blocks from Stanley Park in the other. Stanley Park is a 1,000-acre nature preserve with an aquarium, a zoo, a seawall promenade, beaches, a bird sanctuary, rose gardens, and miles and miles of foot and bicycle paths. Built in 1906 by the Edwards family, proprietors of the first photography business in Vancouver, the West End Guest House features some of the family's first photographs.

When the house was renovated in 1985, the goal was to "create a bright, cheerful, and, above all, comfortable atmosphere without losing a sense of the home's Victorian origins." Charles is actively interested in heritage preservation, travel, and bicycling; George shares his love of travel and, with just the slightest encouragement, will sit down to his lovely Weinbach piano to play for you.

Sunnymeade House Inn

1002 FENN AVENUE, VICTORIA, BRITISH COLUMBIA V8Y 1P3

Tel: **(604) 658-1414**
Best Time to Call: **Mid-morning; evenings**
Host(s): **Jack and Nancy Thompson**
Location: **1½ mi. from Rte. 17**
No. of Rooms: **4**
Max. No. Sharing Bath: **4**
Double/sb: **$50–$53**
Single/sb: **$38**
Suites: **$75 for 3**

Open: **All year**
Reduced Rates: **25%, Nov. 15–Apr. 15**
Breakfast: **Full**
Other Meals: **Available**
Pets: **No**
Children: **Welcome (crib)**
Smoking: **No**
Social Drinking: **Permitted**
Airport/Station Pickup: **Yes**

Take the scenic route into Victoria and discover this inn on a winding country road by the sea. The Thompsons designed, built, decorated, and custom furnished the English-style house. Nancy, a former professional cook, will prepare your choice of breakfast from a choice of seven. You'll be steps away from the beach and within walking distance of tennis courts. All bedrooms have vanity sinks.

V.I.P. Bed and Breakfast ✪

1786 TEAKWOOD ROAD, VICTORIA, BRITISH COLUMBIA, V8N 1E2

Tel: **(604) 477-5604**
Best Time to Call: **7 AM–10 PM**
Coordinator: **Helen J. Ridley**
State/Regions Covered: **Victoria, Sidney**

Rates (Single/Double):
Average: **$30** **$40**
Luxury: **$40** **$60**
Credit Cards: **No**

You have a wide choice of B&Bs on Helen's roster, including traditional older homes close to the city center, a contemporary home near the University of Victoria, a country home near Butchart's Gardens, or waterfront homes near the ferry terminals. Family and weekly rates are often available, and some homes welcome children and your well-behaved pet. Beacon Hill Park, Butchart's Gardens, Craigdarroch Castle, Maritime Museum, and Provincial Museum are some of the major attractions.

Beachside Bed and Breakfast ✪

4208 EVERGREEN AVENUE, WEST VANCOUVER, BRITISH COLUMBIA V7V 1H1

Tel: **(604) 922-7773**
Host(s): **Gordon and Joan Gibbs**
Location: **4 mi. W of Vancouver**
No. of Rooms: **3**
No. of Private Baths: **2**
Max. No. Sharing Bath: **3**
Double/pb: **$75**
Double/sb: **$65**
Single/sb: **$50**

Open: **All year**
Breakfast: **Full**
Credit Cards: **AMEX, MC, VISA**
Pets: **Sometimes**
Children: **Welcome**
Smoking: **No**
Social Drinking: **Permitted**
Airport/Station Pickup: **Yes**
Foreign Languages: **French**

Guests are welcomed to this beautiful waterfront home with a fruit basket and fresh flowers. The house is a Spanish-style structure, with stained-glass windows, located at the end of a quiet cul-de-sac. Its southern exposure affords a panoramic view of Vancouver. A sandy beach is just steps from the door. You can watch the waves from the patio or spend the afternoon fishing or sailing. The hearty breakfast features homemade muffins, French toast, and Canadian maple syrup. Gordon and Joan are knowledgeable about local history, and can gladly direct you to Stanley Park, the site of Expo 86, hiking, skiing, and much more.

NEW BRUNSWICK

Note: All prices listed in this section are quoted in Canadian dollars.

Oakley House ✪

LOWER JEMSEG, NEW BRUNSWICK, CANADA E0E 1S0

Tel: **(506) 488-3113**
Host(s): **Max and Willi Evans Wolfe**
Location: **33 mi. E of Fredericton; 3 mi. from Trans-Can. Hwy.**
No. of Rooms: **3**
Max. No. Sharing Bath: **6**
Double/sb: **$38–$40**
Single/sb: **$24**
Open: **All year**
Breakfast: **Full**
Other Meals: **Available**
Credit Cards: **VISA**
Pets: **Sometimes**
Children: **Sometimes**
Smoking: **No**
Social Drinking: **Permitted**
Airport/Station Pickup: **Yes**
Foreign Languages: **French, Russian, Spanish**

Max and Willi's home is set right in the heart of strawberry country; their 20-acre property borders the Jemseg River, the waterway that connects Saint John and Grand Lake. The 150-year-old house is surrounded by lilacs, acacias, and old apple trees. Whatever the season, there's plenty to do nearby—cycling, swimming, and sailing in summer; canoeing in fall; and cross-country skiing and ice skating in winter. Bird-watching is excellent, especially in migratory season—loons, osprey, and eagles nest nearby. Thanks to a Jersey cow and a large organic garden, your hosts produce most of their own food. Breakfasts are bountiful—buckwheat pancakes with maple syrup, hot muffins, eggs and sausages, and more. Gagetown—just a short ferry ride away—is a favorite, with its craft shops, restaurants, marina, and historic sites.

NOVA SCOTIA

Note: All prices listed in this section are quoted in Canadian dollars.

Bute Arran ✪

P.O. BOX 75, BADDECK, NOVA SCOTIA, CANADA B0E 1B0

Tel: **(902) 295-2786**
Best Time to Call: **After 6 PM**
Host(s): **Donald and Margot MacAulay**
Location: **2 mi. from Hwy. 105**
No. of Rooms: **3**
No. of Private Baths: **1**
Max. No. Sharing Bath: **6**
Double/pb: **$37**
Single/pb: **$37**
Double/sb: **$32**
Single/sb: **$27**
Open: **June 15–Oct. 1**
Breakfast: **Full**
Credit Cards: **AMEX, DC, MC, VISA**
Pets: **Sometimes**
Children: **Welcome (crib)**
Smoking: **Permitted**
Social Drinking: **Permitted**

This rambling Cape Cod cottage is on the shore of Bras d'Or Lake, convenient to the famed Cabot Trail, a scenic 185-mile drive around northern Cape Breton. It is one mile east of the Alexander Graham Bell National Historic Park. It is furnished in a comfortable blend of antique and modern pieces, with lots of books and games for guests of all ages. Breakfast features hearty oatcakes and scones. The MacAulays serve tea in the evening.

Confederation Farm ✪

RR3, PARRSBORO, DILIGENT RIVER, NOVA SCOTIA, CANADA B0M 1S0

Tel: **(902) 254-3057**
Best Time to Call: **Evenings**
Host(s): **Bob and Julia Salter**
Location: **45 mi. S of Amherst**
No. of Rooms: **4**
No. of Baths: **2**
Max. No. Sharing Bath: **4**
Double/sb: **$30**
Single/sb: **$24**
Open: **May 15–Oct. 31**
Reduced Rates: **No**
Breakfast: **Full**
Pets: **Sometimes**
Children: **Welcome (crib)**
Smoking: **Permitted**
Social Drinking: **Permitted**
Airport/Station Pickup: **Yes**

This peaceful berry and fruit farm overlooks Cape Split on the Bay of Fundy. Breakfast often features blueberry pancakes, bacon and eggs, homemade breads, jams, and sausages. Prices are modest and portions are hefty. Be sure to ask to see Bob's Horse and Buggy Days museum containing a collection of family memorabilia from way back when. The highest tides in the world may be viewed here, and it is a rock buff's paradise. The Salters have three housekeeping cottages as well as a picnic park on their property.

ONTARIO

Note: All prices listed in this section are quoted in Canadian dollars.

Bed & Breakfast—Kingston ✪

10 WESTVIEW ROAD, KINGSTON, ONTARIO, CANADA K7M 2C3

Tel: **(613) 542-0214**
Coordinator: **Ruth MacLachlan**
Best Time to Call: **9 AM–6 PM Mon.–Sat.**
States/Regions Covered: **Ontario—Bath, Gananoque, Kingston, Morrisburg, Newboro, Seeley's Bay, Sydenham, Verona, Westport**

Rates (Single/Double):

	Single	Double
Average:	**$30**	**$40–$45**
Luxury:	**$35**	**$45–$60**

Credit Cards: **No**

Situated at the eastern end of Lake Ontario, at the head of the St. Lawrence River, Kingston has much to offer besides gorgeous scenery. There's Old Fort Henry, boat cruises through the Thousand Islands, historic sites, museums, and sports activities of every sort; the Rideau Nature Trail starts here and heads northeast toward Ottawa. Send $1 for the detailed directory.

The Webster House ✪

37 JAMES STREET E., BROCKVILLE, ONTARIO K6V 1K3

Tel: **(613) 345-4707**
Host(s): **Doli and Peter Darrach**
Location: **68 mi. S of Ottawa**
No. of Rooms: **3**
Max. No. Sharing Bath: **3**
Double/sb: **$50**
Single/sb: **$40**
Open: **All year**

Breakfast: **Full**
Pets: **No**
Children: **No**
Smoking: **No**
Social Drinking: **Permitted**
Airport/Station Pickup: **Yes**
Foreign Languages: **Spanish**

The Webster House has been painstakingly preserved—the formal parlor has ten-foot windows and an original ceiling medallion; the less-formal second parlor is the perfect spot to work on the jigsaw puzzles or read any of the books and magazines available to guests. The outdoors is as beautiful as the indoors, with its terraced garden shaded by an ancient tree, and a Victorian porch where guests may "take tea" surrounded by wicker and chintz. Convenient to a parklike waterfront, excellent shopping, and many fine restaurants, the Webster House is a perfect stopping point for anyone visiting the Thousand Islands.

Knechtel's Guest House ✪

7 PARK AVENUE WEST, ELMIRA, ONTARIO N3B 1K9

Tel: **(519) 669-2066**
Best Time to Call: **Evenings**
Host(s): **Marguarite and Ross Knechtel**
Location: **10 mi. NE of Waterloo; ½ mi. from Hwy. 86, Elmira Exit**
No. of Rooms: **3**
Max. No. Sharing Bath: **3**
Double/sb: **$40**
Single/sb: **$35**
Open: **All year**
Breakfast: **Full**
Pets: **Sometimes**
Children: **Welcome (crib)**
Smoking: **Permitted**
Social Drinking: **Permitted**
Foreign Languages: **French**

You may sit on the porch and watch the Mennonites' horse-drawn buggies pass by on the tree-lined street. Guests at this 75-year-old Queen Anne home, with its stained-glass windows and spiral staircase, enjoy strolling in the garden or through town and visiting the horse-racing track at the end of the street. Ross and Marguarite and their teenage son and daughter enjoy having guests. Tea and cookies are served in the evening.

Cedarlane Farm B&B ✪

R.R. 2, IROQUOIS, ONTARIO, CANADA K0E 1K0

Tel: **(613) 652-4267**
Best Time to Call: **Before 9 AM; after 7 PM**
Host(s): **Don and Patsy Henry**
Location: **55 mi. S of Ottawa**
No. of Rooms: **3**
Max. No. Sharing Bath: **6**
Double/sb: **$30**
Single/sb: **$20**
Open: **All year**
Breakfast: **Full**
Other Meals: **Available**

Pets: **No**
Children: **Welcome**
Smoking: **No**
Social Drinking: **Permitted**
Airport/Station Pickup: **Yes**

Relax in a lovely 150-year-old stone farmhouse set on 15 acres, off a quiet country road. The house is furnished with antiques and handmade quilts, with original pine floors throughout. Guests are welcome to read in the living room beside the fieldstone fireplace, or to walk around the farm and visit the ducks, geese, and chickens. The kids will enjoy the swing set, wading pool, and toys that belong to the Henrys' three children. Breakfast specialties include pancakes and sausage served with local maple syrup, ham and eggs, muffins, rolls, and homemade preserves. Snacks are offered in the evening, and additional meals and picnic lunches can be arranged. Your hosts can direct you to local beaches, the pool, museums, and boat tours of the Thousand Islands. They will also be glad to baby-sit for the kids if you go out on the town.

Rose's B&B ✪

526 DUFFERIN AVENUE, LONDON, ONTARIO N6B 2A2

Tel: **(519) 433-9978**
Host(s): **Betty and Doug Rose**
Location: **1 mi. from 401**
No. of Rooms: **3**
No. of Private Baths: **1**
Max. No. Sharing Bath: **4**
Double/pb: **$35**
Double/sb: **$25**
Open: **All year**
Reduced Rates: **Weekly**
Breakfast: **Full**
Pets: **No**
Children: **Welcome, over 8**
Smoking: **No**
Social Drinking: **Permitted**

Situated midway between Detroit, Michigan, and Toronto, Ontario, this fully renovated 120-year-old Victorian home is located in the exclusive downtown area. It is less than an hour to the famed Stratford Festival Theatre, where Shakespeare reigns supreme. Local diversions include a children's museum, an Indian museum, and parks with every variety of recreational activity.

Hiebert's Guest House ✪

BOX 1371, 275 JOHN STREET, NIAGARA-ON-THE-LAKE, ONTARIO, CANADA L0S 1J0

Tel: **(416) 468-3687**
Host(s): **Otto and Marlene Hiebert**
Location: **10 mi. N of Niagara Falls**
No. of Rooms: **3**
Max. No. Sharing Bath: **3**
Double/sb: **$50**

Single/sb: **$45**
Open: **All year**
Reduced Rates: **$5 less, Jan.–Apr.**
Breakfast: **Full**
Pets: **No**
Children: **Welcome**
Smoking: **No**
Social Drinking: **No**

We wish we could share with you the many letters of reference attesting to "the cleanliness," "the warm Mennonite hospitality," "the delicious food," "the friendliness of the Hieberts." Their home is 10 miles from Niagara Falls, Ontario, and the U.S. border. The Shaw Festival Theatre and all of the area's points of interest are within walking distance. The breakfast bran muffins are a special treat.

Ottawa Area Bed & Breakfast ✪

P.O. BOX 4848, STATION E, OTTAWA, ONTARIO, CANADA K1S 5J1

Tel: **(613) 563-0161**
Best Time to Call: **10 AM–10 PM**
Coordinators: **Robert Rivoire and R. G. Simmens**
States/Regions Covered: **Ontario—Kanata, Nepean, Gloucester, Ottawa; Quebec—Hull**
Rates (Single/Double):
Average: **$30** **$40**
Credit Cards: **No**

If you are seeking an interesting but inexpensive holiday, then Canada's capital, Ottawa, is the place for you. The city is packed with free activities including museums, the House of Parliament, art galleries, and historic sites. You can skate on the Rideau Canal or bike on miles of parkways and trails.

Levere's Guest Home ✪

611 RUBY STREET, BOX 1233, PORT ELGIN, ONTARIO N0H 2C0

Tel: **(519) 832-5520**
Host(s): **Terry and Janet Levere**
Location: **100 mi. N of Toronto**
No. of Rooms: **3**
No. of Private Baths: **1**
Max. No. Sharing Bath: **6**
Double/pb: **$35**
Double/sb: **$30**
Single/sb: **$25**
Guest Cottage: **$350 (week); sleeps 6**
Open: **All year**
Breakfast: **Full**
Pets: **No**
Children: **Welcome, over 10**
Smoking: **No**
Social Drinking: **Permitted**
Airport/Station Pickup: **Yes**

Experience warm hospitality in this modern home located in a quiet residential area just five minutes from Lake Huron. The guest suite features a private entrance to two large double bedrooms and a single bedroom. Adjacent is a family room with a stereo and cable television, a game room with a pool table, and guest refrigerator. A hearty breakfast is served with homemade goodies. Complimentary tea and muffins are graciously served in the evening.

Toronto Bed & Breakfast ✪

P.O. BOX 74, STATION M, TORONTO, ONTARIO, CANADA M6S 4T2

Tel: **(416) 233-3887 or 233-4041**
Best Time to Call: **Evenings; weekends**
Coordinator: **Randy Lee**
States/Regions Covered: **Toronto**

Rates (Single/Double):

Modest:	**$35**	**$45**
Average:	**$40**	**$50**
Luxury:	**$45**	**$55**

Credit Cards: **No**
Minimum Stay: **2 nights**

Toronto, located on Lake Ontario, is a sophisticated city, but the hosts in Randy's network of homes are warm, friendly, and helpful. Accommodations vary from a bedroom in a British Colonial to a terraced penthouse suite in a luxury condo; full breakfast is included. All homes are convenient to public transportation, so that you can easily visit the CN Tower, the Ontario Science Centre, Fort York, and the exciting Harbourfront with its craft galleries and ethnic restaurants. Send $3 for the descriptive directory and make your reservations directly with the host of your choice.

PRINCE EDWARD ISLAND

Note: All prices listed in this section are quoted in Canadian dollars.

Woodington's Country Inn ✪

RR 2, KENSINGTON, PRINCE EDWARD ISLAND, C0B 1M0 CANADA

Tel: **(902) 836-5518**
Best Time to Call: **Noon**
Host(s): **Marion and Claude "Woody" Woodington**
No. of Rooms: **5**
Max. No. Sharing Bath: **5**
Double/sb: **$34**
Single/sb: **$17**

Open: **All year**
Reduced Rates: **10%, after Aug. 25**
Breakfast: **Full**
Other Meals: **Available**
Pets: **Welcome**
Children: **Welcome**
Smoking: **Permitted**
Social Drinking: **Permitted**

Relax on the spacious lawns surrounding this immaculate Victorian farmhouse or stroll to the private beach. You'll feel at home immediately. Marion is a fabulous cook and her table reflects all that is fresh and wholesome. Woody hand-carves the most realistic duck decoys you've ever seen. Marion's spare time is spent making gorgeous quilts. A wood carving or quilt would make a memorable souvenir to take home.

Smallman's Bed and Breakfast

KNUTSFORD, O'LEARY, RR 1, PRINCE EDWARD ISLAND, CANADA C0B 1V0

Tel: **(902) 859-3469**
Host(s): **Arnold and Eileen Smallman**
Location: **7½ mi. from Rte. 2**
No. of Rooms: **4**
Max. No. Sharing Bath: **6**
Double/sb: **$25**
Single/sb: **$15**
Suites: **$30**
Open: **All year**
Breakfast: **Full**
Pets: **Sometimes**
Children: **Welcome**
Smoking: **Permitted**
Social Drinking: **No**
Airport/Station Pickup: **Yes**

This comfortable split-level home is just 10 minutes from the beach. The kids will enjoy the backyard sandbox as well as a private track where the family racehorses train. Your hostess is a dedicated baker, always ready with coffee and a homemade snack. Breakfast specialties include homemade biscuits and cereals. Many local restaurants serve fresh lobster, clams, and oysters in season. Your hosts can direct you to the better buys in town, as well as the Gulf of St. Lawrence, golf courses, mills, and museums.

Dyment Bed & Breakfast

RR 3, WILMOT VALLEY, SUMMERSIDE, PRINCE EDWARD ISLAND, CANADA C1N 4J9

Tel: **(902) 436-9893**
Best Time to Call: **Before noon; after 6 PM**
Host(s): **Earle and Wanda Dyment**
Location: **32 mi. W of Charlottetown**
No. of Rooms: **3**
Max. No. Sharing Bath: **6**
Double/sb: **$26**
Single/sb: **$20**
Open: **May 20–Oct. 31**
Breakfast: **Full**
Pets: **Sometimes**
Children: **Welcome (crib)**
Smoking: **No**
Social Drinking: **Permitted**

This spanking-clean house is set in a picturesque farming area overlooking the Wilmot River. Wanda delights in having people stay, and allows you to use her kitchen for light snacks. There is much to do and see, including swimming, golf, deep-sea fishing, and going to the racetrack.

QUEBEC

Note: All prices listed in this section are quoted in Canadian dollars.

Montreal Bed & Breakfast ✪

4912 VICTORIA, MONTREAL, QUEBEC, CANADA H3W 2N1

Tel: **(514) 738-9410 or 738-3859**
Coordinator: **Marian Kahn**
States/Regions Covered: **Montreal, Ste. Adele (Laurentian Mountains), Sutton**

Rates (Single/Double):

	Single	Double
Modest:	**$30**	**$40**
Average:	**$35–$40**	**$45–$55**
Luxury:	**$45**	**$60–$100**

Credit Cards: **MC, VISA (deposits only)**

Marian has a list of lovely homes in Montreal and surrounding countryside. Many hosts are French Canadian, and the full breakfasts included in the rate often reflect a gourmet's touch. Visit Old Montreal and The Harbor for a glimpse of history, the Museum of Fine Arts, Place Des Arts for a touch of culture. McGill University, Mount Royal Park, St. Helen's Island, and the Laurentian Mountains are all worth a visit too. There are marvelous restaurants, wonderful shops, and the people are warm and friendly.

Montrealers at Home, A Downtown B&B Network ✪

3458 LAVAL AVE., MONTREAL, QUEBEC, CANADA H2X 3C8

Tel: **(514) 289-9749**
Best Time to Call: **9 AM–9 PM**
Coordinator: **Robert Finkelstein**
State/Regions Covered: **Montreal, Westmount, Outremont, Quebec City**

Rates (Single/Double):

	Single	Double
Modest:	**$25**	**$35**
Average:	**$30**	**$45–$50**
Luxury:	**$35–$40**	**$55–$65**

Credit Cards: **MC, VISA**

Bob specializes in downtown accommodations with hosts ready to introduce you to good shopping, diverse restaurants, and places of special interest with an experienced eye on good value. After a day of hectic activity that might include a *calèche* ride through the cobbled streets of the Old Quarter, or a visit to the futuristic high-fashion urban area, and samples of excellent cuisine from all over the world, your hosts look forward to having you return to relax in their homes.

7

PUERTO RICO

Larsen's Bed and Breakfast ✪

GUERRERO NOBLE #3, PUNTAS LAS MARIAS, SAN JUAN, PUERTO RICO 00913

Tel: **(809) 727-0033**
Hosts: **Swen and Geri Larsen**
No. of Rooms: **3**
No. of Private Baths: **1**
Max. No. Sharing Bath: **4**
Double/pb: **$45**
Double/sb: **$35–$40**
Open: **All year**
Reduced Rates: **Available**
Breakfast: **Continental**
Pets: **No**
Children: **Welcome, over 12**
Smoking: **Permitted**
Social Drinking: **Permitted**
Foreign Languages: **Spanish**

Larsen's is located in a quiet residential neighborhood on one of San Juan's best beaches. Handmade red bricks frame the arches of this Spanish-style house, which is surrounded by flowering shrubs and fruit trees. The rooms have fresh flowers and are furnished with many antiques from years of living and traveling in Europe. Relax with a cocktail on a large shaded patio, which runs the length of the house. Swimming and sunning are just steps away, and beach towels are provided. Shops and a park with a jogging track are within walking distance, and your hosts will gladly provide sightseeing information on this beautiful Caribbean island.

Appendix: *UNITED STATES AND CANADIAN TOURIST OFFICES*

Listed here are the addresses and telephone numbers for the tourist offices of every U.S. state and Canadian province. When you write or call one of these offices, be sure to request a map of the state and a calendar of events. If you will be visiting a particular city or region, or if you have any special interests, be sure to specify them as well.

State Tourist Office

Alabama Bureau of Tourism
and Travel
532 South Perry Street
Montgomery, Alabama 36104
(205) 261-4169 or (800) 252-2262
(out of state) or (800) 392-8096
(within Alabama)

Alaska Division of Tourism
P.O. Box E
Juneau, Alaska 99811
(907) 465-2010

Arizona Office of Tourism
1480 East Bethany Home Road
Suite 150
Phoenix, Arizona 85014
(602) 255-3618

Arkansas Department of Parks
and Tourism
1 Capitol Mall
Little Rock, Arkansas 72201
(501) 371-7777 or (800) 643-8383
(out of state) or (800) 482-8999
(within Arkansas)

California Office of Tourism
1121 L Street, Suite 103
Sacramento, California 95814
(916) 322-1396

Colorado Office of Tourism
625 Broadway
Suite 1700
Denver, Colorado 80202
(303) 592-5410 or (800) 255-5550

Connecticut Department of Economic
Development-Vacations
210 Washington Street
Hartford, Connecticut 06106
(203) 566-3948 or (800) 243-1685
(out of state) or (800) 842-7492
(within Connecticut)

Delaware State Travel Service
99 Kings Highway, P.O. Box 1401
Dover, Delaware 19903
(302) 736-4271 or (800) 441-8846
(out of state) or (800) 282-8667
(in Delaware)

Washington, D.C. Convention
and Visitors' Bureau
Suite 250
1575 I Street, N.W.
Washington, D.C. 20005
(202) 789-7000

Florida Division of Tourism
101 East Gaines Street
Tallahassee, Florida 32399-2000
(904) 487-1462

Georgia For Information
Tourist Division
Department of Industry and Trade
Box 1776
Atlanta, Georgia 30301
(404) 656-3590

Hawaii Visitors Bureau
2270 Kalakaua Avenue, Suite 801
Honolulu, Hawaii 96815
(808) 923-1811
or
New York Office
441 Lexington Avenue, Room 1407
New York, N.Y. 10017
(212) 986-9203

Idaho Department of Commerce
Capitol Building, Room 108
Boise, Idaho 83720
(208) 334-2470 or (800) 635-7820

Illinois Office of Tourism
310 South Michigan Avenue
Suite 108
Chicago, Illinois 60604
(312) 793-2094 or (800) 252-8987 (within Illinois) or (800) 637-8560 (neighboring states)

Indiana Tourism Development Division
1 North Capitol, Suite 700
Indianapolis, Indiana 46204-2288
(317) 232-8860 or (800) 2 WONDER

Iowa Development Commission
Visitors Group
200 East Grand
Des Moines, Iowa 50309-2882
(515) 281-3679

Kansas Department of Economic Development—Travel and Tourism Division
400 West 8th Street
Fifth Floor
Topeka, Kansas 66603
(913) 296-2009

Kentucky Department of Travel Development
22 Floor Capitol Plaza Tower
Frankfort, Kentucky 40601
(502) 564-4930 or (800) 225-8747 (out of state)

Louisiana Office of Tourism
Inquiry Department
P.O. Box 94291
Baton Rouge, Louisiana 70804-9291
(504) 925-3860 or (800) 231-4730 (out of state)

Maine Publicity Bureau
97 Winthrop St.
Hallowell, Maine 04347
(207) 289-2423

Maryland Office of Tourist Development
45 Calvert Street
Annapolis, Maryland 21401
(301) 269-3517

Massachusetts Division of Tourism
Department of Commerce and Development
100 Cambridge Street—13th Floor
Boston, Massachusetts 02202
(617) 727-3201 or (800) 343-9072 (out of state)

Michigan Travel Bureau
Department of Commerce
P.O. Box 30226
Lansing, Michigan 48909
(517) 373-1195 or (800) 543-2 YES

Minnesota Tourist Information Center
375 Jackson Street
Farm Credit Service Building
St. Paul, Minnesota 55101
(612) 296-5029 or (800) 328-1461 (out of state) or (800) 652-9747 (in Minnesota)

Mississippi Division of Tourism
P.O. Box 22825
Jackson, Mississippi 39205
(601) 359-3414 or (800) 647-2290 (out of state) or (800) 962-2346 (within Mississippi)

Missouri Division of Tourism
P.O. Box 1055
Jefferson City, Missouri 65102
(314) 751-4133

Montana Promotion Division
1424 9th Avenue
Helena, Montana 59620
(406) 444-2654 or (800) 548-3390

Nebraska Division of Travel and Tourism
P.O. Box 94666
Lincoln, Nebraska 68509
(402) 471-3796 or (800) 228-4307

Nevada Commission on Tourism
Capitol Complex
Carson City, Nevada 89710
(702) 885-4322

New Hampshire Office of Vacation Travel
P.O. Box 856
Concord, New Hampshire 03301
(603) 271-2343 or (800) 258-3608 (in the Northeast outside of New Hampshire)

New Jersey Division of Travel and Tourism
C.N. 826
Trenton, New Jersey 08625
(609) 292-2470

New Mexico Travel Division
Joseph Montoya Building
1100 St. Francis Drive
Santa Fe, New Mexico 87503
(505) 827-0291 or (800) 545-2040

New York State Division of Tourism
1 Commerce Plaza
Albany, New York 12245
(518) 474-4116 or (800) 225-5697 (in the Northeast except Maine)

North Carolina Travel and Tourism Division
430 North Salisbury Street
Raleigh, North Carolina 27611
(919) 733-4171 or (800) VISIT N.C. (out of state)

North Dakota Tourism Promotion
State Capitol Grounds
Bismarck, North Dakota 58505
(701) 224-2525 or (800) 472-2100 (within North Dakota) or (800) 437-2077 (out of state)

Ohio Office of Tourism
P.O. Box 1001
Columbus, Ohio 43266–0101
(614) 466-8844 or (800) BUCKEYE (out of state)

Oklahoma Division of Tourism
215 N.E. 28th Street
Oklahoma City, Oklahoma 73105
(405) 521-2409 or (800) 652-6552 (in neighboring states)

Oregon Economic Development Tourism Division
595 Cottage Street, N.E.
Salem, Oregon 97310
(503) 378-3451 or (800) 547-7842 (out of state) or (800) 233-3306 (within Oregon)

Pennsylvania Bureau of Travel Development
Department of Commerce
416 Forum Building
Harrisburg, Pennsylvania 17120
(717) 787-5453 or (800) 847-4872

Rhode Island Department of Economic Development
Tourism and Promotion Division
7 Jackson Walkway
Providence, Rhode Island 02903
(401) 277-2601 or (800) 556-2484 (East Coast from Maine to Virginia, also West Virginia and Ohio)

South Carolina Division of Tourism
Edgar Brown Bldg.
Room 106
1205 Pendleton Street
Columbia, South Carolina 29201
(803) 734-0127

South Dakota Division of Tourism
Capitol Lake Plaza
711 Wells Avenue
Pierre, South Dakota 57501
(605) 773-3301 or (800) 843-1930

Tennessee Tourist Development
P.O. Box 23170
Nashville, Tennessee 37202
(615) 741-2158

Texas Tourist Development
P.O. Box 12008
Capitol Station
Austin, Texas 78711
(512) 463-7400

Utah Travel Council
Council Hall
Capitol Hill
Salt Lake City, Utah 84114
(801) 533-5681

Vermont Travel Division
134 State Street
Montpelier, Vermont 05602
(802) 828-3236

Virginia Division of Tourism
202 North 9th Street
Suite 500
Richmond, Virginia 23219
(804) 786-4484

Washington State Department of Commerce and Economic Development
Tourism Promotion and Development Division
101 General Administration Building
Olympia, Washington 98504
(206) 753-5600 or (800) 544-1800 (out of state) or (800) 562-4570 (within Washington)

Travel West Virginia
West Virginia Department of Commerce
State Capitol
2101 Washington Street
Charleston, West Virginia 25305
(304) 348-2286 or (800) CALL W.VA

Wisconsin Division of Tourism
P.O. Box 7606
Madison, Wisconsin 53707
(608) 266-2161 or (800) 372-2737 (within Wisconsin and neighboring states)

Wyoming Travel Commission
Frank Norris, Jr. Travel Center
Cheyenne, Wyoming 82002
(307) 777-7777

Canadian Province Tourist Office

Travel Alberta
15th Floor
10025 Jasper Avenue
Edmonton, Alberta, Canada T5J 3Z3
(403) 427-4321 (from Edmonton area) or 1-800-222-6501 (from Alberta) or 1-800-661-8888 (from the U.S. and Canada)

Tourism British Columbia Parliament Buildings
Victoria, British Columbia, Canada V8V 1X4
(604) 387-1642

Travel Manitoba
Dept. 6020
7th Floor
155 Carlton Street
Winnipeg, Manitoba, Canada R3C 3H8
1-800-665-0040 (from mainland U.S. and Canada)

Tourism New Brunswick
P.O. Box 12345
Fredericton, New Brunswick, Canada E3B 5C3
1-800-442-4442 (from New Brunswick) or 1-800-561-0123 (from mainland U.S. and Canada)

Tourism Branch
Department of Development
P.O. Box 2016
St. John's, Newfoundland, Canada A1C 5R8
(709) 576-2830 (from St. John's area) or 1-800-563-6353 (from mainland U.S. and Canada)

TravelArctic
Yellowknife
Northwest Territories, Canada X1A 2L9
(403) 873-7200

Department of Tourism
P.O. Box 130
Halifax, Nova Scotia, Canada B3J 2M7

Nova Scotia Tourist Information Office
136 Commercial Street
Portland, Maine 04101
U.S.A.
1-800-341-6096 (from mainland U.S. except Maine) or 1-800-492-0643 (from Maine)

Ontario Travel
Queen's Park
Toronto, Ontario, Canada M7A 2E5
1-800-268-3735 (from mainland U.S. and Canada—except Yukon and the Northwest Territories)

Department of Finance and Tourism
Visitor Services Division
P.O. Box 940
Charlottetown, Prince Edward Island, Canada C1A 7M5
(902) 892-2457 or 1-800-565-7421 or (from New Brunswick and Nova Scotia—May 15 to October 31)

Tourisme Québec
C.P. 20 000
Québec (Québec), Canada G1K 7X2
1-800-443-7000 (from 26 Eastern States) or (514) 873-2015 Collect from all other U.S. locations.

Tourism Saskatchewan
2103—11th Avenue
Regina, Saskatchewan, Canada S4P 3V7
(306) 787-2300 or 1-800-667-7191 (from mainland U.S. except Alaska)

Tourism Yukon
P.O. Box 2703
Whitehorse, Yukon, Canada Y1A 2C6
(403) 667-5340

BED AND BREAKFAST RESERVATION REQUEST FORM

Dear ____
Host's Name

I read about your home in *Bed & Breakfast U.S.A. 1988,* and would be interested in making reservations to stay with you.

My name: ____

Address: ____
street

____
city state zip

Telephone: ____
area code

Business address/telephone: ______________________________

____

Number of adult guests: ______________________________

Number and ages of children: ______________________________

Desired date and time of arrival: ______________________________

Desired length of stay: ______________________________

Mode of transportation: ______________________________
(car, bus, train, plane)

Additional information/special requests/allergies: ______________

____

____

____

____

____

I look forward to hearing from you soon.

Sincerely,

APPLICATION FOR MEMBERSHIP
(Please type or print)
(Please refer to Preface, pages xx for our membership criteria.)

Name of Bed & Breakfast: ______________________________

Address: ______________________________

City: __________ State: _____ Zip: _____ Phone: (   ) ______

Best Time to Call: ______________________________

Host(s): ______________________________

Located: No. of miles ____ compass direction ____ of Major

City ____________________ Geographic region __________

No. of miles _______ from major route _______ Exit: _______

No. of guest bedrooms with private bath: ______________
No. of guest bedrooms that share a bath: ______________
How many people (including *your* family) must use the shared bath? ______________________________
How many bedrooms, if any, have a sink in them? __________

Room Rates:
$____ Double—private bath $____ Double—shared bath
$____ Single—private bath $____ Single—shared bath
$____ Suites
Separate Guest Cottage $____ Sleeps ____

Are you open year-round? ☐ Yes ☐ No
If "No," specify when you are open: ______________________

Do you require a minimum stay?______________________

Do you discount rates at any time? ☐ No ☐ Yes If "Yes," specify (i.e., 10% less during March, April, November; 15% less than daily rate if guests stay a week; $10 less per night Sunday through Thursday).______________________________

Do you offer a discount to senior citizens? ☐ No ☐ Yes: ____%

Do you offer a discount for families? ☐ No ☐ Yes: ____%

Breakfast: Type of breakfast included in rate:
☐ Full ☐ Continental
Breakfast is not included: ☐ cost: $ ______

Describe breakfast specialties: ______________________________
____

Are any other meals provided? ☐ No ☐ Yes
Lunch ☐ cost: $__________ Dinner ☐ cost: $ __________
Meals are included in rate quoted with room ☐ Yes ☐ No

Do you accept Credit Cards? ☐ No ☐ Yes:
☐ AMEX ☐ DINERS ☐ MASTERCARD ☐ VISA

Will you GUARANTEE your rates from January through December, 1989? ☐ Yes ☐ No

Note: This Guarantee applies only to those guests making reservations having read about you in *Bed & Breakfast U.S.A., 1989*.

Do you have household pets? ☐ Dog ☐ Cat ☐ Bird

Can you accommodate a guest's pet?
☐ No ☐ Yes ☐ Sometimes

Are children welcome? ☐ No ☐ Yes If "Yes," specify age restriction ______________________________

Do you permit smoking anywhere in your house? ☐ No ☐ Yes

Do you permit social drinking? ☐ No ☐ Yes

Guests can be met at ☐ Airport ____ ☐ Train ____ ☐ Bus ____

Can you speak a foreign language fluently? ☐ No ☐ Yes

Describe on a separate sheet of paper:

GENERAL AREA OF YOUR B&B (i.e., Boston Historic District; 20 minutes from Chicago Loop):

GENERAL DESCRIPTION OF YOUR B&B (i.e., brick Colonial with white shutters; Victorian mansion with stained-glass windows):

AMBIENCE OF YOUR B&B (i.e., furnished with rare antiques; lots of wood and glass):

THE QUALITIES THAT MAKE YOUR B&B SPECIAL ARE:

THINGS OF HISTORIC, SCENIC, CULTURAL, OR GENERAL INTEREST NEARBY (i.e., 1 mile from the San Diego Zoo; walking distance to the Lincoln Memorial):

YOUR OCCUPATION and SPECIAL INTERESTS (i.e., a retired teacher of Latin interested in woodworking; full-time hostess interested in quilting):

If you do welcome children, are there any special provisions for them (i.e., crib, playpen, high chair, play area, baby-sitter)?

Do you offer snacks (i.e., complimentary wine and cheese; pretzels and chips but BYOB)?

Can guests use your kitchen for light snacks? ☐ No ☐ Yes

Do you offer the following amenities: ☐ Guest Refrigerator
☐ Air-conditioning ☐ TV ☐ Piano ☐ Washing Machine
☐ Dryer ☐ Hot tub ☐ Pool ☐ Tennis Court Other ______

What major college or university is within 10 miles?

____

Please supply the name, address, and phone number of three personal references from people not related to you (please use a separate sheet).

Please enclose a copy of your brochure, if possible, along with color photos including exterior, guest bedrooms, baths, and breakfast area. Use a label to identify the name of your B&B on each. If you have a black-and-white line drawing, send it along too. If you have an original breakfast recipe that you'd like to share, send it along too. (Of course, credit will be given to your B&B.) **Nobody can describe your B&B better than you, so please do. Limit your description to 100 words and submit it typed, double spaced, on a separate sheet of paper. We will of course reserve the right to edit.** As a member of the Tourist House Association of America, your B&B will be described in the next edition of our book, *Bed & Breakfast U.S.A.*, published by E. P. Dutton and distributed to bookstores and libraries throughout the U.S. The book is also used as a reference for B&Bs in our country by major offices of tourism throughout the world.
Note: If the publisher or authors receive negative reports from your guests regarding a deficiency in our standards of CLEANLINESS, COMFORT, and CORDIALITY, and/or failure to honor the rate guarantee, we reserve the right to cancel your Membership.

This Membership Application has been prepared by:

____

(Signature)

Please enclose your $20 Membership Dues. Date: ________________

Yes! ☐ Send information on Group Liability Insurance.
No ☐ I am insured by __________________________

Return to:
Tourist House Association of America
R.D. 2, Box 355A
Greentown, Pennsylvania 18426

To assure that your listing will be considered for the 1989 edition of *Bed & Breakfast U.S.A.*, we MUST receive your completed application by March 31, 1988. Thereafter, listings will be considered only for the semiannual supplement. (See page 698.)

APPLICATION FOR MEMBERSHIP FOR A BED & BREAKFAST RESERVATION SERVICE

NAME OF BED & BREAKFAST SERVICE: ____________________

ADDRESS: ____________________

CITY: ________ STATE: ____ ZIP: ____ PHONE: (   ) ______

COORDINATOR: ____________________

BEST TIME TO CALL: ____________________

Do you have a telephone answering ☐ machine? ☐ service?

Names of State(s), Cities, and Towns where you have Hosts (in alphabetical order, please, and limit to 10):

Number of Hosts on your roster: _________

THINGS OF HISTORIC, SCENIC, CULTURAL, OR GENERAL INTEREST IN THE AREA(S) YOU SERVE:

Range of Rates:

Modest:	Single $__________	Double $__________
Average:	Single $__________	Double $__________
Luxury:	Single $__________	Double $__________

Will you GUARANTEE your rates through December 1989?
☐ Yes ☐ No

How often do you re-inspect listings? ____________________
Do you require a minimum stay? ____________________
Surcharges for one-night stay? ____________________
Do you accept Credit Cards? ☐ No ☐ Yes:
☐ AMEX ☐ DINERS ☐ MASTERCARD ☐ VISA

Is the guest required to pay a fee to use your service?
☐ No ☐ Yes—The fee is $____________________

Do you publish a directory of your B&B listings?
☐ No ☐ Yes—The fee is $____________________

Are any of your B&Bs within 10 miles of a university? Which? ____
____

Briefly describe a sample Host Home in each of the above categories: e.g., A cozy farmhouse where the host weaves rugs; a restored 1800 Victorian where the host is a retired general; a contemporary mansion with a sauna and swimming pool.

Please supply the name, address, and phone number of three personal references from people not related to you (please use a separate sheet of paper). Please enclose a copy of your brochure.

This Membership Application has been prepared by:

____
(Signature)

Please enclose your $20 Membership Dues. Date: ______________

If you have a special breakfast recipe that you'd like to share, send it along. (Of course, credit will be given to your B&B agency.) As a member of the Tourist House Association of America, your B&B agency will be described in the next edition of our book, *Bed & Breakfast U.S.A.*, published by E. P. Dutton. Return to: Tourist House Association, RD 2, Box 355A, Greentown, PA 18426.

To assure that your listing will be considered for the 1989 edition, we must receive your completed application by March 31, 1988. Thereafter, listings will be considered only for the semiannual supplement. (See page 698.)

WE WANT TO HEAR FROM YOU!

Name: ______________________________

Address: ______________________________
street

____
city state zip

____

Please contact the following B&Bs; I think that they would be great additions to the next edition of *Bed & Breakfast U.S.A.*

Name of B&B: ______________________________

Address: ______________________________
street

____
city state zip

Comments:

Name of B&B: ______________________________

Address: ______________________________
street

____
city state zip

Comments:

____

The following is our report on our visit to the home of:

Name of B&B: ____________________ Date of visit: __________

Address: ____________________ I was pleased. ☐

____________________ I was disappointed. ☐

Comments:

Just tear out this page and mail it to us. It won't ruin your book!

Return to:
Tourist House Association of America
R.D. 2, Box 355A
Greentown, Pennsylvania 18426

INFORMATION ORDER FORM

We are constantly expanding our roster to include new members in the Tourist House Association of America. Their facilities will be fully described in the next edition of *Bed & Breakfast U.S.A.* In the meantime, we will be happy to send you a list including the name, address, telephone number, etc.

For those of you who would like to order additional copies of the book or perhaps send one to a friend as a gift, we will be happy to fill mail orders. If it is a gift, let us know and we'll enclose a special gift card from you.

ORDER FORM

To:
Tourist House Association
R.D. 2, Box 355A
Greentown, PA 18426

From: ______________________
(Print your name)

Address: ______________________

____
City State Zip

Date: ____________

Please send:

☐ List of new B&Bs ($2.00); available July to December.

☐ ____ copies of *Bed & Breakfast U.S.A.* @ $11 each (includes 4th class mail)

Send to: ______________________

Address: ______________________

____
City State Zip

☐ Enclose a gift card from:

Please make check or money order payable to Tourist House Association.